Ecuador
& the Galápagos Islands

a Lonely Planet travel survival kit

Rob Rachowiecki

Ecuador & the Galápagos Islands

4th edition

Published by
    Lonely Planet Publications
    Head Office: PO Box 617, Hawthorn, Vic 3122, Australia
    Branches: 155 Filbert St, Suite 251, Oakland, CA 94607, USA
                     10a Spring Place, London NW5 3BH, UK
                     71 bis rue du Cardinal Lemoine, 75005 Paris, France

Printed by
    The Bookmaker Pty Ltd
    Printed in China

Photographs by
    Rob Rachowiecki (RR)   Tony Wheeler (TW)   Jeff Williams (JW)

    Front cover:
    Title page: David Peevers, Cuenca locals
    Galápagos Wildlife Guide title page: Nigel French

Published
    January 1997

Although the author and publisher have tried to make the information as accurate as possible, they accept no responsibility for any loss, injury or inconvenience sustained by any person using this book.

National Library of Australia Cataloguing in Publication Data

Rachowiecki, Rob, 1954-.
    Ecuador & the Galápagos Islands.

    4th ed.
    Includes index.
    ISBN 0 86442 348 9.

    1. Ecuador – Guidebooks. 2. Galápagos Islands – Guidebooks.
    I. Title. (Series: Lonely Planet travel survival kit).

918.660474

text & map keys © Rob Rachowiecki 1997
maps © Lonely Planet 1997
photos © photographers as indicated 1997
climate charts compiled from information supplied by Patrick J Tyson, © Patrick J Tyson, 1997

Rob Rachowiecki

Rob was born near London and became an avid traveler while still a teenager. He has visited countries as diverse as Greenland and Thailand. He spent most of the 1980s in Latin America, traveling, mountaineering and teaching English, and he now works part time in Ecuador and Peru as a leader for Wilderness Travel, an adventure travel company. He is the author of Lonely Planet's travel survival kits to Peru, Costa Rica and Southwest USA and has contributed to Lonely Planet's shoestring guides to South America and Central America, as well as to books by other publishers. When not traveling, he lives in Arizona with his wife, Cathy, and their three children: Julia (age 9), Alison (age 7) and Davy (age 4).

Dedication

For Julia, because she's great!

From the Author

Many people provided invaluable input for this update. As always, all the staff at the South American Explorers Club deserve a big hand for their useful suggestions, not least of which was where to go for a drink in the evening. Club member Jane Letham helped immensely with checking information in Quito. My friend Randy Galati traveled the entire coast and provided me with copious and thorough notes that were much appreciated, as were his detailed opinions about Ecuadorian beer.

David Sutherland, Head of Interpretation at the Charles Darwin Research Station, sent me much valuable information about the Galápagos Islands, and naturalist guide Mauricio García helped keep me up to speed in the islands. Divemaster Francisco Zembrano helped me obtain hotel and other information in the Galápagos.

Oswaldo Muñoz, president of the Ecuadorian Ecotourism Association, kindly reviewed the last edition of this book and made many useful suggestions, as well as provided hospitality in Quito. Sacha Lodge guide Cherise Miller sent copious notes of her travels in Ecuador, with an emphasis on sensitive travel in the Oriente. La Selva guide Judy Meltzer was also a source of useful information in the Oriente. Robert and Daisy Kunstaetter, publishers of the *Latin American Travel Advisor*, took me on a memorable drive to explore the area south of Quito.

Steven Wille, of Centro de Estudios Interamericanos in Cuenca, and Beto and Teresa Chico, of Cabañas Yanuncay, also in Cuenca, all provided much insight into that region. Jean Brown and David Gayton, of Safari Tours in Quito, spent time with me suggesting changes, additions and improvements to the book. Rodrigo Mora allowed me access to his detailed notes on Otavalo. Luis Meneses F sent me his tourist map of San Gabriel. Adam McLellan provided most of the Tulcán updates. Antonio Alarcón, of the Hostal Villantigua, sent me Mitad del Mundo information. Michel Leseigneur, of Hostal Plantas y Blanco in Baños, sent useful updates on that town, and Renee Turolla mailed me a video of the Hacienda Manteles in the Baños area. John Ivanko sent ecotourism information for various parts of the country. Jason Spensley of FUNDECOL, Director Eric Horstman of Bosque Protector Cerro Blanco and ecologist Rik Pennartz of Manglares Churute all sent useful facts about their areas of expertise.

I acknowledge and thank all these great folks. Many other readers wrote super-useful letters that were among my greatest aids in researching this new edition. Readers names are acknowledged on the page before the introduction.

My wife and children, as always, put up with my long sessions at the computer, especially as the deadline came and went. I couldn't ask for a more supportive and loving family. And I appreciate my editors allowing me to send the last few chapters a couple of weeks late – I'll try not to do it again!

You can contact me via electronic mail at robrachow@aol.com with updates and suggestions, but I regret that I cannot plan your trip for you!

From the Publisher

This edition of *Ecuador & the Galápagos Islands* was born in Lonely Planet's office in Oakland, California. Don Gates coordinated the editing, with ample assistance from Carolyn Hubbard. Don, Carolyn and Sandra Lopen Barker edited and proofread the book, with Sacha Pearson making neat bows out of every loose end thrown her way. *Ramilletes de flores* to Tom Downs, Michelle Gagné, Kate Hoffman, Caroline Liou and Laini Taylor for further proofing and general support.

Hayden Foell was responsible for layout, and Hugh D'Andrade added illustrations and advice. Rini Keagy and Chris Salcedo created the maps under the guidance of Alex Guilbert. Scott Summers lent his production expertise to all.

Thanks are also due to the following: Michele Matter, her mother Ligia Andino and uncle Germán Andino; Paul Clifton and the cartos of Oz; John Fadeff and his poison-arrow frog; Juan Carlos Blum Baquero, director general of INEC; Juan Gallegos Herrera, forestry engineer at INEFAN; Mirka J Negroni and the International Gay and Lesbian Human Rights Commission in San Francisco; and the good people of the Ecuadorian embassy in Los Angeles. *Muchísimas gracias a todos.*

Warning & Request

Things change – prices go up, schedules change, good places go bad and bad places go bankrupt – nothing stays the same. So, if you find things better or worse, recently opened or long since closed, please tell us and help make the next edition of this book even more accurate and useful.

We value all of the feedback we receive from travelers. Julie Young coordinates a small team that reads and acknowledges every letter, postcard and email, and ensures that every morsel of information finds its way to the appropriate authors, editors and publishers. Everyone who writes to us will find their name in the next edition of the appropriate guide and will also receive a free subscription to our quarterly newsletter, *Planet Talk*. The very best contributions will be rewarded with a free Lonely Planet guide.

Excerpts from your correspondence may appear in updates (which we add to the end pages of reprints); new editions of this guide; in our newsletter, *Planet Talk*; or in the Postcards section of our website. Please let us know if you don't want your letter published or your name acknowledged.

Thanks

Many thanks to the travelers who used the last edition and wrote to us with helpful hints, useful advice and interesting anecdotes. Your names appear on the page before the introduction.

Contents

Map Legend

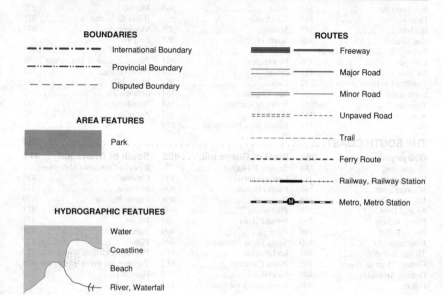

BOUNDARIES

— · — · — · — International Boundary

— · · — · · — Provincial Boundary

— — — — — Disputed Boundary

AREA FEATURES

Park

HYDROGRAPHIC FEATURES

Water

Coastline

Beach

River, Waterfall

Swamp, Spring

ROUTES

Freeway

Major Road

Minor Road

======= ------- Unpaved Road

- - - - - - - - Trail

Ferry Route

Railway, Railway Station

Ⓜ Metro, Metro Station

SYMBOLS

❂	**NATIONAL CAPITAL**	✈	Airfield		🅟	Gas Station
◉	**Provincial Capital**	✈	Airport	⛳	Golf Course
●	**City**	∴	Archaeological Site, Ruins	⊕	Hospital, Clinic
●	City, Small	Ⓢ	Bank, ATM	❶	Information
●	Town	✕	Battlefield	🛆	Lighthouse
■	Hotel, B&B	🍷	Beach	✳	Lookout
▲	Campground	◒	Bus Depot, Bus Stop	⚒	Mine
⌂	Chalet, Hut	▦	Cathedral	🯅	Monument
⌂	Hostel	∩	Cave	▲	Mountain
⌂	Shelter	†	Church	🏛	Museum
▼	Restaurant	○	Embassy	♪	Music, Live
🍴	Bar (Place to Drink)	⤜	Fishing, Fish Hatchery	—	One-Way Street
☕	Café	⤢	Foot Bridge	⌂	Observatory
		❈	Garden	🅟	Parking

☂	Park
)(	Pass
⌐	Picnic Area
★	Police Station
▭	Pool
✉	Post Office
⚓	Shipwreck
❖	Shopping Mall
🏛	Stately Home
☎	Telephone
◼	Tomb, Mausoleum
🯅	Trailhead
⚘	Winery
🐘	Zoo

Note: Not all symbols displayed above appear in this book.

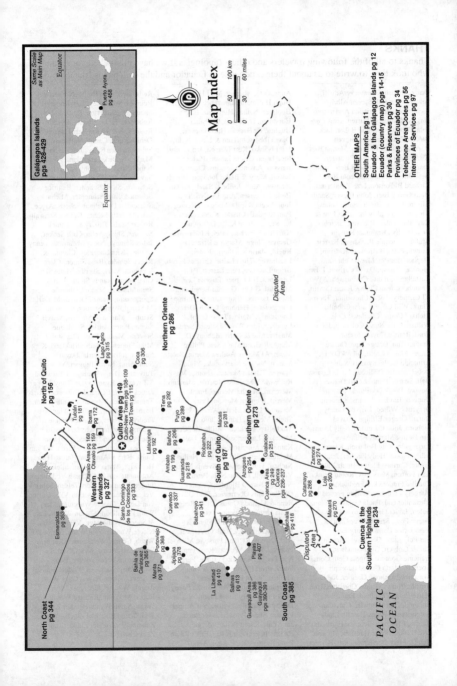

THANKS

Thanks to all of the following travelers and others (apologies if we have misspelled your name) who took time to write to us about their experience in Ecuador and the Galápagos Islands.

Omar Abbosh, Genevieve Adjedj, Anurag Agrawal, Steven Albright, Eleanor Allen, Christina Andersson, Jorg Andratschbe, Darren Armstrong, John B Babbs Jr, Julie Baker, Jack Bakker, Vanessa Bals, Steven Bammel, Fiona Barltrop, Marian Bart, Ninke Bautmans, Juliu Belanger, Patrice Bélie, Suzanne S Bell, Brinley Best, Joel Benzimra, Nicola Berk, Richard Bidkerton, L & T Biderstal, Hans Georg Bier, John Biever, Sarah Bilson, Vivian Birch-Jones, James Bird, Rev David Blanton, Dr Lou & Kay Blas, Adam Blejwas, Gretchen Bowder, Eva Braiman, Kerstin Brandes, Jacquie Briskham, Barrett Brown, Patricia Browne, JC Brun, Stephen Bunton, Mario Cabrera, Monica Canova, David Carlson, Edwin Castellanos, Judith Cavanaugh, AW Chambers, Jean Chang, Jonah Chasin, CJ Chenery, J & C Chevallier, Thorne Clark, Will Clive, Laura Cobelli, Richard Colby, Charles R Cole, Wilham Cole, Steve Coleman, John Cord, Ranald Coyne, Joseph Crapanzano, Doug Cripe, Chiare Crotti, Marco Crotti, John J David, Armando DeBeraradinis, Sabine Debel, Martin Dedicoat, Linda Louisa Dell, Sharon Dennis, Carl Denzen, A Devora, Frank Dominick, Ramito Donoso, Jim Dos Santos, Kenneth Dreyfuss, Willem Drijver, Jimmy Duran, Gregor Effinger, David Eichorn, Julie C Emrich, Sally Evans, Jim Evans, Markus Falk, Sue Farrington, Kate Feibusch, Klever Alban Flores, Hedy Fischer, Jennette Fisher, Carmen Flores, Heinz Flück, Kari Fortun, Mary Fox, Robin Frank, Camille Frederick, J Fredrickson, Margery Freeman, Marion Freundlieb, Alexander Gal, Paola Galasso, Solana Galen, Javier Galparsoro & Club Marco Polo, Sari & Peter Gantzel, Jesus Uribe Garcia, Mary Jane Gasdick, Luisa Georgov, Petra Giger, Rainer Golgert, Glen Goodwin, Francine Gordon, Angela Gott, Corine Goubert, Marta Grajeda, Joseph Grasmick, Anthony Greiner, Joe E Griffith, Nancy Grona, Christine Grua, Marie-Pierre Guicherd, Francois Guinand, Don Gurewitz, Christian Hafenrichter, Peggy Hamill, Linda Hardie, J Harring, Beatrice Hartmann, Eric Haskell, Peter Hausner, Micaela Heintz, Mark Henderson, Eric Herrera,

Andreas Hessberger, Ms J Hofman, Hugh Hoffmann, Lawrence Honnier, S Hooliger, Nathan Horowitz, Eric Horstman, D Howell, Christina Hughes, Dr Hannes Hutzelmeyer, David Ibbotson, Tom & Susan Isgar, John Ivanko, Kurt Iverson, Jan Jacobs, Inge Jager, Gisela Janson, Pieter Janssen, Amanda Jenkins, Charlene Jewell, Mary & Blake Johnson, Wendy Johnson, Alain Jolibert, Sandy Jordan, Helle Jorgensen, Ann Joselyn, Trine Juul, Neeta Kapila, Margaret Keefe, Paul Kendall, Charles Kineke, Jack Kineke, Leslie P King, Dr Lothar Kirsch, J Kirscher, Jacek Klamrowski, George Kluge, Marjorie Kriz, JD Kuehl, Marie Kuieborg, Jeroen Laarhoven, Tiina Laine, Charles Lamb, Brigit Lanckes, Pete Larrett, Pam Leamons, H Learner, Eugene Lee, Meredith G Lee, Gudrun Leonhard, Daniel Levine, Bjorn Linzer, Philippe Longepierre, Henning Losch, Derek Lounsbury, Markus Low, Carol Lundeen, Lisa Woo Maclean, Bernard Magier, Mal & Chris Mahony, D Major, Richard Manasseh, Phillip Mann, Al Marro, Andrea Martin, Scott Martin, Nicolle Martindale, Yigal Master, Tilman Matzat, Thomas Mayr, Rolfe McAfee, Julie McCole, Mariano Merchan, Martha Merino, Frank Merritt, Stephen Merson, Petra Mertens, Linda Mertz, Arnold & Sheila Metcalf, Hanne Elmo Mikkelsen, Nicholas Millhouse, Craig Moeckel, Laurence Monnier, Dale & Katharina Morrison, Markus Muehlbacher, Sally Mullard, Nellie Nathan, Trui Naeyaert, Svenja Noh, Volker Noll, Dellon Nolt, Petra Nuding, Tore O Bjordal, Cecilia Oballe, Hans Obermeier, Paul Oliver, Rene & Colinda Ooms, DP O'Reagan, Sonia Ortubay, Eveline Otten, Christian Otto, Arthur Oudendijk, Renske Ouweneel, Ruth Overstreet, Kirk Owens, Richard Parsons, Michael Pearson, Ronald Pelton, Rene Pepin, Nan Periog, Antonio Perrone, Ferga Perry, Fritli Pfyffer, Janet & Doug Phillips, Susan Pinnell, Sigrid Pomplun, Thomas Popp, Susan Povey, Peter Prak, Mary Anna Prentice, Debby Prigal, Paul Prior, Prof Anibal Proano, Shani Prosser, Janet Pugh, June Pull, Karen Pullar, Margie Radenich, Prakash A Raj, Erika Rasch, Peter Rasmussen, C Raul, Anne

Redston, Sharon Reilly, Norbert Reintjes, Silvia Rey, Kay Roberts, Shaunagh Robertson, Keith & Judy Robinson, Jackie Rogers, Gerard Rooney, E & M Rotsaert-Haezebrouck, Denise Ruck, Camila Valasco Sabando, Fien Sabre, Jose JL Sadaba, Markus & Dirk Saher, James Salmon, Nancy Sanders, Debby Sas, John Savage, Nicole Schafer, Sabine Schauch, Silvia Scheiter, Beatrice Schmied, Julia Schneider, Michael Schneider, Dr Helmut Schops, Alyce Schultz, Jutta Schutz, Devore Schwalb, Robert Seals, Thierry & Yannick Seguret, Shelly Selin, Cath Senker, Juliet Serenyi, Nicky Shearman, Penny Shelley, Kim Shockley, Claudia & Roger Schulte, Babs Simon, Clare Sixsmith, Marie Skertiz, Mette Skov, Greg Smith, Randy Smith, James Smurfit, Kiran Soma, Catherine Speckmann, Heinz Stachelheid, Carla M Stangl, Petra Stattler, Christian Stauber, Marcia M Stavros, Marcia Steere, Petra Stettler, Stephanie Stevens, Manuel Stoll, Ilka Stolze, Mike Stoneman, Judi Strickland, Kent Sugnet, Johanna Surla, David Sutherland, Norm Taggart, Vesa Taiveaho, Diego Tamayo, J Tarwood, S Tavenier, Ryan Taylor, Tony Tepper, James Terry, Bertrand Thibonnet, Rich Thom, Carien Tibosch, Ursula Tisljar, Barbara Toffani, Jim Tompkins, Frederick Toms, Mike & Pauline Truman, Nadine Tschanz, Conrad Tuerk, Dirk van Damme, Carl van Denzen, Arthur van den Elzen, WJ van Gulik, Bart & Arno van Haren, H van Heeswijk, Maria von Keirsbilck, Antoinette van Zijl, Rajesh Vedanthan, Jurgen Veeuler, Albert Velsen, Sabrina Vergari, Pascale & Arthur Vila, Clifton von Jaeger, Connie Waechter, Mary Wall, P Wallbudge, Alan Waller, Pete & Sheena Wallbridge, Vera Walters, Nicole Wanner, Paul Watts, Mercedes Webb, Conrad Weichmann, Kenneth Weir, Carl-Martin Weiss, Nathalie Wermuth, Marcus Wieser, Edo Wijtenburg, Kathleen Wilder, Louise & Steve Wilson-Hayes, Gary Winter, Angela Wischet, Georgina Woern, Robert M Wolin, Richard Wood, Anne Wyatt, Sarah Wyatt, Heather Zavod, Wei Zhang, Eberhard Zloch, Teresa Zuberbuhler, Achim Zubke, Ralf Zuckschwerdt

Introduction

Ecuador is the smallest of the Andean countries, and in many ways it is the easiest and most pleasant to travel in.

From the beautifully preserved colonial capital of Quito, located in the highlands at 2850 meters (9300 feet) above sea level, you can travel by frequent buses to Andean Indian markets, remote jungle towns and warm Pacific beaches. In fact, starting from Quito, you can get to most points in this tropical country in less than a day by public transport.

The highlands have many colorful Indian markets – some world famous and deservedly so, and others that are rarely visited by foreigners but are no less interesting. Any journey in the highlands is dominated by magnificent volcanoes such as Cotopaxi – at 5897 meters (19,348 feet), one of the highest active volcanoes in the world – and many others.

Jungle travel in Ecuador is easier than in most countries because the distance between jungle sites and cities is far less; you can be in the jungle after just a day's bus travel from Quito. There are many exciting opportunities to hire local guides or to strike out on your own from jungle towns such as Misahuallí and Coca on the Río Napo, a tributary of the Amazon.

The coast, too, has much to offer. Go to a picturesque fishing village and watch the fishers expertly return their traditional balsa-wood rafts through the ocean breakers to the sandy shore, or help them pull in their nets in return for some of the catch.

Laze on the beach in the equatorial sun, swim in the warm seas and in the evening listen to salsa music in a local bar.

The Galápagos Islands, 1000 km off the Pacific coast of Ecuador, are high on the list of destinations for travelers interested in wildlife. Here you can swim with penguins and sea lions, or walk along beaches while pelicans flap by and huge land or marine iguanas scurry around your feet. The wildlife is so unafraid of humans that at times it's difficult to avoid stepping on the animals.

This book tells you everything you'll need to know about traveling through this enchanting country. The most interesting sights, the best-value hotels and restaurants and practical advice on taking all forms of public transport, from air flights to dugout canoes, set off by a host of background details will make this guide an indispensable part of your trip.

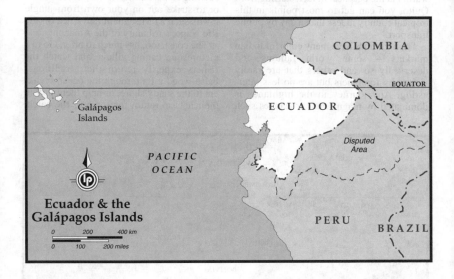

COLOMBIA

EQUATOR

Galápagos Islands

ECUADOR

PACIFIC OCEAN

Disputed Area

Ecuador & the Galápagos Islands

0   200   400 km
0   100   200 miles

PERU

BRAZIL

Facts about the Country

HISTORY

Most histories of Ecuador begin with the expansion of the Incas from Peru in the 1400s. Archaeological evidence, however, indicates the presence of people in Ecuador for many thousands of years before then. There are two theories explaining where the earliest inhabitants came from.

It is generally accepted that Asian nomads crossed what is now known as the Bering Strait some 25,000 years ago and began reaching the South American continent by about 12,000 BC. It is believed that several thousand years later, trans-Pacific colonization by the island dwellers of Polynesia added to the population.

Although Stone Age tools found in the Quito area have been dated to 9000 BC, the oldest signs of a more developed culture date back to 3200 BC. These belong to the Valdivia period and consist mainly of ceramics, especially small figurines, found in the central coastal area of Ecuador. Examples of these can be seen in the major museums of Quito and Guayaquil.

Early Tribes

The history of pre-Inca Ecuador is lost in a tangle of time and legend. Generally speaking, the main populations lived either on the coast or in the highlands. The earliest historical details we have date to the 11th century AD when there were two dominant tribes: the expansionist Caras in the coastal areas and the peaceful Quitus in the highlands.

The Caras, led by Shyri, conquered the Quitus, but it seems to have been a peaceful expansion rather than bloody warfare. The Cara/Quitu peoples became collectively known as the Shyri nation and were the dominant force in the Ecuadorian highlands until about 1300, by which time the Puruhá of the southern highlands had also risen to power under the Duchicela lineage.

Conflict was avoided by the marriage of a Shyri princess, the only child of a King Caran of the Shyris, to Duchicela, the eldest son of the King of the Puruhás. This Duchicela/Shyri alliance proved successful and the Duchicela line ruled more or less peacefully for about 150 years.

The Inca Empire

At the time of the Inca expansion, the Duchicela descendants still dominated the north and the south was in the hands of the Cañari people. The Cañari defended themselves bitterly against the Inca invaders and it was some years before the Inca, Tupac-Yupanqui, was able to subdue them and turn his attention to the north. During this time he fathered a son, Huayna Capac, by a Cañari princess.

The subjugation of the north took many years, and Huayna Capac grew up in Ecuador. He succeeded his father to the Inca throne and spent years traveling all over his empire, from Bolivia to Ecuador, constantly putting down uprisings from all sides. Wherever possible, he strengthened his position by marriage; his union with Paccha, the daughter of the defeated Cacha Duchicela, produced a son, Atahualpa.

The year 1526 is a major one in Ecuadorian history. The Inca Huayna Capac died and left his empire not to one son, as was traditional, but to two: Huáscar of Cuzco and Atahualpa of Quito; thus the Inca Empire was divided for the first time. In the same year, on September 21, the first Spaniards landed in northern Ecuador near what is now Esmeraldas. They were led south by the pilot, Bartolomé Ruiz de Andrade, on an exploratory mission for Francisco Pizarro, who himself remained further north. Pizarro was not to arrive as conqueror for several years.

Meanwhile, the rivalry between Huayna Capac's two sons grew. The Inca of Cuzco, Huáscar, went to war against the Inca of Quito, Atahualpa. After several years of

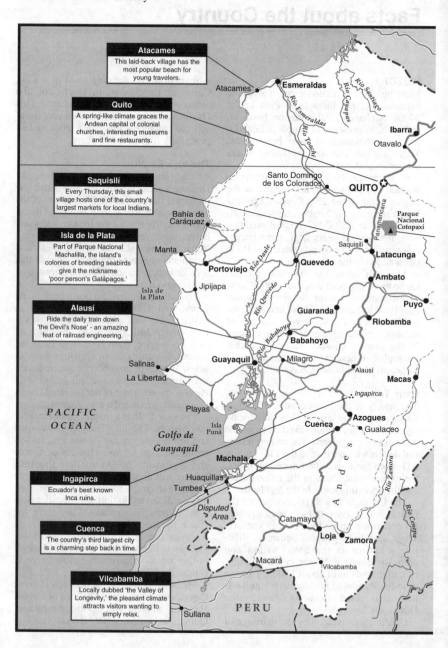

Atacames
This laid-back village has the most popular beach for young travelers.

Quito
A spring-like climate graces the Andean capital of colonial churches, interesting museums and fine restaurants.

Saquisilí
Every Thursday, this small village hosts one of the country's largest markets for local Indians.

Isla de la Plata
Part of Parque Nacional Machalilla, the island's colonies of breeding seabirds give it the nickname 'poor person's Galápagos.'

Alausí
Ride the daily train down 'the Devil's Nose' - an amazing feat of railroad engineering.

Ingapirca
Ecuador's best known Inca ruins.

Cuenca
The country's third largest city is a charming step back in time.

Vilcabamba
Locally dubbed 'the Valley of Longevity,' the pleasant climate attracts visitors wanting to simply relax.

Atacames · **Esmeraldas**

Río Santiago
Río Cayapas
Río Esmeraldas
Río Toachi
Ibarra
Otavalo
Santo Domingo de los Colorados
QUITO
Bahía de Caráquez
Panamericana
Parque Nacional Cotopaxi ▲
Manta
Saquisilí
Latacunga
Río Daule
Quevedo
Portoviejo
Ambato
Jipijapa
Puyo
Isla de la Plata
Guaranda
Riobamba
Río Quevedo
Río Babahoyo
Babahoyo
Salinas
Guayaquil
Milagro
La Libertad
Río Babahoyo
Alausí
Macas
Ingapirca
Playas
Isla Puná
Azogues
Gualaceo
PACIFIC OCEAN
Cuenca
Golfo de Guayaquil
A n d e s
Machala
Huaquillas
Tumbes
Río Zamora
Disputed Area
Catamayo
Loja **Zamora**
Macará
Vilcabamba
Río Cenepa
Sullana
PERU

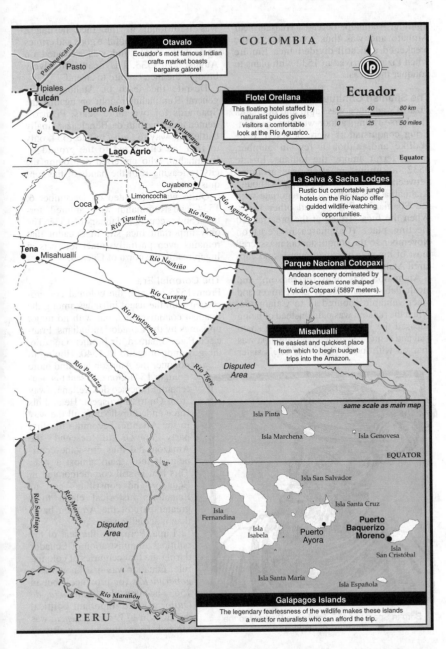

COLOMBIA

Ecuador

Equator

Otavalo
Ecuador's most famous Indian crafts market boasts bargains galore!

Pasto
Ipiales
Tulcán
Puerto Asís

Flotel Orellana
This floating hotel staffed by naturalist guides gives visitors a comfortable look at the Río Aguarico.

0   40   80 km
0   25   50 miles

Río Putumayo

Lago Agrio

Cuyabeno
Coca
Limoncocha
Río Aguarico

La Selva & Sacha Lodges
Rustic but comfortable jungle hotels on the Río Napo offer guided wildlife-watching opportunities.

Río Tiputini
Río Napo

Tena
Misahuallí
Río Nashiño

Parque Nacional Cotopaxi
Andean scenery dominated by the ice-cream cone shaped Volcán Cotopaxi (5897 meters).

Río Curaray

Misahuallí
The easiest and quickest place from which to begin budget trips into the Amazon.

Río Pintoyacu

Río Pastaza

Río Tigre

Disputed Area

Río Santiago
Río Morona

Disputed Area

Río Marañón

PERU

same scale as main map

Isla Pinta
Isla Marchena
Isla Genovesa

EQUATOR

Isla San Salvador
Isla Santa Cruz
Isla Fernandina
Isla Isabela
Puerto Ayora
Puerto Baquerizo Moreno
Isla San Cristóbal
Isla Santa María
Isla Española

Galápagos Islands
The legendary fearlessness of the wildlife makes these islands a must for naturalists who can afford the trip.

fighting, Atahualpa defeated Huáscar near Ambato and was thus sole ruler of the weakened and still-divided Inca Empire when Pizarro arrived in 1532 with plans to conquer the Incas.

The Spanish Conquest

Pizarro's advance was rapid and dramatic. His horse-riding, armor-wearing, cannon-firing conquistadors were believed to be godlike and, although few in number, spread terror among the Indians. In late 1532, a summit meeting was arranged between Pizarro and Atahualpa. Although Atahualpa was prepared to negotiate with the Spaniards, Pizarro had other ideas. When the Inca arrived at the prearranged meeting place (Cajamarca in Peru) on November 16 the conquistadors massacred most of his poorly armed guards and captured Atahualpa.

Atahualpa was held for ransom, and incalculable quantities of gold, silver and other valuables poured in to Cajamarca. When the ransom was paid, instead of being released the Inca was put through a sham trial and sentenced to death. Atahualpa was charged with incest (marrying one's sister

was traditional in the Inca heritage), polygamy, worship of false gods and crimes against the king, and was executed on August 29, 1533. His death effectively brought the Inca Empire to an end.

Despite the death of Atahualpa, his general Rumiñahui fought on against the Spaniards for two more years. Pizarro's lieutenant Sebastián de Benalcázar finally battled his way to Quito in late 1534, only to find the city razed to the ground by Rumiñahui, who preferred destroying the city to leaving it in the hands of the conquistadors.

Quito was refounded on December 6, 1534, and Rumiñahui was captured, tortured and executed in January of 1535. The only important Inca site in Ecuador that remains even partially intact today is at Ingapirca, to the north of Cuenca.

The Colonial Era

From 1535 onward, the colonial era proceeded with the usual intrigues among the Spanish conquistadors, but with no major uprisings by the Ecuadorian Indians. Francisco Pizarro named his brother, Gonzalo, the governor of Quito in 1540. Hoping to conquer the Amazon and find more gold, in 1541 Gonzalo sent his lieutenant, Francisco de Orellana, away from Quito to prospect. He and his force ended up floating all the way to the Atlantic, becoming the first party known to descend the Amazon and thus cross the continent. It took them almost a year. This feat is still commemorated in Ecuador and constitutes part of Ecuador's historical claim to a greater part of the Amazon basin than it actually has.

Lima, Peru, was the seat of the political administration of Ecuador during the first centuries of colonial rule. Ecuador was first known as a *gobernación* (or province), but in 1563 became the *Audiencia de Quito*, a more important political division. In 1739 the *audiencia* was transferred from the viceroyalty of

Born in Spain in 1475, Francisco Pizarro led the conquest of the Incas.

Peru, of which it was a part, to the viceroyalty of Colombia (then known as Nueva Grenada).

Ecuador remained a peaceful colony during these centuries, and agriculture and the arts flourished. Various new agricultural products were introduced from Europe, including cattle and bananas, which still remain important in Ecuador today. There was prolific construction of churches and monasteries, which were decorated with unique carvings and paintings resulting from the blend of Spanish and Indian art influences. This so-called 'Quito school of art,' still admired by visitors today, has left an indelible stamp on the colonial buildings of the time.

Life was comfortable for the ruling colonialists, but the Indians (and later *mestizos*, or people of mixed Spanish/Indian blood) were treated abysmally under their rule. A system of forced labor was not only tolerated but encouraged, and it is no surprise that by the 18th century there were several uprisings of the Indians against the Spanish ruling classes. Both poor and rich died in violent fighting.

One of the best remembered heroes of the early revolutionary period is Eugenio Espejo, born in Quito in 1747 of an Indian father and a mulatto mother. Espejo was a brilliant man who obtained his doctorate by the age of 20 and became a major literary voice for independence. He wrote political satire, founded a liberal newspaper and spoke out strongly against colonialism. He was imprisoned several times and died in jail in 1795.

Independence

The first serious attempt to liberate Ecuador from Spanish rule was by a partisan group led by Juan Pío Montúfar on August 10, 1809. The group managed to take Quito and install a government, but this lasted only 24 days before royalist troops (loyal to the king of Spain) were able to regain control.

Independence was finally achieved by Simón Bolívar, the Venezuelan liberator who marched southward from Caracas, freed Colombia in 1819 and supported the people of Guayaquil when they claimed independence on October 9, 1820. It took almost two years before Ecuador was entirely liberated from Spanish rule. The decisive battle was fought on May 24, 1822, when one of Bolívar's best officers, Field Marshal Sucre, defeated the royalists at the Battle of Pichincha and took Quito.

Bolívar's idealistic dream was to form a united South America, and he began by amalgamating Venezuela, Colombia and Ecuador into the independent nation of Gran Colombia. This lasted only eight years, with Ecuador becoming fully independent in 1830. In the same year a treaty was signed with Peru, drawing up a boundary between the two nations. This is the boundary shown on all Ecuadorian maps. (In 1942, after a war between the two countries, the border was redrawn in Rio de Janeiro. It is this border that is found on non-Ecuadorian maps, though officially it is not acknowledged by Ecuadorian authorities.)

Simón Bolívar, 'El Libertador,' freed Venezuela, Colombia and Ecuador from Spanish colonial rule.

Political Development

Independent Ecuador's internal history has been a typically Latin American turmoil of political and open warfare between liberals and conservatives. Quito has emerged as the main center for the church-backed conservatives, while Guayaquil has traditionally been associated with liberal and socialist beliefs. This rivalry continues on a social level today; Quiteños have nicknamed Guayaquileños *monos* (monkeys) and the lively coastal people think of the highland inhabitants as very staid and dull.

The rivalry between the political groups has frequently escalated to extreme violence; conservative President García Moreno was shot and killed in 1875 and liberal President Eloy Alfaro was killed and burned by a mob in Quito in 1912. The military began to take control, and the 20th century has seen as many periods of military rule as of civilian.

Ecuador's most recent period of democracy began in 1979 when President Jaime Roldos Aguilera was elected. He died in an airplane crash in 1981 and his term of office was completed by his vice president, Osvaldo Hurtado Larrea.

In 1984 the conservative León Febres Cordero was elected to the presidency. In the elections of 1988 a social democrat, Rodrigo Borja, was elected and the government leaned to the left. The following elections, in 1992, resulted in the victory of another conservative, Quiteño Sixto Durán Ballén of the Partido Unidad Republicano (Republican Unity Party). The most recent elections took place in July 1996 (see Government & Politics, below). These, like previous elections, were not easy to follow: In addition to about 15 political parties in Ecuador, there are also a number of communist, socialist and revolutionary political movements that are not officially recognized. These groups do have a certain amount of political power, which they exercise by forming alliances among the official parties.

Since the 1942 Rio de Janeiro treaty with Peru there have been numerous border incidents, some escalating into deadly battles or minor wars. These usually flare up in January, the month during which the treaty was signed. The most recent serious incidents, resulting in dozens of casualties among the armed forces on both sides, were in 1981 and 1995. The expenses of the latter war led to a government tax on all motor vehicles to help offset the costs.

Despite intense and bloody rivalry between liberals, conservatives and the military during the earlier part of this century, Ecuador has remained internally peaceful in recent years, although there are often demonstrations, marches and strikes that may occasionally shut down public transport for a day or two.

GEOGRAPHY

Ecuador is one of the world's most varied countries despite its small size, which at 283,520 sq km is about the size of either New Zealand or the US state of Nevada, or somewhat larger than either the UK or the Australian state of Victoria. Ecuador straddles the equator on the Pacific coast of South America and is bordered by only two countries: Colombia to the north and Peru to the south and east.

The country is divided into three regions. The backbone of Ecuador is the Andean range, with Chimborazo (6310 meters) its highest peak. The mountains run from north to south, splitting the country into the western coastal lowlands and the eastern jungles of the upper Amazonian basin, known in Ecuador as the Oriente. In only 200 km, as the condor flies, you can climb from the coast to snowcaps over six km above sea level, and then descend down to the steaming rainforest on the eastern side.

The central highlands are composed of two volcanic mountain ranges, about 400 km long, with a valley nestled between them. This valley was appropriately dubbed 'The Avenue of the Volcanoes' by the German explorer, Alexander von Humboldt, who visited Ecuador in 1802. Within the valley are the capital, Quito – at 2850 meters above sea level, the second highest national capital in the world after La Paz, Bolivia – and many other towns and tiny villages often of great interest to the traveler for their Indian markets and fiestas. This is the region with the highest population density in the country.

The western coastal lowlands used to be heavily forested, but most of the natural vegetation has now been destroyed for agriculture and the mangroves have been hacked out for shrimp ponds. The western provinces of Los Ríos, Manabí and El Oro are the most intensively farmed in Ecuador. The eastern lowlands of the Oriente still retain much of their virgin rainforest, but oil exploitation and colonization are beginning to seriously threaten this habitat. The population of the Oriente has more than tripled since the late 1970s.

In addition to the mainland, Ecuador owns the Galápagos Islands which also straddle the equator, about 1000 km west of the coast.

CLIMATE

Ecuador's climate follows a pattern very different from the one travelers from temperate regions are used to. Instead of the four seasons, there are wet and dry seasons, and weather patterns also vary greatly between different geographical regions.

The Galápagos and coastal areas are influenced by ocean currents. The warm equatorial countercurrent from the central Pacific causes a hot and rainy season from January through April. It doesn't rain all the time, but you can expect torrential downpours that often disrupt communications. Daytime temperatures average about 30°C (86°F), but are often much higher; this time of year is generally an unpleasant time to be traveling in the coastal regions (although it is also the time when locals hang out at the beach to cool off). From May to December both the cool Humboldt and Peru currents from the south keep temperatures a few degrees lower and it rarely rains, though it is often gray, damp and overcast, especially in July and August.

If you plan to travel in the Oriente, bring your rain gear, as it rains during most months, especially during the afternoon and evening. August and December through March are usually the driest months, and April through June are the wettest – with regional variations. It's usually almost as hot as the coast.

The dry season in the highlands is from June through September and a short dry season also occurs during the month around Christmas. It doesn't rain daily in the wet season, however. April, the wettest month, averages one rainy day in two.

El Niño

At irregular intervals of every few years, the warm central-Pacific currents of January through April are more pronounced and may flow for a longer period, causing the *El Niño* phenomenon. This is characterized by abnormally high oceanic temperatures during the coastal rainy season; much marine life (seaweed, fishes) is unable to survive. This in turn creates problems for other species – ranging from marine iguanas to seabirds to human beings – that rely on the marine life as food.

A particularly extreme El Niño occurred from late 1982 through early 1983, causing severe problems for the wildlife of the Galápagos Islands and for the coastal fishing industry.

The climatological phenomenon is named El Niño (the baby boy) because it usually gets underway at year's end, or about the time the Christ child was born.

El Niño, for all its disruptiveness, is still far from being fully understood by climatologists. However, the US National Oceanographic and Atmospheric Administration (NOAA) now posts a website explaining what is known about the El Niño phenomenon and making some attempt at forecasting future events. Readers with Internet access can contact: http://www.pmel.noaa.gov/toga-tao/el-nino/home.html. ■

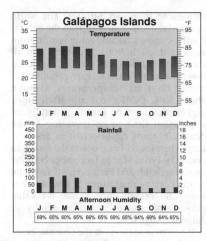

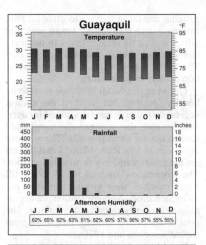

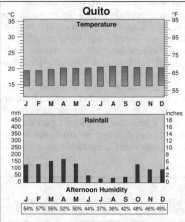

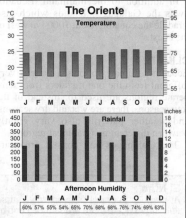

Daytime temperatures average a high of 20°C to 22°C (68°F to 72°F) and a low of 7°C to 8°C (45°F to 48°F) year round, though you should expect more extreme variations on occasion. These figures are based on climatic data from Quito.

Despite all these statistics, you should remember the Ecuadorian adage that they can experience all four seasons in one day. Without a doubt, the most predictable aspect of the weather in Ecuador is its unpredictability.

ECOLOGY & ENVIRONMENT

Deforestation is Ecuador's most severe environmental problem in all three of its major physiographic regions – the western coastal lowlands, the central Andean highlands and the eastern Amazonian lowlands.

In the highlands almost all of the natural forest cover has disappeared – only a few pockets remain protected, mainly in private nature reserves. Along the coast the once-plentiful mangrove forests have all but vanished, too. These harbor a great diversity of marine and shore life but have been cut down in order to make artificial ponds in which shrimp are reared for export.

About 95% of the forests of the western slopes and lowlands have disappeared to become agricultural land, with banana plantations accounting for much of this. The ecological importance of this area has only recently been identified. The western lowlands harbor a greater number of different species than almost anywhere on the planet and a large number of these are endemic (found nowhere else on earth). Countless species have become extinct even before they have been identified; an effort is now being made to conserve what little there is left in both private and national reserves. Some observers estimate that the remaining western forests will disappear by the first decade of the 21st century unless a concerted effort is made to preserve them.

Although much of the rainforest in the Ecuadorian Amazon remains standing, it is seriously threatened by fragmentation. Since the discovery of oil, roads have been built into the area, colonists have followed and the destruction of the forest has increased exponentially. The main drive behind the destruction is logging for short-term timber sales, followed by cattle ranching.

Clearly, these problems are linked very tightly with Ecuador's economy. Oil, bananas and shrimp are the nation's top three exports, between them accounting for about two-thirds of the value of Ecuador's exports. However, the serious environmental damage caused by the production of these and other products requires that their value be carefully examined. All of these products are subject to the whims of world markets and volatile economic pressures. Oil reserves are not expected to last more than a few decades. Banana crops could be wiped out by catastrophic diseases or climatic factors.

Apart from the direct loss of tropical forest and the plants and animals that depend on it (see the sidebar Why Conserve the Rainforest?), deforestation also leads to severe degradation in other ways. The loss of forest cover leads to erosion of the soil, which is then washed into rivers. The increased amount of silt in the rivers make them less able to support microorganisms and this effects the rest of the food chain.

Attempts to combat erosion and desertification using artificial fertilizers also contribute to the pollution of rivers, as do oil spills in the rainforest. Many indigenous inhabitants of the rainforest use the rivers as an essential source of drinking water and food, and their livelihoods are directly threatened by these and other pollutants. Unfortunately, government policies allow oil exploration and encourage colonization and clearing of the land, with little regard for the forests, rivers, wildlife or people living there.

Other water-related problems are caused by poorly regulated and improper mining in the coastal areas and inadequate sewage disposal facilities in the major cities.

Despite the environmental problems outlined above, Ecuador's beautiful and often unique scenery and wildlife, combined with fascinating people – particularly the Indians of the highlands – attract hundreds of thousands of international visitors annually. This makes tourism the country's fourth or fifth (depending on which statistics you want to follow) most important source of revenue. The tourist industry is aware of the potential problems of uncontrolled tourism and various successful efforts have been made to benefit from the industry while controlling potential damage.

In the ever-popular Galápagos Islands, for example, attempts to build large resort hotels have been averted and all visitors are accompanied by trained guides. On the mainland, various ecotourism operations provide lodge accommodations and guides in areas of forest that are then protected. In 1990 the Asociación Ecuatoriana de Ecoturismo (ASEC) was founded and officially recognized by the government in 1992. Today, several dozen travel agencies, outfitters and hotel and lodge operators are members of ASEC and work to sustainably

Why Conserve the Rainforest?

The loss of tropical forests is a problem that has become acute in recent years. Deforestation is happening at such a rate that most of the world's tropical forests will have disappeared by early in the 21st century; loss of other habitats is a less publicized, but equally pressing concern. With this in mind, two important questions arise: why are habitats such as the tropical rainforests so important, and what can be done to prevent their loss?

Much of Ecuador's remaining natural vegetation is tropical forest and there are many reasons why this particular ecosystem is important. Roughly half of the 1.6 million known species on earth live in tropical rainforests such as those found in Parque Nacional Yasuní (see the Northern Oriente chapter). Scientists predict that millions more life forms remain to be discovered, principally in the world's remaining rainforests which have the greatest biodiversity (numbers of different species) of all the habitats known on the planet. This incredible array of plants, animals and insects cannot exist unless the rainforest that they inhabit is protected – deforestation results not only in the loss of the rainforest, but in countless extinctions as well.

The value of tropical plants is more than simply providing habitat and food for animals, and it is more than the esthetic value of the plants themselves. Many types of medicines have been extracted from forest trees, shrubs and flowers. These range from anesthetics to antibiotics, from contraceptives to cures for heart disease, malaria and various other illnesses. Countless medicinal uses of plants are known only to the indigenous inhabitants of the forest. Much of this knowledge is lost as the various indigenous cultures are assimilated into the Western way of life, or when tribal groups are destroyed by disease or genocide. Undoubtedly, other pharmaceutical treasures remain locked up in tropical forests, unknown to anybody; they may never be discovered if the forests are destroyed.

Many tropical crops are monocultures that suffer from a lack of genetic diversity. In other words, as agriculturalists breed strains that are high yielding, easy to harvest, taste good, etc, the plants they produce become genetically almost identical. If these monocultures are attacked by a new disease or pest epidemic they may be wiped out if resistant strains have been bred out of the population. Plants such as bananas (Ecuador's most economically important agricultural product) are also found in the wild in tropical forests. In the event of an epidemic scientists could seek out disease-resistant wild strains to breed into the commercially raised crops. Deforestation leads not only to species extinction, but also to loss of the genetic diversity which may help species adapt to a changing world.

While biodiversity for esthetic, medicinal and genetic reasons may be important to us, the survival of tropical rainforests is even more important to the indigenous peoples who live within them. In Ecuador there are Huaorani, Shuar, Cofan, Secoya, Cayapa and other Indian groups still living in a more or less traditional manner. These tribes rely on the rainforest to maintain their cultural identity and a way of life that has lasted for centuries. Accelerated deforestation has led to the demise of tribal groups, their traditional cultures being

and responsibly develop the industry both within their own operations and through public education and political pressure.

Further information is available from Oswaldo Muñoz, the English-speaking president of ASEC, at: La Asociación Ecuatoriana de Ecoturismo, Amazonas 2468, 2nd floor, PO Box 402-A, Quito (☎ 552 617, fax 565 261).

FLORA & FAUNA

Part of the reason that Ecuador is among the most species-rich nations on the globe is that it is a tropical country. Scientists have for many years realized that the tropics harbor a much greater diversity of living organisms than do more temperate countries, but the reasons for this variation are still a matter of debate and research. The most commonly held belief is that the tropics acted as a refuge for plants and animals during the many ice ages affecting more temperate regions – the much longer and relatively stable climatic history of the tropics has enabled speciation to occur. This may well be part of the answer, but lost to modernity. They are as unable to survive in a Western world as we would be if forced to survive in the jungle.

Rainforests are important on a global scale because they moderate climatic patterns worldwide. Scientists have recently determined that the destruction of rainforests is a major contributing factor to global warming, which will, if left unchecked, lead to disastrous changes to our world. These changes include melting of ice caps causing rising ocean levels and flooding of major coastal cities, many of which are only a scant few meters above present sea level. Global warming would also make many of the world's 'breadbasket' regions unsuitable for crop production.

While these are all good reasons for the rainforest and other habitats to be preserved and protected, the reality of the economic importance of their utilization by the developing nations that own the forests must also be considered. It is undeniably true that rainforests provide resources in the way of lumber, pasture land and possible mineral wealth, but this is a short-sighted view.

The long term importance of the rainforest – both from a global view and as a resource of biodiversity, genetic variation and pharmaceutical wealth – is recognized both by the countries that contain forest as well as by the other nations of the world that will be effected by their destruction. Efforts are now underway to show that the economic value of the standing rainforest is greater than wealth realized by deforestation.

One important way of making a tropical forest an economically productive resource without cutting it down is by protecting it in national parks and reserves and making it accessible to tourists and travelers from all over the world. This type of ecotourism is becoming increasingly important for the economy of Ecuador and other nations with similar natural resources.

More people are likely to visit Ecuador to see monkeys in the forest than to see cows on pasture. The visitors spend money on hotels, transport, tours, food and souvenirs. In addition, many people who spend time in the tropics become more understanding of the natural beauty within the forests and of the importance of preserving them. As a result, visitors return home and become goodwill ambassadors for tropical forests.

Other innovative projects for sustainable development of tropical forests are being organized. Conservation International has developed the sustainable harvesting of the tagua nut – this rainforest product is as hard as ivory and is being used to carve souvenir ornaments and even to make buttons for North American clothing manufacturers. Brazil nuts are harvested for 'Rainforest Crunch' snack products. 'Debt for nature' swaps have been initiated by conservation organizations (see Conservation, below). Iguana farms, orchid plantations, wicker work from aerial roots and harvesting seeds of ornamental plants are some of the other projects that are being explored. Whatever the methods used to preserve the rainforests, it is essential that the forests are protected. ∎

ecologists offer various other more technical theories.

A better understood reason for Ecuador's biodiversity is simply that there are a great number of different habitats within the borders of this small country. Obviously, the cold, high Andes will support very different species from the low tropical rainforests, and when all the intermediate habitats are included and the coastal areas added, the result is a wealth of habitats, ecosystems and wildlife. Ecologists have labeled Ecuador as one of the world's 'megadiversity hotspots.' This has attracted increasing numbers of nature lovers from all over the world.

Habitats

Ecologists use a system called Holdridge Life Zones, presented by LR Holdridge in 1947, to classify the type of vegetation found in a given area. Climatic data such as temperature, rainfall and their variation throughout the year are analyzed and combined with information on latitudinal regions and altitudinal belts to give roughly 116 life zones on earth. Some two dozen tropical life zones are found in Ecuador. These are often named according to forest type and altitude, and so there are dry, moist, wet and rain forests in tropical, premontane, lower montane, montane and subalpine areas. Within each life zone several types of habitat may occur. Thus Ecuador has many habitats, each with particular associations of plants and animals. Some of the most important or interesting are described here.

The coastal lowlands have a variety of habitats, of which one of the most remarkable is **mangrove swamp**. Mangroves are trees that have evolved the remarkable ability to grow in salt water. The red mangrove is the most common in Ecuador and, like other mangroves, has a broadly spreading system of intertwining stilt roots to support the tree in the unstable sandy or silty soils of the shoreline.

Mangroves form forests and are good colonizing species – their stilt roots trap sediments and build up a rich organic soil which in turn supports other plants. In between the roots, a protected habitat is provided for many types of fish, as well as mollusks, crustaceans and many other invertebrates. The branches provide nesting areas for a variety of seabirds, such as pelicans, frigatebirds and others. Mangroves are found primarily in the far northern and southern coastal regions of the country – the shrimp industry has extensively destroyed the mangroves on most of Ecuador's coastline, endangering the breeding grounds of many species. (See also The Mangroves of Muisne in the North Coast chapter.)

Another fast-disappearing habitat, the **tropical dry forest**, is found in hot areas with well-defined wet and dry seasons, as on the coast. Tropical dry forest trees lose their leaves during the dry season and tend to grow in a less concentrated pattern than those in the rainforest, creating a more open habitat. It is estimated that only about 1% of tropical dry forest remains undisturbed. The best and only extensive example in Ecuador is found on the central Pacific

coast in Parque Nacional Machalilla, and tropical dry forest is further described in that section.

In remote valleys at higher elevations, **tropical cloud forests** are found – one of the least known types of tropical forest. They are so named because they trap (and help create) clouds which drench the forest in a fine mist, allowing some particularly delicate forms of plant life to survive. Cloud forest trees are adapted to steep rocky soils and a harsh climate. They have a characteristic low, gnarled growth; dense, small-leaved canopies and moss-covered branches supporting a host of plants, such as orchids, ferns, bromeliads and many others. These aerial plants, which gather their moisture and some nutrients without ground roots, are collectively termed epiphytes.

The dense vegetation at all levels of this forest gives it a mysterious and delicate fairy-tale appearance. It is the home of such rare species as the woolly tapir, Andean spectacled bear and puma. This habitat is particularly important as a source of fresh water and to control erosion.

Above these forests lies the *páramo*, or high-altitude grass- and shrubland. This is the natural 'sponge' of the Andes – it catches and gradually releases much of the water that is eventually used by city dwellers in the highlands. The páramo covers over 10% of Ecuador's land area and is characterized by a harsh climate, high levels of ultraviolet (UV) light and wet peaty soils. It is a highly specialized highland habitat unique to the neotropics (tropical America), and found only from the highlands of Costa Rica at 10°N to northern Peru at 10°S. Similarly elevated grasslands in other parts of the world differ in their climates and evolutionary history, and have different assemblages of plants and animals.

The páramo has a fairly limited flora dominated by hard grasses, cushion plants and small herbaceous plants. These have adapted well to the harsh environment and consequently the vegetation looks strange and interesting. Major adaptations include the development of small, thick leaves which are less susceptible to frost; the development of curved leaves with heavy, waxy skins to reflect extreme solar radiation during cloudless days; the growth of a fine, hairy down as insulation on the plant's surface; the arrangement of leaves into a rosette to prevent them shading one another during photosynthesis and to protect the delicate center of the plant; and the compacting of the plant so it grows close to the ground where the temperature is more constant and the wind less strong. Thus many páramo plants are characteristically small and compact, sometimes resembling a hard, waxy, green carpet.

Not all páramo plants are so compacted, however. The giant *Espeletia*, members of the daisy family, are a weird sight as their loosely arranged stands float into view in a typical páramo mist. They are as high as a person, hence the local nickname of *frailejones*, meaning 'gray friars.' They are an unmistakable feature of the northern Ecuadorian páramo, particularly in the El Angel region near Tulcán. Further south, the páramo becomes rather drier and the bromeliads called *puyas* are found – plants with a rosette of spiky leaves growing out of a short trunk.

Another attractive plant of the central and southern Ecuadorian páramo is the *chuquiragua*, which resembles a thistle topped with orange flower heads and with stems densely covered with tough, spiky leaves. This plant has medicinal properties and is used locally to soothe coughs, and to treat liver and kidney infections.

The páramo is also characterized by dense thickets of small trees. These are often *Polylepis* species, or *quinua* in Quichua, members of the rose family. With the Himalayan pines, they share the world altitudinal record for trees. They were once considerably more extensive, but fire and grazing have pushed them back into small pockets. Instead, grasses are more common. A spiky, resistant tussock grass, locally called *ichu*, is commonly encountered. It grows in large clumps and makes walking uncomfortable.

Over half a million Ecuadorians live on the páramo, so it is of considerable importance to the inter-Andean economy. It has been used for growing a large variety of potatoes and other tubers for centuries, while the great increase in cattle grazing is a more recent phenomenon.

In order to manage the land for cattle, burning is carried out to encourage the growth of succulent young shoots. This does not favor older growth and, combined with erosion caused by overgrazing, poses considerable threats to this fragile habitat.

Of all the tropical habitats found in Ecuador, it is the **rainforest** that seems to attract the most attention from visitors.

A walk through a tropical forest shows that it is very different from the temperate forests that many North Americans or Europeans may be used to. Temperate forests, such as the coniferous forests of the far north or the deciduous woodlands of milder regions, tend to have little variety. It's pines, pines and more pines, or interminable acres of oaks, beech and birch. Tropical forests, on the other hand, have great variety. If you stand in one spot and look around, you see scores of different species of trees, and you often have to walk several hundred meters to find another example of any particular species.

Visitors to the rainforest are often bewildered by the huge variety of plants and animals found there. With the exception of those for mammals and birds, there are few useful field guides to what there is to be seen. For this reason, it is worth investing in a guided natural-history tour if you are particularly interested in learning about the fantastic flora and fauna – not that any guide will be able to answer all your questions!

One thing that often astounds visitors is the sheer immensity of some trees. A good example is the ceiba tree (also called the kapok), with huge flattened supports, or buttresses, around its base, which may easily reach five or more meters across. The smooth gray trunk often grows straight up for 50 meters before the branches begin. These spread out into a huge crown with a slightly flattened appearance; the shape is distinctive and the tree is often the last to be logged in a ranching area. When you see a huge, buttressed, flattened-looking tree in a pasture in the Amazonian lowlands, very often it is a ceiba. This is also one of the few trees in the rainforest to shed its leaves, which it does before flowering to enable the wind to better distribute the pollen. Most other trees in the rainforest are pollinated by animals and don't need to shed their leaves to allow the wind to do the job.

Some rainforest trees have strange roots looking like props or stilts supporting them. These trees are most frequently found in rainforest that is periodically flooded – the stilt roots are thought to play a role in keeping the tree upright during the inundations. Various types of trees use this technique – in the Oriente, palms are often supported by this kind of root system; on the coast look for mangroves with stilt roots.

In areas that have been cleared – often naturally, as by a flash flood which may remove the trees on the riverbanks, or simply by an ancient forest giant falling during a storm – various fast-growing pioneer species appear. These may grow several meters a year in areas where abundant sunlight is suddenly available. Some of the most common and easily recognized of these are in the genus *Cecropia*, which has a number of species. Their gray trunks are often circled by ridges at intervals of a few centimeters, but are otherwise fairly smooth, and their branches tend to form a canopy at the top of, rather than all along, the trunk. The leaves are very large and palmate (like a human hand with spread fingers), with the underside a much lighter green than the top surface. This is particularly noticeable when strong winds make the leaves display alternately light and dark green shades in a chaotic manner.

These are just a few of the most common sights in the forest. The incredible variety of plants is correlated with the high biodiversity of the animals which live within the forests. Terry Erwin of the Smithsonian Institution has spent much time in Amazonian rainforests and reports that 3000 species of beetles were found in five different areas of rainforest – but each area was only 12 meters square! Erwin estimates that each species of tree in the rainforest supports over 400 unique species of animals. Given the thousands of known tree species, this means that there are millions of species of animals living in the rainforest, many of them insects and most unknown to science. These complex interrelationships and high biodiversity are among the reasons why many people are calling for a halt to the destruction of tropical forests. Despite this, Ecuador has one of the highest rates of deforestation in South America (see Why Conserve the Rainforest?, above).

Plants

There are about 25,000 species of vascular plants in Ecuador, and new species are being discovered every year. This number is exceptionally high when compared to the 17,000 species found in the entire North American continent. An introduction to some of the most common plants of Ecuador is given in Habitats, above.

Birds

Birdwatchers from all over the world come to Ecuador because of the great number of species recorded here – over 1500, or approximately twice the number found in any one of the continents of North America, Europe or Australia. The South American continent has almost 3000 species of birds, although it is impossible to give a precise number for either the continent or the countries within it. Noted ornithologist Robert Ridgely is working on a field guide to the birds of Ecuador; he estimates that several species are added to the Ecuadorian list every year. Paul Greenfield, the Quito-based artist and ornithologist who is illustrating Ridgely's forthcoming guide, recently reported 1550 species for the country.

Most birds added to the Ecuadorian list are already known from other South American countries. Occasionally, however, a species new to science is discovered – a very rare event in the world of birds. The most recent Ecuadorian bird to be discovered, described, scientifically named and accepted by the ornithological community is the El Oro parakeet *(Pyrrhura orcesi)*. This bird was discovered west of Piñas in El Oro Province by Ridgely, Greenfield and Rose Anne Rowlett in 1980 (it takes years for the full process from discovery to acceptance to occur). The zigzag heron, one of the world's rarest herons, was found nesting near La Selva Jungle Lodge (see the Northern Oriente chapter) in 1984 and 1990, which were the first nesting records of that species in Ecuador. This heron continues to be seen near La Selva and some 500 other species have been recorded in this small area alone. It is likely that other bird species exist in Ecuador that have never been described by scientists.

Many visitors are less interested in observing a newly described species and are more interested in seeing the birds typical of Ecuador. One of these is the Andean condor, often called the largest flying bird in the world. With its three-meter wingspan and 10-kg weight, it is certainly magnificent. In 1880 the British mountaineer Edward Whymper noted that he commonly saw a dozen on the wing at the same time. Today there are only a few hundred pairs left in the highlands. I have seen condors only half a dozen times in several years of travel in Ecuador, so you shouldn't expect to see them very frequently. Condors are best recognized by their flat, gliding flight with fingered wing tips (formed by spread primary feathers), silvery patches on the upper wing surface (best seen when the bird wheels in the sun) and a white neck ruff and unfeathered, pinkish head. Otherwise the bird is black.

Other birds of the highlands include the carunculated caracara, a large member of the falcon family. It has bright orange-red facial skin, yellowish bill and legs, white thighs and underparts and is otherwise black. This bird is often seen in the páramos of Parque Nacional Cotopaxi (see the South of Quito chapter). Also frequently sighted here is the Andean lapwing, unmistakable with its harsh and noisy call, reddish eyes, legs and bill, and brown/white/black striped wing pattern particularly noticeable in flight.

Most towns, both in the highlands and the lowlands, are host to the ubiquitous rufous-collared sparrow. The well-known house sparrow of Europe, Asia, Australia and North America is a rarely seen recent arrival in South America. Instead, the similarly sized rufous-collared sparrow, readily identified by the chestnut collar on the back of the neck, takes the place of the house sparrow in Ecuador and most of the continent.

For many visitors, the diminutive hummingbirds are the most delightful birds to observe. About 120 species have been recorded from Ecuador, and their exquisite beauty is matched by extravagant names such as green-tailed goldenthroat, spangled coquette, fawn-breasted brilliant and amethyst-throated sunangel, to name a few.

Hummingbirds beat their wings in a figure-eight pattern up to 80 times per second, thus producing the hum for which they are named. This exceptionally rapid wingbeat enables them to hover in place when feeding on nectar, or even to fly backwards. These tiny birds must feed frequently to gain the energy needed to keep them flying. Species like the Andean hillstar, living in the páramo, have evolved an amazing strategy to survive a cold night; they go into a state of torpor – like a nightly hibernation – by lowering their body temperature by about 25°C, thus lowering their metabolism drastically.

For visitors interested in birds, a trip to the Galápagos Islands is very rewarding. This is partly because about half of the 58 resident species are endemic to the islands. Also, most of the Galápagos birds have either lost, or not evolved, a fear of human visitors. Therefore travelers can walk among colonies of blue-footed boobies or magnificent frigatebirds without causing them to fly off.

Some other exciting birds (on the mainland) include brightly colored blue-and-yellow macaws and 44 other parrot species;

19 different toucans with their incredibly large and hollow bills; the huge and very rare harpy eagle that is capable of snatching monkeys and sloths off branches as it flies past; and a large array of other tropical birds such as flycatchers (167 species), tanagers (133 species), antbirds (110 species) and cotingas (43 species).

Mammals

Mammals, too, are well represented with some 300 species recorded in the country. These vary from monkeys in the Amazonian lowlands to the rare Andean spectacled bear in the highlands. The most diverse mammals are the bats, with well over 100 species in Ecuador alone.

Visitors to protected areas of the Amazonian lowlands may see one or more of the several species of monkeys found in Ecuador, including the howler, spider, woolly, titi, capuchin and squirrel monkeys, as well as tamarins and marmosets. The monkeys of the new world (the Platyrrhini) differ markedly from the monkeys of the old world, including ourselves (the Catarrhini). New world monkeys have, comparatively, been little studied and their names are still under constant study and revision.

The male howler monkeys are heard as often as they are seen; their eerie vocalizations carry long distances and have been likened to a baby crying or the wind moaning through the trees. Many visitors are unable to believe they are hearing a monkey when they first listen to the mournful sound.

Other tropical specialties include two species of sloths. The diurnal three-toed sloth is quite often sighted, whereas the two-toed sloth is nocturnal and therefore rarely seen. Sloths are often found hanging motionless from tree limbs, or progressing at a painfully slow speed along a branch towards a particularly succulent bunch of leaves, which are their primary food source. Leaf digestion takes several days and sloths defecate about once a week.

Mammals commonly seen in the highlands include deer, rabbits and squirrels.

Toilet Habits of Sloths

Sloths are most fastidious with their toilet habits, always climbing down from their tree to deposit their weekly bowel movement on the ground. Biologists do not know why sloths do this; one suggested hypothesis is that by consistently defecating at the base of a particular tree, the sloths provide a natural fertilizer that increases the quality of the leaves of that tree, thus improving the sloth's diet. ■

Foxes are also occasionally sighted. There are far fewer species of mammals in the highlands than in the lowlands. The mammals most commonly associated with the Andes are the cameloids – the llamas, alpacas, guanacos and vicuñas. Of these, only the llama lives in Ecuador, and in far fewer numbers than in Peru or Bolivia. Nevertheless, llamas can even be seen occasionally on the outskirts of Quito, and there is a huge experimental flock near the entrance of Parque Nacional Cotopaxi. Llamas are exclusively domesticated and are used primarily as pack animals, although their skin and meat is occasionally used in remote areas.

Other possible mammal sightings include anteaters, armadillos, agoutis (large rodents), capybaras (even larger rodents, some weighing up to 65 kg), peccaries (wild pigs) and otters. River dolphins are occasionally sighted on Amazonian tributaries. Other exotic mammals such as ocelots, jaguars, tapirs, pumas and spectacled bears are very rarely seen.

Insects

Many thousands of species of insects have been described from Ecuador; undoubtedly, many thousands more remain undiscovered.

Butterflies, of which there are some 4500 species, are among the first insects that the visitor to the tropics notices. Perhaps the most dazzling butterflies are the morphos. With their 15-cm wingspan and electric blue upper wings, they lazily flap and glide along tropical rivers in a shimmering display. When they land, however, their wings close and only the brown underwings are visible. In an instant they have changed from outrageous flaunting to a modest camouflage.

Camouflage plays an important part of many insects' lives. Some resting butterflies look exactly like green or brown leaves, others like the scaly bark of the tree on which they are resting. Caterpillars are often masters of disguise. Some species mimic twigs, another is capable of constricting certain muscles to make itself look like the head of a viper, and yet another species looks so much like bird droppings that it rarely gets attacked by predators.

Any walk through a tropical forest will almost invariably allow the observer to study many different types of ants. Among my favorites are the *Atta* leaf cutter ants, which can be seen marching in columns along the forest floor, carrying pieces of leaves like little parasols above their heads. The leaf segments are taken into the ants' underground colony and there the leaves are allowed to rot down into a mulch. The ants tend their mulch gardens carefully, and allow a certain species of fungus to grow there. The fruiting bodies of the fungus are then used to feed the colony, which can exceed a million ants. The fungus has lost its ability to reproduce itself and relies on the ants to propagate it, which they do by taking some fungus with them when they start a new nest.

Other insect species are so tiny as to be barely visible, yet their lifestyles are no less esoteric. The hummingbird flower mites are barely half a millimeter in length, and live in flowers visited by hummingbirds. When the flowers are visited by the hummers, the mites scuttle up into the birds' nostrils and use this novel form of air transport to disperse themselves to other plants. Smaller still are mites which live on the proboscis of the morpho butterflies.

From the largest to the smallest insects – there is a world of wonder to be discovered in the tropical forests.

Amphibians & Reptiles

These creatures form a fascinating part of the Ecuadorian fauna. The approximately 360 species of amphibians include tree frogs that spend their entire life cycle in trees. Some of them have solved the problem of where to lay their eggs by doing so into the water trapped in cup-like plants called bromeliads, which live high up in the forest canopy.

Perhaps more bizarre still are the marsupial frogs. The females carry their eggs in pouches under their skins – sometimes 200 or more at a time. The eggs are pushed into the pouches by the male immediately after fertilization. Hatching occurs in the pouches and the tadpoles eventually emerge from under their mother's skin.

Dendrobatids, better known by their colloquial name of poison-arrow frogs, are among the most brightly colored of frogs. Some are bright red with black dots, others red with blue legs and still others are bright green with black markings. Some species have skin glands exuding toxins that can cause paralysis and death in many animals, including humans. It is well known that dendrobatids have long been used by Latin American forest Indians to provide a poison with which to dip the tips of their hunting arrows. It should be mentioned that the toxins are most effective when introduced into the blood stream (as with arrows), but have comparatively little effect when a frog is casually touched.

There are nearly 350 species of reptiles recorded in Ecuador, which is about 100 more than are found in the whole of North America. Snakes – much talked about but seldom seen – make up roughly half of Ecuador's reptiles. Snakes usually slither away into the undergrowth when they sense that people are coming, so only a few fortunate visitors are able to catch a glimpse of one. Perhaps Ecuador's most feared snake is the fer-de-lance, which is very poisonous and sometimes fatal to humans. It often lives in overgrown, brushy fields, so the gricultural workers clearing these fields are the most frequent victims. Tourists are rarely bitten.

Fish

Recent inventories of Amazonian fish have shown surprisingly high biodiversity. There are about 2500 species in the whole Amazon basin, and roughly 1000 species in Ecuador. Some of these are fearsome and feared. The electric eel can produce shocks of 600 volts; a school of piranha can devour a large animal in minutes; stingrays can deliver a crippling sting; and the tiny candirú catfish can swim up the human urethra and become lodged there by erecting its sharp spines. Despite these horror stories, most Amazonian rivers are safe to swim in. Follow the example of the locals:

Shuffle your feet as you enter the water to scare off the bottom-dwelling stingrays; wear a bathing suit to avoid having a candirú swim up your urethra; and don't swim with open, bleeding cuts or in areas where fish are being cleaned – piranhas are attracted to blood and guts.

National Parks

Ecuador's first *parque nacional* (national park) was the Galápagos, formed in 1959, but it was not until the mid to late 1970s that a comprehensive national park system began to be established on the mainland. The first mainland park was

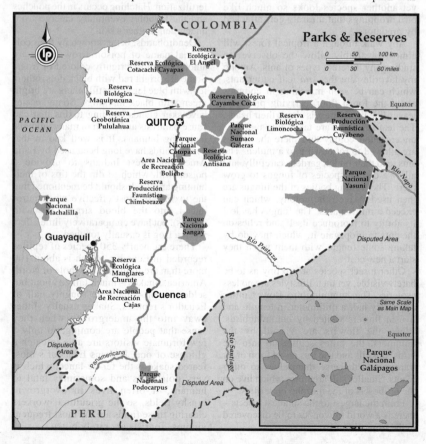

Cotopaxi, established in 1975, followed by Machalilla, Yasuní and Sangay in 1979, and Podocarpus in 1982. The Sumaco Galeras forest reserve was elevated to national park status in the early 1990s. Apart from these seven national parks, there are nine *reservas* (reserves) of various kinds, about half of which were created in 1979, and a few national monuments and recreation areas. New reserves are added every few years. In addition, local conservation organizations, such as the Fundación Natura, the Jatun Sacha Foundation and others, have begun to set aside private nature reserves.

Together, these areas cover almost 16% of the national territory. All of Ecuador's major ecosystems are partly protected in one (or more) of these areas.

The national parks do not have the tourist infrastructure that one may be used to in other parts of the world. There are almost no hostels, drive-in campgrounds, restaurants, ranger stations, museums, scenic overlooks or information centers. Many are inhabited by native peoples who had been living in the area for generations before the area achieved park or reserve status. Some of the parks and reserves are remote, difficult to reach and lack almost all facilities.

Nevertheless, the adventurous traveler can visit most of them and details are given in the appropriate sections of this book. Entrance fees vary, with Ecuadorians paying only a small fraction of the fee charged to foreign visitors. On the mainland, most highland parks charge US$10 and most lowland parks charge US$20 per visitor, but these fees are valid for a week and allow in-and-out privileges. In the Galápagos Islands, the park fee is US$80 (plus another US$30 that goes to the island towns). These are all official rates, but, as of this writing, if you pay in sucres you'll save roughly 20% in some mainland parks – a disparity that may change by the time you read this. In the Galápagos, you must pay in US dollars.

Some of the funds are used to better protect the parks by paying for and equipping park rangers and so forth. All of these

areas are susceptible to interests that are incompatible with full protection: oil drilling, logging, mining, ranching and colonization. Despite this, the national parks do preserve large tracts of pristine habitat and many travelers visit at least one park or reserve during their stay in Ecuador.

The national park system is administered by *Instituto Ecuatoriano Forestal y de Areas Naturales y Vida Silvestre* (INEFAN; or the Ecuadorian Institute of Forestry, Natural Areas and Wildlife), which is part of *Ministerio de Agricultura y Ganadería* (MAG; or the Ministry of Agriculture and Ranching). The head office of INEFAN (☎ 548 924) is at Ministerio de Agricultura y Ganadería, 8th floor, Amazonas y Eloy Alfaro, in Quito. Unfortunately, MAG is unable to properly protect the national park system. Oil has been removed from the Reserva de Producción Faunísta Cuyabeno for several years and, in 1991, the government gave permission to Conoco to begin oil exploration in Parque Nacional Yasuní. Because of protests from all over the world, Conoco sold its oil concessions to MAXUS, an international company, which is continuing with oil exploration and extraction. Continued pressure on this company has caused it to at least moderate some of the worst and most environmentally damaging extraction techniques.

Conservation

Various international agencies such as Conservation International, The Nature Conservancy, Natural Resources Defense Council, the World Wildlife Fund and World Wide Fund for Nature have provided much needed expertise and economic support. They developed programs such as the 'debt for nature' swaps whereby parts of Ecuador's national debt was paid off in return for local groups receiving Ecuadorian funds for preserving crucial habitats. These swaps are not as popular or as successful as they used to be, and the focus of conservation work nowadays is financial support to train and equip local park rangers, educate the population, fund research and develop low-impact and sustainable practices such as responsible tourism.

By far the biggest environmental NGO (non-government organization) within Ecuador is the Fundación Natura. In the absence of a specific government department for the environment, the Fundación has been most involved in improving the system of protected areas in the country and has developed its own cloud forest reserve, Pasochoa, near Quito. The Fundación also has a large environmental education program and arranges campaigns on specific conservation issues. Because it is Ecuador's biggest and best known NGO, it tends to receive a large share of international funding and has been criticized by smaller, grassroots NGOs as having a top-heavy bureaucracy.

Local conservation groups have blossomed since the late 1980s. Groups on the coast are particularly concerned with the protection of the mangrove forests and have been forging cooperative links with shell and crab collectors who are being affected by mangrove destruction. Some groups have been quite successful in providing legal protection for these forests. Other groups have concentrated on improving environmental data collection and training members in the disciplines needed to create a strong information base for national conservation research.

The Amazon region has been an important focus for small NGOs in recent years. They focus not only on the environment, but also on the protection of the rights of indigenous inhabitants. In the mid-1990s, organizations protecting the fast-diminishing and unique forests on the western slopes of the Ecuadorian Andes have become important.

Several small groups have been established to protect specific natural areas. These groups then go on to involve communities around these reserves through environmental education, agroforestry and community development projects. Such community involvement at the grassroots level is essential for viable conservation in Ecuador.

The role of indigenous organizations should also be recognized as an effective voice in environmental protection. The struggle they have been engaged in to secure land rights, particularly in the Amazon regions, has gone a long way to secure the future of the tropical forests in that area.

In the Galápagos Islands, the Charles Darwin Foundation is a long-established and tireless protector of the archipelago. Conservation, scientific research and education of both local people and international visitors are among its main goals.

Most of these organizations rely on support from the public. Even large entities such as the World Wildlife Fund receive the bulk of their income not from government agencies or corporate contributions, but from individual members. The Nature Conservancy, for example, reports that 78.7% of its 1990 revenue came from individual members. The vital work of these and other agencies requires every assistance possible. Ecuadorian conservation groups are particularly in need of assistance. If you visit Ecuador and would like to help conserve it, please obtain further information from and contribute whatever you can to the following addresses. These are a selection of the best known organizations. Other, more local ones are listed in the text.

Acción Ecológica
    Calle Lérida 407 and Pontevedra, Quito
    (☎ 542 182, ☎ /fax 547 516)
Charles Darwin Foundation
    6 de Diciembre 4757, PO Box 17-01389,
    Quito (☎ 244 803, fax 443 935, see also
    Online Services)
    100 N Washington St, Suite 311,
    Falls Church, VA 22046, USA
    (☎ (703) 538 6833, fax 538 6835)
Consejo Ecuatoriano para Conservación y
Investigación de Aves
    Avenida de los Shyris 2030, PO Box
    17-17906, Quito (☎ /fax 468 876)
Conservation International
    1015 18th St NW, Suite 1000,
    Washington DC 20036, USA
    (☎ (202) 429 5660, fax 887 0193)
EcoCiencia
    Tamayo 1339 and Colón, PO Box 17-
    12257, Quito (☎ 526 802, 548 752)

Top: Giant Tropical Snail, Western Lowlands (RR)
Left: Scarlet Macaw (RR)
Right: Lorenzo Criollo in traditional Cofan regalia (RR)

Top: Miguel Andrango of Tahuantinsuyo Weaving Workshop, Agato, near Otavalo (RR)

Bottom: Beads for sale at Otavalo Market (RR)

Fundación Ecuatoriana de Mamíferos Marinos
    Vélez 991, 5th floor, Guayaquil (☎ 524 608)
Fundación Jatun Sacha
    Río Coca 1734, PO Box 17-12867, Quito
    (☎ /fax 441 592, see also Online Services)
Fundación Maquipucuna
    Baquerizo 238 y Tamayo, PO Box 17-
    12167, Quito (☎ 507 200/1, fax 504 571)
Fundación Natura
    Avenida América 5653 and Voz Andes,
    PO Box 17-01253, Quito
    (☎ 447 341/2/3/4, fax 434 449)
    Sarmiento 188 and Portete, Quito
    (☎ 246 072, 443 026)
Galápagos Conservation Trust
    PO Box 50, Shaftesbury,
    Dorset SP7 8SB, UK
International Union for the Conservation of
Nature and Natural Resources
    Atahualpa 955 y República, 4th floor, Quito
    Avenue Mont Blanc, 1196 Gland,
    Switzerland
Nature Conservancy, The
    Latin America Division, 1815 N Lynn St,
    Arlington, VA 22209, USA
    (☎ (703) 841 2711, fax 841 1283)
World Wildlife Fund
    1250 24th Street NW,
    Washington DC 20037, USA
    (☎ (202) 293 4800, fax 293 9211)
    Panda House, Godalming,
    Surrey, GU7 1XR, UK

GOVERNMENT & POLITICS

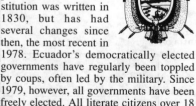

Ecuador is a republic
with a democratic gov-
ernment headed by a
president. The first con-
stitution was written in
1830, but has had
several changes since
then, the most recent in
1978. Ecuador's democratically elected
governments have regularly been toppled
by coups, often led by the military. Since
1979, however, all governments have been
freely elected. All literate citizens over 18
have the right to vote, and the president
must receive over 50% of the vote to be
elected. With about 15 different political
parties, 50% of the vote is rarely achieved,
in which case there is a second round
between the top two contenders. A president governs for four years and cannot be

reelected as of this time, though a change
of this law has been considered.

The president is also the head of the
armed forces and appoints his own cabinet
ministers. There are 12 ministries forming
the executive branch of the government.

The legislative branch of government
consists of a single Chamber of Representatives (or congress) which has 77 members
(this number will increase to 113 according
to a recent internal vote of the chamber). Of
these, 12 national representatives are
elected for four years; the remainder are
elected on a provincial level for two-year
terms. The congress appoints the justices of
the Supreme Court.

There are 21 provinces, each with democratically elected prefects and a governor
appointed by the president. The provinces
are subdivided into smaller political units
called *cantones*; each canton has a democratically elected *alcalde*, or mayor.

The elections in 1992 had several candidates running for president. In the first
round, Sixto Durán Ballén of the Partido
Unidad Republicano and Jaime Nebot
Saadi of the Partido Social Cristiano
respectively achieved 32.9% and 25.2% of
the votes. In the runoff, Durán received a
58% majority and was elected. Nine candidates declared their intent to run for president in 1996, with the first round of voting
beginning in May.

The political parties change often, with
new ones formed and old ones abandoned
on a regular basis. They have positions
including left-wing, center, populist and
right-wing, with the latter being the most
frequently accepted by the voters. President Durán's right-wing government has
attempted to tackle the deficit and reduce
inflation, but has run into strong opposition
from trade unions who oppose privatization
proposals, and from indigenous and environmental groups who oppose the destruction of their homelands and the flora and
fauna of the Amazon rainforest by oil
exploration. Widespread protests have
created major problems for the administration. The conservative government has also
been plagued with corruption scandals, one

of which involving Vice President Alberto Dahik who was accused of depositing state funds into private bank accounts. Dahik resigned in October 1995 and is seeking political asylum in Costa Rica.

The short border war with Peru in January 1995 temporarily gained the president popular backing and united the political parties. Neither the acclaim nor the unity lasted into 1996. During the first round of presidential elections in May, none of the nine candidates from various political parties achieved the 50% of the vote necessary for election. The second

round of voting took place on July 7, 1996, to elect one of the two candidates who received the most votes in the first round.

The contenders in the July election were two firebrand politicians from Guayaquil, both known for their brash macho attitudes. Neither had enjoyed much support in the staid political circles of Quito. The right-wing Jaime Nebot, a wealthy rancher and a former governor of Guayaquil Province, is famous for parliamentary antics including a drunken exchange in congress during which he threatened to piss upon a political opponent. In his less wild moments, Nebot

plans free-market reforms designed to boost economic growth. His opponent, Abdala Bucaram, a populist former mayor of Guayaquil, is remembered for alleging that a political opponent had inferior sperm. Bucaram supports the poor and opposes the privatization of state enterprises. The contest promised to be a lively one.

The victor was the 44-year-old Bucaram, who received about 54% of the vote and earned the nickname 'El Loco' (the madman) for his fiery, curse-laden style of oration. This was his third run for the Ecuadorian presidency. Bucaram's campaign promised cheap public housing, lowered costs of staple food products and free medicine, which made him popular with the poor. He also intends to slow or stop many of the country's free market reforms, which worries conservative businesspeople and analysts, who fear that his policies will lead to economic instability. It is perhaps telling that Nebot won the vote in both Quito and Guayaquil, while Bucaram won everything else.

ECONOMY
Until recently Ecuador was the archetypal 'banana republic.' Indeed, in the early 1970s bananas were the single most important export, and almost all Ecuador's exports were agricultural. This changed very rapidly with the discovery of oil. Petroleum exports rose to first place in 1973, and by the early 1980s accounted for well over half of the total export earnings.

The newfound wealth produced by oil export has improved standards of living to some extent. Nevertheless, Ecuador remains a poor country. Distribution of wealth has been patchy, and much of the rural population continues to live at the same standard as in the 1970s. About 40% of the national income goes to the richest 5% of the population. However, education and medical services have improved.

Despite the income from oil exports, the 1980s were a difficult decade for the Ecuadorian economy. In 1982-83 El Niño floods caused severe disruptions in agriculture, and exports of bananas and coffee

were roughly halved. This was followed by a drop in world oil prices in 1986. In that year, oil exports dropped from about US$1820 million in 1985 to US$910 million in 1986. In 1987 a disastrous earthquake wiped out about 40 km of the oil pipeline, severely damaging both the environment and the economy. Oil exports in 1987 totaled only US$645 million.

After oil was discovered, Ecuador began borrowing money in the belief that profits from oil exports would enable the country to repay its foreign debts. This proved impossible in the mid-1980s with the sharp decline in Ecuador's oil exports. Although the pipeline has been repaired and oil exports have increased, their value (US$875 million in 1988, US$1030 million in 1989, US$1250 million in 1993) is still well short of the levels of the early 1980s. Ecuador's foreign debt stands at about US$13 billion. About 25% of the budget is used to pay for the foreign debt. Ecuador continues to rely on oil as its economic mainstay, though reserves are not as large as had been anticipated. Estimates range from 10 to 15 years until the remaining reserves are depleted at the current rates of extraction.

According to the Banco Central del Ecuador, total exports in 1994 were US$3717 million, of which 32% was oil, 17% bananas, 14% shrimp and 9% coffee. The main trading partner is the USA, which bought 43% of Ecuador's exports and accounted for over 25% of the US$3642 million of goods imported during 1994. Asia, Europe and Latin America all are important trading partners as well. Tourism continues to develop as a source of international income, and revenues from this industry were estimated at US$230 million in 1993.

Annual inflation had been about 20% in the early 1980s, but reached nearly 100% in the problem years of the mid-1980s. This has dropped to about 50% in the early 1990s.

Per capita GDP (Gross Domestic Product) was US$1110 in 1992. This compares with US$16,700 for Australians, US$15,900 for British citizens, and US$23,400 for US citizens in the same year.

POPULATION & PEOPLE

The estimated population of Ecuador in 1996 is 11,500,000. This is approximately 10 times the number of Indians estimated to have been living in the area at the time of the Spanish conquest.

The population density of about 42 people per sq km is the highest of any South American nation. About 40% of this total are Indians, and another 40% are mestizos. It is difficult to accurately quantify how many pure-blooded Indians and how many mestizos there are – some sources give figures of 25% Indian and 55% mestizo. About 15% are white and most of the remainder black, with a small number of people of Asian descent.

Of the Indians, the majority are Quichua-speaking and live mainly in the highlands. Among the Quichua-speakers, various subgroups have been isolated from one another for centuries and, consequently, the language they speak varies markedly from province to province. Sometimes the Indians themselves have a difficult time in understanding the dialects of the Indians of a different region.

The Quichua Indians of each region also have distinctive differences in clothing – it is possible to tell where an Indian is from by the color of his poncho or by the shape of her hat. Some of the best known highland groups are the Otavaleños, Salasacas, Cañaris and Saraguros. Many Indians now live in towns and cities.

The province of Chimborazo has the largest population of rural Quichua Indians – some 250,000 living in 431 legally recognized communities and villages in the páramo.

A few other small groups live in the Amazonian lowlands. These groups include about 60,000 Quichuas, about 40,000 Shuar (formerly called Jivaro), about 1000 Huaoranis and about 600 each of the Cofan and Siona-Secoya peoples. There are also about 5000 Chachi (formerly Cayapas) Indians living near the coast in the rainforests of northern Esmeraldas Province, and about a thousand Tchatchilas (Colorado) Indians living near

Santo Domingo de los Colorados in the western lowlands.

All these groups have their own languages, often completely unrelated to one another.

Approximately 48% of the Ecuadorian population lives on the coast (and the Galápagos) and about 46% in the highlands. The remainder lives in the jungle region of the Oriente, and colonization of this area is slowly increasing.

The birth rate is 26.5 per 1000 inhabitants and the annual population increase is 2%, which means that the population will double in 34 years. This is significantly lower than five years ago (31 per 1000 and 2.4% and 29 years). Life expectancy is 67.1 years for males and 72.3 years for females.

About 37% of the population is under 15, or roughly twice as many as in Europe and North America.

The urban population is 55%. The remaining rural population is mainly indigenous. People living in the country are often referred to as *campesinos* (peasants or farmers). An indigenous person is called an *indígena*, but never *indio,* which is considered extremely insulting.

EDUCATION

Elementary education (two years of kindergarten and six grades of school) is mandatory, although about 50% of children drop out of school before completing elementary education. Of those continuing on to the six grades of secondary education, about a further 50% drop out.

A student must satisfactorily complete a grade (normally taking a year) before being allowed to continue with the next grade. A high school diploma is issued to those students completing secondary education. The diploma is a basic requirement for higher education. There are about 20 universities and technical colleges in Ecuador.

In the highlands, the school year is from September to June. In the coast, however, the school year is from May to January.

Adult literacy rates were reported in 1990 as 86.2% for females and 90.5% in males.

ARTS

A visit to any archaeology museum in Ecuador will testify to the artistic excellence of the pre-Columbian peoples. Their pottery shows fine painting and sculpture, and their metallurgy, particularly gold and silver work, was highly developed. Because the names of the artists have long been forgotten, their work is thought of as archaeology rather than fine art. Nevertheless, some of this archaeological work formed the basis of what became known as the Quito school of art.

Colonial Art

The Spaniards arriving in the 16th century brought their own artistic concepts with them. These often revolved around Catholic religious themes. The Spaniards soon began to train the local indigenous artists to produce the colonial religious art that can now be seen in many churches and art museums. Religious statues were carved, painted then embellished with gold leaf – sculpture, painting and gold work were all techniques with which the Indians had long been familiar. Paintings, too, had liberal amounts of gold leaf included. And so arose the *Escuela Quiteña*, or Quito school of art: Spanish religious concepts as executed and heavily influenced by Indian artists.

The Quito school lasted through the 17th and 18th centuries. Some of the best known artists of this period include the sculptor Manuel Chili, better known by his Quichua nickname, 'Caspicara,' meaning 'pockmarked.' Some of his work can be seen in the church of San Francisco in Quito. This church also contains a famous sculpture of the Virgin by Bernardo Legarda. Notable painters include Miguel de Santiago, whose huge canvases grace the walls of Quito's church of San Agustín, and Manuel Samaniego, Nicolás Goríbar and Bernardo Rodríguez.

Many of Quito's churches were built during this colonial period, and their architects were also somewhat influenced by the Quito school. In addition, churches often had Moorish (Arab) influences (Spain had been under Arab rule for centuries). The overall appearance of the architecture of colonial churches is overpoweringly ornamental, and almost cloyingly rich – in short, baroque. The houses of the middle and upper class of that period were elegant and simple, often consisting of rooms with verandahs around a central courtyard.

Many of the houses were two storied, the upper floors bearing ornate balconies. The walls were whitewashed and the roofs were of red tile. Quito's colonial architecture has been well preserved and led to UNESCO declaring old Quito *Patrimonio de la Humanidad* (Patrimony of Humanity) in 1978. Several other towns, notably Cuenca, have attractive colonial architecture.

Post-Colonial Art

The Quito school died out with the coming of independence. The 19th century is called the Republican period and its art is characterized by formalism. Its favorite subjects are heroes of the revolution and important members of high society in the new republic. Rather florid landscapes are another popular theme.

The 20th century has seen the rise of the indigenist school, which is characterized by subject matter rather than style. The oppression and burdens of Ecuador's indigenous inhabitants are the unifying theme. Important indigenist artists include (among many others) Eduardo Kingman, Endara Crow, Camilo Egas and Oswaldo Guayasamín. These and other artists have works in modern galleries and museums in Quito; Egas (died 1962) and Guayasamín (still alive) have museums in their homes.

Literature

Ecuador has not produced any writers that have become household names outside the country. Nevertheless, there are several notable literary figures.

Juan Montalvo (1832-89) was a prolific essayist from Ambato who frequently attacked the dictatorial political figures of the time, particularly President Gabriel García Moreno. His best known work is *Siete Tratados* (1882), or 'Seven

Treatises,' which includes a comparison between Simón Bolívar and George Washington. Juan León Mera (1832-94), also from Ambato, is famous for his novel *Cumandá* (1891) describing Indian life in the 19th century.

Perhaps the most notable writer of the 20th century was the Quiteño, Jorge Icaza (1906-79). He was profoundly influenced by the indigenist school and his most famous novel is *Huasipungo* (1934), translated as *The Villagers* (1973). This is a brutal story about Indians – how their land is seized and the savage massacre of those who protested. The book is made all the more horrifying by the knowledge that the story is based on the real problems facing the Indians. Icaza was also known as a playwright, actor and writer of short stories.

There are many contemporary Ecuadorian writers. A good introduction to Ecuadorian literature is *Diez Cuentistas Ecuatorianos* (1990, Libri Mundi, Quito), a book of short stories by 10 Ecuadorian writers born in the 1940s. The stories are in Spanish with English translations. My favorite recent book by an Ecuadorian is Pablo Cuvi's *In the Eyes of My People* (1988, Dinediciones, Quito). The book is illustrated with 121 superb color photographs, most by the author, and is available in Spanish or English. It is an informed and informal travelogue about Ecuador, written in a distinctive and evocative style that reminds me of a cross between Kerouac's *On the Road* and Steinbeck's *Travels with Charley*.

Performing Arts

The performing arts are important in Ecuador although, as with literature, there are no artists whose names are known to most visitors. There are several theaters, especially in Quito, where performances range from street theater to mime to political satire to more traditional plays. There are occasional symphony concerts, but it is the more traditional music, with pre-Columbian influences, which is of the greatest interest to many visitors.

Music

Traditional Andean music has a distinctive and haunting sound which has been popularized in western culture by songs like Paul Simon's version of *El Condor Pasa* and the score of the excellent natural history TV series *The Flight of the Condor*. Two main reasons contribute to the other-worldly quality of traditional music. The first is the scale: it is pentatonic, or consisting of five notes, compared to the eight note octaves we are used to. The second is the fact that string and brass instruments were imported by the Spanish – pre-Columbian instruments consisted of wind and percussion which effectively portrayed the windswept quality of páramo life.

The most ancient traditional instruments include the *rondador*, or bamboo panpipe; the *quena* and *pingullo*, or large and small bamboo flutes; *conchas*, or conch shells played like a horn; as well as a variety of drums, rattles and bells.

The Spanish brought stringed instruments (guitars, harps and violins). Some of these were incorporated into Andean music and others were modified to produce the typical *charango*, a very small instrument with five double strings. The sounding box was often made of an armadillo shell, but fortunately for the armadillos, wood is being increasingly used.

Most traditional music is a blend of pre-Columbian and Spanish influences. It is best heard in a *peña*, or *música folklórica* club (see Entertainment in Facts for the Visitor). Traditional music can also be heard on the streets during fiestas, but increasingly often fiesta ensembles are cacophonous brass bands.

Crafts

In Ecuador, indeed in much of Latin America, there is a bridge between fine arts and crafts: *artesanía*. This literally means artisanship and refers to textile crafts ranging from finely woven ponchos to hammocks, as well as well-made Panama hats, basketwork, leatherwork, jewelry, woodcarving and ceramics.

These items are discussed in more detail under Things to Buy in the Facts for the Visitor chapter.

CULTURE

By 'culture' here, I refer to some of the habits, attitudes and values of Ecuadorian society, particularly as they may apply to foreign travelers who may not be aware of what may be considered appropriate behavior by Ecuadorians. Culture in the sense of intellectual and artistic pursuits is discussed in the Arts section, above.

Greetings are important to Ecuadorians, especially in the highlands. Strangers conducting business will, at the minimum, exchange a cordial 'Buenos días, cómo está?' before launching into whatever they are doing. Male friends and casual acquaintances meeting one another in the street shake hands at the beginning and end of even a short meeting; women kiss one another on the cheek in greeting and farewell. Men often kiss women decorously on the cheek, except in a business setting where a handshake is more appropriate. Close male friends hug one another in the traditional *abrazo*. Indians, on the other hand, don't kiss; and their handshakes, when offered, are a light touch rather than a firm grip. In all situations, politeness is a valued habit.

Ecuadorians are used to less personal space than many North Americans and Europeans. Conversations tend to take place face to face, streets and public transport are very crowded and homes have little individual space. Frequent kissing and hugging on a nonsexual basis, such as described above, is another example of this. Noise seems part of the way of life. Radios and TVs in hotel rooms are turned on early in the morning and late at night without thought as to whether guests in neighboring rooms can hear. Don't expect anyone to take you very seriously if you ask to have the volume turned down; carry earplugs instead.

Clothing is important to Ecuadorians, and even poor people will try and dress in their best. The casually unkempt look is out; the well-pressed suit or attractive skirt

and blouse are in. That is not to say that Ecuadorians don't like to dress informally – they do – but a neat and conservative turnout is preferred, especially in the highlands. Shorts are not worn in the highlands except by athletes and extremely gauche travelers. Wear long pants or a skirt.

Spitting is common, particularly in the lower socioeconomic classes; however, belching or burping in public is considered the absolute height of bad manners by everyone.

The concept of smoking being a hazard to one's health is not very big in Ecuador. Nonsmoking areas are very rare, and most restaurants allow diners to smoke wherever they please. The same applies to public transport, including airplanes.

When calling someone over to you, don't crook your finger up and beckon, as people may do in North America or Europe. This is considered very rude. A better way to call someone over from a distance is to give a flat, downward swipe of the open hand. Body language using hands and facial expressions is hard to describe but an important part of interpersonal communications. Watch to see how Ecuadorians do it.

Begging is a fact of life in Ecuador. If you drive on the back roads in the highlands at certain times, you may see campesinos literally lined up along the roads with their hands out in supplication. This is particularly true on Sunday and the period around Christmas. At those times, it's considered OK to give the people something, but please, do so in a manner which shows some basic human respect. I once saw a busload of tourists throw candy through the windows of the bus and onto the ground. They then filmed the ensuing scramble and roared off without any interaction with the people begging. It is difficult to say which were the more pathetic – the tourists or the beggars.

Begging children are becoming more common in the cities. Particularly sad is the sight of little girls, of only four or five years of age, walking the main drag of Quito (Avenida Amazonas) trying to sell roses to tourists at all hours of the night. These kids are often forced to work the streets until the early hours of the morning. While giving them money may help them on an immediate level, the long term problem of homeless kids working the streets and not receiving an education is exacerbated. I suggest donations to one of the many charities, like Save the Children, that help homeless children all over the world. You can specify that you wish the money to be spent in Ecuador. In Quito, you can make donations to *Centro del Muchacho Trabajador* (Working Boy's Center) on the Plaza San Martín at the intersection of Pichincha and Chile in La Marín. People interested in the work being done to help and educate shoeshine boys and other homeless kids can arrange a tour – this is free, but a donation of several dollars would be appreciated.

Legally and morally, everyone is equal in Ecuador, irrespective of race or gender. In reality, blacks and indigenous people are discriminated against and treated as second class citizens. This is particularly true of indigenous people. The term *indio* (Indian), while having few negative connotations in English, is considered an insult in Spanish.

The Indian population frequently stages protests about their unfair and inhumane treatment. In 1990 Indians barricaded themselves into a church (Santo Domingo) and demanded their rights. Their demands ranged from autonomy of Indian groups to providing basic services, such as running water, to indigenous communities. While autonomy could be considered a debatable issue, the right to running water seems basic. These kinds of issues continue to be problems.

Graffiti of the *Vayase Yanqui* (Yankee, go home) type is frequently seen in Ecuador. While many Ecuadorians display some anti-American sentiment, this is directed against the interventionist policy of the USA in Latin America, and not against the individual US traveler.

Indeed, US citizens often remark how friendly the Ecuadorian people are. This is partly because of Ecuadorians' inherent politeness, and partly because US travelers are the second most frequent visitors (after neighboring Colombians) to Ecuador, and thus contribute an important amount to the nation's economy.

RELIGION

As is common with other Latin American countries, Ecuador's predominant religion is Roman Catholicism. Some of the older towns have splendid 16th- and 17th-century Catholic churches. Although churches of other faiths can be found, they form only a very small minority. The Indians, while outwardly Roman Catholic, tend to blend Catholicism with their traditional beliefs.

LANGUAGE

For the traveler in Ecuador, Spanish is the most useful language. Although Spanish is translated as *español*, the form used in Ecuador is more frequently and correctly called *castellano*. Most Indians are bilingual, with Quichua being their preferred language and Spanish their second tongue. As well as the Quichua-speaking Indians of the highlands, there are several small lowland groups speaking their own languages. It is rare to encounter Indians who understand no Spanish at all, although they certainly exist in the remoter communities. Although English is understood in the best hotels, airline offices and tourist agencies, it is of little use elsewhere.

If you don't speak Spanish, take heart. It is an easy language to learn. Courses are available in Quito (see the Quito chapter) or you can study books, records and tapes while you are still at home and planning your trip. These study aids are available for free from many public libraries, or you might want to consider taking an evening or college course. Once you have learned the basics, you'll find that you'll be able to travel all over Latin America because, apart from Brazil which is Portuguese-speaking, most of the countries use Spanish.

Spanish is easy to learn for several

reasons. First, it uses Roman script, and secondly, with few exceptions, it is spoken as it is written and vice versa. Imagine trying to explain to someone learning English that there are seven different ways of pronouncing 'ough.' This isn't a problem in Spanish. Thirdly, many words are similar enough to English that you can figure them out by guesswork. *Instituto Geográfico Militar* means the Military Geographical Institute, for example.

Even if you don't have time to take a course, at least bring your phrasebook and dictionary. A good phrasebook is *Latin American Spanish Phrasebook* by Anna Cody (Lonely Planet). Don't dispense with the dictionary, because the phrasebook limits you to asking where the bus station is and won't help you translate the local newspaper.

Although the Spanish alphabet looks like the English one, it is in fact different. 'Ch' is considered a separate letter, for example, so *champú* (which simply means 'shampoo') will be listed in a dictionary after all the words beginning with just 'c.' Similarly, 'll' is a separate letter, so *llama* is listed after all the words beginning with a single 'l.' The letter 'ñ' is listed after the ordinary 'n.' Bear this in mind also when using telephone directories or other reference works. Vowels with an accent are accented for stress and are not considered separate letters. Recently, however, the Academia Real de la Lengua Española (in Spain) has decided to eliminate ch and ll as separate letters, which means that new Spanish dictionaries will list champú and llama in the same word order that English speakers are used to. Whether this will spread to Latin American Spanish remains to be seen.

Spanish pronunciation is generally more straightforward than English, and if you say a word the way it looks like it should be said, chances are that it will be close enough to be understood. You will get better with practice, of course. A few notable exceptions are *ll* which is always pronounced 'y' as in 'yacht,' the *j* which is pronounced 'h' as in 'happy,' and the *h* which isn't pronounced at all. Thus the phrase *hojas en la calle* (leaves in the street) would be pronounced 'o-has en la ka-yea.' Finally, the letter *ñ* is pronounced as the 'ny' sound in 'canyon.'

Grammar

Word order in Spanish is generally similar to English sentence construction with one notable exception. Adjectives follow the nouns they qualify instead of preceding them as they do in English. Thus 'the white house' becomes *la casa blanca.*

Articles, adjectives and demonstrative pronouns must agree with the noun in both gender and number. Nouns ending in *a* are generally feminine and the corresponding articles are *la* (singular) and *las* (plural). Those ending in *o* are usually masculine and require the articles *el* (singular) and *los* (plural). Common exceptions to this rule are *el mapa, el problema, el dentista, el idioma* and *la mano.*

There are hundreds of other exceptions to these guidelines that can only be memorized or deduced by the meaning of the word. Plurals are formed by adding *s* to words ending in a vowel and *es* to those ending in a consonant.

In addition to using all the familiar English tenses, Spanish also uses the imperfect tense and two subjunctive tenses (past and present). Tenses are formed either by adding a myriad of endings to the root verb or preceding the participle form by some variation of the verb *haber* (to have/to exist).

There are verb endings for first, second and third person singular and plural. Second person singular and plural are divided into formal and familiar modes. If that's not enough, there are three types of verbs – those ending in *ar, er* and *ir* – which are all conjugated differently. There are also a whole slough of stem-changing rules and irregularities that must be memorized. This sounds a lot more complicated than it really is – you'll be surprised at how quickly you'll pick it up.

Greetings & Civilities

Good morning.	*Buenos días.*
Good afternoon (or good evening).	*Buenas tardes.*
yes	*sí*
no	*no*
hello	*hola*
See you later.	*Hasta luego.*
Good-bye!	
(formal)	*¡Adios!* or
(informal & popular)	*¡Chao!*
How are you?	
(familiar)	*¿Cómo estás?*
(formal)	*¿Cómo está?*
Please.	*Por favor.*
Thank you.	*Gracias.*
It's a pleasure.	*Con mucho gusto.*
Excuse me!	*¡Perdone!*
You're welcome.	*De nada.*

Some Useful Phrases

Do you speak Spanish?
  ¿Habla usted castellano?
Where (What country) do you come from?
  ¿De dónde (De qué país) es usted?
Where are you staying?
  ¿Dónde estás alojado?
What is your profession?
  ¿Cuál es su profesión?
What time do you have?
  ¿Qué hora tiene?
Don't you have smaller change?
  ¿No tiene sencillo?
Do you understand? (casual)
  ¿Me entiende?
Where can I change money/traveler's checks?
  ¿Dónde se cambia monedas/cheques de viajeros?
Where is the . . . ?
  ¿Dónde está el/la . . . ?
How much is this?
  ¿A cómo?, ¿Cuánto cuesta esto?
¿Cuánto vale esto?
too expensive
  demasiado caro
cheaper
  más barato
I'll take it.

Lo llevo.
What's the weather like?
  ¿Qué tiempo hace?
Buy from me!
  ¡Cómprame!
to the right
  a la derecha
to the left
  a la izquierda
Continue straight ahead.
  Siga derecho.
Go ahead.
  Siga, no más.
  (very popular Ecuadorian idiom)
I don't understand.
  No entiendo.
more or less
  más o menos
when?
  cuándo?
how?
  cómo?
How's that again?
  ¿Cómo? or *¿Mande?*
  (very popular Ecuadorian idiom)
why?
  por qué?
where?
  dónde?
What time does the next plane/bus/train leave for . . . ?
  ¿A qué hora sale el próximo avión/ómnibus/tren para . . . ?
where from?
  ¿de dónde?
around there
  por allá
around here
  por aquí
It's hot/cold.
  Hace calor/frío.

Some Useful Words

airport	*aeropuerto*
altitude sickness	*soroche*
bank	*banco*
block (in a city)	*cuadra*
bus station	*terminal terrestre*
cathedral, church	*catedral, iglesia*

city	*ciudad*
downhill	*por abajo*
exchange house	*casa de cambio*
friend	*amigo/a*
here	*aquí*
husband/wife	*marido/esposa*
Indian/peasant	*indígena/*
	campesino
	(never *indio*)
mother/father	*madre/padre*
people	*la gente*
police	*policía*
post office	*correo*
rain	*lluvia*
snow	*nieve*
there	*allí*
town square	*plaza*
train station	*estación de*
	ferrocarril
uphill	*por arriba*
wind	*viento*

Time

What time is it?
¿Qué hora es? or *¿Qué horas son?*
It is one o'clock.
Es la una.
It is two o'clock.
Son las dos.
midnight
medianoche
noon
mediodía
in the afternoon
de la tarde
in the morning
de la mañana
at night
de la noche
half past two
dos y media
quarter past two
dos y cuarto
two twenty-five
dos con veinticinco minutos
twenty to two
veinte para las dos

Sunday	*domingo*
Monday	*lunes*
Tuesday	*martes*
Wednesday	*miércoles*
Thursday	*jueves*
Friday	*viernes*
Saturday	*sábado*
January	*enero*
February	*febrero*
March	*marzo*
April	*abril*
May	*mayo*
June	*junio*
July	*julio*
August	*agosto*
September	*se(p)tiembre*
October	*octubre*
November	*noviembre*
December	*diciembre*
rainy season (winter)	*el invierno*
dry season (summer)	*el verano*
today	*hoy*
tomorrow	*mañana*
yesterday	*ayer*

Numbers

1	*uno/una*	30	*treinta*
2	*dos*	40	*cuarenta*
3	*tres*	50	*cincuenta*
4	*cuatro*	60	*sesenta*
5	*cinco*	70	*setenta*
6	*seis*	80	*ochenta*
7	*siete*	90	*noventa*
8	*ocho*	100	*cien(to)*
9	*nueve*	101	*ciento uno*
10	*diez*	200	*doscientos*
11	*once*	201	*doscientos uno*
12	*doce*	300	*trescientos*
13	*trece*	400	*cuatrocientos*
14	*catorce*	500	*quinientos*
15	*quince*	600	*seiscientos*
16	*dieciseis*	700	*setecientos*
17	*diecisiete*	800	*ochocientos*
18	*dieciocho*	900	*novecientos*
19	*diecinueve*	1000	*mil*
20	*veinte*	100,000	*cien mil*
21	*veintiuno*	1,000,000	*un millón*

Facts for the Visitor

PLANNING

When to Go

Travelers can visit Ecuador year round. Certain areas are better at certain times of the year, but there are no general cut-and-dried rules. If visiting the Galápagos, you'll find the warm rainy season, from January to April, has the warmest water for snorkeling, but the waved albatrosses are out at sea. During the rest of the year the water is cooler (typically around 20°C) and the weather drier, but it's mistier. The roughest water for sailing seems to be around August and September, though even then it's not too bad. The busiest seasons in the Galápagos are around Christmas and June to August, coinciding with North American and European vacation time.

The coast has a similar weather pattern – hot and wet from January to May (when tropical rainstorms may make some of the poorer roads impassable) and drier and cooler during the rest of the year. January to April, although rainy, coincides with coastal school vacations and the beaches are crowded. July and August are gray, damp and overcast. Locals don't visit the coast much then, though gringos do because those may be the only months during which they can get away!

The dry season in the highlands is normally June to August, which coincides with the wettest months in the Oriente, when roads may be closed. So there is no perfect time for a general tour of the country. The high seasons are generally considered to be mid-December through January and June to August, as that is when the most foreign visitors arrive.

Maps

Bookstores have a limited selection of Ecuadorian maps. The best selection is to be had from the Instituto Geográfico Militar (IGM), on top of a hill on Avenida T Paz and Miño, off Avenida Colombia in Quito. The building can be recognized by a map of Ecuador painted on one of its outside walls. There are no buses; walk (maybe not on your first day at this altitude) or take a taxi. Permission to enter the building is given to you at the main gate in exchange for your passport. Opening hours are from 8 am to 3 pm Monday to Thursday and 8 am to noon on Friday.

Few city maps are published, and except for detailed city maps of the whole of Quito, Guayaquil and Cuenca, you'll find the city maps in this book are generally the best available. The IGM does have some excellent large-scale maps of the whole country, ranging from a 1:1,000,000 one-sheet Ecuador map to 1:50,000 topographical maps. These occasionally go out of print, but most maps are freely available for reference. Some areas, especially the Oriente and parts of the western lowlands, are inadequately mapped. Bradt Publications (of the UK) has Ecuadorian maps for sale.

The best map is the 1:1,000,000 scale sheet published by International Travel Maps (☎ (604) 879 3621, fax 879 4521), 345 W Broadway, Vancouver BC, Canada V5Y 1P8. These are available in specialist map and travel bookstores in North America and Europe.

What to Bring

As an inveterate traveler and guidebook writer, I've naturally read many guidebooks. I always find the What to Bring section depressing, as I'm always told to bring as little as possible; I look around at my huge backpack, my two beat-up duffel bags bursting at the seams, and I wonder sadly where I went wrong. I enjoy camping and climbing, so I carry tent, ice ax, heavy boots and so on. I'm an avid birdwatcher, and I'd feel naked without my binoculars and field guides. And of course I want to photograph these mountains and birds, which adds a camera, lenses, tripod and other paraphernalia. In addition, I enjoy relaxing just as much as leaping around mountains taking photographs of birds, so I always have at least two books to read as well as all my indispensable guides and maps.

After confessing to the amount of stuff I travel with, I can't very well give the time-honored advice of 'travel as lightly as possible.' I suggest you bring anything that is important to you; if you're interested in photography, you'll only curse every time you see a good shot (if only you'd brought your telephoto lens), and if you're a musician you won't enjoy the trip if you constantly worry about how out of practice you are getting.

A good idea once you're in Quito is to divide your gear into two piles. One for what you'll need for the next section of your trip, the rest to stash in the storage room at your hotel (most hotels have one). Ecuador is a small country, so you can use Quito as a base and divide your traveling into, say, coastal, highland and jungle portions, easily returning to Quito between sections and picking up the gear you need for the next.

There's no denying that traveling light is much less of a hassle, so don't bring things you can do without. Traveling on buses and trains is bound to make you slightly grubby, so bring one change of dark clothes that won't show the dirt, rather than seven changes of nice clothes. Many people go overboard with changes of clothes, but one change to wash and the other to wear is the best idea. Bring clothes that wash and dry easily (jeans take forever to dry).

Remember that clothes can be bought cheaply in Ecuador. T-shirts are popular souvenirs, and heavy wool sweaters and long-sleeved cotton shirts can be bought inexpensively at Indian markets. A shopping mall will yield underwear and socks. In fact, you can outfit yourself quite well in Ecuador. This is very useful if you are arriving in the country on a cheap air-courier ticket, when you are allowed only carry-on luggage. You can buy clothes of almost any size if you need them, but shoes only go up to size 43 Ecuadorian, which is about 10½ North American. Suffice it to say that I have US size 12 feet (don't laugh, they're not that big!) and I can't buy any footwear at all in Ecuador. This is true of most Latin American countries, so bring a spare pair if you're planning a long trip.

The highlands are often cold, so bring a wind-proof jacket and a warm layer to wear beneath, or plan on buying a thick sweater in Otavalo. A hat is indispensable; it'll keep you warm when it's cold, shade your eyes when it's sunny and keep your head dry when it rains (a great deal!). A collapsible umbrella is great protection against sun and rain as well. Cheap highland hotels often lack heat in their rooms – usually, they will provide extra blankets on request, but a sleeping bag is very useful, though not essential.

I believe clothing is a personal thing and what works for one person is unsuitable for another. Therefore, I don't provide an exhaustive clothing list. The following is a checklist of small items you will find useful and probably need:

- pocket flashlight with spare bulb and batteries
- travel alarm clock
- Swiss Army-style pocketknife
- sewing and repairs kit (dental floss makes strong, colorless emergency thread)
- a few meters of cord (useful for clothesline and spare shoelaces)
- sunglasses
- plastic bags
- soap and dish, shampoo, tooth brush and paste, shaving gear, towel
- toilet paper (rarely found in cheaper hotels and restaurants)
- ear plugs for sleeping in noisy hotels or buses
- insect repellent (containing a high concentration of Deet)
- suntan lotion (quality lotions are expensive and hard to find in Ecuador)
- address book
- notebook
- pens and pencils
- paperback book (easily exchanged with other travelers when you've finished)
- water bottle
- first-aid kit (see Health, below)

Optional items include:

- camera and film
- Spanish-English dictionary and phrasebook
- small padlock
- large folding nylon bag to leave things in storage
- snorkeling gear (for the Galápagos)
- water purification tablets or filter
- binoculars and field guides (highly recommended if you plan on visiting the Amazon)

Tampons are available in Ecuador, but only in the major cities and in regular sizes, so make sure you stock up with an adequate supply before visiting smaller towns, the jungle or the Galápagos. Some tampons are sold without applicators and are relatively expensive – sanitary pads are cheaper. If you use contraceptives, then you'll also find them available in the major cities. Condoms are widely sold, but their quality may be questionable. Spermicidal jelly is hard to find. The choice of oral contraceptives is limited, so if you use a preferred brand you should bring it from home.

You need something to carry everything around in. A backpack is recommended because carrying your baggage on your back is less exhausting than carrying it in your hands, which are left free. On the other hand, it's often more difficult to get at things inside a pack, so some travelers prefer a duffel bag with a full-length zipper.

Whichever you choose, ensure that it is a good, strongly made piece of luggage, or you'll find that you spend much of your trip replacing zippers, straps and buckles. Hard traveling is notoriously hard on your luggage, and if you bring a backpack, I suggest one with an internal frame. External frames snag on bus doors, luggage racks and airline baggage belts, and are liable to be twisted, cracked or broken.

TOURIST OFFICES

The government tourist information agency is called CETUR and they have offices in the major cities; the location of each of these is listed under the appropriate towns. CETUR seem mostly geared to affluent tourists wishing to see the standard tourist

sights and I rarely found them of much help when it came to information about budget hotels, buses to remote villages or inexpensive nightclubs where the locals go. English was spoken sometimes, but not always. Usually they were friendly and tried to help as much as their limited resources allowed, but at other times I found them uninterested and bored.

It's still worth trying them if you have a problem, because at times they really do go out of their way to be of assistance. I remember complaining to a man at one tourist office that I couldn't find a bank that would change money for me. He took me to a bank and personally introduced me to a submanager he knew, told him I was a personal friend of his and made sure that I got some dollars changed. I've never been elevated from the status of complete stranger to personal friend so quickly!

There are no CETUR offices outside of Ecuador, but your local Ecuadorian consulate may have some basic information.

See also Useful Organizations, below.

VISAS & DOCUMENTS
Passport
All nationals entering as tourists need a passport that must be valid for at least six months after your arrival. Check the expiration date on your passport – it's easy to forget. If you run out of pages in your passport, new ones can be added more cheaply than getting a new passport. This can be done at your embassy, if you are already traveling, or at your passport office at home. Allow several days at your embassy and several weeks at your home passport office.

You should always carry your passport, as there are occasional document checks on public transport. You can be arrested if you don't have identification. Immigration checks go through periodic swings. You can be in Ecuador for three months without anyone asking to see your passport or you can be stopped in the street for no reason and asked for your documents twice in one week. Failure to produce a visa and tourist card (see below) can result in deportation.

Visas

Most travelers entering Ecuador as tourists do not require visas. Some older guidebooks report that Australians and New Zealanders require a tourist visa, but when I called the Ecuadorian consulate in Los Angeles they assured me this was not true. Nuclear testing in the Pacific in 1995-6 by France has led to visas being required of French citizens traveling to nations on the Pacific, including Ecuador, so French travelers should check before they travel. Otherwise, only citizens of Cuba, a few Asian countries (China, Taiwan, North and South Korea, Vietnam) and several Middle Eastern countries currently require a tourist visa. These regulations are subject to change; it's worth checking with an Ecuadorian consular office for current requirements.

All travelers who do not wish to enter as tourists require visas. Nonimmigrant visas are available for diplomats, refugees, students, laborers, religious workers, business people and cultural exchange visitors. Various immigrant visas are also available. Obtaining a visa is time consuming so commence the process as far ahead of your visit as possible. This does not apply to travelers entering as tourists.

One traveler reports that he tried to obtain a six-month visa to teach English; the consul in San Francisco made this difficult by requiring police records and various other official letters and documents. He tried again at the Los Angeles consulate and was able to obtain a visa with no problem just by presenting his airline ticket home and a valid passport. Obviously, the situation varies from consulate to consulate, so if at first you don't succeed, try again elsewhere. See Embassies, below, for a partial list of Ecuadorian embassies.

Tourist Cards

Tourists need a passport and a T-3 tourist card which is obtainable on arrival in Ecuador. There is no charge for this card, but don't lose it as you will need it for stay extensions, passport checks and leaving the country. If you should lose it, you can get another at the immigration office in Quito

or Guayaquil, or at the point at which you exit the country.

On arrival, you are normally asked how long you want to stay. If you show your outbound ticket, you should get as many days as you need. You are given an identical *Entrada* (entrance) stamp on both your passport and T-3 tourist card which indicates how long you can stay. The maximum is 90 days, but usually less is given. There is no set pattern in this; sometimes there are periods when everyone got 30 days irrespective of whether they wanted to stay for three days or three months. Whatever happens, keep cool. If you argue with the official who gave you only 30 days when you wanted 45, he could hassle you further. It's easy and quick to get a stay extension in Quito at Avenida Amazonas 2639 – allow a few hours for this.

Check your immigration stamp carefully before you leave the immigration area. Make sure it is properly dated. I know of one case when a person had a stamp for *JUN 1*, when in fact they arrived on July 1. Also make sure your stamp is legible to avoid problems when you leave.

There are also T-1 and T-2 tourist cards. These are for short visits only and may be issued to travelers in transit through the country, or who are staying for less than 72 hours.

The main problem with staying in Ecuador is undoubtedly the 90-day rule. This means that you can't stay in the country for more than 90 days in any 12-month period. Ecuador isn't a large country and 90 days is more than enough for most people. A longer stay with a tourist card is flatly refused and the only official way to stay on is with an appropriate nonimmigrant or immigrant visa. Obtaining one in Ecuador is often a time-consuming, frustrating and costly process, and it's usually better to apply for a visa at your nearest Ecuadorian consulate if you are a bona fide businessperson or whatever.

The one exception to the 90-day rule (and don't ask me why) is British passport holders who are reportedly allowed to stay for 180 days per 12-month period.

If you are a tourist and want to stay longer than 90 days, simply leaving the country (across to Peru, for example) and returning a few days later doesn't work. The officials check your passport for entry and exit dates and are quick to notice if your 90 days have been used up. Should you go to Peru and get a new passport at your embassy because your previous one was lost, severely damaged, stolen or expired, then returning to Ecuador is another story. With no Ecuadorian stamps in your brand new passport you have no problem.

If you leave Ecuador with, say only 60 of your 90 days used, you will receive your balance of 30 days upon re-entry with no problem.

Onward Tickets

In addition to your passport and tourist card, you officially need a ticket out of the country and evidence of sufficient funds for your stay (US$20 per day). This is the law and if you turn up at the border stoned or looking as if you haven't washed or eaten for a week, the law will be enforced. However, during my many trips to Ecuador, I was never asked for an onward ticket and was only asked to show sufficient funds once. They didn't count it too carefully – I just waved a bunch of traveler's checks.

I have heard a story of passengers on a flight from Miami to Quito being refused entry without an onward ticket. If you're flying in, it's safest to buy an onward ticket. Make sure it can be refunded if you don't use it. In Ecuador this can take a couple of weeks, but they'll give you the money in dollars. Don't worry about an onward ticket at the land borders; it's very unlikely that the rule will be mentioned if you arrive looking reasonably respectable.

Leaving the Country

If you have a valid T-3 tourist card and leave overland, you need to turn in your T-3 card and receive a *Salida* (exit) stamp in your passport – this is done at the border. If you leave by air, the same applies and, in addition, you must pay a US$25 airport

departure tax. Make sure you have both Entrada and Salida stamps in your passport when you leave.

If you have some other kind of visa, you need to get an exit permit from the immigration authorities in Quito before you leave the country. Travelers with a visa also need to pay an exit tax and obtain police clearance.

Photocopies

It's a good idea to have a photocopy of the important pages of your passport (the ones with your personal data and entry stamp or visa) kept separate from your passport. This will make it much easier to prove you are who you say you are in the event that your passport is lost or stolen. The photocopy is often enough of an ID to satisfy hotel clerks or money changers who need your passport number for their records. On the back of the photocopy, it is wise to list emergency phone numbers and numbers of your airline tickets, traveler's checks, credit cards and other important documents. Also, make photocopies of your airline ticket and insurance policies.

Travel Insurance

No matter how you're traveling, make sure you take out travel insurance. This should cover you not only for medical expenses and luggage theft or loss, but also for unavoidable cancellation or delays in your travel arrangements, and everyone should be covered for the worst possible case, such as an accident that requires hospital treatment and a flight home. Coverage depends on your insurance and type of ticket, so ask both your insurer and your ticket-issuing agency to explain the finer points. Some policies will not cover you if something happens to you while you are at a 'notorious' trouble spot. STA Travel (see Getting There & Away) offers a variety of travel insurance options at reasonable prices. Ticket loss is also covered by travel insurance. Make sure you have a separate record of all your ticket details – or better still, a photocopy of it. Also, make copies of your policy in case the original is lost.

Buy travel insurance as early as possible. If you buy it the week before you fly, you may find, for instance, that you're not covered for delays to your flight caused by strikes or other industrial action that may have been in force before you took out the insurance.

Driver's License

If you plan on renting a car, a valid driver's license from your home country is normally accepted if it is of the type that has a photograph on it. Some Ecuadorian car rental companies want an international driver's license, so if you know that you will be driving, it's best to apply for one in your home country before you leave. This is normally straightforward if you already have a driver's license.

Student Cards

Students might receive discounts of about 15% on flights to the Galápagos, and have in the past saved 50% of the US$80 Galápagos park entrance fee. Other discounts may be possible, but the Galápagos ones are the biggest. International student cards are not accepted because false ones have been issued in Ecuador and officials no longer trust them. Bring the student card from your home school, college or university, and make sure that the photo on it looks like you and that it has not expired. Generally, student cards are less useful in Ecuador than in many other countries.

International Vaccination Certificates

While these are not required by law, vaccinations are advisable. See the Health section in this chapter.

EMBASSIES
Ecuadorian Embassies Abroad

Though some countries have consular representation in several cities, these are their main offices. Many other countries have Ecuadorian embassies or consular representation; addresses and telephone numbers can be found in telephone directories.

Canada
    50 O'Connor St, Suite 1311, Ottawa, Ontario
    K1N 6L2 (☎ (613) 563 8206, fax 235 5776)
France
    34 avenue de Messine, 75008 Paris
    (☎ (01) 45 61 10 21, fax 42 89 22 09)
Germany
    Koblenzerstrasse 37, 53173 Bonn
    (☎ (228) 35 25 44)
Switzerland
    Helvetiastrasse 19-A, 3005 Bern
    (☎ (131) 351 1755, fax 351 2771)
UK
    Flat 3B, 3 Hans Crescent, Knightsbridge,
    London SW1X OL5
    (☎ (0171) 584 1367, fax 823 9701)
USA
    2535 15th St NW, Washington, DC 20009
    (☎ (202) 234 7200, fax 667 3482)

Foreign Embassies in Ecuador

Many countries have embassies or consulates in Quito, Guayaquil or both. These are listed under the respective city. It is a good idea to register with your embassy, especially if you plan to stay in the country for any extended period.

CUSTOMS

Each traveler is allowed to import a liter of spirits, 300 cigarettes and an unspecified 'reasonable' amount of perfume into Ecuador, duty free. There is no problem in bringing in the usual personal belongings, but if you plan on bringing in several cameras, a computer or something else that might not be considered a 'usual personal belonging,' you should check with an Ecuadorian consulate.

Pre-Columbian artifacts are not allowed to be taken out of Ecuador or imported into most other countries. Bringing endangered animal products home is also illegal.

MONEY
Costs

Costs in Ecuador are among the lowest in Latin America. In over a decade of traveling in Ecuador, I've noticed that the price of travel basics such as hotels, meals and transportation can almost double or halve (in US$ terms) from year to year, but are still cheap by Western standards. Because prices tend to vary even more in terms of sucres than in US dollars, I've used the latter in all my price quotes in this book.

During the past few years, Ecuador has developed a two-tier pricing system in which foreign visitors pay a lot more than Ecuadorians do for some services. This applies mainly to the following: Train rides are US$10 for foreigners compared to less than US$1 for Ecuadorians. Some airplane flights (to the Amazon and the Galápagos at time of writing, but not to highland and coastal towns, though this may change) cost roughly twice as much for foreigners. National park entrance fees are much higher for foreigners (US$10 or US$20 on the mainland, US$80 in the Galápagos, per person, valid for a week or two weeks). Many top-end hotels charge foreigners as much as twice what they charge nationals.

Travelers on a budget can save money by using buses and staying in bottom-end and midrange hotels, none of which are currently subject to the so-called 'gringo tax.' Restaurants should also provide meals at the same price for everyone.

If you're on a very tight budget, you'll find that you can easily manage on a bare-bones budget of US$10 per day, including the occasional luxury such as a bottle of beer or a movie. If you're really economical, you could manage on as little as US$6 per day if you stay in the very cheapest and most basic hotels and eat the meal of the day in restaurants.

If you can afford to spend a little more, however, you'll probably enjoy yourself more. The luxury of a simple room with a private hot shower and a table on which to write letters home can be had for as little as US$5 per person if you know where to go – this book will show you where.

Saving time and energy by flying back from a remote destination which took you several days of land travel to reach is also recommended. At present, the most expensive internal flight on the Ecuadorian mainland is about US$51 (for foreigners flying from Quito to the Amazon) and most flights are much cheaper. A taxi, particularly when you're in a group, isn't expensive and usually costs less than US$1 for short but convenient rides. Even if you demand the very best available, in most parts of Ecuador it will cost much less than wherever home may be.

I sometimes meet travelers who spend most of their time worrying over how to make every penny stretch further. It seems to me they spend more time looking at their finances than looking at the places they're visiting. Of course, many travelers are on a grand tour of South America and want to make their money last, but you can get so burned out on squalid hotels and bad food that the grand tour becomes an endurance test. I'd rather spend eight months traveling comfortably and enjoyably than a full year of strain and sacrifice.

There is one major stumbling block for budget travelers and that is the Galápagos. Getting there is expensive and staying there isn't particularly cheap, either. I suggest you read the Galápagos chapter before you decide whether you want to go.

Carrying Money

Pickpockets prey on easy targets, and unsuspecting tourists are a prime choice. Avoid losing your money by following a few basic precautions: Carry money in inside pockets, money belts or pouches beneath your clothes. Don't carry a wallet in a pocket or a purse, as these are the first places pickpockets look. Divide your money and carry it in several places, so that if you are pickpocketed you don't lose all your cash.

It is a good idea to carry an emergency packet somewhere separate from all your other valuables. This emergency packet could be sewn into a jacket (don't lose the jacket!) or even carried in your shoe. Aside from money, it should contain a photocopy of the important pages of your passport in case it is lost or stolen. On the back of the photocopy, list the serial numbers of all your traveler's checks, airline tickets, credit cards and bank accounts, as well as any important telephone numbers. Also keep one high-denomination bill in with this emergency stash. You will probably never have to use it, but it's a good idea not to put all your eggs into one basket. Divide the rest of your money – some in an inside pocket and some in a money pouch, for example. In most decent hotels, you can leave money and valuables in a safe deposit box, though this is not very reliable in the most basic hotels.

Cash vs Traveler's Checks

There is not very much difference between exchange rates for cash and traveler's checks. Occasionally, US$100 bills are looked upon with suspicion, because these have been counterfeited the most often. Once in a while, you are asked to produce proof of purchase (ie a receipt) when cashing traveler's checks. These hassles are rarely major problems, and if it happens you can always try somewhere else.

There isn't much advantage in carrying all your money in cash. Traveler's checks are much safer because they are refunded if they are lost or stolen. I've had no difficulty in exchanging major brands of traveler's checks in Ecuador. Don't bring all your money in traveler's checks, however. It's always useful to have a supply of cash dollars for the occasions when only cash is accepted. Note that cash bills are likely to be refused if they have tears in them, so bring a supply of bills in good condition.

Change Don't expect to be able to pay for inexpensive services with large bills, because change is often not available. Cab drivers may say they don't have change simply to try and make a bit of extra money. It's worth asking drivers '¿Tiene cambio de diez mil sucres?' ('Do you have change for S/10,000?' – or whatever the size of your bill), to make sure you're not stuck with this. If traveling to small towns, bring a supply of small-denomination bills.

ATMs

Ecuadorian ATMs have only recently become compatible with foreign credit cards. The following banks are worth trying: Banco de los Andes, Banco de

Guayaquil and Filanbanco for Visa; Banco del Pacífico, Banco de Préstamos, Banco Popular and Banco General de Crédito for MasterCard. These are new and growing facilities; ask locally for more information.

Credit Cards

Credit cards are also useful and most major cards are accepted, particularly in first class restaurants, hotels, gift shops and travel agencies. Cheaper hotels, restaurants and stores don't want to deal with credit cards. Even if an establishment has a credit card sticker in the window, don't assume that they will accept that card. The sticker may be for embellishment only – ask.

Visa, MasterCard and Diners Club are the most widely accepted. AmEx (American Express) is less popular. Despite this, AmEx and Diners Club are the only ones with Ecuadorian offices (see under Quito and Guayaquil) that can help you replace them quickly if they are lost or stolen. If you use the other cards, you have to call home (collect calls are usually accepted) to report their loss and arrange for another card to be sent to you. Find out what telephone number you need to call before you leave home.

Credit card transactions usually cost a small percentage of the bill. In North America and Europe, this cost is borne by the merchant and you just pay what you are charged for. In Ecuador, the merchant will often add about 6% or 8% to your cost in order to cover the transaction fee. Check this carefully – paying cash is often better value.

Another good use for credit cards is buying dollars from a bank or withdrawing sucres from an ATM (see ATMs, above). Note that cash advances on credit cards, either from a bank or through an ATM, are charged the normal rate of interest (usually 15% to 20%) from the day you obtain the money. One way of avoiding this is to overpay your credit card bill, thus leaving a positive balance in your account.

Not all bank branches will give cash advances.

International Transfers

If you run out of money, it is a simple matter to have more sent to you assuming, of course, that there's someone at home kind enough to send you some. A bank transfer is most quickly done by fax, although this will take at least three days. All you need to do is pick an Ecuadorian bank that will cooperate with your bank at home (eg Bank of America, Bank of London & South America, Banco del Pacífico) and fax your family, friend or bank manager to deposit the money in your name at the bank of your choice. Commissions are likely to be charged by the bank sending the money, so find out about this from your bank at home before you go.

Unlike many Latin American countries, Ecuador allows you to receive the money in the currency of your choice (US dollars are the most readily exchanged). If you are planning on traveling throughout Latin America, you'll find that Ecuador is one of the best countries to have money sent to.

Recently, Western Union offices have opened in major cities and offer a faster and more convenient way of receiving cash, but also more expensive. For example, receiving US$1000 in Quito costs US$75.

Currency

The currency in Ecuador is the sucre, usually written as S/. It has nothing to do with sugar; in fact it is named after General Sucre, who defeated the Spanish colonialists at the Battle of Pichincha on May 24, 1824, thus opening the way to independence for Ecuador. There are bills of 10,000, 5000, 1000, 500, 100, 50, 20, 10 and five sucres – though bills smaller than S/100 are rarely seen any more. Bills of S/50,000 were due to come into circulation in mid-1996, and there are plans to introduce S/100,000 bills within the next year or two. There are coins of one, five, 10, 20 and 50 sucres; larger-denomination coins are planned.

Currency Exchange

There are two rates of exchange; the lower one is used in international business trans-

actions and is of no concern to the traveler. The higher rate is available at all banks, *casas de cambio* (exchange houses) and for credit card transactions. The sucre is frequently devalued, so it is impossible to give accurate exchange rates. The following table gives some idea:

1981	30	sucres per US dollar
1985	120	sucres per US dollar
1988	515	sucres per US dollar
1992	1230	sucres per US dollar
1996	3020	sucres per US dollar

Other major currencies were worth approximately the following in 1996:

590	sucres per French franc
2030	sucres per German mark
2200	sucres per Canadian dollar
2340	sucres per Australian dollar
2500	sucres per Swiss franc
4500	sucres per pound sterling

Although all of the above hard currencies are exchangeable in Quito, Guayaquil and, perhaps, Cuenca, outside of these cities you should try to travel with US dollars, which are by far the easiest to exchange.

Changing Money

Banks are open for business from 9 am to 1:30 pm Monday to Friday. In some cities banks may stay open later or are open on Saturday, mainly if Saturday happens to be market day. Casas de cambio are usually open from 9 am to 6 pm Monday to Friday and until noon on Saturday. There is usually a lunch hour, which varies from place to place.

In Quito and Guayaquil, the international airport and major hotels have exchange facilities outside of the usual hours.

It is best to try to exchange as much money as you need in the major cities, as exchange rates are lower in the smaller towns. In some places, notably the Oriente, it is very difficult to exchange any money at all.

If you are stuck in a small town and are out of sucres, try the banks. Even if they don't officially do foreign exchange, the bank manager may be persuaded to change a small amount of US cash dollars from his personal account, or he may know of someone who will do so. Also ask at the best hotels, restaurants, travel agents and stores in town.

Where you should exchange your money varies from month to month. On a visit to Ecuador in the mid-1980s, I found there was an embargo on foreign exchange at all banks, so I had to change at casas de cambio. For several years the banks have again been dealing in foreign currency, but you'll have to check the latest situation upon your arrival. Casas de cambio usually involve less paperwork and are quicker than banks.

Normally, all exchange rates are within 2% of one another, so it's not worth hassling all day for the best deal unless you're changing a sizable sum. Good places to change money are indicated under each town in this book.

Should you change more money than is actually necessary, you can buy back dollars at international airports when leaving the country. The loss depends on fluctuations of the dollar, but you rarely get back more than you paid. If you aren't flying out, you can change money at the major land borders.

Black Market

There are street changers at the land borders and, when leaving or arriving overland, these are usually the best way to buy or sell sucres. Recently, there have also been street changers outside the main exchange houses of Quito and Guayaquil – their operation is supposedly illegal, but authorities have been turning a blind eye. Street rates are not any better than bank or exchange house rates. They are mainly interested in cash dollars, and forged currency and cheating have been reported. Therefore changing on the street is not recommended, except at land borders where you have no choice. In any case, be wary of forged notes, fixed calculators and erroneous exchange rates.

Tipping & Bargaining

Better restaurants add 10% tax and 10% service charge to the bill – if the service has been satisfactory, you can add another 5% for the waiter (there are few waitresses in better restaurants). Cheaper restaurants don't include tax or service charge. If you want to tip your server, do so directly – don't just leave the money on the table.

Tip porters at the airport about US$0.25 per bag, bellboys at a first-class hotel about US$0.50 per bag. Hairdressers receive about US$0.50 or more for special services. Taxi drivers are not normally tipped, though you can leave them the small change from a metered ride.

If you go on a guided tour a tip is expected. Unfortunately, some Ecuadorian tour companies pay their guides low wages, and they make more in tips than in wages. If you are in a group, tip a top-notch guide about US$2 to US$3 per person per day – less for a half-day tour. Tip the driver about half as much as the guide. If you engage a private guide, think about US$10 per day. These suggestions are for professional, bilingual guides – tip more if you feel your guide is exceptional, less if they aren't that great.

If going on a long tour that involves guides, cooks, crew (eg in the Galápagos), tip about US$25 to US$50 per client per week, distributed among all the personnel.

If you are driving and park your car on the street, boys or men will offer to look after your car. Give them about US$0.20 for several hours, a few cents for a short time.

Bargaining is accepted and expected in markets when buying crafts and occasionally in other situations. If you're not sure whether bargaining is appropriate, try asking for a *descuento* (discount). These are often given in hotels, at tour agencies, in souvenir shops and other places where tourists spend money.

Taxes

A total of 20% (10% tax and 10% service charge) is added to bills in the best hotels and restaurants, though the cheapest hotels and restaurants don't add anything. Ask if you aren't sure.

POST & COMMUNICATIONS

Post offices often have a number of kiosks next to them. These are often good places to buy postcards, aerograms, envelopes etc.

Sending Mail

Most of the letters and postcards I've sent from Ecuador have arrived at their destinations, sometimes in as little as a week to the USA or Europe, though closer to two weeks is normal.

I like to use aerograms because they contain no enclosure and are more likely to arrive safely. For a few cents extra, you can send mail *certificado*, and although I haven't experienced a loss this way, there isn't much you can do if it doesn't arrive.

I suggest that you ask to see each letter postmarked at the post office. I once left a pile of stamped postcards with the clerk at the Puerto Ayora post office in the Galápagos – not one of the postcards arrived! Dishonest postal workers will sometimes steam off the stamps to resell, and throw away your mail.

The post office in each town is marked on the town maps. In some smaller towns it is often just part of a house or a corner of a municipal office. In Quito and Guayaquil there are several post offices dotted around town. The hours are usually 9 am to 5 pm Monday to Friday. In the bigger cities they're open a half-day on Saturday.

For reasons I don't understand, letters to the same destination, but mailed from different towns are often charged different postage. It appears that some post offices aren't sure what the correct postage is, or perhaps they don't have the correct denomination stamps. Recently, mail to the USA was about US$0.35 for postcards or aerograms.

Sending Parcels

Ecuadorian air-mail rates for parcels have soared in the last few years, so Ecuador is no longer a cheap place from which to mail your extra souvenirs home.

Parcels weighing less than two kg can be sent from most post offices. Heavier parcels should be mailed from the post office at Ulloa and Dávalos, in Quito. Regulations change, so check in advance whether the parcel should be sealed or unsealed (for customs inspection) when you bring it to the post office. Recently, parcels had to be open, and you had to seal it up in front of the postal official, so bring tape or strong string. The South American Explorers Club (see Useful Organizations, below) in Quito is usually up-to-date on this.

The large grain sacks available from many hardware stores or in public markets are good for mailing clothes and weavings. Cardboard boxes are often available from SuperMaxi supermarkets first thing in the morning. Box dimensions must be less than 70 x 30 x 30 cm; bags can be a little bigger. The maximum weight is 20 kg. You should bring a list of the contents and your passport to the post office. On the customs slip, mark the box for 'Gifts' rather than 'Samples' to minimize customs duties.

Recent (approximate) postal rates for airmail parcels under 10 kg were US$46 to the USA and US$122 to other countries; parcels under 15 kg were US$66/180 to the USA/others. There is a cheaper system which combines air and surface delivery. This costs US$28/38 for under 10 kg, or US$38/52 for under 15 kg. Sea mail is available for *Impresos* (books or printed matter) – very slow, but very cheap.

Courier companies in Quito and Guayaquil can send important parcels quickly to major airports in the world, but the addressee must come to the airport to pick up the parcel. This is a fast, reliable, but expensive service – about US$57 to the USA for a parcel weighing under one kg.

Receiving Mail

Incoming mail is somewhat less reliable. A few letters may take as long as two months to arrive and occasionally never make it. Ask your friends to photocopy important letters and to send two copies.

Most travelers use either the post office's *lista de correos* (poste restante/general delivery) or American Express for receiving mail. Sometimes embassies will hold mail for you, but some embassies refuse to do so and will return it to the sender. Ask before using your embassy. You can also have mail sent to the care of (c/o) your hotel, but it's liable to get lost. The best place for travelers to receive mail is c/o South American Explorers Club (see Useful Organizations, below) – this service is available to members only.

If you have mail sent to the post office, you should know that letters are filed alphabetically; so if it's addressed to John Gillis Payson, Esq it could well be filed under 'G' or 'E' instead of the correct 'P.' It should be addressed to John PAYSON, Lista de Correos, Correos Central, Quito (or town and province of your choice), Ecuador. Ask your loved ones to clearly print your last name and avoid having witticisms such as 'World Traveler Extraordinaire' appended to your name.

American Express (☎ 560 488) will also hold mail for their clients if addressed in the following way: John PAYSON, c/o American Express, Apartado 2605, Quito, Ecuador. Their street address is Avenida Amazonas 339 (in the Ecuadorian Tours building), and they are open from 8 am to 5 pm Monday to Friday.

Receiving small packages is usually no problem. If the package weighs more than 2 kg, however, you will have to go to customs to retrieve it and perhaps pay duty.

Telephone
Telephone service is erratic and expensive if calling abroad. Christopher Isherwood described the Quito telephone service as 'about as reliable as roulette' (*The Condor and the Cows*, 1949), and it still has a long way to go. With a little patience you can usually place calls to anywhere, although long-distance and international calls from small or remote towns can be a problem. There is a phone service on the Galápagos, but this is as likely to fail as it is to get through.

EMETEL is the place to go for long-distance national and international telephone, telex and telegram services. Their offices are required by law to be open from 8 am to 10 pm on a daily basis, except in

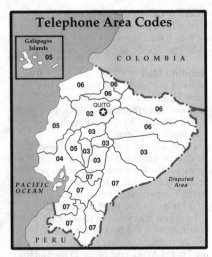

the case of offices in small and remote towns where they can keep shorter hours if they have a dispensation from the government. In a few places, EMETEL offices are open before 8 am.

I checked up on the EMETEL office in every town I visited and found that in places of any size they were indeed open during the specified hours. Calls must be placed by 9:30 pm. You will find the EMETEL office locations marked on all the street plans in this book. The bigger towns have telex and telegram services; the smaller towns have only the phone.

Calls within Ecuador There are few public phone booths, except in EMETEL offices and on a few major city streets. For local calls within a city, you can often borrow a phone in a store – they will dial the call for you (to make sure you are not calling your mum in London) and will charge you a few cents for the call. All but the most basic hotels will allow you to make local city calls.

Intercity calls can be dialed through the operator at EMETEL offices. Some EMETEL offices sell *fichas* (tokens) with which you can direct dial to other parts of the country. Telephones accepting telephone cards have recently appeared; you can buy the cards at EMETEL offices. A few telephones will accept coins.

If you need a national operator, dial ☎ 105. If you need information, dial ☎ 104.

Local numbers have six digits. Area codes are divided by province:

Azuay	07
Bolívar	03
Cañar	07
Carchi	06
Chimborazo	03
Cotopaxi	03
El Oro	07
Esmeraldas	06
Galápagos	05
Guayas	04
Imbabura	06
Loja	07
Los Ríos	05
Manabí	05
Morona Santiago	07
Napo	06
Pastaza	03
Pichincha (including Quito)	02
Sucumbíos	06
Tungurahua	03
Zamora Chinchipe	07

Dial ☎ 09 for mobile phones. Don't use area codes unless calling a number outside of the area you are calling from. If you need to dial an area code, you normally have to dial ☎ 0 first, unless you are calling from abroad.

One of the worst places to make a call is in the Quito International Airport. Service here is pathetic. They have a telephone office open from 8 am to 10 pm where you can line up and arrange for a call to be put through. Outside of these hours, there are public telephones that don't accept anything but Ecuadorian fichas or telephone cards, which you can't buy because the EMETEL office is closed. This means travelers arriving on an international flight can't make a local phone call except during EMETEL business hours. I complained about this to the tourist office at the airport and they smiled sympathetically, telling me that I wasn't the first person to have complained about this and

they had passed the complaints on to the telephone company. EMETEL has done nothing about it yet.

International Calls Even the most remote villages can often communicate with Quito and connect an international call. These cost about US$8 for three minutes to the US, about US$11 to Europe, if you call from an EMETEL office. Waiting time can sometimes be as short as 10 minutes, though it can also take an hour or more to get through. Rates are 20% cheaper on Sunday and after 7 pm on other days.

The best hotels can connect international calls to your room at almost any time, though these are often heavily surcharged by the hotel. Collect or reverse-charge calls are possible to a few countries which have reciprocal agreements with Ecuador; these agreements vary from year to year so you should ask at the nearest EMETEL office. Recently, you could call collect only to the UK, USA, Argentina, Brazil, Colombia and Spain. Direct dialing to a North American or European operator (eg AT&T USADirect ☎ 119) is technically possible, but EMETEL and hotels don't like to deal with these calls because they don't make any money on them! One EMETEL operator told me that she would allow me just five minutes on an AT&T USADirect call and then cut me off!

If you are calling from a private phone, you can call the international operator (☎ 116) to place a call. After you have given the operator the number you want to call, hang up. They will call you back when the call gets through – anywhere from five minutes to over an hour. They will also call you back and tell you the charges. These operator-assisted calls are the most expensive.

The country code for Ecuador is 593. To call a number in Ecuador from abroad, call the international access code (011 from North America, 00 from Britain, 0011 from Australia), the country code (593), the area code *without* the 0 (2, 3, 4, 5, 6 or 7, depending on the area), and the six-digit local telephone number.

ONLINE SERVICES

Accommodations

Alandaluz Ecocultural Tourist Center
admin@amingay.ecx.ec
admin@amingay.ecx.apc.org
Café Cultura (Quito)
sstevens@pi.pro.ec
Hotel Sebastián (Quito)
hsebast1@hsebastian.com.ec
La Casa Amarilla (Baños)
posada@explorer.ecx.ec
Luna Runtún (Baños)
runtun@ecua.net.ec

Airlines

AeroPerú
http://ichu.rcp.net.pe:80/aeroperu
Air France
http://www.airfrance.fr
Alitalia
http://www.alitalia.it
American Airlines
http://www.amrcorp.com
British Airways
http://www.british-airways.com
Continental Airlines
http://www.flycontinental.com
KLM Royal Dutch Airlines
http://www.klm.nl
LAN Chile
http://www.lanchile.com
Lufthansa
http://www.lufthansa.de
Varig Brazilian Airlines
http://freesun.be/varig

Language Schools

Academia de Español Quito
edalvare@pi.pro.ec
Bipo & Toni's
bipo@pi.pro.ec
Instituto Superior de Español
institut@superior.ecx.ec
http://www.qni.com/~mj/ise
South American Spanish Institute
mlramire@srv1.telconet.net
http://www.qni.com/~mj/samerica

General Information

El Niño Information
http://www.pmel.noaa.gov/toga-tao/el-nino/home.html ∎

Organizations

American Birding Association
abasales@abasales.com
Charles Darwin Foundation
nzpcdf01@sivm.si.edu
Corporación de Conservación y Desarollo (CCD)
ccd@ccd.org.ec
The Earth Preservation Fund/Wildland Adventures
wildadve@aol.com
The Ecotourism Society
ecotsocy@igc.apc.org
Fundación Jatun Sacha
jatsacha@jsacha.ecx.ec
Fundación para la Educación y Desarrollo de las Nacionalidades Indígenas (FUNEDESIN)
dtm@pi.pro.ec
Latin American Travel Advisor
lata@pi.pro.ec
http://www.amerispan.com/latc
http://www.greenarrow.com/latc.htm
South American Explorers Club
(Quito) explorer@saec.org.ec
(Lima) montague@amauta.rcp.net.pe
(New York) explorer@samexplo.org
http://www.samexplo.org

Travel Agencies & Outfitters

Angermeyer's Enchanted Expeditions
angerme1@angermeyer.com.ec
Council Travel
http://www.ciee.org/cts/ctshome.htm
Galasam Economic Tours
galapagos@galasam.com.ec
Galápagos Adventure Tours
100762.1616@compuserve.com
Nuevo Mundo Expeditions
hsebast1@hsebastian.com.ec
Ríos Ecuador
kayak@riosecua.ecx.ec
Safari Tours
admin@safari.ecx.ec
Wilderness Travel
info@wildernesstravel.com

Fax, Telegram & Email

EMETEL will send faxes for you, but this is expensive. Rates are about US$9 per page to the USA, so 10 pages are US$90, even though it only takes about 10 minutes to send them. A 10-minute phone call is about US$25. I have found it cheaper to send faxes from first-class hotels. They charge by the minute instead of by the page and even with a high hotel surcharge, it's still half the price of EMETEL. This is fine if you are staying at the hotel; if you aren't, they might do it for you if you pay cash. Major cities have private companies that will send and receive faxes for you, which may also be cheaper than EMETEL.

Telegrams and telexes can be sent from EMETEL offices or from better hotels, as well.

Email is beginning to make an appearance in Ecuador. As of this writing, a few companies have email addresses and some hotels allow you to connect your laptop to their phone lines. Email access is available to South American Explorers Club members at their Quito clubhouse. This is obviously a recent development everywhere in the world; Ecuador is a little behind but is catching up. People using this form of communication will need to check out the situation themselves – anything I write today will be obsolete in a few months.

BOOKS

See the Books appendix.

BOOKSTORES

There are two particularly well-known and very good bookstores in Ecuador that sell a wide selection of books in English (French and German, too). In Guayaquil go to the Librería Científica on Luque 223. In Quito there is Libri Mundi, the best known bookstore in Ecuador. It is at Juan León Mera 851, with branches at Hotel Colón and Hotel Oro Verde. Both shops also have a good selection of Spanish books.

Perhaps the best source of books about Latin America is the South American Explorers Club – stop by their Quito clubhouse or write to their US office for a catalogue. In Europe, an excellent source of books is Bradt Publications, 41 Nortoft Rd, Chalfont St Peter, Bucks SL9 0LA, UK (☎ (02) 407 3478). They also have a catalogue.

NEWSPAPERS & MAGAZINES

Although Ecuador is a small country, there are literally dozens of newspapers available. Most towns of any size publish a local newspaper, which is useful for finding out what's screening in the town cinemas or catching up on the local gossip, but has little national news and even less international news. A better selection is available in Quito and Guayaquil.

The best newspapers are independent *El Comercio* and the more liberal *Hoy* published in Quito, and independent *El Telégrafo* and *El Universo* in Guayaquil. These are about US$0.40 each in the city of publication. The further away from the city you are, the more you pay. For example, a day-old *El Comercio* in a small jungle town will be about 50% more expensive.

The above are morning papers – *Últimas Noticias* and *La Razón* are afternoon tabloids which allow readers to catch up with the latest news. There are also a few sensationalist rags that luridly portray traffic accident victims on the front page while relegating world affairs to a few columns behind the sports section.

Ecuador's best known news magazine is *Vistazo*, published every two weeks. It is popular, widely read and covers most of what is going on in Ecuador – politics, sports, economy etc. The monthly *Hogar* is also a popular news magazine, along with several others. Most of these tend to report local political stories with the same slant. Obviously, you need a basic groundwork in Spanish to read these magazines.

Current information about the continent is available through two quarterly newsletters: the *South American Explorer*, published by the South American Explorers Club, and *The Latin American Travel Advisor*. (See Useful Organizations, below.)

Foreign newspapers and magazines are available at Libri Mundi bookstore, the reading rooms of the luxury hotels in Quito and Guayaquil, and at the international airports. The foreign edition of the *Miami Herald* is often available in the evening of the day it is published, but costs about US$2. Other newspapers are usually a few days late. Latin American editions of *Time* and *Newsweek* are also readily available at about US$2 each, and *The Economist* for US$4. All foreign editions are in English, but have more space devoted to Latin American news.

Free English language newspapers that come out at various intervals (supposedly monthly) include *Q* and *Inside Ecuador*. There are also two small free weekly magazines called *City* and *The Explorer*. These are available most often in Quito and can provide useful information about current events.

RADIO & TV

There are 10 television channels, though not all can be picked up throughout the country. Some remote towns receive only one or two channels. The programming leaves much to be desired. I remember one evening when Ecuador was playing Peru in a soccer match; every channel was carrying coverage of the match. If you're not much interested in sports, you can watch very bad Latin American soap operas or reruns of old (and equally bad) North American sitcoms. The nightly news broadcasts are quite good, especially for local news. Occasionally a National Geographic special makes its way to the screen; these kinds of programs are advertised days ahead in the better newspapers.

There is a cable network that offers US satellite stations such as CNN, ABC, NBC, CBS and others.

If you carry a portable radio when you travel, you'll find plenty of stations to choose from. There is more variety on radio than TV, and you can listen to programs in Quichua as well as Spanish. There are some 300 stations, including about 10 cultural and 10 religious ones. HCJB (89.3 FM in Quito and 102.5 FM in Guayaquil) is a missionary radio station with programming in English and a nightly world-news roundup at 8:50 pm. Owners of portable shortwave radios can easily pick up BBC World Service, Voice of America and Radio Australia.

In 1991, about 3.4 million radios and 910,000 TVs were estimated to be in use throughout the country.

PHOTOGRAPHY & VIDEO
Film & Equipment

Definitely bring everything you'll need. Camera gear is very expensive in Ecuador and film choice is limited. Some good films are unavailable, such as Kodachrome slide film. Ektachrome and Fujichrome slide films are available. Ordinary print film, such as Kodacolor and Fujicolor, is the most widely available, reasonably priced (about the same as in the US) and is usually the best buy. Slide film is more expensive. Film is hard to find in small towns – buy it in the big cities. Rolls may be kept in hot storage cabinets and are sometimes sold outdated, so if you do buy any film in Ecuador, check its expiration date.

Developing

Don't have slide film developed in Ecuador if you can help it, as processing is mediocre (though amateur photographers find print developing to be OK). On the other hand, carrying around exposed film for months is asking for washed-out results. It is best to send it home as soon after it's exposed as possible.

To avoid problems with the mail service, send film home with a friend. You'll often meet people heading back to whichever continent you're from and they can usually be persuaded to do you this favor, particularly if you offer to take them out to dinner. I always buy either process-paid film or prepaid film mailers so I can place the exposed film in the mailer and not worry about the costs. The last thing you want to do on your return from a trip is worry about how you're going to find the money to develop a few dozen rolls of film.

Photography

Equatorial shadows are very strong and come out almost black on photographs. Often a bright but hazy day makes for better photographs than a very sunny one. Photography in open shade or using fill-in flash will help. The best time for shooting is when the sun is low – the first and last two hours of the day. If you are heading into the Oriente you will need high-speed film, a flash and a tripod to take photographs within the jungle. The amount of light penetrating the layers of vegetation is surprisingly very low.

Photographing People

The Ecuadorian people make wonderful subjects for photos. From an Indian child to the handsomely uniformed presidential guard, the possibilities of 'people pictures' are endless. However, most people resent having a camera thrust in their faces and people in markets will often proudly turn their backs on pushy photographers. Ask for permission with a smile or a joke, and if this is refused don't become offended. Some people believe that bad luck can be brought upon them by the eye of the camera. Others, more sophisticated, are just fed up with seeing their pictures used in books, magazines and postcards; somebody is making money at their expense. Sometimes a 'tip' is asked. Be aware and sensitive of people's feelings – it is not worth upsetting someone to get your photograph.

It is worth bringing some photographs from home – your family, home, place where you live, work or go to school. They will be of interest to the Ecuadorian friends you make, and a great icebreaker if your Spanish is limited.

Video Systems

Videos sold in Ecuador are compatible with North American systems, but don't work with the systems used in other continents.

TIME

The Ecuadorian mainland is five hours behind Greenwich Mean Time and the Galápagos are six hours behind. Mainland time is equivalent to Eastern Standard Time in North America. Because of Ecuador's location on the equator, days and nights are of equal length year round and there is no daylight-saving time.

It is appropriate to mention here that punctuality is not one of the things that Latin Americans are famous for.

ELECTRICITY

Ecuador uses 110 volts, 60 cycles, AC (the same as in North America, but not compatible with Britain and Australia). Plugs have two flat prongs, as in North America.

WEIGHTS & MEASURES

Ecuador uses the metric system, and I have done so in this book. For travelers who still use miles, ounces, bushels, leagues, rods, magnums, stones and other quaint and arcane expressions, there is a metric conversion table at the back of this book.

LAUNDRY

There are no self-service laundry machines in Ecuador. Most laundries (lavanderías) only do dry cleaning, though there are a few in Quito and Guayaquil where you can have your clothes washed and dried. You have to leave the clothes for several hours – it's not self-service.

Many hotels will have someone to do your laundry; this can cost very little in the cheaper hotels (about a dollar for a change of clothes). The major problem is that you might not see your clothes again for two or three days, particularly if it is raining and they can't be dried. There are faster laundry services in the better hotels, but rates are charged by the piece and are often very expensive. Then tax is added!

If you wash the clothes yourself, ask the hotel staff (in budget hotels) where to do this. Most cheaper hotels will show you a huge cement sink and scrubbing board which is much easier to use than a bathroom washbasin. Often there is a well-like section next to the scrubbing board and it is full of clean water. Don't dunk your clothes in this water as it is often used as an emergency water supply in the case of water failure. Use a bowl or bucket to scoop water out instead, or run water from a tap.

HEALTH

It's true that most people traveling for any length of time in South America are likely to have an occasional mild stomach upset. It's also true that if you take the appropriate precautions before, during and after your trip, it's unlikely that you will become seriously ill. I've lived and traveled in Latin America every year since 1980, and I'm happy to report that I've picked up no major illnesses.

Travel Health Guides

There are a number of books on travel health. The following are among the best:

Staying Healthy in Asia, Africa & Latin America (Moon Publications) is probably the best all-around guide to carry, as it's compact, but very detailed and well organized.
Travelers' Health by Dr Richard Dawood (Random House) is comprehensive, easy to read, authoritative and highly recommended, although it's rather large to lug around.
Where There is No Doctor by David Werner (Macmillan) is a very detailed guide intended for someone, like a Peace Corps worker, going to work in an underdeveloped country, rather than for the average traveler.

Vaccinations

Vaccinations are the most important of your predeparture health preparations. Although the Ecuadorian authorities do not, at present, require anyone to have an up-to-date international vaccination card to enter the country, you are strongly advised to read the following list and receive the ones appropriate for your trip. Pregnant women should consult with their doctor before taking these vaccinations.

The **yellow fever** vaccination is very important if you are planning a trip to the jungles of the Oriente or the coastal lowlands, but not necessary if you intend to stay in the highlands and Galápagos. This vaccination lasts 10 years.

The **typhoid** vaccination consists of two injections taken four weeks apart, so you have to think ahead for this one. The typhoid vaccine makes some people feel unwell and often gives you a sore arm, so try not to schedule the last shot for the day you're packing. You should get a booster shot every three years, but this doesn't normally feel so bad.

Also known as Hepatitis A, **infectious hepatitis** is the most common travel-acquired illness that can be prevented by vaccination. Protection can be provided either with the antibody gamma globulin or with a new vaccine called Havrix, also known as Hepatitis A vaccine.

Havrix provides long-term immunity (possibly more than 10 years) after an initial course of two injections and a booster at one year. It may be more expensive than gamma globulin, but it certainly has many advantages, including length of protection and ease of administration. It takes about three weeks to provide satisfactory protection, so plan carefully prior to travel.

Gamma globulin is an antibody that reduces the chances of hepatitis infection. Because it may interfere with the development of immunity, it should not be given until at least 10 days after administration of the last vaccine needed; it should also be given as close as possible to departure, as it is most effective during the first few weeks after administration (its effectiveness gradually lessens within three and six months).

Since the outbreak of **cholera** in Latin America in 1990, many travelers have expressed interest in a vaccine for the disease. These are available but are not very good. Protection is estimated at about 50% to 80% efficient and only lasts for a maximum of six months. The disease is best prevented by clean eating habits (see Cholera, below).

In addition, most people in developed countries get a **diphtheria-tetanus** injection and oral **polio** vaccine while they are in school. You should get boosters for these every 10 years.

Medical Insurance

However fit and healthy you are, *do* take out medical insurance, preferably one with provisions for flying you home in the event of a medical emergency. Even if you don't get sick, you might be involved in an accident. Shop around for the best policy and be sure to read the fine print. Some policies will not cover 'dangerous activities' such as scuba diving, climbing or motorcycle riding - try to avoid this type of policy. (See also Travel Insurance under Visas & Documents, above.)

First-Aid Kit

The scope of your first-aid kit should depend on your knowledge of first-aid procedures, where and how far off the beaten track you are going, how long you will need the kit and how many people will be sharing it. The following is a suggested checklist, which you should amend as you require.

- your own prescription medications
- antiseptic cream
- antihistamine or anti-itch cream for insect bites
- aspirin or similar painkiller
- Pepto-Bismol and/or Lomotil for diarrhea
- antibiotics such as ampicillin and tetracycline (only if you plan on going far off the beaten track. These are available by prescription only; carry the prescription and know what you are doing. Some people are extremely allergic to antibiotics.)
- water purification tablets or iodine
- powdered rehydration mixture for severe diarrhea – particularly useful if traveling with children
- throat lozenges
- ear and eye drops
- antacid tablets
- motion-sickness medication
- alcohol swabs
- lip balm
- foot and groin (antifungal) powder
- unbreakable thermometer
- assorted sticky bandages (Band-Aids), surgical tape, gauze, butterfly closures
- scissors
- first-aid booklet
- sunburn salve (aloe vera gel works well)
- moleskin and/or corn pads (if you plan on hiking)

A convenient way of carrying your first-aid kit so that it doesn't get crushed is in a small plastic container with a sealing lid, such as Tupperware.

Don't use medications indiscriminately and be aware of their side effects. Some people may be allergic to things as simple as aspirin. Antibiotics such as tetracycline can make you extra sensitive to the sun, thus increasing the chance of severe sunburn. Antibiotics are not recommended for prophylactic use – they destroy the body's natural resistance to diarrhea and other diseases. Lomotil will temporarily stop the symptoms of diarrhea, but will not cure the problem. Motion sickness or antihistamine medications can make you very drowsy.

Although many drugs can be easily bought in Ecuadorian pharmacies, you should be aware that some drugs that have been banned in North America or Europe are still sold in third world countries (including Ecuador) where regulations are lax. Make sure you buy the drug you need and not some strange mixture which may not be good for you. Check expiration dates on over-the-counter medicines.

Health Precautions

Several other things must be considered before leaving home. If you wear prescription glasses, make sure you have a spare pair and the prescription. The tropical sun is strong, so you may want to have a prescription pair of sunglasses made.

Also buy sunblock lotion, because the lotions available in Ecuador are not very effective. A minimum sunblocking factor of 15 is recommended, or 30 if you are fair or burn easily.

Ensure that you have an adequate supply of the prescription medicines you use on a regular basis. If you haven't had a dental examination for a long time, you should have one rather than risk a dental problem in Ecuador.

Finally, frequent hand-washing with soap (especially before eating) goes a long way toward preventing the spread of infections and diseases.

Water Purification

If you use tap water for drinking or washing fruits and vegetables, you should purify it first. The most effective method is to boil it continuously for 20 minutes, which is obviously inconvenient.

Various water-purifying tablets are available, but most of them aren't wholly effective – the hepatitis virus may survive. Also, they make the water taste strange and are not recommended for frequent or long-term use.

The most effective method is to use iodine. Some water-purifying tablets have iodine as their active ingredient – check the label. You can use a few drops of prepared iodine solution, but the problem is that it's difficult to know exactly how strong the solution is in the first place and how many drops you should use. The South American Explorers Club can often advise you. I suggest buying a supply of iodine tablets at home before you leave for your trip – only use them when you have to. Drink bottled water or beverages instead of always purifying possibly contaminated water.

A variety of portable filters have recently come on the market. They are available from camping stores and tend to be expensive.

Tooth-brushing and iced drinks are subjects of frequent debate. The safest way is to use bottled or purified water for brushing teeth and to avoid drinks with ice in them. However, if you are on an extended trip, you will tend to build up resistance over the months, and the minute amount of tap water ingested in tooth-brushing becomes increasingly less likely to hurt you. In first-class hotels and restaurants, the waiter may tell you that the water used for ice has been purified. This may be true, but you can never really be sure. It's a risk you either decide to take or not – depending on how much you want ice in your drink.

Diarrhea

Drastic changes in diet experienced while traveling can often make you susceptible to minor stomach ailments, such as diarrhea. After you've been traveling in South America for a while you seem to build up some sort of immunity, which just goes to show that most of the stomach problems you get when you first arrive aren't serious.

The major problem when you have diarrhea is fluid loss leading to severe dehydration – you can actually dry out to the point of death if you go for several days without replacing the fluids you're losing – so drink plenty of liquids. Caffeine is a stomach irritant and a diuretic, so the best drinks are weak herbal tea, mineral water and caffeine-free soft drinks. Avoid milk and, if you can, fast. If you are hungry, stick to a light, bland diet such as crackers, toast and yogurt. Cultured yogurt helps repopulate your intestine with beneficial organisms; other dairy products are not recommended. By giving your body plenty of fluids and little food, you can often get rid of diarrhea naturally in about 24 to 36 hours. Rest as much as you can.

If you need to make a long journey you can stop the symptoms of diarrhea by taking Lomotil or Imodium. These pills will not cure you, however, and it is likely that your diarrhea will recur after the drug wears off. Pepto-Bismol is also effective. Resting, fasting and drinking plenty of fluids is the most benign treatment.

Most people get diarrhea during a trip, but in most cases it lasts only a few hours or a day and is a mild inconvenience rather than a major problem. You never know when it may hit you though, so it's worth carrying some toilet paper with you – many Ecuadorian toilets lack TP just when you need it the most.

If you have recurring diarrhea, a course of antibiotics may help, but get a stool sample checked and talk to a doctor first.

Dysentery

If your diarrhea continues for several days and is accompanied by nausea, severe abdominal pain and fever, and you find blood in your stool, it's likely that you have contracted dysentery. Although many travelers suffer from an occasional bout of diarrhea, dysentery is fortunately not very

Top: Basketware, Saquisili (RR)
Left: Animal Market, Otavalo (RR)
Right: Inspecting weavings in Otavalo Market (RR)

Top: Río Cuchipamba raft ferry near Gualaquiza (RR)
Bottom: Disembarking from the panga, Galápagos (RR)

common. There are two types: amoebic and bacillary. It is not always obvious which kind you have. Although bacillary responds well to antibiotics, amoebic – which is rarer – involves more complex treatment. If you contract dysentery, you should seek medical advice.

Hepatitis

Most serious diseases are relatively uncommon. A depressingly common disease is hepatitis A, which is caused by ingesting contaminated food or water. Salads, uncooked or unpeeled fruit, unboiled drinks and dirty syringes (even in hospitals) are the worst offenders. Infection risks are minimized by using bottled drinks, washing your own salads with purified water and paying scrupulous attention to your toilet habits.

If you get the disease, you'll know it. Your skin and especially the whites of your eyes will turn yellow, and you literally feel so tired that it takes all your effort to go to the toilet. There is no cure except bed rest. If you're lucky, you'll be on your feet in a couple of weeks; if you're not, expect to stay in bed for months.

If you do get hepatitis A, it's not the end of the world. You may feel deathly ill, but people almost never suffer from permanent ill effects. If you're on a long trip, you don't have to give up and go home. Find a hotel that has a decent restaurant and get a room that isn't two flights of stairs and three hallways away from the nearest bathroom. Arrange with the hotel staff to bring you meals and drinks as you need them, and go to bed. Chances are that you'll be fit enough to travel again within a month.

Cholera

Cholera is transmitted orally, by the ingestion of impure water or contaminated food. It is suggested that drinking only bottled drinks or purified water and avoiding all uncooked food is the best prevention – better than taking vaccinations. Talk to your physician if you are concerned about this. The bacteria that causes cholera is easily killed by boiling.

Cholera symptoms appear one to three days after infection, beginning with an extremely sudden, explosive onset of diarrhea that rapidly empties the gastrointestinal tract. The patient continues to produce a watery, mucus-like diarrhea, which is often accompanied by severe bouts of vomiting. Blood is not normally found in the stool. The main problem is rapid dehydration which, if left untreated, can lead to death in a few days. Treatment is by oral or intravenous replacement of fluids and is simple and very effective.

Although thousands of cholera victims died in Latin America during the outbreak in the early 1990s, they were generally extremely poor people who either could not afford or were too far away from medical treatment. Very few cases of cholera have been reported in travelers, and I have not heard of any deaths resulting from these cases. If you maintain clean toilet and eating habits, you are more likely to get killed in a transport accident than die from cholera.

Malaria

This is another disease to think about before leaving. Malarial mosquitoes don't live above 2500 meters, so if you plan on staying in the highlands you needn't worry about malaria. (I've been told they don't live much above 500 meters in the Oriente.) If you plan on visiting the lowlands, you should purchase anti-malarial pills in advance because they have to be taken from two weeks before until six weeks after your visit. Dosage and frequency of pill-taking varies from brand to brand, so check this carefully.

Chloroquine (called Aralen in Ecuador) is recommended for short-term protection. Long-term use of chloroquine *may* cause side effects and travelers planning a long trip into the lowlands should discuss this risk against the value of protection with their physician. Recently, chloroquine-resistant strains of malaria have been found in Ecuador – the new recommended drug is mefloquine (Lariam), but this is less widely available and more expensive than chloroquine. Pregnant women are at a higher risk when taking anti-malarials. Fansidar is now known to cause sometimes fatal side effects; this drug should be used only under medical supervision.

Protection Against Mosquitoes If you are going to spend a great deal of time in tropical lowlands and prefer not to take antimalarial pills on a semipermanent basis, remember that malarial mosquitoes bite at night. You should wear long-sleeved shirts and long trousers from dusk till dawn, use frequent applications of an insect repellent and sleep under a good mosquito net. Sleeping under a fan is also effective; mosquitoes don't like wind. Also, only some *Anopheles* species carry the disease and they generally bite standing on their heads with their back legs up – mosquitoes that bite in a position horizontal to the skin are not malarial mosquitoes.

A woman traveler suggests that changing clothes for dinner is not a good idea in mosquito-prone areas, as dusk is a particularly bad time for mosquitoes, and that dressy skirt does little to keep the insects away. Keep the long pants and bug repellent on!

Dengue Fever
There is no prophylactic available for this mosquito-spread disease; the main preven- tative measure is to avoid mosquito bites (see Malaria, above). The carrier is *Aedes aegypti* – a different species from that which carries the malarial parasite, but it is avoided in the same way.

A sudden onset of fever, headaches and severe joint and muscle pains are the first signs before a pink rash starts on the trunk of the body and spreads to the limbs and face. After about three or four days, the fever will subside and recovery will begin. A shorter, less severe second bout may occur about a day later. There is no treat- ment except for bed rest and pain killers. Aspirin should not be taken. Be sure to remain hydrated and drink plenty of fluids.

Serious complications are not common, but full recovery can take up to a month or more. Quite common in some Latin Amer- ican countries, dengue fever is less common in Ecuador. Less than 3% of cases in the Americas are of the more dangerous hemorrhagic dengue fever, which may be lethal. It's not easy to tell the difference, so medical help should be sought.

Sexually Transmitted Diseases (STDs)
Heterosexual and homosexual prostitutes are quite active in the major cities, and the incidence of sexually transmitted diseases

---

Insect Repellent
The most effective ingredient in insect repellents is *diethyl-metatoluamide*, also known as Deet. You can buy repellent with 90% or more of this ingredient; many brands (including those available in Ecuador) contain less than 15%, so buy it ahead of time. I find that the rub-on lotions are the most effective, and pump sprays are good for spraying clothes, especially at the neck, wrist, waist and ankle openings.

Some people find that Deet is irritating to the skin – they should use lower strengths. Everyone should avoid getting Deet in the eyes, on the lips and in other sensitive regions. This stuff can dissolve plastic, so keep it off plastic lenses etc. I know of someone who put plenty of Deet onto his face and forehead, then began sweating and got Deet-laden sweat in his eyes resulting not only in eye irritation, but also in clouding his plastic contact lenses!

Deet is toxic to children and shouldn't be used on their skin. Instead, try Avon's Skin So Soft, which has insect-repellent properties and is not toxic – get the oil, not the lotion. Camping stores sometimes sell insect repellents with names such as 'Green Ban' – these are made with natural products and are not toxic, but I find them less effective than repellents with Deet.

Mosquito spirals (coils) can sometimes be bought in Ecuador. They work like incense sticks and are fairly effective at keeping mosquitoes away. ■

(including AIDS) is increasing among them. There are two effective ways to avoid contracting an STD: Have a monogamous relationship with a healthy partner or abstain from sexual activity.

Travelers without an exclusive sexual partner and who are unwilling to abstain are strongly advised against using prostitutes. Having sex with a person other than a prostitute is somewhat safer, but still far from risk-free. The use of condoms minimizes, but does not eliminate, the chances of contracting a STD. Condoms are widely available in Ecuadorian pharmacies.

Diseases such as syphilis and gonorrhea are marked by rashes or sores in the genital area and burning pain during urination. Women's symptoms may be less obvious than men's. These diseases can be cured relatively straightforwardly by antibiotics. If not treated they can become dormant, only to emerge in much more difficult to treat forms a few months or years later. Ecuadorian doctors know how to treat most STDs – if you have a rash, discharge or pain go see a doctor.

Herpes and AIDS are incurable as of this writing. Herpes is not fatal.

HIV/AIDS

HIV, the Human Immunodeficiency Virus, may develop into AIDS, Acquired Immune Deficiency Syndrome (SIDA in Spanish). HIV is a significant problem in Brazil, and the virus is spreading in other South American countries, particularly among prostitutes of both sexes. Any exposure to blood, blood products or bodily fluids may put the individual at risk. Transmission in Ecuador is predominantly through heterosexual sexual activity, unlike many other countries where transmission is mainly through contact between homosexual or bisexual males, or via contaminated needles shared by IV drug users. Apart from abstinence, the most effective preventative is to always practice safe sex using latex barriers, such as condoms and dams. Condoms (preservativos) are available in some Ecuadorian pharmacies, although they are expensive and of low quality, and I am told it's worth wearing

two. It is impossible to detect the HIV-positive status of an otherwise healthy-looking person without a blood test.

HIV/AIDS can also be spread through infected blood transfusions; if you need a transfusion, go to the best clinic available and make sure they screen blood for transfusions. It can also be spread by dirty needles – vaccinations, acupuncture, tattooing and ear or nose piercing can potentially be as dangerous as intravenous drug use if the equipment is not clean. If you do need an injection, ask to see the syringe unwrapped in front of you, or better still, buy a needle and syringe pack from a pharmacy – it is a cheap insurance package against infection with HIV.

Fear of HIV infection should never preclude treatment for serious medical conditions. Although there may be a risk of infection, it is very small indeed.

Altitude Sickness

This occurs when you ascend to high altitudes quickly, for example if you fly into Quito (at 2850 meters) from sea level. The best way to prevent altitude sickness is to spend a day or two traveling slowly to high altitudes, thus allowing your body time to adjust. Even if you don't do this, it is unlikely that you will suffer greatly in Quito because it is still relatively low. A very few people do become seriously ill, but most travelers experience no more than some shortness of breath and headache. If, however, you travel higher than Quito you may experience more severe symptoms, including vomiting, fatigue, insomnia, loss of appetite, a rapid pulse and irregular or Cheyne-Stokes breathing during sleep.

The best thing you can do upon arriving at high altitude is to take it easy for the first day, and to avoid cigarettes and alcohol. This will go a long way to helping you acclimatize. If you feel sick, the best treatment is rest, deep breathing, an adequate fluid intake and a mild pain killer such as Tylenol to alleviate headaches. If symptoms are very severe, the only effective cure is oxygen. The best way to obtain more oxygen is to descend to a lower elevation.

Heat & Sun

The heat and humidity of the tropics make you sweat profusely and can also make you feel apathetic. It is important to maintain a high fluid intake and to ensure that your food is well salted. If fluids and salts lost through perspiration are not replaced, heat exhaustion and cramps frequently result. The feeling of apathy that some people experience usually fades after a week or two.

If you're arriving in the tropics with a great desire to improve your tan, you've certainly come to the right place. The tropical sun will not only improve your tan, it will also burn you to a crisp. I know several travelers who have enjoyed themselves in the sun for an afternoon, and then spent the next couple of days with severe sunburn. An effective way of immobilizing yourself is to cover yourself with sunblock, walk down to the beach, remove your shoes and badly burn your feet, which you forgot to put lotion on and which are especially untanned.

The power of the tropical sun cannot be overemphasized. Don't spoil your trip by trying to tan too quickly; use strong sunblock lotion frequently and put it on all exposed skin. It is hard to find strong sunblock – bring it from home. Wearing a wide-brimmed sun hat is also a good idea.

Bites & Stings

Insects Insect repellents go a long way in preventing bites, but if you do get bitten, avoid scratching. Unfortunately this is easier said than done. To alleviate itching, try applying hydrocortisone cream, calamine lotion or soaking in a baking-soda bath. Scratching will quickly open bites and cause them to become infected. Skin infections are slow to heal in the heat of the tropics and all infected bites as well as cuts and grazes should be kept scrupulously clean, treated with antiseptic creams, and covered with dressings on a daily basis.

Another insect problem is infestation by lice (including crabs), which crawl around in your body hair and make you itch. To get rid of them, wash with a shampoo that contains benzene hexachloride, or shave the

affected area. To avoid being reinfected, wash all your clothes and bedding in hot water and the shampoo. It's probably best to just throw away your underwear. Lice thrive on body warmth; clothing that isn't worn will cause the beasties lurking within to die in about 72 hours.

Arachnids Scabies are mites that burrow into your skin and cause it to become red and itchy. To kill scabies, wash yourself with a benzene benzoate solution, and wash your clothes too. Both benzene hexachloride (for lice) and benzene benzoate are obtainable from pharmacies in Ecuador.

Scorpions and spiders can give severely painful – but rarely fatal – stings or bites. A common way to get bitten is to put on your clothes and shoes in the morning without checking them first. Develop the habit of shaking out your clothing before putting it on, especially in the lowlands. Check your bedding before going to sleep. Don't walk barefoot, and look where you place your hands when reaching to a shelf or branch. It's extremely unlikely that you will get stung, so don't worry too much about it.

Reptiles Being bitten by a snake is also extremely unlikely. Should you be bitten, the snake may be a nonvenomous one. In any event, follow this procedure: First, kill the offending creature for identification if you can do so safely. If not, make note of the snake's markings, size etc, and try to keep the snake away from other people. Second, don't try the slash-and-suck routine. One of the world's deadliest snakes is the fer-de-lance, and it has an anticoagulating agent in its venom. If you're bitten by a fer-de-lance, your blood coagulates twice as slowly as the average hemophiliac's and so slashing at the wound with a razor is a good way to help someone bleed to death. The slash-and-suck routine does work in some cases, but this should be done only by someone who knows what they are doing. Third, get the victim to a doctor as soon as possible. Fourth, reassure the victim and keep calm. Even the deadly fer-de-lance only succeeds in killing a small percentage of its bite victims. Fifth, while reassuring and evacuating the victim, apply a tourniquet just above the bite if it is on a limb. Release pressure for 90 seconds every 10 minutes, and make sure that the tourniquet is never so tight that you can't slide a finger underneath it. If circulation is cut off completely, worse damage will result.

In Australia, a country with a fair amount of snakebite experience, a new method of treatment is now recommended: Simply immobilize the limb where the bite took place and bandage it tightly (but not with a tourniquet) and completely. Then, with the minimum of disturbance, particularly of the bound limb, quickly get the victim to medical attention.

Mammals Rabid dogs are more common in Latin America than in more developed nations. If you are bitten by a dog, try and have it captured for tests. If you are unable to test the dog, you must assume that you have rabies, which is invariably fatal (if untreated) so you cannot take the risk of hoping that the dog was not infected. Treatment consists of a series of injections. Rabies takes from five days (exceptionally) to several weeks to develop, so if you are bitten, don't panic. You've got plenty of time to get treated. Ensure that any bite or scratch is cleaned immediately and thoroughly with soap and running water or swabbed with alcohol to prevent potential infections or tetanus.

Rabies is also carried by vampire bats, who actually prefer to bite the toes of their sleeping human victims rather than necks as in popular folklore. So don't stick your toes out from your mosquito net or blanket if you're sleeping in an area where there are bats. Other carriers are monkeys, cats . . . in fact, many mammals. A rabies vaccine is now available and should be considered if you are in a high-risk category, like if you intend to explore caves (with bats) or work with animals.

Medical Attention
If you've taken the precautions mentioned in the previous sections you can look forward to a generally healthy trip. Should something go wrong, however, you can get good medical advice and treatment in the major cities – addresses and directions are given in the appropriate city sections. Guayaquil and Quito have the most comprehensive medical facilities in Ecuador. For straightforward procedures, costs are lower than in the USA. You will be expected to pay for services when you receive them, and can then file a claim with your insurance company later.

TOILETS
Ecuadorian plumbing is poor and has very low pressure. Putting toilet paper into the bowl seems to clog up the system, so a waste receptacle is often provided for the paper. This may not seem particularly sanitary, but it is much better than clogged bowls and water overflowing onto the floor. A well-run hotel, even if it is cheap, will ensure that the receptacle is emptied and the toilet cleaned every day. The same applies to restaurants and other public toilets. The better hotels have adequate flushing capabilities.

Public toilets are limited mainly to bus terminals, airports and restaurants. Lavatories are called *Servicios Higiénicos* and are usually marked 'SS.HH' – a little confusing until you learn the abbreviation. People needing to use the lavatory will often go into a restaurant and ask to use the *baño*; toilet paper is not always available, so the experienced traveler learns to carry a personal supply. Used toilet paper is usually placed in a waste basket, as the water pressure is often too poor to properly flush the toilet. Travelers are urged to follow suit – a basket of used toilet paper is a lot less unpleasant than an overflowing toilet.

Because of the lack of public lavatories, men tend to urinate outdoors much more than visitors may be used to, particularly in areas lacking restaurants or similar facilities. Behind trees, against walls, behind buses, up alleys – it is a common, discreet but unremarkable sight. Women in towns are likely to ask a restaurant if they can use the facilities and in the country, local campesino women may urinate outdoors simply by squatting down with their voluminous skirts around them.

WOMEN TRAVELERS

Generally, women travelers will find Ecuador safe and pleasant to visit. This is not to say that machismo is a thing of the past. On the contrary, it is very much alive and practiced. Ecuadorian men generally consider *gringas* to be more liberated (and therefore to be easier sexual conquests) than their Ecuadorian counterparts. Local men will often make flirtatious comments, whistle and hiss at single women – both Ecuadorian and foreign. Women traveling together are not exempt from this attention. Ecuadorian women usually deal with this by looking away and completely ignoring the man, which works reasonably well for gringas, too. Women who firmly ignore unwanted verbal advances are often treated with respect.

Women who speak Spanish find that it is easier to deal with traveling and the persistent (and often well-meaning) questions: 'Where are you from? How old are you? What do you study/do for work? Are you married/have a boyfriend?' The pattern is always the same. Some single women claim to be married or have steady boyfriends. Some wear a wedding ring. A useful phrase in Spanish is *¡No me molestas!* (Don't bother me!)

Traveling with another woman gives you some measure of psychological support. Traveling with a man tends to minimize the attention that Ecuadorian men may direct towards women travelers. Increasing numbers of Ecuadorian men are becoming sensitive to the issue of machismo – they may practice it with their buddies, but won't hassle every gringa they see.

Occasionally, you hear of a woman traveler being raped. A rape prevention counselor who works with women in the US Peace Corps suggests that a lone woman should never wander around poorly lit areas at night or remote places (empty looking beaches) at any time. Don't assume that a deserted tropical beach is really deserted – walk with friends. Other suggestions include carrying a metal whistle (in your hand, not in your backpack). This produces a piercing blast and will startle off most would-be rapists long enough for a woman to get away.

I have met many women who have traveled safely, and alone, throughout Ecuador. Just because machismo exists does not mean that all single women travelers are going to have their entire trip ruined by unwanted advances or worse. Many women have made friends with Ecuadorian men and found them charming and friendly. However, unless you are attracted to a local man, you should avoid going somewhere with him alone, as that indicates that you are interested in sleeping with him and you will be pressured to do so. Friendships are best developed in public group settings.

Macho behavior is often exacerbated when men are in groups of their buddies and have been drinking. This is particularly true at fiestas, especially the kind that have lots of street dancing and drinking. Single women are definitely perceived as available and will be subject to harassment or worse. Women accompanied by a man at a fiesta will experience much less hassle.

Resources

Unfortunately, there is not much in the way of local resources for women travelers. In 1995 there was the Centro Ecuatoriano para la Promoción y Acción de la Mujer (CEPAM; ☎ 230 844, 546 155), Los Ríos 2238 and Gandara (a block south of the Parque Alameda in Quito), but it may well be closed by now. Occasionally, a coffee shop for women or a women's group opens, but there aren't enough financial resources to keep them open long. Ask around.

The South American Explorers Club in Quito is often staffed by women – these friendly and wonderful people can tell you like it is. Safari Tours in Quito has opened a women-only hostal (see Quito); its codirector Jean Brown can provide no-nonsense information if needed (though her primary position is as the repository of an awesome brain-bank of travel information).

Two books that I have seen that appear to be useful are *Women Travel – Adventures, Advice & Experience* by Natania Jansz and Miranda Davies (Prentice Hall) and the *Handbook for Women Travelers* by Maggie and Jemma Moss (Piatkus Publishers).

I would be very pleased to receive practical advice for women from women travelers.

GAY & LESBIAN TRAVELERS

Gay rights in a political or legal context don't even exist as an issue for most Ecuadorians. Homosexuality remains illegal within the country, and this anti-gay bias is mirrored in the media. As in most Latin countries, sexuality is more stereotyped than it is in Europe or North America, with the man playing a dominant macho role and the woman tagging along with that. This attitude spills over into the perception of homosexuality. A straight-acting macho man will seldom be considered gay, even if he is, while an effeminate man, regardless of his sexual orientation, will be called a *maricón*, a mildly derogatory term for a homosexual man.

Relatively few gay men in Ecuador are exclusively homosexual; bisexuality is more common. This means that AIDS is often transmitted heterosexually and is a growing problem (see Health).

Ecuadorian gay and lesbian groups seldom promote themselves as such in order to avoid any organized backlash. Police harassment of individual homosexuals, although illegal, is a regular occurrence. Lesbians, often unwilling to associate themselves with larger, less politically compromised activist groups, are an almost ignored segment of the population. Same-sex couples traveling in Ecuador should be wary of showing affection in public. I've heard reports of a small underground social scene, but no significant movement has developed. The various gay-oriented travel guides rarely have much information about Ecuador.

The only place I know of that is openly gay-friendly is mentioned in the Quito chapter.

DISABLED TRAVELERS

Unfortunately, Ecuador's infrastructure for disabled travelers is virtually nonexistent, as is the case with most third world countries. Wheelchair ramps are few and far between, and pavements are often badly potholed and cracked. Bathrooms and toilets are often barely large enough for an able-bodied person to walk into, and very few indeed are accessible to wheelchairs. Features such as signs in Braille or telephones for the hearing-impaired are practically unknown. Nevertheless, there are disabled Ecuadorians who get around, mainly through the help of others. It is not particularly unusual to see disabled travelers being bodily carried to a seat on a bus, for example. Buses are (legally) supposed to carry disabled travelers for free. Local city buses, already overcrowded, won't do that, but long-distance city buses sometimes will.

For some general advice, a good starting point is *Nothing Ventured: Disabled People Travel the World* edited by Alison Walsh (1991, Rough Guides). One disabled traveler writes that the best resource is the many other disabled people who you will see in Ecuador. If you take the time to learn Spanish, you will find that local disabled people will be very helpful.

SENIOR TRAVELERS

Though many seniors travel in Ecuador, I am aware of no special discounts available to them. Seniors still pay full fare on transport, full price in hotels and museums, etc.

For discounted fares and packaged tours, contact Elderhostel (☎ (617) 426 8056), 75 Federal St, Boston, MA 02110, USA, or Grand Circle Travel (☎ (617) 350 7500, (800) 995 5689, fax 423 0445), 347 Congress St, Boston, MA 02210, USA. Grand Circle was begun by the founder of the American Association of Retired Persons (AARP). Begin your search at your local senior citizens' center.

TRAVEL WITH CHILDREN

Children pay full fare on buses if they occupy a seat, but often ride for free if they sit on a parent's knee. Children under 12 pay half fare on domestic airline flights and get a seat, while infants under two pay 10% of the fare, but they don't get a seat.

In hotels, the general rule is simply to bargain. Children should never have to pay as much as an adult, but whether they stay for half price or free is open to discussion.

While 'kids meals' (small portions at small prices) are not normally offered in restaurants, it is perfectly acceptable to order a meal to split between two children or an adult and a child.

Foreigners traveling with children are still a curiosity in Ecuador (especially if they are gringos) and will meet with extra, generally friendly, attention and interest.

For more advice and suggestions, see Lonely Planet's *Travel with Children* by Maureen Wheeler et al (3rd edition, 1995).

USEFUL ORGANIZATIONS
South American Explorers Club

This club was founded in 1977 in Lima, Peru, by Don Montague and Linda Rojas. A Quito office was founded by Betsy Wagenhauser in 1989, and there is also a US office in Ithaca, NY. The club functions as an information center for travelers, adventurers, scientific expeditions etc, and provides a wealth of advice about traveling anywhere in Latin America. Anyone considering a trip to Ecuador would do well to join this organization.

Both the Quito and Lima clubhouses have an extensive library of books, maps and trip reports left by other travelers. Many maps and books are for sale. Useful current advice can be obtained about travel conditions, currency regulations, weather conditions and so on.

The club is an entirely member-supported, nonprofit organization. Annual membership dues are US$40/60 per individual/couple, and include four quarterly issues of the informative and enjoyable *South American Explorer* magazine. (Membership dues are tax deductible in the US. Members from other countries must add US$7 for postage.)

In addition, members receive full use of both Quito and Lima clubhouses with the following facilities: an information service and library; introductions to other travelers and notification of expedition opportunities; storage of excess luggage (anything ranging from small valuables to a kayak); storage or forwarding of mail addressed to you at the club; use of the club's computer and email equipment; a relaxing place in which to read and research, or just to have a cup of tea and a chat with the friendly staff; a book exchange; buying and selling of used equipment; a notice board; discounts on the books, maps and gear sold at the club; and other services. The storage facilities are particularly useful if you plan on returning to Ecuador; I leave heavy camping/climbing gear here from year to year.

Nonmembers are welcome to visit the club, but are asked to limit their visit to about half an hour, and are not eligible for membership privileges until they cough up their US$40. Paid-up members can hang out all day – the club is highly recommended. You can join when you get to Ecuador, or you can join in advance by writing to the US office. For information on how to reach them by email or log onto their website, see Online Services.

Lima
   Avenida Portugal 145, Breña
   mail: Casilla 3714, Lima 100, Peru
   (☎ /fax 425-0142)
Quito
   Jorge Washington 311 and Leonidas Plaza
   mail: Apartado 21-431, Quito, Ecuador
   (☎ /fax 225 228)
USA
   126 Indian Creek Rd, Ithaca, NY 14650
   (☎ (607) 277 0488, fax 277 6122)

FEPROTUR

The Fundación Ecuatoriana de Promoción Turística (FEPROTUR) was formed in 1989 and is a private nonprofit organization whose function is to promote and develop tourism in Ecuador at both the national and international level. FEPROTUR works with INEFAN, travel agents, scientists, indigenous people etc, in an effort to develop socially and environmentally sound ecotourism practices. The organization has organized seminars and prepared training courses for guides, and has published some useful booklets. Contact FEPROTUR at JL Mera 130 and Patria, Edificio CFN, 5th floor, Quito (☎ 509 860, 506 566).

Fundación Natura

This is Ecuador's largest and best known nongovernment organization (NGO) dedicated to conservation, environmental advocacy and environmental education. They also manage the protected Pasochoa Forest Reserve, which is one of the few remaining inter-Andean humid forests left in the country. The reserve is described at the end of the Quito chapter. Contact the Fundación Natura at Avenida América 5663 and Voz Andes, Quito (☎ 447 342/343/344).

Latin American Travel Advisor

You can get up-to-date information on safety, political and economic situations, health risks, costs etc for all the Latin American countries from *The Latin American Travel Advisor*. This is an impartial, 16-page quarterly newsletter published in Ecuador. Four issues are US$39, the most recent issue is US$15 and back issues are US$7.50, sent by airmail. The Latin American Travel Advisor is reachable at PO Box 17-17-908, Quito, Ecuador (fax 562 566, see also Online Services).

Indigenous Issues

The year 1992 marked the 500th anniversary of Columbus' arrival in the Americas. For native peoples from Alaska to Argentina, this was not an anniversary to celebrate. There are various organizations supporting indigenous rights throughout the Americas. More information (in Spanish) on the indigenous point of view is available from the following organizations.

CONAIE (Confederación Nacional Indígena del Ecuador)
    Los Granados 2553 and 6 de Diciembre,
    El Batan, Quito
    mail: Casilla 92-C, Sucursal 15,
    El Batan, Quito, Ecuador
    (☎ 248 930, fax 442 271)
Fundación Pueblo Indio
    Ruiz de Castilla 216 and Sosaya, Quito
    (☎ 529 361, fax 235 098)

DANGERS & ANNOYANCES

Although rip-offs are a fact of life in Latin America, you'll find Ecuador is safer than the worst offenders, Peru and Colombia. Unfortunately, Ecuador is not as safe to travel in as when I first visited in 1980. This is probably related to the recently depressed economic situation (see Economy in Facts about the Country) combined with the increase in tourism to Ecuador over the past decade. You should, therefore, take some simple precautions to avoid being robbed.

Theft Armed robbery is still rare in Ecuador, although parts of Quito, Guayaquil and some coastal areas do have a reputation for being dangerous (specific information is given under those towns). Sneak theft is more common, and you should remember that crowded places are the haunts of pickpockets. This means poorly lit bus stations, crowded city streets or bustling markets. What often happens is that travelers get so involved in their new surroundings and experiences that they forget to stay alert, and that's when something is stolen. It could happen in New York City or London as well.

Thieves look for easy targets. Tourists who carry a wallet or passport in a hip pocket are asking for trouble. Leave your wallet at home; it's an easy mark for a pickpocket. Carrying a roll of bills loosely wadded under a handkerchief in your front pocket is as safe a way as any of carrying your daily spending money. The rest should be hidden. Always use at least an inside pocket or preferably a body pouch, money belt or leg pouch to protect your money and passport.

Thieves often work in pairs or groups. While one distracts your attention, another thief is robbing you. This can happen in a variety of ways: a bunch of kids fighting in front of you, an old lady 'accidentally' bumping into you, someone dropping something in your path or spilling something on your clothes, several people closing in around you on a crowded city bus . . . the possibilities go on and on. The only thing you can do is to try, as much as possible, to avoid very tight crowds and to stay alert, especially when something out of the ordinary happens.

To worry you further, there are the razor-blade artists. No, they don't wave a blade in your face and demand 'Your money or your life!' They simply slit open your luggage with a razor when you're not looking. This includes a pack on your back or luggage in the rack of a bus or train, or even your trouser pocket.

Many travelers carry their day packs in front of them to avoid having them slashed during trips to markets etc. Some travelers buy large grain sacks from hardware stores or markets and put their packs or luggage in them when they travel. This makes their bag look less obviously like a tourist's bag – many locals use grain sacks to transport their belongings. Also, the sacks will keep your luggage clean and more protected.

When walking with my large pack, I move fast and avoid stopping, making it difficult for anyone intent on cutting the pack. If I have to stop (at a street crossing, for example), I tend to gently swing from side to side and look around a lot. I don't feel paranoid – walking fast and looking around as I walk from bus station to hotel has become second nature to me. Taking a taxi from the bus station to a hotel is a safer alternative in some cities (this is mentioned in the text under the appropriate city). I never put my bag down unless I have my foot firmly on it.

One of the best solutions to the rip-off problem is to travel with a friend and to watch out for one another. An extra pair of eyes makes a lot of difference. I often see shifty-eyed looking types eyeing baggage at bus stations or pockets in busy markets, but they notice if you are alert and are far less likely to bother you. They'd rather pick the wallet from some gawker who isn't paying attention.

Drugs Definitely avoid any conversation with someone who offers you drugs. In fact, talking to any stranger on the street can hold risks. It has happened that travelers who have talked to strangers have been stopped soon after by plain-clothes 'police officers' and accused of talking to a drug dealer. In such a situation, never get into a vehicle with the 'police,' but insist on going to a bona fide police station on foot.

Scams Be wary of false or crooked police who prey on tourists. On the other hand, a uniformed official who asks to see your passport in broad daylight in the middle of a busy street is probably just doing a job – a few friendly words and a compliment on how you are enjoying this beautiful country will usually ensure that your passport will be examined quickly and returned politely.

A recent report indicates that there are false policemen around who will stop you and claim that they are narcotics officers and that there is a drug tax that foreigners must pay to help eliminate the drug trade. An official-looking document is produced listing different countries and how much their citizens are required to pay. This is a complete scam – ignore it and walk away.

Don't accept food from strangers. I know of one person who ate some cookies given to him by some smooth-talking 'friends' on a bus – he woke up two days later in an alley with just his shirt and trousers. I've heard of several reports of this; Ecuadorian authorities claim that it's Colombians who do it. Unopened packages of cookies and other foods are injected with horse tranquilizers using hypodermic syringes. I know it sounds weird, but it's true.

Robbery Every year or so, you hear of a couple of night bus robberies in the

Guayaquil area. Night buses are simply held up at a road block and robbed by armed men. These are always long-distance buses, so you should avoid taking night buses that go through Guayas Province unless you have to. It happens to one bus in many thousands so don't get paranoid if your schedule demands a night bus through the area.

If you are driving a car, never park it unattended. Never leave any valuables in sight in the car – even attended cars will have their windows smashed by hit-and-run merchants.

There has been a rash of recent problems for climbers and hikers. Armed gangs have robbed tourists hiking up Quito's backyard volcano, Pichincha. Others have robbed and raped small groups staying in some of the more remote mountain huts, such as on Iliniza and Tungurahua. Never leave gear unattended in a mountain hut while you are hiking. Some huts, eg on Cotopaxi or Chimborazo, have guardians and a place to lock up gear when you climb and are relatively safe. I suggest inquiring at the South American Explorers Club for up-to-date information on these problems. Also, climb and hike in a sizable group in questionable areas.

Take out travelers' insurance if you're carrying really valuable gear such as a good camera. But don't get paranoid; Ecuador is not an extremely dangerous country, and after dozens of trips during the past decade, I have yet to be robbed.

If you are robbed, you should get a police report as soon as possible. This is a requirement for any insurance claims, although it is unlikely that the police will be able to recover the property. In Quito you should go to the police at Mideros and Cuenca in the old town between 9 am and noon. You could try the *Servicio de Investigaciones Criminales de Pichincha* (SICP) which is at the intersection of Montúfar and Esmeraldas in the old town, to see if your stolen camera or whatever has shown up (not likely). In other towns go to the main police headquarters.

LEGAL MATTERS

If you get into legal trouble and are jailed, your embassy can offer only limited assistance. This may include an occasional visit from an embassy staff member to make sure that your human rights have not been violated, letting your family know where you are and putting you in contact with an Ecuadorian lawyer (whom you must pay yourself). Embassy officials will not bail you out and you are subject to the laws of Ecuador, not to the laws of your home country.

Drug penalties in Ecuador for possession of even small amounts of illegal drugs are much stricter than in the USA or Europe. Defendants often spend many months in jail before they are brought to trial and, if convicted (as is usually the case) can expect sentences of several years in jail.

Businesspeople should be aware that legal disputes which may be of a civil nature in their home countries may be handled as a criminal proceeding in Ecuador. This may mean that you are not allowed to leave Ecuador while your dispute is being settled, and could possibly lead to arrest and jailing until the case is settled.

Drivers should carry their passport as well as driver's license. In the event of an accident, unless extremely minor, the vehicles should stay where they are until the police arrive and make a report. This is essential for all insurance claims. If the accident results in injury and you are unhurt, you should take the victim to obtain medical help, particularly in the case of a pedestrian accident. You are legally responsible for the pedestrian's injuries and will be jailed unless you pay, even if the accident was not your fault. Drive as defensively as you can.

BUSINESS HOURS

Banks are open from 9 am to 1:30 pm Monday to Friday.

In Quito and Guayaquil most stores, businesses, exchange houses and government offices are open from about 9 am to

5:30 pm Monday to Friday with an hour off for lunch. In smaller towns, lunch breaks of two (or even three) hours are not uncommon. On Saturday, many stores and some businesses are open from 9 am to noon.

Restaurants tend to remain open late in the big cities, where 10 pm is not an unusual time to eat an evening meal. In smaller towns, restaurants often close by 9 pm or much earlier in villages. Restaurants often close on Sunday, when the selection of available eating places can be quite limited.

HOLIDAYS & SPECIAL EVENTS

Many of the major festivals are oriented to the Roman Catholic liturgical calendar. These are often celebrated with great pageantry, especially in highland Indian villages where a Catholic feast day is often the excuse for a traditional Indian fiesta with much drinking, dancing, rituals and processions. Other holidays are of historical or political interest, for example Independence Day on August 10. On the days of the major holidays, banks, offices and other services are closed and transportation is often very crowded, so book ahead if possible.

The following list describes the major holidays, but they may well be celebrated for several days around the actual date. Those marked by an asterisk (*) are official public holidays when banks and businesses are closed; others are more local holidays. If an official public holiday falls on a weekend, offices may be closed on the nearest Friday or Monday. If an official holiday falls midweek, it may or may not be moved to the nearest Friday or Monday to create a long weekend.

January 1
    *New Year's Day**
January 6
    *Epiphany**
February 27
    National Community Spirit Day
March or April
    *Carnival** (Held the last few days before Lent, Carnival is celebrated with water fights. Ambato has its fruit and flowers festival.)
    *Easter** (Palm Sunday, Holy Thursday, Good Friday, Holy Saturday and Easter Sunday are celebrated with religious processions. Holy Saturday is a public holiday, but many businesses close earlier in the week.)
May 1
    *Labor Day** (A day of workers' parades)
May 24
    *Battle of Pichincha** (National holiday celebrates the decisive battle of independence from the Spanish in 1822)
June
    Corpus Christi (A movable religious feast day combined with traditional harvest fiesta in many highland towns. Usually the 9th Thursday after Easter, it features processions and street dancing.)
June 24
    Saint John the Baptist (Fiestas in Otavalo area)
June 29
    Saints Peter and Paul (Fiestas in Otavalo area and other northern highland towns)
July 24
    *Simón Bolívar's Birthday** (National holiday to celebrate the liberator's birthday)
July 25
    Founding of Guayaquil (A major festival for the city of Guayaquil, it combines with the national holiday of July 24 and the city closes down and parties.)
August 10
    *Quito Independence Day**
October 9
    *Guayaquil Independence Day** (This combines with the October 12 national holiday and is an important festival in Guayaquil.)
October 12
    *Columbus Day** (National holiday to celebrate the 'discovery' of America, also known as Americas Day or *Día de la Raza*.)
September 1-15
    Fiesta del Yamor (Otavalo's annual festival)
November 1
    *All Saints' Day**
November 2
    *All Souls' Day** (Celebrated by flower-laying ceremonies in cemeteries. Especially colorful in rural areas, where entire Indian families show up at the cemeteries to eat, drink and leave offerings in memory of their departed relatives. The atmosphere often becomes festive rather than somber.)
November 3
    *Cuenca Independence Day** (This combines with the national holidays of November 1 and 2 to give Cuenca its most important fiesta of the year.)

December 6
  Founding of Quito* (Celebrated in Quito throughout the first week of December with bullfights, parades and street dances.)
December 24
  Christmas Eve*
December 25
  Christmas Day*
December 28-31
  End-of-year celebrations (Parades and dances culminate in the burning of life-size effigies in the streets on New Year's Eve.)

In addition to these major festivals, there are many smaller ones. Most towns and villages have their own special day. In addition, many towns and villages have important weekly market days (see Main Market Days in the Things to Buy section).

ACTIVITIES & HIGHLIGHTS

Where to begin? There are so many exciting things to do, see and experience in Ecuador that any list of suggestions will certainly be inadequate. In this section, I try to outline the main reasons that the majority of travelers come to Ecuador – I apologize to those travelers (philatelists and numismatists, athletes and Zen Buddhists, cyclists and boaters, and many others) whose varied and worthwhile interests are not discussed here. You should still come!

Where I mention a place name, you should refer to that section for further information.

Indian Markets

These are often a success story for everyone – gringos go home with beautiful souvenirs, artisans make a living selling their crafts and local buses, hotels and restaurants benefit as well. There are plenty of great markets; Otavalo is the most famous, but markets at Saquisilí and many other highland towns and villages are well worth visiting.

Climbing & Hiking

Tents, sleeping bags and other gear can be rented in Quito and some other towns. Adventures in Parque Nacional Cotopaxi, the Baños area, Area Nacional de Recreación Las Cajas (near Cuenca) and around Chimborazo (Ecuador's highest mountain) are all worthwhile and described in this book. For dedicated outdoor adventurers, read *Climbing & Hiking in Ecuador* (see the Books appendix).

Wildlife

The first thought here is **birds**. Half of the birds in South America are found in Ecuador – and little Ecuador has twice as many birds as all of North America. See the Books appendix at the end of the book for listings of birdwatching guides. Pasochoa Forest Preserve near Quito, operated by the Fundación Natura, is one of the best places in the highlands to see many species of hummingbirds.

The **Galápagos Islands** is the second thought here. I place them second because they are becoming increasingly overvisited by curiosity seekers and are becoming prohibitively expensive to visit – go if you are really interested, don't bother if wildlife is not your thing. The Galápagos are a bunch of relatively recent volcanic rocks stuck in the middle of the Pacific; many of the plants and animals on them are endemic to the islands. If you don't know what endemic means, perhaps you should go elsewhere.

Thirdly, think **Amazon**. Various trips can be taken into the rainforest. I remember talking to a traveler who thought the Amazon would be a cross between Hawaii and the African plains – she was disappointed not to see more wildlife in a luxuriantly tropical setting. The wildlife is there, but the luxuriant vegetation masks much of it. Many areas of the Ecuadorian rainforest have been colonized and you won't see jaguars in these areas (which are, of course, the easiest to get to). Having said this, I recommend Ecuador as being as good a country as any to visit the rainforest. See the Oriente chapters for more details.

Finally, don't neglect the wildlife of the **highlands** – the páramo habitats of the Tulcán area, Parque Nacional Cotopaxi and Area Nacional de Recreación Las Cajas are all recommended.

History

Many highland towns have Spanish colonial architecture dominating their city centers. Quito's old town has been designated Patrimonio de Humanidad by UNESCO. Flying from Quito to Cuenca gives an unforgettable aerial glimpse of the beautiful colonial center of Cuenca. Many other highland towns have interesting colonial architecture.

Fiestas

From the capital's annual fiesta during the first week in December to the local festivities in small towns and villages – these are a chance to mingle with local people and have fun. All Souls' Day (November 2) is particularly recommended in the highlands; Bolívar's Birthday (July 24) and the Founding of Guayaquil (July 25) are particularly recommended in Guayaquil. Carnaval time (the weekend preceding Ash Wednesday) is celebrated all over Latin America – in Ecuador, it takes the form of water-throwing in most areas, and a festival of fruit and flowers in Ambato.

Hang Out

Travelers needing a place to relax and hang out for a week or two will find several good spots. Vilcabamba in the Southern Highlands and Alandaluz on the central coast are both very laid back. Otavalo in the highlands, Baños on the edge of the highlands/jungle, Misahuallí in the jungle and Atacames on the coast are all popular travelers' destinations, all accompanied by a certain amount of hype and frenzied activity. If you want to meet people on the gringo trail, these are the places to go. Cuenca is the big city to quietly hang out in – the third largest Ecuadorian town, it is nevertheless very traditional and attractive. Quito is a better capital city to spend time in than many other capitals.

Travel

There are numerous interesting, unusual and fun ways to travel, though I can't guarantee luxurious comfort! Ride on the roof of the train as it zigzags down *El Nariz del Diablo* (the Devil's Nose) – a dizzying descent from Alausí in the highlands to Guayaquil on the coast. Voyage along a tropical river in a dugout canoe from Borbón on the coast or Misahuallí in the Oriente. Pack yourself into a bus full of locals and take the high road around Chimborazo. Take a flight along the Andes in a TAME jet or fly along the coast or over the Oriente in a light aircraft – don't forget your camera. Cross the Río Guayas by passenger ferry to see the busy traffic on Ecuador's widest river. Amble around the Vilcabamba or Baños area by horseback.

COURSES

Various colleges and organizations in the USA can provide you with information on studying in Ecuador. Most of these courses are available for academic credit. You have to pay for tuition and room and board, but student grants, awards and other financial aid can often be arranged. Students should talk to their college advisors to see if their institution has further contact.

Most foreign students come simply to learn Spanish, and there are a plethora of schools to help them at any level. With many courses, accommodations with local families can be arranged, and also include intensive one-on-one instruction for several hours a day. Costs are reasonable. Most schools are found in Quito, but there are also schools in Cuenca, Baños and other towns. These are listed under the specific towns.

WORK

Officially you need a workers visa to be allowed to work in Ecuador. Tourists have, however, obtained jobs teaching English in language schools, usually in Quito. Schools often advertise for teachers on the bulletin boards of travelers' hotels and restaurants. You are expected to be a native English speaker, but I know of one Dutchman fluent in English who got a job. Pay is low, but it's enough to live on if you're broke. It's best to start looking soon after you arrive, because it's not easy to get a work visa and you may have to leave in 90 days.

If, in addition to speaking English like a native, you actually have a bona fide teaching credential, so much the better. Schools such as the American School in Quito will often hire teachers of mathematics, biology and other subjects, and may often help you get a work visa if you want to stay on. They also pay much better than the language schools. I don't know of other jobs that are readily available without a working visa.

The following schools may employ qualified teachers. The schools are listed in order from those paying the least (and more likely to hire unqualified people) to those paying the most (and expecting teachers to have proper qualifications).

Academia Benedicts
    Avenida América 3811, Quito (☎ 432 729)
Bahía International School
    Guayaquil (☎ 691-440)
British Council
    Amazonas 1646 and La Niña, Quito
    PO Box 1197, Quito (☎ 540 225)
    RSA diploma required
Fulbright Commission
    Almagro 916 and Colón, Quito (☎ 222-103)
Harvard
    10 de Agosto and Riofrío, Quito
    (☎ 568 870)
Lingua Franca
    Salazar 429 and Coruña (☎ 546 075)
The Experiment
    Avenida de Salazar 635 and Portugal, Quito
    (☎ 242 993)
Universidad de San Francisco
    Quito (☎ 459 137)

Another way of making money, if you're in that unfortunate position of needing it, is by selling good-quality equipment such as camping and climbing gear or camera items. Good used gear can be sold for about 50% to 60% of its new price.

ACCOMMODATIONS
There is no shortage of places to stay in Ecuador. It is almost unheard of to arrive in a town and not be able to find somewhere

to sleep, but during major fiestas or the night before market day, accommodations can be rather tight. For this reason, I have marked as many places to stay as possible on the town maps. Most of the time, many of these will be superfluous, but every once in a while you'll be glad to have the knowledge of as many lodgings as possible.

Youth Hostels & Camping
A youth hostel system has recently appeared and holders of youth hostel cards often get a small discount. The cheapest hostels are about US$8 per person, but are clean and well run. Cheaper hotels can, however, be found. Details are given in the text under individual cities.

There are climbers' refuges *(refugios)* on some of the major mountains or you can camp in the countryside. If you're carrying a tent or want to hike up to a mountaineering refuge, I suggest you get a copy of *Climbing & Hiking in Ecuador* (see The Outdoors in the Books appendix). There are rarely campsites in the towns; the constant availability of cheap hotels makes town campsites redundant.

Hotels
Hotels go by a variety of names. A *pensión* or a *hospedaje* is usually an inexpensive boarding house or place of lodging, often family run. A *hostal* can vary from inexpensive to moderately priced, depending on whether the owner thinks of the place as a cheap hostel or an up-market inn. A *hostería* tends to be a mid-priced, comfortable country inn. *Cabañas* are cabins found both on the coast and in the Oriente. They can range from basic and cheap little boxes to pleasant mid-priced bungalows. *Hotel* is a catch-all phrase for anything from a flea-ridden brothel to the most luxurious place in town. A *lodge* tends to be in remote rural areas and usually provides complete service (meals, guides and transportation arrangements) as well as lodging, which is often rustic, though comfortable enough if kerosene lanterns and cold showers aren't a deterrent.

Budget Travel The fact that a hotel is marked on a city map does not necessarily imply that I recommend it. They are listed because they may be all that is available in your price range. If you are going to a town specifically for a market or fiesta, try to arrive a day early, or at least by early afternoon the day before the market. I've included telephone numbers for many hotels, but the cheaper ones may not accept phone reservations, and even if they do, they may not honor them if you arrive late in the day. The use of the telephone in these cases is to call from the bus station to see if they have a room available; if you then intend to, head over right away.

Sometimes it's a little difficult to find single rooms, and you may get a room with two or even three beds. In most cases, though, you are only charged for one bed and don't have to share, unless the hotel is full. Ensure in advance that you won't be asked to pay for all the beds or share with a stranger if you don't want to. This is no problem 90% of the time. Some of the cheapest hotels will ask you to take a bed in a room with other travelers. These 'dormitory-style' accommodations may save you a little money, but don't assume that every traveler is as honest as you are and leave your valuables lying around unattended.

If you are traveling as a couple, or in a group, don't automatically assume that a room with two or three beds will be cheaper per person than a room with one bed. Sometimes it is and sometimes it isn't. If I give a price per person, then usually a double or triple room will cost two or three times a single. If more than one price is given, this indicates that double and triples are cheaper per person than singles.

Couples sharing one bed *(cama matrimonial)* are usually, though not always, charged the same as a double room with people in separate beds.

Look around the hotel if possible. The same prices are often charged for rooms of widely differing quality. Even in the US$3-a-night cheapies, it's worth looking around. If you get shown into a horrible airless box with just a bed and a bare light bulb, you can ask to see a better room without giving offense simply by asking if they have a room with a window, or explaining that you have to write some letters home and is there a room with a table and chair. You may be amazed at the results.

Never rent a room without looking at it first. In most hotels, even the cheapest, they'll be happy to let you see the room. If they aren't, then it usually means that the room is filthy anyway. Also ask to see the bathroom and make sure that the toilet flushes and the water runs if you want a wash. If the shower looks and smells as if someone threw up in it, the staff obviously don't do a very good job of looking after the place. There's probably a better hotel at the same price nearby.

Pricing In the smaller towns, I usually lump accommodations together in one section. In larger towns, I separate them into groups.

'Bottom end' hotels are the cheapest, but not necessarily the worst. Although rooms are usually basic, with just a bed and four walls, they can nevertheless be well looked after, very clean and amazing value for the money. They are often good places to meet other travelers, both Ecuadorian and foreign. Prices in this category range from US$2 to very approximately US$10 per person (less in small cities, or up to US$10 in large cities which are more expensive.) Every town has hotels in this price range, and in smaller towns hotels aren't any more expensive. Although you'll usually have to use communal bathrooms in the cheapest hotels, you can sometimes find rooms with a private bathroom for as little as US$4 or US$5 per person.

'Middle' category hotels usually cost from about US$8 to US$40 per person (depending on the city), but are not always better than the best hotels in the bottom-end price range. On the whole, however, you can find some very good bargains here. Even if you're traveling on a budget, there are always special occasions (your birthday?) when you can indulge in comparative luxury for a day or two.

'Top end' hotels are absent from many towns. In major cities, hotels in this price category may be luxurious and have a two-tiered pricing system. In Guayaquil and Quito, for example, a luxury hotel may charge a foreigner well over US$100 for a double, but an Ecuadorian gets the room for half the price or less. This system stinks, but is legal and there's not much you can do about it other than avoid staying in luxury hotels. Apart from the expensive luxury hotels, I include some very good hotels in this category where rates are still very cheap by western standards – from about US$50 a double and up.

Bathroom Facilities These are rarely what you may be used to at home. The cheapest hotels don't always have hot water, or it may only be turned on at certain hours of the day. Ask about this if you're planning on a hot shower before going out to dinner. Often there's hot water only in the morning.

Another intriguing device you should know about is the electric shower. This consists of a single cold-water shower head hooked up to an electric heating element that is switched on when you want a hot (more likely tepid) shower. Don't touch anything metal while you're in the shower or you may discover what an electric shock feels like. The power is never high enough to actually throw you across the room, but it's unpleasant nevertheless. I managed to shock myself once by simply picking up the soap which I had balanced on a horizontal water pipe.

Some hotels charge extra for hot showers and a rare few simply don't have showers at all.

Security Most hotels will give you a key to lock your room, and theft from your hotel room is not as frequent as it is in some other countries. Nevertheless, carrying your own padlock is a good idea if you plan on staying in the cheapest hotels. Once in a while you'll find that a room doesn't look very secure – perhaps there's a window that doesn't close, or the wall doesn't come to the ceiling and can be climbed over. It's worth finding another room. This is another reason why it's good to look at a room before you rent it.

You should never leave valuables lying around the room. It's just too tempting for a maid who earns only US$2 or US$3 a day for her work. Money and passport should be in a secure body pouch; other valuables can usually be kept in the hotel strongbox. (Some cheaper hotels might not want to take this responsibility.) Don't get paranoid though. I haven't had anything stolen from my room in years of traveling in Ecuador, and rarely hear of people who have.

Many small hotels lock their door at night, which may make it difficult for late night revelers to return to their rooms. Usually, there is a doorbell, but this is often located in some not very obvious position. Normally, there is a night guard who will let you in, but if the guard is asleep it may take several minutes of ringing, knocking or yelling to get attention. It's worth asking at what time the hotel locks up if you are planning on a night out – then at least someone might expect you.

Staying in Villages
If you're traveling really far off the beaten track, you may end up in a village that doesn't have even a basic pensión. You can usually find somewhere to sleep by asking around, but it might be just a roof over your head rather than a bed, so carry a sleeping bag or at least a blanket.

The place to ask at first would probably be a village store – the store owner usually knows everyone in the village and would know who is in the habit of renting rooms or floor space. If that fails, you can ask for the *alcalde* (mayor) or at the *policía*. You may end up sleeping on the floor of the schoolhouse, the jail or the village community center, but you're likely to find someplace if you persevere. People in remote areas are generally hospitable.

FOOD
If you're on a tight budget, food is the most important part of your trip expenses. You can stay in rock-bottom hotels, travel 2nd

class and never consider buying a souvenir, but you've got to eat well. This doesn't mean expensively, but it does mean that you want to avoid spending half your trip sitting on the toilet.

The worst culprits for making you sick are salads and unpeeled fruit. With the fruit, stick to bananas, oranges, pineapples and other fruit that you can peel yourself. With unpeeled fruit or salads, wash them yourself in water that you can trust (see Health, above). It actually can be a lot of fun getting a group together and heading out to the market to buy vegetables and preparing a huge salad. You can often persuade someone in the hotel to lend you a suitable bowl, or you could buy a large plastic bowl quite inexpensively and sell or give it away afterwards.

As long as you take heed of the salad warning, you'll find plenty of good things to eat at reasonable prices. You certainly don't have to eat in a fancy restaurant; their kitchen facilities may not be as clean as their white tablecloths. A good sign for any restaurant is if the locals eat there – restaurants aren't empty if the food is delicious and healthy.

If you're on a tight budget you can eat from street and market stalls if the food looks freshly cooked, though watch to see if your plate is going to be 'washed' in a bowl of cold, greasy water and wiped with a filthy rag (it's worth carrying your own bowl and spoon). Alternatively, try food that can be wrapped in paper, such as pancakes.

A *comedor* is literally a dining room, but the name is often applied to a cheap restaurant where the locals eat. Comedores are good places for a cheap meal.

Local Dishes

The following is a list of local dishes worth trying at markets, street stands and restaurants.

Caldo – Soups and stews are very popular and are often served in markets for breakfasts. Soups are known as *caldos, sopas* or *locros*. Chicken soup, or *caldo de gallina*, is the most popular. *Caldo de patas* is soup made by boiling cattle hooves and, to my taste, is as bad as it sounds.

Cuy – Whole roasted guinea pig. This is a traditional food dating back to Inca times. It tastes rather like a cross between rabbit and chicken. The sight of the little paws and teeth sticking out and eyes tightly closed is a little unnerving, but cuy is supposed to be a delicacy and some people love it.

Lechón – Suckling pig. Pigs are often roasted whole and are a common sight at Ecuadorian food markets. Pork is also called *chancho*.

Llapingachos – Fried mashed-potato-and-cheese pancakes often served with *fritada* – scraps of fried or roasted pork. These are my favorite.

Seco – Stew. The word literally means 'dry' (as opposed to a 'wet' soup). The stew is usually meat served with rice and can be *seco de gallina* (chicken stew), *de res* (beef), *de chivo* (goat), or *de cordero* (lamb).

Tortillas de maíz – Tasty fried corn pancakes.

Yaguarlocro – Potato soup with chunks of barely congealed blood sausage floating in it. I happen to like blood sausage and find this soup very tasty; many people prefer just straight *locro* which usually has potatoes, corn and an avocado or cheese topping.

Restaurants

In a restaurant, there'll be other dishes to choose from. For breakfast, the usual eggs and bread rolls or toast are available. *Huevos fritos* are fried eggs, *revueltos* are scrambled, and *pasados* or *a la copa* are boiled or poached. These last two are usually semiraw, so ask to have them *bien cocidos* (well cooked) or *duros* (hard) if you don't like your eggs runny. *Tostadas* are toast and *panes* are bread rolls, which go well with *mantequilla y mermelada* (butter and jam). A good local change from eggs are sweet corn tamales called *humitas*, often served for breakfast with coffee, mainly in the highlands.

Lunch is the biggest meal of the day for many Ecuadorians. If you walk into a cheap restaurant and ask for the *almuerzo* or lunch of the day, you'll get a decent meal for US$1 to US$2. An almuerzo always consists of a sopa and a *segundo* (second dish), which is usually a seco with plenty of rice. Sometimes the segundo is *pescado* (fish) or a kind of lentil or pea stew *(lenteja, arveja)*, but there's always rice. Many, but not all, restaurants will give you a salad (often cooked), juice and a *postre* (dessert) as well as the two main courses.

The supper of the day is usually similar to lunch. Ask for the *merienda*. If you don't want the almuerzo or merienda, you can choose from the menu, but this is always more expensive. However, the set meals do tend to get a little repetitious after a while and most people like to try other dishes.

A *churrasco* is a hearty plate with a slice of fried beef, one or two fried eggs, vegetables (usually boiled beet slices, carrots and beans), fried potatoes, a slice of avocado and tomato and the inevitable rice. If you get *arroz con pollo* then you'll be served a mountain of rice with little bits of chicken mixed in. If you're fed up with rice, go to a *Pollo a la Brasa* restaurant where you can get fried chicken, often with fried potatoes on the side. *Gallina* is chicken that has usually been boiled, as in soups, while *pollo* is more often spit-roasted or fried. Pollo tends to be under-done, but you can always send it back to have it cooked longer.

Parrilladas are steak houses or grills. These are recommended if you like meat, and a complete loss if you don't. Steaks, pork chops, chicken breasts, blood sausages, liver and tripe are all served on a grill, which is placed on the table. Every time I order a parrillada for two people, I find there's enough for three (they'll give you a plastic bag for the leftovers). If you don't want the whole thing, choose just a chop or a steak. Although parrilladas aren't particularly cheap, they are reasonably priced and a very good value.

Seafood is very good, even in the highlands, as it is brought in fresh from the coast and iced. The most common types of fish are a white sea bass called *corvina* and trout *(trucha)*. Ceviche is popular throughout Ecuador; this is seafood marinated in lemon and served with popcorn and sliced onions, and it's delicious. Unfortunately, improperly prepared ceviche has recently been identified as a source of the cholera bacteria. However, most restaurants in Ecuador are aware of this and do a good job of clean preparation, so if the restaurant is popular and looks clean, the ceviche will most likely be both delicious and safe to eat. Ceviche can be *de pescado* (fish), *de camarones* (shrimp) or *de concha* (shell-fish, such as clams or mussels). A *langosta* (lobster dinner) costs from about US$10 – a bargain by western standards.

Most Ecuadorian meals come with *arroz* (rice), and some travelers get fed up with it. Surprisingly, one of the best places to go for a change from rice is a Chinese restaurant. These are known as *chifas* and are generally inexpensive and a good value. Apart from rice, they serve *tallarines*, which are noodles mixed with your choice of pork, chicken, beef or vegetables *(legumbres, verduras)*. Portions tend to be filling.

Vegetarians will find that chifas offer the best choice for meatless dishes, or you can go to a *cevichería* if you don't consider seafood to be meat. Vegetarian restaurants are rare in Ecuador. If you have any kind of strict diet, you would be advised to bring a camping stove with you and cook your own. Most hotels don't mind this, especially the cheapest ones. Just don't burn the place down.

If you want inexpensive luxury, go for breakfast at the fanciest hotel in town (assuming they have a restaurant or cafeteria). You can relax with coffee and rolls and the morning paper, or get a window seat and watch the world go by. Despite the elegant surroundings and the bow-tied waiter, you are only charged an extra few cents for your coffee. Makes an nice change and the coffee is often very good.

Cities big enough to have first-class hotels also have good but expensive (by Ecuadorian standards) international restaurants, often right in the hotels themselves.

DRINKS
Water

I don't recommend drinking tap water anywhere in Latin America. *Agua potable* means that the water comes from the tap, but it's not necessarily healthy. Even if it comes from a chlorination or filtration plant, the plumbing is often old, cracked and full of crud. One suggestion is to carry a water bottle and purify your own water (for more about this, see the Health section).

If you don't want to go through the hassle of constantly purifying water, you can buy bottled mineral water very cheaply. Don't ask for mineral water, ask for Güitig (pronounced Weetig), which is the best known brand, although there are other equally good ones. They come in a variety of sizes and are available in restaurants and, more cheaply, in grocery stores. Güitig and others are usually highly carbonated and rather salty. Some people prefer *Agua Linda,* which is less fizzy and salty. This often comes in large two-liter plastic bottles which are disposable, but can be reused for your own purified water. Buying water in a glass bottle means you have to pay a deposit on the bottle.

Soft Drinks

The advantage of buying a bottled drink in a store is that it is very cheap; the disadvantage is that you have to drink it at the store because the bottle is usually worth more than the drink inside (canned drinks cost up to three times more than bottles). You can pay a deposit, but you have to return the bottle to the store you bought it from; a different store won't give you any money for it. What many travelers do is pay a deposit on, or effectively buy, a bottle of pop, beer or mineral water and then trade it in every time they want to buy a drink someplace else.

All the usual soft drinks are available, as are some local ones with such endearing names as Bimbo or Lulu. Soft drinks are collectively known as *colas* and the local brands are very sweet. 7-Up is simply called *seven,* so don't try calling it 'siete arriba' as no one will have any idea what you're talking about. You can also buy Coca-Cola, Pepsi Cola, Orange Fanta or Crush (called *croosh)* and Sprite – the latter pronounced *essprite!* Diet soft drinks are

becoming available in the fancier hotels, restaurants and supermarkets.

Ask for your drink *helada* if you want it out of the refrigerator or *al clima* if you don't. Remember to say *sin hielo* (without ice) unless you really trust the water supply.

Fruit Juices

Juices *(jugos)* are available everywhere and are usually better than colas to my taste, but they cost more. Make sure you get *jugo puro* and not *con agua.* The most common kinds are *mora* (blackberry), *naranja* (orange), *toronja* (grapefruit), *piña* (pineapple), *maracuya* (passion fruit), *sandía* (watermelon), *naranjilla* (a local fruit tasting like bitter orange) or papaya.

Coffee & Tea

Coffee is available almost everywhere, but may be disappointing. Coffee beans may be roasted and ground fine, then compacted into a small perforated metal cup over which boiling water is slowly poured. The result is a thick syrup which is then poured into cruets and diluted with hot milk or water. Sometimes it tastes OK, but sometimes it's poor. It looks very much like soy sauce, so always check before pouring it into your milk (or over your rice)! Instant coffee is also served. 'Real' filtered coffee is becoming more available. Espresso is available only in the better restaurants. *Café con leche* is milk with coffee, and *café con agua* or *café negro* is black coffee.

Tea, or *té,* is served black with lemon and sugar. If you ask for tea with milk, British style, you'll get a cup of hot milk with a tea bag to dunk in it. Herb teas and hot chocolate are also popular.

Alcohol

Finally we come to those beverages that can loosely be labeled 'libations.' The selection of beers is limited, but they are quite palatable and inexpensive. Pilsner usually comes in large 650 ml bottles and is my drink of choice. Club is slightly more expensive, has a slightly higher alcohol content (3.9% as opposed to 3.5%, if you're interested), and comes in small 330 ml bottles. Other beers are imported and available only in the more expensive restaurants or at specialty liquor stores.

Local wines are truly terrible and should not be experimented with. Imported wines from Chile, Argentina or Peru are good, but cost much more than they do in their country of origin – nevertheless, these are the best deals for wine drinkers. Californian and European wines are available, but are more expensive still, and Australian wines haven't made it to Ecuador yet.

Spirits are expensive if imported and not very good if made locally, with some notable exceptions. Rum is cheap and good. The local firewater, *aguardiente* or sugarcane alcohol, is an acquired taste, but is also good. It's very cheap; you can get a half bottle of Cristal aguardiente for about US$1. A popular fiesta drink that is made and sold on the streets is a *canelita* or *canelazo* – a hot toddy made with hot water, aguardiente, lemon and *canela* (cinnamon). If you're desperate for gin, vodka or whisky, try the Larios brand – probably the best of a bad bunch.

ENTERTAINMENT

The most typical nightlife is a peña, or Ecuadorian *música folklórica* club (see Music in Facts about the Country for a description of traditional folkloric music). This is a popular form of entertainment for all Ecuadorians, from cabinet ministers to campesinos. Concerts are informal affairs, usually held late of a weekend night, and accompanied by plenty of drinking. They are not held everywhere – Quito and Otavalo often have good ones.

Apart from peñas, there are the usual nighttime activities: Cinemas are popular and cheap, with shows for well under a dollar. There are theater productions and symphonies in the main cities. Discotheques and dance clubs are popular in the main cities too. Some of these are great fun if you like dancing to Latin rhythms like salsa or merengue. In the smaller towns, there isn't much to do apart from going to the local cinema, except during the annual fiesta.

SPECTATOR SPORTS

The national sport is *fútbol* (soccer) which is played in every city, town and village. Major-league soccer games are played in Quito and Guayaquil on Saturday afternoons and Sunday mornings. Soccer in Ecuador, as in all Latin America, can be quite passionate, and going to a game is usually exciting. The best Ecuadorian teams recently were Emelec and Barcelona, both of Guayaquil, but of course this is likely to change.

Volleyball is popular, but more as an amateur game played in parks than as a professional sport. Golf and tennis are becoming increasingly popular – Ecuadorian tennis player Andres Gomez won the US Open Men's Doubles (with Slobodan Zivojinovic) in 1986, and the French Open in 1990. Gomez is arguably Ecuador's most internationally famous athlete.

Typically Latin sports activities such as bullfighting and cockfighting are very popular. The main bullfighting season is during the first week in December in Quito, when bullfighters from Mexico and Spain may take part. Other highland towns have occasional bullfights, but this sport is less popular in the lowlands. Cockfighting is popular nationwide, and most towns of any size will have a *coliseo de gallos* (cockfighting arena). A variety of strange ball-games are also played. One of these is a sort of paddleball called *pelota de guante*, where players hit a rubber ball with large, spiked paddles. Another is a marbles games called *cocos*, which is played with giant steel ball bearings.

THINGS TO BUY

Souvenirs are good, varied and cheap. Although going to villages and markets is fun, you won't necessarily save a great deal of money. Similar items for sale in the main cities are often not much more expensive, so if you're limited on time you can shop in Quito or Guayaquil. If you only have the time or inclination to go on one big shopping expedition, you'll find the Saturday market at Otavalo has a wide variety and is convenient – this makes it very popular.

Many other markets are colorful events for locals rather than tourists.

In markets and smaller stores, bargaining is acceptable, indeed expected, though don't expect to reduce the price by more than about 20%. In 'tourist stores' in Quito, prices are usually fixed. Some of the best stores are quite expensive; on the other hand, the quality of their products is often superior. Shopping in markets is more traditional and fun – though remember to watch your pockets.

Clothing

Woolen goods are popular and are often made of a pleasantly coarse homespun wool. Otavalo is good for these, as well as for sweaters, scarves, hats, gloves and vests. The price of a thick sweater will begin at around US$10, depending on size and quality; fashionable boutique sweaters can fetch US$50. If you're planning trips high into the mountains, these make good, warm additions to your wardrobe. Wool is also spun into a much finer and tighter textile that is used for making ponchos. Otavaleño Indian ponchos are amongst the best anywhere.

Clothing is also made from Orlon, which is cheaper than wool but looks garish and unattractive. Some can tell the difference just by looking, but if you're not sure, try the match trick: Take a tiny piece of lint from the material and set fire to it. If it melts, it's Orlon; if it burns, it's wool. (Perhaps the match trick is not the wisest idea – storekeepers may not appreciate it.) Many people think that only woolen items are traditional, earthy, cool, ethnic etc. While that may be true, if you see an Orlon sweater that you like, there's nothing to stop you buying it, and it'll be one of the cheapest sweaters you've ever bought.

Hand-embroidered clothes are also attractive, but it's worth getting them from a reputable shop; otherwise they may shrink or run. Cotton blouses, shirts, skirts, dresses and shawls are available.

Ecuadorian T-shirts with designs featuring Galápagos animals are very popular; many other bold and distinctive motifs are available. If you're a T-shirt collector, you'll find all sizes and colors to choose from.

Panama hats are worth buying. A good Panama is so finely made that it can be rolled up and passed through a man's ring, though it's unlikely that you'll find many of that quality. They are made from *toquilla*, a palmlike bush that grows abundantly in the coastal province of Manabí. Montecristi and Jipijapa are major centers. The hat's name dates back to the 1849 California gold rush, when prospectors traveling from the eastern US to California through the Isthmus of Panama bought the hats, but they are originally Ecuadorian.

Weavings

A large variety of mainly woolen weavings are to be found all over the country, with Otavalo, as usual, having a good selection. They range from sq-foot weavings that can be sewn together to make throw cushions or shoulder bags, to weavings large enough to be used as floor rugs or wall hangings. Designs range from traditional to modern; MC Escher styles are popular.

Bags

Apart from bags made from two small weavings stitched together, you can buy

---

Main Market Days

The more important markets are asterisked.

Saturday
Otavalo*, Latacunga*, Riobamba*, Cotacachi, Guano, Azoguez
Sunday
Sangolquí*, Machachi*, Pujilí*, Peguche, Cuenca, Santo Domingo de los Colorados, Salcedo, Tulcán
Monday
Ambato*
Tuesday
Latacunga, Riobamba, Guano
Wednesday
Pujilí
Thursday
Saquisilí*, Cuenca, Riobamba, Tulcán ■

shigras or shoulder bags made from agave fiber that are strong, colorful and eminently practical. They come in a variety of sizes and are expandable. Agave fiber is also used to make macramé bags.

Leather
A famous center for leatherwork is Cotacachi, north of Otavalo. Prices are cheap in comparison to those in more developed countries, but quality is very variable, so examine possible purchases carefully. Although the best leatherwork in Ecuador is supposedly done in the Ambato area, it's much easier to find leather goods for sale in Cotacachi. Leatherwork items range from full suits to coin purses, and wide-brimmed hats to luggage bags.

Products from Trees
The major woodworking center of Ecuador is San Antonio de Ibarra, and any items bought elsewhere are likely to have been carved there. Items range from the utilitarian (bowls, salad utensils, chess sets, candlesticks) to the decorative (crucifixes, statues, wall plaques). Again, prices are very low, but quality varies.

Balsa-wood models are also popular. They are made in the jungles of the Oriente and sold in many of Quito's gift stores. Brightly painted birds are the most frequently seen, but other animals and boxes are also sold.

Tagua-nut carvings are common souvenirs. The nut is actually the seed of a coastal palm *(Phytelephas macrocarpa).* The egg-sized seed is carved into a variety of novelty items such as napkin rings, egg cups and chess pieces.

Jewelry
Ecuador isn't famous for its gemstones, but it does have good silverwork. Chordeleg near Cuenca has beautifully filigreed silver items. The Amazon area produces necklaces made from nuts and other rainforest products.

Bread Figures
Painted and varnished ornaments made of bread dough are unique to Ecuador and are best obtained in Calderón, a village just north of Quito. Some of the most inexpensive ones are designed as (and make) great Christmas tree ornaments. Designs are imaginative and fun – Christmas stockings with a mouse peeking out, giant green cacti vaguely suggestive of a Christmas tree, animals, candles . . . the designs go on and on. For a few dollars, you can buy decorations for everyone on your gift list.

Other Purchases
Baskets made of straw, reeds or agave fibers are common everywhere. Onyx (a pale, translucent quartz with parallel layers of different colors) is carved into chess sets and other objects. Miniature blowpipes modeled after those used by Amazonian Indians are also popular, and you'll find plenty of other choices.

Getting There & Away

There are three ways of getting to Ecuador: by air from anywhere in the world, by land from either Colombia or Peru and by sea. However, very few people even consider the ocean route these days as it is more expensive and less convenient than flying.

AIR

Airports & Airlines

There are two major international airports serving Ecuador: Guayaquil on the coast and Quito in the highlands. Remember that a flight between these two cities only costs about US$31 if you buy the internal ticket in Ecuador.

Ecuador's main international airline at present is Saeta (☎ (800) 827 2382 in the USA or Canada), providing service to Los Angeles, New York, Miami and several Latin American capitals. TAME, almost exclusively a domestic airline, has recently begun service from the Ecuadorian towns of Tulcán and Esmeraldas to Cali in southern Colombia.

American Airlines has the most frequent services to Ecuador from the USA, with the most gateway cities. Continental flies to Ecuador from Houston. Both airlines stop at or continue to other Latin American cities. Several major Latin American carriers fly from Ecuador to Latin America and the USA.

Major carriers from Europe, usually stopping in Miami or somewhere in the Caribbean en route to Ecuador, include Iberia, KLM and Lufthansa. Other European carriers provide flights connecting with North and Latin American airlines.

These and other international airlines have offices in Quito and Guayaquil, and are listed in the Getting There & Away sections under those towns.

If you plan to fly to Ecuador, bear in mind that the main hub for flights to and from western South America is Lima, Peru. You may be able to fly more cheaply to Lima and finish your journey to Ecuador by land. Bus travel from Lima to the Ecuadorian border takes about 24 hours and costs about US$20. If you prefer to travel directly to Ecuador, frequent international flights arrive and depart from either Quito or Guayaquil.

For a list of the major airlines' website addresses, see Online Services in Facts for the Visitor.

Buying Tickets

The ordinary tourist or economy-class fare is not the most economical way to go. It is convenient, however, because it enables you to fly on the next plane out and your ticket is valid for 12 months. If you want to economize further, there are several options. Students and people under 26 qualify for discounts with most airlines.

Whatever your age, if you can purchase your ticket well in advance and stay a (variable) minimum length of time, you can usually spend about 30% to 40% less than a full economy fare. These are called APEX, excursion or promotional fares, depending on the country from which you are flying and the rules and fare structures that apply there.

Normally the following restrictions apply: You must purchase your ticket at least 21 days (sometimes more) in advance, and you must stay away a minimum period (about 14 days on average) and return within 180 days (sometimes less). Individual airlines have different requirements and these change from time to time. Most of these tickets do not allow stopovers and there are extra charges (penalties) if you change your dates of travel or destinations. These tickets are often sold out well in advance of departure, so book early whenever possible.

It is worth bearing in mind that roundtrip fares are always cheaper than two one-way tickets. They are also cheaper than an 'open jaws' fare, which would enable you to fly into one city (say Quito) and leave via another (say Lima).

There is also a 10% tax on all international flights originating in Ecuador. This must be paid before boarding the aircraft. For example, if you purchase a Miami-Caracas ticket and a Quito-Miami ticket (intending to travel overland from Caracas to Quito), you will be charged 10% of the Quito-Miami fare at the airport because this flight originates in Ecuador. This does not apply to the return portion of a Miami-Quito-Miami ticket, because it does not originate in Ecuador. Check this carefully if you are buying a ticket originating in Ecuador.

If, because of a late flight (though not a rescheduled one) you lose a connection or are forced to stay overnight, the carrier is responsible for providing you with help in making the earliest possible connection and paying for a room in a hotel of their choice. They should also provide you with meal vouchers. If you are seriously delayed on an international flight, ask for these services.

The cheapest tickets are those sold by companies specializing in discount airfares (the so-called 'bucket shops,' although this term is little used these days). These companies are legally allowed to sell discounted tickets to help airlines and charter companies fill their flights. These tickets often sell out fast, and you may be limited to only a few available dates and have other restrictions. While APEX, economy and student tickets are available direct from the airlines or from a travel agent, discounted tickets are available only from the discount ticket agencies themselves. Most of them are good, reputable, bonded companies, but once in a great while, a fly-by-night operator comes along, taking your money for a supercheap flight and giving you an invalid or unusable ticket. Check what you are buying carefully before handing over your money.

Discount ticket agencies often advertise in newspapers and magazines; there is much competition and a variety of fares and schedules are available. Fares to South America have traditionally been relatively expensive, but ticket agencies have recently been able to offer increasingly economical fares to that continent.

Courier travel is another possibility, if you are flexible with dates and can manage with only carry-on luggage. For Latin American destinations, courier travel is most practical from the USA (see The USA, below). Couriers are hired by companies who need to have packages delivered to Ecuador (and other countries) and will give the courier exceptionally cheap tickets in return for using his or her baggage allowance. These are legitimate operations – all baggage to be delivered is completely legal. And it is amazing how much you can bring with only carry-on luggage! I have heard of couriers boarding an aircraft wearing two pairs of trousers, two shirts under a sweater and a rain jacket with the pockets stuffed with travel essentials. Bring a folded plastic shopping bag and, once you have boarded the aircraft, you can remove the extra clothes and place them in the plastic bag. (Try not to have metal objects in inside pockets when you go through the metal detector at the airport! Also bear in mind that most courier companies want their couriers to look reasonably neat, so don't overdo the 'bag lady' routine.) Remember, you can buy things like T-shirts, a towel and soap after you arrive at your destination, so traveling with just carry-on is certainly feasible.

Baggage & Other Restrictions

These vary depending on the airline and the class of service you have chosen. The airline or your travel agent will be able to explain restrictions to you. As a minimum, you will be allowed two pieces of luggage totaling 20 kg, plus a carry-on bag that fits under the seat in front of you. On some airlines or in business and first class, you will be allowed more.

Restrictions on cheaper tickets usually mean that you cannot get a refund, and if you change your dates of travel you must pay an additional charge.

The USA

In recent years 'consolidators' (as discount ticket agencies in the US are called) have begun to appear. The travel sections in major newspapers such as *The Los Angeles Times* and *The New York Times* sometimes advertise cheap fares to South America, although these may be no cheaper than APEX fares. A useful book about this is *Consolidators: Air Travelers Bargain Basement* by Kelly Monaghan.

One agency that can help you find the best deal to Ecuador (or anywhere else in the world) is Council Travel Services, a subsidiary of the Council on International Educational Exchange (CIEE). You can find their address and telephone numbers in the telephone directories of many North American cities, particularly those with universities. Their head office (☎ (212) 661 1414/50, (800) 226 8624, fax 972 3231) is at 205 E 42nd St, New York, NY 10017. Call them for the office nearest you. Another good choice is STA Travel (☎ (213) 937 8722, (800) 777 0112, fax 937 2739), 5900 Wilshire Blvd, Los Angeles, CA 90036. They also have subsidiaries in other towns.

There are flights to Ecuador from New York, Los Angeles, Houston and Miami. Flights from other cities connect with one of these, usually Miami. Prices depend mainly on two things: when you go and how long you want to stay. The low season is mid-August through November, and January through June. December, July and the first half of August are the high season. Fares for short visits (up to 21 days) are the cheapest; fares for longer visits are more expensive. If you are planning on spending several months in South America and want to visit several countries, Caracas, Venezuela, is often the cheapest flight destination from the USA. From there you can travel overland through Colombia, Ecuador, Peru and Brazil, and then back to Venezuela for your return flight.

Recent low-season fares from Miami have been US$492 for stays of less than 21 days, US$515 (up to 60 days) and US$680 (up to 150 days). High-season fares are a little more. From New York, add about US$120 to each Miami fare. From Los Angeles, fares start at US$750 for under 21 days. At press time, the airline Servivensa was offering 'special fares' from Miami or New York for US$400 and US$550 respectively – substantially cheaper than the other airlines, but harder to book. These fares will probably not be available by the time you read this, but it does pay to shop around. All prices above include an obligatory US$18 tax and are liable to change – downwards as well as up.

People are often surprised that fares from Los Angeles in southern California are so much higher than from northerly New York. A glance at the world map soon shows why. New York at 74° west is almost due north of Miami at 80° and Quito at 78°. Thus planes can fly a shorter, faster and cheaper north-south route. Los Angeles, on the other hand, is 118° west and therefore much further away from Quito than New York is.

Another possibility, for travelers wishing to visit several Latin American countries, is to fly with AeroPeru (☎ (800) 777 7717 in the US and Canada). They offer 'Around South America Airpasses' from Miami to Peru, plus other Latin American countries, including Ecuador.

Courier travel is another good option. Recently, Linehaul Services (☎ (305) 477 0651) in Miami required couriers for flights from Miami to Ecuador. Roundtrip tickets cost about US$200 and were good for 30 days. This is a good option for people flying from New York or Miami. For up-to-date information, contact Travel Unlimited, PO Box 1058, Allston, MA 02134, which publishes a monthly newsletter listing courier flights to Ecuador and many other countries. A year's subscription costs US$25 in the USA, US$35 elsewhere. You can get a single issue for US$5. For a general overview there are several books including the *Courier Air Travel Handbook* by Mark Field (Thunderbird Press).

Travelers wishing to tour the Galápagos will find that Saeta sells 'tied-in' tickets from Miami to Ecuador and on to the

Galápagos. These fares are about US$100 cheaper than buying your Galápagos portion in Ecuador. The problem is you need to make your arrangements in advance, as the tickets are valid for only certain dates. It may be possible to change the dates, but check first. Unless you are going on an organized tour with reliable boat departures, these 'tied-in' tickets may be more hassle than they are worth. Saeta uses SAN airline to Isla San Cristóbal and, though there are tours available from that island if you book ahead, the cheapest tours are usually from Puerto Ayora on Isla Santa Cruz, which is reached by the TAME domestic flights. The two islands are half a day's boat ride apart and ferry service is infrequent, so you are stuck on the island you fly to. If you do book a tour in advance and fly with Saeta, make sure that the tour begins and ends in Isla San Cristóbal.

Canada

There are no direct flights from Canada to Ecuador; travelers must connect through one of the gateway cities in the USA. Particularly recommended Canadian travel agencies include Travel CUTS (☎ (416) 977 3703, fax 977 4796), 171 College St, Toronto, ON, M5T 1P7, with other offices in major Canadian cities.

Europe

Discount ticket agencies ('bucket shops') generally provide the cheapest fares from Europe to South America. Fares from London are often cheaper than from other European cities, even though your flight route may take you from London through a European city! Don't ask me why. Many European (especially Scandinavian) budget travelers buy from London ticket agencies, as cheap fares are difficult to find in their own countries. Discounted tickets available from these agencies are often several hundred dollars cheaper than official fares, and while they usually carry certain restrictions, they are valid and legal.

In London competition is fierce. Discount flights are advertised in the classi-

fied sections of newspapers ranging from the *Times* to *Time Out*. I have heard consistently good reports about Journey Latin America (JLA; ☎ (0181) 747 3108 for flights, fax 742 1312), 16 Devonshire Rd, Chiswick, London W4 2HD. They specialize in cheap fares to anywhere in Latin America as well as arranging itineraries for both independent and escorted travel. They will make arrangements for you over the phone or by fax. Ask for their free magazine, *Papagaio*, full of helpful information.

Another reputable budget travel agency is Trailfinders (☎ (0171) 938 3366) 42-50 Earl's Court Rd, London W8 6EJ. The useful travel newspaper *Trailfinder* is available for free. STA Travel (☎ (0171) 938 4711), Priory House, 6 Wrights Lane, London W8 6TA, and Council Travel (☎ (0171) 437 7767), also in London, both specialize in fares for students and those under 26. Also worth a try is Passage to South America (☎ (0171) 602 9889, fax 602 4251), 113 Shepherd's Bush Rd, London, W6 7LP. The cheapest fares from London may start at UK£500, which is an incredible deal considering the distance. Restrictions usually involve leaving only on certain days, and tickets may be valid for only 90 days, with penalties for changing your return date. A UK£10 departure tax is added. Fares depend on how long you want to stay (longer stays are more expensive), which airline you choose and when you travel. The (expensive) high seasons are December, early January, July and August.

Most airlines from Europe will take you to Miami, Colombia, Venezuela or the Caribbean, where you connect with other flights to Ecuador. Note that fares, routes and low/high seasons change frequently and that the best information is to be had from travel professionals.

Courier flights are also possible from Europe. Look in the classified sections of Sunday newspapers.

European agents selling cheap flights to South America from outside of the UK include the foliowing.

Globetrotter
    Renweg, 8001, Zurich, Switzerland
Uniclam
    63 Rue Monsieur le Prince, Paris 75006,
    France
Hajo Siewer Tours
    Martinstrasse 39, Olpe 57462, Germany

Council Travel has offices in Munich, Germany (☎ 089 395 022), and Paris, France (☎ 01 44 55 55 65). STA Travel also has offices in European cities. The cheapest fares, however, are usually to be had in London. The British agencies will sell tickets to other European nationals, but you often have to pick them up in person in London (or have them mailed to a UK address).

Central America
There are direct flights from Mexico City, Panama City, and San José, Costa Rica, to Ecuador. Other Central American countries have connecting flights from their capitals via San José or Panama on to Ecuador. There are no particularly cheap deals here – you pay whatever the going economy rate is. This is about US$260 one way from Panama or US$370 from San José.

South America
Again, there are no particularly cheap deals. One-way economy-class fares to Ecuador are about US$150 from Bogotá, Colombia; US$310 from Caracas, Venezuela; US$180 from Lima, Peru; US$450 from Santiago, Chile; US$340 from La Paz, Bolivia; US$590 from Buenos Aires, Argentina; and US$730 from Río de Janeiro, Brazil.

If you want to fly and are not in a desperate hurry, you can often go somewhat cheaper by taking internal flights. For example, you could fly Guayaquil-Machala for US$18, take a bus across the border to Tumbes, Peru (about four hours and a couple of dollars), then take internal Peruvian flights Tumbes-Lima and Lima-Tacna (about US$100 each leg), take a bus from Tacna across the border to Arica, Chile (a

couple of hours), and fly Arica-Santiago (about US$110). The combined cost is better than the direct fare of US$450, but expect to travel for about three days to make all connections.

Australia & New Zealand
There is little choice of routes between Australia and South America and there are certainly no bargain fares available. If you are going on to Europe or Asia, Round-the-World (RTW) tickets probably work out a better value for the money. Many travelers fly to the west coast of the USA and then overland through Mexico and Central America, returning to the USA to pick up their RTW flight. Alternately, you can continue on to Miami and then take a return flight to your desired South American destination from there. Miami-Quito-Lima-Miami is one route that has been used. There are usually strict conditions – such as a five-month limit – applying to discount tickets, so be careful.

Aerolíneas Argentinas flies from Sydney via Auckland to Buenos Aires where passengers must overnight before continuing to Ecuador.

Check the ads in the travel pages of papers like Melbourne's *The Age* or the *Sydney Morning Herald*.

Asia
There is also very little choice of direct flights between Asia and South America apart from Japan, and there certainly won't be any bargains there. Council Travel has an office in Tokyo, Japan. STA Travel has offices in Tokyo and some other Asian cities.

LAND
From South America, traveling by public transport through Peru or Colombia – the only two countries having land borders with Ecuador – is no problem.

SEA
Occasionally you can find a ship going to Guayaquil, Ecuador's main port, though

this is a very unusual way to arrive in Ecuador. It's certainly cheaper and more convenient to fly, but the 'romance' of crossing the world the old way is still a draw to some.

Very few cruise ships use Guayaquil as a port of call as they head down the Pacific coast of South America. A few cargo lines will carry passengers.

The Polish Ocean Lines has passages from several European ports to many South American ones; prices vary depending on the destination, but expect to pay roughly US$2000 from Europe to Ecuador. A reader reports that he recently made a passage on a Polish Ocean Lines vessel sailing from Gdynia, Poland via Hamburg, Germany to Guayaquil, continuing to Peru and Chile before returning to Rotterdam, Holland. He suggests that in Ecuador you don't pay at the shipping offices (which are friendly but chaotic), but pay the captain on board to avoid problems. In Europe, a good contact for trans-Atlantic cargo vessels is Klaus Holz (☎ (046) 42 66 86), Frachtschiff Touristik International, Marschall 2, 24376 Hasselberg, Germany.

The Chilean Ocean Line has passages from several US ports to Chile stopping at Guayaquil en route. Lykes Line and Egon Oldendorff also carry passengers from the USA to Guayaquil and other South American ports. Fares are very roughly US$1500 from the USA to Ecuador. These are all one way – most shipping lines prefer to sell roundtrips, however.

It is possible to arrive in Ecuador on your own sailing boat or, if you don't happen to have one, as a crew member. Crew members don't necessarily have to be experienced because many long ocean passages involve standing watch and keeping your eyes open. You should be able to get along with people in close quarters for extended periods of time, as this is the most difficult aspect of the trip. If you get fed up with someone, there is nowhere else to go. Crew members are often (but not always) asked to contribute towards expenses, especially

food. Still, this is usually much cheaper than traveling overland. Check the notice boards around marinas for vessels looking for additional crew members.

Atulyo and Preyasi, owners of the sailing vessel S/V *Wailana*, sailed from California to Ecuador in the early 1990s. They report that the following are good places to hang out and meet 'yachties.' In Mexico: Papi's Deli, Cabo San Lucas, Baja California; Phil's Restaurant, Melaque, Bahía Navidada, near Manzanillo; La Sirena Gorda Restaurant, Zihuatanango; Acapulco Yacht Club, Acapulco. In Costa Rica: Playa de Cocos, Bahía Ballena (near Montezuma), Puntarenas and Golfito are all good. The Jungle Club, also known as Captain Tom's Place, on an island opposite Golfito, is one of the best places. The Balboa Yacht Club is a good place in Panama. In Ecuador, Salinas is the port most frequented by international yachts.

A possible source of information is *The Hitchhikers Guide to the Oceans* by Alison Muir Bennett and Clare Davis (1990, Seven Seas Press).

DEPARTURE TAXES

There is a hefty US$25 departure tax on international flights from Ecuador. This is payable in sucres or in cash US dollars at the exchange rate of the day.

If you leave by land, you don't have to pay the departure tax.

ORGANIZED TOURS

Many kinds of organized tours are available. These range from hotel-based visits of the highlands to strenuous mountaineering expeditions, from camping in the rainforest to staying at a luxurious jungle lodge and, of course, tours to the Galápagos.

Many varieties of tours can be arranged within Ecuador and are described in the main body of the book. Other tours can be arranged in advance from home (especially if you live in the USA). There are many operators to choose from. The following are recommended operators, but there are certainly others.

Responsible Tourism

Whether you go with an organized tour or arrange your trip by yourself, you are encouraged to travel in a culturally and environmentally sensitive manner. Try to be a positive force rather than a drain on the resources of the country you are visiting.

Some suggestions: interact with local people – don't just take photos and run – and don't make promises you cannot keep. Accept and respect local customs and lifestyles rather than imposing your own. Don't buy illegal artifacts, such as pre-Columbian pieces or items made from endangered animals, like cat skins or jewelry made from sea turtle or black coral. Support local artisans by buying locally made handicrafts and artwork. Learn a few words of Spanish, try local food and stay in small, locally run hotels.

For further information about responsible traveling, contact the following organizations:

Center for Responsible Tourism
    2 Kensington Rd, San Anselmo, CA 94960, USA (☎ (415) 843 5506)
La Asociación Ecuatoriana de Ecoturismo
    Avenida Amazonas 2468, PO Box 402-A, Quito (☎ 552 617, fax 565 261)
The Earth Preservation Fund
    c/o Wildland Adventures, 3516 NE 155th, Seattle, WA 98155, USA (☎ (206) 365 0686,
    (800) 345 4453, fax 363 6615, see also Online Services)
The Ecotourism Society
    PO Box 755, North Bennington, VT 05257, USA (☎ (802) 447 2121, fax 447 2122,
    see also Online Services)
Tourism Concern
    Froebel College, Roehampton Lane, London SW15 5PU, UK (☎ (0181) 878 9053) ■

Elderhostel
    75 Federal St, Boston, MA 02110, USA (☎ (617) 426 8056). Excellent educational tours for travelers over 60 (younger companions are permitted).
Field Guides
    PO Box 160723, Austin, TX 78716, USA (☎ (512) 327 4953, fax 327 9231). These tours are only for dedicated birdwatchers.
Galápagos Adventure Tours
    29 Palace View, Bromley, Kent BR1 3EJ, UK (☎ (0181) 460 8107, fax 289 3266, see also Online Services). Fully escorted tours to the Galápagos on the best boats. Scuba diving and jungle excursions are available.
Galápagos Travel
    PO Box 1220, San Juan Bautista, CA 95045, USA (☎ (408) 623 2920, (800) 969 9014, fax 623 2923). Galápagos tours on the better small boats.
Inca Floats
    1311 63rd St, Emeryville, CA 94608, USA (☎ (510) 420 1550, fax 420 0947). Mainly Galápagos tours on small boats with some mainland tours.
International Expeditions
    One Environs Park, Helena, AL 35080, USA (☎ (205) 428 1700, (800) 633 4734, fax 428 1714). General natural history tours.

Journey Latin America
    14-16 Devonshire Rd, Chiswick, London W4 2HD, UK (☎ (0181) 747 8315, fax 742 1312). Flight and tour specialists to Latin America with many years of experience.
South American Experience
    47 Causton St, London SW1P 4AT, UK (☎ (0171) 976 5511, fax 976 6908). Similar to Journey Latin America.
University Research Expeditions Program (UREP)
    University of California, Berkeley, CA 94720, USA (☎ (510) 642 6586). Visit Amazon villages to learn and record local knowledge and to help develop sustainable activities. Open to the public.
Wilderness Travel
    801 Allston Way, Berkeley, CA 94710, USA (☎ (510) 548 0420, (800) 368 2794, fax 548 0347). One- and two-week Galápagos tours, Amazon tours and combinations; cultural and environmental awareness is their specialty.
Wildland Adventures
    3516 NE 155th St, Seattle, WA 98155, USA (☎ (206) 365 0686, (800) 345 4453, fax 363 6615, see also Online Services). This agency offers general tours with an emphasis on responsible tourism.

WARNING

The information in this chapter is particularly vulnerable to change: Prices for international travel are volatile, routes are introduced and canceled, schedules change, special deals come and go, and rules and visa requirements are amended. Airlines and governments seem to take a perverse pleasure in making price structures and regulations as complicated as possible. You should check directly with the airline or a travel agent to make sure you understand how a fare (and ticket you may buy) works. In addition, the travel industry is highly competitive and there are many lurks and perks.

The upshot of this is that you should get opinions, quotes and advice from as many airlines and travel agents as possible before you part with your hard-earned cash. The details given in the chapter should be regarded as pointers and are not a substitute for your own careful, up-to-date research.

Getting Around

Ecuador has a more efficient transportation system than most Andean countries. Also, it is a small country, which means you can usually get anywhere and everywhere quickly and easily. The bus is the most frequently used method of transportation; you can take buses from Tulcán, on the Colombian border, to Huaquillas, on the Peruvian border, and arrive in only 18 hours. Airplanes and boats (especially in the Oriente and in the Galápagos) are also frequently used, but trains less so.

Whichever form of transportation you use, remember to have your passport with you – do not leave it in the hotel safe or packed in your luggage. To board many planes and boats, you need to show your passport.

Buses may go through a transit police check upon entering any town and, although your passport is not frequently asked for, it's as well to have it handy for those times when you are asked to show it. Passport controls are more frequent when traveling by bus in the Oriente. If your passport is in order, these procedures are no more than cursory.

AIR

Even the budget traveler should consider the occasional internal flight. With the exception of flying to the Galápagos, internal flights are comparatively cheap, and even the most expensive flight is currently under US$55. There is a two-tier pricing system on a few flights, on which foreigners pay more than Ecuadorians. These include flights to and from the Oriente towns of Macas, Lago Agrio and Coca (US$50 one way to or from Quito for foreigners, which is about twice what locals pay) and to the Galápagos (US$333/377 roundtrip from Guayaquil/Quito, about twice what Ecuadorians pay and four times what island residents pay). Despite the extra costs, foreigners are not treated to any better in-flight service! Other flights cost

the same for Ecuadorians and foreigners, though this may change in the future.

Domestic Airports
The main airports are shown on the accompanying Air Services Map. Almost all flights originate or terminate in Quito or Guayaquil, so a useful way for the traveler to utilize these services is by taking a long overland journey from one of these cities and then returning quickly by air.

Domestic airports do not charge a departure tax on internal flights (but don't forget the US$25 international departure tax charged if you leave Ecuador on an international flight).

Domestic Airlines
Ecuador's most important domestic airline is TAME, which flies to almost all the destinations in the country. Its competitors are SAN and Saeta, which has flights between Quito, Guayaquil and Cuenca, and to the Galápagos. Although SAN and Saeta are technically separate airlines, they operate essentially as one airline, with Saeta doing international flights into Ecuador and also Quito-Guayaquil connecting flights, and SAN being their domestic arm. SAN-Saeta share reservations offices and airport counters. Prices are the same for all companies so, if traveling between the major cities, use the one whose schedule most closely matches yours.

There are also various small airlines, most of which fly along the coast in small aircraft carrying five to nine passengers. Chartered flights can be arranged into the Oriente. The military has been known to provide flights, as have the missions and the oil companies, however, you hear about this less and less. These days, with improving air services, it's usually easier to pay a few extra dollars for a scheduled flight than to spend several days lining up a flight with someone else.

Internal Air Services

— Regular TAME or SAN Flights
--- Seasonal TAME Flights
········ Regular Flights with Small Airlines

TAME flies from Quito to and from Guayaquil, Cuenca, Loja, Macas, Coca, Lago Agrio, Tulcán, Esmeraldas, Manta, Portoviejo, Bahía de Caráquez and Baltra in the Galápagos. TAME used to fly to Tarapoa in the Oriente and may resume flights there. TAME also flies from Guayaquil to and from Cuenca, Loja, Machala and Baltra, Galápagos. There are seasonal TAME flights from Guayaquil to Salinas. In the past TAME has flown from Guayaquil to Macará and from Cuenca to Loja and Macas, but these flights have been suspended for some time due to a lack of

aircraft. Flights are frequently suspended for this reason; if an airplane needs maintenance, flights to places like Machala and Tulcán (which are relatively easy to reach by bus) are the first to be cut.

SAN-Saeta schedules flights to and from Quito and Guayaquil, Cuenca, and San Cristóbal, Galápagos. SAN-Saeta has been known to give a discount (variously reported as 10% to 25%) on their Galápagos flights to bona fide students with a student card from their home college. TAME have, in the past, given 10% discounts, but recent reports are that they are

Ecuador from Above

Once in a while you may be treated to a special mountain fly-by when flying in Ecuador. This happened to me on the flight from Macas to Quito. We flew by Cotopaxi and the pilot decided to give us a closer look. Banking sharply, he did a complete circuit of the volcano. For over a minute we enjoyed a wonderful view of the top of the mountain and a rare look directly into the crater. TAME scored a lot of points that day!

I also remember a spectacular Quito-Cuenca flight I chanced to take one cloudless morning in June. As we took off, Cayambe (Ecuador's third highest peak) was briefly visible behind the aircraft. Almost immediately, the majestic bulk of Antisana (fourth highest) appeared, it's four lumpy peaks rising from the edge of the Amazon basin. After a few minutes, we passed the ice-cream cone of Cotopaxi (second highest), and then Tungurahua (10th highest) with the town of Baños nestled in a valley to the north of the mountain. Soon after, we saw the rarely clear, jagged peaks of El Altar (fifth highest), and the famous sulfur-yellow lagoon in the middle of its blown-away crater, followed by the smoking volcano, Sangay (seventh highest).

After a wonderful 40-minute flight, we descended, flying low over the red-tiled colonial roofs of Cuenca, with a good look at the blue-domed cathedral in the central plaza. The view I describe was from the left of the aircraft; on the right passengers could see Iliniza Norte and Iliniza Sur (eighth and sixth highest) followed by the highest mountain in Ecuador, Chimborazo, and the nearby Carihuairazo (ninth highest). As this flight costs only around US$31, if the weather looks clear it's worth heading down to the airport just to joy-ride.

Flying from Quito to Guayaquil, the most spectacular mountain views are from the left-hand side; flying to Macas, the view is to the right. Many other flights have mountains on either side. Decide which peaks you prefer to see, and also consider the time of day so that you won't be looking into the sun. A topographical map will help you see which side of the plane will be best for you. ■

hard to get and the hassle involved in a 10% reduction is not worth it.

Between them, the airlines provide about 10 to 12 flights a day between Quito and Guayaquil. There are one to three flights a day between Quito and Cuenca, daily flights to Baltra and several flights a week to other towns. There are no Sunday flights to the Oriente. For more details, see the Getting There & Away sections under the appropriate cities.

Flights are frequently late, but not by very much. Flights first thing in the morning are more likely to be on time, but by the afternoon things tend to have slid half an hour behind schedule. You should show up about an hour early for domestic flights, as baggage handling and check-in procedures tend to be rather chaotic. After one particularly bad overbooking incident where the plane 'grew smaller,' a frustrated foreigner quipped that TAME must stand for 'Try Again Mañana, Extranjera.'

If you show up early for your flight between Quito and Guayaquil, you can often get on an earlier flight if there is room. If you paid for your ticket with cash (not credit card), then TAME will accept your SAN-Saeta ticket and vice versa.

There are no seating assignments on domestic flights – you choose your seat aboard on a first-come, first-served basis. There are no separate sections for smokers and nonsmokers. Many flights give extraordinary views of the snow-capped Andes; it is worth getting a window seat even if the weather is bad, as the planes often rise above the clouds, allowing spectacular views of volcanoes riding on a sea of cloud (see also the sidebar Ecuador from Above).

Wherever you want to fly, don't despair if you can't get a ticket. It's always worth going to the airport in the hope of someone not turning up for the flight. Make sure that you're there early and get yourself on a waiting list if there is one. If you do have a reservation, make sure you confirm it. And reconfirm it. And reconfirm it again. As a general rule, I would confirm flights both 72 and 24 hours in advance, as well as when you arrive in Ecuador. Ecuadorians are notorious for bumping you off your flight if you don't reconfirm. Since the first edition of this book the situation has improved somewhat, but still, reconfirm. If it's impossible for you to do so, tell them beforehand so that they know. Try to have it on the computer if possible. And try to find someone to reconfirm for you.

BUS
Long Distance
Ecuador is developing a system of central bus terminals in each city – especially in the highlands and increasingly in the lowlands – which means that if you have to change buses you don't have to go looking for different terminals. All buses arrive and depart from the same place. Once you have located the central bus terminal, often referred to as the *terminal terrestre*, it is a simple matter to find a bus to take you where you want to go. Some towns still haven't completed their main bus terminals, and may still have several smaller ones.

When waiting in bus terminals, watch your luggage very carefully. Snatch-theft is common and razor-blade artists abound. Keep luggage where you can see it and stay alert. I hear stories depressingly often of theft in bus terminals. Thieves are looking for an easy rip-off and won't bother you if you look on top of things. See Dangers & Annoyances in Facts for the Visitor for more information on playing it safe.

Throughout this book, I indicate the location of bus terminals on the city maps. The accompanying text gives the most important destinations served by the terminal, the approximate cost of the journey, about how long it takes to get there and how frequently buses leave.

I have refrained from giving exact schedules, as that is a sure way to make this book obsolete even before it is published. Timetables change frequently and are not necessarily adhered to. If a bus is full, it might leave early. Conversely, an almost empty bus will usually spend half an hour giving *vueltas* (driving laps between the terminal and the main plaza), with the driver's assistant yelling out of the door in hopes of attracting more passengers. This is less likely to happen in cities, but is the norm in smaller towns.

Various types of buses are used; they can be roughly grouped into two types. *Busetas* (small buses) usually hold 22 passengers and are fast and efficient. Although standing passengers are not normally allowed, the seats can be rather cramped. Larger coaches, called *autobuses* or *buses grandes*, have more space but often allow standing passengers, so they can get rather crowded. These are generally slower than the busetas, at times taking almost twice as long to reach their destinations because they drop off and pick up so many standing passengers. Increasing numbers of buses have installed video players and so if the passing countryside is not enough to entertain you, you can watch a film.

Although they're slow, the big coaches are sometimes more fun, as passengers get on and off all the time, perhaps accompanied by chickens or a few hundredweight of potatoes. If you're in any hurry, make sure that you take a buseta.

Getting around Ecuador by bus is easy, but here are some tips to make your travels more enjoyable. If you go to the terminal the day before your bus trip, you can usually buy tickets in advance. This means you can choose your approximate time of departure, and often you can choose your seat number too. I'm over six feet tall, and one of my pet hates is being squished in the tiny back seat of a bus. I think it's worth buying tickets in advance so that I can get a front-row seat, which generally means more leg room, much better views and a more exciting trip.

Some people prefer second-row seats, to avoid being jostled by passengers getting on and off. In the event of a serious accident, the front row is usually the most lethal (though I don't think it's as dangerous as some people make out.) Try to avoid those rows over the wheels – usually the third row from the front and the third from the back in the busetas, and the fourth or fifth rows from the front and back in larger buses. Ask about the position of the wheels when buying your ticket. Also remember that the suspension at the back of a bus is usually far worse than anywhere else, so try to avoid the back rows.

Some bus companies don't sell tickets in advance. This is usually when they have frequent departures (twice an hour or more). You just arrive and get on the next bus that's going your way. If the next bus out has only uncomfortable seats, you can miss it and be first on the next one (assuming the wait is not too long).

If traveling during long holiday weekends or special fiestas, you may find that buses are booked up for several days in advance, so book early if you can.

If you're traveling very light, it's best to keep your luggage inside the bus with you. If I'm off on a trip for a few days, I often leave much of my luggage at the South American Explorers Club (or in a hotel storage room) and travel with a bag small enough to fit under the seat or between my legs. Local people get away with taking fairly large pieces of luggage aboard, so you don't have to put yours on the outside luggage rack, even if the driver tells you to.

If your luggage is too big to fit in your seat, it will have to go on top or in a luggage compartment. Sometimes the top is covered with a tarpaulin, but not always, so pack your gear in large plastic bags (garbage bags are good) in case of rain. The luggage compartment is sometimes filthy, and your luggage can get covered with grease or mud. Placing your luggage in a large protective sack is a good idea. Many locals use grain sacks as luggage; you can buy them for a few cents in general stores or markets. I have heard of a few incidents of theft from luggage inside luggage compartments, and even of whole pieces of luggage being stolen. This is not a frequent occurrence, but minimize the risk by securely locking checked luggage and keeping your eye on it as it is loaded into the luggage compartment. Check on it during stops.

Often when a bus stops on the main routes, vendors selling fruit, rolls, ice cream or drinks suddenly appear, so you won't starve. Long-distance buses usually stop for a 20-minute meal break at the appropriate times. The food in the terminal restaurants may be somewhat basic, so if you're a picky eater you should bring food with you.

Fares for tickets bought in bus terminals are a set price. The larger terminals often have traveler information booths that can advise you about this, but normally I find that you get charged the correct fare. The booths can give you information on all the routes available from the larger terminals.

If you're only going part of the way, or you get on a bus in a small town as it comes by between larger towns, the bus driver will charge you appropriately. About 90% of the time you are charged honestly, although once in a while they try to overcharge you.

Once I was charged US$1 for a ride that I paid US$0.40 for going the other way. I pointed this out to the driver who was adamant that the fare was US$1. The Latin American machismo meant that he didn't want to admit that he was wrong. Although there's little point in getting uptight about a few cents, this particular example was too blatant for me to ignore. I told him he could have US$0.40 or we could go talk to the transit police; he didn't want to talk to the transit police.

This sort of thing doesn't happen very often; however, the only way to guard against it is to know roughly the correct fare beforehand.

If you want to travel somewhere immediately, just go to the terminal and you'll usually find the driver's assistant running around trying to hustle up some passengers for his bus. Often, on frequently served routes, you'll be on a bus going your way within a few minutes of arriving at the terminal. Before boarding a bus, make sure it's going where you want to go.

Occasionally drivers will say that they are going where you want to go and then take you only part of the way and expect you to change buses. If you want a direct bus, make sure you ask for it. Also make sure that it is leaving soon, and not in two hours.

Finally, if the bus looks too slow, too fast, too old, too cramped or you just don't like it for whatever reason, there is usually another bus leaving soon if you're going to a major destination. Most places are served by several bus companies and you can make the choice that's best for you.

One last word about Ecuadorian buses: toilets – there usually aren't any. A recent exception is the Panamericana company's bus routes from Quito to Guayaquil, Huaquillas, Manta, Loja, Esmeraldas and Cuenca. Their fares are more expensive. Other long-distance buses have rest stops every three or four hours. Try not to get onto a bus with a full bladder or you may join the famous traveler who had to pee in his boot. A reader wrote to encourage me to state that small children may piss or vomit on you on buses. I get some off-beat letters from people on the road . . . .

Trucks

In remote areas, trucks often double as buses. Sometimes they are flatbed trucks with a tin roof, open sides and uncomfortable wooden plank seats. These curious-looking buses are called *rancheras* and are especially common on the coast.

In the remoter parts of the highlands, ordinary trucks or pickups *(camionetas)* are used to carry passengers; you just climb in the back. If the weather is OK, you get fabulous views and can feel the refreshing wind (dress warmly). If the weather is bad, you hunker down underneath a dark tarpaulin with the other passengers. It certainly isn't the height of luxury, but it may be the only way of getting to some remote rural areas, and if you're open-minded about the minor discomforts, you may find that these rides are among the most interesting you have in Ecuador.

Payment for these rides is usually determined by the driver and is a standard fare depending on the distance. You can ask other passengers how much they are paying; usually you'll find that the trucks double as buses and charge almost as much.

TRAIN

Ecuador's rail system was severely damaged by landslides and flooding during the extremely heavy rains of the 1982-83 El Niño wet season. Many kilometers of track were totally destroyed, but since many roads and bridges were also badly damaged, available repair money was channeled into the more important road network; the railway system had to wait until funds become available.

After the 1982-83 disaster Ecuador noticed a decline in the amount of tourist revenue entering the country. This was partly attributed to the loss of the Quito-Durán (a suburb of Guayaquil) railway line. The dramatic descent from Alausí in the mountains to Guayaquil on the coast is one of the most spectacular train rides in the world, and was one of the main reasons some tourists visited Guayaquil. The ride was made famous by a British TV series on the world's greatest train journeys.

The fantastic line from Alausí to Guayaquil reopened in the early 1990s. Trains run on this route every day. The section from Quito to Alausí reopened in the mid-1990s. Service from Quito to Riobamba runs only once a week (Saturdays), but daily from Riobamba to Alausí and on to Guayaquil. The Quito-Riobamba service may become more frequent in future.

There used to be trains running from Cuenca to Sibambe (on the Alausí-Durán line), but these have been suspended and it is not known if they will start again.

In the north an *autoferro* runs most days between Ibarra and San Lorenzo, but its service is subject to frequent cancellations and delays. Space is limited on the auto-ferro – which is like a bus mounted on a railway chassis – and you are advised to buy tickets ahead of time. It is not as comfortable as a normal train, but on this route, ordinary trains are not used. See Getting

There & Away under Ibarra in the North Coast chapter for more information.

ENAFER is the government-run national railway company, but there is no central telephone number to reach them. You must go to individual towns to buy tickets. Departure times and other rail-service information are given under the appropriate town headings. Note that since the reopening of the Quito-Riobamba-Alausí-Durán line, a two-tier fare system has been operating. Foreigners pay US$12 or US$14 for any of the train trips outlined in this section, regardless of how far they travel on it. Locals pay about US$1.

Although many readers have written to me complaining about this two-tier price system which they perceive as discrimination, the reality is that the elevated fares for foreigners are the only thing which can keep these scenic and exciting railway routes open. If you don't want to pay US$14, the bus is a much cheaper alternative. Note that these train journeys are normally all-day affairs.

Metropolitan Touring (see Organized Tours in Quito) also has a very pricey private train trip from Quito to Riobamba aboard comfortable carriages, accompanied by bilingual guides and including meals. Book trips in Quito.

TAXI

Ecuador is an oil-producing country and it keeps down the price of gasoline (petrol) for domestic consumption. Depending on the grade, gas is approximately US$1.20 to US$1.40 per gallon (for some reason gas is not dispensed in liters). This price combined with low wages means that taxis in Ecuador are very cheap.

Ecuadorian taxis come in a variety of shapes and sizes, but they are all yellow. Most have a lit sign on top reading 'Taxi' – those that don't have a taxi sticker in the windshield. Taxis often belong to cooperatives; the name and telephone number of the cooperative is usually printed on the door.

The main rule for taking taxis is to ask the fare beforehand, or you'll be over-charged more often than not. Meters are rarely seen, except in Quito where they are obligatory. Even if there is a meter, the driver may not want to use it. This can be to your advantage, because with the meter off the driver can avoid interminable downtown traffic jams by taking a longer route. This saves both you and him time and the extra cost in gas is negligible. A long ride in a large city (Quito or Guayaquil) shouldn't go over US$4 and short hops can cost under US$1. In smaller towns fares vary from about US$0.50 to US$2. Fares from international airports (Quito and Guayaquil) can be exorbitantly high – see those towns for tips on how to avoid getting gouged. At weekends and at night fares are always about 25% to 50% higher. Taxis can be hard to flag down during rush hours.

You can hire a taxi for several hours. A half day might cost about US$10 to US$15 if you bargain. You can also hire pickup trucks that act as taxis to take you to remote areas (such as a climbing hut or a refuge). If you hire a taxi to take you to another town, a rough rule of thumb is about US$1 for every 10 km. Remember to count the driver's return trip, even if you're not returning. If you split the cost between four passengers, you'll each be paying between two and three times the bus fare for a roundtrip.

CAR & MOTORCYCLE
Rental

Renting a car in Ecuador is more expensive than full-price car rental in Europe or the US. Cheap car rentals aren't found. If the price seems reasonable, check to see for what extras you have to pay; often there is a per kilometer charge and you have to buy insurance. Some cars are not in very good condition.

It is difficult to find any kind of car rental outside of Guayaquil, Quito, Cuenca and a few other towns. I checked several places in Quito and was told that I had to have a credit card to be able to rent, as they would not accept a cash deposit. Renters normally have to be 25 years old (a few companies may accept 23- or 21-year-old drivers). A valid driver's license from your home country is usually accepted if it has your photograph on it. Some companies require an international driver's license, so if you know that you will be driving, it's best to apply for one in your home country before you leave.If you already have a standard driver's license, this is normally a straight-forward process.

Typical rates start around US$35 per day for a subcompact car but can go over US$100 for a large 4WD vehicle. Weekly rentals are the best deals. Weekly rates – including insurance, tax and unlimited distance allowances – ranged in 1996 from US$215 for a Suzuki subcompact to about US$800 for a Mitsubishi Montero 4WD. Most companies' prices are comparable.

Automobile insurance policies can carry a hefty deductible – as much as US$1000, depending on the company. Some international rental agencies (Budget, Avis, Hertz) will make reservations for you from your home country, but, according to one reader, this is more expensive still than renting in Ecuador.

Generally, car rental places are honest, though I have received a few warnings and complaints. Have everything put into writing to avoid confusion or misunderstandings. This document should include prices; distance allowances *(kilometraje)*; any applicable discounts, taxes or surcharges; and the place and time of vehicle return. Make sure any existing damage to the vehicle (scratches etc) are noted on the rental form. Rental cars are often rather old and beat-up but reasonably well serviced. Make sure there is a spare tire and jack (if only to know where they are stored in case of a flat tire).

If you are driving, bear in mind Ecuador's system of road signs is very poor. A sign may point to your destination several kilometers before the turn-off, then when you reach the turn-off there may be no sign at all. Large potholes, narrow roads and drivers passing on curves, speeding or going too slow are all part of the adventure. Even so, a car does allow you the freedom

to choose where you go . . . *if* you can figure out how to get there!

Rental cars are targets for thieves. Don't leave your car parked with bags or other valuables in sight. When leaving your car for any period, park in a guarded lot.

Motorcycle rental is hard to find in Ecuador.

Your Own Vehicle
Few travelers arrive with their own vehicle, although with the recent opening of the car ferry between Panama and Colombia (around the roadless Darien Gap) this is likely to change.

I have recently talked to someone who bought a motorcycle in Santiago, Chile, who tells me it's the best place in South America to buy your own vehicle, be it motorcycle or car, new or used. People who prefer to drive a vehicle of their own might consider buying one in Santiago and continuing from there.

BICYCLE
Each year a handful of cyclists attempt to ride from Alaska to Argentina, or any number of shorter long-distance rides, and manage to get through Ecuador OK. They report that coastal areas are flat and relatively boring, while cycling in the Andes is more fun and visually rewarding, though strenuous. Mountain bikes are recommended, as road bikes don't stand up to the poor road quality.

Renting bikes has only recently become an option in Ecuador. Try Baños, where bikes are used for the day's descent to Puyo, their riders returning that afternoon by bus. See Organized Tours in Quito for mountain biking tours. Otherwise, rental is uncommon and the quality of the bicycles is poor. Bikes for sale tend to be of the one-speed variety, so dedicated bikers are probably better off bringing their own. Most airlines will allow bikes to be checked at no extra cost if they're in boxes. However, boxes give baggage handlers little clue as to the contents and the box is liable to be roughly handled, possibly damaging the bike. An alternative is wrapping your bike in heavy-duty plastic. Airline's bicycle carrying policies vary, so shop around.

Bicycle shops are scarce in Ecuador and their selection of parts is often completely inadequate. Bring important spare parts from home.

HITCHHIKING

Hitching is never entirely safe in any country in the world, and is not recommended. Travelers who decide to hitch should understand that they are taking a small but potentially serious risk. However, many people do choose to hitch, and the advice that follows should help to make their journeys as fast and safe as possible. If you do choose to hitch, travel in pairs and let someone know where you are planning to go.

Hitching is not very practical in Ecuador for three reasons: there are few private cars, public transportation is relatively cheap and trucks are used as public transportation in remote areas, so trying to hitch a free ride on one is the same as trying to hitch a free ride on a bus. Many drivers of *any* vehicle will pick you up but will also expect payment. If the driver is stopping to drop off and pick up other passengers, ask them what the going rate is. If you are the only passenger, the driver may have picked you up just to talk with a foreigner, and he may wave aside your offer of payment. If you do decide to try hitching, make sure in advance of your ride that you and the driver agree on the subject of payment.

WALKING

Ecuador has several options for adventurous treks in the Andes, although the trails are not as well known as those in Peru. Some excellent hiking and climbing guidebooks have been published specifically for foot travelers; see Books appendix at the end of the book for a listing of the better ones.

Walking around cities is generally safe, even at night, if you stick to the well-lit areas. Always be on the alert for pickpockets, though, and make inquiries before venturing into an area you don't know.

BOAT

Boat transportation is common in Ecuador and can be divided into four types. The most common is the motorized dugout canoe, which acts as a water taxi or bus along the major rivers of the Oriente and parts of the coast. In the Galápagos there are medium-sized motor cruisers and sailboats that are used by small groups to move between the islands of the archipelago. Third, there are large vessels used either for carrying cargo and a few passengers, or as cruise ships for many passengers.

Finally, many rivers are crossed by ferries that vary from a paddled dugout taking one passenger at a time to a car ferry capable of moving half a dozen vehicles. These are sometimes makeshift transportation to replace a bridge that has been washed out, is being repaired or is still in the planning stages.

Dugout Canoes

Dugout canoes often carry as many as three dozen passengers and are the only way to get around many roadless areas. If you hire one as a personal taxi, they are expensive. However, taking a regularly scheduled ride with other passengers is quite affordable, though not as cheap as a bus for a similar distance. An outboard engine uses more fuel per kilometer than a bus engine and dugouts travel more slowly than a bus.

The only places between which you are likely to travel any distance in dugouts are from Misahuallí or Coca in the jungles of the Oriente and San Lorenzo to La Tola on the northwest coast.

Most of these boats are literally dugouts, with a splashboard sometimes added to the gunwales. These are long in shape and short on comfort. Seating is normally on hard, low, uncomfortable wooden benches which accommodate two people each. Luggage is stashed forward under a tarpaulin, so carry hand baggage containing essentials for the journey. You will be miserable for hours if you don't take the following advice, which alone is worth the cost of this book: *Bring seat padding.* A folded sweater or towel will make a world of difference on the trip.

Pelting rain and glaring sun are major hazards and an umbrella is excellent defense against both. Bring suntan lotion or wear long sleeves, long pants and a sun hat – I have seen people literally unable to walk because of second-degree burns on their legs after a six-hour exposure to the tropical sun. The breeze as the boat motors along tends to keep insects away and also tends to cool you, so that you are not likely to notice the burning effect of the sun. If the sun should disappear or the rain begin, you can become quite chilly, so bring a light jacket.

Insect repellent is useful during stops along the river. A water bottle and something to snack on will complete your hand baggage. Don't forget to stash your spare clothes in plastic bags or they'll get soaked by rain or spray.

A final word about dugout canoes: they feel very unstable! Until you get used to their motion, you might worry about the whole thing just rolling over and tipping everybody into the shark, piranha or boa constrictor-infested waters. Desperately gripping the side of the canoe and wondering what madness possessed you to board in the first place doesn't seem to help. I've ridden in many dugouts and have never had a problem, even in rapids and ocean waves. Dugouts are much more stable than they feel, so don't worry about a dunking.

Yachting

The idea of sailing your own yacht to the Galápagos sounds romantic. Unfortunately, to sail in the Galápagos you need a license and these are all limited to Galápagos boats. If you arrive in the islands in your own boat, you will have to moor the boat in Puerto Ayora and hire one of the local boats to take you around. The Ecuadorian authorities give transit permits of seven days for sailors on their own boats (this is a recent ruling and is subject to change; previously it was only 72 hours). I have heard that longer stays are possible if you are moored and not sailing.

Other Boats

In the Galápagos, you have a choice of traveling in anything from a small sailboat taking four passengers to a cruise ship complete with air-conditioned cabins with private baths. More information on these boats is given in the Galápagos chapter.

In addition to the dugout canoes of the Oriente, one cruise ship makes a relatively luxurious passages down the Río Aguarico. The *Flotel Orellana* is described further in the Northern Oriente chapter.

There are a few ratty steamers plying coastal routes. These are mainly cargo boats and are rarely used by travelers.

A few boats travel between the Galápagos and Guayaquil, but it's easier to fly there and sail between the islands once you arrive. Again, there is more information under the appropriate coastal towns.

LOCAL TRANSPORTATION

There are no underground or surface trains used in Ecuadorian cities. Local transportation is by bus or taxi.

Local buses are usually slow and crowded, but are also very cheap. You can get around most towns for about US$0.10. Local buses often travel to nearby villages, and riding along is a good, inexpensive way to see the area. Just stay on the bus until the end of the line, pay another US$0.10 and head back again. If you make friends with the driver you may even end up with an entertaining tour director, as he points out the local sights in between collecting other passengers' fares.

When you want to get off a local bus, yell ¡Bajada!, which means 'Down!' (as in 'The passenger is getting down.'). Telling the driver to stop will make him think you're trying to be a back-seat driver, and you will be ignored. He's only interested if you're getting off, or down from the bus. Another way of getting him to stop is to yell ¡Esquina! (which means 'Corner!'). He'll stop at the next one. Adding *por favor* doesn't hurt, and makes everyone think you speak excellent Spanish. If you don't actually speak Spanish and someone tries to converse after your display of linguistic brilliance, a smile and a sage nod should suffice until you get down from the bus.

ORGANIZED TOURS

Many kinds of tours are available, from hotel-based excursions to the highlands to strenuous mountaineering expeditions, from camping in the rainforest to staying at a luxurious jungle lodge and, of course, tours to the Galápagos.

Many tours can be arranged within Ecuador and are described in the main body of the book under the appropriate cities. Others can be arranged in advance from home, especially if you live in the USA. See Getting There & Away for more details.

Quito

Quito is my favorite Latin American capital. At about 2850 meters above sea level, it has a wonderful spring-like climate, despite the fact that it is only 22 km south of the equator. It is in a valley flanked by majestic mountains and, on a clear day, several snow-capped volcanoes are visible from the capital. As well as being in a beautiful location, it is rich in history and much of the old colonial town is well preserved.

In 1978 UNESCO declared Quito's colonial center a world cultural heritage site. Now, development and other changes in Quito's old town are strictly controlled. This is not to say that progress has stopped – on the contrary, the old center bustles with life. But the buildings are unchanged, and to walk down colonial Quito's streets late at night, after the rush hour traffic has finished, is to step into a bygone era. There are no modern buildings discordantly built next to centuries-old architecture, and no flashing neon signs to disrupt the ambiance of the past.

History

The site of the capital dates from pre-Columbian times. Early inhabitants of the area were the peaceful Quitu people, who gave their name to the city. The Quitus integrated with the coastal Caras, giving rise to the Indian group known as the Shyris. About 1300 AD the Shyris joined with the Puruhás through marriage, and their descendants fought against the Incas in the late 1400s.

By the time the Spanish arrived in Ecuador (1526), Quito was a major Inca city. Rather than allow it to fall into the hands of the Spanish conquerors, the city was razed by Rumiñahui, a general of Atahualpa, shortly before their arrival. There are no Inca remains. The present capital was founded atop the ruins by Spanish lieutenant Sebastián de Benalcázar on December 6, 1534. Many colonial-era buildings survive in the old town.

Orientation

Quito's population of about 1,200,000 makes it the second largest city in Ecuador (Guayaquil is the largest). It is located along the central valley in a roughly north-south direction and is approximately 17 km long and four km wide. It can conveniently be divided into three segments.

The center (el centro) is the site of the old town with its whitewashed, red-tiled houses and colonial churches; this is the area of greatest cultural interest to the traveler, and also has the cheapest hotels used by backpackers.

The north is modern Quito, the new town, with its major businesses, airline offices, embassies, shopping centers and banks. The best hotels and restaurants are found here. The north end contains the airport and middle- and upper-class residential areas. Avenida Amazonas is the best-known street, though Avenida 10 de Agosto and Avenida 6 de Diciembre are the most important thoroughfares.

The south, consisting mainly of working-class housing areas, is of less interest.

Addresses in Quito, and throughout Ecuador, are given by placing the building number after the street name. Often, the nearest intersecting street name is also added, eg: Jorge Washington 311 and Leonidas Plaza Gutiérrez.

Information

Tourist Offices The main CETUR tourist information office is at Eloy Alfaro 1214 (☎ 225 101). There is also one at the airport's domestic terminal and one at Venezuela 914 (☎ 514 044) in the old town. Hours are 9 am to 5 pm Monday to Friday.

They can provide you with brochures, maps and tourist information, and there is often someone available who speaks

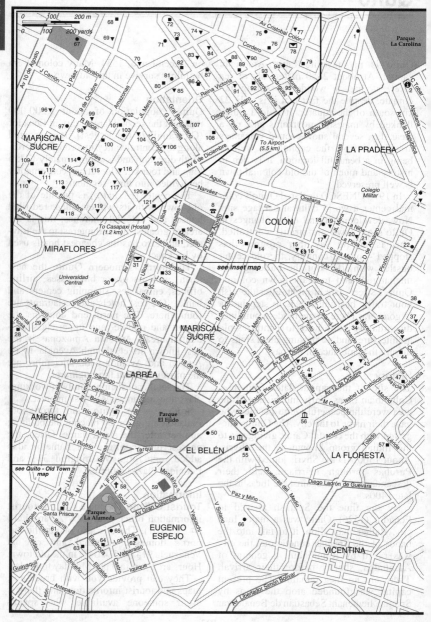

0　100　200 m
0　100　200 yards

Parque La Carolina

MARISCAL SUCRE

LA PRADERA

Av Cristóbal Colón

Cordero

To Airport (5.5 km)

COLÓN

MIRAFLORES

To Casapaxi (Hostal) (1.2 km)

see inset map

Universidad Central

Av América

LARRÉA

MARISCAL SUCRE

AMÉRICA

Parque El Ejido

EL BELÉN

LA FLORESTA

see Quito - Old Town map

Parque La Alameda

EUGENIO ESPEJO

VICENTINA

Av Libertador Simón Bolívar

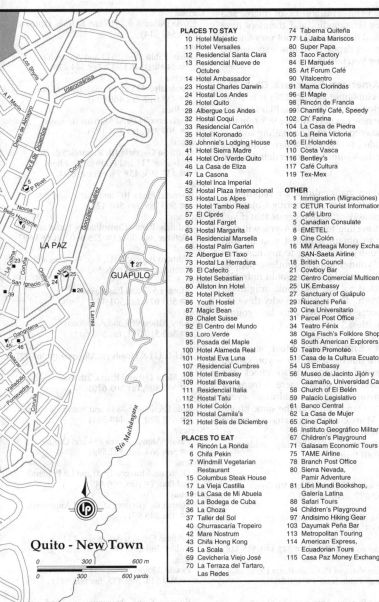

PLACES TO STAY
10 Hotel Majestic
11 Hotel Versalles
12 Residencial Santa Clara
13 Residencial Nueve de Octubre
14 Hotel Ambassador
23 Hostal Charles Darwin
24 Hostal Los Andes
26 Hotel Quito
28 Albergue Los Andes
32 Hostal Coqui
33 Residencial Carrión
35 Hotel Koronado
39 Johnnie's Lodging House
41 Hotel Sierra Madre
44 Hotel Oro Verde Quito
46 La Casa de Eliza
47 La Casona
49 Hotel Inca Imperial
52 Hostal Plaza Internacional
53 Hostal Los Alpes
55 Hotel Tambo Real
57 El Ciprés
60 Hostal Farget
63 Hostal Margarita
64 Residencial Marsella
68 Hostal Palm Garten
72 Albergue El Taxo
73 Hostal La Herradura
76 El Cafecito
79 Hotel Sebastian
80 Allston Inn Hotel
82 Hotel Pickett
86 Youth Hostel
87 Magic Bean
89 Chalet Suisse
92 El Centro del Mundo
93 Loro Verde
95 Posada del Maple
100 Hotel Alameda Real
101 Hostal Eva Luna
107 Residencial Cumbres
108 Hotel Embassy
109 Hostal Bavaria
111 Residencial Italia
112 Hostal Tatu
118 Hotel Colón
120 Hostal Camila's
121 Hotel Seis de Diciembre

PLACES TO EAT
4 Rincón La Ronda
6 Chifa Pekin
7 Windmill Vegetarian Restaurant
15 Columbus Steak House
17 La Vieja Castilla
19 La Casa de Mi Abuela
20 La Bodega de Cuba
36 La Choza
37 Taller del Sol
40 Churrascaría Tropeiro
42 Mare Nostrum
43 Chifa Hong Kong
45 La Scala
69 Cevichería Viejo José
70 La Terraza del Tartaro, Las Redes

74 Taberna Quiteña
77 La Jaiba Mariscos
80 Super Papa
83 Taco Factory
84 El Marqués
85 Art Forum Café
90 Vitalcentro
91 Mama Clorindas
96 El Maple
98 Rincón de Francia
99 Chantilly Café, Speedy
102 Ch' Farina
104 La Casa de Piedra
105 La Reina Victoria
106 El Holandés
110 Costa Vasca
116 Bentley's
117 Café Cultura
119 Tex-Mex

OTHER
1 Immigration (Migraciónes)
2 CETUR Tourist Information
3 Café Libro
5 Canadian Consulate
8 EMETEL
9 Cine Colón
16 MM Arteaga Money Exchange, SAN-Saeta Airline
18 British Council
21 Cowboy Bar
22 Centro Comercial Multicentro
25 UK Embassy
27 Sanctuary of Guápulo
29 Ñucanchi Peña
30 Cine Universitario
31 Parcel Post Office
34 Teatro Fénix
38 Olga Fisch's Folklore Shop
48 South American Explorers Club
50 Teatro Promoteo
51 Casa de la Cultura Ecuatoriana
54 US Embassy
56 Museo de Jacinto Jijón y Caamaño, Universidad Católica
58 Church of El Belén
59 Palacio Legislativo
61 Banco Central
62 La Casa de Mujer
65 Cine Capitol
66 Instituto Geográfico Militar
67 Children's Playground
71 Galasam Economic Tours
75 TAME Airline
78 Branch Post Office
80 Sierra Nevada, Pamir Adventure
81 Libri Mundi Bookshop, Galería Latina
88 Safari Tours
94 Children's Playground
97 Andisimo Hiking Gear
103 Dayumak Peña Bar
113 Metropolitan Touring
114 American Express, Ecuadorian Tours
115 Casa Paz Money Exchange

Quito - New Town
0 — 300 — 600 m
0 — 300 — 600 yards

English. (The availability of maps and brochures is sporadic, and travelers have complained that the staff is not very knowledgeable – it depends on how experienced the person you talk to is.)

South American Explorers Club The SAEC's clubhouse (☎ 225 228) is at Jorge Washington 311 and Leonidas Plaza Gutiérrez in the new town. Hours are 9:30 am to 5 pm Monday to Friday. The mailing address is Apartado 21-431, Eloy Alfaro, Quito. See Facts for the Visitor for further details about the club.

Visas Many nationalities are required to have visas to enter neighboring Colombia. A US embassy official suggests that if you plan on traveling to the USA you will find it easier to obtain a tourist visa in your home country. According to my nameless source, 'young, single, rootless people, such as the travelers who would normally be expected to use the book, might get turned down.' Don't ask me why this official expects my readers to be 'young, single, rootless.'

Foreign Embassies Most consular offices are not open all day – you should call ahead for hours. Also check the address and how to get there – many of these consulates change addresses every year or two but often keep the same phone number. Many countries also have consular representation in Guayaquil.

Edificio in the following addresses means 'Building.'

Argentina
    Amazonas 477 and Robles, 5th floor
    (☎ 562 292, fax 568 177)
Austria
    Coruña 1224 and San Ignacio
    (☎ 503 456)
Belgium
    JL Mera 863 and Wilson (☎ 545 340, 545 348)
Bolivia
    Edificio Vizcaya II, César Borja Lavayen
    and Juan Pablo Sanz (☎ 458 863)
Brazil
    Edificio España, Amazonas 1429 and
    Colón, 10th floor (☎ 563 086)

Canada
    6 de Diciembre 2816 and J Orton, Office 4N
    (☎ 543 214)
Chile
    Juan Pablo Sanz 3617 and Amazonas
    (☎ 249 403, 453 327, fax 444 470)
Colombia
    Atahualpa 955 and República, 3rd floor
    (☎ 458 012, fax 460 054)
Costa Rica
    Inglaterra 712 and Mariana de Jesús
    (☎ 504 450, fax 504 195)
Denmark
    Edificio Gabriela III, República de El
    Salvador 733 and Portugal, 3rd floor
    (☎ 437 163, 458 786, fax 436 942)
France
    General Plaza 107 and Patria
    (☎ 560 789, fax 566 424)
Germany
    Edificio Banco Consolidado, Patria and 9 de
    Octubre, 6th floor (☎ 225 660, fax 563 697)
Holland
    Edificio Banco BHU, 9 de Octubre and
    Orellana (☎ 567 606, 563 853)
Ireland
    Montes 577 and Las Casas
    (☎ 503 674, fax 501 444)
Israel
    Eloy Alfaro 969 and Amazonas
    (☎ 565 510/511, fax 504 635)
Italy
    La Isla 111 & Humberto Albornoz (☎ 561 077)
Japan
    JL Mera 130 and Patria, 7th floor
    (☎ 561 899, fax 503 670)
Mexico
    6 de Diciembre 4843 and Naciones Unidas
    (☎ 457 820, fax 448 245)
Norway
    Pasaje Alonso Jerves 134 and Orellana
    (☎ 566 364, fax 502 593)
Panama
    Diego de Almagro 1550 and La Pradera,
    3rd floor (☎ /fax 566 449)
Paraguay
    Gaspar de Villaroel 2013 and Amazonas
    (☎ /fax 245 871)
Peru
    Edificio España, Amazonas 1429 and
    Colón, 2nd floor (☎ 527 678, 549 255)
Sweden
    Pasaje Alonso Jerves 134 and Orellana
    (☎ 509 514, 509 423, fax 502 593)
Switzerland
    Edificio Xerox, Amazonas 3617 and Juan
    Pablo Sanz, 2nd floor (☎ 434 948, 449 314)

UK
>González Suárez 111 and 12 de Octubre
>(☎ 560 670, fax 560 730)
USA
>Patria and 12 de Octubre
>(☎ 562 890, fax 502 052)
Uruguay
>Edificio Invescor, Tamayo 1025 and L
>García, 5th floor (☎ 561 181)
Venezuela
>Coruña 1733 and Belo Horizonte
>(☎ 564 626, fax 502 630)

Immigration & Documents There are two immigration offices: One is for tourist card extensions and the other is for visas. Most travelers will only need the tourist card extension, but if you want to stay longer than 90 days you will need a student, business, work or residence visa. Visas are usually expensive and complicated, while the tourist card extension is free and straightforward as long as you haven't used up your 90 days.

Tourist card extensions can be obtained from Migraciónes (☎ 454 122/099), at Avenida Amazonas 2639 (also numbered 3149 for some strange reason) and República, from 8 am to 12:30 pm Monday to Friday. It takes anywhere from 10 minutes to two hours depending on how busy they are on the day you go. Although an onward ticket out of Ecuador and 'sufficient funds' are legally required, they are seldom requested. It's still worth bringing any airline tickets or traveler's checks you may have, just in case. I have received a report that women in shorts are not allowed into the building.

For visas go to the Extranjería at Páez 552 and Colón. They are open 9 am to noon Monday to Friday.

Student Cards If you sign up for a Spanish course at the university you can get a student card there. Otherwise, try Ecuadorian Tours (US$16) – they will ask to verify your student status unless you look very young and student-like. Students flying from Quito to the Galápagos can get a discount of 10% to 25% with Saeta, or a much smaller discount with TAME. Other-

wise, a student card does not save you much money in Ecuador. But if you're heading south to Peru you'll find it entitles you to substantial discounts there. I have heard that student cards issued in Ecuador to foreign students are sometimes looked upon with suspicion and that the card from your home college is much more likely to be accepted.

Money Banks are open from 9 am to 1:30 pm (later in some branches). They will handle money wired from your home bank and pay you in US dollars. Most bank offices are on Avenida Amazonas. Banks may pay slightly better rates than casas de cambio, but the latter are open longer (9 am to 6 pm on weekdays plus Saturday mornings) and require less paperwork. Rates shouldn't vary by more than 2% or 3% – shop around if you are trying to make your money stretch. Exchange rates for the previous day are usually in the newspaper, but rates can change from hour to hour.

Casa Paz is the best-known casa de cambio with branches at Amazonas 370 and Robles (☎ 563 900, 564 500) in the new town and on Sucre near Venezuela (☎ 511 364) in the old town. MM Jaramillo Arteaga is also good, with an office at the northwest corner of Amazonas and Colón (☎ 504 030) in the new town and at Mejía 401 and Venezuela (☎ 350 574) in the old town. Others that have been recommended include Multicambio (☎ 561 734) on Avenida Colón near Reina Victoria, and Casa de Cambio Delgado at Amazonas 1225. There are a number of other exchange houses.

If you want to change money on Sunday, you will find the Casa Paz airport office open. Also, their office at the Hotel Colón is open on Sunday and they are often open until 7 pm on weekdays.

If you change more money than you need, it is easy to buy back dollars at a rate about 2% below what you sold them for.

Credit cards are widely accepted in first-class restaurants, hotels, travel agents and stores. Make sure you are getting a good exchange rate. Visa is the most widely accepted, followed by MasterCard. The main credit card offices are:

American Express
    Ecuadorian Tours, Avenida Amazonas 339 and Jorge Washington, 5th floor (☎ 560 488)
Diners Club
    Avenida República 710 and Eloy Alfaro (☎ 221 372)
MasterCard
    Naciones Unidas 825 and Los Shyris (☎ 462 770)
Visa
    Banco de Guayaquil, Avenida Colón and Reina Victoria (☎ 566 824)
    Filanbanco, Amazonas 530 and Roca

A new Western Union office (☎ 565 059) has opened at República 396. Reportedly, the major hotels and travel agencies can contact them. They provide instant but pricey money transfers from anywhere there is a Western Union office (all over North America, less common elsewhere). A US$1000 transfer from the USA costs US$75.

Post & Communications The central post office is at Espejo 935 and Guayaquil in the old town. Hours are 7:30 am to 5:30 pm on weekdays and 8 am to 2 pm on Saturday. Currently, this is where you pick up your general delivery *(lista de correos)* mail, though there is talk of moving the office to the new town. Another branch post office (☎ 508 890) in the new town is on Avenida Colón at Reina Victoria, with the same hours. If you are mailing a package of over two kg, use the office at Ulloa 273 and Dávalos (☎ 521 730).

American Express clients can receive mail sent to them c/o American Express, Apartado 2605, Quito, Ecuador. Their street address is Avenida Amazonas 339, 5th floor, and hours are 8 am to 5 pm Monday to Friday.

There are several air courier services: DHL (☎ 565 059), Avenida República 396 and Diego Almagro; IML (☎ 567 112), 9 de Octubre 114 and Colón; MACOB (☎ 549 200), 10 de Agosto 645. There are others. Rates are very high.

The main EMETEL office for international calls is in the new town at 10 de Agosto and Colón (☎ 507 691, 509 025). The old town office (☎ 612 112) is on Benalcázar at Mejía. Other EMETEL offices are at the Terminal Terrestre de Cumandá and at the airport (☎ 580 582 or 451 858, respectively). These offices are open from 8 am to 10 pm (last call at 9:30 pm) daily. Cheap rates for international calls are after 7 pm.

The area code for Quito and the province of Pichincha is 02.

Bookstores Libri Mundi is the best bookstore, with a good selection of titles in English, German, French and Spanish. They have books about Ecuador as well as those of a more general nature. Their main shop (☎ 234 791) is at JL Mera 851 near Veintimilla and is open from 8:30 am to 7 pm Monday to Friday, and 9:30 am to 1:30 pm and 3:30 to 6:30 pm on Saturday. A smaller branch is in the Hotel Colón shopping mall (☎ 550 455). LibroExpress, on Amazonas 816 and Veintimilla, is good for maps, magazines, and some books. The other bookstores in Quito mainly sell books in Spanish.

The best maps are available from the Instituto Geográfico Militar (IGM), which is on top of a hill at the end of Paz y Miño, a small street a few blocks southeast of Parque El Ejido in the new town. There are no buses, so walk or take a taxi. The map sales room is open from 8 am to 3 pm Monday through Friday. You need to leave your passport at the gate to be allowed in. I suggest going in the morning to buy maps as it can take a while and afternoon hours are erratic.

They have a good selection of country and topographical maps to look at or buy, but their selection of city maps is very limited and you'll be better off with the city maps in this book. Country maps are also available from street vendors and the Libri Mundi bookstore, but they are more expensive than at the IGM.

The most useful map of Quito is the *Guía Informativa de Quito* by Nelson Gómez, published every few years. This slim blue book has about a dozen fold-out maps that cover Quito, and an alphabetical street index. It is available at most bookstores and is recommended for anyone wishing to spend time outside of the city center.

Cultural Centers The British Council (☎ 540 225, 508 282), Amazonas 1646 and Orellana, has a library open 8:30 am to 12:45 pm and 2 to 7 pm Monday to Friday. There are British newspapers to read, and books (in English) may be borrowed for a US$20 annual fee. There is also a café on the premises. They screen free movies on Wednesdays at 8 pm. Get there early for a good seat.

The Alianza Francesa, Eloy Alfaro 1900 and 6 de Diciembre, shows free French movies several times a week.

Laundry At the following places, they will wash, dry and fold your clothes within 24 hours:

Opera de Jabón/Soap Opera
    Pinto 325 and Reina Victoria (☎ 543 995)
Lava Hotel Self Service
    Almagro 818 and Colón (☎ 506 129)
Lavalimpio
    Tamayo 420 and Roca
Superlavado
    Pinto 305 and Reina Victoria
Wash and Go
    Pinto 340 and JL Mera (☎ 230 993)

The first two are the only places I found with machines available to wash and dry your own clothes if you wish. Usually, clothes must be left with a *lavandería* and picked up the following day. Most hotels will wash and dry your clothes, but this gets quite expensive in the first-class hotels (less so in more modest establishments). Most cheaper hotels provide facilities for hand washing laundry.

Photography Cameras are expensive in Quito. If yours breaks, a recommended repairman is Gustavo Gómez (☎ 230 855), Edificio Molino, Asunción 130 and 10 de Agosto, Office 1.

There are several places along Amazonas in the new town and around Plaza Santo Domingo in the old town where print film is processed within a day. The results are usually satisfactory but not top quality. Fotomania (☎ 520 346), 6 de Diciembre 921 and Patria, has been recommended for good quality processing and instant passport photos. (See also Photography & Video in Facts for the Visitor.)

Medical Services An American-run hospital with an outpatient department and emergency room is Hospital Voz Andes, Juan Villalengua 267 (☎ 241 540) near the intersection of Avenidas América and 10 de Agosto. The No 1 Iñaquito bus passes close by. Fees start at about US$8 for an office visit. A newer hospital which has been recommended as the best is the Metropolitano (☎ 431 457/520), Avenida Mariana de Jesús and Occidental. A private clinic specializing in women's medical problems is Clínica de la Mujer (☎ 458 000), Amazonas 4826 and Gaspar de Villarroel. Clínica Pichincha (☎ 561 643, 562 296), Veintimilla 1259 and Páez, does lab analysis for parasites, dysentery etc.

The following individual doctors have been recommended. Dr Steven Contag, gynecologist, (☎ 561 690, 560 408), Cordero 410 and 6 de Diciembre, 4th floor, speaks English. Dr John Rosenberg, internist and tropical medicine, (☎ 223 333), Foch 467 and Almagro, speaks English and German. Dr José A Pitarque, ophthalmologist, (☎ 441 360), at the Hospital Metropolitano, speaks English. Your embassy or the SAEC can recommend others.

There are many dentists in Quito. Some recommended dental clinics include the Clínica de Especialides Odontológicas (☎ 521 383, 237 562), Orellana 1782 and 10 de Agosto; Clínica Dental Arias Salazar (☎ 524 582), Amazonas 239 and 18 de Septiembre; and Clínica Dental Dr Pedro Herrera (☎ 554 316), Amazonas 353 and Jorge Washington.

Note that foreign medical insurance, if it covers your hospital visit, normally does not reimburse the hospital. Pay your own medical fees directly to the doctor or hospital, and then bill your insurance company for reimbursement of the covered portions. Doctors and hospitals normally accept credit card payments. (See also Health in Facts for the Visitor.)

Women Travelers There are few resources or centers for women. La Casa de Mujer (☎ 230 844), Los Ríos 2238 and Gándara, is a block southwest of the Isidro Ayora Maternity Hospital near La Parque Alameda. This provides emergency beds, showers and kitchen facilities for women for about US$1 per night. This is geared towards Ecuadorian women, but might be of some assistance to other women in an emergency. Hostal Eva Luna (see Places to Stay) is a hostal specifically for women. The Carcel de Mujeres (Women's Prison) on Calle de Las Toronjas off Avenida El Inca at the north end of Quito, has several foreign women imprisoned for drug offenses. Women from the USA, Russia, Israel and the Dominican Republic have all requested visitors to chat with and keep up with the outside world. Inexpensive care packages – stuff like shampoo, tampons, books, fruit, cassette tapes, magazines etc – are welcomed though not expected. Visiting hours are 10 am to 2 pm Wednesday and weekends, and 1 to 4 pm weekdays.

I would be pleased to hear about other women's resources from travelers who encounter them.

Emergency Some helpful numbers to have in an emergency are:

police	☎ 101
fire department	☎ 102
general emergency	☎ 111
Red Cross ambulance	☎ 131, 580 598
emergency rescue	☎ 199

Dangers & Annoyances The elevation of about 2850 meters will make you feel somewhat breathless if you first arrive from sea level. This is a mild symptom of altitude sickness and will disappear after a day

or two. It is best to take things easy on arrival. Don't overexert yourself, eat lightly and cut back on cigarettes and alcohol to minimize the symptoms.

Quito is a safer city than the neighboring capitals of Bogotá or Lima, but unfortunately crime has been on the increase over the last few years. Be aware that pickpockets work crowded areas, such as public buses, markets and church plazas. (See also Dangers & Annoyances in Facts for the Visitor.)

The old town, where there are plenty of sightseeing, camera-laden tourists, is becoming increasingly attractive to groups of thieves. Plaza San Francisco in particular has recently had a rash of thefts, and the old town as a whole is a place to be careful. I suggest going on a tour or in a group to take photographs – and keep alert. If you dress inconspicuously and don't carry a valuable camera, you can wander around freely. After you have identified the areas you want to photograph, return with some friends and your camera.

One place you should definitely avoid is the steps of García Moreno heading from Ambato to the top of El Panecillo. I have received repeated reports of armed thieves on this climb. Take a taxi or a tour to the top and, once there, stay within the paved area around the statue of the Virgin. You won't have any problem there, and can take good photos of Quito and the surrounding mountains, but don't wander off down the grassy slopes or you stand a good chance of being robbed. I have also read that a taxi with tourists was stopped by robbers on the drive up. It is possible that the driver was in cahoots with the thieves. Take a taxi from a cab rank.

Generally, the new town is safer than the old town, but you should still stay alert, especially at night. The area bounded by Avenidas Patria, Amazonas, Colón and 12 de Octubre contains many of the better hotels, restaurants, gift shops and travel agencies – it is, therefore, popular with tourists and is also becoming the haunt of pickpockets, particularly at night. I hang out here at night and have never had a

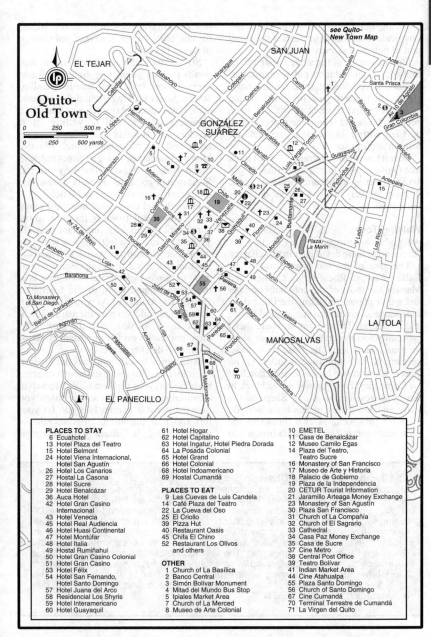

see Quito-
New Town Map

EL TEJAR

Quito-
Old Town

0   250   500 m
0   250   500 yards

SAN JUAN

GONZÁLEZ
SUÁREZ

Santa Prisca

LA TOLA

MANOSALVAS

EL PANECILLO

To Monastery
of San Diego

PLACES TO STAY
6 Ecuahotel
13 Hotel Plaza del Teatro
15 Hotel Belmont
24 Hotel Viena Internacional,
    Hotel San Agustín
26 Hotel Los Canarios
27 Hostal La Casona
28 Hotel Sucre
29 Hotel Benalcázar
36 Auca Hotel
42 Hotel Gran Casino
    Internacional
43 Hotel Venecia
45 Hotel Real Audiencia
46 Hotel Huasi Continental
47 Hotel Montúfar
48 Hotel Italia
49 Hostal Rumiñahui
50 Hotel Gran Casino Colonial
51 Hotel Gran Casino
53 Hotel Félix
54 Hotel San Fernando,
    Hotel Santo Domingo
57 Hotel Juana del Arco
58 Residencial Los Shyris
59 Hotel Interamericano
60 Hotel Guayaquil

61 Hotel Hogar
62 Hotel Capitalino
63 Hotel Ingatur, Hotel Piedra Dorada
64 La Posada Colonial
65 Hotel Grand
66 Hotel Colonial
68 Hotel Indoamericano
69 Hostal Cumandá

PLACES TO EAT
9 Las Cuevas de Luis Candela
14 Café Plaza del Teatro
22 La Cueva del Oso
25 El Criollo
39 Pizza Hut
40 Restaurant Oasis
45 Chifa El Chino
52 Restaurant Los Olivos
    and others

OTHER
1 Church of La Basílica
2 Banco Central
3 Simón Bolívar Monument
4 Mitad del Mundo Bus Stop
5 Ipiales Market Area
7 Church of La Merced
8 Museo de Arte Colonial

10 EMETEL
11 Casa de Benalcázar
12 Museo Camilo Egas
14 Plaza del Teatro,
    Teatro Sucre
16 Monastery of San Francisco
17 Museo de Arte y Historia
18 Palacio de Gobierno
19 Plaza de la Independencia
20 CETUR Tourist Information
21 Jaramillo Arteaga Money Exchange
23 Monastery of San Agustín
30 Plaza San Francisco
31 Church of La Compañía
32 Church of El Sagrario
33 Cathedral
34 Casa Paz Money Exchange
35 Casa de Sucre
37 Cine Metro
38 Central Post Office
39 Teatro Bolívar
41 Indian Market Area
44 Cine Atahualpa
55 Plaza Santo Domingo
56 Church of Santo Domingo
67 Cine Cumandá
70 Terminal Terrestre de Cumandá
71 La Virgen del Quito

problem, but I dress casually and don't carry valuables that might attract the attention of potential thieves.

Should you be unfortunate enough to be robbed, you should file a police report, particularly if you wish to make an insurance claim. The place to go is the police station at Mideros and Cuenca in the old town between 9 am and noon. The report should be filed within 48 hours of the theft for insurance purposes.

Despite the above warnings, I don't think that Quito is particularly dangerous. If you avoid attracting undue attention to yourself it's very unlikely that you'll have any problems at all.

Walking Tour

All sights mentioned in this section are described in more detail later in this chapter.

The area of the old town bounded by Calles Flores, Rocafuerte, Cuenca and Manabí has most of the colonial churches and major plazas, including the Plaza de la Independencia, with the Presidential Palace and cathedral. There is no set route that I especially recommend, but, if you are short on time, see at least the Plaza de la Independencia and continue southwest on García Moreno two blocks to the church of La Compañía. From here it is one block to the northwest (right) along Sucre to the Plaza and Monastery of San Francisco. Be alert for pickpockets. Two blocks to the southeast (left) of La Compañía brings you

to Calle Guayaquil; turn southwest (right) for one block to see the Plaza and Church of Santo Domingo.

Stroll along the old-town streets and you'll pass an interesting sight on almost every block. It is well worth spending several hours walking around this historic area, if not several days. It's also a bustling commercial area, full of yelling street vendors and ambling pedestrians, tooting taxis and belching buses, and whistle-blowing policemen trying to direct traffic in the narrow, congested one-way streets. Sunday is a good day to walk around the old center for some peace and quiet.

From the old town, head northeast along Calle Guayaquil towards the new town. Guayaquil runs into the important Avenida 10 de Agosto – turn left and you will pass the Banco Central on your left. Opposite the Banco Central is an impressive monument to Simón Bolívar; the monument is at the southernmost point of the triangular Parque La Alameda. As you head north through the park you pass the astronomical observatory. As you leave the park, continue northward on the important street of Avenida 6 de Diciembre.

After three blocks you pass the modern Palacio Legislativo (legislative congress building) on your right on Calle Montalvo. Continuing on 6 de Diciembre takes you past the popular Parque El Ejido on your left and past the huge, circular, mirror-walled Casa de la Cultura (with museums)

The Times, They are a'Changin'

Although set opening hours for colonial churches and museums are routinely given, these hours are rarely firm. Museums change their hours for reasons varying from a national holiday to staff sickness, so the opening hours in the following sections are meant only as guidelines. If possible, call ahead to verify hours. Monday is generally the worst day to visit museums, as many of them are closed.

Churches are open every day but are crowded with worshippers on Sunday. Hours are variable and changeable. The earthquake of 1987 damaged and closed several churches – most were open as of 1996, but hours seem to be different every time I go. Early morning seems to be a good time to visit churches. They sometimes remain open until after 6 pm, but are often closed for parts of the day. It's unpredictable. Good luck! ■

on your right. Past the Casa de la Cultura, turn left for three blocks along Avenida Patria, with Parque El Ejido to your left, and you reach the small stone arch that is the beginning of Quito's most famous modern street, Avenida Amazonas.

It is about three km from the heart of the old town to the beginning of Amazonas. Walk along Amazonas for banks, boutiques, souvenir stands and sidewalk cafés. On the parallel street of JL Mera you'll find the best bookstores and craft stores. Almost 1½ km away from Parque El Ejido, Amazonas crosses Calamá, which has several of Quito's best restaurants (to the right or southeast). There is much more to see outside of the old town, but it is scattered around Quito; you can walk, but many people take a bus or taxi to the places they are most interested in.

Museums – old town

Museo de Arte y Historia This museum (☎ 214 018, 210 863), at Espejo 1147 and Benalcázar, is in an old building in the center – it's also called Museo Municipal Albert Mena Caamaño. It used to be a Jesuit house until 1767, when it became an army barracks. The present museum contains a wealth of early colonial art dating from the 16th and 17th centuries, as well as more modern art. The basement has gory waxworks showing the assassination of local patriots who were killed by royalist forces in 1810, over a decade before independence was achieved.

The building is just off the Plaza de la Independencia, and is a little difficult to find because the sign is not obvious. The museum was closed for restoration in 1995 and 1996, but may reopen by the time you read this.

Casa de Sucre Several historical buildings in the center are now museums. A good one to visit is Casa de Sucre (☎ 512 860), which is well restored with period (1820s) furniture and has a small museum. Mariscal (field marshal) Antonio José de Sucre, the hero of Ecuadorian independence (and the man after whom Ecuadorian currency is named), lived here.

The house is on Venezuela 573 and Sucre. Hours are from 8 am to noon and 1:30 to 4 pm Tuesday to Friday, and 8 am to 1 pm on Saturday and Monday – but they change frequently (as do many of these places). Admission is US$1.25. They have a small gift shop with books about Ecuador.

Casa de Benalcázar The Casa de Benalcázar (☎ 218 102), located at Olmedo 968 and Benalcázar, dates from 1534 and was restored by Spain in 1967. Entrance is free during business hours. Sometimes classical piano recitals are held here – it's a delightful site for such entertainment. Check the newspapers or inquire at the house.

Museo de Arte Colonial This museum (☎ 212 297), on the corner of Cuenca and Mejía, reopened in the late 1980s after a long period of restoration. The building dates from the 17th century and houses

Casa de Sucre –
a hero's welcome home

what many consider to be Quito's best collection of colonial art from the 16th to the 18th centuries. Many famous sculptors and painters are represented, and there is also a collection of period furniture. Hours are 10 am to 6 pm Tuesday to Friday, and from 10 am to 2 pm Saturday and Sunday. Admission is US$2/1 for adults/students.

Museo Camilo Egas Another Ecuadorian painter who has a museum in his name is Camilo Egas (1889-1962). Some 40 of his works as well as other pieces are displayed in the Museo Camilo Egas (☎ 514 511), now under the auspices of the Banco Central. The collection has been recently restored. The museum is open 9 am to 1 pm and 3 to 5 pm Monday to Friday. Hours are subject to frequent change and the museum may be closed when they are setting up a special exhibition; admission is US$0.35. The address is Venezuela 1302 and Esmeraldas.

La Cima de la Libertad This museum is housed in a modern building on the flanks of Volcán Pichincha, west of the old town. It is best reached by taxi. The museum was built on the hill where Marshal Sucre fought the historical and decisive battle of Independence on May 24, 1822. There is a collection of historical and military artifacts and a huge and impressive mural by Kingman. Upon surrender of your passport, a soldier will guide you around. Photography is prohibited inside the museum. Outside the museum, however, photography is recommended – great views of the city below. I forgot my camera and regretted it.

Hours are from 9 am to 4 pm daily except Monday; admission is free.

Museums – new town
Museo del Banco Central This is Quito's best archaeology museum (☎ 223 259) and is now housed in the Casa de la Cultura (see below). It houses well-displayed pottery, gold ornaments (including the gold mask that is the symbol of the Museo del Banco Central), skulls showing deformities and early surgical methods, a mummy and many other objects of interest. There is also

a display of colonial furniture and religious art and carving.

Entrance is about US$2 (US$1.25 for students). Hours are from 9 am to 5 pm Tuesday through Friday, and 10 am to 3 pm on Saturday and Sunday.

Casa de la Cultura Ecuatoriana This large, circular glass building at the corner of Avenidas Patria and 12 de Octubre, to the east of the Parque El Ejido, has several collections (☎ 565 808, 522 410).

There is a fascinating display of traditional musical instruments, many several centuries old. The instruments are mainly Ecuadorian, but there are also Asian, African and European oddities. Also on display are examples of traditional Ecuadorian regional dress. The large art collection contains both contemporary Ecuadorian work and 19th-century pieces. The contemporary work exhibit includes canvases by Ecuador's most famous artists, Guayasamín and Kingman, among others.

Hours are 10 am to 6 pm Tuesday to Friday and 10 am to 2 pm on weekends. Admission is US$2/1 for adults/students.

There is also a movie theater that often shows international movies of note, and an auditorium where classical and other music is performed – check the newspapers or posters up in front of the building.

Museo de Jacinto Jijón y Caamaño Across the traffic circle from the Casa de la Cultura and northeast along Avenida 12 de Octubre is the Catholic University, which has an interesting private archaeology museum (☎ 521 834, 529 240) on the 3rd floor of the library. The museum is named after an Ecuadorian archaeologist and much of the collection was donated by his family after his death. The entrance to the museum is on 12 de Octubre near the intersection with Calle J Carrión.

Hours are from 9 am to 4 pm Monday through Friday (although they have, in the past, closed for lengthy lunch breaks). Admission is US$0.40 and you can get a guided tour (sometimes available in English) of the small archaeological collec-

A Late Night at the Museum

A friend and I got a little more than we bargained for on a recent visit to the art museums in the Casa de la Cultura. We arrived soon after 4 pm and felt that we had enough time before the 6 pm closing to have a worthwhile visit. By the end of the afternoon we were perusing the modern Ecuadorian art collection and noticed that lights were being turned off at one end of the hall, so we began drifting slowly toward the exit.

When we arrived, we found the door locked and a man standing there. It turned out that he was a museum office worker but that he did not have the key to the door – we were locked in and there was no one else there. Apparently, the guard was in a hurry to get home that night and he had left promptly at 6 pm without checking to see if there was anyone left inside the museum.

I briefly considered how many objets d'art I could hide under my coat before asking how we were going to get out. The office worker shrugged and volunteered that the night guard would probably be here by 8 pm and he would have a key. Probably! I suggested that there must be someone whom we could phone to bring a key, but found that all the offices with a phone in them had been locked for the night. Finally, we managed to attract the attention of someone outside and, explaining our predicament, got him to call the night guard to make sure that he would indeed show up, and perhaps a bit earlier than usual. He finally arrived at a few minutes before 8 pm and released us from our enforced museum visit. Next time I'll try to get locked into a bar after hours – that might be a lot more fun! ∎

---

tion. There is also a collection of colonial art exhibiting some of the masters of the Quito school.

Museo Guayasamín Modern art can be seen at the Museo Guayasamín (☎ 242 779, 244 373), the home of Oswaldo Guayasamín, an Ecuadorian Indian painter born in 1919 and now famous throughout the world. Guayasamín's collection of pre-Columbian and colonial pieces can also be seen.

The museum is at Calle Bosmediano 543 in the residential district of Bellavista to the northeast of Quito. It's an uphill walk or you can take a bus along 6 de Diciembre to Eloy Alfaro, then a Bellavista bus up the hill (make sure the bus has a Bellavista placard, or ask the driver). The bus can drop you about a block from the museum (or take a taxi). Hours are from 9:30 am to 1 pm and 3 to 6 pm Monday to Friday and 9:30 am to 1 pm on Saturday; entrance is US$1. You can buy original artwork here – beautiful and not cheap. Posters are available at a reasonable cost.

Museo Amazónico Formerly the Museo Shuar, this museum (☎ 562 633) run by the Salesian Mission has a small display of jungle Indian artifacts collected by the missionaries. Indian cultural publications (in Spanish) are sold. The museum is at 12 de Octubre 1436. Hours are from 11:30 am to 12:30 pm and 1 to 5 pm Monday to Friday, and 11:30 am to 12:30 pm Saturday. Admission is US$0.50.

Instituto Geográfico Militar Apart from selling maps to the public (see above for details), the IGM (☎ 522 066) has a geographical museum and planetarium open to the public. The IGM is at the end of the steep climb up Calle Paz y Miño, southeast of the Parque El Ejido.

Museum hours are 8 am to noon and 2 to 4 pm Tuesday to Friday; they have been open at weekends in the past but were closed on my last visit. Check locally. Shows in the planetarium last 30 minutes and are screened several times a day. Admission is US$0.35. You have to leave your passport at the IGM entrance gate to be allowed in.

Museo de Ciencias Naturales This museum (☎ 449 824) houses a natural history collection, which has previously been exhibited in a military college and at the Casa de la Cultura. The current display is at Parque La Carolina, on the Avenida Los Shyris side, opposite Avenida República de El Salvador. This is the best natural history museum in Ecuador and worth a visit if you want to acquaint yourself with Ecuador's flora and fauna.

Hours are 8:30 am to 1 pm and 1:30 to 4:30 pm Monday to Friday, and 9 am to 1 pm Saturday. Admission is US$1 or US$0.80 for students.

Vivarium (☎ 452 280, 210 863) This museum was recently opened by the Gustavo Orces Herpetological Foundation, which itself was created in 1989 to study and teach about Ecuadorian reptiles and amphibians. The Vivarium has a number of live animals including the highly poisonous fer-de-lance snake, boa constrictors, iguanas, turtles and tortoises. The (new) address is Reina Victoria 1576 and Santa María. Call ahead to arrange a tour. Admission is about US$2 – donations to support this research and educational institution are gratefully accepted.

Fundación Sinchi Sacha Sinchi Sacha is Quichua for 'powerful forest,' and this foundation (☎ 230 609, 527 240) exhibits the artwork and everyday utensils of the peoples of the Oriente. A nonprofit organization supporting Amazonian cultures, the foundation publishes a variety of literature about the rainforest and its peoples. There is also a good gift shop. The museum, at Reina Victoria 1780 and La Niña, is open from 8 am to 7 pm Monday to Saturday.

Churches

There is a wealth of churches, chapels, convents, monasteries, cathedrals and basilicas in Quito. The old town especially has so many of them that you can hardly walk two blocks without passing a church. Photography is not normally permitted because the intensity of the flash has a detrimental effect on the pigment in the many valuable religious paintings. Slides and postcards can be bought at the post office. There are signs asking tourists not to wander around during religious services – at such times you can enter and sit in a pew.

Monastery of San Francisco Ecuador's oldest church is the Monastery of San Francisco, on the plaza of the same name. Construction began only a few weeks after the founding of Quito in 1534, but the building was not finished until 70 years later. It is the largest colonial structure in Quito. The founder is commemorated by a statue at the far right of the raised terrace in front of the church. He is the Franciscan missionary Joedco Ricke, who is also credited with being the first man to sow wheat in Ecuador.

Although much of the church has been rebuilt because of earthquake damage, some of it is original. Go to the chapel of Señor Jesús del Gran Poder to the right of the main altar to see original tilework. The main altar itself is a spectacular example of baroque carving, and the roof and walls are also wonderfully carved and richly covered in gold leaf. Much of the roof shows Moorish influence.

The church contains excellent examples of early religious art and sculpture; unfortunately it is often too dark to see them properly. Tour guides turn lights on periodically so keep your eyes open for this. The bells are rung every hour, and often on the quarter hour. You can see the bell-ringer at work in his cubbyhole just to the right of the main door. To the left of the monastery is the Cantuña chapel, which houses an excellent collection of Quiteño art. Visiting hours recently were from 7 am to 11 am daily, and from 3 to 6 pm Monday to Thursday; admission is free.

To the right of the main entrance is the **Museo Franciscano** (☎ 211 124), which contains some of the monastery's finest artwork. Here you can see paintings, sculpture and furniture dating back to the 16th century. One of the oldest signed paintings is a Mateo Mejía canvas dated 1615. Some of the woodcarvings are even older and are covered with gold leaf, paint, period clothing or a fine porcelain finish. Some of the furniture is fantastically wrought and inlaid with literally thousands of pieces of mother-of-pearl.

The museum costs US$0.50 to visit, and Spanish-speaking guides are available. Hours are from 9 to 11 am and from 3 to 6 pm Monday to Saturday.

La Compañía Looking out across the plain, cobblestoned plaza of San Francisco, you see the ornate green and gold domes of the church of La Compañía de Jesús, just two blocks away. The construction of this Jesuit church began in 1605, the year that San Francisco was completed, and it took 163 years to build. The church is famous as the most ornate in Ecuador; it has been claimed that seven tons of gold were used to gild the walls, ceilings and altars. Quiteños call La Compañía the most beautiful church in the country, although some visitors find its splendor a little too rich. Note the Moorish influence in the intricate designs carved on the magnificent red-and-gold columns and ceilings. There is a beautiful cupola over the main altar. The remains of the Quiteño saint, Mariana de Jesús, who died in 1645, are kept here.

This church has suffered some settling of the foundations and was one of the most severely damaged in the 1987 earthquake. Restoration work continues but opening hours are changeable. A sign just inside the door gives visiting hours as 9:30 to 11 am and 4 to 6 pm daily, but don't rely on it. A small fire (apparently arson) caused minor damage in early 1996, which made the opening hours even less predictable. The church normally opens for services at 7 am. Admission is free.

Cathedral One block away from the ornate Jesuit church is the Plaza de la Independencia with the stark cathedral. Although not as rich in decoration as some of the other churches, the cathedral has several points of historical interest. Plaques on the outside walls commemorate Quito's founders and Marshal Sucre, the leading figure of Quito's independence, is buried in the cathedral. To the left of the main altar is a statue of Juan José Flores, Ecuador's first president. Behind the main altar is the smaller altar of Nuestra Señora de los Dolores; the plaque there shows where President Gabriel García Moreno died on August 6, 1875. He was shot outside the Presidential Palace (just across the plaza) and was carried, dying, to the cathedral. The cathedral contains paintings by several notable artists of the Quito school. Visiting hours are erratic; supposedly from 8 to 10 am and 2 to 4 pm daily except Sunday. Admission is free.

El Sagrario The main chapel of the cathedral was begun in 1657 and was finished 49 years later, but it is now a separate church, El Sagrario. This church was being renovated by Poland's University of Warsaw before the 1987 earthquake, and was damaged during that quake. Renovation continues and it is interesting to visit if you want to see how restoration work is done. El Sagrario is on García Moreno, next to the cathedral.

San Agustín Two blocks away from the Plaza de la Independencia (at Chile and Guayaquil) is the church where many of the heroes of the battles for Ecuador's independence are buried. This is the site of the signing of Ecuador's declaration of independence on August 10, 1809. The church is another fine example of 17th-century architecture.

The **Museo de San Agustín** (☎ 515 525, 580 263) is in the convent to the right of the church (at Chile and Flores). It houses many canvases of the Quito school, including a series depicting the life of Saint Augustine painted by Miguel de Santiago. The museum was recently restored and hours have been changeable. Try 9 am to 1 pm and 3 to 6 pm.

Santo Domingo The church of Santo Domingo, on the plaza at the southwest end of Flores, is especially attractive in the evening, when its domes are floodlit. It too dates back to early Quito. Construction began in 1581 and continued until 1650. An exquisite statue of the Virgen del

Rosario, a gift from King Charles V of Spain, is now one of the church's main showpieces. The statue is in an ornately carved baroque-style side chapel. In the busy Plaza Santo Domingo in front of the church is a statue of Marshal Sucre pointing in the direction of Pichincha, where he won the decisive battle for independence on May 24, 1822.

La Merced One of colonial Quito's most recent churches is that of La Merced (at Cuenca and Chile), which was begun in 1700 and completed in 1742. Its tower has the distinction of being the highest (47 meters) in colonial Quito and it contains the largest bell of Quito's churches.

The church has a wealth of fascinating art. Paintings show volcanoes glowing and erupting over the church roofs of colonial Quito, the capital covered with ashes, Marshal Sucre going into battle, and many other scenes. The stained-glass windows also show various scenes of colonial life such as early priests and conquistadors among the Indians of the Oriente. It is a surprising and intriguing collection. Recent hours were 3 to 8 pm Monday to Saturday, but I'll bet they'll be different by the time you visit.

San Diego This monastery, museum and cemetery are to the east of El Panecillo hill, between Calicuchima and Farfán. The monastery is an excellent example of 17th-century colonial architecture and the building (including the monk's living areas) can be toured. There is a treasure of colonial art, including a pulpit by the notable Indian woodcarver, Juan Bautista Menacho, which is considered one of the country's finest pulpits. The cemetery, with its numerous tombs, mausoleums and other memorials, is also worth a visit. The monastery should be visited with a guide, available daily except Monday from 9 am to 1 pm and 3 to 6 pm – ring the doorbell. A tour costs about US$1.

Other Churches Moving out of the old town, you can still find several interesting churches. High on a hill on Calle Venezuela

is the new church of **La Basílica**, which is still unfinished, though work on it began in 1926. Obviously, the tradition of taking decades to construct a church is still alive. At the north end of Parque La Alameda is the small church of **El Belén**, which was built on the site of the first Catholic mass to be held in Quito.

Finally, in a precipitous valley on the east side of town, is the **Sanctuary of Guápulo**, built between 1644 and 1693. The best views of this delightful colonial church are from behind Hotel Quito at the end of Avenida 12 de Octubre. Here, there is a statue of Francisco de Orellana looking down into the valley that was the beginning of his epic journey from Quito to the Atlantic – the first descent of the Amazon by a European. From the statue there is a steep footpath that leads down to Guápulo and it's a pleasant walk, though somewhat strenuous coming back. The local No 21 Santo Domingo-Guápulo bus goes there. Hours are 8 to 11 am and 3 to 6 pm Monday to Saturday. If it is closed, try asking at the caretaker's house next to the church to have it opened up. There is an excellent collection of Quiteño colonial art and sculpture, and the pulpit, carved by Juan Bautista Menacho in the early 1700s, is particularly noteworthy.

This is just a selection of Quito's most interesting and frequently visited churches. There are dozens more.

Other Sights

La Virgen del Quito The small, rounded hill that dominates the old town is called El Panecillo (the little bread loaf) and is a major Quito landmark. It is topped by a huge statue of the Virgin of Quito with a crown of stars, eagle's wings and a chained dragon atop the world. Read the Bible (Revelations, Chapter 12) for some ideas about why the Virgin was built as she is.

From the summit, there are marvelous views of the whole city stretching out below, as well as views of the surrounding volcanoes. The best time for volcano views, particularly in the rainy season, is early morning before the clouds roll in.

Although you can get there from the old town by climbing the stairs at the end of Calle García Moreno (it takes about half an hour) this is dangerous and strongly discouraged. Unfortunately, I have received numerous reports of travelers being robbed on the climb. The thieves may work in gangs and are sometimes armed. A taxi from the old town costs about US$2 or US$3; they will wait and bring you back.

Markets At the bottom of El Panecillo is Avenida 24 de Mayo. This used to be a major open-air Indian market. An indoor market was opened in 1981 at the upper end of 24 de Mayo. Nonetheless, some outdoor selling still takes place, especially on Calle Cuenca and the streets to the northwest of it, and at the intersection with 24 de Mayo. Saturday and Wednesday are the main market days, but the area is busy on other days as well. Nearby is the so-called Ipiales Market, up the hill from Imbabura along Chile. Anything from stolen cameras to smuggled Colombian goods to underwear can be bought here. This is a fascinating area to visit, but there are many pickpockets and bag/camera snatchers, so go to look rather than photograph.

The most popular produce market in the new town is the Santa Clara market on Ulloa and Versalles, just south of Colón.

La Ronda Just off Avenida 24 de Mayo between Calles García Moreno and Venezuela and on to Maldonado is the historic alley now called Calle Juan de Dios Morales, but known to most people by its traditional name of La Ronda. This street is perhaps the best preserved in colonial Quito and is narrow enough so cars rarely drive along it, which adds to its charm. It is full of old, balconied houses and you can enter several of them. Just walk along the street and you'll see which ones are open to visitors; they usually have handicrafts for sale.

Plaza de la Independencia While wandering around the churches of colonial Quito you'll probably pass through the Plaza de la Independencia several times.

Apart from the cathedral you can see the Palacio del Gobierno, also known as the Palacio Presidencial. It is the low white building on the northwest side of the plaza with the national flag flying atop it. The entrance is flanked by a pair of handsomely uniformed presidential guards.

The president does indeed carry out business in this building, so sightseeing is limited to the entrance area. Inside you can see a mural depicting Francisco de Orellana's descent of the Amazon. Ask the guard at the gate for permission to view the mural (not often given, though you can see inside from the gate).

The Archbishop's Palace, now a colonnaded row of small shops, can be seen on the northeast side of the Plaza. The interior patios can be visited.

Plaza del Teatro At the junction of Calles Guayaquil and Flores is the tiny Plaza del Teatro, where you'll find Teatro Sucre, built in 1878. This is Quito's most sophisticated theater with frequent concerts and plays.

Parque La Alameda Leaving the old town, you'll see the long, triangular Parque La Alameda with an impressive monument to Simón Bolívar at the apex. There are several other interesting monuments in the park. On the southeast side there is a relief map of Ecuador and further in toward the center there are statues of the members of the 1736-44 French Académie des Sciences expedition that surveyed Ecuador and made the equatorial measurements which gave rise to the metric system of weights and measures. Look for the statues of the leader, Charles-Marie de La Condamine, and for one of the Ecuadorian expedition members, Pedro Vicente Maldonado, who traveled to Europe after the expedition and died in London in 1748 at the age of 44. Quite by chance, I found a plaque dedicated to Maldonado at the rear of St James Church in Piccadilly when I was walking around London recently.

In the center of the park is the Quito Observatory, which was opened by President García Moreno in 1864 and is the

QUITO

oldest in the continent. It is used both for meteorology and astronomy and can be visited on Saturday morning.

At the north end of the park are a pair of ornamental lakes where rowboats can be hired for a few sucres. Nearby is a small monument with a spiral staircase and a view of the church of El Belén. This part of the park is filled with picnicking families on weekends.

Palacio Legislativo The legislative palace is the equivalent of the Houses of Parliament or Congress. This is where the elected members of congress carry out the nation's affairs. A huge sculpted panel stretching across the north side of the building on Calle Montalvo, just off 6 de Diciembre, represents the history of Ecuador and is worth a quick look.

Parque El Ejido A few blocks beyond Parque La Alameda is the biggest park in downtown Quito, the pleasant, tree-filled Parque El Ejido. This is a popular venue for ball games and you can usually see impromptu games of soccer and volleyball, as well as a strange, giant marbles game typical to Ecuador. It is played with golf-ball-sized steel balls. At the north end of the park open-air art shows are held at weekends.

Avenida Amazonas From the center of the north end of the park runs modern Quito's showpiece street, Avenida Amazonas. Here are modern hotels and airline offices, banks and restaurants. It is a wide avenue with plenty of room for pedestrians. Trucks and most buses are prohibited (except for a few buses bound for the airport and the north end of the city). There are a number of outdoor restaurants where you can have a coffee or a snack and watch modern Quito go by.

Language Courses
Spanish schools are a large and growing industry in Quito. There are dozens of schools where you can learn Spanish and new ones open every month, while others

fold. Classes are available at various levels; courses are offered for almost any length of time you want; classes can be individual or group; accommodations with local families can be arranged. With so many possibilities, it is easy to arrange classes once you arrive in Quito. Make sure you get what you want by visiting several schools to see which is best for you. Some people find that seven hours of one-on-one practice is too demanding, while others think this total immersion system is great. Choose what is best for you. Rates vary from about US$3 per hour to almost US$7 per hour. The South American Explorers Club is a good source of recommendations. The following schools have been recommended by readers or SAEC members – the cheapest ones may be noisy or cramped, and are usually in the old town, but the teachers are OK.

Academia de Español Quito
  Marchena 130 and 10 de Agosto, PO Box 39-C, Quito (☎ 553 647, fax 506 474) – expensive, but accommodations with local families included
Bipo & Toni's
  Carrión 300 and Leonidas Plaza Gutiérrez (☎ 547 090) – not cheap but lots of extracurricular social activities
Colonial Spanish School
  Sucre 518 and Benalcázar (☎ 582 237, fax 568 664) – one of the cheaper recommended schools
Experiment in International Living
  Hernando de la Cruz 143 and Mariana de Jesús (☎ 229 596, 447 090) – expensive but respected, with international connections
Instituto Superior de Español
  Ulloa 152 and Carrión (☎ 223 242, 523 813) – mid-priced and popular, with SAEC-member discounts
Israel Spanish School
  Olmedo 552 and Flores, 2nd floor – inexpensive and enthusiastic
La Lengua
  Colón 1001 and JL Mera, 8th floor (☎ 501 271) – mid-priced and has had several recommendations
Madre Tierra
  Guayaquil 1258 and Manabí, 3rd floor (☎ 218 416) – reasonable prices and caters to all levels

New World Spanish School
  290 Gangotena and Orellana (☎ 371 176,
  fax 435 654) – family operated
South American Spanish Institute
  Amazonas 1549 and Santa María
  (☎ 544 715, fax 226 348) – expensive, very
  good and can help with visa extensions
Start Right
  Amazonas 662 and Carrion, 5th floor
  (☎ 236 129) – fairly inexpensive

If you prefer group classes and can find your own accommodations, try the Catholic University (Universidad Católica) at Avenida 12 de Octubre and Robles. They have six-week classes for about US$100. The university also has classes in Quichua. The best time for classes is August and September – they don't always have them at other times of year.

Signing up for classes could help you get a student visa (see Information).

Work

Teaching English is the most usual way in which travelers are able to earn money in Ecuador. The best jobs are for bona fide teachers who obtain work in advance – see the Facts for the Visitor chapter. If you have no job lined up, the best bet is at one of the local 'English as a second language' schools. These occasionally advertise in the 'gringo' hotels or in the newspapers when they need teachers.

Organized Tours

Most travel agents in Quito will sell you both domestic and international airline tickets (adding the obligatory 10% tax), make hotel reservations, and arrange guided trips to hike in the mountains, climb the snow-capped volcanoes, explore the jungle or visit the Galápagos. But be warned that most guide services are not cheap. It is usually better to deal directly with the agency supplying the services you want. The following is a list of agencies and the particular services that they provide. Most companies will provide city tours and standard excursions to Otavalo, Cotopaxi and other places.

Note that it is often cheapest to book a

tour close to where you will be touring. Therefore some travelers try to arrange a tour in the Galápagos or the Oriente after they get there. This works, but there are several problems. During the Galápagos' high seasons many boats are full and it may be difficult to find one available. During the low seasons (and anytime in the Oriente) it may take several days to get a group of people together who are all interested in doing the same thing. This is OK if you have a week or two to kill, but if you want to be sure of leaving on a trip soon after you arrive, you should book in advance, especially for the Galápagos. (Several readers have written that they have been able to get on a Galápagos tour within two or three days at a good price, but a few report waiting over a week.)

For trips to the Oriente, a good tactic is to gather a group of budget travelers by advertising in your hotel or at the South American Explorers Club, then go to the Oriente altogether to look for a guide. This is advice for travelers on a shoestring budget and not much limited by time. If you are on a short trip, by all means book a tour in Quito. Good guides and tours are available, and you can leave quickly, although you'll pay a bit more for this convenience.

I do not give prices for Galápagos trips, because they are not fixed. As a rough guide, the cheapest trips are around US$500 per person per week in the low season, medium-priced trips are around US$1000 and luxury trips can reach over US$2000 per person per week.

Ecuadorian Tours (☎ 560 488), Amazonas 339 and Jorge Washington, is the American Express agent and is a good all-purpose travel agent.

The biggest and best-known travel agency is Metropolitan Touring (☎ 560 650, 560 801, fax 564 655), Amazonas 239, and (☎ 463 680, 464 780, fax 464 702, 465 868), República de El Salvador 970 (mail: PO Box 17-12-0310, Quito). They run medium-priced to luxury tours in the Galápagos, on both yachts and cruise ships. Their naturalist guides are very good. They run the first-class (by Oriente standards)

Flotel Orellana on the Río Aguarico (see The Northern Oriente chapter), operate expensive but luxurious train trips in their own specially modified coaches and hire Ecuador's best-known mountaineer, Marco Cruz, to head their climbing program. They are good with their preset itineraries but not as good at customizing tailor-made travel (according to two readers who tried this).

Nuevo Mundo Expeditions (☎ 552 617/839, fax 565 261, see also Online Services), Avenida Coruña and San Ignacio (mail: PO Box 402-A, Quito), are a small but very professional outfit with strong conservation interests (they are founding members of the Ecuadorian Ecotourism Association, in which they play a leading role). Their tours and prices are nearer the top end of the market and they have excellent guides. They are the only company to visit the unique and fascinating Solar Museum during their equator tour. They also organize Galápagos tours, visit the Reserva Producción Faunística Cuyabeno in the Oriente and do a variety of Andean trekking and horseback trips.

A company that does expensive but very good luxury yacht trips in the Galápagos is Quasar Nautica (☎ 446 996/7, 441 550, fax 436 625), Shyris 2447 and Gaspar de Villaroel. Slightly cheaper, but still at the top end of the market, is Angermeyer's Enchanted Excursions (☎ 569 960, fax 569 956), Foch 769 and Amazonas. They run some of the best and most popular boats in the Galápagos – if you can get on one of them. Angermeyer's also arranges excursions to the Oriente and Andes. Other recommended agencies include Etnotur (☎ 563 380, 230 552, fax 502 682), L Cordero 1313 and JL Mera; Andes Discoveries (☎ 228 520, fax 550 952), Amazonas and Dávalos; and Seaman Tour on Amazonas.

Galasam Economic Tours (☎ 507 079/080, fax 567 662, see also Online Services), Amazonas and Cordero (head office in Guayaquil) has a variety of boats ranging from inexpensive to mid-range prices. Their inexpensive boats are among the cheapest Galápagos tours available, but

their better tours have, with a few exceptions, been recommended. The cheapest of all are arranged by César Gavela, Jr of the Hotel Gran Casino Internacional (☎ 514 905), Avenida 24 de Mayo and Bahía de Caráquez in the old town. As these are the cheapest trips available (in advance), don't expect much comfort. I have received several reports stating that these are a good value. On the other hand, I also have received several letters from travelers complaining that the trips were very poor, that the itinerary was not as advertised and that the guides were unknowledgeable. This is what happens when you deal in the very bottom end of the price market. The Gran Casino also has information about cheap tours to the jungle.

There are several agencies offering rental equipment and guiding services for ascents of Ecuador's snow peaks. These mountains are well in excess of 5000 meters and require some basic mountaineering skills. The weather can turn bad quickly in the Andes, and inexperienced climbers have been killed. Some 'guides' have climbed a mountain a couple of times, and then offer their services for very low prices – these people are not listed here. I recommend you hire an experienced climbing guide and climb in safety. Expect to pay very roughly US$100 per person to climb a major peak – this is for a group of three climbers with one guide. Climbs of minor peaks not requiring technical equipment are cheaper partly because the climb is easier and partly because a guide can take a larger group, so the cost can be split more ways.

The following are reputable adventure-travel and climbing agencies: Sierra Nevada (☎ 553 658, fax 554 936), JL Mera 741 and Veintimilla, does climbing, river rafting and mountain biking. Pamir (☎ 542 605, fax 547 576), next door at JL Mera 721, has very experienced climbing and trekking guides. Agama Expediciones (☎ 518 191, fax 518 196), Venezuela 1163 and Manabí, run by Eduardo Agama in the old town, has climbing and Oriente trips. Campo Abierto (☎ 230 029), 6 de Diciembre and Roca, is a climbing store with gear, advice, a climbing magazine, and occasional organized treks and climbs. For river rafting and kayaking in the Oriente, Rios Ecuador is recommended (see under Tena for more details).

For buying or renting climbing and/or camping equipment, check out Andisimo, 9 de Octubre 427 and Roca, Altamontaña Expediciones, Washington 425 and 6 de Diciembre, and Equipos Cotopaxi (☎ 500 038, 526 725), 6 de Diciembre 927 and Patria. Both have good information, but neither leads guided climbs. Climbers should read *Climbing & Hiking in Ecuador* (4th edition due in 1997), by Rob Rachowiecki et al (Bradt Publications).

Recommended mountain-bike tours are offered by Flying Dutchman (☎ 542 806, fax 449 568), Foch 714 and JL Mera. They have good bikes and guides, and offer one-to five-day tours. Another outfit to try is Aventour (☎ 524 715, fax 223 720), Calamá 339 and Reina Victoria. They offer river rafting and mountain biking tours, though I haven't had any feedback on their trips from readers yet.

For jungle trips, apart from the top-end operators listed at the beginning of the section, I recommend Emerald Forest (☎ 526 403, fax 568 664), Amazonas 1023 and Pinto, which specializes in tours to the Río Napo and the Parque Nacional Yasuní area – several readers have recommended them. Another jungle outfitter with a good reputation and several reader recommendations is Native Life (☎ 550 836, fax 229 077), Pinto 446 and Amazonas. They specialize in the Cuyabeno, among other areas. Both of these strive to be environmentally and culturally responsible. I appreciate readers' comments on this subject.

Fundación Golondrinas (☎ 226 602), Isabel La Católica 1559, is a conservation project with volunteer opportunities. They arrange four-day walking tours in the páramo and forests west of Tulcán. Costs are US$50 per day and they have been well recommended.

Finally, one company providing in-depth information and services – ranging from volcano climbs to jungle trips to personalized off-the-beaten-track expeditions – is Safari Tours (☎ 552 505, 223 381, fax 220 426), Calamá 380 and JL Mera. One of the owners, Jean Brown, is a walking encyclopedia of travel information. They provide 4WD transport to just about anywhere, maintain a database of available Galápagos trips at very good prices and have contacts with a host of hotels, lodges and guides. They have a paperback book exchange, too.

Places to Stay

As befits a capital city, Quito has well over a hundred hotels and it would be pointless to list every one. The following selection will give you plenty of choice. As a general guideline, hotels in the old town tend to be less comfortable, older and much cheaper than those in the new town. That is not to say that there are no cheap hotels in the new town. In fact, a big increase in the incidence of thefts in the old town and a concomitant increase in cheap hotels in the new town means that more budget travelers are staying in the new town than before. The more expensive hotels add a 10% or 20% tax – my quotes below include taxes, but ask the better hotels whether the tax is included in the rates they give you.

December is a busy month in Quito. The founding of Quito is celebrated on the 6th, and the Christmas-New Year period is also busy. Try not to arrive in the evening without a reservation if you wish to stay in a particular hotel.

July and August are the busy season with vacationers from North America and Europe – hotel prices may go up a bit then.

Places to Stay – bottom end

Old Town Many cheap hotels are at the south end of the old town, on the streets heading towards the bus terminal. Here, you'll find a score of cheap hotels within a few blocks of one another. Some foreign budget travelers and many locals stay in the area but watch your belongings on the streets and ensure your room is always locked. Some travelers (particularly single women) do not feel comfortable staying in this area.

The *Hotel Grand* (☎ 210 192, 519 411), Rocafuerte 1001, is popular with international budget travelers and has been recommended by them. Basic but clean rooms are US$4.50/8 for singles/doubles or US$6/10 with private bath. The hotel is family-run and friendly, and has hot water, a laundry service and a restaurant. A block away, *La Posada Colonial* (☎ 212 859), Paredes 188, is also a popular choice with similar facilities at US$3.50 per person or US$4.50 with private bath. Another well-liked travelers' place is the *Hotel Belmont* (☎ 516 235), Antepara 413, between the old and new town. This clean, safe, family-run hotel charges US$4 per person.

The legendary *Hotel Gran Casino* (☎ 516 368), García Moreno 330, once widely known as the 'Gran Gringo,' used to be a classic backpackers' dive in a poor area of town. It's still there, but the basic and beat up rooms are a poor value, even at the US$2.40 price. Instead, stay opposite in the newer and much nicer *Hotel Gran Casino Colonial* (☎ 211 914) with a pleasant colonial courtyard, restaurant and doubles with bath at US$6. Two blocks away is the *Hotel Gran Casino Internacional* (☎ 211 214), at 24 de Mayo and Bahía de Caráquez. They have decent rooms with private hot bath for about US$3.50 per person (mostly doubles and triples). They also have a travel agency for the cheapest Galápagos tours.

On the Plaza Santo Domingo is the *Hotel Santo Domingo* (☎ 512 810, 211 958), Rocafuerte 1345, charging US$3 per person or US$3.50 with private hot bath. It's noisy but OK. Next door, the similarly priced *Hotel San Fernando* is grimy. The pleasant, friendly but noisy *Hotel Juana del Arco* (☎ 214 175, 511 417), Rocafuerte 1311, has hot water and charges US$4 each or US$6/10 with bath. Some rooms have plaza views (these are the noisiest). The viewless back rooms are much quieter. Just off the plaza, *Hotel Félix* (☎ 514 645), Guayaquil 431, has pretty flowers on the balconies. There is reportedly only one hot shower for about 30 basic rooms, but the place is clean and secure – ring the bell to

get in. It's a good deal for US$2 per person. The nearby *Hotel Venecia* (☎ 211 403), Rocafuerte 1514, is basic but clean. The electric showers deliver only lukewarm water, writes one traveler, but that's about par for those contraptions. Rates are US$3/4.50 with communal bath or US$6 for a double with private bath. *Ecuahotel* (☎ 515 984), Chile 1427 and Cuenca, is another budget option that has a few rooms with good views.

There are several cheap and basic hotels on the historic street of La Ronda (officially called Juan de Dios Morales). The best is *Residencial Los Shyris* (☎ 515 536), La Ronda 691, at US$3 per person or US$9 for a double with private bath. There are cheaper but worse places on this street, which can be unsafe after dark.

There are many hotels on Maldonado heading toward the bus terminal. Some are shown on the map. While these are convenient for the terminal, the street attracts pickpockets, so don't dally. The following are OK and have hot water. The basic but secure *Hotel Ingatur* (☎ 216 461), Maldonado 3226, is just US$2.25/3.50 for rather dank rooms or US$3.50/5 with bath. The slightly better *Hotel Guayaquil* (☎ 211 520), Maldonado 3248, has varied rooms, some quite spacious, for US$4 for a double or US$5/6 with bath. Also basic but decent is the *Hotel Capitalino* (☎ 513 433), Maldonado 3235, at US$2.50/4. The *Hotel Indoamericano* (☎ 515 094), Maldonado 3022, isn't bad for the basic dives by the terminal. They charge US$4/7.50 or US$6/10 with bath. The *Hotel Colonial* (☎ 510 338), down an alley from Maldonado 3035, is quiet and has hot water in the morning. Basic but clean rooms are US$5/8. The *Hotel Interamericano* (☎ 214 320), Maldonado 3263, charges US$5 to US$9 for a single and US$9 to US$15 for a double, depending on whether or not you have a bathroom, telephone or TV in your room. The best bottom-end hotel in this area is the *Hotel Piedra Dorada* (☎ 517 460), Maldonado 3210, which charges about US$12 for a clean double, and has plenty of hot water in the private showers.

Going from Plaza Santo Domingo along Calle Flores, there's the friendly *Hotel Huasi Continental* (☎ 517 327), Flores 332, with spartan but clean rooms for US$4/6.50 or US$6/10 with private hot bath. The nearby *Hotel Montúfar* (☎ 211 419), Sucre 160, is recommended for those on a tight budget. It's basic but clean and quiet, has warm water and is only US$2 per person or US$5 for a double with bath. Further down Flores is the better *Hotel San Agustín* (☎ 216 051, 212 847), Flores 626, at US$6/8 or US$8/12 with private bath, and the *Hotel Los Canarios* (☎ 519 103), Flores 856, which is US$5/8 with bath.

The *Hotel Hogar* (☎ 218 183), Montúfar 208, is US$9 for a clean double with bath and hot water in the mornings. *Hostal Rumiñahui* (☎ 211 407), Montúfar 449, is US$8 for a clean double with bath. Nearby the friendly *Hotel Italia* (☎ 518 643), Junín 765, has clean but basic rooms for US$3.50 per person.

Another budget hotel in the old town is the *Hotel Sucre* (☎ 514 025), on Cuenca at the corner of Plaza San Francisco. The hotel is attractive from the outside, but has only basic rooms inside, though some have excellent plaza views, which alone are worth the US$2 per person. Showers are cold. Also on this plaza is the *Hotel Benalcázar* (☎ 518 302), Benalcázar 388, at US$3 per person or US$3.50 with private bath.

The *Hotel Plaza del Teatro* (☎ 512 980, 514 293, fax 519 462), Guayaquil 1373, in a nice old house by the theater plaza. Rates here are about US$10/14 in good rooms with private bath and there is a coffee shop on the premises. Nearby, the pleasant old *Hostal La Casona* (☎ 514 764), Manabí 255, has clean rooms for US$11/16, including breakfast.

Casa Patty (☎ 510 407), Iquique 233 and Manosalvas, (in the La Tola district, six blocks east of Plaza Marín along Chile to Iquique, then three blocks south – a steep walk) is run by the same family that has Pensión Patty in Baños. The large house has double rooms for US$5. Kitchen facilities are available and the management is friendly. Call ahead to see if there's room.

New Town A popular (and often full) budget hotel just east of the Parque La Alameda, *Residencial Marsella* (☎ 515 884), Los Rios 2035 and Castro, has clean rooms, hot water and a roof with a view. I have received a few comments that everything is fine until you have a complaint, and then the management becomes unhelpful. Rates are about US$3 to US$6 per person; rooms vary quite widely in quality, from comfortable doubles with bath to a few airless singles with shared bath. If this is full, try the newer *Residencial Margarita* (☎ 512 599, 510 441), around the corner at A Elizalde 410 and Los Rios, with clean rooms at US$3 each, or more with bath.

The small, family-run *Residencial Italia* (☎ 224 332), 9 de Octubre 237, has plenty of kids running around. Basic rooms are US$4 per person or US$5 with bath, and are often full.

Several small, family-run hostals have opened over the past few years and cater to backpackers, budget travelers of all ages and students. They are very popular places to stay and most of the following would be where I would stay if I were economizing. Hot showers, kitchen and laundry facilities, luggage storage, living room (often with TV or books), notice board and information are available in a friendly and relaxed environment. These are good places to meet travelers interested in hiking or off-the-beaten-track travel. They normally have a few double and triple rooms and a larger dormitory-style room. Single rooms are less common. Showers are usually shared. Because they are small places, it is best to phone ahead for availability and price. The following are all in the small hostal category.

Casapaxi (☎ 542 663, 551 401), Pasaje Navarro 364 near Avenida La Gasca, is about one km north of Avenida América up a hill; the No 19 bus passes by. It is friendly, clean and helpful, and costs about US$5 for one night, with long-stay discounts given (as is true for most of hostals). *Hostal Tatu* (☎ 544 414), 9 de Octubre 275, is also recommended and charges US$4.50 per person in dorms or US$12 for a double.

La Casa de Eliza (☎ 226 602), Isabel La Católica 1559, is US$6.50 per person. Owners Eliza and Piet arrange excellent treks through northern Ecuador in association with the Cerro Golondrinas Cloudforest Conservation Project (see the sidebar in the North of Quito chapter). If La Casa de Eliza is full, try Eliza's sister's house a few blocks away.

La Casona (☎ 230 129, 544 036), Andalucia 213, is US$6.50 per person, and is in a lovely house. A new arrival on the scene is *El Centro del Mundo* (☎ /fax 229 050), Lizardo García 569 and Reina Victoria. It's run by travelers (an Ecuadorian/French Canadian couple) for travelers, and features cable TV and home cooking. Rates are US$4 or US$5 in dorm rooms and US$12/15 in doubles and triples.

Other good ones at US$6 or US$7 per person include: *Johnnie's Lodging House*, Caamaño 145 and Colón; *El Cafecito* (☎ 234 862), Luis Cordero 1124, over the restaurant of the same name (see Places to Eat) has a few doubles and several rooms with four or six beds and is very popular; *El Ciprés* (☎ /fax 549 558, 549 561), Lérida 381 and Toledo, is in a quiet neighborhood and has dorm rooms, a big garden and complimentary continental breakfast; *Albergue Los Andes* (☎ 521 944, fax 508 639), Santa Rosa 163 and Avenida Universitaria, has dorm beds at US$5 and doubles for US$14; *Hostal La Herradura* (☎ 226 340), Pinto 570, has individual rooms at US$6/10, or US$12 with bath.

The *Magic Bean* (☎ 566 181), Foch 681, above the popular restaurant of that name (see Places to Eat), is a great meeting place. It's US$7 in dorm rooms, US$20 for a double or US$24 for a double with bath. *Hostal Eva Luna* (☎ 220 426), Roca Pasaje 405 and Amazonas, is down a little alley off Roca and Amazonas. It is a hostal for women, opened by Safari Tours in late 1995. Rates are US$8 each. *Albergue El Taxo* (☎ 225 593), Foch 909, is run by artists who charge US$9 each and have local information. The *Hostelling International* youth hostel (☎ 543 995, fax 226 271), Pinto 325, has spotless rooms with three or four beds at US$9.50 per bed (private bath) or US$8.50 (shared bath). Hostel members pay about US$8/7.

Parque Italia (☎ 224 393, fax 564 901), Narvaez 802 and Carvajal (a couple of long blocks west of Avenida América – covered by the enlargement on the New Town map) is a recently opened B&B run by an Ecuadorian/Austrian couple. They have pleasant rooms with terraces for one to three people at US$8 per person, and offer weekly and monthly discounts.

The clean *Hotel Viena* (☎ 235 418), Tamayo 879, has good hot private showers. It's good value for US$7/11. The similarly priced *Hotel Koronado* (☎ 565 643), Cordero 779, is another reasonable choice. The clean and friendly *Hostal Coqui* (☎ 223 148, ☎ /fax 565 972), Versalles 1075, is good at US$10/13 for rooms with bath or US$6/10 without. There is also a café. The *Hotel Versalles* (☎ 547 321), Versalles 1442, is adequate for US$10/15 with bath. The *Residencial Santa Clara* (☎ 541 472), Darquea Teran 1578, is clean, quite pleasant-looking, friendly and OK for US$8/16 with bath. Meals are available. Others in this area are the *Residencial Carrión* (☎ 234 620, 548 256) at Carrión 1250 and Versalles. This residencial is popular, geared to long-staying guests and is often full. Rates are about US$14/16.50 for rooms with phone and TV, and there is a restaurant. *Hotel Majestic* (☎ 543 182) at Mercadillo 366 and Versalles has pleasant, clean rooms with private baths, TV and telephone for US$14/20. They have friendly staff and a bar/restaurant.

The *Loro Verde* (☎ 226 173), Rodríguez 241, has a great central location and spacious rooms with bath for US$12/18. Nearby, the *Posada del Maple* (☎ 544 507), Rodríguez 148, is a pleasant and friendly little hotel charging US$15/20 with bath, a little less with shared bath, and US$8 per bed in a dorm. Breakfast is included and it's on a quiet street. The centrally located *Hotel Pickett* (☎ /fax 541 453, 551 205) at Presidente Wilson 712 and JL Mera charges US$12/16 for basic rooms with telephone and bath with plenty of hot water. The new and clean *Hostal Farget* (☎ 570 066), Santa Prisca at Farget 109, has nice rooms for US$14/18.

Private Homes If you would like to stay in a local home, families interested in hosting travelers can be found through the SAEC or by reading the classified ads in the newspapers. If you are taking Spanish courses, ask also at your school. Prices average between US$6 and US$13 per person per day, sometimes including meals and laundry service, and may be negotiable if you are staying a long time or have several people sharing. Most families have only one or two rooms available; single rooms may cost a bit more. English is not always spoken.

Places to Stay – middle
Old Town The best hotel near the terminal terrestre is the *Hostal Cumandá* (☎ 516 984, 513 592) at Morales 449, right behind the bus terminal. Clean, carpeted rooms with bathrooms and hot water are US$10.50/16 with TV and a telephone available in some rooms. Avoid rooms on the terminal side as it can get noisy – otherwise it's a value.

The *Hotel Viena Internacional* (☎ 213 605, 211 329), Flores 600, is popular with travelers wanting comfort in the old town. Large carpeted rooms, some with balconies and all with telephones, bathrooms and hot water, are US$10 per person. There's a book exchange and restaurant.

The *Auca Hotel* (☎ 512 240) at Venezuela 625 and Sucre looks spartan but has clean but cramped rooms with private bath, TV and telephone for US$16/22. The nearby *Hotel Real Audiencia* (☎ 512 711, fax 580 213), on the corner of the Plaza Santo Domingo at Bolívar 220 and Guayaquil, is the best hotel in the old town. It has clean rooms with bath, phone and TV for US$22/30. There is also a bar and restaurant.

New Town The centrally located *Allston Inn Hotel* (☎ 508 956, 229 955, fax 222 721), JL Mera 741 and Baqueadano, has been recommended for clean, comfortable rooms with private hot showers for US$17/24. The similarly priced and fairly new *Hostal Bavaria* (☎ 509 401), Páez 232 and 18 de Septiembre, looks quite pleasant with comfortable rooms with TV and phone. *Hotel Nueve de Octubre* (☎ 552 424/524), 9 de Octubre 1047 and Colón, has simple rooms with carpeting and telephone for US$16/24. There is a restaurant and the place is OK, though they aren't really much better than some hotels in the bottom-end section charging several dollars less. The *Hostal Charles Darwin* (☎ 592 384), Colina 304 and Orellana, is a small and intimate hotel on a quiet side street. Double rooms with private bath are US$25, including breakfast and kitchen facilities. The *Hostal Los Andes* (☎ 550 839), Muros 146 and González Suárez, is in an upper-class residential area near the British embassy. It is very clean and recommended, has a friendly, English-speaking staff and is a good value at US$18/24, though the walls are a bit thin, according to one reader. Welcome to Latin America, where sound-proof walls are few and far between.

Opposite the Quito Airport is the *Hotel Aeropuerto* (☎ 458 708) at Amazonas 7955 (the north end of the Avenida), where rooms go for US$20/25 with bath, hot water and telephone. They are definitely overpriced – there is little to recommend it other than its proximity to the airport (most other hotels are seven to 11 km away).

Between the old and new towns, a couple of blocks west of Parque El Ejido, is the *Hotel Inca Imperial* (☎ 524 800) at Bogotá 219. This hotel is recommended for friendly and helpful English-speaking management and there is a restaurant. Rooms are US$20/30 with private bath and hot water. Another good choice is the *Hostal Plaza Internacional* (☎ 524 530, fax 505 075), Leonidas Plaza Gutiérrez 150 and 18 de Septiembre, which is a friendly place in a lovely older house; it's often full. The rates are US$28/42, and the staff speaks English. Another attractive hotel in a converted mansion with a garden is the *Café Cultura* (☎ /fax 224 271), above the restaurant of the same name (see Places to Eat). Pleasant rooms are about US$35/45.

The *Hotel Embassy* (☎ 561 990, fax 563 192), in the heart of a quiet residential district at Presidente Wilson 441 and 6 de Diciembre, is motel-like and rather lacks character. Still, its comfortable rooms (around US$30/35) are spotless and complete with carpeting, telephone and bathroom, some with a kitchenette. Their restaurant is recommended. This hotel is used by some airlines and smaller tour agencies to accommodate groups, and independent travelers have occasionally had problems with reservations. One reader reports being overcharged. Some readers have recommended the *La Estancia Inn* (☎ 235 993), a block away at Wilson 508 and Almagro. It's attractively decorated and a few dollars cheaper than the Embassy. A few blocks away is *Hostal Camila's* (☎ 546 880, fax 225 412) at 6 de Diciembre 1329 and Roca. This small hostal is in a recently renovated Spanish-style house, and has comfortable, spacious rooms with telephone, TV and bathroom for US$19/26 including breakfast.

The *Hotel Ambassador* (☎ 561 777, 562 054, fax 503 712), 9 de Octubre 1052 and Colón, has rather small rooms, many with TV and telephone, for US$28/34, and there is a pricey restaurant and bar. Nearby, the small and pleasant *Hostal Palm Garten* (☎ 523 960, 526 263, fax 568 944), in a converted mansion at 9 de Octubre 923 and Cordero, has comfortable and attractive rooms with TV and telephone for US$48/62. A recommended small hotel is the *Hostal Villantigua* (☎ 227 018, 528 564, fax 545 663), Jorge Washington 237 and Tamayo. Built in 1940 when the area was still largely rural, it is now one of the most comfortable houses in modern Quito. There are twelve rooms furnished with colonial-style furniture ranging in price from US$22 to US$40 for singles and US$35 to US$55 for doubles, all with private bath, and some with fireplaces and minibars. A breakfast room is open from 7:30 to 9:30 am. A couple of readers recommend the 14-room *Hotel Sierra Madre* (☎ 505 687, 505 688, 224 950, fax 505 715), Veintimilla 464 and Tamayo, also in

this price range. Rooms are described as immaculate, some with a balcony, and the staff speaks English and is very helpful. Breakfast is included.

There are a couple of smaller first-class hotels that are reasonably economical, but are often booked up well ahead. One of the best is *Hostal Los Alpes* (☎ 561 110) in a beautiful old house at Tamayo 223 and Jorge Washington. Comfortable carpeted rooms with spotless bathrooms and a telephone are about US$54/70, including breakfast. Their restaurant is excellent and the hotel enjoys a lot of repeat business, so reservations are advised. Also good and in the same price range is *Residencial Cumbres* (☎ 562 538, 560 850, fax 562 702) at Baqueadano 148 near 6 de Diciembre. Breakfast is included. Both hotels have friendly English-speaking management.

Places to Stay – top end
All the top-end hotels are in the new town. These hotels are very good and compare well with first-class hotels anywhere in the world. Unfortunately, nearly all suffer from the habit of charging non-Ecuadorian guests approximately twice as much as residents of Ecuador. (I give the higher rates below.) Though luxury hotels are popular with businesspeople and tour groups, their inflated rates place them beyond the price range of most independent travelers.

Among the best (because they charge foreigners almost the same as Ecuadorians) luxury hotels for independent travelers is the *Hotel Sebastián* (☎ 222 400, 222 300, fax 222 500, see also Online Services), Almagro 822 and Cordero. There are about 50 good-sized rooms and seven suites, many with balconies and some with great views. Apart from the usual features – cable TV, direct dial phones, room service, writing desks, attractive furnishings – there are several thoughtful touches: Water has been filtered and so you can drink it out of the tap, and ozone-purified water is available at the cafeteria. Towels and sheets are washed on request using environmentally safe soap (a rarity in Ecuador). Fruits and vegetables served in the coffee shop and restaurant are organically grown. All in all, this is my personal top-end choice. Rates are US$72/84, or US$90/101 in suites.

The similarly priced *Chalet Suisse* (☎ 562 700, fax 563 966), Reina Victoria 312 and Calamá, has 50 rooms, a small casino, a sauna and exercise room. Their restaurant is Swiss-influenced. The *Hotel Tambo Real* (☎ 563 820, fax 554 964) at 12 de Octubre and Queseras del Medio (opposite the US Embassy) is one of the cheapest of the larger luxury hotels and also has a casino as well as 24-hour room services. Their 90 large rooms go for US$95/110, and some have minibars.

There are two large luxury hotels on Amazonas in the heart of the new town. The *Hotel Alameda Real* (☎ 562 345, fax 565 759), Roca 653 and Amazonas has 150 very large rooms, many with balconies, wet bars or kitchenettes, renting for US$122/140. They have a good restaurant, bar, coffee shop and casino.

The biggest hotel in town is the *Hotel Colón* (☎ 561 333, 560 666) at Amazonas and Patria. This hotel has everything you might need for a luxurious stay – pool, sauna, massage parlor, exercise room, discotheque, casino, barber and hairdressing salons, a small shopping mall, a 24-hour coffee shop, two restaurants, two bars and numerous meeting rooms. The Colón is one of the capital's main social centers and this is where many visiting dignitaries stay. Its central location also makes it one of upper-class Quito's most lively meeting places. Almost all of the 450 rooms have good views of Quito – head up to the 20th floor and walk out onto the roof for a really great view. Rooms here vary in size and range from about US$150 to US$200. All rooms have cable TV.

If you want a luxury hotel away from the center, try the *Hotel Quito* (☎ 544 600, 567 284) at González Suárez 2500 and 12 de Octubre. They have a panoramic view of both Quito and the Guápulo valley and attractive gardens with a pool. This hotel features many of the facilities of the Colón but is more out of the way and therefore

quieter and a little cheaper than the Colón. Also in this price range is the newer *Akros Hotel* (☎ 430 600, fax 431 727), way north of town at 6 de Diciembre 3986 and Checoslovaquia, with 200 large, modern and comfortable rooms and the usual hotel services. Also away from the center is the new *Crowne Plaza Hotel* (☎ 251 666, 445 305, fax 251 958, 445 180), Los Shyris 1757 and Naciones Unidas (at the northeast corner of Parque La Carolina). This is a businessperson's hotel with excellent facilities for executives, but not geared towards tourists.

The *Hotel Oro Verde Quito* (☎ 566 497, 567 128, fax 569 189) at 12 de Octubre 1820 and Cordero is the city's most expensive hotel. It too has all the amenities you could possibly want (including pool, gym, excellent restaurants and a casino), if you don't mind paying about US$250 for one of its 240 rooms. More expensive suites are available.

Places to Stay – apartments

Visitors wanting to stay for a longer time may want to rent an apartment or suite with a kitchen for self catering. Often, apartments require a one-month minimum stay and are often full. One of the least expensive is *Residencial Casa Oriente* (☎ 546 157), Yaguachi 824 and Llona, behind the Hospital Eugenio Espejo. They charge US$100/120 a month in simple rooms with one bed. Daily rates are US$5 per person, and there are kitchen privileges and a rooftop terrace overlooking the city. *Apartamentos Calima* (☎ 524 036), Cordero 2028 and 10 de Agosto, charges US$260 per month for two people; they have no daily rates. The *Apart Hotel Mariscal* (☎ 528 833, fax 222 446), Robles 958 and Valdivia, charges US$40 a day or US$475 a month per double. These last two have kitchen facilities. The *Apart Hotel Panorámico* (☎ 542 425), San Ignacio 1188 and González Suárez, is in an expensive neighborhood and charges US$330 per person per month for nice little apartments with great views. These apartments are often booked solid well in advance.

Other places charge by the day only. These include *Apartamentos Colón* (☎ 563 183, fax 561 985), Leonidas Plaza 326 and Roca, with double apartments for US$30 a day; *Amaranta Apart Hotel* (☎ 527 191, fax 560 586), Leonidas Plaza 194 and Jorge Washington, for US$56 a day; and *Antinea Apart Hotel* (☎ 506 838, fax 504 404), Rodríguez 175 and Almagro, which has lovely furnished apartments for US$66 a day for two people.

Places to Eat
If you are economizing, it is best to stick to the almuerzos or meriendas (set lunches and dinners) which are sold in many restaurants, particularly those used by workers and businesspeople. These set meals often cost well under US$2 and may not be listed on the menu – ask. Almuerzos and meriendas are more difficult to find at weekends because these meals are aimed at working people. Many restaurants are closed on Sunday.

The fancier restaurants add 10% tax plus 10% service charge to the bill. This does not necessarily happen in the cheaper places. In even the most expensive restaurants, however, two people can dine well for about US$30 or US$40, not including wine, which adds from about US$10 a bottle.

Places to Eat – old town
There are few restaurants of note in the old town, although this is where the cheapest places are found. There are several cheap restaurants on the 1400 block of Rocafuerte near the Plaza Santa Domingo. The *Restaurant Los Olivos* (☎ 514 150) at Rocafuerte 1421 is one – big helpings for under US$2. That doesn't mean this is the best choice – there are equally good places within a block.

Other cheap places that have been recommended include the *Restaurant Oasis* at Espejo 812, and the good Chinese restaurant, *Chifa El Chino*, on Bolívar near Guayaquil. A *Pizza Hut* (☎ 583 764) on Espejo near the Cine Bolívar serves decent Italian food, but is not very cheap – about US$3 to US$4 for an individual pizza.

The *Fuente de Soda* at Sucre 258 and Venezuela serves snacks and ice cream. Also good for desserts, snacks, cappuccino and juices is *Pastelería El Torreón* on the Plaza del Teatro at Guayaquil and Manabí – a place for rest and refreshment during your busy sightseeing visit to the old town.

The more expensive *El Criollo* (☎ 219 828) at Flores 825 has good food in pleasant surroundings, but expect to pay about US$8 for a meal. *La Cueva del Oso* (☎ 583 826), Chile 1046 and Venezuela, looks upscale but is reasonably priced and has Ecuadorian specialties as well as musicians at times. It is one of the best places in the old town. Another top-notch place is *Las Cuevas de Luis Candela*, a Spanish restaurant at Benalcázar and Chile. It is rather more expensive than the other places. (A recent unconfirmed report indicates that it has moved to Orellana near Coruña in the new town.)

Places to Eat – new town
Just because you are in the new town doesn't mean you can't eat economically. The trick to finding cheap meals in the new town is to avoid eating on Amazonas and Calamá, where most restaurants are excellent but not inexpensive. Look for little places tucked away on side streets offering set meals for local office workers – the food is usually unexciting but a good value.

If you want inexpensive fast food walk down Calle Carrión, east of Amazonas. This block has earned the nickname of 'Hamburger Alley' and has about a dozen places serving burgers, etc. It is very popular with students. Make sure that your burger is thoroughly cooked and hot – the hygiene is questionable in these joints.

Vegetarian Quito is probably the best place in Ecuador for a choice of vegetarian food. A great find is *El Holandés* (☎ 522 167), Reina Victoria 600 and Carrión. They serve filling international vegetarian food – Indonesian, Indian, Dutch, Japanese etc. Meals are well worth every penny of their US$3 tag – I found myself returning here, even though I am a dedicated carnivore. (It's run by the owners of the Flying Dutchman bicycle tours.) Another popular place is *Vitalcentro* at Lizardo García 630 and Reina Victoria. Hearty vegetarian lunches are about US$2 and are served between noon and 2 pm. A cafeteria and health food store is open from 10 am to 5 pm. *El Maple* (☎ 520 994), Páez 485 and Roca, uses organically grown vegetables and washes its salads in purified water. The restaurant is pleasant, with meals in the US$2 to US$3 range.

El Cafecito (☎ 234 862), Luis Cordero 1124, under a popular budget hotel (see Places to Stay) serves inexpensive, mainly vegetarian meals and snacks all day long. There is a bar with a fireplace – a relaxing place for an evening drink. The *Windmill Vegetarian Restaurant* (☎ 222 575), Colón 2245 and Versalles, has also been recommended and adjoins a Health Food Store. *El Marqués*, Calamá 443 and Amazonas, has good set vegetarian lunches for US$2 – a good price in a pricey area of town.

Various Italian restaurants, such as *Pizza Hut*, serve meatless meals and have salad bars. Many Chinese restaurants *(chifas)* also have vegetarian choices on their menus.

Seafood Ecuador is justly famous for its ceviches made of marinated seafood. One of the best cevicherías is *Las Redes* (☎ 525 691) at Amazonas 845 and Veintimilla. Have the ceviche mixta; it's huge and delicious and costs about US$9.

Other excellent seafood restaurants (in ascending order of price) are *La Jaiba Mariscos* (☎ 543 887) at Avenida Colón 870 and Reina Victoria, *El Cebiche* (☎ 526 380) at JL Mera 1232 and Calamá, and the currently popular *Mare Nostrum* (☎ 237 236, 563 639), Foch 172 and Tamayo. Expect to pay about US$6 to US$12 for a main course in these restaurants.

There are several cheaper, though less elegant seafood restaurants. I have eaten consistently well at *Cevichería Viejo José* (☎ 540 187) at Veintimilla 1254 and Páez – just a block and a half from Amazonas.

Despite the name, they serve meat dishes as well as seafood. The restaurant is run by people from the coastal province of Manabí, the service is friendly, they are open every day and you can get a decent meal for about US$3. A recent report says that they have been so successful that they have opened another branch (☎ 225 187) at Reina Victoria 84 and La Patria. Another seafood restaurant that has US$3 meals is *Puerto Manabí* (☎ 226 206), Lizardo García 1238 and JL Mera – I haven't looked into this one.

Most restaurants in Quito have at least some seafood on the menu.

Steak & Meat A good place to go if you are hungry, especially for meat, is the Brazilian *Churrascaría Tropeiro* (☎ 548 012) at Veintimilla 546 and 6 de Diciembre. US$8 buys an 'all-you-can-eat' meal. Waiters keep coming round with beef, pork, lamb, chicken and other goodies, and there is a help-yourself salad bar.

My favorite steak house, the *Casa de Mi Abuela* (☎ 565 667) at JL Mera 1649 and La Pinta, is excellent and popular. Steaks are huge and delicious. A set steak meal is about US$8. Slightly cheaper and locally popular is the *Columbus Steak House* (☎ 551 857, 231 811) at Avenida Colón 1262 and Amazonas. It's good, but don't expect anything but meat. Their barbecues *(parrilladas)* are recommended, though note that the complete meal comes with liver, heart and kidneys, so ask for just beef if you don't like organs. They have recently opened some new branches.

Others that have been recommended to me but which I haven't tried are the moderately priced *Shorton Grill* (☎ 523 645), Calamá 216 and Almagro; *La Casa de Piedra* (☎ 502 318), Roca 562; and *Martín Fierro* (☎ 243 806), Inglaterra 1309 and República, a block west of Parque La Carolina.

Dedicated carnivores should know that, although these are all good choices by Ecuadorian standards, even their best cuts cannot compare to a tender steak from the US Midwest.

Ecuadorian Budget travelers should check out *Mama Clorindas* (☎ 544 362) at Reina Victoria 1144 and Calamá. This is a good, cheap place to try traditional local food, particularly at lunch time – meals are about US$2 to US$3.

Good, typical Ecuadorian food served in elegant surroundings can be found at *La Choza* (☎ 230 839) at 12 de Octubre 1821 and Cordero. They were closed when I tried to eat there on a Saturday night, so call ahead for hours and reservations. Expect to pay about US$15 for a complete meal. A little more expensive, but well recommended for typical Ecuadorian dishes is *Rincón La Ronda* (☎ 540 459) at Belo Horizonte 400 and Almagro. They often have live music in the evenings and are popular with international tour groups as well as affluent Ecuadorians. The interior is beautifully decorated and the service is good, though the waiters will encourage you to order expensive wines. Another place to try 'safe' Ecuadorian food is at the *Taberna Quiteña* (☎ 230 009) at Amazonas 1259 and Cordero. This is a low-roofed cellar bar with musicians wandering around at night – the food is OK, but check the prices before you order. Meals should be around US$6.

Italian There are many Italian restaurants but most are not very cheap. A popular and reasonably priced one is *Ch' Farina* (☎ 434 481), Carrión 619 and JL Mera. They serve a variety of pastas, lasagnas and pizzas, and have carry-out service. The newly opened *Ristorante Il Risotto* (tell 220 400), Pinto 209 and Almagro, is run by an Italian couple and is the latest favorite for Italian-food fans. Pasta meals start around US$5, and they are open every night, including Sundays. *La Scala* (☎ 229 502), Salazar 958 and 12 de Octubre, is one of the more popular upscale places. On Roca, east of Amazonas, *Veccia Roma* (☎ 230 876) continues to be recommended, and *La Gritta* (☎ 567 628) at Santa María 246 and Reina Victoria is one of the best (and priciest) Italian restaurants in town.

Cheaper Italian food is available in the many pizza restaurants. *Pizza Hut* (☎ 526 453) at JL Mera 566 and Carrión is fairly standard. There is also a Pizza Hut at Naciones Unidas and Amazonas (☎ 441 762) and one in the old town. *Equus* (☎ 452 346), Los Shyris 1578 and Naciones Unidas, on the Parque La Carolina, is a 24-hour pizzeria with a big video screen that is predictably popular with local young people. Other recommended places are *Pizza Pizza* (☎ 228 251), Santa María 126 and Almagro; *El Hornero* (☎ 542 518), at Veintimilla 1149 and Amazonas, and (☎ 563 377) at González Suárez 1070; and *Roy's Pizzeria* (☎ 460 028), Amazonas 1663 and Orellana, with a bar playing American country-western music. Most of these places will deliver to your hotel if you feel like eating in. El Hornero is particularly good for take out.

Chinese Chifas are popular in Ecuador, and Quito has several good, medium-priced places. The *Chifa Mayflower* (☎ 540 510, 507 854), Carrión 442 and 6 de Diciembre, is good and charges from about US$3 for a meal. They are planning on opening a couple of other branches. Another recommended one at similar prices is the *Chifa Pekin* (☎ 520 841) at Belo Horizonte 197 and 6 de Diciembre. A little more expensive, but very good Chinese food is served at *Chifa Hong Kong* (☎ 226 374), L García 235 and 12 de Octubre. *Casa China* (☎ 522 115), Cordero 613 and Tamayo, is also good and reasonably priced. There are plenty of others.

French There are several popular French restaurants, all of which are rather pricey, but serve fine cuisine in elegant surroundings. Reservations are a good idea at all of these, and although tourists can get by with informal wear, expect the locals to be very dressed up. One of the best-known and most reasonably priced restaurants is the *Rincón de Francia* (☎ 554 668) at Roca 779 and 9 de Octubre. Here a full meal will cost about US$12 to US$15. Also good and a little pricier are the following: *La Belle Epoque* (☎ 233 163) at Whimper 925 and 6 de Diciembre; *Rincón de Borgoña*

(☎ 446 627, 439 576), Eloy Alfaro 2712 and Portugal; and *Normandie* (☎ 233 116), L Plaza 1048.

Spanish Excellent Spanish food is served in a number of restaurants – as with the French places they tend to be elegant, pricey and popular with well-dressed businesspeople on an expense account or Quito's upper class. One of the best is *La Vieja Castilla* (☎ 566 979) at La Pinta 435 and Amazonas. *Costa Vasca* (☎ 564 940), 18 de Septiembre 553 and Páez, is also excellent and has an intriguing and unusual decor. Other good choices are *La Paella Valenciana* (☎ 239 681) at Almagro 1727 and República, which has big portions; and *La Rana Verde* (☎ 223 954/5/6) at JL Mera 639 and Veintimilla, which has tapas (Spanish snacks and hors d'oeuvres).

German & Swiss As with French and Spanish places, these restaurants are good, but not very cheap. *Mucki's Restaurant* (☎ 563 022), JL Mera 639 and Carrión, is one of the best, and *El Ciervo* (☎ 543 116), Dávalos 270 and Páez, is also worth trying (and it has German newspapers). *Le Péché Mignon* (☎ 230 709), at Belo Horizonte 338 and Almagro, has tasty fondues.

Mexican A few Mexican restaurants have opened in recent years. Note that Mexican food tends to be spicy and hot – it is nothing like Ecuadorian food, despite both countries being Latin American. One of the oldest is *La Guarida del Coyote* (☎ 503 292) at Carrión 619 and Amazonas, with meals around US$10; another is *Tex-Mex* (552 790) at Reina Victoria 235 and 18 de Septiembre. Meals here cost about US$4 or US$5 each, and are of the 'Americanized' version (Tex is for Texas, for non-US readers), but that doesn't detract from their tastiness. Opposite Tex-Mex is the more expensive but also more authentic *El Sabor Mexicano*, with good food and, occasionally, live *mariachis* (Mexican musicians). Friday night is usually good for mariachis. Also try the *Taco Factory* (☎ 543 956), as of press time at Foch and JL Mera, with

less expensive meals and large margarita pitchers. They are planning to move to larger premises in late 1996 – ask around. The new *Speedy* (☎ 538 431), at Roca 750 and Amazonas, also looks good. Another choice for decent Mexican food is *La Fonda del Cuervo* (☎ 243 287), Avenida América and La Prensa (in the north end at the 'Y' on the way to the airport).

Cafés Avenida Amazonas is a good place to come and watch the world go by, and to see and be seen. There are four or five popular pavement cafés on the 400 and 500 blocks of Amazonas (near Roca). They serve a decent cup of coffee and don't hassle you if you sit there for hours. These are extremely popular meeting places and are not very expensive.

Currently the most popular café is *Magic Bean* (☎ 566 181), Foch 681 and JL Mera. The bean in question is coffee, and they open around 7 am for excellent Colombian coffee and good breakfasts, and stay open all day, serving a variety of light meals. Their garden dining area and bar are usually packed with international travelers. There is live music on some nights. Above the café is an equally popular budget hotel (see Places to Stay) that goes by the same name. The *Art Forum Café*, JL Mera 870 and Wilson, opposite the Libri Mundi bookstore, is recommended for a light snack out of doors, with less of the hustle and bustle of Amazonas or Magic Bean. They serve good cappuccino and also have an art gallery. The British-run *Café Cultura*, Robles 513 and Reina Victoria, in the hotel of the same name, is recommended for excellent breakfasts. They also serve English afternoon tea – a somewhat pricey affair, considering that their scones were just ordinary Ecuadorian bread rolls when I stopped in. Perhaps they were having an off day; the tea was nice.

The *Colón Coffee Shop* at Amazonas and Jorge Washington is reasonably priced considering that it is in one of the capital's most luxurious hotels. It is open 24 hours and serves meals as well as snacks. For delicious pastries and desserts, or for a light lunch, the elegant *Chantilly Café* (☎ 528 226) at Roca 736 and Amazonas is recommended. This place is very popular for business lunches and is open only Monday to Friday. It is at the back of the building.

Other cafés which have been recommended, but which I haven't seen and which aren't on the map include *Los Bocadillos*, Cordero 1444 and Amazonas, for cappuccino and sandwiches; *Bangalo* (☎ 520 499), Carrión 185 and Tamayo, for specialty teas; and *El Pobre Diablo* (☎ 224 982), Santa María 338 and JL Mera, which is a café by day and a bar with (recorded) jazz in the evening.

Bars There are several bars that serve food. American-run *Adam's Rib* at Calamá 329 and JL Mera serves ribs and a variety of other American-style dishes at medium prices. They have a pool table. *El Pub* (☎ 523 589) at González Suárez 135 (opposite the Hotel Quito) serves pub food and is popular with Ecuadorians looking for a touch of something British. (The British embassy is nearby). My favorite bar for a quiet drink and darts is the American/ British-owned *La Reina Victoria* (☎ 226 369) at Reina Victoria 530 near Roca. They are only open in the evening from Monday to Saturday and serve light meals (pizzas, sandwiches, chili etc) and bar snacks from Monday to Friday, except on special holidays when full meals are made. This place is popular with expatriates who find it reasonably priced; budget travelers find it expensive.

Hotels Quito's luxury hotels have excellent international restaurants. Three of the very best are *El Techo del Mundo* in the Hotel Quito (superb views), the elegant and expensive *Le Gourmet* in the Hotel Oro Verde, and *El Conquistador* at the Hotel Colón. The Colón serves a delicious and varied all-you-can-eat lunch buffet in the lobby every Sunday from noon till 2:30 pm. It costs US$12 and is well worth it if you are looking for a luxurious splurge. They also have an excellent daily all-you-can-eat breakfast buffet for US$5.50. The

Oro Verde also has a Japanese restaurant which has been recommended.

Other Restaurants One of my favorite places is *La Terraza del Tartaro* (☎ 527 987) on the top floor of the Edificio Amazonas building at Veintimilla 1106 and Amazonas. An elevator at the back of the lobby will take you up (press button 2 and you automatically get taken to the top floor). This is a classy place and you can expect to pay about US$10 each for a full meal with a great view of Quito. Steaks are the specialty, though they also serve good chicken and seafood. *Bentley's* (☎ 238 684) at JL Mera 404 and Robles, is also a good choice for steaks, chicken and seafood in elegant surroundings.

At JL Mera 741 and Veintimilla, *Super Papa* (☎ 508 956) serves hot baked potatoes stuffed with a variety of hot or cold fillings – they're absolutely delicious – from 7 am to 9:30 pm daily. They also serve breakfasts. This small restaurant is popular with travelers and is a good meeting place. One wall is covered with notices ranging from personal notes to recommendations for new places to stay, eat, drink or visit.

Taller del Sol (☎ 550 417), Salazar 1063 and Destruge, has a good selection of Latin American food from a variety of countries. Meals start at about US$5. Also in this price range is *La Bodega de Cuba* (☎ 542 476), Reina Victoria 1721 and La Pinta, for good Cuban meals in a nice atmosphere. The *Kontiki* (☎ 565 602), Whymper 1094 and Almagro, is Quito's only Hawaiian restaurant. *Crepes & Waffles* (☎ 500 658), Orellana 461 and Rabida, is a modern restaurant that is popular but pricey – a bowl of salad is about US$3, ice creams are about US$2 – but their salads are organically grown and the ice cream selection is one of the most varied in Quito. Various fresh sandwiches and snacks are also sold.

On the 300 block of Calamá (same block as Safari Tours on the map) there are several good places to eat. *La Creperie* (☎ 226 780), Calamá 362, serves both dinner and dessert crepes, as well as other dishes such as goulash and steak. Meals are around US$5 to US$9. The *Excalibur* (☎ 541 272, 552 502) at Calamá 380 is an elegant and cozy restaurant considered one of the best in Quito, as well as one of the priciest. They serve international food.

La Casa de Al Lado and the *Café Kubata* are both dinner theaters (see Plays, Dance & Concerts, below).

Entertainment

Quito doesn't appear to be the world's most exciting capital for nightlife, but there's a fair amount happening if you search it out. Read the newspapers for exact details. *El Comercio* has the most thorough coverage. The English-language newspapers *Q* and *Inside Ecuador* also cover culture and entertainment.

Fiestas Entertainment reaches its height during the various fiestas. The founding of Quito is celebrated throughout the first week of December and there are bullfights at the Plaza de Toros, just beyond the intersection of Avenida América and 10 de Agosto. There is also street-dancing on the night of December 6.

New Year's Eve is celebrated by erecting life-sized puppets in the streets and burning them at midnight. These puppets are often very elaborate and usually represent politicians. Carnival, a movable Catholic feast, is celebrated by intense water fights – no-one is spared. Colorful religious processions are held during Easter week.

Cinemas On a day-to-day basis, films provide cheap and good entertainment. There are some 20 cinemas and movies range from pornography to kung fu to terminally violent, but at least some of them show good English-language films with Spanish subtitles. The best theaters for comfort and quality are the Colón, República, San Gabriel and Universitario. Entrance is US$1.50 in the better cinemas and under US$1 in others.

In addition, good films are sometimes shown at the *Casa de la Cultura*. The *British Council* shows good movies on Wednesdays at 8 pm, and the *Alianza Francesa* shows several French movies a week. Recently, screening times were 10 am on Saturday, 5:30 pm on Sunday and 7:30 pm on Tuesday, but these are subject to change. The British and French films are free, so get there early for a good seat.

The following theaters advertise their films in the daily newspapers:

Alameda
    Arenas 140 near La Parque Alameda
    (☎ 553 853)
Alhambra
    Guayaquil 1613 (☎ 214 261)
América
    América 648 (☎ 224 201)
Atahualpa
    Venezuela and Bolívar (☎ 212 557)
Benalcázar
    6 de Diciembre and Portugal
Bolívar
    Espejo 847 and Guayaquil
    (☎ 210 960, 215 778)
Capitol
    Gran Colombia 338 on La Parque Alameda
    (☎ 224 121)
Colón
    10 de Agosto 2436 and Colón (☎ 224 081)
Cumandá
    Maldonado 3035 near 24 de Mayo
    (☎ 210 657)
Granada
    Chile and Cuenca (☎ 210 220)
Hollywood
    Guayaquil 828 (☎ 211 308)
Iñaquito
    Avenida Naciones Unidas, Edificio Casa del
    Médico (☎ 452 660)
Metro
    Venezuela & Sucre (Pasaje Royal) (☎ 213 034)
México
    Tomebamba 463 near 1000 block of
    Maldonado (☎ 266 140)
República
    Avenida de La República 476 and Almagro
San Gabriel
    América and Mariana de Jesús (☎ 453 587)
Universitario
    Plaza Indoamérica, Universidad Central,
    América and Pérez Guerrero
Variedades
    Flores 930 at Plaza del Teatro (☎ 211 060)
24 de Mayo
    Granaderos and 6 de Diciembre

QUITO

Plays, Dance & Concerts Metropolitan Touring with the Ministerio de Turismo has organized a spectacular Ballet Folklórico called *Jacchigua*, which is presented in the San Gabriel cinema (see above) at 7:30 pm on Wednesday and Friday (subject to change). Admission is US$8 to US$16, depending on the seat. For information and reservations, call ☎ 506 650 or 464 780.

If your Spanish is up to it, you can see a play at the *Teatro Nacional Sucre* in the old town – this is the oldest of Quito's cultural spots, and part of the fun is seeing the elegant building. Classical music concerts are also presented at this theater – sometimes the National Symphonic Orchestra plays for no charge. This theater was being renovated and may be closed until 1997. Meanwhile, the National Symphonic Orchestra (information in Spanish at ☎ 244 358) is playing at the *Teatro Politécnico*. Entrance is free or inexpensive (about US$4). Mid-August to mid-September there are no symphony shows.

Other possibilities include the *Teatro Prometeo*, which is inexpensive and sometimes has mime performances that anyone can understand. They also have modern dance shows. The *Patio de Comedias* has also been recommended for plays, which are often presented on Sunday nights. The *Pichincha Playhouse* presents plays in English by an expatriate theater company – amateur, but of a high standard. The two *universities* in Quito present a variety of performances – political satire is high on the list of Ecuadorian students' theater.

The *Teatro Bolívar* presents classical and opera concerts every once in a while. The *Casa de la Cultura* has concerts and, occasionally, plays. Concerts are also presented in the Conservatorio Nacional de la Música, the auditorium of the Corporación Financiera Nacional, and in the basement theater of the Las Cameras Centro de Comercio y Industria. These last two often have free concerts.

Latin American rock concerts are occasionally presented – the *Plaza de Toros* and the Casa de la Cultura are popular venues.

Contemporary dance is presented at the *Humanizarte* art gallery. Interesting modern plays are performed at the Teatro Fénix and at the *Casa de Al Lado* – the latter is a dinner/theater place that also shows innovative films and may have live jazz or Latin music. Cover is about US$6 to US$10. The *Café Kubata* is another restaurant that frequently has dramatic productions.

These cultural events are advertised in the daily newspapers and on posters at the venues themselves. There is usually more going on in the rainy season.

Café Kubata
    L García and Diego de Almagro (☎ 547 255)
Casa de la Cultura Ecuatoriana
    Patria and 12 de Octubre
    (☎ 565 808, 522 410)
Conservatorio Nacional de la Música
    1159 Madrid (☎ 564 790)
Corporación Financiera Nacional
    JL Mera and Patria
    (behind the Hotel Colón) (☎ 561 026)
Humanizarte
    Amazonas 1167 and Orellana (☎ 523 319)
La Casa de Al Lado
    Valladolid 1018 and Cordero (☎ 226 398)
Las Cameras Centro de Comercio y Industria
    República and Amazonas (☎ 433 787)
Patio de Comedias
    18 de Septiembre 457 and Amazonas
    (☎ 561 902)
Pichincha Playhouse
    Colón 758 (☎ 543 689, 213 321)
Teatro Bolívar
    Espejo 847 and Guayaquil
    (☎ 210 960, 215 778)
Teatro Nacional Sucre
    Flores and Manabí, at Plaza del Teatro
    (☎ 216 668, 211 644)
Teatro Politécnico
    Diego Ladrón de Guevara, at the west end
    opposite the Rumiñahui Coliseum
Teatro Prometeo
    6 de Diciembre 794 and Tarquí,
    behind the Casa de la Cultura
    (☎ 230 505, 565 808)
Universidad Católica
    12 de Octubre and Robles
    (☎ 529 240, 521 834)
Universidad Central
    América and Pérez Guerrero
    (☎ 521 590, 236 988)

Nightlife Peñas have traditional *música folklórica* shows and are very popular among Ecuadorians. They are usually quite expensive. Often there is a cover charge (up to US$8 per person) or a minimum consumption, and you may be expected to wear a jacket or skirt. They don't open until 9 pm and entertainment might not begin till 10 or 11 pm – and continue till the early hours. Friday and Saturday nights are the busiest nights. Peñas serve drinks and often snacks. The audience does not usually dance at peñas.

The *Nucanchi Peña* (☎ 540 967) at Avenida Universitaria 496 and Armero in front of the Universidad Central is a fairly inexpensive place with a US$4 cover. It's popular with students and families, and is probably the best choice for travelers wanting to see a peña show. There are performances from Tuesday to Saturday.

Some peñas are held in small, crowded bars such as the *Dayumak Peña Bar* (☎ 553 274) at JL Mera 555, which is popular with young people and has folklórica shows on Thursdays and Fridays. Other peñas are *Rincón Andino Peña* at JL Mera and Roca, the expensive (US$8 per person cover) *Paccha Camac* (☎ 469 553) on Jorge Washington and JL Mera and the *Taberna Quiteña* (☎ 230 009; see under Places to Eat – Ecuadorian).

Dancing is also popular – again, there is often a cover charge or a drinks minimum. For dancing to Latin American salsa music go to one of the *salsatecas*, which generally have a lower cover charge than the discotheques that play North American-style music. Salsatecas are friendly and lively; they are especially popular with Ecuadorians and Latin American tourists, though there's usually a sprinkling of slightly more adventurous gringos. The discotheques tend to attract rich young Ecuadorians who dress up and think it's cool to disco – *plásticos* is a slightly disparaging term occasionally heard to describe some of the clientele.

The best salsateca is generally said to be the *Seseribó* in Edificio El Girón at Veintimilla and 12 de Octubre. Another good one is *Ramón Antigua*, a few blocks away at Veintimilla 139 and Isabel La Católica. A third place to go salsa dancing is the *Cali Salsateca* at Orellana and Reina Victoria.

Possible discotheques include *Blues Bar* at La Granja 112 and Amazonas, and the very upper-class *Club 330* at Whimper and Coruña. The *Licorne* in the Hotel Colón has also been recommended, but it is expensive – its popularity waxes and wanes. Other currently popular bars, usually with loud rock/Latin music, dancing on tiny floors, plenty of boozing and young international travelers (even some Ecuadorians), include the *Arribar*, JL Mera 1238 and García, and *No Bar* (☎ 546 955), Calamá 442 and Amazonas. These are not good places for a quiet drink and a chat. The formerly popular *Papillón* has been boycotted by travelers recently after an incident in which the manager beat up his English girlfriend. *Reggae Bar* (☎ 540 906), Amazonas 1691 and Orellana, plays reggae and is popular late at night.

If your idea of a night out is to hang out in a bar for a drink and a chat, you'll find plenty of good places. Several are British or American bars that have a pub-like atmosphere. They are not cheap by Ecuadorian standards. Some of these serve food and are described under Places to Eat – Bars. They are all good, but my choice is *La Reina Victoria* (☎ 233 369) at Reina Victoria 530 and Roca. Owned and managed by a friendly US/British couple, Dorothy and Gary, this is a real home away from home for the homesick traveler. There is a fireplace, dart board, bumper pool and excellent pub ambiance. Cheers!

Other bars worthy of note are *Hopp y Ex* (☎ 522 779), Reina Victoria 854 y Baquedano, which is gay-friendly and a nice spot with occasional art exhibits. *Jazzoo* at the Hotel Quito features live music with an emphasis on jazz every Thursday, Friday and Saturday after 9 pm. The US$6 cover includes your first drink. The *Magic Bean* (see Places to Eat) sometimes has live open-mike evenings. *El Pobre Diablo* (☎ 224 982), Santa María 338, is a new place with a nice ambiance – fireplace, jazz music, tea and coffee, as well as beer. Also try the quiet little *Rumors Bar* on JL Mera and Veintimilla, and the *Cowboy Bar* on the 1100 block of Almagro at La Pinta, which plays exclusively country-western tapes.

Café Libro (☎ 526 827), Diego Almagro 1500 and La Pradera, has live jazz on Thursdays, 'spontaneous' peñas on Fridays and poetry readings, drama, and arty happenings on other nights. *Café y Arte* (☎ 234 148), Coruña 1365 and Orellana, is similar.

These night spots and drinking holes come and go – ask around about the latest 'in' place.

Things to Buy

There are many good stores for souvenir hunters in the new town along and near Avenida Amazonas. If buying on the streets (there are street stalls and ambulatory vendors) you should bargain. In the fancier stores, prices are normally fixed, though bargaining is not out of the question, particularly if you are buying several things. The better stores are usually more expensive, though not necessarily exorbitant, and the items for sale are often top quality.

Some stores sell pre-Columbian ceramics and colonial antiques. It is legal for Ecuadorian residents only to buy these items. You are not allowed to export archaeological or antique items and they will be confiscated at the customs upon departure from Ecuador or arrival at your home country. Another thing to avoid buying is anything made from animals – this includes black coral jewelry and mounted butterflies, as well as the more obvious things like animal skins. These are protected and it is illegal to import animal products into most countries.

The following is a list of recommended stores selling a wide selection of goods at a variety of price levels. Folklore (☎ 563 085) at Colón 260 is the store of legendary designer Olga Fisch (who died in 1991). This is the place to go for the very best and the most expensive items. They also have a branch at the Hotel Colón

(☎ 526 667) and the Hotel Oro Verde (☎ 569 003). The Productos Andinos Indian cooperative at Urbina 111 and Cordero (near the intersection of Avenidas Colón and 6 de Diciembre) has much cheaper but still highly recommended goods. Also relatively inexpensively priced are the government-run OCEPA stores at a variety of locations: Jorge Washington 718 and Amazonas (☎ 236 334), Carrión 1236 and Versalles (☎ 541 992), Coruña 1632 and 12 de Octubre (☎ 568 067), Amazonas 2615 y República (☎ 449 671) and Venezuela 976 and Mejía (☎ 512 105) in the old town.

Most other stores won't be much more expensive than Folklore, nor much cheaper than OCEPA or Productos Andinos, and yet maintain a decent quality. The following are all reliable. Galería Latina (☎ 540 380), JL Mera 833 and Veintimilla next to the Libri Mundi bookstore (itself a great place to shop), has superb Andean textiles. Nearby is the Centro Artesanal (☎ 548 235), at JL Mera 804, which is known for canvases painted by local Indian artists, and for other products. A block away is La Bodega (☎ 225 844), at JL Mera 614, with a wide and wonderful selection of souvenirs. MCCH, JL Mera and Robles, is a women artisan cooperative store with a fine selection.

Other places nearby that have been recommended include El Aborigen at Jorge Washington 536 and JL Mera, and Ecuafolklore (☎ 524 315) at Robles 609 and JL Mera. Amor y Café (☎ 226 847), Foch 721 and JL Mera, is recommended for professionally designed ethnic clothing. Travel Co (☎ 542 345) JL Mera and L García, and (☎ 221 841), JL Mera 517 and Roca, is good for postcards, T-shirts, maps and books, among other things.

There are many other stores in the area and their exclusion does not imply that they aren't any good! Wander around, and remember that many are closed on Sunday.

Excellent Amazonian crafts are sold at the Fundación Sinchi Sacha, which also has a museum (see Museums). Profits benefit indigenous groups. For expensive modern art, see the Museo Guayasamín described earlier under Museums.

Note that souvenirs are a little cheaper outside of Quito if you have the time and inclination to search them out – it is more convenient to shop in the capital.

For more ordinary shopping, to buy groceries, batteries, stationery, soap and other travelers' essentials, a number of places can be recommended. A cheap general store with a large selection is El Globo at 10 de Agosto and Roca.

There are many supermarkets. One of the best in the old town is La Feria at Bolívar and Venezuela. In the new town, the Supermaxi is good – there are branches at several shopping centers, including Multicentro and Centro Comercial Iñaquito. Shopping centers are similar to North American shopping malls – many small stores selling all kinds of things. They are often called a *centro comercial*, abbreviated to CC. The most important are:

Centro Comercial Caracol
    Amazonas and Naciones Unidas – opposite
    the Centro Comercial Iñaquito
Centro Comercial El Bosque
    Occidental and Carvajal
Centro Comercial El Espiral
    Amazonas and Jorge Washington – convenient to downtown, but with a limited
    selection of stores and products
Centro Comercial El Jardín
    Amazonas and Avenida de la República –
    opposite Immigration, this is Quito's newest
    and glitziest. Mall rats will love it.
Centro Comercial Iñaquito (CCI)
    Amazonas and Naciones Unidas – opposite
    the CC Caracol
Centro Comercial Multicentro
    6 de Diciembre and La Niña
Centro Comercial Naciones Unidas (CCNU)
    Naciones Unidas and Japón
Centro Comercial Quicentro
    6 de Diciembre and Naciones Unidas

Most stores and shopping centers are closed on Sunday. One exception is the new CC El Bosque on the northwestern outskirts of town. Note that the CCI, CCNU and CC Caracol are all clustered together. Convenience counts for something.

Getting There & Away

Air There is one airport with a domestic and international terminal side by side. You can walk from one to the other in about 60 seconds.

Services at the airport terminal include tourist information, money exchange, post office, cafeteria/bar, EMETEL international telephone office (only from 8 am to 10 pm – very difficult to call at other times unless you have a local calling card) and gift shops. For airport information, call ☎ 430 555.

The airport is about 10 km north of the city center. See Getting Around, below, for bus and taxi information.

Air – domestic There is no departure tax for internal flights, most of which are run by TAME. In addition SAN-Saeta has flights to Guayaquil and Cuenca. The airlines will accept one another's tickets for Guayaquil and Cuenca if their flights aren't full and if you paid for the ticket with cash. Internal flights (except for the Galápagos) are fairly inexpensive – prices and schedules change frequently and the following are approximate. The most expensive mainland flights are to the Oriente, where foreigners must pay twice as much as locals. Fares below are one way and subject to change, as are the flight details.

Flights to Guayaquil (US$29) leave from eight to 14 times a day, most often on weekdays. If you don't have a ticket and are in a hurry, you can often just show up at the airport and get on the next available flight to Guayaquil. Flights to Cuenca (US$29) leave one to three times a day.

Only TAME operates services to the following cities: Tulcán (US$19) Monday to Friday at noon; Esmeraldas (US$21) Monday to Friday mornings and Sunday afternoons; Portoviejo (US$26) Monday, Wednesday and Friday afternoons; Manta (US26) Monday to Saturday mornings and Sunday afternoons; Bahía de Caráquez (US$26) Friday and Sunday afternoons; Macas (US$45) Monday, Wednesday and Friday afternoons; Coca (US$46) two flights most mornings except Wednesday

QUITO

(one flight) and Sunday (no flights); Lago Agrio (US$46) Monday to Saturday mornings; Loja (US$32) Monday to Saturday mornings at 6 am. Machala (US$38) can be reached from Quito with connections at Guayaquil from Monday to Friday.

These schedules can change frequently – a broken-down airplane can cause a city simply to be removed from the itinerary for a week or more until a needed part is obtained and replaced. Lack of passenger demand often leads to canceled flights. But, despite these frustrations, flying from Quito is generally straightforward and economical. Return flights to Quito are usually the same planes that flew out.

Baltra Island in the Galápagos is reached from Quito by TAME flights every morning (no Sunday flight in the low season). There may be a change at Guayaquil, but your luggage is transferred. The return cost is about US$377 for non-Ecuadorian residents. These flights to Baltra Airport are the normal way to go for travelers heading to the main port of Puerto Ayora on Isla Santa Cruz. SAN-Saeta also has morning flights to Isla San Cristóbal (sometimes changing at Guayaquil) daily except Thursday and Sunday (same price).

In the old town TAME is at Manabí 635 and Venezuela (☎ 512 988), and in the new town at Avenida Colón 1001 and Rábida (☎ 554 905) and 10 de Agosto 239 and La Parque Alameda (☎ 583 939, 510 305). SAN-Saeta share an office at Guayaquil 1228 and Olmedo in the old town (☎ 211 431), and Santa María and Amazonas in the new town (☎ 502 706, 564 969). In addition, you can buy domestic air tickets from Ecuadorian travel agents at the same cost as direct from the airlines.

Finally, Icaro (Instituto Civil Aeronautico) (☎ 448 626) sometimes has sightseeing flights or even flying lessons available. For about US$650/1100 you can hire a seven/13-passenger airplane for an hour. This can be for sightseeing or to get somewhere.

Air – international Several international airlines have offices in Quito – many on or near Avenida Amazonas. There is an inter-

national airport departure tax of US$25 payable in either US dollars or sucres. If you are flying internationally, confirm 72 hours in advance, reconfirm 24 hours in advance and arrive at the airport two hours before your flight. You might take off late, but at least you'll be on the flight. Flights are frequently overbooked, so if you don't reconfirm, you'll get bumped – 'Sorry, you're not on the computer.'

The following airlines have offices in Quito. Those marked with an asterisk (*) have direct flights into and out of Ecuador. Their country of origin follows in parentheses (where it isn't obvious). Some airlines fly only into and out of Guayaquil but it is a simple matter to connect to Quito with one of the many daily domestic flights. Only the more important airlines are listed; look in the telephone book for lesser-known ones. Expect addresses and phone numbers to change; see also Online Services in Facts for the Visitor.

Aeroflot (Russia)
    18 de Septiembre and Amazonas
    (☎ 220 982, 545 454)
Aerolíneas Argentinas*
    Amazonas 1188 and Calamá
    (☎ 568 262, 543 257)
AeroPerú*
    Jorge Washington 718 (☎ 561 699/700/703)
Air France*
    18 de Septiembre 368 and Amazonas
    (☎ 524 201, 523 596)
Alitalia
    Ernesto Noboa 474 and 6 de Diciembre,
    Office 202 (☎ 545 652, 509 061)
American Airlines* (USA)
    Amazonas 367 and Robles
    (☎ 561 144, 561 526)
Avianca* (Colombia)
    6 de Diciembre 511 and 18 de Septiembre
    (☎ 508 843/844/846)
British Airways
    Amazonas 1429 and Colón (☎ 540 000/902)
Continental Airlines* (USA)
    Naciones Unidas and Amazonas, Edificio
    Banco La Previsora (☎ 461 485/6/7)
Iberia* (Spain)
    Amazonas 239 and Jorge Washington
    (☎ 560 546/7/8)
Icelandair
    Almagro 1822 and Alpallana (☎ 561 820)

JAL Japan Airlines
9 de Octubre 410 and Chile (☎ 310 818)
KLM* (Holland)
Amazonas 3623 and Catalina Herrera,
Edificio Xerox (☎ 455 233)
Ladeco* (Chile)
18 de Septiembre 238 and Reina Victoria
(☎ 508 396)
Lacsa* (Costa Rica)
12 de Octubre 394 (☎ 505 213/4)
Lufthansa* (Germany)
18 de Septiembre 238 and Reina Victoria
(☎ 541 300, 508 396)
Saeta* (Ecuador)
Santa María and Amazonas (☎ 502 706/12)
Swissair
10 de Agosto 6116 (☎ 241 555)
Varig* (Brazil)
Amazonas 1037 and Pinto (☎ 561 584/5/6)
Viasa* (Venezuela)
Amazonas 1188 and Calamá
(☎ 543 257, 543 269)

Bus Quito's bus station, the Terminal Terrestre de Cumandá, contains the offices of several dozen bus companies at Maldonado 3077, a few hundred meters south of the Plaza Santo Domingo in the old town. The terminal can be reached by walking down the steps from Maldonado (see map). Buses will drop you off on Maldonado by the steps, or you may prefer to walk down from Plaza Santo Domingo – the traffic along Maldonado is snail-paced. This route, however, does have problems with pickpockets and bag snatchers. Taxi drivers often take an alternate route that enters the terminal from the south side.

The terminal serves most destinations from Quito. There is an information window (☎ 570 529) where staff will tell you which company goes where, although it's fairly obvious. Walk around and compare departures.

Usually there are several companies serving the same destination at different times. For the most popular towns, you'll find ticket sellers yelling out their destinations, even though each window is clearly labeled. Only buses departing within a few minutes are allowed to park outside the terminal, so you can often be on your way within minutes of arriving. Usually it is

easy enough to get onto the bus you want, but if you plan on traveling during holiday periods or just before the weekend, it's best to go to the terminal and book in advance. If you do find you have to wait, there are several snack bars. There is also a post office, EMETEL office, banking machines and small stores. Watch your luggage carefully inside the terminal if you don't want someone else to walk off with it.

With literally hundreds of buses departing during the day, it is impossible to give accurate timetables. There are several buses a day to most destinations, and some places – such as Ambato or Otavalo – may have several departures an hour.

Here is a list of the major destinations served and the approximate cost and length of a journey. US$0.10 is added to each ticket as a terminal departure tax. These fares below are subject to change, but this gives an idea of the comparative costs of the trips. Fares tend to remain the same, in sucre terms, for a year or so. Then they might jump up 50% because of a year's inflation combined with increased gas prices. This means if they have just gone up, their cost in US dollar terms will be high – if they haven't gone up in a while, costs can be almost half the price they were a year ago.

Destination	Cost (US$)	Duration (hrs)
Ambato	2.70	2½
Bahía de Caráquez	6.00	8
Baños	2.80	3½
Coca	11.00	13
Cuenca	6.50	8
Guaranda	3.30	5
Guayaquil	6.20	8
Ibarra	2.40	3
Lago Agrio	9.00	10
Latacunga	1.40	1½
Loja	11.00	14
Machala	7.50	11
Manta	6.00	8
Otavalo	2.00	2¼
Portoviejo	6.00	8
Puyo	4.40	8
Riobamba	3.30	4
Santo Domingo	2.40	2½
Tena	4.80	6
Tulcán	4.70	5½

QUITO

For other destinations, you may have to go to the nearest major city and change. Inquire at the bus offices.

With several companies serving most destinations, you have a choice. If the first company you talk to doesn't have a bus leaving when you want, ask at the next counter. Companies serving the same destination tend to be clustered together in one part of the terminal. Also, find out whether the bus will be a slow old one, which may give a more interesting ride, or a newer fast one, which may be small and cramped, but will get you there faster. If the bus isn't almost full, the ticket seller will often show you which seats are available so you can choose where you sit.

There is a small bus terminal at Villa Flora, about two km south of the Terminal Terrestre de Cumandá. Buses from here go to nearby small towns like Machachi, though it is possible that these buses will eventually move to the Cumandá terminal. Any southbound city bus that is marked 'Villa Flora' will get you to the Villa Flora terminal.

Panamericana has opened a terminal in the new town at Colón and Reina Victoria. They have comfortable long-distance buses with on-board bathrooms and reclining seats to Guayaquil, Huaquillas, Manta, Loja, Esmeraldas and Cuenca. Their prices are about US$3 to US$4 higher than the normal services. Some companies at the terminal terrestre are introducing their own 'luxury' buses to compete with this.

There are companies that will sell international bus tickets to Peru or Colombia. Avoid these. The tickets are very expensive and you still have to change buses at the border. Once across the border you often find that only one company will accept your ticket and you can wait for hours until they depart. It's much cheaper and far more convenient to buy tickets as you go.

Train The famous Quito-Guayaquil train has recently reopened after a decade-long suspension caused by the 1982-83 El Niño floods. There are now trains at 8 am on Saturday (I have heard that a Wednesday

service was added, and there may be more in the future) that go through Latacunga and Ambato to Riobamba. These are old-fashioned and uncomfortable trains with primitive bathroom facilities. Some passengers ride on the roof (great views but very cold). The journey to Riobamba costs US$10 (much less for Ecuadorians, but there's not much that foreigners can do about this except for ride the bus) and takes until mid-afternoon. On Sundays, there is a roundtrip from Quito to Cotopaxi National Park for US$20. Safari Tours (see Organized Tours) is planning on opening a hostel at the train station near Cotopaxi.

The Quito train station (☎ 656 142) is on Avenida Sincholagua and Vicente Maldonado, about two km south of the old town. The train station booking office is open the day before trains depart. You can also buy advance tickets and get information from ENAFER, the government-run train company, at their office (☎ 513 422) at Bolívar 443 and Benalcázar in the old town. Travelers have reported that you can buy tickets at the station on the morning of departure with no problem (but this is a newly reopened service and this could change).

Metropolitan Touring (see Organized Tours) operates a train trip for tourists that includes an overnight at a first-class Riobamba hotel. The specially renovated autoferro car is comfortably furnished with clean bathrooms, a bar and dining area. Tours depart by train and return by bus, with stops at markets, villages and other sites of interest. Guides are bilingual. Two-day/one-night tours including meals and accommodations are about US$260 per person.

Getting Around
To/From the Airport The Quito International Airport is at the north end of Avenida Amazonas where it intercepts with Avenida de la Prensa, about 11 km north of the old town center. Many of the northbound buses on Amazonas and 10 de Agosto go to the airport. Some have *Aeropuerto* placards

and others say *Quito Norte*. A taxi from the new town should be under US$4, or US$5 from the old town. From the airport, taxi drivers try to overcharge – bargain hard.

If you are going from the airport into town, you will find bus stops on Avenida 10 de Agosto, about 150 meters away from the front entrance of the terminal. If you have a pile of luggage, taxi drivers charge anything they can get away with (US$10!) from in front of the international terminal, a little less from in front of the national terminal. Bargain to get the fare down or walk out to Avenida 10 de Agosto and flag down a cab on the street.

Bus The crowded local buses have a flat fare of about US$0.10 that you pay as you board. They are safe enough and rather fun, but watch your bags and pockets. There are also *Ejecutivo* and *Selectivo* buses, which don't allow standing and charge about US$0.25. Generally speaking, buses run north-south and have a fixed route. The ejecutivo and selectivo buses, particularly, can be found on 10 de Agosto and 6 de Diciembre. Buses have destination placards in their windows, and drivers are usually helpful and will tell you which bus to take if they are not going to your destination. Traffic in the old town is very heavy and you may often find it faster to walk than to take a bus, especially during the rush hours. Buses have both a name and a number, and although they usually have a fixed route, this may vary because of heavy traffic, road repair or the whim of the driver.

The narrow streets of downtown are usually one way. Calles Guayaquil and Venezuela are one way into the old town towards El Panecillo, and Calles García Moreno and Flores are one way out of the old town and away from El Panecillo. There are about 40 different bus routes. The IGM published a Quito Bus Routes map in 1976 – this has now been out of print for many years and there seems to be little interest in publishing a new one. Since it was published, routes have changed quite a bit and it is beyond the scope of this chapter to give them all. If you have a spe-

cific place you want to get to by local bus, ask at your hotel, bus drivers, passers-by or the tourist office. The locals know where the buses go. It's not difficult to get around if you ask and are prepared to put up with very crowded buses and watch your belongings carefully.

In mid-1996 Quito's long-awaited trolley system began operation. The line runs between the Estación Trolebús Sur, on Avenida Maldonado south of Villaflora, and the Estación Trolebús Norte, on 10 de Agosto just north of Avenida de La Prensa. Cars run along Maldonado and 10 de Agosto about every 10 minutes from 6 am to 12:30 am and the fare is US$0.25. They stop every couple of blocks. The result of this new line opening is that fewer buses now use the major thoroughfare of 10 de Agosto. As part of the trolley project, the government has restricted the number of buses allowed to run city routes and this is expected to result in an overall improvement in air quality, especially in the Old Town.

Car Car rental in Quito, as elsewhere in Ecuador, is expensive. There are car rental offices at the airport. Expect to pay at least US$30 per day for a seven-day rental (a basic car) and make sure that mileage and adequate insurance are included. See the Getting Around chapter for more car rental information.

The following companies are found in Quito. Ecuacar and Localiza have been recommended as reliable and competitively priced. Major international companies are also here. I do not recommend renting a car for getting around Quito because taxis and buses are much cheaper and more convenient. A rental car is a possibility for getting around the country. However, if you plan on visiting the main towns and travelers' destinations, you will find buses fast, efficient and reliable in most cases – and very cheap. Rental vehicles are useful for visiting some out-of-the-way areas that don't have frequent bus connections (in which case a more expensive 4WD vehicle is a good idea).

Avis
    Colón 1741 and 10 de Agosto (☎ 550 238)
    Airport (☎ 440 270)
Budget
    Colón and Amazonas (☎ 237 026)
    Hotel Colón (☎ 525 328)
    Airport (☎ 240 763, 459 052)
Dollar
    Airport (☎ 439 922)
Ecuacar
    Colón 1280 and Amazonas
    (☎ 529 781, 540 000)
    Airport (☎ 247 298)
Hertz
    Veintimilla 928 and Amazonas (☎ 238 932)
    Airport (☎ 246 381)
Localiza Rentacar
    6 de Diciembre 1570 and Wilson
    (☎ 505 974, 505 986)
Los Carritos Diligentes
    Airport (☎ 544 999)

Taxi Taxi cabs are all yellow and have red
'TAXI' stickers in the window. Usually,
there are plenty available, but rush hour can
leave you waiting for 10 or 15 minutes for
an empty cab. Rainy afternoons are particularly
difficult times to hail a cab.

A law was passed in 1984 requiring
Quito cabs to have meters and almost all
drivers now use them, although occasionally
they will ask to arrange a price with
you beforehand. Sometimes this is to your
advantage as it enables the driver to take a
roundabout route to avoid traffic, thus
saving both of you time. Generally, though,
you should have the driver use the meter.
Late at night they will ask for a higher fare,
which is fair enough, but it shouldn't be
more than twice the metered rate. Some
drivers will say the meter is broken – you
can always flag down another cab.

Taxis can be hired for several hours or
for a day. If you bargain hard, you could
hire a cab for a day for about US$50 if you
don't plan on going very far. Cabs hired
from the better hotels have set rates for
long trips and are a bit more expensive but
also more reliable. Short journeys downtown
cost from about US$1 to about US$5
for a long trip. From Avenida Amazonas to
the top of the Panecillo, with a one hour
wait and return, is about US$10.

Around Quito

Many excursions can be made from Quito
using the city as a base. Below, I describe
those which are done from Quito as a day
trip rather than as part of an overnight tour.

LA MITAD DEL MUNDO

The most famous local excursion is to the
equator at La Mitad del Mundo ('the
middle of the world') in the village of San
Antonio, about 22 km north of Quito. This
is the place where, in 1736, Charles-Marie
de La Condamine's expedition made the
measurements which showed that this was,
indeed, the equator. The measurements also
gave rise to the metric system and proved
that the world was not perfectly round, but
bulged at the equator.

The center of the Mitad del Mundo
complex is a massive 30-meter-high **monument**
topped by a brass globe, 4½ meters
in diameter. The stone trapezoidal monument
is built on the equator. Visitors take
an elevator to the top, where there is a
viewing platform, and then descend by
stairs winding through the excellent
Museo Etnográfico, which is housed
within the monument. The museum has
interesting and well-displayed exhibits
showing the many different Indian tribes
that make up the indigenous population of
the country. The museum and monument
are open from 10 am to 4 pm Tuesday to
Friday and 10 am to 5 pm Saturday and
Sunday. Admission is about US$0.40.

Also at Mitad del Mundo is a realistic
looking 1:200 scale **model of colonial
Quito**. This is housed in a building to the
left (west) of the monument and costs
US$0.80 to visit. It is worth the effort.
Nearby, there is a **planetarium** run by the
IGM with a variety of shows to do with
astronomy. Shows are hourly from 11 am
to 3 pm Tuesday to Friday, and till 4 pm
Saturday and Sunday. Admission is inexpensive.
To the southeast of the monument
is a 'colonial village' that was recently built
as part of the complex. There are plazas,

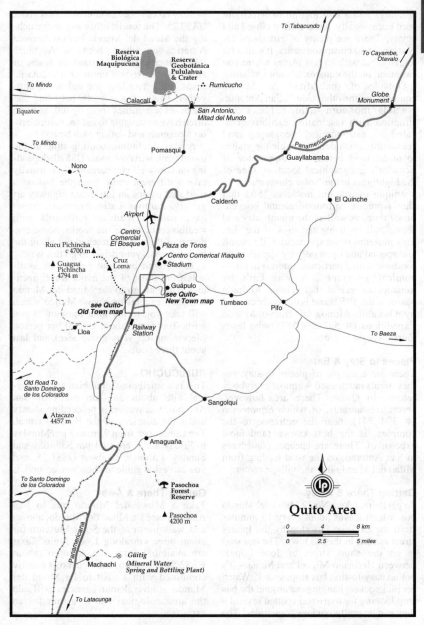

Quito Area

0   4   8 km

0   2.5   5 miles

buildings and a bullring, all of which are used occasionally, but are often closed and empty. There are plenty of gift shops for postcards and cheap souvenirs. It's all a bit touristy, but with so few places where you can stand on the equator, it's not too bad.

Outside of the Mitad del Mundo complex, on the other side of San Antonio, is a **solar museum** – a tiny, red brick construction with fascinating exhibits dedicated to astronomical geography and containing much data to enable the visitor to understand better the importance of Ecuador's geographical location. One of the highlights is the 'solar chronometer' – a unique instrument made in 1865 that shows precise astronomical and conventional time, as well as the month, day and season, all by using the rays of the sun. This museum is not spectacular, it is small and special and open only by appointment for those with a particular interest in astronomical geography. It was built by Ecuadorian scientist Luciano Andrade Marín in the 1950s and is currently curated by Oswaldo Muñoz of Nuevo Mundo Expeditions (☎ 552 839/617), who leads tours there on request.

Places to Stay & Eat

There are a couple of places to stay, but they aren't much used – almost everybody returns to Quito. There are, however, several restaurants, of which *Equinoccio* (☎ 394 741), near the entrance to the complex, is the best known (and most expensive). There are cheaper comedores in San Antonio, on the road leading from Mitad del Mundo into the village center.

Getting There & Away

To get there, take a No 22 Mitad del Mundo bus, which leaves about every 15 minutes from the El Tejar bus stop by the Ipiales street market in the old town. The bus stop is on the short street of José López, between Hermano Miguel and Mejía – it's not an easy-to-find bus stop, so ask. Watch for pickpockets hanging out around the bus stop looking for tourists. I spotted several – they can be pretty obvious sometimes! The

journey takes about an hour and costs about US$0.25. The tourist office suggests catching the Mitad del Mundo bus on Avenida América anywhere between Avenidas Pérez Guerrero and Mariana de Jesús, or along 10 de Agosto north of Mariana de Jesús, thus avoiding the old town altogether. This is a possibility, but I find that the buses sometimes come by full, and you often have to struggle to get on, particularly on weekends and during rush hours.

A taxi, including waiting time at the monument, will cost about US$20, depending on how well you bargain. Taxis usually take a different route from the bus on a road that passes an intriguing highway art gallery. Famous Latin American artists have painted roadside billboards with weatherproof paint; the works, some two dozen of them, are stretched out along the highway. Ask your driver to go this way.

Tours, with bilingual guides, are available from most of the major travel agencies. They all go to the Mitad del Mundo complex, except for Nuevo Mundo which will take you to the solar museum if you wish. Tours cost about US$20 per person (depending on your group size) and last about three hours.

RUMICUCHO

This is a small pre-Columbian archaeological site about 3½ km north of San Antonio. Excavation is proceeding slowly under the auspices of the Banco Central. The site is open from 9 am to 3 pm Monday to Friday and 8 am to 4 pm Saturday and Sunday. Entrance is about US$1.25, and you can ask a guide to show you around.

Getting There & Away

Take a Mitad del Mundo bus to San Antonio (see La Mitad del Mundo, above) and walk north of the Solar Museum for about three km along 13 de Junio. Taxis are available from San Antonio (about US$2.50) or Quito. Rumicucho is usually combined with a visit to La Mitad del Mundo – several tour agencies will add the archaeological site to a tour for an extra fee.

RESERVA GEOBOTÁNICA PULULAHUA

This small 3300-hectare reserve lies about four km north of San Antonio and is often visited in conjunction with a visit to Mitad del Mundo. The most interesting part of the reserve is the volcanic crater of the extinct Pululahua. This was apparently formed in ancient times when the cone of the volcano collapsed, leaving a huge crater some 300 meters deep and four km across (some guidebooks claim 500 meters deep and nine km in diameter – I think that is an exaggeration). The flat and fertile crater bottom is used for agriculture. Within the crater there are two small cones, the larger Loma Pondoña (2975 meters) and the smaller Loma El Chivo.

The crater is open to the west side, through which moisture-laden winds from the Pacific blow dramatically. It is sometimes difficult to see the crater because of the swirling clouds and mist. The moist winds, combined with the crater's steep walls, create a variety of microclimates, and the vegetation on the fertile volcanic slopes is rampant and diverse. Because the walls are much too steep to farm, the vegetation grows undisturbed and protected. There are many flowers and, of course, a variety of birds.

The crater can be entered on foot by a steep trail on its southeast side. There is also a rough track (suitable for 4WD vehicles) on the southwest side. The steep trail is the best way to see the birds and plants because most of the flat bottom is farmed. There is no official entrance or fee for the reserve.

Getting There & Away

Take a Mitad del Mundo bus (see Mitad del Mundo, above). From the monument, a paved road continues to the village of Calacalí, about 7½ km away. There are occasional buses from San Antonio to Calacalí, particularly at weekends. About four km beyond Mitad del Mundo on the road to Calacalí, there is a paved road to the right – the first one. Ask the driver to drop you off here. About one km along this road there is

a small parking area – the crater is just beyond. The trail descends from the parking area to the crater bottom.

Alternatively, continue on the road to Calacalí for about a further 2½ km. A dirt road on your right leads into the crater. You can return the way you came, perhaps stopping at the picturesque little village of Calacalí (no facilities).

Taxis from San Antonio or Quito will take you to the rim and tours can be arranged from Quito in combination with a visit to Mitad del Mundo.

POMASQUI

This village is passed about six km before reaching Mitad del Mundo on the way from Quito. It is worth a stop to see the two churches on the Plaza Yerovi (the main plaza) two blocks east of the gas station on the main highway. On the south side of the plaza is the church of El Señor del Árbol (the Lord of the Tree), which has a noted sculpture of Christ in a tree – the branches of the tree look like Christ's arms raised above His head in a boxing champion's salute. Various miracles have been ascribed to this image by devotees. On the east side of the plaza is the parish church with a variety of religious paintings, some of which are slightly bizarre (the miraculous intervention of the Virgin to save a believer from certain death), and various statues including a carved and poly-chromed Santa Clara who is the patron saint of Pomasqui.

The Fiesta of El Señor del Árbol is normally the first Sunday in July. Santa Clara Day is July 27, and so the whole month is a busy one for the citizens of Pomasqui, who have processions, games, bull fights etc.

CALDERÓN

This village is about 10 km northeast of Quito on the Panamericana (not the road to Mitad del Mundo). Calderón is a famous center of a unique Ecuadorian folk art: Here the people make bread-dough decorations ranging from small statuettes to colorful Christmas tree ornaments, such as stars, parrots, Santas, tortoises, candles and tropical fish. The ornaments make practical gifts as they are small, unusual and cheap (buy a handful for US$1). These decorative figures are inedible – preservatives are added so that they'll last many years.

Some figurines are used for All Souls' Day (November 2) ceremonies in Calderón and many other Andean villages. It is thought that the figurines represented animal or human sacrifices in preconquest times. The cemetery here is a good place to visit from Quito on All Souls' Day.

Calderón is a small village, so you won't have any difficulty finding stores on the one main street. There is nowhere to stay and only basic restaurants.

Getting There & Away
Buses run along 10 de Agosto toward Calderón and beyond. The corner with Avenida Colón is supposed to be a good place to flag one down. Buses going as far as Otavalo or beyond may possibly give you a ride if they aren't full (which they often are). Local city buses don't go as far as Calderón. Somewhere in between are buses that go there – keep trying and you'll eventually find one.

If you wanted to visit just Calderón from Quito, you could hire a cab for under US$20 including some waiting time for you to shop. Most tours to Otavalo stop at Calderón briefly.

SANGOLQUÍ
The Indian market nearest the capital is the Sangolquí Sunday morning market. There is a smaller market on Thursday. Frequent local buses go there from Plaza Marín at Chile and M de Solanda in the old town. Sangolquí is about 15 km southeast of the old town.

PASOCHOA FOREST RESERVE
This is a private reserve operated by the Fundación Natura (☎ 246 072, 443 026), Sarmiento 188 and Portete (near the stadium in Quito), Ecuador's major non-governmental conservation organization. The reserve is roughly 30 km southeast of Quito and has one of the last remaining stands of undisturbed humid Andean forest

left in the central valley. Over 100 species of birds and many rare plants have been recorded here.

The forest is luxuriant and contains a wide range of highland trees and shrubs. These include the Podocarpaceae, which are the only conifers native to the Ecuadorian Andes (the pines seen elsewhere are introduced), various species of mountain palm trees, the Andean laurel, the huge-leaved *Gunnera* plant (nicknamed 'the poor folks' umbrella') and many more. Orchids, bromeliads, lichens, ferns and other epiphytic plants contribute to the forest's attractions. The prolific birdlife includes hummingbirds, of which at least 11 species are present, and which are one of the main attractions. Various other tropical birds such as furnarids, tapaculos, honeycreepers and tanagers may be seen along the nature trails. Mammals such as rabbits, squirrels and deer are sometimes observed, and, more rarely, foxes and even pumas. The reserve is very highly recommended to any naturalist and birdwatcher.

The reserve is a small one, only 400 hectares in size, located on the northern flanks of the extinct volcano of Pasochoa at elevations of 2700 to 3800 meters. The area is within the collapsed volcanic caldera (crater) and there are good views of other peaks. There are several trails ranging from easy half-hour loops to fairly strenuous all-day hikes. The shorter trails are self-guiding; guides are available for

Once common in Ecuador, the number of Andean condors is declining dramatically.

the longer walks. One trail leads out of the reserve and to the summit of Pasochoa (4200 meters) – this takes about six hours.

Apart from protection and conservation of this unique habitat for recreational use, the Fundación Natura also encourages scientific research in the area and has set up an educational program. This last is particularly designed to teach local schoolchildren about their environment – information that has hitherto been lacking for most students. These worthwhile programs are funded, to a great extent, by contributions to the Fundación Natura, particularly the entrance fee that is charged to visitors.

Information

A daily entrance fee of US$7 is charged to foreign visitors. Overnight camping is permitted in designated areas, the fee for which is US$2 per person. There are latrines, picnic areas, barbecue grills and water. There is also a simple hostal with 20 bunk beds for US$5 per person. You need to bring a sleeping bag. Hot showers and kitchen facilities are available. During weekends, a small restaurant is open; otherwise, bring your own food. The reserve is open every day from dawn till dusk. The Fundación Natura asks visitors to check with their offices to obtain maps, information and camping permits, and pay fees for reservations at weekends, especially during the dry season when the hostal can be full. Normally, however, the hostal is well-nigh empty, particularly midweek, and you can pay when you get there.

Getting There & Away

Buses leave from Quito about twice an hour for the village of Amaguaña, about one hour away. These buses leave from near the Plaza La Marín in the old town (ask for the exact location). Ask the driver to let you off near the 'El Ejido' and from the church nearby there is a signed cobblestone road to the reserve, about six or seven km away. You have to walk this. Alternately, go all the way into Amaguaña (about a km beyond El Ejido) and go by truck to the reserve entrance and information center for

about US$7 or US$8 (the truck can take several people). The locals are used to people visiting the reserve and can help give directions – it's not hard to find.

Taxis from Quito can also get you there, but not all the drivers know where to go. If you can't find a driver who knows the way, ask at the Fundación Natura for help in finding a knowledgeable driver. You might want to arrange a driver on the day before you visit to get there early – the best birding is in the early hours.

VOLCÁN PICHINCHA

Quito's closest volcano is Pichincha, looming over the western side of the city. The volcano has two main summits, the closer Rucu Pichincha (about 4700 meters) and the higher Guagua Pichincha (4794 meters). Guagua is active and is monitored by volcanologists. A major eruption in 1660 covered Quito in 40 cm of ash; there were three minor eruptions in the 1800s. The most recent bout of activity began in 1981 with a few puffs of smoke. It is unlikely that any serious activity will occur in the near future and the topography of the volcano is such that, even if a major eruption were to occur, the lava would flow into the almost unpopulated areas north, west and south of the volcano, sparing Quito which lies to the east.

Climbing either of the summits is strenuous, but technically straightforward, and no special equipment is required. By heading west on one of the streets leaving Quito and continuing upward, an ascent of Rucu Pichincha can be done in a long day, returning to the city by nightfall. Unfortunately, this is easier said than done. One main street of access, 24 de Mayo, has been the scene of frequent attacks and robberies of hikers, and this route is strongly discouraged. Another main access, through El Tejar, does not have as many robbery problems – instead, vicious dogs have often bitten hikers. Once out of the city, the route goes past the TV antennas on the hill named Cruz Loma – several attacks, robberies and rapes have been reported in this area in recent years.

These warnings should not be taken lightly – walking through some of the poor suburbs on the western edges of the city is not a good idea if you are laden with good warm clothes and camera gear. The best solution is to go in a large group and check for the latest information before you go. The South American Explorers Club is always an excellent source of up-to-date information. They can tell you the best route to take through the ever-changing and expanding western outskirts of town, and recommend a guide if you wish. The climbing guides listed in Organized Tours, above, can also be of assistance. Guides will usually have a jeep available to drive you past all the problem areas to a point high up on the mountain (even so, the shortened climb to the summit is a strenuous affair taking most of a day). Many people continue to climb Rucu Pichincha because the views are superb, but get information before you go and plan your trip with care to avoid having a problem.

Climbing the smoking Guagua Pichincha is a longer trip, but less beset with non-mountainous hazards. A southbound No 8 Tola-Pintado bus will take you past Avenida Chilibulo shortly before the end of the run. Occasional buses head out along Avenida Chilibulo to the village of Lloa. From here, there is a track that takes about half a day of walking to reach a hut just below the crater summit of Guagua. This track can also be negotiated in a sturdy 4WD vehicle to just below the refuge. The refuge is very basic – a few bunks and, usually, a caretaker who can look after your gear and let you use the kitchen facilities. From the hut, reaching the crater rim and descending within takes about two to three hours. Again, check with the South American Explorers Club or a climbing guide for the latest information before you go.

North of Quito

The Andean highlands north of Quito are one of the most popular destinations in Ecuador. Few travelers spend any time in the country without visiting the famous Indian market in the small town of Otavalo, where you can buy a wide variety of weavings, clothing and handicrafts. Though many travelers limit their visit to just Otavalo, there is much more to see in the region.

The dramatic mountain scenery is dotted with shining white churches set in tiny villages, and includes views of Cayambe, the third highest peak in the country, as well as a beautiful lake district. Several small towns are noted for specialty handicrafts such as woodcarving or leatherwork.

Ibarra is a small, charmingly somnolent colonial city worth visiting, both in its own right and as the beginning of the Ibarra-San Lorenzo railway linking the northern highlands with the coast. If you are traveling overland to or from Colombia, it's almost impossible to avoid this region.

NORTH TO CAYAMBE

About 10 km north of Quito on the Panamericana is the village of Calderón (see Around Quito in the Quito chapter). Beyond Calderón the road descends in a series of magnificent sweeps towards the village of **Guayllabamba**, in a fertile river valley of the same name that is famous for its produce. Roadside stalls offer huge avocados and that strangely reptilian-looking Andean fruit, the *chirimoya*. It's a member of the custard apple family and perhaps the nearest translation is the 'sweetsop' – I prefer the Spanish name. You discard the knobbly green skin is discarded and you eat the white pulp inside. The chirimoya definitely tastes better than it looks or sounds.

Some three km beyond Guayllabamba, the road forks and you can take either road as they both end at Cayambe.

About 10 km along the right-hand road you pass a turnoff to the south that leads back to Quito via a roundabout route. This takes you through **El Quinche**, famous for its Virgin and paintings inside the impressive church, and on through pretty countryside and tiny hamlets to Pifo. Here you can turn right and return to Quito via Tumbaco. A few kilometers northeast of El Quinche turnoff, the Panamericana crosses the equator. Here you'll find a **monument** consisting of a large concrete globe that is much less visited than the ever-popular Mitad del Mundo monument north of Quito. A few kilometers beyond is the turnoff to the historical **Hacienda Guachala**, which is described below under Cayambe. Soon you cross the railway tracks of the now-defunct Quito-Ibarra train, and 60 km from Quito you reach Cayambe.

The left-hand route, although a little shorter, is somewhat more twisting and slower than the right-hand route, and therefore some drivers avoid it. It also crosses the equator, but there is no marker. The region is generally less inhabited and has more barren countryside than the other road. I prefer it for the exciting drive and wild scenery. The only village of any size on this road is **Tabacundo**.

COCHASQUÍ

Heading toward Tabacundo from Quito, you'll find a turnoff to the left as few kilometers before Tabacundo. That road leads to Tocachi and the ruins of Cochasquí. These were built by the Cara Indians before the Inca conquest and had been largely forgotten until recently. The area was declared a national archaeological site in 1977 and is currently being excavated and investigated.

There are 15 low, truncated, grass-covered pyramids, some of which are almost 100 meters long, and there are about 30 other mounds are also present.

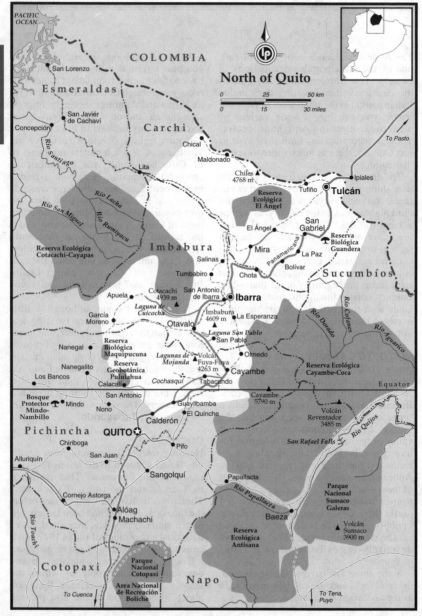

PACIFIC
OCEAN

COLOMBIA

North of Quito

0   25   50 km

0   15   30 miles

San Lorenzo

Esmeraldas

Carchi

To Pasto

San Javier
de Cachaví

Concepción

Río Santiago

Chical

Maldonado

Lita

Chiles
4768 m

Tufiño

Ipiales

Tulcán

Río Lacha

Reserva
Ecológica
El Ángel

Río San Miguel

Río Rumiyacu

El Ángel

San
Gabriel

Reserva
Biológica
Guandera

Reserva Ecológica
Cotacachi-Cayapas

Imbabura

Salinas

Mira

Panamericana

La Paz

Tumbabiro

Chota

Bolívar

Sucumbíos

Apuela

Cotacachi
4939 m

San Antonio
de Ibarra

Ibarra

García
Moreno

Laguna de
Cuicocha

Imbabura
4609 m

La Esperanza

Río Cofanes

Río Aguarico

Otavalo

Laguna San Pablo

Río Dorado

Nanegal

Reserva
Biológica
Maquipucuna

San Pablo

Lagunas de
Mojanda

Volcán
Fuya-Fuya
4263 m

Olmedo

Reserva Ecológica
Cayambe-Coca

Nanegalito

Reserva
Geobotánica
Pululahua

Cochasquí

Cayambe

Los Bancos

Calacalí

Tabacundo

Equator

San Antonio

Bosque
Protector
Mindo-
Nambillo

Mindo

Nono

Guayllabamba

Cayambe
5790 m

Volcán
Reventador
3485 m

El Quinche

Pichincha

Calderón

QUITO

San Rafael Falls

Río Quijos

Chiriboga

San Juan

Pifo

Alluriquín

Sangolquí

Papallacta

Parque
Nacional
Sumaco
Galeras

Cornejo Astorga

Río Papallacta

Volcán
Sumaco
3900 m

Río Toachi

Alóag
Machachi

Baeza

Reserva
Ecológica
Antisana

Cotopaxi

Parque
Nacional
Cotopaxi

Napo

Area Nacional
de Recreación
Boliche

To Cuenca

To Tena,
Puyo

The remarkable panoramic view from the site (you can see El Panecillo of Quito if you have good binoculars) has led archeologists to assume that Cochasquí was built for strategic purposes. Additionally, the alignments of the pyramids and some of the structures associated with them point to ceremonial and astronomical uses. Note that the site is not as dramatic as the Inca ruins are elsewhere – some readers have been disappointed.

There is a small on-site museum, and local Spanish-speaking guides give tours of the museum and site. If you are pressed for time, ask for a short tour – longer tours may last a couple of hours. Although entrance to the site and tours are officially free, I encourage visitors to tip guides because their wages are inadequate. The site and museum are open from 9 am to 3 pm daily except Monday.

The guides can also show you life-size houses modeled after indigenous architectural styles (houses still look like this in the more remote parts of the Sierra). These are built entirely from local materials using ancient methods – you won't see nails or electrical outlets! Inside you'll see indigenous furnishings and cooking utensils, while guinea pigs (a traditional delicacy of the Incas) scurry around. Outside, a garden teems with a cornucopia of Andean plants used for food, medicinal, ceremonial and utilitarian purposes. Many of these plants and their traditional uses as folk remedies are dying out in the highlands. One purpose of this project is to preserve them despite competition from today's monocultural agricultural practices and the ubiquitous panacea, aspirin. (See the 'Why Conserve the Rainforest?' sidebar in Facts about the Country for more on conservation.)

Getting There & Away
There is no public transport. Some buses (try Transportes Lagos) between Quito and Otavalo take the Tabacundo road and can drop you at the turnoff. There is a sign. From there, a dirt road climbs about nine km to the site. The site workers and guides usually drive up to the ruins about 9 am and can

give you a lift, but otherwise you have to walk. Hitching opportunities are few due to the lack of traffic. Taxis can be hired from Cayambe and will do the roundtrip, including waiting time, for about US$10.

CAYAMBE
Cayambe (population about 15,000) is the most important town on the way to Otavalo. It is famous for its dairy industry, and there are many stores and restaurants selling a variety of local cheeses and cheese products. Salt crackers called *bizcochos* are also produced here. The local Salesian Monastery reportedly has an excellent library on indigenous cultures.

Places to Stay & Eat
Although this is the only town of any size so close to the equator, few people stay here, preferring instead to buy some cheese and continue to Otavalo. Centrally located, the *Youth Hostal Cayambe* (☎ 360 007), Bolívar 23 and Ascázubi, is the cheapest place to stay. Bunks are about US$5 per person. The clean *Hostería Mitad del Mundo* (☎ 360 226) at the south end of town charges about US$6 per person.

The *Hostería Napoles* (☎ 360 231) is about one km north of town on the Panamericana. They sell cheese products and have one of the best restaurants in Cayambe. There is also a garden with a miniature 'zoo' (a few caged parrots, etc). Cabins with private bath, hot water and TV are US$9/15 for singles/doubles.

A few kilometers south of Cayambe is the *Hacienda Guachala*, founded in 1580 and said to be the oldest hacienda in Ecuador. The hacienda has housed Ecuadorian presidents and visiting luminaries during its four centuries of existence. In 1993, it opened as a hotel and offers 14 comfortable rooms with private bath. There is a swimming pool, and two colonial chapels are on the landscaped grounds. Horseback riding, hiking and jeep tours are available. There is a restaurant and bar, and the main building contains many artifacts and antiques. Rates are about US$40/50 and reservations can be made in Quito (☎ /fax 563 748), Reina Victoria 1138 and Foch, Office 4. The hacienda is about 1½ km along the Cangahua road, which heads southeast from the Panamericana about seven km south of Cayambe. Several readers have recommended this place.

Getting There & Away

Any bus between Quito and Otavalo can drop you in Cayambe.

Some buses run to Cayambe (as well as Calderón, Guayllabamba and Tabacundo) direct from Quito, but they don't leave from the Terminal Terrestre de Cumandá. Rather, you should stand next to the road and flag them down. A good place to wait is on Avenida 10 de Agosto at its intersection with Avenida Juan de Ascaray, near the bullring. Flag down any bus that has a sign indicating it's going to your destination, or one that looks like it could use some passengers. Start early in the day so that you don't get stuck somewhere at nightfall – you'll probably have plenty of adventures.

FROM CAYAMBE TO OTAVALO

From Cayambe it is 31 km along the Panamericana to Otavalo. The snow-capped mountain east of the road is the extinct **Volcán Cayambe**. At 5790 meters, it is Ecuador's third highest peak. For trivia buffs it is also the highest point in the world through which the equator directly passes – at about 4600 meters on the south side. There is a climbing refuge (refurbished in 1994) that costs US$10 to stay in, though you need 4WD to reach it. From the refuge, the climb is more difficult than the more frequently ascended peaks of Cotopaxi and Tungurahua, but climbing guides in Quito can get you up there.

The Panamericana climbs from the Pichincha to Imbabura Province, a region known for its indigenous inhabitants and pretty lake district. Soon you see the largest of these lakes, Laguna San Pablo, stretching away to your right, with the high peak of Volcán Imbabura (4609 meters) behind it. The area is dotted with villages inhabited by the Otavaleño Indians.

OTAVALO

This small town of some 22,000 inhabitants is justly famous for its friendly people and their Saturday market. The market dates back to pre-Inca times when jungle products were brought up from the eastern lowlands and traded for highland goods. Today's market serves two different groups: locals who buy and barter animals, food and other essentials, and tourists looking for crafts.

The story of the phenomenal success of the Otavaleño weavers is an intriguing one. The backstrap loom has been used in the area for some 4000 years. The Indians' proficiency as weavers was harshly exploited by the colonialists beginning in 1555 and later by the Ecuadorian landowners who forced them to labor in *obrajes* (sweatshops), often for 14 or more hours a day. Miserable though this was, it did have the effect of instilling a great knowledge of weaving in the Otavaleño people.

In 1917 a local weaver had the idea of copying the Scottish tweeds that were then in vogue, and this was so successful that it again led to recognition of the skill of the Otavaleño weavers. This ability, combined with the Agrarian Reform of 1964 and the people's shrewd business sense, has made the Otavaleños the most prosperous Indian group in Ecuador and perhaps on the continent. It is difficult to find a town of any size that does not have an Otavaleño store. They also make frequent business trips to neighboring countries and even to North America and Europe.

The goods they sell are undeniably oriented towards the tourist market and this has led to recent complaints from 'real travelers' that the market is too 'touristified.' This seems to me a kind of inverse snobbism that reveals a lack of concern for the well-being of the weavers. Their prosperity in a changing and difficult world is only to be applauded, but a truer measure of their success is their continuing sense of tribal identity and tradition.

One of the most evident features of the Otavaleños' cultural integrity is their traditional way of dress. Not just some costume

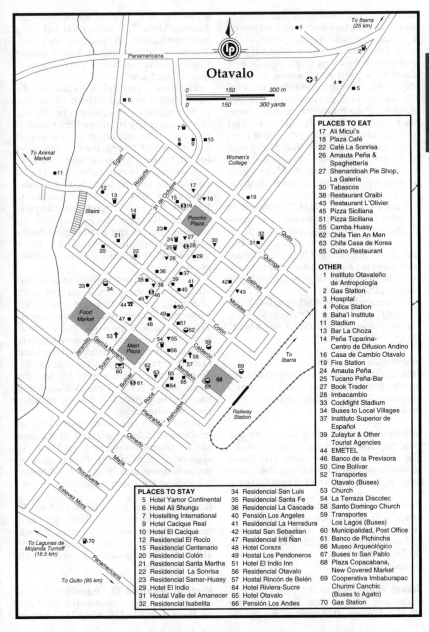

Otavalo

To Ibarra
(25 km)

Panamericana

0   150   300 m

0   150   300 yards

To Animal
Market

To Quito (95 km)

To Lagunas de
Mojanda Turnoff
(16.5 km)

To Quito (95 km)

Women's
College

Poncho
Plaza

Food
Market

Main
Plaza

Railway
Station

To
Ibarra

Stairs

PLACES TO EAT
17 Ali Micui's
18 Plaza Café
22 Café La Sonrisa
26 Amauta Peña &
     Spaghetteria
27 Shenandoah Pie Shop,
     La Galería
30 Tabascos
38 Restaurant Oraibi
43 Restaurant L'Olivier
45 Pizza Siciliana
45 Pizza Siciliana
55 Camba Huasy
62 Chifa Tien An Men
63 Chifa Casa de Korea
65 Quino Restaurant

OTHER
1   Instituto Otavaleño
     de Antropología
2   Gas Station
3   Hospital
4   Police Station
8   Baha'i Institute
11 Stadium
13 Bar La Choza
14 Peña Tuparina-
     Centro de Difusion Andino
16 Casa de Cambio Otavalo
19 Fire Station
24 Amauta Peña
25 Tucano Peña-Bar
27 Book Trader
28 Imbacambio
33 Cockfight Stadium
35 Buses to Local Villages
37 Instituto Superior de
     Español
39 Zulaytur & Other
     Tourist Agencies
44 EMETEL
46 Banco de la Previsora
50 Cine Bolívar
52 Transportes
     Otavalo (Buses)
53 Church
54 La Terraza Discotec
58 Santo Domingo Church
59 Transportes
     Los Lagos (Buses)
60 Municipalidad, Post Office
61 Banco de Pichincha
66 Museo Arqueológico
67 Buses to San Pablo
68 Plaza Copacabana,
     New Covered Market
69 Cooperativa Imbaburapac
     Churimi Canchic
     (Buses to Agato)
70 Gas Station

PLACES TO STAY
5   Hotel Yamor Continental
6   Hotel Ali Shungu
7   Hostelling International
9   Hotel Cacique Real
10 Hotel El Cacique
12 Residencial El Rocío
15 Residencial Centenario
20 Residencial Colón
21 Residencial Santa Martha
22 Residencial La Sonrisa
23 Residencial Samar-Huasy
29 Hotel El Indio
31 Hostal Valle del Amanecer
32 Residencial Isabelita
34 Residencial San Luis
35 Residencial Santa Fe
36 Residencial La Cascada
40 Pensión Los Angeles
41 Residencial La Herradura
42 Hostal San Sebastian
47 Residencial Inti Ñan
48 Hotel Coraza
49 Hostal Los Pendoneros
51 Hotel El Indio Inn
56 Residencial Otavalo
57 Hostal Rincón de Belén
64 Hotel Riviera-Sucre
65 Hotel Otavalo
66 Pensión Los Andes

put on for the tourists at the Saturday market, traditional attire is worn on normal workdays in their homes, villages and fields. Otavaleño men are immediately distinctive with their long single pigtails, calf-length white pants, rope sandals, reversible gray or blue ponchos, and dark felt hats. The women, too, are very striking, in their beautifully embroidered blouses, long black skirts and shawls, and interesting folded head cloths, which Otavaleños interpret in various ways. The women also wear bright jewels, the most obvious being the many strings of gold-colored blown-glass beads around their necks, and bracelets of long strands of red beads.

The majority of the 22,000 inhabitants of the town of Otavalo are whites or mestizos. Of the 40,000 Indians, most live in the many nearby villages and come into Otavalo for market day. Quite a few Indians own stores in Otavalo, however, where you can buy most items if you are unable to come for the market.

For detailed cultural information, I recommend Lynn Meisch's *Otavalo: Weaving, Costume and the Market* (Libri Mundi, Quito, 1987).

Information

Tourist Offices There is no official tourist information office, but there are travel agencies (see below) that are helpful with local information.

Money Casas de cambio (see map) give good rates and also change traveler's checks. The Banco de la Previsora gives cash advances on credit cards. You can sometimes buy souvenirs with US cash dollars.

Post & Communications The post office is in the Municipalidad and is best entered from the back of the Municipalidad on Piedrahita. The EMETEL office is at Calderón and Sucre. The area code for Otavalo is 06.

Travel Agencies At the east corner of Sucre and Colón, 2nd floor, Zulaytur (☎ 921 176, fax 922 969) is run by the knowledgeable, English-speaking Señor Rodrigo Mora. This agency has had many recommendations and only one complaint. The people at Zulaytur are known to give tourist information even if you don't go on one of their tours.

There are several other agencies on the same block. I've received letters from each of them telling me that they are the best and that all the others are illegal! Each agency provides similar tours at competitive prices; visit them and choose the one that most appeals to you. They are all quite good.

A variety of inexpensive guided tours enable you to visit local Indian homes, learn about the entire weaving process, buy products off the loom and take photographs. Rodrigo Mora's emphasis on anthropological and sociological background information makes his tours very worthwhile. Most other agencies are following suit.

The most popular tour visits several local villages and lasts all day. Tours cost about US$10 per person with a maximum of ten passengers – more with fewer passengers. Transportation is included, but lunch is extra. More expensive tours take travelers to visit the beautiful Andean lakes around Otavalo or to trek in the local countryside. Some agencies have horses for rent for about US$20 per half-day. Various other tours can be arranged. Ask at the agencies for more information.

If you have a reasonably large group, an informative slide presentation of the area can be arranged with Rodrigo Mora. At appropriate times of year, visits to some of the local fiestas may be possible (although not all fiestas are open to outsiders).

Bookstores The Book Trader, Salinas 5-03 on the Poncho Plaza, buys, sells and trades books in English, German, French and perhaps some other languages. They also sell maps, posters, postcards and music cassettes.

Medical Services The following doctors have been locally recommended. Dr Patricio Buitrón (☎ 921 159, 921 678), on Roca

Top: Monastery of San Francisco, Quito (RR)
Left: Presidential Palace guard, Quito (RR)
Right: Independence Plaza, Quito (RR)

Top: Climbing Cotopaxi (RR)
Left: Old Quito and Mt Cayambe (RR)
Right: Virgin of Quito, Panecillo (RR)

> **The Volcanoes of Otavalo**
> Two extinct volcanoes can be seen from Otavalo on clear days: the massive bulk of Volcán Imbabura (4609 meters) to the east and the sharper, more jagged Volcán Cotacachi (at 4939 meters, Ecuador's 11th highest mountain) to the northwest. The locals refer to these peaks as Taita ('Daddy') Imbabura and Mama Cotacachi. Legend has it that when it's raining in Otavalo, Taita Imbabura is pissing in the valley.
>   Another legend suggests that when Mama Cotacachi awakes with a fresh covering of snow, she has been visited by Taita Imbabura during the night. ■

near Quiroga, speaks some English, and Dr Klaus Fay (☎ 921 203, Tuesday through Saturday), on Sucre near Morales, speaks German and English.

The hospital is on Sucre, about 400 meters outside of town.

The Market

The main market day is Saturday. There are three main plazas, with the overflow spilling out onto the streets linking them. The **Poncho Plaza** is where the items of most appeal to tourists are sold. Here you can buy woolen goods such as ponchos, blankets, scarves, sweaters, tapestries and gloves as well as a variety of embroidered blouses and shirts, shawls, string bags, rope sandals etc.

Bargaining for every purchase is the norm. If you buy several items from the same person, you can expect a discount of 20% or even more if you are good at bargaining. Some people aren't good at it and feel uncomfortable trying to knock a few sucres off an already cheaply priced item. Just remember that it is expected and make an offer a little below the first asking price (assuming you want to buy the thing).

This market gets underway soon after dawn and continues until about noon. You are advised to spend Friday night in Otavalo and get to the market early. It can get rather crowded in midmorning when the big tour groups arrive and prices are higher. If you come in the early morning, you'll find a greater selection at better prices. Note that there are increasing numbers of pickpockets and bag snatchers at the market – keep your eyes open and your valuables hidden.

The **food market** sells produce and household goods for the locals, and there is an **animal market** that begins in the predawn hours (5 to 9 am) on the outskirts of town. These are not oriented toward tourists, but you are welcome to visit them; many people find the sight of poncho-clad Indians quietly bartering for a string of screaming piglets much more interesting than the scene at Poncho Plaza. The animal market is over by early morning, so plan on an early arrival. It lies over a kilometer out of town; cross the bridge at the end of Morales and follow the crowds to get there.

The popularity of the market is such that there is a smaller market is held on Wednesday (mainly for tourists), and selling goes on every day during the peak visitor months of June to August. During these months, some travelers prefer the Wednesday market, which is less crowded and has as good a selection of crafts as the Saturday market. Stores selling crafts are open daily year-round.

Museums

The **Instituto Otavaleño de Antropología** houses a small archaeological museum of the area, a library and a bookstore selling books (in Spanish) about the anthropology and culture of Otavalo. The museum is just off the Panamericana north of town. It is free and open from 8 am to noon Tuesday to Saturday and from 2 to 6 pm Tuesday to Friday. It was recently refurbished and hours may change.

There is a small **Museo Arqueológico** in the Pensión Los Andes on Montalvo near Roca. This is free for guests of the pension and there is a modest admission charge for others.

Language Courses

The Quito-based Instituto Superior de Español has Spanish language classes at Sucre 11-10 and Morales.

Special Events

Some small village fiestas date back to pre-Columbian rituals and can last as long as two weeks, with much drinking and dancing. They are not much visited by outsiders, and, in some cases, it would be dangerous for tourists to just show up. One little-known annual event involves ritual battle between rival villages at which locals are sometimes killed. The authorities turn a blind eye, and outsiders are not tolerated.

June 24 is Saint John the Baptist Day, and June 29 is the Day of Saints Peter and Paul. These and the intervening days are an important fiesta for Otavalo and the surrounding villages. There is a bullfight in Otavalo and a boating regatta on Laguna San Pablo, as well as celebrations in nearby Ilumán.

A few kilometers southeast of Otavalo, on the southern shores of Laguna San Pablo, in the villages around San Rafael, there is a fiesta called Corazas on August 19. Also in some of the south shore villages is the Pendoneros Fiesta on October 15.

Otavalo's best-known fiesta is held in the first two weeks of September. The Fiesta del Yamor consists of plenty of music, processions and dancing as well as fireworks displays, cockfights and an election of the Queen of the Fiesta.

Precise dates of these can vary from year to year, but they are usually well publicized and you can find out what's going on from posters. In addition, there are the usual feast days celebrated throughout the land.

Places to Stay

Because Otavalo is such a popular destination, there are many more places to stay than in other bigger but less interesting towns. Despite this, it can get rather crowded on Friday night, so arrive early for the best selection. Most places are quite cheap, and new hotels open regularly. If you arrive midweek and plan to stay a few days, you can often negotiate a cheaper price. Conversely, late Friday night isn't a good time to expect any favors. Prices may rise at weekends, especially during the high season or for one-night stays.

Note that the best hotels are in country haciendas out of town. A car is the most convenient way to get to these.

There have been several reports of theft from hotel rooms in Otavalo. Keep your room door locked, even if leaving for just a little while.

Places to Stay – bottom end

Currently, the most popular budget choice is the clean and helpful *Hostal Valle del Amanecer* (☎ 920 990, fax 920 286), Roca and Quiroga. They charge about US$4.50 per person or US$6.50 with bath and hot water. There's a café and they rent mountain bikes at US$7 a day. Also good and recommended is the very clean and friendly *Residencial El Rocío* (☎ 920 584), Morales 11-70, which charges US$3.50 per person and has a couple of rooms with private bath for US$9 a double. There is hot water and the view from the roof is nice.

The clean *Hotel Riviera-Sucre* (☎ 920 241), G Moreno 3-14, is in an old house with a courtyard. It has hot water and is popular with budget travelers. Rates are about US$4.50 per person. The similarly priced *Residencial La Sonrisa*, Colón 6-10, has a games room and a decent, inexpensive café. Other OK places at US$4 to US$5 per person, with hot water in shared baths, include the *Residencial Santa Fe* (☎ 920 161), Colón 5-07; the family-run *Residencial San Luis* (☎ 920 614), Calderón 6-02; and the friendly little *Residencial Inti Ñan* (☎ 921 373), J Montalvo 6-02, which is often full.

The cheapest is the very basic but friendly *Pensión Los Andes*, Montalvo 3-75, at about US$2.25 per person. It has cold water and a private archaeology museum! For about US$3.25 per person, the *Residencial Samar-Huasy*, Jaramillo 6-11, has clean, small rooms. Hot showers are available at times. Other adequate places at US$3 to US$4 include the *Residencial*

Otavalo (☎ 920 739), J Montalvo 4-44 (not to be confused with the more expensive Hotel Otavalo); the *Residencial Santa Martha* (☎ 920 568), Colón 7-04 (I've received reports of theft here, though others say it's safe); the friendly *Residencial La Herradura* (☎ 920 304), Bolívar 10-05; the clean *Residencial La Cascada* (☎ 920 165) at Colón near Sucre; and the *Residencial Isabelita*, Roca 11-07. Other cheapies include the *Pensión Los Angeles*, Colón 4-10, and the *Residencial Colón*, Colón 7-13.

The *Residencial Centenario* (☎ 920 467), Pasaje Saona 7-03 (an alley just off the Poncho Plaza) is clean and looks good for US$5.50 per person or US$6.50 with private bath. The *Hostal San Sebastián* (☎ 920 208), Roca 9-05, is friendly and has large but slightly overpriced rooms at US$7/10 or US$9/13 with private bath. The *Hostal Los Pendoneros* (☎ 921 258), Calderón 5-10, is good and clean. Singles are US$6.50 with shared bath, and doubles with hot bath are US$14. The restaurant downstairs is popular.

The *Hotel El Cacique* and *Hotel Cacique Real* (☎ 922 303, 922 438, 921 740), opposite one another on the north end of 31 de Octubre, have nice carpeted rooms with TV for US$17 a double. Nearby is the Hostelling Internacional *Jatun Pacha* (☎ 921 168, 922 223), which looks nice from the outside (it was temporarily closed the morning I stopped by).

The *Hotel El Indio* (☎ 920 601), Sucre 12-14, is clean and has hot water and a restaurant. There are only 10 rooms at US$18 a double with bath, some with a balcony. You have to book these early for the weekend – they are usually full by Wednesday afternoon with guests staying for the rest of the week. (Don't confuse this with the more expensive Hotel El Indio Inn.)

The *Hotel Otavalo* (☎ 920 416), Roca 5-04, is very clean – in fact, last time I was in there the smell of wax polish was overpowering. It has rooms with private bath and hot water for about US$11/16 or US$8/11 with shared bath. They have a pizzeria and breakfast restaurant, and they recommend reservations for the weekend. The new *Hostal*

Rincón de Belén (☎ 920 171, 921 860), Roca 8-20, has simple but clean rooms with TV and hot showers for US$14/18. They have a decent restaurant.

On the western shores of Laguna San Pablo is the *Hostal Chicapan* (☎ 920 331), which has rooms for about US$11 a double with bath. They have a restaurant.

Places to Stay – middle

The quite new and clean *Hotel El Indio Inn* (☎ 922 922, ☎ /fax 920 325), Bolívar 9-04, has nice large rooms with TV and telephone and a good restaurant downstairs. Rooms cost about US$20/28. Newer still, the *Hotel Coraza* (☎ 921 225, fax 920 459), Sucre near Calderón, has over 50 modern carpeted rooms with TV and telephone. There is a decent restaurant, bar, coffee shop, gift shop and parking garage, and it seems like a fair value for US$30 per double.

The *Hotel Yamor Continental* (☎ 920 451, 920 848, fax 920 982) has clean and spacious rooms in a hacienda-like building set in charming flower-filled gardens at the northeast end of town. There is a small (unheated) pool, a games area with a miniature golf course, a beat-up tennis court, and a pricey restaurant and bar. Rooms with private bath, TV and phone are about US$30 for either one or two people but go up to almost US$40 at weekends.

The best hotel in Otavalo itself is the *Hotel Ali Shungu* (☎ 920 750), at the northwest end of Calle Quito; it's owned and operated by a couple of former US residents now residing in Otavalo. There is a large and attractive patio and flowery garden, and the views of Volcán Imbabura are very fine. The rooms are appealingly decorated with local crafts and flowers, and there are plenty of lights. The 16 spacious and comfortable rooms with private baths and plenty of hot water rent for about US$30/40 (high season weekends), and a couple of huge suites cost US$60 to US$100 for two to six people. A very good restaurant serving vegetarian and meat dishes is on the premises, and it has live *música folklórica* at weekends, when a two-day stay is required. There is also a fireplace, book exchange and laundry service. The hotel prefers to receive adult guests. I have received more readers' recommendations for this hotel than any other in Ecuador – many write that it was their favorite hotel on their trip. To be fair, I also received two criticisms, one from a woman traveling with a group of children who found that the hotel didn't want to have anything to do with them, and another from a fellow who had the room rates misquoted and then had the owner argue with him.

Another possibility is the *Cabañas del Lago* (☎ 918 001, 918 108; reservations in Quito ☎ 435 936, fax 461 316), on the east side of Laguna San Pablo two or three km north of the village of San Pablo. They have some 15 modern and comfortable cabins with private bath, and there's a restaurant on the premises. Small boats are available for rides or hire, and horseback riding and miniature golf are offered. Rates are about US$45 for a double room with TV, breakfast included.

Places to Stay – top end

The very popular *Hostería Cusín* (☎ 918 013, fax 918 003; in Quito ☎ /fax 253 341) is an excellent hotel on the southern outskirts of San Pablo (about 10 km southeast of Otavalo). It is in a beautiful converted 17th-century hacienda with all the trimmings. The oldest part of the hacienda dates to 1602, though it was completely remodeled in 1990. There is a cozy bar with a roaring fireplace, a games room (snooker, darts, table tennis), a well-stocked video room, a reading room, beautiful gardens, a squash court and horses and mountain bikes available for guests. The Andrango family from Agato (see below) have an exclusive crafts shop on the premises.

The hostería is usually booked well in advance for weekends, though it is less busy midweek. It costs US$66/96 for attractively furnished rooms with bath, many with fireplaces. Continental breakfast is included. Some rooms are in the main building, while others are in smaller cottages in the grounds. Complete packages including three delicious home-cooked set meals are US$96 per person. Lunches are especially good, with traditional soups and local dishes attracting daytrippers from Quito.

On the approach to the hostería is *El Monasterio de Cusín*, under the same ownership as the Hostería Cusín. There are 16 large rooms with fireplaces and beamed ceilings set around two attractive courtyards. A tower reading room offers lovely views and extensive gardens are filled with perennial flowers. There is a dining room and conference room – the monastery is used for meetings and conferences.

Reservations for Monasterio de Cusín can be made in the US at Casamolina, 53 E 66th St, New York, NY 10021 (☎ (212) 988 4552, fax 988 4935), or in the UK (☎ (0181) 788 7542, fax 788 8620). The owner, Nick Millhouse, is British, and the manager, Marcia Simón, is Ecuadorian; one or the other is usually on the premises. The Cusín office also has information about and can make reservations for several other highland haciendas.

Right on the lake, about five km southeast of Otavalo on the Panamericana, is the *Hostería Puerto Lago* (☎ 921 901/902, fax 920 900), which has also been recommended. There is a good restaurant with fine lake views, and boats are available. Rates are about US$70 per double including dinner.

Places to Eat

There are many restaurants aimed at the ever-present gringo visitor to Ecuador's most famous market. On the Poncho Plaza the Ecuadorian/Austrian-run *La Galería* is a good café serving vegetarian dishes and decent espresso. The nearby *Shenandoah* pie shop is also popular, though it seems to have gone downhill in quality recently. *Ali Micui's*, on the north corner of the Poncho Plaza, serves both vegetarian and non-vegetarian food at inexpensive prices. Across the street, the more upmarket *Plaza Café*, open from 8 am to 10 pm, has delicious and innovative dinners for around

US$5. Readers have recently reported some other new restaurants on this plaza.

Just off the Poncho Plaza on Salinas, *Tabascos* has pricey Mexican food, decent breakfasts and a rack of magazines in English. For good breakfasts and cheap pizzas, the German-run *Café La Sonrisa* in the Residencial Sonrisa has been recommended.

The *Pizza Siciliana*, with two locations, is said to have the best pizzas. One is at Sucre 10-03 and the other is under the Hotel El Indio Inn. The *Quino Restaurant*, Roca 7-40 near the Hotel Otavalo, is popular and has good seafood. (The restaurant in the Hotel Otavalo has good ice cream and snacks, though their pizza isn't quite as good as the Siciliana.)

Restaurant Oraibi on Colón near Sucre has cheap vegetarian food and a pleasant atmosphere. *Restaurant L'Olivier*, Roca 9-08, has medium-priced French food. *SISA* next to the Hotel Coraza is mid-priced. It has a wide variety of dishes and is one of the better restaurants in town.

There are several chifas, of which the best are the *Tien An Men* and the *Casa de Korea*, both on García Moreno just off the Main Plaza. If you're after fried chicken, try the *Camba Huasy* on Bolívar just off the Main Plaza. All these are reasonably priced.

The *Hotel El Indio* serves good local food, particularly fritada (not always available). The *Hotel Ali Shungu* has, I think, the best food in town, and it's worth the extra few dollars. Get there early on Friday when they have live music.

Entertainment

Otavalo is a quiet place during the week, but it gets livelier on the weekend. The *Cine Bolívar* on Bolívar and Colón sometimes screens English-language films.

On Friday and Saturday nights there's the popular *Amauta Peña* (☎ 920 967), Jaramillo 6-14, near the west corner of the Poncho Plaza. They open around 8 pm, but music doesn't begin until after 10 pm and costs about US$1 cover. The music and ambiance can vary from abysmal to enjoyable – take your chances. This place has

spawned the *Amauta Peña & Spaghettería* around the corner – eat pasta, then party!

The *Peña Tuparina – Centro de Difusion Andino*, on Morales near 31 de Octubre, is similar and has received several recommendations from travelers – the cover here is about US$0.50. The *Tucano Peña-Bar* at Morales 5-10 and Sucre has both folklórica and salsa music, and often has live or recorded music midweek as well as on weekends. The *Restaurant Oraibi* may have a peña during high-season weekends. Other places to check out include the *Bar La Choza* on Morales near Egas and *La Terraza Discotec*, upstairs on Bolívar just off the main plaza.

Finally, the weekly cockfight is held in the ring at the west end of 31 de Octubre, every Saturday afternoon about 3 pm. I don't like cockfights, but they certainly play an important part in the local macho culture. Admission is US$0.60.

Getting There & Away

Bus Getting from Quito to Otavalo is totally straightforward. There are several companies at the Terminal Terrestre de Cumandá, and the buses leave frequently. They all charge about US$2 for the two to three-hour ride. The best companies are Transportes Otavalo and Transportes Los Lagos – they take you into the town center. The others tend to go on to Ibarra and will drop you off on the Panamericana, forcing you to walk about a kilometer into town.

From the northern towns of Ibarra or Tulcán, you'll find buses leaving for Otavalo every hour or so from their respective terminals.

In Otavalo, the main bus terminal area is near the strangely named Plaza Copacabana, where you'll probably arrive if coming from Quito on Transportes Los Lagos. There is a taxi rank if you need it; US$0.80 will take you to most hotels. From this plaza you can also catch old local buses to some of the villages south of Otavalo, such as San Pablo del Lago. The delicious-sounding Cooperativa Imbaburapac Churimi Canchic has buses from here to Agato every hour or so.

A couple of blocks away on Avenida Calderón, you'll find Transportes Otavalo, which has frequent buses to Ibarra (about US$0.30), where you change for buses farther north. There were no direct buses to Tulcán at press time. Transportes Otavalo also has many Quito-bound buses as well as buses to Apuela and García Moreno.

Farther down Calderón, at the intersection with 31 de Octubre, you'll find a bunch of rather decrepit buses in which people are waiting expectantly. This is a good place to find out about bus services to Cotacachi, Apuela and many of the remoter towns and villages. Transportes Cotacachi and 6 de Julio go to Cotacachi – 6 de Julio is the faster and charges about US$0.25. Transportes Cotacachi has some buses continuing to Apuela and García Moreno. A truck leaves for these villages every morning except Tuesday at about 7 am. Transportes 8 de Septiembre goes to Ilumán. There is no strict schedule to any of these towns, and prices are low. Adventurous travelers might just want to get aboard and see what happens, but leave yourself enough time to get back to a hotel, as most of these villages have no formal accommodations.

Reaching the villages of Calderón, Guayllabamba and Cayambe is not straightforward. The companies running buses between Otavalo and Quito normally won't sell tickets to intermediate points. You can buy a full-price ticket to Quito and get off where you want, discarding the rest of the ticket. Alternately, if there are only a few passengers, just board the bus as it leaves and pay the driver for where you want to go. You'll be dropped off at the turnoff from the main road, and will have to walk several hundred meters to the village.

Train There is a railway station, though trains have not run to Quito for many years. Trains to Ibarra run sporadically. They were not operating in 1995, but in 1996 several trains a day to and from Ibarra were reported. The fare is marginally cheaper than the bus, and you might want to ride the train just for the experience. It takes about one hour to reach Ibarra, and you can get off in the villages of Peguche or Ilumán if you want.

Taxi You can always hire a taxi from Quito for a few hours and have them take you exactly where you want to go. A taxi for the day can be hired for about US$50 or US$60 if you have any bargaining ability – not too bad if you split it three or four ways.

AROUND OTAVALO
Many of the Indians live and work in the nearby villages of Peguche, Ilumán and Agato. These are loosely strung together on the east side of the Panamericana, a few kilometers northeast of Otavalo, and can be reached by bus or taxi, on foot or with a tour. There are many other Otavaleño villages in the area, and a visit to the tourist agencies in Otavalo will yield much information. The villages southwest of Laguna San Pablo are known for the manufacture of fireworks, tortora reed mats and other reed objects.

Although people are generally friendly, bear in mind that on Saturday afternoon after the market, as well as on Sunday, some of the Indians get blind drunk (as happens throughout the Andes); you may, therefore, find this an inopportune time to visit.

Unfortunately, I have also received a report of armed robberies of people hiking in the area, especially to the Cascadas de Peguche. Ask for local advice before going out on foot, and go with friends or a group.

Peguche
A popular walk heads out of Otavalo to the north and then east off the main highway – you'll be in Peguche in about an hour. Some people go in the hopes of being invited into the Indians' houses and buying the best weavings direct from the loom at bargain prices. That's wishful thinking. Prices aren't much (if at all) lower than in Otavalo, and people have better things to do than invite curious gringos into their

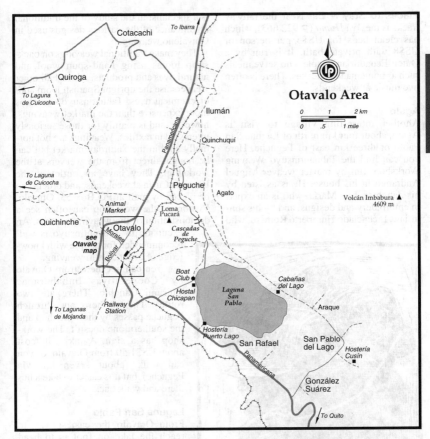

Otavalo Area

NORTH QUITO

houses. On the other hand, the locals are friendly and you might be lucky – especially if you speak Spanish (or Quichua!). One place that may allow visits is Tejidos Mimahuasi, owned by weavers José María Cotacachi and Luz María Fichabamba. (On Saturday you can find them at stall No 61 in Otavalo.)

On the central plaza of Peguche, the Centro Pachacutic sometimes has folklórica concerts.

Another way of reaching Peguche from Otavalo is simply by taking a train or walking northeast along the railway tracks for about three km. The Coopera-

tiva Imbaburapac Chirumi Canchic has some buses that go through Peguche en route to Agato.

You can continue northeast on foot to Ilumán, four or five km away, or east to Agato, three or four km from Peguche. About one or two km southeast of Peguche are some waterfalls, **Las Casacadas de Peguche**, that are reportedly managed by the Fundación Natura in Quito. Near the falls are some pre-Columbian ruins in poor condition. A small entry fee may be charged at weekends. A trail leads to the falls from the railway line. Ask locals for directions and advice.

Places to Stay & Eat Near the railway tracks is the *Aya Huma* (☎ 922 663), which has clean beds for US$5 per person or US$8 with private bath. It is run by a Dutch-Ecuadorian couple who serve meals such as homemade pancakes. There is often live music at weekends.

Agato

Another interesting village to visit is Agato, about four km north of Laguna San Pablo or three km east of Peguche. Here you can find the Tahuantinsuyo Weaving Workshop, run by master weaver Miguel Andrango in his house. He is assisted by his daughter, Luz María, who is an expert in embroidery and designs, and by his son-in-law, Licenciado Humberto Romero, who is a specialist in the study of the traditional significance of the various designs used in Otavaleño weaving.

They make traditional weavings on back-strap looms using hand-spun wool and natural dyes and products. Almost all other weavers use the upright Spanish loom and/or chemical dyes. Tahuantinsuyo's work is more expensive than the market weavings, however, and is mainly for those seriously interested in textiles. Weavings are not normally sold in the Saturday market but can be bought direct from the weavers at the workshop. They have an outlet at the Hostería Cusín at weekends, and orders can be placed by mail at PO Box 53, Otavalo. Visitors to the workshop can often see a demonstration of the weaving process. An excursion to Tahuantinsuyo is well recommended for people with knowledge of or interest in weaving.

You can get there from Otavalo by Cooperativa Imbaburapac Chirumi Canchic. There are two routes: The northern one through Peguche passes by the workshop and the southern one doesn't. The workshop has a sign. A taxi will cost about US$1.50 from Otavalo, or you can walk (about seven km via Peguche), but it is easier to take a bus there and walk back.

Laguna San Pablo

From Otavalo the easiest way to reach the lake on foot is to head roughly southeast on any of the paths heading over the hill behind the railway station. When you get to the lake you'll find a (mostly paved) road encircling it, with beautiful views of the Volcán Imbabura to the northeast. You pass through the village of San Pablo del Lago and end up on the Panamericana.

Ilumán

This village is just off the Panamericana, about seven km northeast of Otavalo. This is another place to see weavers at work. The Conterón family runs a small handicrafts store, Artesanías Inti Chumbi, on the 2nd floor of their house on the Parque Central. Apart from weavings and embroidered work, one of their specialties is very attractive Otavaleño dolls. Weaving demonstrations can be arranged. Cuy can be ordered and prepared here if you order it a day in advance. This village is reputedly a good destination during Otavaleño fiesta times because there are few tourists.

The easiest way to get here is to take the Transportes 8 de Septiembre bus from Otavalo. Alternately, walk out along the Panamericana or along the railway tracks past Peguche.

Lagunas de Mojanda
These beautiful lakes are set in high páramo scenery about 17 km almost due south of Otavalo. Camping is possible on the south side of the biggest lake and there is a basic stone refuge (bring sleeping bag and food). Fuya Fuya, a jagged, extinct volcano (4263 meters), is nearby. You can walk to the lakes or get there by taxi; there is a dirt road from Otavalo, and a taxi charges about US$10 roundtrip. You can make a good day trip by taking a taxi first thing in the morning and hiking back.

From the lakes, it is possible to hike across the páramo about 20 km due south to the ruins of Cochasquí. The views are fantastic on clear days. The useful 1:50,000 topographical map of the Mojanda area, numbered ÑII-F1, 3994-III, is available from the IGM in Quito.

COTACACHI
This small village, some 15 km north of Otavalo and just west of the Panamericana, is famous for its leatherwork. Stores are strung out all along the main street, and you can find almost anything you might want in the way of leather goods. Market day is Saturday. Most tourists just pay a quick visit to the stores and return to Ibarra or Otavalo, but if you wander around to the right of the main street, you'll find an attractive main plaza.

Places to Stay & Eat
The hotel *El Mesón de las Flores* (☎ 915 009/264, fax 955 270, 915 828), at García Moreno and Sucre, is in a lovely building over two centuries old. Both US$30 and US$60 have been quoted for a double with private bath (I suspect 'gringo pricing'), and there is a good bar and restaurant.

The elegant *Hostería La Mirage* (☎ 915 237, fax 915 065) is an attractive country hotel with antique furniture, bar, restaurant, fireplace, exercise room, sauna, small swimming pool, tennis court, horseback riding and tame birds. The hotel is in pleasant gardens almost a kilometer out of town. There are about two dozen spacious rooms, each with a fireplace (the staff will light a fire on request) and attractively carved furniture. This place is definitely romantic. Rates are US$170 for a double, including taxes, dinners and breakfasts (served in bed, if you wish). The hotel is often full at weekends, so reservations are recommended. The restaurant is also very good; Saturday lunch is packed with shoppers from the Otavalo market.

There's also a cheaper restaurant at the corner of the small plaza on the main road. The *Restaurant La Estancia* is next to the hospital and open at weekends. You can eat cuy here.

There are reportedly a couple of cheap hotels, which I didn't get the chance to check out. Ask around.

A few kilometers away near the turn to Cotacachi just off the Panamericana, the 200-year-old *Hacienda Pinsaquí* is an elegant country home with seven lovely guest rooms and a renowned riding stable. One report claims that the owner has been known to lead his favorite stallion through the French doors of the lounge to the fireplace to meet the guests! Rooms are US$72/96; reservations can be made through the Hostería Cusín (see Places to Stay in Otavalo) or major travel agents.

Getting There & Away
From Otavalo there are buses at least every hour. *Camionetas* (pickups or light trucks) can be hired from the market at the far end

of town to take you to various local destinations, such as Laguna de Cuicocha.

RESERVA ECOLÓGICA COTACACHI-CAYAPAS

This huge reserve protects western Andean habitats ranging from Volcán Cotacachi down to the northwestern coastal lowlands (see the North Coast chapter for more details). One cannot travel from the highland to lowland part of the reserve except by very difficult bushwhacking. Most visitors either visit the lowlands from San Miguel on the Río Cayapas or the highlands around Laguna de Cuicocha, described below.

LAGUNA DE CUICOCHA

Driving west some 18 km from the town of Cotacachi, you come to an ancient, eroded volcanic crater famous for the deep lake found within. The crater is on the lower southern flanks of Volcán Cotacachi. Just before arriving at the lake, you will pass the entrance to the Reserva Ecológica Cotacachi-Cayapas. In the past, a nominal entrance fee was charged, but there was no fee recently.

At the lake, cheap boat rides are available to take you on a half-hour trip around the islands in the middle. On sunny weekends it is often popular with the locals, but at other times this facility may not be operating. Just watching everyone hanging around waiting for a boat can be more interesting than the ride itself. The view of the three-km-wide deep blue lake and the extinct Volcán Cotacachi behind it is quite impressive.

A path follows the edge of the lake, sometimes along the shore and often inland because of cliffs. A profusion of flowers, including orchids, attracts hummingbirds. Views of the lake and surrounding mountains are excellent when the weather is good. The trail begins near the reserve entrance booth and circles the lake counterclockwise. Ask the guards at the booth for details. Allow about six hours for the complete circuit and bear in mind that the path becomes rather faint in places, particularly

on the far side of the lake. Consider going as far as the trail is easy to follow and backtracking.

Note that the blue berries growing around the lake are poisonous.

Places to Stay & Eat

On the lakeshore *Parador Cuicocha* was once a hotel, but today there is a nowhere to stay. Instead it houses a basic restaurant that is open intermittently. Prices are medium to high. Camping is allowed near the lake; inquire at the guard booth for directions.

Getting There & Away

A group can hire a taxi or pickup from Cotacachi for about US$10, including waiting time at the lake and the return trip. One-way fares by taxi or truck cost about US$4 from Cotacachi. Buses pass the lake en route to Apuela from Otavalo.

You can avoid the main roads (the Panamericana from Otavalo to the Cotacachi turnoff, and then the paved road through Cotacachi to the lake) either by hiking along the more direct, unpaved road between the lake and Cotacachi, or by taking the old road between the lake and Otavalo (a long day hike). The 1:50,000 Otavalo map numbered ÑII-F1, 3994-IV is recommended for this region.

APUELA

West of Laguna de Cuicocha the road reaches its highest point and begins to drop down the western slopes of the Andes. The scenery is splendidly rugged, and this is an opportunity to see some of the remoter, less-visited parts of the highlands. Some 40 km west of Cuicocha you reach the village of Apuela, set in subtropical forests at about 2000 meters above sea level. The people are very friendly and will direct you to thermal springs, about an hour's walk away from the village along the main road to the west.

Places to Stay & Eat

There are two cheap and very basic pensiones. The *Hostal Veritas* is on the plaza and the friendly *Residencial Don Luis* is a couple of blocks away up the hill. There is a simple restaurant across the street from the Residencial Don Luis.

Near the thermal springs are the *Cabañas Río Grande,* with rustic cabins sleeping four for about US$20. Zulaytur in Otavalo can make a reservation.

In the nearby little village of Santa Rosa (not marked on most maps), look for a house with a 'Tourism Cabins' sign. They can direct you to **Bosque Nublado de Santo Tomás**, set in cloud forest similar to that at the Intag reserve (see below). It's about a one-hour walk from Santa Rosa, and you can stay there for US$20 per person per day, including meals.

Getting There & Away
There are two or three buses per day from Otavalo, more on Saturday, and these are often crowded. Try Transportes Otavalo and Transportes Cotacachi. Beyond Apuela there are more remote villages including Santa Rosa; inquire in Apuela about transportation between them.

INTAG CLOUD FOREST RESERVE
This private 500-hectare reserve is in part a working 200-hectare farm and in part primary and secondary forest. It lies between 1850 to 2800 meters in the western Andes near Apuela, a two-hour ride followed by a one-hour hike from Otavalo. The surrounding subtropical cloud forest is rich in flora and fauna, and birdlife is prolific; a list of the most common species is available. Orchids bloom during the dry season (from July to September). The rainy season – Intag gets about 250 cm of rain annually – is from October to May, with most rain falling in the afternoons and evenings; mornings are usually sunny. Much of the surrounding forest is threatened, and some has already been logged. The owners of the reserve, who are active in the local conservation movement, can fill you in on the details.

A rustic lodge provides clean, simple rooms (no electricity) that may have to be shared. Bathrooms are separate, and the showers are solar heated. The meals consist mainly of local produce, with a vegetarian emphasis, though chicken and dairy products are also available.

Up to 12 guests can be accommodated at a cost of US$45 per person per day with a minimum of six people. Smaller groups are charged US$67 per person per day. There is a two-night minimum stay. All meals and the services of a bilingual guide are included. Activities include horseback riding, fishing and hiking. Reservations are essential and should be made two months in advance with Carlos Zorrilla/ Sandy Statz, Intag Cloud Forest Reserve, Casilla 18, Otavalo, Imbabura, Ecuador. Alternately, Safari Tours in Quito can help by forwarding reservations. Most guests have strong interests in conservation and natural history.

If you are unable to make a reservation, the owners suggest you try the nearby Bosque Nublado Santo Tomás (see Apuela). Travelers are not encouraged to drop in at Intag.

IBARRA
Just 22 km north of Otavalo and 115 km north of Quito is the attractive colonial town of Ibarra. With a population of about 80,000, it is the provincial capital of Imbabura. The elevation at the train station is 2210 meters, making Ibarra several hundred meters lower than most highland cities, which results in a pleasant climate. One main reason travelers come here is to take the train from Ibarra to San Lorenzo on the coast. Others choose to stay here as a base for explorations of the Otavalo area. It's certainly less touristy than Otavalo.

There's not much to do in Ibarra itself, but I enjoy the town because it's picturesque and old fashioned. Horse-drawn carts clatter along cobbled streets flanked by colonial buildings, dark-suited old gentlemen sit in the shady parks discussing the day's events and most good folks are in bed by 10 pm. It's a relaxing sort of place. Many of Ibarra's houses are in the colonial style. Red-tiled and whitewashed, they have given Ibarra the nickname of *la ciudad blanca* (the white city).

NORTH QUITO

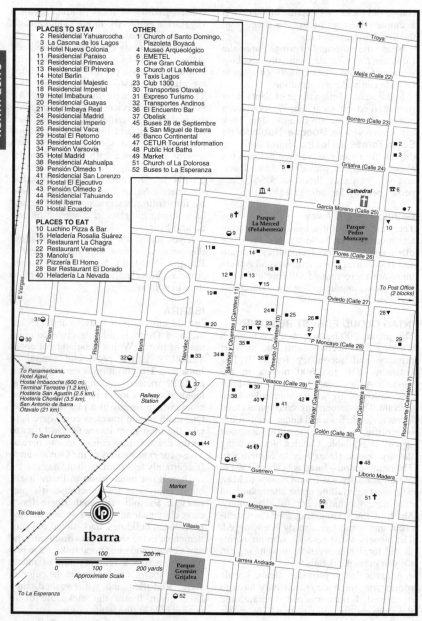

PLACES TO STAY
2 Residencial Yahuarcocha
3 La Casona de los Lagos
5 Hotel Nueva Colonia
11 Residencial Paraíso
12 Residencial Primavera
13 Residencial El Príncipe
14 Hotel Berlín
16 Residencial Majestic
18 Residencial Imperial
19 Hotel Imbabura
20 Residencial Guayas
21 Hotel Imbaya Real
24 Residencial Madrid
25 Residencial Imperio
26 Residencial Vaca
29 Hostal El Retorno
33 Residencial Colón
34 Pensión Varsovia
35 Hotel Madrid
38 Residencial Atahualpa
39 Pensión Olmedo 1
41 Residencial San Lorenzo
42 Hostal El Ejecutivo
43 Pensión Olmedo 2
44 Residencial Tahuando
49 Hotel Ibarra
50 Hostal Ecuador

PLACES TO EAT
10 Luchino Pizza & Bar
15 Heladería Rosalía Suárez
17 Restaurant La Chagra
22 Restaurant Venecia
23 Manolo's
27 Pizzería El Horno
28 Bar Restaurant El Dorado
40 Heladería La Nevada

OTHER
1 Church of Santo Domingo,
   Plazoleta Boyacá
4 Museo Arqueológico
6 EMETEL
7 Cine Gran Colombia
8 Church of La Merced
9 Taxis Lagos
23 Club 1300
30 Transportes Otavalo
31 Expreso Turismo
32 Transportes Andinos
36 El Encuentro Bar
37 Obelisk
45 Buses 28 de Septiembre
   & San Miguel de Ibarra
46 Banco Continental
47 CETUR Tourist Information
48 Public Hot Baths
49 Market
51 Church of La Dolorosa
52 Buses to La Esperanza

Ibarra

0   100   200 m
0   100   200 yards
Approximate Scale

Market day is Saturday, and as most tourists go to Otavalo on Saturday, the Ibarra market is full of locals. After the market, the local men play *pelota de guante*, an Ecuadorian paddleball game. It's a strange game played with a small, soft ball and large, spiked paddles that look like medieval torture implements. I couldn't figure out the rules.

Ibarra's annual fiesta is held during the last weekend in September, when the hotels are often booked ahead.

Orientation

Ibarra can be roughly divided into two areas. The southeast area around the railway station is the busiest and has the bulk of the cheap hotels, while to the north are the main plazas and the older buildings, in a generally quieter and more pleasant area.

Streets in Ibarra are both numbered and named. Roughly, north-south streets are numbered calles, and east-west streets are numbered carreteras. Both numbers and names appear on the street signs, but names seem more widely in use. I use names throughout this section.

Information

Tourist Offices The CETUR information office is at Colón 7-43 and Olmedo. Hours are erratic.

Money The Banco Continental, Olmedo 11-67 and Colón, will change US cash dollars and traveler's checks, at rates a little below Quito's. There used to be a casa de cambio, which is now closed, but there may be another open by the time you visit Ibarra. It's best to bring enough sucres with you to last throughout your stay.

Post & Communications The post office is at Juan de Salinas 6-64, two blocks east of the map. The EMETEL office is half a block north of Parque Pedro Moncayo on Sucre. The area code for Ibarra and the province of Imbabura is 06.

Note that Ibarra has slowly changed its telephone prefixes from 950 and 951 to 955, 956 and 957. A few places still have the old prefixes, but this may change by the time you read this. If you have problems with the 950 or 951 prefixes, try the others and see if that helps.

Things to See & Do

The **Parque La Merced** (also known as Peñaherrera) has a small museum and a church with a representation of the Virgin – **Virgin of La Merced** - a huge statue on top of the building. Inside, there is an ornate altar. In the middle of the park there is a bust of Victor Manuel Peñaherrera (1865-1930), the Ibarra-born university professor who was deacon of the Faculty of Law in the Central University and a judge on the Supreme Court during his lifetime.

The larger, tree-filled **Parque Pedro Moncayo** is dominated by the cathedral. Pedro Moncayo (1807-88) was an Ibarra-born journalist and diplomat.

Out at the north end of Bolívar is the quaint little **Plazoleta Boyacá** with a monument to Simón Bolívar to commemorate his victory at the Battle of Ibarra on July 17, 1823. It depicts the incongruous scene of an Andean condor attacking an African lion.

Behind this small square, the modern concrete-block church of **Santo Domingo** is topped by a huge statue of Saint Dominic with a giant rosary swinging in the wind. Some people may enjoy viewing the paintings in the rather garish interior. A few of the paintings seem rather tongue-in-cheek: An old-fashioned representation of Jesus throwing the moneylenders out of the temple depicts one of the throng clutching a bag marked '$1000 Petroleo.' The church also has a museum of religious art (open 9 am to noon, and 3 to 6 pm, Monday to Saturday; there is a small admission charge).

Also of interest is the church of **La Dolorosa** on Sucre and Mosquera. This was built in 1928, but the domed roof collapsed completely during the earthquake of 1987. It has since been rebuilt.

Apart from visiting these plazas and churches, there's not much to do. The small, private **Museo Arqueológico** on the Plaza La Merced is open occasionally.

Language Courses

The Imbabura Spanish Center (☎ 959 429), directed by Miguel and Bernarda Ponce, Apartado 1001505, Ibarra, Imbabura, arranges one-on-one tuition for US$3 an hour and homestays with meals for US$15 a day. Study-tour packages are also available. Call them for directions to their school, which is in a private house away from the center, at Urbanización La Victoria, Manzana 33, Casa 10.

Places to Stay – bottom end

There are many cheap hotels in Ibarra. The highest concentration of places to stay is near the railway station. Many cost only US$2 or US$3, but are not particularly attractive – basic, noisy with train traffic, and usually with only cold water. There are a few decent budget hotels, however. Generally speaking, Ibarra has some of the cheapest accommodations anywhere in Ecuador.

Hotels charging just under US$2 per person include the *Residencial San Lorenzo*, Olmedo 10-56, and *Residencial Paraiso*, Flores 9-53, which sometimes have warm showers. These two are the best of the super-cheapies.

Other very basic places charging under US$2 are the *Pensión Varsovia*, *Residencial Guayas* and *Residencial El Principe*. At about US$2.25 per person are *Pensión Olmedo 1*, which looks OK from the outside but is pretty basic inside; the *Pensión Olmedo 2*; the *Residencial Tahuando*; the *Hotel Berlin*; and the *Residencial Atahualpa*. A recent guest at the Berlin reports that it's a reasonable value for the low price, and a few rooms have plaza views. The *Residencial Majestic*, Olmedo 7-63, has pretty reliable hot water and charges US$2.25 per person, or US$3 with private bath.

The friendly *Hotel Imbabura*, Oviedo 9-33, has a pretty little courtyard with flowers. The best rooms are on the quiet street; inner rooms can be dark. There are warm showers. Rates are a decent value at US$2.75 per person. Similarly priced and also a fair value is the *Residencial Imperial*, Bolívar 6-22, which has rooms with

private baths. Others at this price are the *Residencial Primavera*, where rooms vary from poor to OK, and the *Residencial Yahuarcocha*; both have hot water. The *Residencial Vaca*, Bolívar 7-53, has basic rooms with private bath and warm water for US$3.20 per person, as does the *Residencial Imperio*, which is not as clean.

The popular (but often full by 3 pm) *Residencial Colón* (☎ 950 093), at Narváez 8-62, is clean, friendly, pleasant and has hot showers at times. Rooms with bath are US$4.50 per person, and a little less for standard bath. They have laundry service. The newer *Hostal El Retorno* (☎ 957 722), P Moncayo 4-32, has fair-size rooms with private bath and 24-hour warm showers, some with TV, at about US$4 per person – a good deal. They have a restaurant, as does the *Hostal Ecuador* (☎ 956-425), Mosquera 5-54. This is currently the best budget value at US$5 per person for clean, spacious rooms with private hot shower. Another place in this price range is the *Hostal Imbacocha* (☎ 950 800), out of town on the Panamericana, across the street from the expensive Hotel Ajaví.

For something a bit more upmarket, try the *Residencial Madrid* (☎ 951 760), Olmedo 8-57, which has carpeted rooms with TV; the *Hotel Madrid* (☎ 956 177), Moncayo 7-41, with a restaurant attached; and the *Hostal El Ejecutivo* (☎ 956 575), Bolívar 9-69. All these have doubles with private hot shower for about US$14, but they have only a few singles. The El Ejecutivo also has some rooms with shared bath for US$6/9.

Places to Stay – middle

The best hotels in the town center include the nice-looking *Hotel Nueva Colonia* (☎ 952 918, 955 543), Olmedo 5-19 and Grijalva. They charge US$11/16 for carpeted rooms with private bath and telephone. There is a restaurant. The *Hotel Imbaya Real* (☎ 953 993, 959 729), P Moncayo 7-44, also has nice-looking rooms at about this price. The *Hotel Ibarra* (☎ 955 091), Mosquera 6-158 and Sánchez y Cifuentes, has adequate rooms with private bath and telephone for US$10 per person, and it has a restaurant. The best place in this price range is *La Casona de los Lagos* (☎ 957 844, fax 951 629), Sucre 3-50 and Grijalva. They have a nice-looking restaurant and a sauna. Clean, pleasant rooms are US$14/21.

The better hotels are west of town, on or just off of the Panamericana south toward Otavalo. The first-class (by Ibarra standards) *Hotel Ajaví* (☎ 955 221/787/555, fax 952 485) is halfway between town and the terminal terrestre, just under one km west of the town center. The hotel is modern and boasts a good restaurant and bar, swimming pool, and sauna. Rooms are clean and spacious but unexciting. Singles/doubles with TV, telephone and mini-fridge cost about US$40/50. A kilometer beyond the terminal terrestre is the *Hostería San Agustín* (☎ 955 888) in a pretty site 200 or 300 meters off the Panamericana. The pleasant rooms for about US$22/30, and there's a decent restaurant.

Almost four km west of Ibarra is the best hotel in the area, the *Hostería Chorlaví* (☎ 955 777, fax 956 311; 522 703 in Quito). With plenty of Old-World charm, it is in a converted hacienda and has pretty gardens, a (cold) swimming pool and an excellent restaurant/bar. They have a famous buffet-style lunch with folklórica at weekends, which is very popular with well-off Ecuadorians and tour groups after the Otavalo market – perhaps a bit too touristy for some travelers' tastes. There are both rooms in the old hacienda building and cabins on the grounds. Rates are about US$35/45 depending on the room. Meals are about US$8. If this hotel is full, the smaller and similarly priced *Hostería Rancho de Carolina* (☎ 953 215, ☎ /fax 955 215) is almost next door and has been recommended as clean and comfortable.

The good hotels are often booked well in advance, particularly at weekends. Make reservations if possible.

Places to Eat
The *Restaurant La Chagra*, Olmedo 7-48, has large helpings and reasonable prices. It is popular with the locals, maybe because it has a large-screen TV. There are also several good and cheap chifas on this street – look around and take your pick. *Luchino Pizza & Bar*, on the Parque Pedro Moncayo, has Italian food and snacks and has been recommended by several travelers for its pizzas. Another reasonable choice is the good *Pizzería El Horno*, Moncayo 6-30. The *Restaurant Venecia*, P Moncayo 7-28, has also been recommended for inexpensive food.

Manolo's at the corner of P Moncayo and Olmedo is popular with students and young people. It serves snacks and beer, and has a friendly English-speaking owner. For desserts, juices and ice cream, try the *Heladería Nevada* on Velasco 8-37. Locals say that the best ice cream is in the traditional *Heladería Rosalia Suárez*, Oviedo 7-82. Doña Rosalia reportedly started the ice cream shop when she was 16 and was reputed to be 105 years old when she died in 1985. Her granddaughter runs it now using the old-fashioned *helados de paila* technique in which cream is spun in a copper pail on a bed of straw and ice.

The *Bar Restaurant El Dorado*, on Oviedo near Sucre, is trying to be the best place in town, judging by the white tablecloths and shining silverware. The meals, especially the seafood dishes, are good and medium priced. The better hotels (out of town) serve excellent meals.

Entertainment
Ibarra is a quiet city and even on Saturday nights there is little going on. There are a couple of cinemas. A popular bar to hang out in is *El Encuentro* at Olmedo 9-35 near Velasco. They have a rustic ambiance (old leather saddles and strange implements hang from the walls) and music occasionally. Both *Luchino Pizza & Bar* and *Club 1300* (in Manolo's) are also nice places for a beer. Occasionally peñas are advertised, but locals are more likely to go into Otavalo for weekend nightlife.

Getting There & Away
Bus Buses from Quito depart from the

Terminal Terrestre de Cumandá all day, once or twice an hour. The trip can take from 2½ to four hours, depending on the company. The fastest is Transportes Andinos, but the buses are small and uncomfortable and you may conclude that the driver has suicidal tendencies. Other companies will take you more slowly and safely. They all charge about US$2. There are also frequent buses from Otavalo and Tulcán.

Ibarra's terminal terrestre, on the Panamericana just over a kilometer west of the town center, has been closed since 1994. It should reopen by the time you read this; meanwhile, buses leave from the places shown on the map.

There are frequent departures for Quito, Tulcán (US$2; three hours) and Otavalo (30 minutes). Buses to Otavalo run from 5:30 am to 9:30 pm.

Several times a day there is direct bus service to several other major towns. These trips usually involve a stop in Quito but save you from having to look for another bus terminal in the capital. If you can't get on the train to San Lorenzo, there are five daily buses to Esmeraldas (US$6; eight hours). Several buses go to Guayaquil (US$6 to US$8; 10 hours). Reportedly, during the 1996 dry season a twice-daily bus service to San Lorenzo was begun on the newly constructed road.

There are also buses to less important towns such as Tumbabiro – ask around.

Train It used to be that you could get from Quito to Ibarra by train, but this service has been discontinued for years now. An autoferro runs irregularly between Ibarra and Otavalo; in 1995 there were no trains, but in 1996 there were four or five daily departures for the one-hour ride. This is likely to continue to change.

The train service of most interest to travelers is the Ibarra-San Lorenzo railway, which links the highlands with the coast. The scenery en route is quite spectacular. You drop from Ibarra at 2210 meters to San Lorenzo at sea level 193 km away. Thus you see a good cross-section of Ecuador's western Andean foothills.

The train is usually an autoferro. Most days there is only one departure at 7 am, so seats are limited. A second train is occasionally added. Sometimes, trains run every other day, or, worse still, a variety of problems may close the tracks for weeks on end. Be prepared for disappointment.

If the train is running, it is worth trying to make a reservation on the previous day, although normally you are told that you must buy tickets on the day of departure. This is notoriously difficult, especially around the weekend – huge crowds of people push and shove to try and get their money into the tiny opening in the ticket window, and you have to be pretty obnoxious to obtain a ticket. There are always thieves working the crowds – keep valuables well hidden on your body. If you try the day before and are told 'No reservations,' slipping the clerk 2000 sucres or so (approximately US$1) often results in a ticket. Of course it's not ethical, but the dual pricing system has also been criticized as unethical. Foreigners pay US$15 while locals pay about US$2 – there's not much you can do about that. In 1996 the road from Ibarra to San Lorenzo reportedly has been completed, though buses don't yet go all the way. Soon they will, rendering the train journey obsolete. Charging foreigners inflated rates may be the only way to keep the service economically feasible.

The journey is scheduled to take about seven hours, but in reality it often takes twice as long. Delays caused by landslides, breakdowns and cows on the track are the norm. If there are two trains leaving, try to get on the first one – most of the line is single track, so a disabled train blocks the way. Every few weeks, a landslide (be prepared to help dig if it's only a small slide!) will close the track for a few days, and getting tickets for the next available train isn't easy. In short, it can be an exciting or a frustrating trip, depending on your point of view.

En route to San Lorenzo most of the drop in elevation occurs during the first half of the trip as you descend along the Río Mira valley, with good white-water views on the right side of the train. This is the steepest section and the most prone to closure. When the section is closed, the train company may provide buses to a station farther down the track. At several stops fruit and other food can be purchased, but bringing a water bottle and some emergency food is advised. Once in San Lorenzo you can continue along the north coast by boat. There are no roads except the recently constructed one from Ibarra, which may be open.

If the weather looks at all reasonable, ride up on the roof of the train for excitement and great views. It can be a struggle to get on, but try.

Taxi If you are in a real hurry to get back to Quito, you could use Taxis Lagos (☎ 955 150) on the Parque La Merced. They charge about US$6 per person and cram six passengers into a large taxi. The taxis leave five or six times a day for the 2¼-hour ride.

Getting Around
Local buses with the companies 28 de Septiembre and San Miguel de Ibarra (see map) provide service to the terminal terrestre when it is open. Some of their buses continue to San Antonio de Ibarra. Different buses leave from the same street for several other local destinations. An exception is the bus to La Esperanza, which leaves about once an hour from Parque Germán Grijalva near the east end of Avenida Sánchez y Cifuentes.

SAN ANTONIO DE IBARRA
This village, which is almost a suburb of Ibarra, is famous for its woodcarving. There's little wood found in the Ibarra area, so most of it comes from the Ecuadorian jungles. Cedar and walnut are among the more frequently used woods. The village has a pleasant main square, around which stands a number of stores, poorly disguised as 'workshops' or 'factories.' The most famous is the Galería Luís Potosí, which has some of the best carvings.

Señor Potosí is famous throughout Ecuador and his work sells all over the world.

Some of his best pieces – selling for hundreds of dollars – are on display in the upstairs section of his gallery. The atmosphere is totally relaxed; no high-pressure salesperson breathes down your neck while you inspect the work.

A warning, though: Should you decide to purchase a large carving and have it shipped home, it's best to arrange for the shipping yourself. Some friends of mine bought a carving, left a deposit for it to be shipped back, and found out many months later that their carving had been sold to someone else a few days later. They received their deposit back, but were very disappointed – their once-in-a-lifetime art investment had been sold to someone who paid cash and carried it out.

Not all the pieces are expensive, and you can buy small, mass-produced carvings for a couple of dollars. Various subjects are depicted, but the favorites seem to be beggars, religious statues and nude women.

Some people recommend that the best deals and selections are to be found on the streets away from the main square. Frankly, I couldn't see any difference.

Places to Stay & Eat
The only accommodations are at is the *Hostería Los Nogales* (☎ 955 000), with rooms from US$3 per person. Most visitors stay in Ibarra or Otavalo. There are no proper restaurants in San Antonio de Ibarra; one place, a block off the main plaza, serves greasy hamburgers and hot dogs.

Getting There & Away
Transportation from Ibarra is frequent during daylight hours. Buses drop you off at the main plaza. The 15-minute ride costs just a few cents. Or you could walk the five km or so west on the Panamericana from Ibarra.

LA ESPERANZA
This is a pretty little village in the country six or seven km due south of Ibarra. It is a good place for budget travelers looking for peace and quiet to stay. There's nothing to do except talk to the locals and take walks

in the surrounding countryside. It's supposed to be a good area to look for the San Pedro cactus.

Volcán Imbabura (4609 meters) is about nine km to the southwest as the crow flies. It is easier to climb this mountain from La Esperanza than from the Laguna San Pablo side. The nine km look deceptively close – remember that you are not a flying crow and that the summit is about 2000 meters higher than La Esperanza. There is a maze of tracks heading towards the summit, but you'll have to scramble the last bit – ask the locals for directions. Allow about 10 hours for the roundtrip including time at the top for photographs of Laguna San Pablo way below you.

If Imbabura seems like too ambitious of a climb, try Loma Cubilche (3836 meters). This hill is about eight km almost due south of La Esperanza. It's an easier climb and also offers good views. If climbing doesn't appeal to you at all, you can take the cobbled road through pretty countryside to the south – buses go along here occasionally.

Places to Stay & Eat
There is only one very basic but friendly hotel which costs about US$3 per person – the *Casa Aida*. You can get good, simple and cheap meals here. This is a good place to get information and directions for local walks. There is also the small *Restaurant María*, which rents a basic room.

Getting There & Away
Buses from the Parque Germán Grijalva in Ibarra serve the village frequently along a cobbled country road and irregularly continue farther south through Olmedo to Cayambe. Buses are crowded at weekends.

NORTH OF IBARRA
As you drive north from Ibarra on the Panamericana you soon pass the highly touted tourist site of **Lago Yaguarcocha** (Quichua for 'lake of blood'). It was so called after a battle between the Incas and the Caras, when the latter's bodies were supposedly thrown into the lake, turning the water red. There's not much to see

except for a racetrack around the lake; it is used for auto racing during the annual fiesta at the end of September. You can walk to the lake in a couple of hours from Ibarra – head east on Oviedo to the edge of town, cross the river, and head north – or take a taxi. There is a hotel on the edge of the lake, the *Cabañas Conquistador* (☎ 955 500). Rooms are about US$20 for a double with bath and there is a restaurant.

The Panamericana soon drops quite steeply to the Río Chota valley at about 1565 meters before beginning the long climb to San Gabriel at almost 2900 meters. The warm and dusty **Chota** area is inhabited by reserved but friendly black people, whose ancestors were originally brought in as slaves in the 17th century. They now make their living growing fruit. Chota is less than an hour from Ibarra and can be visited on day trips. Fiestas and concerts in Chota may occasionally be advertised in Ibarra – the music is a weird and wonderful mix of plaintive Andean and driving African sounds. It's worth hearing if you get the chance.

After leaving Chota, the Panamericana crosses the provincial line from Imbabura into Carchi. The road passes the little town of Bolívar capital of the canton of the same name, and a few kilometers farther by the village of La Paz. Near La Paz are thermal springs and waterfalls, as well as a grotto containing stalactites and a famous statue of the Virgin. There are buses to the springs from Tulcán, or you can walk about five km southeast of the Panamericana from La Paz on a road signed for the 'Grutas.' The complex (thermal springs, pool and grotto) is open from Thursday to Sunday. There is reportedly a hotel open sporadically near the grotto, though I haven't checked it personally (send me a postcard if you go there). The road in this area is steep, winding and rather slow, and the scenery is wild.

SAN GABRIEL
This is the next town of any size north of Ibarra along the Panamericana. It's almost 90 km away from Ibarra but only 38 km from the border town of Tulcán. It's not a

particularly interesting place, but I mention it here because Tulcán hotels are occasionally full and this is the nearest place to stay. It's also a good place to go if you want to be the only gringo in town.

At San Gabriel there is a bus stop on the Panamericana; many buses don't enter the town. Walk up the hill on Calle Montalvo for two blocks and then turn right onto Calle Bolívar, which is the main street. Walk three blocks, passing the church, until you reach the Plaza Central. Here there is a startling nude statue of Bolívar, the liberator – imagine a nude George Washington in a small US town.

Three and four km north of town (head north on Calle Bolívar and keep going) there are the two Cascadas (waterfalls) de Paluz on the Río San Gabriel. One of the falls is about 60 meters high.

Heading west out of town on Calderón brings you to the old (unpaved) road to the village of El Angel, which bicyclists have recommended as a good three-hour ride along which many *frailejones* (tall páramo plants) grow. It's approximately 20 km.

Places to Stay & Eat

Hotels are basic. The *Residencial Montúfar* (☎ 290 385) is on the plaza at Colón 03-44 and Bolívar. The better-looking *Residencial Ideal* (☎ 290 265) is on Calle Montúfar 08-26 and Sucre, half a block from the plaza. It charges US$2 per person or US$3 with private bath and hot water. Also on the plaza are two or three simple restaurants.

Getting There & Away

The Ciudad de San Gabriel bus company (☎ 290 185) is on the plaza at Montúfar and Colón. It has buses to Quito every 45 minutes from 3 am to 6:30 pm. The five-hour ride costs about US$3.50. For buses to Tulcán it's best to wait on the Panamericana. Alternately, take a jeep colectivo taxi from the plaza; these leave as soon as all the seats are filled.

EL ANGEL

This village is about 20 km west of the Panamericana at San Gabriel. It's an entrance point to the Páramos de El Angel, a wild area of highland vegetation and mists. Among the most notable plants in the páramo are the *frailejones*, a giant member of the daisy family that can grow to two meters in height – an amazing sight. The páramo is one of the few areas in Ecuador where Andean condors are seen, and there are many other intriguing plants and animals.

In 1992 this area became protected by the formation of the **Reserva Ecológica El Angel**, which covers almost 16,000 hectares of páramo. Day tours (about US$10 per person depending on group size) reportedly can be arranged at Grijalva 04-26 in El Angel. The best way to visit the páramo is with the Cerro Golondrinas Project (see the sidebar).

Market day on Monday enlivens El Angel, which is otherwise a very quiet little town.

Places to Stay & Eat

Ofelia López Peñaherrera, Grijalva 02-59 (no sign), rents *basic rooms*. There are no showers and the water is cold, but the family is friendly. Also try the basic *Residencial Viña del Mar* on the main plaza. There is also a restaurant on this plaza.

Getting There & Away

Transportes Espejo on the main plaza goes to Quito, via Ibarra, about once an hour during the day. Buses to Tulcán leave only in the early morning.

RESERVA BIOLÓGICA GUANDERA

This 400-hectare tropical wet montane forest reserve was founded in 1994 by the Fundación Jatun Sacha (see the Western Lowlands and Northern Oriente chapters). The reserve lies between 3100 and 3600 meters on a transitional ridge (forest to páramo) about 11 km east of San Gabriel, near the village of Mariscal Sucre (not found on most maps). Andean spectacled bears and high-altitude parrots and toucans are among the attractions. From the village it is 90 minutes on foot to the reserve, where construction of a station with sleeping rooms began in 1996. Until the building

The Cerro Golondrinas Project

The Cerro Golondrinas area lies west of the new Reserva Ecológica El Angel and encompasses various ecosystems, including páramo and, in its lower elevations, temperate and subtropical montane cloud forest. There are areas of primary forest and páramo interspersed with small local farms. Similar forests on the western slopes of the Ecuadorian and Colombian Andes have been deforested at an alarming rate. The Cerro Golondrinas Project aims to conserve some of the remaining forests while improving the living standards of the farmers who reside in the area.

The project is one of the most successful grassroots conservation undertakings in Ecuador. It involves the cooperation of a small local NGO called Fundación Para El Desarrollo Alternativo (FUNDEAL, Foundation for Alternative Development); the people from a popular budget travelers' hostal in Quito, La Casa de Eliza (see Places to Stay in Quito); and local campesinos.

Cerro Golondrinas has a two-pronged approach to conserving the area. Sustainable agricultural techniques, including (but not limited to) tree nurseries, orchid farms, reforestation projects and seed banks, are being developed as an alternative to the prevalent and highly destructive logging/cattle ranch cycles (see also Ecology & Environment in Facts about the Country). Tourists are encouraged to visit, trek through the area, enjoy the plants and animals, and stay with local families. The local families, in turn, work in sustainable agriculture and as hosts, guides and interpreters for visitors. This ecologically, environmentally and socially responsible form of tourism benefit the locals, protects the forests and provides visitors with an in-depth immersion into this remote region of Ecuador.

Travelers can become involved both as tourists and as volunteers or researchers in the tree nurseries and seed banks, among other possibilities. Four-day treks on foot or horseback led by local guides traverse a cross-section of Andean habitats and offer excellent opportunities for birdwatching and nature study, as well as interaction with local families. The treks cost US$50 per person per day, including all food, accommodations and guiding services. They have been well recommended by a number of readers. During the wet months of October to May, the trails can get very muddy; the best time to go is during the dry season, when departures occur weekly.

Further information is available from Piet Sabbe, Cerro Golondrinas Project Coordinator, c/o La Casa de Eliza (☎ 226 602, fax 566 076), Isabel La Católica 1559, Apartado 17-21-1786, Quito. ∎

is operational, visitors can camp or stay in Mariscal Sucre with the reserve guard, José Cando Rosero (☎ 986 322), who can guide you. A bed is US$4, meals are US$4 (or you can cook for yourself) and guiding service is US$4. Mariscal Sucre is reached from San Gabriel's Plaza Central by school bus at 6 am and 1 pm when school is in session. Otherwise, there are buses on Saturday morning in San Gabriel for the Mariscal Sucre Saturday market, or a taxi costs about US$6. Volunteers and researchers are needed, and natural history buffs are welcome. Reservations should be made at the Jatun Sacha office in Quito (☎ / fax 250 976, 441 592, 253 266), Río Coca 1734, Casilla 17-12-897, Quito.

TULCÁN

This small city of about 40,000 inhabitants is the provincial capital of Carchi. As you drive through, the northernmost province of the Ecuadorian highlands, you see plenty of farms and ranches, particularly as you get close to Tulcán. It is therefore an important market town, but for most travelers its main importance is as the gateway into Ecuador from Colombia, some six km away. In fact, Tulcán is not a particularly interesting town, and most travelers continue on to Colombia or south into Ecuador. There are, however, some interesting trips in the vicinity, described at the end of this chapter.

With the present favorable rate of exchange of the Colombian peso against the

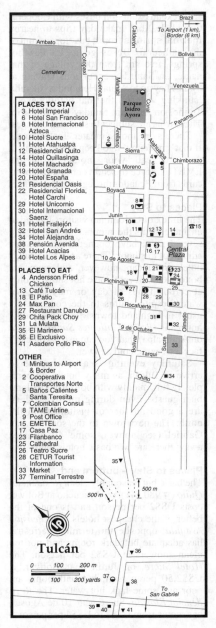

PLACES TO STAY
3 Hotel Imperial
6 Hotel San Francisco
8 Hotel Internacional Azteca
10 Hotel Sucre
11 Hotel Atahualpa
12 Residencial Quito
14 Hotel Quillasinga
16 Hotel Machado
19 Hotel Granada
20 Hotel España
21 Residencial Oasis
22 Residencial Florida, Hotel Carchi
29 Hotel Unicornio
30 Hotel Internacional Saenz
31 Hotel Frailejón
32 Hotel San Andrés
34 Hotel Alejandra
38 Pensión Avenida
39 Hotel Acacias
40 Hotel Los Alpes

PLACES TO EAT
4 Andersson Fried Chicken
13 Café Tulcán
18 El Patio
24 Max Pan
27 Restaurant Danubio
29 Chifa Pack Choy
31 La Mulata
35 El Marinero
36 El Exclusivo
41 Asadero Pollo Piko

OTHER
1 Minibus to Airport & Border
2 Cooperativa Transportes Norte
5 Baños Calientes Santa Teresita
7 Colombian Consul
9 Post Office
15 EMETEL
17 Casa Paz
23 Filanbanco
25 Cathedral
26 Teatro Sucre
28 CETUR Tourist Information
33 Market
37 Terminal Terrestre

Ecuadorian sucre, Tulcán has become very popular for Colombian weekend bargain hunters. There is a Sunday street market (few tourist items), and the hotels are often filled with Colombian shoppers on Saturday night.

At almost 3000 meters above sea level Tulcán has a rather cold climate. It is the highest provincial capital or town of its size in the country.

Orientation
The town is long and narrow, with most activity happening on or near the parallel streets of Bolívar and Sucre. There appear to be two numbering systems for street addresses; to avoid confusion I will not give street numbers in this section, but will refer to the nearest street intersections instead.

Information
Tourist Offices The CETUR information office is at Pichincha and Bolívar. Basic information is also available at the border crossing point, six km away.

Colombian Consulate The consul is on Bolívar at García Moreno, though the hours are sporadic. It's better to check the consulate in Quito for visa requirements.

Money Money exchange is best in Tulcán rather than at the border, except at weekends when you are at the mercy of the street changers. (The bus running between Tulcán and the border accepts both Colombian and Ecuadorian currency.) Filanbanco, on Sucre and 10 de Agosto, is reputedly the only bank doing foreign exchange. Faster service is available at the casas de cambio on Ayacucho, northwest of the central plaza. Casa Paz is the best known; they exchange both pesos and dollars (including traveler's checks at a discount). Rates are normally a little lower than in Quito. There are several other exchange offices nearby; most give rates within 1% of one another.

There are also street changers with their little black attaché cases full of money. They hang out around the border, the banks and the bus terminal. Because there is no real black market, you won't get much better rates from them than from the exchange houses, but they are useful when the other places are closed.

If you are leaving Ecuador, try to change sucres to US dollars, and then change the dollars to pesos when you get to Colombia. If arriving, cash dollars are your strongest currency.

Post & Communications The post office is on Bolívar near Junín. The main EMETEL telephone office is on Olmedo near Junín and there is also a branch at the terminal terrestre, southwest of town. The area code for Tulcán and the province of Carchi is 06.

Things to See & Do
The big tourist attraction in town is the **topiary garden** in the cemetery. Topiary is a form of gardening in which bushes and trees are trimmed and sculpted into animal or geometrical shapes. The Tulcán cemetery is the most striking example of this work in Ecuador and one of the best in Latin America. Behind the cemetery the locals play a strange Ecuadorian paddle-ball game, *pelota de guante* (see the description under Ibarra) at weekends.

Parque Isidro Ayora has a rather striking white **statue** of Abdón Calderón riding a horse. Calderón was a battle-hardened 18-year-old lieutenant fighting against the Spanish Royalists at the decisive Battle of Pichincha, which cemented Ecuador's independence on May 24, 1822. He is famous not only for his youthfulness, but for his tenacity during the battle. Historians report that he was shot in the right arm, causing him to wield his sword with his left hand. A second bullet in the left arm made him drop his sword, but he continued fighting after having one of his soldiers tie the sword to his arm. A third shot in the left leg didn't stop him either. Finally, a bullet tore apart his right leg just as the battle was ending victoriously. He died the next day and was promoted to captain posthumously.

Weekend excursion buses with Cooperativa 11 de Abril make day trips to nearby **thermal springs** from a bus stop in front of the cathedral. Buses go to La Paz hot springs, five km from the village of that name, on Saturday excursions leaving at 8 am. They go to Aguas Hediondas (literally 'stinking waters') thermal baths, beyond Tufiño, on an 8 am Sunday morning trip. These trips are subject to seasonal changes.

There's one movie theater, Teatro Sucre. If that's not enough to keep you enthralled, you can call your mother from the EMETEL office or send your first/last postcards from Ecuador through the post office.

Places to Stay
The influx of Colombian visitors has led to an increase in the number of hotels, and several more have opened since the last edition of this book. There aren't any fancy hotels in Tulcán, however, and many are bottom-end. Several have hot showers only at certain times of day or may lack hot water despite claims to the contrary. As usual in highland towns, there are public hot baths (*Baños Calientes Santa Teresita* on Atahualpa) that you can use if you can't face a freezing cold shower.

Saturday evening is a rotten time to arrive in Tulcán, as many hotels are completely full, mainly with boisterous Colombian guests. Even during midweek, there are a good number of visitors from the north. The next town to the south is San Gabriel (see above), some 40 minutes away; there are two basic hotels there.

Places to Stay – bottom end
The basic but reasonably clean *Residencial Quito* (☎ 980 541), on Ayacucho at Bolívar, costs US$2 per person and is one of the better of the cheapest hotels. The *Pensión Avenida*, opposite the terminal terrestre, has adequate but dark rooms and not too clean showers at US$2 per person. The *Hotel Sucre*, on Junín near Bolívar, is US$2.50 per person, but bathrooms are poor and some lack hot water. The *Residencial Florida*, Sucre near 10 de Agosto, has rooms from US$2 to US$4 per person –

only the US$4 ones have hot water. Next door, the *Hotel Carchi* has clean rooms with shared bath at US$4 per person. The *Hotel Atahualpa*, on Bolívar near Junín, has basic rooms at US$3 per person.

Two decent places near the bus station are the *Hotel Acacias*, where some rooms have a balcony, and the *Hotel Los Alpes*, which also has a restaurant. Both have clean rooms with private bath and TV for US$4.50/7.50. The *Hotel Granada*, on Bolívar near 10 de Agosto, is just OK for US$3.50 per person with shared bath, and the *Residencial Oasis* (☎ 980 342), on 10 de Agosto at Sucre, is reasonable at US$4 per person with private bath. The *Hotel Imperial* (☎ 981 094), on Bolívar at Panama, has nice, light rooms with shared showers at US$4 per person, and the *Hotel San Francisco* (☎ 980 760), Bolívar at García Moreno, seems OK at the same price but with private showers.

Nice places for about US$12 a double (with bath, of course) include the *Hotel Unicornio* (☎ 980 638), Pichincha at Sucre, which has some rooms with TVs or balconies; the *Hotel Quillasinga* (☎ 981 892), Ayacucho on the central plaza, which has TVs, a restaurant and a weekend disco; the *Hotel Alejandra* (☎ 981 784), Sucre at Quito, with a restaurant; and the *Hotel San Andrés*, Sucre and 9 de Octubre, which also has some singles with shared bath for US$4.

Places to Stay – middle

The *Hotel España* (☎ 983 860), Pichincha near Sucre, charges about US$4.50 for singles with shared bath and US$7 per person in nice, light rooms with private bath. The *Hotel Frailejón* (☎ 998 129), Sucre at Rocafuerte, was the first of Tulcán's 'better' hotels. Rooms come with towels, soap and bottled water for US$8/14 and rooms with TV are an extra US$5. Some rooms are rather dark. The hotel is built on different levels and some steps are uneven, so be careful not to trip. Their restaurant is quite good. The *Hotel Internacional Saenz* (☎ 981 916, fax 983 925), across the street, is a newer choice at

US$8.50 per person in clean rooms with TV and telephone. There is a restaurant/bar downstairs, and the management is friendly.

The *Hotel Internacional Azteca* (☎ 981 899, 981 447, fax 980 481), Bolívar near Boyacá, is reputedly the town's 'best' hotel, with a pizzeria, discotheque and bar. Rates are US$12/21 for rooms with TV and phone, but the rooms seem rather worn. A better bet at this price (unless you don't mind a disco) is the new *Hotel Machado*, Bolívar at Ayacucho.

With the increase in the number of hotels in recent years, I would not be surprised if more mid-range hotels opened in the near future.

Places to Stay – near the border

The priciest place to stay in the Tulcán area is near the border, six km away from town. The *Complejo Turístico Rumichaca* (☎ 980 372, 980 276, fax 982 893) is about 300 meters away from the border, and offers a swimming pool (which recently lacked water), restaurant, bar and a discotheque (if you can find someone to open it). Prices are US$18/24 with bath, TV and phone. Rooms are no better than the ones in town, but it is a bit quieter out here.

Places to Eat

Tulcán isn't one of this planet's culinary centers. Many restaurants are only open for lunch and supper, closing in midafternoon. Monday night is a particularly poor night to go out in search of gastronomic adventures, as most of the restaurants are closed.

New *El Patio*, Bolívar 13-91, has large portions and good breakfasts – it's one of Tulcán's best restaurants. *Café Tulcán* has ice cream, pastries and decent breakfasts. *Max Pan* has also been recommended for breakfasts.

Another among the best restaurants is the pricey *La Mulata* in the Hotel Frailejón, serving good Ecuadorian food. In the town center there are the usual chifas, of which the *Chifa Pack Choy* beneath the Hotel Unicornio is the best, according to several travelers. There is a pizzeria in the Hotel Internacional Azteca. For very cheap

Ecuadorian-style food, the *Restaurant Danubio*, on Pichincha near Bolívar, is OK but has a limited menu. *Andersson Fried Chicken* and *El Marinero* aren't bad for chicken and ceviche, respectively.

There is a basic café in the terminal terrestre, but it's not always open. In case it's not, head for the inexpensive *Asadero Pollo Piko* across the street. A block from the terminal is the not-very-exclusive *El Exclusivo*; at least it's clean and seems to have a reasonable selection of food.

Out by the border a bunch of stalls sell snacks, but there are no restaurants, except in Complejo Turístico Rumichaca (see Places to Stay).

Getting There & Away
Air The airport is two km northeast of the town center. TAME has an office in the Hotel Internacional Azteca (☎ 980 675) and another at the airport (☎ 982 850). Their flights from Quito to Tulcán leave at noon, Monday to Friday, and return to Quito at 1 pm (or 4:50 pm on Tuesday and Thursday). The 30-minute flight saves you five or six hours on the bus and costs only US$19. There are also flights to Cali, Colombia, on Tuesday and Thursday afternoons (US$79, plus US$25 international departure tax).

Note that flights from Tulcán to Quito are often full and are also among the first to be canceled when TAME is having aircraft problems.

Bus Buses to and from Ibarra (three hours; US$2.20) and Quito (5½ hours; US$4.70) leave and arrive via the terminal terrestre. There are frequent departures, but the selection of times is better in the mornings. There are also several daily direct departures for Santo Domingo de los Colorados or Guayaquil, if you enjoy the slow form of torture provided by cramped Ecuadorian buses during journeys taking 10 hours or longer. Note that there can be a very thorough customs/immigration check between Tulcán and Ibarra.

If you wish to travel west of Tulcán along the border to Tufiño, Maldonado and

Chical, take the Cooperativa Transportes Norte buses leaving from Sierra and Arellano near the town center. There is a bus to Tufiño (one hour; US$0.50) every one or two hours until midafternoon. There is also one daily bus that leaves about 11 am and continues on to Maldonado (4½ hours; US$2) and Chical. There may be more buses to Maldonado; check with Cooperativa Transportes Norte.

Cooperativa 11 de Abril buses leave from a stop in front of the cathedral.

Getting Around
Airport To get to the airport take the border-crossing bus (see Crossing the Colombian Border), which will leave you by the entrance for the same price as going to the border. A taxi will cost about US$1.50, or it's a two-km walk from the city center. If flying into Tulcán, you have to take a taxi or walk because there are no airport buses.

Bus The terminal terrestre is inconveniently located 2½ km southwest of the town center. City buses (US$0.10) run southwest from the center along Bolívar and will deposit you at the terminal. If arriving at Tulcán, cross the street in front of the terminal and take the bus from the other side to get to the town center.

Crossing the Colombian Border
You don't need to obtain an exit or entry stamp in the town of Tulcán. All formalities are taken care of at the Ecuador-Colombia border, six km away at Rumichaca. Fourteen-seat minibuses to the border leave as soon as they are full all day long from Parque Isidro Ayora. They cost about US$0.30 (Ecuadorian or Colombian currency).

Return buses from the border will charge the same to the town center, but you can usually persuade the driver to charge double and take you to the Tulcán bus terminal some 1½ km away if you are in a hurry to head south. Taxis between the bus terminal and the border are about US$3.

The border is open daily from 6 am to 9 pm. It has, in the past, been closed for lunch from noon to 2 pm, but this may no longer apply. With the heavy traffic from Colombia, entrance formalities (into Ecuador) are usually no problem. Almost nobody needs a visa, and tourist cards (which you must keep until you leave) are issued at the border. Unless you look like a bum, an exit ticket and sufficient funds are rarely requested. You might not be given the full 90 days that you are allowed, but extensions in Quito are normally fast and straightforward. Make sure that both your tourist card and passport are correctly stamped and dated.

If leaving Ecuador, you must get a *Salida* (exit) stamp in your passport and turn in your tourist card. Try not to lose your tourist card, but if you do, they should give you another one free if your passport is in order. If your documents aren't in order, several things might happen. If you've merely overstayed the time allowed by a few days, you can pay a fine that is usually about US$10 – this really is a fine, not a bribe. If you've overstayed by several months, you may well have to pay a hefty fine or be sent back to Quito. And if you don't have an *Entrada* (entrance) stamp, you will also be sent back.

On the Colombian side, entrance formalities are straightforward, as long as your passport and visa are in order. In the past, Australians, New Zealanders, Canadians and US citizens among others needed a visa, but in recent years this no longer applies. Check with a Colombian consulate to make sure. From the border there is frequent transportation to Ipiales, the first town in Colombia, two km away. There you'll find plenty of hotels and onward connections; see Lonely Planet's *Colombia – travel survival kit* by Krzysztof Dydyński (2nd edition, 1995).

WEST OF TULCÁN

Right on the border to the west of Tulcán, the small villages of **Tufiño, Maldonado** and **Chical** are rarely visited by gringos. A road is planned, which will continue from Chical on to the coast at San Lorenzo, but this won't be completed for many years. (This is not the newly constructed road between Ibarra and San Lorenzo.) Meanwhile, Chical is the end of the road, and adventurous travelers may be intrigued to see what's there; it certainly is a remote area.

At Tufiño there are several **thermal springs**, most of them on the Colombian side of the border. It is easy enough to cross over to Colombia on a day pass to soak in the pools, but you are sent back to Tulcán if you want to enter Colombia properly. However, regulations may have changed.

There is a basic *restaurant* in the village, but no hotels. If you ask around, you could probably find someone who will rent you a bed or floor space, but it's probably easiest to visit Tufiño in the morning and return to Tulcán on an afternoon bus.

The drive beyond Tufiño takes you over the Páramos de El Angel, famous for their strange highland vegetation, especially the giant frailejones. The dirt road climbs to well over 4000 meters as it crosses the wild country at the base of Volcán Chiles (4768 meters), an extinct volcano on the border. The summit is about three or four km away from the road, and the mountain can be climbed in a day with no technical equipment. The bus drivers know where to drop you off; the mountain is the obvious volcano to the north.

From the high mountain pass it is a long descent down the western slopes of the Andes through wild and ever changing scenery into the cloud forests below. Maldonado is in the Río San Juan valley at just over 2000 meters above sea level and almost 90 km west of Tulcán by road. The climate is reportedly pleasant, and swimming in the river invigorating, although I've never been there. There are a couple of small pensions. Chical, about 10 km beyond Maldonado, is the end of the road; one traveler reports that he camped here with no problems.

South of Quito

A glance at a relief map of Ecuador shows the Panamericana heading almost due south of Quito along a long valley flanked by two parallel ranges of high mountains. These two ranges consist for the most part of volcanoes, and several of them are still active. It was this feature that prompted Alexander von Humboldt, the German explorer who visited the country in 1802, to name Ecuador's central valley 'The Avenue of the Volcanoes.' This name is still used today.

The central valley is only a tiny fraction of Ecuador's land surface, yet it contains almost half of its population. Traditionally, Ecuador's Andean Indians farmed the valley's relatively rich volcanic soils, and after the conquest the Spanish found that the central valley made a good communication route between the north and south. Today the same route is used for the Panamericana, and a string of towns stretches south from the capital to Cuenca, Ecuador's third largest city, some 300 km south of Quito by air or 440 km by road.

In between lies some of Ecuador's wildest scenery, with nine of the country's 10 highest peaks and scores of tiny villages of indigenous Andeans leading lives little changed in centuries. Many of these villages are so remote that access is only on foot; some are easier to get to and provide a fascinating glimpse of Andean life. The further south one goes, the larger and more remote are the Indian populations. In Chimborazo Province, for example, there are approximately 250,000 Indians living in 431 small legal communities and villages. Most villages have minor differences in dress that are immediately recognizable to the local people – the pattern, color or shape of a poncho, hat, dress, blouse, trousers or waist-band can all indicate where an Indian is from.

Ecuador's most popular mountain climbs take place in this region, and a handful of local climbers and visiting mountaineers make attempts at scaling these giants year-round. In terms of weather and snow conditions, December and January are considered the best months and March to May the worst. It is beyond the scope of this book to give detailed climbing and hiking information, but it does appear in the books listed in Facts for the Visitor, at the SAEC, or through the climbing guides and outfitters mentioned in Quito and in several towns in this chapter.

Most travelers, however, visit the larger towns that are well connected with one another by road, and travel is generally easy with superb views along the way. Visiting smaller villages is possible, and details are given in the text. Villagers generally come into larger towns on market days, and their traditional and brightly dyed clothing adds splashes of color to the market scenes.

MACHACHI

This small town of 7000 inhabitants is 35 km south of Quito. Its main attraction is the Güitig mineral water bottling plant, which you can visit. It's a four-km walk or you can take a taxi; everyone knows where it is. There's not much else to do.

Places to Stay & Eat

There are two very basic hotels in the center. These are the *Hotel Residencial Mejía*, charging US$3.50 per person, and the *Hotel Miravalle*, at US$2.50 per person. Both are described as dirty. A better choice is the newer *Hotel La Casona* near the Panamericana, at US$5 per person. There are simple restaurants of which the *Pedregal* is the best.

Near Machachi is *La Herreria*, an elegant, rustic retreat dating to 1760. Full of antiques, it is being converted into a top-end hotel that may open in late 1997 or 1998. Meanwhile, guided tours (six people

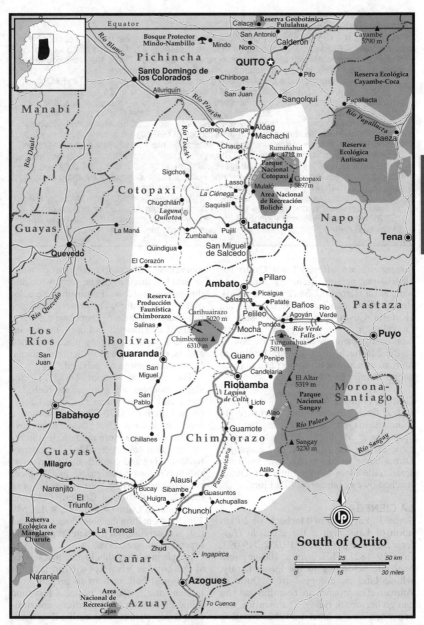

South of Quito

0   25   50 km
0   15   30 miles

Climbing the Ilinizas

The Ilinizas are two mountains about 25 km southwest of Machachi as the condor flies. Iliniza Sur (5263 meters), Ecuador's sixth highest peak, is a difficult ice climb for experienced mountaineers with technical equipment. Iliniza Norte (5126 meters), Ecuador's eighth highest peak, is a rough scramble suitable for fit, acclimatized hikers.

To reach the Ilinizas, take the unsigned turnoff from the Panamericana to El Chaupi; it's about eight km south of Machachi and taxi drivers know it. There are occasional buses from Machachi. The road is cobbled for seven km to El Chaupi village, and continues a further nine km as a dirt road to a parking area (identified by a small shrine to the Virgin), which can be reached by hired pickups (ask for Don Tello in the Machachi plaza, who will take you to the parking area for about US$30). From here, it is a three- to four-hour climb to a refuge where you can spend the night. If you leave Quito at dawn, catch an early bus from Machachi to El Chaupi, and walk hard, you can reach the refuge by nightfall. Part of the climb is up a steep ramp of volcanic scoria. The bulls you see along the way are those bred for the bullring – imagine the strength they attain living up here at 4200 meters! The locals all tell you ¡Cuidado! (beware).

The refuge is in a saddle between the two mountains and has recently been refurbished. There are bunks (bring a sleeping bag), cooking facilities, a guardian and a US$10 per night fee. From the refuge it is a two- or three-hour climb to Iliniza Norte along a fairly well-defined, but at times narrow, steep and slippery trail. ■

---

minimum) are offered from Quito for US$30 per person, including lunch and wine at La Herreria (US$12 with no food). Reservations can be made through the Hostería Cusín (see Places to Stay in Otavalo) or at the better travel agents. Apparently, there are other historic houses in the Machachi area that are turning to tourism as a means of support and maintenance. Inquiry locally.

Getting There & Away

Buses from the Terminal Terrestre de Cumandá in Quito go to Latacunga and can drop you in Machachi, although you will have to pay the full fare to Latacunga. Direct buses to Machachi leave from the small Villa Flora terminal in south Quito, reached by city buses for Villa Flora.

LA CIÉNEGA

Some 30 km south of Machachi or 20 km north of Latacunga is the excellent *Hostería La Ciénega* (☎ (03) 719 052, 719 093, fax 719 182). This is in a 400-year-old hacienda belonging to the Lasso family, whose land once spread from Quito to Ambato. The grounds are beautiful and you can go horseback riding. The mansion was converted into a hotel in 1982, and it is

marvelous. Most rooms having walls several feet thick, as can be seen by looking through the windows. Furnishings are colonial or 19th century. The flower-filled interior courtyard and side chapel are a delight. There is a restaurant and bar – the restaurant is a popular stopping place for lunch and is often crowded with tour groups. Lunch reservations are advised.

The rates are about US$32/42 for singles/doubles, all with private bath, hot water and heater. There is a huge honeymoon suite for US$70. The most attractive rooms are in the original house, but because of demand, some more modern, less interesting rooms have been added in a separate building. Try and confirm that your reservation is in the original house, and get there early to avoid losing your space. You can make a reservation at Cordero 1442 and Amazonas in Quito (☎ 541 337, ☎ /fax 549 126), or try calling the hotel direct. You can risk just arriving, but the hotel is often full, especially at weekends.

People in a hurry should note that service at the hotel is leisurely – it can take the receptionist half an hour to prepare your bill and the restaurant is not a fast-food joint. Early morning departures are difficult; if you want to leave earlier than 8 am, skip breakfast and try to settle your bill the day before.

The hotel is almost two km west of the Panamericana and a little south of the village of Lasso; there is a sign. Bus drivers will drop you at the sign and from there you can walk, or you can hire a car or taxi from Quito or Latacunga.

PARQUE NACIONAL COTOPAXI

Established in 1975, this 34,000-hectare park is mainland Ecuador's most popular and frequently visited national park. That is not to say it is crowded – indeed, it can be almost deserted midweek. Weekends can be crowded, however, particularly with Ecuadorian visitors during the June-to-August dry season.

The centerpiece of the park is undoubtedly the beautifully cone-shaped, snow-capped Cotopaxi (5897 meters), the highest active volcano in the world and Ecuador's second-highest peak. (Chileans claim that their Volcán Tupungato is higher, but controversy exists partly because the active fumaroles are on a lower subsummit.) Present activity is limited to a few gently smoking fumaroles that cannot be seen except by experienced mountaineers, who can climb up to the icy crater and peer within. There have, however, been many violent eruptions in the past few centuries, with three of them literally wiping out the town of Latacunga.

There are also several other peaks within the park, of which Rumiñahui (4712 meters) is the most important. The park gives you a good look at the páramo (see Habitats in Facts about the Country for more details). The forests of pines on the lower slopes are not Ecuadorian; they are imported trees grown for forestry purposes. They have been doing poorly in the last few years; disease seems to be taking its toll.

The wildlife is unusual and interesting. The Andean condor is present, though not often seen. The birds you are likely to see include the caruncled caracara (a falcon with a distinctive orange face); the Andean lapwing; the Andean gull (this 'seagull' is

quite at home in the mountains, 4000 meters above sea level); various highland hummingbirds, such as the Andean hillstar and sparkling violetear; the great thrush (a common black thrush with bright orange bill and feet, and yellow eyes); a number of duck and shorebird species; and other birds whose names are not immediately recognizable to most gringo visitors (cinclodes, solitaires, spinetails, canasteros and others).

The most frequently seen mammals in the park are white-tailed deer and rabbits. The dwarf deer called the little red brocket and the southern pudú are also present – these deer are only about 35 cm high at the shoulder. Their predators are less often seen, but if you are lucky you may catch a glimpse of the *colpeo* (Andean fox) or puma (mountain lion). The rare Andean spectacled bear lives in the remote and infrequently visited eastern slopes of the park. Near the park entrance is a captive herd of llamas that is being studied to understand better how these animals should be managed. In the wetter areas keep your eyes open for the distinctive *Atelopus* frog, which has an orange belly and black back – they are most likely to be seen near water during the wet season, although their numbers have recently been declining (see the sidebar).

There are excellent hiking and mountaineering possibilities within the park. A popular place to camp is near **Limpiopungo**, a large Andean lake at about 3800 meters above sea level, a few kilometers beyond the information center. There are simple cabins (roof and walls, no facilities) in the area between the information center and the lake. Another popular camping place is in the **Area Nacional de Recreación Boliche**, which abuts the national park to the west. You can camp for a night, or bring plenty of food and hike all the way around Cotopaxi – this takes about a week. Information is available at the entrance booth and finding these places is straightforward.

Mountaineers and the curious like to go up to the José Ribas Refugio, at about 4800 meters above sea level on the northern

Where Have All the Frogs Gone?

During a recent international conference of herpetologists (scientists who study reptiles and amphibians) it was noted that a puzzling loss was occurring in frog and toad species all over the world. Amphibians that once were common are now severely depleted in number or are simply no longer found at all. The scientists were unable to agree upon an explanation for the sudden demise of so many amphibian species in so many different habitats.

One theory is that worldwide air quality has depreciated to the extent that amphibians, who breathe both with primitive lungs and through their perpetually moist skin, are more susceptible to airborne toxins because of the gas exchange through their skin. Another theory is that frog skin gives little protection against UV light and increasing UV-light levels of recent years has proven deadly to amphibians. Perhaps they are like the canaries that miners once used to warn them of toxic air in the mines. ■

slopes of the mountain. Sleeping in the refuge costs about US$10; bunk beds and cooking facilities are available, but bring a warm sleeping bag. There is a guardian on duty who can show you where you can leave your gear if you need to do so. Climbing beyond the refuge requires stamina, experience, and snow and ice-climbing gear – it is definitely not a climb for the beginner, although it is a relatively straightforward climb for those who know what they are doing. Mountaineering guides are available in Quito and Ambato (see also Books appendix at the end of the book for more details).

The park's management plan was organized in 1983 with the technical and financial assistance of the World Wildlife Fund. It has the most well-developed infrastructure of the mainland parks. There are rangers, a park center (with an administrative building, a small museum and information center), the domesticated llama herd, the refuge, and camping and picnicking areas. Despite this list, facilities are very basic and most nonmountaineering visitors either come on day trips or camp. A restaurant was planned some years ago, but it has yet to materialize.

The entrance fee to the park is US$10 per person for foreign visitors (a little less if paid in sucres), but this doesn't include the US$10 overnight fee at the refuge or fees for camping – about US$1. To some extent, the elevated fees for foreign visitors help to fund the costs of running the park. The main problems facing the park are litter,

poaching and inadequate staff for patrols, information and educational programs.

The entrance gate is open from 7 am to 3 pm, though you can leave until about 6:30. If you are hiking, it is easy to get in or out anytime, because the 'gate' is only a heavy padlocked chain. Drivers can usually find a park guard in one of the nearby houses who will be happy to let you through at odd hours for a tip.

Altitude sickness is a very real danger; acclimatize for several days in Quito before attempting to walk in. Do not attempt to visit the park immediately after arriving in the highlands from a low elevation.

Places to Stay & Eat

The climbers' refuge and camping areas are described above. Just outside the park is a railway station with trains arriving from Quito and Riobamba. This was recently purchased by Safari Tours (of Quito) and has been refurbished as a hostal, with meals and hot showers available. Call Safari Tours (☎ (02) 552 505, 223 381, fax 220 426) for information.

Just within the park is *Hacienda San Agustín de Callo*, an early 19th-century hacienda built on an Inca site. Several ruins remain, and the hacienda's private chapel is inside an Inca building. The hacienda has only recently been opened to guests, and there are three double rooms with fireplaces and private bathrooms, though more are planned. Rates with all meals are US$120 per person per day. Reservations can be made through the Hostería Cusín (see Places to Stay in Otavalo) or through major travel agents.

Getting There & Away

You can drive, walk or hitchhike into the park. There are two roads in from the Panamericana, roughly 20 and 26 km north of Latacunga respectively (or about 16 and 22 km south of Machachi). You can ask any Latacunga-Quito bus driver to let you off at either entrance. The first entrance north of Latacunga has a national park sign. Follow the main dirt roads (also signed) through the entrance point (about eight or 10 km from the Panamericana) to the park center (about 15 km from the Panamericana).

The more northerly road also has a sign for the park and another for CLIRSEN. The road is paved as far as the CLIRSEN satellite-tracking station (previously operated by NASA) and telecommunications towers, about two km from the Panamericana. The road then becomes dirt and soon passes the Río Daule campsite in the Boliche Recreation Area, eventually reaching the entrance station; this latter route is about three km shorter.

The Limpiopungo area for camping and picnicking is about four km beyond the park center, and the refuge 12 km farther. The lake is at 3800 meters and the refuge is 1000 meters higher – it is very hard work walking at this altitude if you are not used to it.

On weekends a fair number of local tourists visit the park and there is a very good chance of getting a lift. Midweek the park is almost deserted and you'll probably end up walking.

Pickup trucks from Latacunga will cost about US$20 to US$30, but you should bargain. Mountaineers wishing to reach the refuge must clearly specify that they want to go up the steep dirt road to the parking lot under the refuge at the end of the road. Most pickups will make it; a few can't. You can arrange for the pickup to return for you on a particular day for another US$20 to US$30. It is almost an hour's walk uphill from the parking lot (at 4600 meters) to the refuge, which looks like it's about a 10-minute stroll away. This is not flat walking at sea level! Any car will get you into the park to visit the museum, see the llamas and picnic by Limpiopungo, where excellent views of the mountain are possible, weather permitting.

The major travel agencies in Quito can arrange tours to Cotopaxi. A day tour, including a picnic lunch, driver and bilingual guide, will visit the park as far as Limpiopungo but not necessarily as far as the parking lot below the refuge. Ask about this. A two-day tour will combine a day trip to Cotopaxi with an overnight at La Ciénega and a visit to local Indian markets. Costs depend on the number of people in your group and the agency you book with. Bicycle tours are also available in Quito.

LATACUNGA

It's worth coming here just for the drive from Quito, which can be magnificent. Like a mammoth ice-cream cone, Cotopaxi looms to the left of the Panamericana as you travel south, and the two Ilinizas, also snow capped, are on your right. Several other peaks are visible during the 90-km drive, including distant Chimborazo, if you are lucky. On one memorable drive, one morning in August 1995, my friends Robert and Daisy Kunstaetter and I saw nine of Ecuador's 10 highest mountains. Wow!

About 50 km south of Quito the highway crosses a pass at over 3500 meters, and soon after there is an entrance road to Parque Nacional Cotopaxi. The road drops and crosses the railway at the small village of Lasso and then continues to Latacunga at about 2800 meters above sea level.

Latacunga (population about 40,000) is the capital of Cotopaxi Province. Although not a particularly exciting town, it has an interesting history and is a good base for several excellent excursions. It was an important center for the Puruhá Indians who lived here before the Incas.

The town's name originates from the Indian words 'Llacta cunani,' which translate rather charmingly into 'land of my choice.' It became an important colonial center immediately after the conquest, but

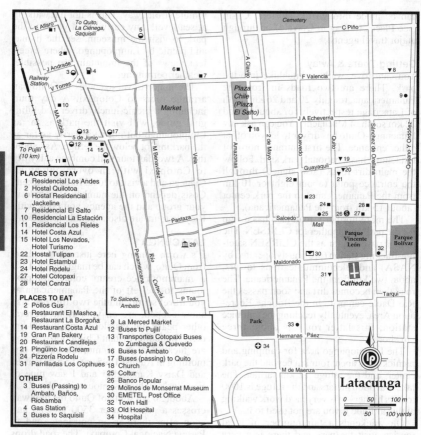

PLACES TO STAY
1 Residencial Los Andes
2 Hostal Quilotoa
6 Hostal Residencial
   Jackeline
7 Residencial El Salto
10 Residencial La Estación
11 Residencial Los Rieles
14 Hotel Costa Azul
15 Hotel Los Nevados,
   Hotel Turismo
22 Hostal Tulipan
23 Hotel Estambul
24 Hotel Rodelu
27 Hotel Cotopaxi
28 Hotel Central

PLACES TO EAT
2 Pollos Gus
8 Restaurant El Mashca,
   Restaurant La Borgoña
14 Restaurant Costa Azul
19 Gran Pan Bakery
20 Restaurant Candilejas
21 Pingüino Ice Cream
31 Pizzería Rodelu
31 Parrilladas Los Copihues

OTHER
3 Buses (Passing) to
   Ambato, Baños,
   Riobamba
4 Gas Station
5 Buses to Saquisilí

9 La Merced Market
12 Buses to Pujilí
13 Transportes Cotopaxi Buses
   to Zumbagua & Quevedo
16 Buses to Ambato
17 Buses (passing) to Quito
18 Church
25 Coltur
26 Banco Popular
29 Molinos de Monserrat Museum
30 EMETEL, Post Office
32 Town Hall
33 Old Hospital
34 Hospital

today there is little evidence of this long and varied history.

This strange absence of historical detail is the result of multiple catastrophes. Cotopaxi, which dominates the town on a clear day, erupted violently in 1742 and destroyed the town, which was rebuilt. Another eruption 26 years later wiped it out again, but the indomitable (or foolhardy) survivors rebuilt it a second time. An immense eruption in 1877 destroyed it a third time, and yet again it was rebuilt on the same site. At present the volcano's activity is minor, and it is extremely unlikely that an eruption will occur within the next several years.

Information
There is no tourist office, but Coltur, a travel agency, provides local tours, guides and information. Bring enough sucres from Quito. There are banks on Parque Vicente León, but changing money is difficult. The best bet is the Banco Popular in the mornings.

EMETEL and the post office are on Quevedo near Maldonado. The area code for Latacunga and the province of Cotopaxi is 03.

Top: San Lorenzo Autoferro, Ibarra (RR)
Left: Church door in Otavalo (RR)
Right: Topiary at Tulcán Cemetery (RR)

Top: Town of Baños (TW)
Left: Aerial view of Cotopaxi crater (RR)
Right: Private Chapel at 400-year-old Hacienda La Cienga, Central Highlands (RR)

The town closes down early, and most restaurants stop serving by 8 or 9 pm.

Things to See & Do
Latacunga is a good center for excursions to Cotopaxi (see above) and to the nearby villages that are described at the end of this section. In the town itself there is little to see, partly because most historic buildings have been wiped out by volcanic eruptions (a thought which I'm sure you'll keep in mind while sightseeing). A small ethnography and art museum, the Molinos de Monserrat, is run by the Casa de la Cultura Ecuatoriana. The museum on Vela near Maldonado is open from 10 am to 5 pm Tuesday through Saturday.

There are several plazas, of which Parque Vicente León is the most attractive, with its well-tended garden and topiary work. At the southeast corner of this plaza is the town hall, topped by a pair of stone condors, and on the south side is the cathedral. Behind the cathedral is a little arcade (Pasaje Catedral) that includes an art gallery. Many of the buildings are light gray and have been built from the local volcanic rock.

Near the south end of town on Quevedo is an old hospital that is a historic landmark – though I couldn't find a way in to visit. The modern hospital is a block away. There is one tiny cinema that shows bad movies and a theater that is usually closed.

Special Events
Latacunga's major annual fiesta is La Virgen de las Mercedes, held September 23 and 24. This is more popularly known as the Fiesta de la Mamá Negra, and there are processions, costumes, street dancing, Andean music and fireworks. This is one of those festivals that, although outwardly Christian, has much pagan Indian influence and is worth seeing. Another big parade in honor of La Mamá Negra is held two weeks later. The Independence of Latacunga is celebrated on November 11 with parades and a bullfight.

There is also a weekly market on Saturday and a smaller one on Tuesday. The markets are colorful but of no special interest, although a few crafts are sold, especially the small string bags known as shigras.

Places to Stay
Many people stay in Latacunga on Wednesday nights for the Thursday morning Indian market at Saquisilí. Hotels are often full by midafternoon on Wednesday, so try to get there early if you're arriving on that day.

A recommended budget-travelers' hotel that has large clean rooms and hot water in the communal showers is the friendly *Hotel Estambul* (☎ 800 354) on Quevedo and Salcedo. Rooms cost about US$8 for a double or US$12 with private bath. A recent recommendation at this price is the helpful *Residencial Santiago* (☎ 800 899, 802 164), 2 de Mayo and Guayaquil, with large rooms with a shared bath, or smaller, darker rooms with private bath and hot water.

For US$3 per person, the basic but friendly *Hostal Residencial Jackeline* (☎ 801 033) and *Residencial El Salto*, both near the northeast corner of the market, have rooms with warm shared showers. Just off the Panamericana on 5 de Junio, the *Hotel Costa Azul* and *Hotel Turismo* both are friendly, have good cheap restaurants and very basic rooms with shared cold showers at US$2 per person. Even cheaper rooms are available at the *Residencial La Estación* near the railway station. It looks pretty run down from the outside, but travelers write that the rooms are clean and there are shared hot showers.

The *Residencial Los Rieles* (☎ 801 254), by the railway tracks, has simple rooms at US$3.50/4.50, or US$7/8 with private bath – there is hot water. The *Hotel Los Nevados* (☎ 800 407), 5 de Junio by the Panamericana, has basic rooms for US$4.50/7, and slightly better ones with bath and hot water for US$7/11. The *Hostal Quilotoa* (☎ 801 866, 800 099, fax 802 090), just off the Panamericana, has good, clean, carpeted double rooms with bath and hot water for US$13. Nearby is the similarly priced *Residencial Los Andes* (☎ 800 933), with comparable though older rooms. Some rooms in these hotels may suffer from road noise coming from the Panamericana.

The *Hotel Cotopaxi* (☎ 801 310), on the northeastern corner of Parque Vicente León, used to be Latacunga's best hotel but has been eclipsed by several better ones. On a recent visit it was full of climbers and backpackers. Rates are US$9 per person in somewhat shabby rooms with private bath and erratic hot water. Some of the rooms have pretty views of the park, but they may be a little noisy. There is a simple restaurant.

Around the corner, the *Hotel Central* (☎ 802 912) charges US$11/18 for clean rooms with hot water. There is a restaurant, and day tours to Cotopaxi are offered (US$80 for four people, plus park fee). Also at this price is the newer *Hotel Tulipan* (also called Tilipulo, ☎ 802 130), Guayaquil at Quevedo. The good-size rooms are clean and have TV and telephones.

The best hotel at this time is the *Hotel Rodelu* (☎ 800 956, 811 264, ☎ /fax 812 341) on Quito just off the Parque Vicente León. Quite comfortable rooms with TV are US$17/25, and there is a restaurant serving breakfast and Italian food.

People looking for some luxury often stay at the *La Ciénega* about 20 km to the north or *Hostería Rumipamba de las Rosas* about 13 km south near Salcedo.

Places to Eat

There are no particularly fine or expensive restaurants in Latacunga. The best places are *Parrilladas Los Copihues*, for steaks and meat dishes; *Restaurant Candilejas*, for 'international' food in a quiet atmosphere; and *Pizzería Rodelu*, which serves pizza and other dishes. Although they are a little more expensive, they certainly won't break the bank. For those on a tight budget, reasonable choices are *Restaurants La Borgoña* and *Costa Azul*, which both serve simple Ecuadorian food, and *El Mashca* for grilled chicken. *Pingüino* is the place to go for ice cream, and *Gran Pan* bakery is good for bread for picnics.

Most restaurants close by 8 pm. *Pollos Gus* on the Panamericana serves fast-food-style hamburgers and roast chicken and is open late. It's hard to find a restaurant for early breakfasts, unless you eat in one of the better hotels.

The Latacunga area is famous for its *allullas*, sold by local women at every bus stop or checkpoint. The women's high-pitched cries of '*aziuuuuzia*' become quite familiar. Allullas are rather dry biscuits made of flour, pork fat and a local unpasteurized cheese, and I'm afraid they taste no better than they sound.

Getting There & Away

Air There is a Latacunga airport, but it is not used for regularly scheduled flights. On rare occasions a plane may be diverted here if it cannot land at Quito. I have heard occasional discussions about expanding the airport into an international one for Quito traffic – I can't see it happening this century.

Bus – long distance There is no main bus terminal. Long-distance buses from Quito's terminal terrestre will usually drop you on the Panamericana at Avenida 5 de Junio before continuing to Ambato. This corner is a good place to stand to catch any north or southbound buses; they pass every few minutes. Some locals prefer to wait by the gas station. Flagging down a bus may be difficult on holiday weekends, as many buses are full and tend to do the Quito-Ambato-Riobamba run without picking up passengers at Latacunga. Be patient and avoid leaving town on holiday weekends.

Slower buses leave from Quito's terminal direct for Latacunga. The bus stop for Quito-bound buses originating in Latacunga is in the Plaza Chile (also popularly known as Plaza El Salto). There is also a bus stop on the Panamericana just south of 5 de Junio for buses originating in Latacunga and going to Ambato. Approximate fares and times are: Quito, US$1.40, two hours; Ambato, US$1, one hour; Riobamba, US$2, 2¼ hours; and Baños, US$1.50, 1¾ hours.

Just half a block from the Panamericana on Avenida 5 de Junio is the bus stop for westbound buses. The road is paved as far as Pujilí beyond which the road deteriorates. This is the roughest, least-traveled, and perhaps most spectacular bus route joining the highlands with the western lowlands. If you're not pressed for time and don't mind the discomfort, riding a beat-up crowded old bus on this dirt road may be the most interesting way of leaving the highlands. The bus climbs to Zumbagua at 3500 meters (US$1.50; two hours) and then drops to Quevedo (US$3.30; 4½ hours) at only 150 meters above sea level. Transportes Cotopaxi runs this route with departures every two hours all day long. Buy tickets on the bus.

Bus – local The buses most frequently used by travelers are the one to Saquisilí (US$0.25; 30 minutes). Departures are every few minutes on market-day mornings, and every hour or so at other times. The buses leave from Benavídez one long block north of the market. Buses departing for various other nearby villages leave from the Plaza Chile. Destinations served by these include Sigchos, Chugchilán and Mulaló. Ask around for other villages. The bus for the village of Pujilí leaves at frequent intervals from MA Subia and 5 de Junio, a block west of the Panamericana.

Train The railway station is on the west side of the Panamericana, one km from the town center. The Riobamba-Quito train passes through about three hours after leaving Riobamba or two hours after leaving Quito; see those towns for further details.

Taxi Plaza Chile (El Salto) is the place to go to hire taxis and pickup trucks for visits to Parque Nacional Cotopaxi and other remote villages (pickups double as taxis on many of the rough roads in the highlands). The manager of the Hotel Estambul will make arrangements for pickups to Cotopaxi. The fare to Cotopaxi is about US$30 one way, but you may have to bargain hard. A taxi or pickup to Zumbagua and Laguna Quilotoa costs a little more.

AROUND LATACUNGA

Ten km west of Latacunga is the easily visited **Pujilí**. It has a basic cheap hotel just off the main plaza and a couple of simple restaurants nearby. The main market day is Sunday, with a smaller market on Wednesday. This is a good town for the All Souls' Day festivities of November 2. It is also one of the best places for Corpus Christi celebrations. During these the colorful *El Danzante* festival takes place, and dancers parade around on stilts and wear costumes covered with tiny mirrors.

Some 57 km further west is **Zumbagua**, a very small village that has an unspoiled, interesting local market on Saturday. The people of the region often use llamas to transport goods to and from the market. The drive there from Latacunga is through beautiful Andean scenery. Food is available but very simple (consider bringing some of your own). Accommodations are currently limited to two small and basic residenciales that fill up fast on Friday, so get there early. The better of the two is the *Hostal Quiroga*, below the market square. Another unnamed place is above the square. There is traditional Andean music, dancing and heavy drinking on Friday night.

About 14 km north of Zumbagua is the famous volcanic lake of **Quilotoa**. The views from the lake are beautiful, but there have been reports of many beggars in the area. Transportation is both infrequent and irregular, except after the Saturday market when vehicles crowded with market-goers head that way. You can hire a taxi in Latacunga or a truck or van in Zumbagua. You can also take a public bus, which leaves only on Friday and Saturday at 10:30 am, from Latacunga or another that leaves mid-morning on Thursday from Zumbagua. You can walk there in about four hours from Zumbagua, but carry water – the lake is alkaline and the road dusty and fringed with cacti. It is also possible to reach the lake from the villages of Sigchos, but there is even less transport.

A few minutes walk from the lake is the new community of **Ponce-Quilotoa** with a few families. Here, look for signs to the

Cabañas Quilotoa operated by artist Humberto Latacunga. There are 20 beds (about US$2 per person), a fireplace, a latrine and a café serving Andean indigenous food, including cuy (guinea pig) on request. You can visit the artist's studio and hire a mule or guide. Performances of Andean music and dancing can be arranged.

Continuing another 14 km north of the lake on a deteriorating road, you can reach the small village of **Chugchilán**, surrounded by wild and spectacular scenery. This is five more hours on foot. The daily bus from Latacunga arrives via a different, more northerly road through Sigchos. At Chugchilán you can sleep in the *Black Sheep Inn*, owned by a couple of North Americans. It's a simple but friendly place, with US$5 beds, good meals available, mules for hire and information for local hikes and treks. There's no phone, but you can write to Apartado 05-01-240, Latacunga, Cotopaxi, Ecuador.

Twenty-three km north of Chugchilán is the bigger village of **Sigchos**, with two or three buses a day to Saquisilí (52 km to the east) and Latacunga. There are a couple of basic places to stay and a small Sunday market here. The best hotel is the *Residencial Cotopaxi*, which charges US$5 per person and reportedly has a hot shower! These villages are all in a very remote area of the Ecuadorian highlands; still more remote communities can be found on foot.

South of Zumbagua is the **Río Tigua valley**. This area is known for the bright paintings of Andean life that are locally made on canvases of leather. The paintings turn up for sale in Quito and at the Cabañas in Quilotoa. The Tigua region is reached by taking the southbound road to the left, about five or six km beyond Zumbagua on the road to Quevedo. The road crosses the Tigua valley, goes past the tiny community of Quindigua and on to Angamarca beyond which the road swings west through the remote cantón capital of El Corazón and, eventually, into Quevedo. This is one of the least accessible parts of the region and forays are not for the inexperienced traveler.

The scenery around all the areas described in this section is quite splendid and the Andean Indian inhabitants somewhat withdrawn and not used to seeing strangers, although they are friendly and helpful once the ice has been broken, especially if you speak Spanish (though many of the Indians speak only Quichua). Travelers wishing to spend any time here should be self sufficient and have some experience in rough travel in strange areas. Transportation cannot be relied upon, and you may have to walk for long distances or wait for hours. Hiring a car is an option, but it limits your contact with the locals. Carry a sleeping bag or blanket, warm clothes, extra water and a snack. The area is photogenic, but please don't be obnoxious with your camera. The people are not keen on being photographed by staring strangers who shoot and move on.

SAQUISILÍ

For many people, the Thursday morning market of Saquisilí is the main reason for coming to Latacunga. Ecuadorian economists consider Saquisilí to have the most important Indian village market in the country, and many travelers rate it as the best they've seen in Ecuador. It is not a tourist-oriented market, though there are the usual few Otavaleño Indians selling their sweaters and weavings. This market is for the inhabitants of remote Indian villages who flood into town to buy or sell everything from bananas to homemade shotguns to herbal remedies to strings of piglets. The majority of the Indians from the area wear little felt porkpie hats and red ponchos.

There are eight different plazas, each of which sell specific goods. One of my favorites is the animal market, a cacophonous affair with screaming pigs playing a major role. Cattle, sheep and a few llamas are also common. The animal market is almost a kilometer out of town – go early and ask for directions.

Along with the travelers, there are thieves – I saw two women with a small child expertly picking tourists' pockets. One woman and the child would stumble in front of an unsuspecting person and, in the ensuing apologies and confusion, the other woman lifted a wallet using her long poncho as a cover for her activities.

The bus from Latacunga drops you off near the Plaza La Concordia, with its many trees surrounded by an iron railing. On Thursday this becomes the market plaza.

Places to Stay & Eat

On the Plaza La Concordia at Bolívar 4-88 and Sucre is the *Pensión La Chabela* (also known as La Chabelita), which provides cheap, basic and none too clean accommodation. There is no sign. A bed can also be found at the marginal *Salón Pichincha*, a couple of blocks away at Bolívar 2-06 and Pichincha. They are likely to be full the night before the market, and most travelers find it best to stay in Latacunga; the bus service begins at dawn, so you won't miss anything.

The German-run *Hostería Rancho Muller* (☎ 721 380, fax 721 103) is on the outskirts of town. Clean, plain rooms with bath cost from US$20 a double to US$45 for six people, but the water was cold when I stopped by. The owner has plans to improve this. There is also a slightly pricey international restaurant, which has the best food in town.

Otherwise, there are no restaurants but plenty of places to eat. I enjoyed breakfast in an unnamed place on the 700 block of Sucre and Bolívar. Inside there was a large smoky kitchen full of Indians and an Elvis Presley poster on the wall. A huge woman supervised the cooking of breakfast over a charcoal brazier, and it was a good opportunity to try dishes such as llapingachos, fritada, caldo de gallina, tortillas de maíz and moté cooked in traditional style – quite a change from bacon and eggs!

There are similar places nearby and also plenty of street stands. One plaza seems to be nothing but food stalls – if you stick to cooked food and don't have a delicate stomach, you'll enjoy it.

Getting There & Away

There are buses returning to Latacunga several times an hour after the market;

there are also trucks and buses going to many of the remote villages in the interior, such as Sigchos and Chugchilán. On market day and sporadically on other days, slow and crowded old buses go direct to and from Quito (US$1.50; two to three hours). Buses leave from near Plaza La Concordia, more or less from where you arrived.

People unwilling to travel by public transport can hire a taxi in Quito (about US$40 for a half day, allowing a couple of hours at the market) or from Latacunga. The bigger tour companies organize one- or two-day tours to Saquisilí and other places. Overnights are usually at La Ciénega.

SAN MIGUEL DE SALCEDO

This small town, usually called Salcedo, is 14 km south of Latacunga on the Panamericana. It has a Sunday market and a lesser one on Thursday. In mid-March it hosts an important Agricultural and Industrial Fair, and there's a big fiesta around November 1. Otherwise, it's of little interest except to ice-cream aficionados, who say that Salcedo has some of the best ice cream in the area.

Places to Stay

There are a couple of cheap and basic hotels in the town center. On the northern outskirts of the town is the *Hostería Rumibamba de las Rosas* (☎ 726 128, 726 306, 727 309, fax 727 103), a fairly modern hotel with comfortable 'log cabin' bungalows furnished with antiques. There is a small private zoo, duck pond, pony rides (and a saddled llama for children!), swimming pool, tennis courts, and games rooms. The whole place has a Disneyland atmosphere. It's rather corny but clean and well run, and the management is very friendly and anxious to please. Rooms are about US$55 for a double.

Places to Eat

There is a very good restaurant and bar at the Hostería Rumibamba. It is a popular place for Ecuadorians on family outings.

AMBATO

Some 47 km south of Latacunga (136 km south of Quito) is the important town of Ambato, the capital of Tungurahua Province. It was badly damaged in a 1949 earthquake, but a modern city was soon rebuilt. It is prosperous and growing, with a population of about 125,000. Its altitude is 2800 meters above sea level.

Apart from the festivals described below (see Special Events), most travelers just pass through Ambato on their way to Baños, which is one of the more popular destinations in the country. It is, however, worth staying in Ambato for a night to see the little-known but interesting museum (see below). The Monday market is a huge affair – the biggest in Ecuador.

Information

Tourist Office CETUR (☎ 821 800), by the Hotel Ambato on Guayaquil and Rocafuerte, is open from 8:30 am to noon and 2 to 5 pm Monday to Friday.

Money Cambiato (☎ 821 008), Bolívar 686, will change both US-dollar traveler's checks and cash at rates close to Quito's. Several banks change foreign currency, but Cambiato is quicker.

Post & Communications EMETEL and the post office are both on Castillo by the Parque Juan Montalvo. The area code for Ambato and the province of Tungurahua is 03.

Travel Agencies & Guides Travel and first-class tour arrangements can be made at Metropolitan Touring (☎ 824 084), Bolívar 471 and Castillo, the head office of which is in Quito.

A recommended adventure-tour operator is Surtrek (☎ 844 448, fax 844 512), L Cordero 2-10 and Los Shyris, just over two km south of the city center. German, English and Spanish are spoken. They rent climbing equipment, provide mountaineering guides for climbing the local snow peaks and also arrange trips to the Oriente. Their mailing address is PO Box 18-01-00865, Ambato, Ecuador.

Walking Tour

Because of reconstruction since the 1949 earthquake, most of the buildings in the center are new and of no great interest. A recommended walk is along Bolívar, southwest of the center, to the pleasant modern suburb of Miraflores on the banks of the Río Ambato (note that Calle Bolívar changes into Avenida Miraflores). The river can be crossed about two km away from town on Avenida Los Guaytambos, which soon leads to the **Quinta de Montalvo**, where that writer's country house stood. It can be visited from 9 am to noon and 2 to 6 pm. This is in the suburb of Ficoa.

Several other famous Ambateños had country houses that survived the earthquake and are worth visiting (☎ 821 024 for information). **Quinta de Mera** belonged to the writer Juan León Mera and can be visited 9 am to noon and 2 to 6 pm. The house is set in an attractive botanical garden on Avenida Los Capulíes in the suburb of Atocha. Close by is the **Quinta La Liria**, the country home of the mountaineer Nicolás Martínez, which is also set in a pleasant garden. Atocha is on the far side of the Río Ambato, about two km northeast of the city center. It can be reached on foot by walking northwest out of town on Montalvo, which soon crosses the river, and then turning right on Capulíes about 200 meters beyond the river. Quinta de Mera is about 1½ km to the northeast, and the Quinta La Liria just beyond it. Local buses go to all these places.

Museo de Ciencias Naturales

This natural history museum (☎ 821 958) is in the Colegio Bolívar on Sucre and Lalama on the northwest side of the Parque Cevallos. There are hundreds of stuffed birds, mammals and reptiles, some of which are quite well done and others rather ratty. In the absence of comprehensive field guides to Ecuadorian wildlife, this is a good museum to visit if you wish to identify species you may have seen in the wild. There's also a rather gruesome display of freaks, such as two-headed calves and six-legged lambs.

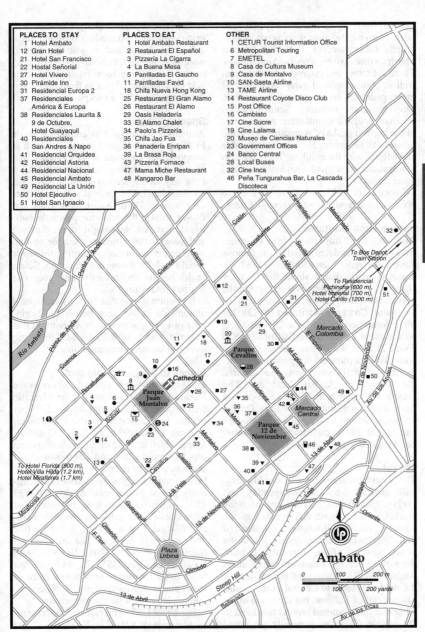

PLACES TO STAY
1 Hotel Ambato
12 Gran Hotel
21 Hotel San Francisco
22 Hostal Señorial
27 Hotel Vivero
30 Pirámide Inn
31 Residencial Europa 2
37 Residenciales
     América & Europa
38 Residenciales Laurita &
     9 de Octubre,
     Hotel Guayaquil
40 Residenciales
     San Andres & Napo
41 Residencial Orquidea
42 Residencial Astoria
44 Residencial Nacional
45 Residencial Ambato
49 Residencial La Unión
50 Hotel Ejecutivo
51 Hotel San Ignacio

PLACES TO EAT
1 Hotel Ambato Restaurant
2 Restaurant El Español
3 Pizzería La Cigarra
4 La Buena Mesa
5 Parrilladas El Gaucho
11 Parrilladas Favid
18 Chifa Nueva Hong Kong
25 Restaurant El Gran Alamo
26 Restaurant El Alamo
29 Oasis Heladería
33 El Alamo Chalet
34 Paolo's Pizzería
35 Chifa Jao Fua
36 Panadería Enripan
39 La Brasa Roja
43 Pizzería Fornace
47 Mama Miche Restaurant
48 Kangaroo Bar

OTHER
1 CETUR Tourist Information Office
6 Metropolitan Touring
7 EMETEL
8 Casa de Cultura Museum
9 Casa de Montalvo
10 SAN-Saeta Airline
13 TAME Airline
14 Restaurant Coyote Disco Club
15 Post Office
16 Cambiato
17 Cine Sucre
19 Cine Lalama
23 Museo de Ciencias Naturales
23 Government Offices
24 Banco Central
28 Local Buses
32 Cine Inca
46 Peña Tungurahua Bar, La Cascada
     Discoteca

Ambato

Apart from the natural history, I particularly enjoyed the fine display of photographs taken around 1910 by Nicolás Martínez (see above), who lived in Ambato. There are street and countryside scenes, as well as photographs of early mountaineering expeditions and Cotopaxi in eruption. The museum curator, Señor Héctor Vásquez, is also a mountaineer with ascents of the highest peaks of Argentina, Peru and Ecuador to his credit. He is knowledgeable and helpful with the exhibits. There are also numismatic, geological, archaeological and other displays.

Entrance is US$2 and hours are 8 am to noon and 2 to 6 pm Monday through Friday.

Parque Juan Montalvo

Ambato's most important plaza is attractively laid out and dedicated to the famous Ambateño writer Juan Montalvo (1832-89; see Arts in the Facts about the Country chapter), of whom there is a statue. On the northwest side of this plaza you can visit his house, **Casa de Montalvo** (☎ 821 024 for information); there is a US$0.40 fee. Next door is the **Casa de Cultura** (☎ 820 338, 824 248), which has a small museum with displays (labeled in Spanish) of journalism, musical instruments, handicrafts, the history of Ambato and art. The museum is open from 8 am to noon and from 2 to 5 pm; entrance is free. On the northeast side of this plaza is the modern and rather bleak **cathedral** with some good stained-glass windows.

Market

The weekly market is held on Monday, with smaller ones on Wednesday and Friday. Established in 1861 the Monday market is the largest city market in the country. Although it has been modernized (buildings rather than outdoors), it is still a huge, bustling affair, attracting Indians from many nearby communities as well as Ambateños. The main spot for produce is the modern Mercado Central at the southeastern end of Lalama, but there are many other markets scattered around town and in the suburbs (these are generally not aimed at tourists). Walking along Cevallos will bring you past Mercado Colombia (also called Modelo), and as you go further northeast along Cevallos you will pass some stalls selling local handicrafts – the best area is about 10 blocks from the center. As always, watch for pickpockets.

Special Events

Ambato is famous for its annual Fiesta de Frutas y Flores (flower festival), which is supposed to coincide with Carnaval but usually is held during the last two weeks in February. Hotels tend to be full at this time, so plan ahead. The festival's 45th anniversary was in 1996. Apart from fruit and flower shows, the festivities include bullfights, parades, late-night street dancing and general fun. Travelers unable to find suitable accommodations during this time should look for rooms in Latacunga, Baños or Riobamba and take the one hour bus journey into Ambato.

It is worth noting that the Carnaval – held nationwide in the week before the beginning of Lent – is unique in Ambato, in that the traditional 'sport' of water-throwing has been banned throughout the city.

Places to Stay – bottom end

The place for basic, cheap hotels is in the Parque 12 de Noviembre and the Mercado Central areas. For about a US$2.50 per person you can stay in the *Residencial América* (☎ 821 092), JB Vela 737 and JL Mera, which has one of those showers that provides tepid water and electric shocks if you touch any of the pipes, but is one of the better super-cheapies. Next door is the similarly priced *Residencial Europa* (☎ 823 459), which claims to have hot water but often doesn't. Some blocks away, *Residencial Europa 2* (☎ 823 196), E Espejo 612 and Sucre, is similar. The *Residencial Nacional* (☎ 823 820), JB Vela and Lalama, charges US$2.75 and has hot water in the morning – sometimes. None of these places are particularly clean or recommended except for the penurious.

For under US$3 you can stay at *Residencial Laurita* (☎ 821 377), JL Mera 333 and

JB Vela, which is reasonably clean and friendly and has hot water. The cheapest rooms are on the top floor with bathrooms below. The similar *Hotel Guayaquil* (☎ 821 194, 823 886), a few doors away at JL Mera 311, is also OK. The *Residencial 9 de Octubre* (☎ 820 018), JL Mera 325, has cold water, even though they also charge about US$3.

Several other very basic and rather grungy-looking hotels in the US$2 to US$3 price range are shown on the map. They include the residenciales *Orquidea, San Andres, Napo* (☎ 824 469), *La Unión* (☎ 824 215), *Ambato* (☎ 822 738) and *Astoria* (☎ 823 196).

If you'd rather stay near the bus terminal, there is the *Hotel Carrillo* (☎ 827 200) right above the terminal for US$3.50 per person. They have hot showers but it's noisy. Walking right from the terminal along Avenida de las Américas to the traffic circle and left on Avenida 12 de Noviembre brings you to the friendly *Residencial Pichincha* (☎ 821 752) on the right-hand side at No 2323 (five minutes from the terminal). They have clean rooms at US$3/5 but only cold water. Just before Residencial Pichincha is the *Hotel Imperial* (☎ 844 837), at 12 de Noviembre 2494. They charge US$5 per person in rooms with private baths and hot water, though the water supply is erratic, as it is in many of the cheaper hotels in Ambato.

The *Hotel San Francisco* (☎ 821 739), M Egüez 837, is quite clean and friendly (though one critic calls it 'seedy'). Rooms cost US$10 a double or US$14 with private hot bath. The *Hotel Ejecutivo* (☎ 820 370), 12 de Noviembre 1230 and E Espejo, has reasonable rooms with shared baths for about US$5 per person, or dark, small rooms with private bath and hot water for US$8/12.

Places to Stay – middle

The new *Hostal Señorial* (☎ 825 124), Cevallos at Quito, has clean, carpeted rooms with bath at US$10 per person. Rooms at the *Pirámide Inn* (☎ 825 252), Cevallos at M Egüez, are US$12/18.

Each has one bed, decent carpeting, bath and TV.

The *Gran Hotel* (☎ 824 119, ☎ /fax 824 235), at Lalama and Rocafuerte, has reasonable carpeted rooms with private hot bath, telephone and TV for about US$14/22. A restaurant and parking are available. Also good is the *Hotel Vivero* (☎ 840 088, 841 000, fax 826 475), JL Mera 504 and Cevallos, which also has rooms with hot water, telephone and TV for about this price. There are cheaper, smaller rooms on the top floor. Another decent place in this price range is the five-story *Hotel San Ignacio* (☎ 824 370), 12 de Noviembre and Maldonado.

Out on Avenida Miraflores, in the suburb of the same name, are three quiet and pleasant hotels, all of which have been recommended. They all have restaurants (limited menus or set meals) and double rooms in the US$30s with private baths and hot water. The closest is the *Hotel Florida* (☎ 823 040/74) at Miraflores 1131, almost one kilometer southwest of where Bolívar becomes Avenida Miraflores on the map. Further along Miraflores is the German-run *Hotel Villa Hilda* (☎ 824 065, 822 730, fax 845 571), which is set in pleasant gardens and has a pool. Finally, you might try the clean and modern *Hotel Miraflores* (☎ 844 395, 843 224) at Miraflores 227.

Places to Stay – top end

By far the best hotel in town is the *Hotel Ambato* (☎ 827 598/9, fax 827 197), Guayaquil and Rocafuerte. They have a casino, good restaurant and bar and comfortable rooms with private bath and hot water, telephone and TV. They charge US$55/70 for rooms with a view.

Places to Eat

The *Chifa Jao Fua* (☎ 829 306), on Cevallos near JL Mera, has good meals for under US$2 and is a good value. Cheaper and almost as good is the *Chifa Nueva Hong Kong*, Bolívar 768 and Martínez. There are several other chifas. You can get supercheap meals around the market. Reasonably priced and tasty chicken is sold at *La*

Brasa Roja on JL Mera at 12 de Noviembre. For breakfast the best bet is one of the cake shops for coffee, juice and rolls or sandwiches. Try the *Panadería Enripan* on JL Mera. *Oasis Heladería*, Sucre near M Egüez, is a popular café. *Mama Miche Restaurant* (☎ 822 913), on 13 de Abril, behind the Centro Comercial Ambato, is quite a good value and open 24 hours. The *Kangaroo Bar*, near the market, serves Mexican snacks and beer and is sometimes a good hangout but not very cheap.

For good medium-priced steak, try *Parrilladas El Gaucho* (☎ 828 969), on Bolívar near Quito, or the slightly cheaper *Parrilladas Favid* on Bolívar near JL Mera. The *Pizzería La Cigarra* (☎ 828 411), at Bolívar 373, cooks a reasonable pizza. *Paolo's Pizzería*, Cevallos at JL Mera, is a quiet place for a light meal or snack. *Pizzería Fornace*, JB Vela at Lalama, has a wider range of good Italian food.

There are three Swiss-run *El Alamo* restaurants: *Restaurant El Gran Alamo* (☎ 820 706), Montalvo 520 and Cevallos, is quite fancy and comparatively expensive; *Restaurant El Alamo* (☎ 821 710), Sucre 660 and JL Mera, is lower priced and good; and *El Alamo Chalet*, Cevallos 612 and Montalvo, I have yet to try.

The Hotel Ambato has the best hotel restaurant; some say it's the best in town. Its most obvious competitor is the nearby *La Buena Mesa* (☎ 822 330), on Quito near Rocafuerte. This is a good French restaurant recommended for its very pleasant atmosphere. *Restaurant El Español*, a block from the Hotel Ambato, is a newer restaurant worth a try.

Entertainment

There is some nightlife but not much. The *Peña Tungurahua Bar*, on Martínez near the Centro Comercial Ambato, has a peña on some weekends that features música folklorica, but it doesn't get underway until about 11 pm. *La Cascada Discoteca* is on the same block. The *Restaurant Coyote Disco Club*, on Bolívar near Quito, is a restaurant popular with young people that has dancing in the evenings. There are a

few cinemas; consult the local newspaper, *El Heraldo*, for what's playing. There is a casino at the Hotel Ambato.

Getting There & Away

Air There is a small airstrip nearby for emergency and military use only. TAME (☎ 826 601, 820 322, 822 595), Sucre 331 and Guayaquil, and SAN-Saeta, Bolívar near Montalvo, only make reservations for flights from other cities.

Bus The terminal terrestre (☎ 821 481) is two km away from the town center, and buses to all destinations leave from here. Get there by heading north on 12 de Noviembre to the traffic circle and then turn right on Avenida de las Américas. The most frequent departures are for Quito (US$2; three hours), Baños (US$0.60; 45 minutes), Riobamba (one hour) and Guayaquil (US$5; six hours). There are several buses a day to Cuenca (US$6; seven hours) and also Guaranda (US$1.60; two hours), some of which continue to Babahoyo and a couple to Chillanes. Several companies run a bus to Tena in the Oriente (six hours, depending on road conditions; note that the road may be closed – see under Baños). There are buses for many other destinations.

For northern destinations it's usually best to take a bus to Quito and change at the terminal there.

Train The train station is near the main bus terminal, two km away from the town center. There are services north to Quito and south to Riobamba, currently only on Saturday, though they have run on other days in the past. Most foreign travelers take the train all the way either from Quito or Riobamba because it costs US$10 for foreigners, regardless of how far you travel. Trains pass through Ambato late in the morning. Inquire at the train station.

Getting Around

Bus The most important local bus service for the traveler is the route between the terminal terrestre and the town center. From the terminal, climb the exit ramp to the Avenida de las Américas, which crosses the railway line on a bridge. On this bridge is a bus stop where a westbound (to your right) bus, often signed 'Centro,' will take you to the Parque Cevallos for US$0.10.

Parque Cevallos is the center for many buses out of town into the suburbs, so it's a good place to ask around if you need to get somewhere. Buses marked 'Terminal' leave from the Calle Martínez side of Parque Cevallos – if in doubt, ask. Buses to the suburb of Ficoa (for the Quinta de Montalvo) also leave from this park. A block away is Calle Bolívar, with buses to Miraflores running along it. Buses to the suburb of Atocha (more quintas) leave from 12 de Noviembre and Sevilla or E Espejo. Buses for several surrounding villages also depart from the Parque Cevallos area.

Taxi Taxis from the terminal terrestre to the center cost about US$1. There are fixed rates for most runs around Ambato and surrounding villages, though attempted overcharging has been reported. There are many taxis at Parque 12 de Noviembre and Parque Cevallos.

AROUND AMBATO

Salasaca and Pelileo (both described later) are the most frequently visited nearby villages because they lie on the good main road to Baños. Other villages are off the main road but are interesting to visit on daytrips. With the exception of Patate, none of them have accommodations and travelers are a rarity. In Ambato, ask at the Parque Cevallos or the terminal terrestre about buses.

Quizapincha, about 10 km west of Ambato, is known for its leatherwork. It can be reached by buses crossing the Puente de Ficoa (bridge) at the northwest end of Montalvo.

Píllaro, some 20 km to the northeast, is in a cereal and fruit growing area. It is known as a center for guitar making and for carvings from animal horns. July to August are big months for fiestas with bullfights, typical highland food and parades. July 15

is the fiesta of Apostolo Santiago (Saint James), and July 25 is cantonization day. August 10, Quito's Independence Day, is also vigorously celebrated with a bullfight and a bull run, in which the bulls charge through the streets; everybody participates.

Píllaro is the entry point for the **Llanganates**, a very remote and difficult-to-reach mountain range in which Atahualpa's treasure is supposedly buried. Many bona fide expeditions have searched for the treasure using ancient maps and documents from the time of the conquest, but nobody has found it yet!

Picaigua, some 10 km southeast of Ambato, is known for ropework, sandals and bags made from the *cabuya* (agave) fiber. Nearby, **Pinllo** is known for its leatherwork. **Patate**, 25 km from Ambato and 5 km northeast of Pelileo, is known for its picturesque location on the Río Patate, the grapes grown in the region, and the production of some of the best aguardiente in the highlands. There are buses from Pelileo to Patate.

Places to Stay

In the pretty village of Patate, the *Hotel Turístico Patate* (☎ 870 177, in Quito ☎ 590 657, 650 486) offers 15 double rooms with private bath and hot water for US$20. There is a restaurant, bar and recreation area, and the management can arrange tours to the Llanganates and local ruins.

At 2900 meters in the mountains northeast of Patate, about 15 km away by road, is the *Hacienda Manteles* (☎ /fax 870 123). This family farm was converted into a delightful country inn in 1992. From the hacienda there are pretty views of the Río Patate valley below and Volcán Tungurahua and other mountains in the distance. The valley is covered by fields spread out like a checkered tablecloth – hence the name 'Manteles,' which is Spanish for tablecloths. Above the inn is an area of cloud forest that can be explored on foot or by horse (US$5 per hour). Guides can be hired to take you to a nearby waterfall, up into the páramo and across the Llanganates, or to visit pre-Columbian remains. Birdwatching, hiking and fishing are other activities.

There are seven good-size rooms, all with private hot shower and sleeping up to three or four people. Rates are US$42/54/66/78 for one to four people in a room. Home-cooked fresh meals are served buffet style and are all-you-can-eat. Breakfast is US$6 and lunch or dinner is US$12. Box lunches are also available. The restaurant/bar has a fireplace and is attractively decorated with Salasacan weavings. Reservations can be made at the Hacienda, in Quito (☎ /fax 505 230) or in the USA (☎ (800) 327 3573, fax (813) 439 2118). Guests with reservations can arrange to be picked up from the bus station in Patate at no extra charge.

SALASACA

As you head southeast from Ambato on the Baños road, the first place of interest is Salasaca about 14 km away. The village and its environs are inhabited by some 2000 Salasaca Indians, who are famous for their tapestries. They are less well known for their history, which is particularly interesting. Originally they came from Bolivia but were conquered by the Incas in the 1400s.

One of the ways in which the Incas controlled the peoples they had conquered was to move them en masse to an area which the Incas had long dominated and where there was less chance of an uprising. Apparently this is what happened to the Salasacas. After the Spanish conquest, they remained where they were but retained an unusually high degree of independence and were almost unknown by outsiders until the middle of the 20th century.

The villagers are recognizable by their typical dress, especially the men who normally wear broad-brimmed white hats, black ponchos, and white shirts and trousers. Traditionally a farming community, they raise their own sheep to obtain wool for their weavings, which are a secondary source of income. Their tapestries are all made by hand and are different from work done by other Indian groups (though

telling the difference may be difficult unless you have spent time examining Ecuadorian weaving).

There is no local produce market in Salasaca; the villagers use the nearby Pelileo Saturday market or go to Ambato. There is a craft market held every Sunday morning near the church on the Ambato-Baños road. Also along this road are several craft stores that are open daily. One of these is a women artisans' cooperative. Nearby is Alonso Pilla's house (as you arrive from Baños it's on the left about 100 meters past the Evangelical church in the center of the village). His house is open from 11 am to 6 pm daily and he gives weaving demonstrations on a backstrap loom using traditional techniques – his work has been well recommended. He puts maps of how to get to his house up in the favorite tourist hotels and restaurants in Baños. Salasacan tapestries are also sold in craft stores in Quito and Cuenca.

The many Indian fiestas in the Salasaca area are worth looking out for. May and June are good months for fiestas all over the highlands. On the Sunday after Easter there is a street dance between Salasaca and Pelileo. On June 15 the Salasacas dress up in animal costumes for Santo Vintio. Corpus Christi (movable date in June) is celebrated in Salasaca and Pelileo. The feast of Saint Anthony is celebrated at the end of November.

All the usual annual holidays (Christmas, Easter, etc) offer interesting fiesta possibilities.

PELILEO

Some six km beyond Salasaca on the Baños road is the larger village of Pelileo. Despite its 400-year history, today's Pelileo is a very modern village. It was founded by the colonialist Antonio Clavijo in 1570 but destroyed by earthquakes in 1698, 1797, 1840 and 1949. The present site is about two km away from the ruins of the old town. It is the market town for nearby villages including Salasaca. Saturday is market day. Pelileo could be dubbed the 'Blue Jeans Capital of Ecuador' – I have never seen so many brands and sizes of jeans for sale, especially on market day.

Pelileo celebrates its cantonization on July 22 with the usual highland festivities: bullfights, parades and plenty of food and drink.

Baños is only 24 km away, but the road drops some 850 meters from Pelileo. The descent along the Río Pastaza gorge is spectacular, and some of the best views of the snow-capped volcano Tungurahua are to be seen on this drive. At 5016 meters, it is Ecuador's 10th highest peak and gives its name to the province.

BAÑOS

The most recent census places the population of this small town at only some 16,000 people, yet there are about 50 hotels in Baños and its outskirts. It is one of the most important tourist spots in the country, popular with Ecuadorians and foreigners alike, and its popularity remains undiminished despite the many thousands of visitors each year. Some people love it and spend a week or more; other travelers think the town too 'touristy' and pass on through. It is in a beautiful spot and there are many attractions in the area – it's worth a visit to decide for yourself whether to love it or leave it. The majority of readers give it a positive review, though several disagree.

Unless you've only just arrived in Latin America, you'll know that Baños means 'baths,' which is precisely what the town is famous for. Some of them are fed by thermal springs from the base of the active Volcán Tungurahua, which means 'little hell' in Quichua. Other baths have melt water running into them from Tungurahua's icy flanks. Locals swear that the baths are great for your health. While that is a debatable point, it is true that the casual atmosphere of this pretty resort town makes it an excellent place to unwind after some hard traveling, and few travelers can resist the opportunity to relax here for a while.

The baths are not the only attraction. Baños' elevation of 1800 meters gives it an extremely agreeable climate, and the surroundings are green and attractive. There are good opportunities for both short walks and ambitious climbs of Volcán Tungurahua as well as El Altar, an even higher extinct volcano some 25 km south of Tungurahua. Both of these are in Parque Nacional Sangay, which is described below.

Baños is also the gateway town into the jungle via Puyo and Misahuallí. East of Baños the road drops spectacularly and there are exceptional views of the upper Amazonian basin stretching away before you. In the town itself there are more attractions: an interesting basilica, a small museum, a little nightlife and restaurants selling typical local food.

There is another much smaller Baños near Cuenca, also with thermal pools.

Information

There is no CETUR tourist office, but (slightly biased) information can be obtained from the many tour operators in town. Owners of hotels and restaurants are used to answering questions. There are always so many travelers in town that they are often your best source of up-to-date information.

Red-tiled roofs are a feature of many Andean villages.

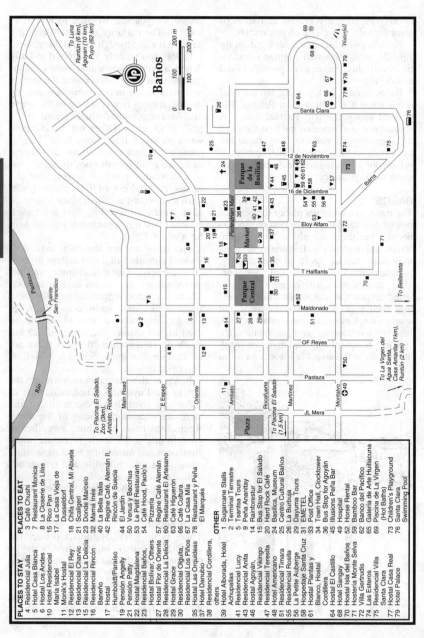

Baños

To Luna
Runtún (6 km),
Agoyán (10 km),
Puyo (62 km)

To Piscina El Salado,
Zoo (3km),
Ambato, Riobamba

Puente
San Francisco

To Piscina El Salado
(1.5 km)

To La Virgen del
Agua Santa,
Casa Amarilla (1km),
Runtún (2 km)

To Bellavista

Waterfall

Santa Clara

Parque
de la
Basílica

12 de Noviembre

16 de Diciembre

Eloy Alfaro

Market

Pedestrian Mall

Parque
Central

T Halflants

Maldonado

OF Reyes

Pastaza

Martínez

JL Mera

Plaza

Ambato

Rocafuerte

Montalvo

Oriente

E Espejo

Main Road

Río

Pastaza

PLACES TO STAY	PLACES TO EAT
4 Residencial Julia	3 Café Chushi
6 Hotel Casa Blanca	7 Restaurant Monica
9 Hostal Los Andes	8 La Closerie de Lilas
10 Hotel Residencial	15 Rico Pan
Maria Isabel	17 La Casa Vieja de
11 Monik's Hostal	Dusseldorf
12 Residencial El Rey	18 Chifa Central, Mi Abuela
13 Residencial Charvic	21 Scaligeri
15 Residencial La Delicia	23 Donde Marcelo
16 Residencial Rincón	32 Mamá Inés
Baneño	40 La Bella Italia
17 Hostal	42 Regine Café, Alemán II,
Humboldt/Paraiso	Rincón de Suecia
19 Pension Angelly	44 El Jardín
21 Pension Patty	50 Venus y Bacchus
22 Hostal Magdalena	53 Le Petit Restaurant
23 Residencial Baños,	54 Café Hood, Paolo's
27 Hostal Bolívar, Others	Pizzería
27 Hostal Flor de Oriente	57 Regine Café Alemán
28 Residencial La Delicia	60 Restaurant El Artesano
29 Hostal Grace	63 Café Higuerón
30 Residencial Olguita,	66 Café Cultura
35 Residencial Los Piños	67 La Casa Mía
38 Hostal Las Orquídeas	78 Restaurant y Peña
38 Hostal Danubio	El Marqués
38 Residencial Cordillera,	
others	OTHER
39 Hotel Alborada, Hotel	1 Sugarcane Stalls
Achupallas	2 Terminal Terrestre
41 Residencial Lucy	5 Tsantsa Tours
43 Residencial Anita	9 Peña Ananitay
46 Hostal Agoyán,	14 Rainforestur
47 Residencial Vikingo	15 Bus Stop for El Salado
48 Residencial Teresita	20 Hard Rock Café
48 Hotel Americano	24 Basílica, Museum
55 Residencial Timara	25 Centro Cultural Baños
55 Residencial Rosita	26 La Burbuja
56 La Petite Auberge	29 Dayuma Tours
58 Hospedaje Santa Cruz	31 EMETEL
61 Hotel Plantas y	31 Post Office
Blanco, Hostal	34 Town Hall, Clocktower
Cordillera	36 Bus Stop for Agoyán
64 Hotel El Castillo	45 Illusions Peña Bar
68 Hotel Sangay	49 Hospital
70 Hotel Isla del Baños	52 Horse Rental
71 Hostería Monte Selva	59 Bamboo Bar
72 Villa Gertrudis	62 Banco del Pacífico
74 Las Esteros	65 Galería de Arte Huillacuna
75 Residencial Villa	69 Piscina de La Virgen
Santa Clara	(Hot Baths)
77 Hotel Casa Real	73 Children's Playground
79 Hotel Palace	76 Santa Clara
	Swimming Pool

SOUTH QUITO

Money The Banco del Pacífico (☎ 740 336/48), Martínez and 12 de Noviembre, changes both US cash dollars and traveler's checks at rates about the same as Quito's. Various stores, restaurants and hotels may also change US dollars.

Post & Communications EMETEL (☎ 740 411) and the post office (☎ 740 901) are both on the Parque Central. (When I used my AT&T Direct calling card at this office, the operator cut me off after five minutes because, she said, EMETEL doesn't make any money from calls charged to a US calling card.) The area code for Baños is 03.

Travel Agencies & Guides There are many 'guides' to provide services for the large numbers of tourists passing through town. Some guides are bad, not very experienced or dishonest. If you hire a guide, make sure that they have recommendations – listen to what other travelers have to say.

Guides should have a *Patente de Operación Turística* license issued by INEFAN and you should be able to examine it. The bottom left box on the license shows the areas the guide is authorized to work in. Natural history guides should also have a CETUR card that ranks them as *Naturalista 1* (lowest ranking), *Naturalista 2* (mid-ranking) or *Nacional* (highest ranking), and states the languages in which they guide.

When going on a tour, find out if any national park will be visited and whether the entrance fees (US$10 per person) are included in the cost. Rather than listing agencies and guides here, I have mentioned them in the appropriate parts of the various activities sections below.

Bookstores The Café Chushi, on E Espejo and PV Maldonado by the bus terminal, has a library of guidebooks and a book exchange for English and German books.

Cultural Centers Centro Cultural Baños, 12 de Noviembre and Ambato, shows classic movies in various languages most nights at 8 pm for US$1.25. It also offers classes in yoga, meditation and the arts. There is a book exchange and various lectures are given. It is run by the owners of the popular Café Hood, who can give you information.

Galería de Arte Huillacuna, Montalvo 2 06 and Santa Clara, has both permanent and changing exhibits of local artists. Many works are for sale. They also have a café.

Medical Services The small local hospital (☎ 740 443/301) is on Montalvo and Pastaza. There are several pharmacies along Ambato.

Emergency The police (☎ 740 251, 101) are on Oriente near JL Mera.

Basilica

Within the town itself, the basilica with the **Santuario de Nuestra Señora de Agua Santa** is worth seeing. This Dominican church is dedicated to the Virgin of the Holy Water, who is credited with several miracles in the Baños area. The annual October celebration in her honor has much street music and many Indian bands playing, but generally she is the object of devout admiration, as exemplified by the many offerings to her and the paintings depicting her miracles.

These paintings are simple but charming, with explanations in Spanish along the lines of 'On January 30, 1904, Sr X fell off his horse as he was crossing the Río Pastaza bridge. As he fell 70 meters to the torrents below, he yelled 'Holy Mother of the Holy Water' and was miraculously saved!' Other paintings show people being miraculously saved from exploding volcanoes, burning hotels, transit accidents and other misfortunes. Reading the explanations is amusing and a great way to practice your Spanish. Please remember, however, that this is a place of worship and act accordingly.

Just above the church is a museum with an eclectic display of stuffed animals, religious paintings, church vestments and local handicrafts. It's open daily from 7:30 am to 4 pm, and entry is US$0.30. There is also a small gift shop.

Zoo

A modest zoo, three km west of town, has local animals exhibited in clean but small cages. The collection includes tapir and the rare harpy eagle. Entrance is US$0.50.

Hot Baths

There are three baths, two in Baños (only one is hot) and a third out of town. All charge a modest entrance fee, for which they provide changing rooms and safe storage for your clothes. Towels and bathing suits may be available for rent, and soap is for sale (nude bathing is prohibited).

The best-known bath is the Piscina de La Virgen, with hot showers and three concrete pools of different temperatures. You can't miss them – they're right under the big **waterfall** at the southeast end of town. You can see the falls from most parts of Baños. Admission is US$0.80. They are open from 4:30 am to 4:30 pm and start getting quite busy soon after sunrise. They are very crowded at weekends when a tepid swimming pool next door (the Piscinas Modernas) opens to take some of the crowds.

Nearby is a cold swimming pool at Santa Clara, which charges US$0.30. They have a sauna available for US$2 per person. Several of the better hotels have swimming pools or saunas.

If you walk up the hill past the cemetery on Martínez, you'll end up on a track that crosses a stream (Quebrada de Naguasco) on a small wooden footbridge. The track continues on the other side to a road in front of Cabañas Bascun, where you turn left to reach the Piscina El Salado, also open from 4:30 am. (There are buses too, which take a different, longer route.) Here there are hot and cold showers, seven concrete pools of varying temperatures and an ice-cold waterfall to stand under if you're the masochistic sort – a real deal for US$0.80. Because these are two or three km of out of town, they're not quite so crowded.

Supposedly, everyone has to take a shower and wear a bathing suit before entering the pools. However, I still receive reports that the locals use the pools for washing themselves, sometimes entering the water wearing clothing, especially on Friday, which is traditionally washing day for the locals (to beat the out-of-town weekend crowds perhaps). If fully clothed people are in the pools, you should avoid putting your head under or getting water in your mouth if you have a sensitive stomach. The baths at El Salado are reportedly emptied every night and filled with clean water, while those at La Virgen are emptied three times a week. Even when freshly filled, the pools look murky because of the mineral content of the water, which is touted for its restorative and healthful properties. Chlorates, sulfates and magnesium are among the principal chemicals found in the baths. The Virgen and El Salado waters supposedly reach temperatures of over 50°C, while the Santa Clara pool is normally about 24°C. The hot pools are better used for soaking rather than swimming.

Hiking

Once you've visited all the pools, there are many walks to take. Plenty of information about these is available in Baños. The following are some suggestions. Note that there have been a few cases of robberies on some trails and near the climbers' refuge. You are advised to seek local updates on this and hike with a group.

The walk down to the Río Pastaza is easy and popular. Just behind the sugarcane stalls by the bus station is a short trail that leads to the **Puente San Francisco** (bridge), which crosses the river. You can continue on trails up the other side as far as you want.

Going south on Calle Maldonado takes you to a footpath that climbs to **Bellavista**, where there is a building with a white cross high over Baños (visible from the town). The path then continues to the tiny settlement of **Runtún** some two hours away. The views are great!

West of town near the zoo, turn right by a religious shrine and walk down to the Puente San Martín and visit the impressive falls of **Cascada Inés María**, a few hundred meters to the right of the bridge. You can also cross the bridge and continue to the village of **Lligua**, about three hours away. From this road, trails climb up the hills to your right.

There are plenty of other possibilities; information is easily available in Baños.

Climbing & Backpacking

Climbers with crampons can ascend Tungurahua (5016 meters) in two days. It's an easy climb for experts, but novices will need an experienced guide to prevent potentially fatal accidents. The volcano is part of Parque Nacional Sangay, so you pay a US$10 entrance fee and US$5 to overnight in the climbers' refuge. A road goes halfway up from Baños – a ride in a truck will cost US$2.50. Ask at Pensión Patty (see Places to Stay) about their 8 am truck departures and their guides, Carlos and José, who have been leading tours and renting equipment for years. They can also arrange for a vehicle to take you part way up the mountain and for mules to carry your gear (ice ax, crampons, etc). Another reputable and recommended climbing outfitter is Expediciones Amazonicas (☎ 740 506), Oriente at T Halflants, which has rental equipment and guides. Willie Navarette (contact him at Café Higuerón), too, has been recommended. US$50 per person is the going rate for the two-day climb with a group. Beware of cheap but inexperienced guides.

The jagged, extinct volcano El Altar (5319 meters) is hard to climb, but the wild páramo surrounding it is a good area for backpacking and camping.

More detailed information about these volcanoes is given below under Parque Nacional Sangay.

Mountain Biking

Several companies rent mountain bikes from about US$4 per day. Check equipment carefully, as maintenance is some-times poor. Expediciones Amazonicas (see above) has been recommended by one source for bike rentals, but there are plenty of other places. I'd look around to find the bike that's best for you. The dramatic descent (mainly) to Puyo, about 70 km east to the edge of the Oriente, is a popular ride. Parts of the road are unpaved, and one section is under construction through 1997, but bikes can be wheeled past. When construction is complete the road may be paved all the way. There is a passport control at Shell, so carry your documents. From Puyo (or earlier) you can simply take a bus back to Baños with the bike on the roof (see Getting There & Away, below). This route into the Oriente is described under The Road to Puyo in the Northern Oriente chapter.

Various other mountain biking options are available, and the outfitters will be happy to tell you about them.

Horseback Riding

Angel Aldáz (☎ 740 175), Montalvo and JL Mera, rents horses for about US$10 per half day or more with a guide. Christián, at Hostal Isla de Baños (see Places to Stay), has half-, full- and two- to nine-day horse trips with guides. Christián speaks English and German. There are other places that rent horses, but these two outfitters have received the best recommendations. Their horses are in good shape and are suitable for both beginners and experienced riders. I have also heard that Caballos José (☎ 740 746), Maldonado and Martínez, is quite good.

Horses can be rented by the hour, though by the time you saddle up and get out of town, it's hardly worth going for such a short period.

Whitewater Rafting

Geoturs (☎ 740 703), on Maldonado half a block south of the bus station, is run by an Ecuadorian/Swiss couple. They offer half-day trips to the Río Patate for US$20, which leave at 8:30 am and 2 pm on demand. Trips last four hours (two hours on the river) and a snack is included. They also offer a full day to the Río Pastaza for US$40, leaving at 8:30 am on demand. This trip is 10 hours, with four hours on the river, and lunch is included. They provide transportation, guide, raft, paddles, life jackets, wet suits and helmets. Experience is not necessary, though you should know how to swim.

Jungle Trips
Many jungle trips from Baños are advertised, but not all guides are experienced or recommended. Guides should have licenses (see Travel Agencies & Guides, above). Much useful general information about jungle trips is given in the Northern Oriente chapter under Misahuallí.

Three- to seven-day jungle tours are about US$30 to US$45 per person depending on destination (three- or four-person minimum). Some focus on Indian culture and plants; others more on wildlife. Don't expect to see many animals in the rainforest – you need patience and luck. June to September is the busy season, when reservations are a good idea if you want to go on a specific date, though if you are loose and just show up, you can usually hook up with a tour. Baños is always full of travelers and is a good town in which to organize a group if you are not already with one.

Rainforestur (☎ 740 423, ☎ /fax 740 743), Ambato near Maldonado, has received several recommendations for their Cuyabeno Reserve tours (US$45 per person per day with a four person minimum and 12 maximum). They also visit other areas of both primary and secondary jungle. Some of their guides speak English, German or French (as well as Spanish). Tours last three days to a week. They will also arrange volcano tours.

Tsantsa Tours (☎ 740 957, fax 740 717), Oriente near Eloy Alfaro, has also been recommended, particularly Sebastian Moya. This is one of the few agencies owned and operated by Indians. Their guides are Shuar Indians who are sensitive to the issues of the local people and environment. Some speak English. Typically trips cost about US$45 per person per day,

and various Oriente destinations are visited. Parts of the proceeds are used to fund education and other projects in local Indian communities.

Dayuma Tours has a Baños office, but it is better to book at their office in Misahuallí. Vasco Tours (☎ 740 017), Eloy Alfaro and Martínez, run by the Vasco brothers, has reportedly moved here recently from Misahuallí. Their guide Juan Medina has been recommended.

Language Courses
There are several places that have been recommended for learning Spanish. The following all charge about US$3 per hour for one-on-one tuition. Spanish School for Foreigners (☎ 740 612), 16 de Diciembre and Espejo; Elizabeth Barrionuevo (☎ 740 314, 740 632), T Halflants 656; and Pepe Eras (☎ 740 232), Montalvo 526. Group classes may be arranged.

Special Events
Baños became the seat of its cantón on December 16, 1944, and an annual fiesta is celebrated on this and the preceding days. There are the usual processions, fireworks, music and a great deal of street dancing and drinking at night. Fun! Also, there are processions and fireworks during the entire month of October as the various barrios of Baños take turns to pay homage to the local icon, Nuestra Señora de Agua Santa.

Places to Stay
There are literally dozens of hotels to choose from, so many of these descriptions are necessarily brief. Most of the hotels are bottom end in that they charge US$5 or less per person, but many are a good value. Some of the cheap hotels have varying quality of rooms – check your rooms before accepting them. Others charge double rates for one night but will drop their prices if you stay longer (negotiate this when you check in, not when you check out). Usually there are plenty of rooms available, but choice can become very limited and prices high if you arrive on a Friday night or if there is a fiesta

underway. Try to arrive early in the day to get the best rooms. The prices given below assume that you are not arriving just before the annual fiestas.

Hotels in Baños can be noisy – it is a vacation town, after all. For some quieter places, see Places to Stay – Around Baños, below.

Places to Stay – bottom end

One of the cheapest places is the basic *Residencial Rincón Baneño* (☎ 740 316), Oriente 662, with hot water and clean doubles for under US$4. The well-known, family-run *Pensión Patty* (☎ 740 202), Eloy Alfaro 556, has friendly management and information on trekking, climbing and horseback riding in the area. It is popular with budget travelers. Basic rooms go for US$2 per person and vary in quality – some of the older ones are pretty funky, but the price is right. There is one hot and several cold showers, and a communal kitchen. Sometimes you'll meet a great group of people – everyone chips in with something to eat or drink, conversations flow, a rum bottle gets opened or a guitar appears. Opposite is the *Pensión Angelly*, which is similarly priced and OK.

Other basic places for about US$2 per person include the *Residencial Olguita* (☎ 740 271) with hot water and front rooms overlooking the Parque Central; *Residencial Julia*, with cold water by the bus station; the nearby *Residencial El Rey*, where three rooms share a hot shower; and the small *Las Esteros*.

The friendly *Residencial Timara* (☎ 740 599), Maldonado near Martínez, is about US$2.80 per person and has hot water and kitchen facilities. The *Residencial Villa Santa Clara* (☎ 740 349), 12 de Noviembre near Ibarra, is popular and has kitchen facilities, hot showers and a garden. Rooms in the old house are US$2 per person and clean new cabins are US$5/8 with hot shower. The friendly *Residencial Lucy* (☎ 740 466) is US$3.50 per person in rooms with private bath and hot water, or US$2.50 with shared bath.

There are several other very basic hotels for about US$3 or less per person. The

friendly *Hotel Americano* (☎ 740 352), 12 de Noviembre near Martínez, has large rooms and a simple restaurant. The *Residencial Teresita* (☎ 740 471), 12 de Noviembre near Rocafuerte, has some rooms overlooking the Parque de la Basílica. Both have hot water and kitchen facilities. Others nearby are the *Hostal Agoyán* and *Residencial Vikingo*. The *Residencial Los Piños* (☎ 740 252) has some rooms with Parque Central views, as do the *Residencial La Delicia 1* (☎ 740 477) and *Residencial La Delicia 2* (☎ 740 537), though both these are grubby, as is the *Hotel Danubio*.

The very popular *Hostal Plantas y Blanco* (☎ /fax 740 044), Martínez at 12 de Noviembre, is attractively decorated with plants, and has a pleasant roof-top terrace (for breakfast) and a steam bath. Clean rooms are US$5 per person with private bath or US$4 with shared bath. There is a laundry and bike rental, and the staff is helpful. Unfortunately they were full both times I stopped by. Next door, the *Hostal Cordillera* is clean and friendly but may lack hot water. Rooms are US$3 per person or US$4 with bath. Around the corner, the *Hospedaje Santa Cruz* (☎ 740 648) is clean and a good value at US$4 per person with bath and hot water. Opposite is the similar *Residencial Rosita*. The good *Hostal Las Orquideas* (☎ 740 911) on the corner of the Parque Central has light, clean rooms, some with balconies, for US$4 per person with private hot shower. These are a good value. The pleasant *Hostal El Castillo* (☎ 740 285), Martínez 255, is also good at US$4 per person for rooms with hot showers most of the time. They provide guests with three meals for US$2.50.

Other accommodations for about US$4 to US$6 per person include the hotels on the busy pedestrian block of Ambato such as the *Residencial Baños* (☎ 740 284), *Residencial Cordillera* (☎ 740 536) and the *Hostal Bolívar* (☎ 740 497). There are others on this block, which tends to be noisy with people partying. Also in this price range are the modern but unremarkable *Hotel Alborada* (☎ 740 814) and *Hotel*

Achupallas (☎ 740 422/389), both on the Parque de la Basílica, and the friendly but quite basic *Residencial Anita* (☎ 740 319). The *Hostal Grace* looks clean and OK, with the top-floor rooms looking like the best. Though one reader reported a theft in 1994, it does not seem to be a regularly occurring problem. The *Hotel Humboldt/ Paraíso* (☎ 740 430/90), Ambato and T Halflants, has clean but rather run-down rooms with private bathrooms and hot water for about the same price; they can provide meals.

Others in the US$4 to US$6 per person price range include the *Hostal Los Andes, Monik's Hostal, Hostal Los Andes, Hotel Residencial María Isabel* and *Le Petite Auberge*.

The following charge about US$6 to US$8 per person. The attractive *Café Cultura* (☎ 740 419), Montalvo and Santa Clara, has six clean double rooms upstairs that share a bathroom with hot water; they also include breakfast. The *Residencial Charvic* (☎ 740 298/113), PV Maldonado and Oriente, is a decent hotel within a block of the bus station. They have small but clean rooms with private bath, hot water and TV. Opposite, the *Hotel Casa Blanca* (☎ 740 092) also looks good. The good, clean, family-run *Hostal Magdalena* (☎ 740 233/364), Oriente 1037 and16 de Diciembre, has rooms with private bath and hot water, and there is a parking lot. It is secure and closes at 10 pm (though you can ring a bell to get in if you let them know you are going out).

Places to Stay – middle

For US$8 to US$10 per person, the *Hostal Flor de Oriente* (☎ 740 418/058, fax 740 717), Ambato and PV Maldonado, has very clean rooms with private bath, hot water and telephone. They have a decent restaurant downstairs and parking is available. Breakfast is included. Another good choice is the German-run *Hostal Isla de Baños* (☎ 740 609), T Halflants 1-31 and Montalvo, with simple but spacious clean rooms with private bath and hot water. The hotel is set in attractive gardens and has a well-recommended restaurant and bar. Both hotels are a good value.

The new *Hostal Casa Real* (☎ 740 215), Montalvo and Santa Clara, has nice clean rooms for US$13/22, and 'suites' for US$44. Their restaurant/bar sometimes has live music. The *Hotel Palace* (☎ 740 470, fax 740 291), Montalvo 20-03 by the waterfall, is clean and pleasant with a good restaurant attached. There is a garden, swimming pool, sauna, spa, Turkish bath, games room and small museum of archaeology and numismatics (coins). Rooms with private bath, TV and telephone are US$22 single plus US$6 for each additional person (up to four) – suitable for families. Rooms in both the old-fashioned house and the annex vary somewhat in quality. The owners are friendly. Rates include use of the facilities that nonguests can use for a few dollars.

The *Hotel Sangay* (☎ 740 490/917, fax 740 056) is opposite the Piscina de La Virgen baths. There are squash and tennis courts, a swimming pool, Jacuzzi and sauna, and restaurant and bar. The (more expensive) rooms in the cabins have TV and are better than rooms in the main building, where the rooms on the ground floor in particular have been criticized as damp and musty (although they have recently been remodeled and may have improved). All rooms have private bathroom, hot water, telephone and cable TV. The hotel is popular with Ecuadorian tour groups, but can seem quite gloomy when there aren't groups to fill up the 72 rooms. Rooms in the hotel building are US$24/34, and rooms in the cabins are US$38/50, including continental breakfast and use of the facilities. Nonguests can use the pool and other facilities for a small fee.

The much quieter, low-key *Villa Gertrudis* (☎ 740 441), Montalvo and V Ibarra, is also set in pretty gardens and has a big pool. They charge US$30 per person, including two meals, but are often full. Nonguests can use the pool for about US$2.

The newest good hotel in town is the *Hostería Monte Selva* (☎ 740 566, 820 068, fax 854 685), at the south end of T Halflants. Attractive wooden cabins are set on a lush hillside just above Baños and the plant-filled gardens have a pool and sauna. It looks nice. Rates are US$25/35, including continental breakfast. There is a bar and restaurant.

Places to Stay – around Baños

About two km from town by footpath or four km by road is the Piscina El Salado, with four nearby hotels that are quieter than most of the places in Baños. There are two basic residenciales right by the baths – *El Salado* and the *Puerto del Salado* with good views of Tungurahua. Rates are about US$4 per person.

About 10 minutes away from the baths are the *Cabañas Bascún* (☎ /fax 740 334), which has both a hot and a cold pool, water slide, sauna, tennis court and restaurant. The pool facilities are open only at weekends and holidays, but the hotel rooms and restaurant are open all week. Clean rooms in cabins are about US$30/40. Family rooms are available on a sliding scale, with the largest sleeping nine people for about US$90. The place is popular as a family weekend getaway. Nonresidents can use the pool and sauna for about US$4.

Between the Bascún and the Piscina El Salado is a B&B, the *Casa Nahuazo* (☎ 740 315), which is run by the friendly Aniko Bahr, who arrived in 1981 with the Peace Corps and somehow never left. The very quiet hotel is a good place to get travel information. There is an English book exchange. The five clean and pleasant double rooms have private bath, hot water, and fresh fruit and flowers. Rates are about US$18/25, including continental breakfast. The kitchen provides snacks or light meals (at a low extra cost) until 5 pm.

The *Casa Amarilla* is a serene escape, about one kilometer south of the hospital on the steep trail leading up towards Runtún. The views of Baños are great. Bed and breakfast accommodations, including kitchen privileges, are US$12/16. The South American Explorers Club in Quito can make reservations.

Finally, high above Baños, is the town's most exclusive hotel, the Swiss-managed *Luna Runtún* (☎ 740 882/3, fax 740 376, see also Online Services). By road, it's six km beyond Baños; follow the signs east of town on the road to Puyo. Luna Runtún can be reached on foot by climbing up from Baños for about three km along either of the main trails. I would guess that 99.9% of the guests do not carry their suitcases up a steep trail but prefer to drive in. The trails are there for a downhill hike back into Baños. Horseback riding and guided hiking can be arranged, with hikes ranging from a gentle botany walk or cultural excursion to more strenuous climbs. On the grounds are a volleyball court and children's playground. The views are gorgeous. The 32 rooms and one suite are spacious and comfortable, with large bathrooms and views. Rates include an American breakfast and a complete à la carte dinner. Standard rooms are US$84/120; superior rooms have a private terrace overlooking Baños and run US$156 per double; the presidential suite, with a fireplace, is US$192.

Places to Eat

There are both Ecuadorian and several European-style restaurants in Baños that are currently enjoying favor.

Donde Marcelo (☎ 740 427), on Ambato near16 de Diciembre, has quite good, though slightly pricey, Ecuadorian food and a very popular bar upstairs. The service is friendly and efficient. This is the heart of Baños' pedestrian street and is always busy. You can sit outside of Marcelo's and people-watch while just having a beer. On the same block, the simpler *Restaurant Latino* and *Restaurant Los Alpes* have decent, cheaper Ecuadorian food. The nearby *Chifa Central* has good-size portions of reasonably priced Chinese and local food. Almost next door, *Mi Abuela* is a recommended little café.

Also on the pedestrian area of Ambato, *Mamá Inés* has a few Mexican dishes and other international food items; it is very popular. Opposite, under the Hotel Humboldt/Paraíso, *La Casa Vieja de Dusseldorf* is also quite good, although the menu is as much local as it is German. On the next block of Ambato, *Rico Pan* (☎ 740 387) is good for breakfast (including granola and yogurt), juices and snacks; they sell some of the best bread in town. There are several other cheap restaurants and bakeries on Ambato and around the market.

The *Café Chushi*, opposite the bus terminal, has a variety of snacks and an English book exchange. The *Restaurant Monica*, Eloy Alfaro and E Espejo, continues to be a gringo hang-out despite its slow and inefficient service. Menus in 12 languages hang on the wall, but the menu prices and what you are charged may differ.

El Jardín, on the Parque de la Basílica, is popular and good for a variety of food and snacks that can be enjoyed in their outdoor patio. The *Café Hood*, 16 de Diciembre and Martínez, features international vegetarian food and has a book exchange, incense, art and music. It's open from 8 to 11 am and 1:30 to 9 pm daily except Tuesday, and is a current favorite among young travelers. One reader writes that it's like a student café in Berkeley, California. The *Café Higuerón* (☎ 740 910), 12 de Noviembre 2-70 and Martínez, has a good variety of meat and vegetarian plates, teas and yummy desserts. It is open from 8 am to 10 pm daily except Wednesday. Though this is one of the town's better restaurants, prices aren't very high. *Restaurant El Artesano*, next to the Hostal Plantas y Blanco, has a variety of food ranging from Arab to Mexican – sounds interesting! I haven't been there, but a reader recommends it. Also worth a look, if you want to get away from standard Ecuadorian restaurants, is the *Venus y Bacchus*, Montalvo and Pastaza, with international teas and coffees, and a variety of unusual sandwiches. The fireplace, sofas and cushions invite you to relax.

The popular *La Closerie de Lilas*, Alfaro 6-20 and Oriente, has good French-influenced meals at very reasonable prices. *Le Petit Restaurant* (☎ 740 936), Eloy Alfaro 2-46 and Montalvo, also has food with a French twist, but is not as cheap as the previous recommendation. Neverthe-

less it's popular with travelers and the food is good, though, as is the way of most French restaurants, portions are modest. The service is leisurely and it's a place to hang out. They show video movies on some days and may have live folklórica bands in the evenings.

Several places serve good-value Italian food; my favorite is the small but friendly *La Bella Italia* (☎ 740 072), Rocafuerte and Eloy Alfaro. The food is freshly made here, so don't come expecting super-fast service. The young Ecuadorian owner lived in New York for several years, speaks English and has a good feel for what North Americans like in their Italian food (I welcome comments from Italian readers!). Some travelers prefer *Paolo's Pizzería* (☎ 740 944), next to the Café Hood – one critic calls this 'one of the hemisphere's best restaurants.' Still other readers recommend *Scaligeri* at Eloy Alfaro and Ambato, next to the Pensión Patty. The *Rincón de Suecia* (☎ 740 365), Rocafuerte and 16 de Diciembre, is more pizzería than Swiss restaurant.

Regine Café Alemán, Montalvo and 16 de Diciembre, has a German menu; it's good for breakfast from 8 am onwards, as well as for light meals, coffee and other drinks. Among other things, they serve tasty potato pancakes and innovative concoctions of tea, coffee and hot chocolate laced with various alcoholic beverages. German newspapers are available. The newer *Regine Café Alemán II*, Rocafuerte at 16 de Diciembre, serves more solid meals (lunch and dinner only), but doesn't seem as popular. Both are closed on Tuesdays. The British-run *Café Cultura* (☎ 740 419), on Montalvo near Santa Clara, features homemade breads, quiches, fruit pies, fresh fish, pastries, fruit juices and various other and delectable items. English magazines are available.

La Casa Mía (☎ 740 248), Montalvo 20-06 and Santa Clara, is an elegant restaurant with a variety of Ecuadorian and Italian food, and occasional live music. Service is good and friendly; prices aren't cheap but seem fair. Almost opposite is the *Restau-*

rant y Peña El Marqués (☎ 740 187), which has good food and good live music some nights. Go over there early and see what's happening.

On certain days (particularly during fiestas) you can buy cuy at some of the market restaurants. They are normally roasted whole, and some people find the sight of their little roasted feet sticking up and their tiny teeth poking out a bit disconcerting. Don't say I didn't warn you! Surprisingly, they taste quite good, a little like a cross between chicken and rabbit. In fact, the local nickname for them in some areas is *conejo*, which means rabbit.

Another local food popular in Baños is toffee. You can see people swinging it onto wooden pegs in the doorways of many of the town's shops – the swinging blends and softens the toffee. You can try a fresh, soft piece for a few sucres, or buy a box of hardened toffees as a souvenir.

Entertainment

Nightlife in Baños consists mainly of chatting with new friends in the restaurants after a strenuous day of soaking in the pools.

Centro Cultural Baños screens classic movies nightly at 8 pm (US$1.25) and has a book exchange.

There are several bars that are frequented by travelers, but their popularity tends to wax and wane from year to year – new ones open and close frequently. Try the *Hard Rock Café* on Eloy Alfaro and Ambato for inexpensive drinks and old rock classics. The somewhat-pricier bar above Donde Marcelo is also popular, and has rock music and a dance floor that can get lively at weekends.

The friendly and hip *Bamboo Bar*, 16 de Diciembre and Martínez, has Latin and rock music with dancing. This is one of the most popular bars in town. The *Peña Ananitay*, Espejo and 16 de Diciembre, has live folklórica late on weekend nights. It is very popular and gets very crowded, but it's one of the best places in town to hear Andean music. El Marqués (see Places to Eat) has weekend peñas with varied music. *Illusions Peña Bar*, Martínez and 16 de

Diciembre, offers a variety of entertainment – videos, live music, a bar.

La Burbuja disco (☎ 740 520), on an alley off the east end of Ambato, is open nights from Wednesday to Saturday, but there's rarely much happening except perhaps weekends after 10 pm (bring all your friends and make it happen). There's a US$2 cover at weekends.

Travelers hang out in the European restaurants mentioned above – they tend to stay open later than most. All of these are suitable for women. Less suitable for women are the many small pool halls (especially on the back streets), which are frequented mainly by men.

Getting There & Away

Buses from Ambato's terminal terrestre leave about every half hour for Baños. The fare is US$0.60 and the ride is about an hour. From Quito and many other towns it's sometimes quicker to catch a bus to Ambato and change, rather than wait for the less frequent direct buses.

The Baños terminal terrestre is within walking distance of most hotels – it's a small town. Buses for Quito (US$2.80; 3½ hours) leave almost every hour, or you can take more frequent buses to Ambato and change for other destinations. There are frequent departures for Riobamba (US$0.80; one hour), but most of these buses go to Riobamba's Oriente terminal, which is several km away from the terminal terrestre. It's inconvenient if you need to make a connection.

Ticket offices in Baños' terminal terrestre will sell you tickets for buses to the Oriente (Puyo or Tena) but usually won't guarantee you a seat or give you a refund if the bus is full (though ask at the terminal in case this has changed). You can, however, buy a ticket from the driver, so it's best to wait for a bus to pass by and then board if there's room.

Note that the road to Puyo is currently closed by construction daily, except from late Sunday night to 6 am Tuesday, and this will probably continue through late 1997. On other days, you can take the bus to the construction site, drag your luggage across a kilometer or more of churned-up mud, then catch another bus to your destination. This *trasbordo* (as the mud-slogging system is euphemistically called) is a frequent occurrence on many roads in the Oriente during the rainy months, so be prepared.

When the bus is running, the two-hour ride to Puyo costs about US$1.50, and the five-hour trip to Tena US$3.50.

Getting Around
Westbound buses leave from the central plaza outside Residencial La Delicia 1. They are marked 'El Salado' and go to the baths of that name. Fares are about US$0.10. A taxi to these baths costs about US$0.80.

PARQUE NACIONAL SANGAY
Stretching for about 70 km south and southeast of Baños, the 272,000-hectare Parque Nacional Sangay is one of the most remote and inaccessible areas in Ecuador. The park was established in 1979 and protects an incredible variety of terrain. Its western boundary is marked by the Eastern Cordillera, and three of Ecuador's highest volcanoes are within the park. The most northerly of these, Tungurahua, can be accessed easily from Baños, while the more southerly volcanoes, El Altar and Sangay, require a much greater effort. The area around the park's namesake Volcán Sangay, in particular, is very rugged and remote, and relatively few people have penetrated it. Nevertheless, the routes to the three volcanoes provide the most frequently used accesses to the park.

From the park's western areas, which climb to over 5000 meters around each of the three volcanoes, the terrain plunges from the high páramos down the eastern slopes of the Andes to elevations barely above 1000 meters at the park's eastern boundaries. In between is terrain so steep, rugged and wet (over 400 cm of rain annually in some eastern areas) that it remains a wilderness in the truest sense. A few small and remote Andean communities (not large

enough to be graced by the title of village) dot the páramos, but the thickly vegetated slopes east of the mountains are the haunt of very rarely seen mammals such Andean spectacled bears, mountain tapirs, pumas, ocelots, jaguarundis and porcupines. Nobody lives there.

Only one road of any importance enters this national park, going from Riobamba to Alao (the main access point to the Volcán Sangay) and petering out in the páramos to the east. Another road is still under construction. When this dirt road is completed it will link Guamote in the highlands with Macas in the southern Oriente, passing the southern extremities of the park. Colonization following in the wake of these roads is the greatest threat to the park, but the inhospitable terrain will probably prevent severe damage to the area's scenic, biological and geological diversity.

Tungurahua
With an elevation of 5016 meters, Tungurahua is Ecuador's 10th highest peak. It is a beautiful cone-shaped volcano with a small cap of snow perched jauntily atop its lush green slopes. The volcano is active but has had no eruption since the beginning of this century. Fumaroles and steam vents can be seen in the crater. Just within the northern boundaries of Parque Nacional Sangay, it is the most frequent access point to at least a small part of the park.

Many travelers like to walk part of the way up the volcano, perhaps as far as the village of Pondoa or to the refuge at 3800 meters. Beyond the refuge the going gets steep, and you should be careful on the slick grassy slopes – a tourist slipped on the grass in 1988 and fell 45 meters to his death. The final section may require crampons and an ice ax, depending on the conditions. The summit is often very cloudy and climbers have become quite disoriented, which has led to other deaths as people lose the trail and head off in the wrong direction. An Israeli attempting a solo climb fell and died in 1992. The mountain is considered one of Ecuador's easier 5000-meter peaks to climb, but don't underestimate it. The 3200-meter vertical ascent from Baños requires plenty of endurance, and the steep and misty upper slopes are not for novices.

Nearly opposite the turn to the zoo and Cascada Inés María at the west end of Baños, a trail to your left climbs to the village of Pondoa (two hours), the climbers' refuge (four to six hours further), and the summit of Tungurahua. There is a dirt road that goes from Baños to Pondoa and then to a point about halfway to the refuge. The road does not, for the most part, follow the trail. Near this halfway point, there is a park entrance station where you pay a fee of about US$10, plus US$5 for use of the refuge. Climbing guides and/or vehicles can be hired in Baños. Mules can be hired in Baños or in Pondoa (where there is a basic store).

The refuge is simply a roof over your head; bring food and sleeping bag. There is a stream for water and basic cooking facilities (ask about this in advance). Do not leave anything in the refuge, as it will probably disappear. The refuge can get very crowded at weekends. The mountain can be climbed at any time of year, but December to early March tend to be best. The wettest months in the Oriente (July and August) tend to influence Tungurahua's weather, often making it rainy and foggy at that time. There have been recent reports of armed robbery at the refuge (which has no guardian). Check in Baños or with the South American Explorers Club in Quito for more information.

El Altar

At 5319 meters this jagged and long-extinct volcano is the fifth highest mountain in Ecuador. It is considered the most technically difficult of Ecuador's peaks and was not climbed until 1963. The wild páramo surrounding the mountain and the greenish lake (Laguna Amarilla, or Yellow Lagoon) within the blown away crater are targets for adventurous backpackers with complete camping gear. Although the area looks almost uninhabited, do not leave any gear unattended or it may disappear.

To get to El Altar, take a bus to Penipe, a village halfway between Baños and Riobamba (any Baños-Riobamba bus can drop you off). From here, go to Candelaria, about 15 km away. There is supposedly a daily bus between Penipe and Candelaria; trucks go there occasionally, or you can hire a pickup truck in Penipe. From Candelaria (which has a very simple store) it is about two km to the Hacienda Releche, near which there is a Parque Nacional Sangay station. You pay the park fee here and can stay the night for a further US$2. The station has cooking and washing facilities; to see if it's open, check with the climbing guides in Baños, Ambato or Riobamba.

From here it is a full-day hike to the crater. Guides and mules can be hired in Candelaria. There are many trails in the area, and it is worth having a guide to show you the beginning of the main trail to El Altar, less than an hour away from the station. On the main trail the going is fairly obvious.

The best times to go are the same as for Tungurahua.

Sangay

This 5230-meter volcano is one of the most active in the Andes, constantly spewing out rocks, smoke and ash. The volcanological situation changes from hour to hour and year to year. The mountain is not technically difficult to climb, but people attempting it run the risk of being killed by the explosions so climbing attempts are rare. You can hike to the base if you wish, although the approach is long and tedious and the best views are from afar.

To get there, take a bus southeast from Riobamba to the villages of Licto or Pungalá, which are next to one another. From there occasional trucks (early mornings on most days) go a further 20 km (one hour) to the village of Alao, where there is a national park ranger station. Here you pay the park fee, get information and are allowed to sleep for a nominal fee. There are a couple of simple stores in Alao.

Guides are available in Alao for the three- or four-day hike to base camp – you'll probably get hopelessly lost without a guide. They charge about US$6 per day plus food for their guiding services. Most guides will watch you climb the mountain from the base camp – very few will go up with you!

Another approach is to take the incomplete highway from Guamote to Macas. The road goes southwest as far as the village of Atillo and then becomes a mule trail dropping down through the eastern Andes to the village of San Vicente, about two or three days away. En route you pass through the southernmost extremity of the national park (see The Southern Oriente chapter). This long and ambitious hike and the approaches and climbs of Sangay and El Altar are described in guides mentioned in the Books appendix at the end of the book. The South American Explorers Club has some recent expedition reports on file.

GUARANDA

Guaranda is the capital of the agricultural province of Bolívar but nevertheless is a small town (population about 15,000). Its name derives from that of the Indian chief Guarango. Guaranda is a quiet, provincial town that has been described as 'dismal.' I found it dignified rather than dismal, and it is pleasantly located with pretty hills all around – there are supposedly seven of these, which inspires locals to call their town 'the Rome of the Andes.' Ecuadorian guidebooks call it 'the authentic provincial city.' It certainly can't be described as exciting, and the main reason you'd want to go there is probably for the bus rides, which offer spectacular views.

The road from Ambato is paved but potholed. The 99-km road climbs from Ambato at 2800 meters to bleak páramo at well over 4000 meters before dropping to Guaranda at 2650 meters, making this the highest paved road in the country. It passes

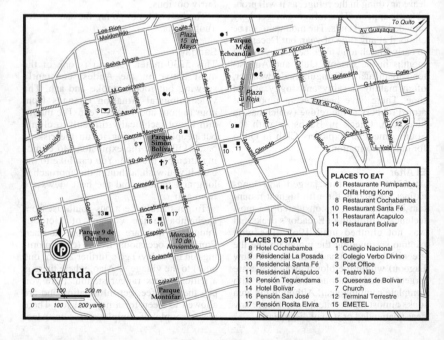

PLACES TO EAT
6   Restaurante Rumipamba, Chifa Hong Kong
8   Restaurant Cochabamba
10 Restaurant Santa Fé
11 Restaurant Acapulco
14 Restaurant Bolívar

PLACES TO STAY
8   Hotel Cochabamba
9   Residencial La Posada
10 Residencial Santa Fé
11 Residencial Acapulco
13 Pensión Tequendama
14 Hotel Bolívar
16 Pensión San José
17 Pensión Rosita Elvira

OTHER
1   Colegio Nacional
2   Colegio Verbo Divino
3   Post Office
4   Teatro Nilo
5   Queseras de Bolívar
7   Church
12 Terminal Terrestre
15 EMETEL

Guaranda

0   100   200 m
0   100   200 yards

within 10 km of Chimborazo (6310 meters) and Carihuairazo (5020 meters).

For the best views of these giants you should get seats on the left of the bus (if going to Guaranda), though the road twists and turns so you do get occasional views from the right side as well. In addition to the mountains, you get a good look at the harsh and inhospitable Andean páramo. Keep your eyes open for flocks of llamas, caracara hawks and, maybe, an Andean condor. The bus ride can get cold, so remember to carry on some warm clothes.

When you leave Guaranda you can take other equally exciting rides. You can continue on down the western slopes of the Andes to Babahoyo and the coast – a spectacular route that was once the most important connection between Quito and Guayaquil, though it is now infrequently used. Or you can head due east to Riobamba on a dizzying dirt road that skirts the southern flanks of Chimborazo and provides fantastic views that are not for the faint-hearted (sit on the left side of the bus).

Information

Cash US dollars can be changed (with difficulty) at a few stores for 5% less than the Quito rate. The banks didn't want to change any foreign currency on my most recent visit, so it's best to bring enough sucres with you.

Guaranda's EMETEL office is on Rocafuerte near Pichincha, and the post office is on Azuay near Pichincha.

The area code for Guaranda and the province of Bolívar is 03.

Things to See & Do

The main market day is Saturday, with a smaller market happening on Wednesday. The best place for the market is Plaza 15 de Mayo, which worth visiting even on ordinary days for its pleasantly quiet, forgotten colonial air (ignore the school on one side). The market at Mercado 10 de Noviembre is held in a modern, ugly concrete building.

If you have nothing to do, go down to the Parque Montúfar and see if one of the statues there still has a bees' nest under its right armpit! (Readers of the 2nd and 3rd editions of this book assure me it does, but please keep me informed.) Walk the streets for a few hours; you'll end up in the last century.

A favorite local activity is the evening *paseo* (stroll) around the Parque Bolívar, from about 6 to 9 pm nightly.

There is one movie theater, Teatro Nilo, which doesn't have shows every day.

The Carnaval is very popular, with people streaming in from all over the province and beyond for such rural festivities as water fights, dances and parades. Some consider this to be one of Ecuador's best festivals.

About three km out of town is a five-meter-high monument, *El Indio de Guarango*, from which you get a good view of Guaranda, Chimborazo and the surrounding countryside. There is a small museum here. A taxi will take you for about US$1, or walk northwest of town for about 30 minutes.

Places to Stay

Most of the hotels in town are basic cold-water cheapies. The water supply is erratic in most of them. They include the *Pensión San José*, on Sucre near Rocafuerte, with large clean rooms at US$1.75 per person. Not as good are the *Pensión Rosita Elvira*, opposite the San José, and the *Residencial La Posada*, Arregon near 10 de Agosto.

The clean *Residencial Acapulco* (☎ 981 953), on 10 de Agosto near 9 de Abril, has hot showers and costs US$4 per person or US$6 with private bath. The similarly priced *Residencial Santa Fé* has an overly amorous manager, according to one female reader, though other travelers have found the place acceptable. The *Pensión Tequendama*, on Rocafuerte near José García, is used by short-stay couples.

On the outskirts of town is the *Hotel Matiaví* (☎ 980 295), at the bus terminal. It has clean rooms with private baths and hot water for about US$4 per person but can be noisy.

The pleasant *Hotel Bolívar* (☎ 980 547), Sucre 7-04 near Olmedo, has clean rooms and hot showers. Rooms with private bath are US$8 per person, US$6 with shared bath or US$10 with TV and phone. The 'best' place in town is the *Hotel Cochabamba* (☎ 981 958, fax 982 125), on García Moreno near 7 de Mayo. Rates are US$8/12 or US$16/20 with private bath, TV and phone. Rooms vary widely in quality.

A 15-minute walk out of town on the Quito road is a 'tourist complex' called *Hotel La Colina* (☎ 980 666) that is often empty. Located on a hill, it has some rooms with good views, a restaurant, bar and small swimming pool. They charge about US$40 for comfortable doubles with private bath and hot water.

Places to Eat

There are few restaurants and they close early – many by 7:30 pm. Several of the best places to eat are in hotels. The best in town is supposedly the pricey *Restaurant Cochabamba* at the hotel of that name, but they have been criticized for serving only a few selections from the rather impressive-looking menu. They are closed on Monday.

Progressively cheaper are the restaurants *Bolívar, Acapulco* and *Santa Fé*, all in the hotels of the same name. The Bolívar has been recommended as having a better selection than the Cochabamba. The Acapulco has cheap food, especially the *chaulafan* (a rice dish).

On the west side of the Parque Bolívar you'll find the reasonably priced *Restaurante Rumipamba*, which is one of the best places to eat outside of the hotels, but is not too special. Nearby, the *Chifa Hong Kong* has cheap set lunches and meriendas, as well as inexpensive à la carte choices. *Queseras de Bolívar*, on the Plaza Roja, sells cheeses from the province and has info about visiting the nearby village of Salinas, where cheese production is an important part of the economy.

Getting There & Away

Most buses leave from the terminal terrestre, 500 meters out of town – head east on García Moreno and EM de Carvajal, and

you can't miss it. Buses depart from 4 am to 5 pm. Afternoon buses can get booked up in advance, so plan ahead.

The most frequent departures are for Ambato (US$1.60; two hours) and Quito (US$3; five hours), with buses for these destinations leaving about once an hour with various companies. Almost as frequently there are buses for Babahoyo (US$2.25; four hours) and Guayaquil (US$3; five hours). There are about six daily buses on the spectacular but poor road to Riobamba (US$2; three hours).

There are also several buses a day to Chillanes, a small town some three hours south of Guaranda. I've never been there nor met anyone who has, but I'm told there's a basic pensión. It certainly would be getting off the beaten track if that's what you want. The Chillanes area produces coffee and aguardiente (sugarcane alcohol). En route to both Babahoyo and Chillanes, you pass through the old town of San Miguel, which still has wooden colonial buildings with carved balconies. Buses for Chimbo and San Miguel leave several times an hour. There are also several buses a day to other villages such as San Luis, Caluma and Echeandia, if you want to explore a remoter area.

SALINAS

About 35 km north of Guaranda in wild and beautiful countryside is the peaceful community of Salinas. It is known for its excellent cheeses, homemade salamis and rough-spun sweaters, and you can visit the small 'factories' that produce them. The people are very friendly and not much used to seeing travelers. It's an interesting destination for people who enjoy venturing off the beaten track and wish to see how people live in a remote rural Ecuadorian community. The countryside around offers pleasant walks. It is definitely very *tranquilo*.

There is a small store on the Salinas plaza that sells the naturally dyed, rough-spun sweaters for well under US$10. Prices are fixed, and other woolen goods are available. There is also a small restaurant and you can buy cheese in 31-kg balls!

Places to Stay

Ask at the store on the plaza about a very inexpensive hostel run by the cheese-making cooperative. There is also the clean and recommended *Hotel El Refuge* (☎ 758 778) on the town's outskirts. Dorm rooms are about US$3 per person, and singles cost a little more. There is a decent restaurant here. Both places have hot showers.

Getting There & Away

A cheese shop called *Queseras de Bolívar* on Guaranda's Plaza Roja has information about getting to Salinas. Trucks for Salinas leave from near this shop on Saturday (to coincide with Guaranda's market) and occasionally other days. The fare is about US$1.

Otherwise, take a bus or truck from the bus plaza about 10 km north on the Guaranda-Ambato road, and get off at Cuatro Esquinas. From here it is about 25 km to Salinas; wait for a passing truck to give you a ride (expect to pay). In Salinas, hang out in the main plaza and flag down any vehicle. Most vehicles leaving town are going to Guaranda. The drive is a spectacular one.

RIOBAMBA

'All roads lead to Riobamba,' proclaims a road sign as you enter this city, and it is indeed true that Riobamba is at the heart of an extensive and scenic road network. Whichever way you arrive or leave, try to plan your journey for daylight hours so as not to miss the great views.

The usual way to arrive is on the Panamericana from Ambato, which is 52 km to the north. The road climbs over a 3600-meter pass, which gives great views of Chimborazo (6310 meters) as well as the nearby Carihuairazo (5020 meters) before dropping to Riobamba at 2750 meters.

An even more spectacular route is the dirt road arriving from Guaranda. There is also a lower road from Baños that follows the Río Chambo valley and passes through numerous small villages. One of these, **Penipe**, is where you'll find the dirt road climbing towards the rugged peak of El Altar. Looking back along this road will also give you views of Tungurahua.

Riobamba, the capital of Chimborazo Province, has a fast-growing population of over 100,000. More or less the geographical center of Ecuador, it has long been an agriculturally important area. Riobamba was a Puruhá Indian center before becoming part of the Inca Empire during the late 15th century long before the Spanish conquest.

The first Spanish colonialists built a city near present-day Cajabamba. This was destroyed in a 1797 earthquake, and the survivors moved to the present site on a large plain surrounded by several snow-capped peaks. The flat terrain of Riobamba enabled it to be built in a regular chess-board pattern, with wide avenues and imposing stone buildings. It has a rather sedate air, and Ecuadorians call it the 'Sultan of the Andes.' One of the main streets through town, with large plazas and government buildings, is called Primera Constituyente in commemoration of the fact that Ecuador's first constitution was written and signed here in 1830.

Information

Tourist Offices The helpful and friendly CETUR tourist information office is on 10 de Agosto, half a block from the Parque Sucre, which is the main plaza. The office is open from 8 am to noon and 2:30 to 5 pm from Tuesday to Saturday.

Money The best and easiest place to change cash and traveler's checks is the Casa de Cambio Chimborazo, next door to the CETUR office. This is open 9 am to 1 pm Monday to Saturday, and 3 to 6 pm Monday to Friday. The banks sometimes change foreign currency but are less reliable.

Post & Communications The post office is in an old-fashioned building at Espejo and 10 de Agosto. There is an EMETEL office downtown at Tarqui and Veloz, and another at the main bus terminal. The area code for Riobamba and the province of Chimborazo is 03.

SOUTH QUITO

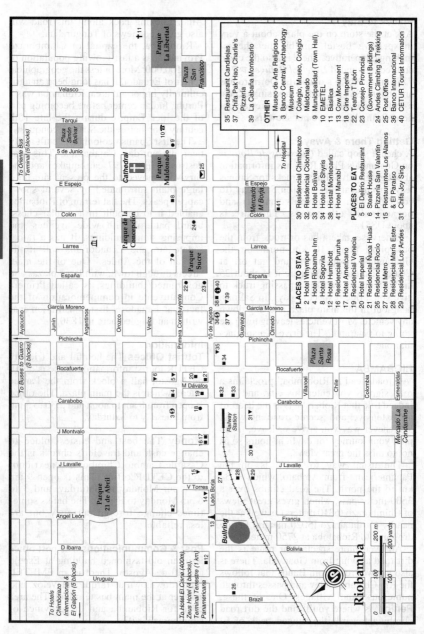

PLACES TO STAY
2 Hotel Whymper
4 Hotel Riobamba Inn
8 Hotel Segovia
12 Hotel Humboldt
16 Residencial Puruha
17 Hotel Americano
19 Residencial Venecia
20 Hotel Imperial
21 Residencial Nuca Huasi
26 Residencial Rocío
27 Hotel Metro
28 Residencial María Ester
29 Residencial Los Andes
30 Residencial Chimborazo
32 Residencial Colonial
33 Hotel Bolivar
34 Hotel Los Shyris
38 Hostal Montecarlo
41 Hotel Manabí

PLACES TO EAT
5 El Delirio Restaurant
6 Steak House
14 Pizzería San Valentin
15 Restaurantes Los Alamos
      & El Paraíso
31 Chifa Joy Sing
35 Restaurant Candilejas
37 Chifa Pak Hao, Charlie's
      Pizzería
39 La Cabaña Montecarlo

OTHER
1 Museo de Arte Religioso
3 Banco Central, Archaeology
      Museum
7 Colegio, Museo, Colegio
      Maldonado
9 Municipalidad (Town Hall)
10 EMETEL
11 Basílica
13 Cow Monument
18 Cine Imperial
22 Teatro T León
23 Consejo Provincial
      (Government Buildings)
24 Andes Climbing & Trekking
25 Post Office
36 Banco Internacional
40 CETUR Tourist Information

Travel Agencies & Guides Several guides are available for climbs or treks on or around any of the local mountains. The best known (and most expensive) is Marco Cruz, who works for Metropolitan Touring in Quito. His Riobamba office is at Expediciones Andinas (☎ 964 915, 962 845), near the Hotel El Galpón at Argentinos 38-60 and Zambrano.

Also very good, experienced and recommended is Marcelo Puruncajas (☎ 940 964, fax 940 963), Andes Climbing & Trekking, Colón 22-21, who guides, rents gear and is among the cheapest of the recommended guides. Silvio Pesantz (☎ 962 681), Argentinas 11-40, Casilla 327, is also experienced and well recommended. Guides charge about US$300 to take two climbers to the summits of Cotopaxi or Chimborazo, everything provided. These trips last two days (one night), and there is no guarantee that the summit will be reached. Several other trips are offered.

Enrique Veloz of Riobamba is the veteran advisor of the Asociación de Andinismo de Chimborazo (☎ 960 916), Chile 33-21 and Francia. He has climbed Chimborazo and the other peaks many times and may be able to guide you. I have received comments that some of the younger, less expensive guides he knows are not very experienced; make sure you get a good guide, as your life depends on it. These trips are not recommended for beginning mountaineers.

Emergency The hospital (☎ 961 705) is at the east end of town at Olmedo 11-01. Contact the police at ☎ 961 913.

Walking Tour
There are several plazas with impressive buildings and churches. A walk along Primera Constituyente will take you past some of them.

On the corner of Primera Constituyente and Rocafuerte you'll find the building in which, on July 5, 1822, Simón Bolívar wrote his famous epic poem about his attempted ascent of Chimborazo (he reached the snow line). The building is now an office, but during work hours you can go in and read his poem and the story of his life.

At Primera Constituyente and Carabobo is the Banco Central (☎ 963 153), which has an archaeology museum that is open only occasionally. The Colegio Maldonado at Primera Constituyente and Larrea has a natural history museum that is occasionally open. Neither of these were open on my last visit.

Finally, the tiled cow monument on León Borja and Angel León is one of the more unusual statues that you'll see in an Ecuadorian town.

Museo de Arte Religioso
This famous museum, in the old church of La Concepción (☎ 952 212) on Argentinos and Larrea, is worth a visit. The building has been beautifully restored, and there are many rooms with a good variety of artwork: paintings, sculptures and religious artifacts. The major piece is a huge, gem-encrusted gold monstrance said to be priceless. Signage is not very good, however, and it is worth hiring a guide. Entrance costs about US$2; the guides work for tips. Hours are from 9 am to noon and 3 to 7 pm Tuesday through Saturday. On Sunday and on holidays the museum may be open in the mornings only; it's closed on Monday.

Parque 21 de Abril
There is an observation platform here, from which the city and surrounding countryside can be appreciated. There is also a tilework representation of the history of Ecuador. The view of snow-capped Tungurahua rising behind the church of San Antonio is especially impressive.

Parque La Libertad
This is another quiet plaza. Its **basilica** is famous as the only round church in Ecuador. Begun in 1883, it took over 30 years to complete and was designed, built and decorated mainly by locals – a source of civic pride. It's often closed; try Sunday and evenings after 6 pm.

Parque Maldonado

This pleasant park is alive with trees, flowers and birds. Riobamba's **cathedral** is on the northeastern side. In the park is a statue of the Ecuadorian geographer Pedro Maldonado (see Parque La Alameda in the Quito chapter).

Market

Saturday is market day and there's much activity in the streets, especially around 5 de Junio and Argentinos, although almost every plaza and park in the city seems to be busy. The market is a colorful affair, with thousands of people from many surrounding villages flocking to barter, buy and sell. It is rather incongruous to see a barefooted Indian woman leading a squealing piglet on a string through the streets of a major town.

New market buildings detract somewhat from the *ambiente*, and many market areas sell mainly food items and plastic consumer goods. Nevertheless, it is the shoppers rather than the shopping that is of interest to travelers. One plaza, however, has plenty of crafts for sale – this is the Parque de la Concepción at Orozco and Colón.

An interesting Riobambeño handicraft is **tagua-nut carving**. These nuts are actually seeds from a type of rainforest palm. The seeds are fairly soft until they are carved, but when exposed to the sun and air they become very hard. The size of small chicken eggs, they are carved into a variety of novelties such as statuettes, miniature cups and rings. By providing economically viable alternatives to cutting the forest down, this industry is starting to become important in the fight to preserve the rainforest. Although the palm grows in many lowland areas, for some reason highland Riobamba has become a carving center.

Another interesting handicraft from the Riobamba area is the **shigra**, a tough woven bag made from *cabuya* (agave, or century plant) fibers. Their durability and practicality make shigras very popular souvenirs for many travelers, who often use them as day bags. Cabuya is also used for rope sandals and, simply, rope.

There are also baskets and mats woven by the Colta Indians from the reeds lining the shores of Lake Colta, a few kilometers south of Riobamba, and many clothing items, such as woven belts, fine ponchos and embroidered shawls.

It should be mentioned that the Otavalo market is a more tourist-oriented, convenient place to shop for souvenirs. At the Riobamba market you'll have to do a lot of searching past stalls of potatoes, plastic buckets and polyester pants – less convenient but perhaps more fun! The tourist office will help further pinpoint which of the many markets and plazas may be of interest to you.

Special Events

Riobamba's annual fiesta celebrates the Battle of Tapi on April 21. On and around that date there is a large agricultural fair with the usual highland events – street parades, dancing and plenty of traditional food and drink. The city and hotels can be particularly crowded then.

Places to Stay – bottom end

Most hotels are in the town center a couple of kilometers away from the terminal terrestre. If you prefer to stay near the terminal, you'll find a few inexpensive places nearby. Opposite the terminal is the friendly and clean *Residencial San Carlos*, which charges about US$3 per person; they have hot water. Nearby, the *Hotel Monterrey* (☎ 962 421) is similarly priced and also OK. In front of the terminal is the comfortable *Hotel Las Retamas* (☎ 965 004/5), which has a restaurant and charges US$6 per person in rooms with private baths and hot water. It is often full.

Most of the cheap hotels are near the train station, but many of these are very run down. *Residencial Ñuca Huasi* (☎ 966 669), 10 de Agosto 10-24, is a very basic place popular with backpackers. The owner has climbing information and arranges transportation to the mountains. Rooms are a bit grimy but the sheets are clean. Rates are US$2.50 per person or US$4 with private bath and hot water (between 7 and

9 am or 7 and 9 pm). Also popular is the clean and friendly (albeit noisy) *Hotel Imperial* (☎ 960 429), Rocafuerte 22-15. Rooms are US$4 per person or US$5 with bath and hot water. The manager will arrange trips to Chimborazo.

Other basic hotels in the US$2 to US$3 per person range include the *Residencial Colonial* and the *Hotel Bolívar* (☎ 968 294) next to the train station; and the *Residencial Venecia*, Dávalos 22-21. These have hot water and seem OK. If they are full, travelers watching their pennies can try the more basic *Hotel Americano* and *Residenciales Puruha, María Ester, Los Andes* and *Chimborazo*.

The *Hotel Metro* (☎ 961 714), León Borja and J Lavalle, and the *Hotel Segovia* (☎ 961 269), Primera Constituyente 22-26, both charge about US$5 per person in adequate rooms with bath and hot water. A better bet at this price is the quiet and clean little *Residencial Rocío*, Brazil 21-68.

For US$6 per person, the friendly and recommended *Hotel Los Shyris* (☎ 960 323), Rocafuerte and 10 de Agosto, has good clean rooms with hot showers. The similarly priced *Hotel Manabí* (☎ 967 967), Colón 19-58, is new and also seems quite a good value. After that, hotel prices jump to over US$10 per person.

Places to Stay – middle
The friendly *Hotel Humboldt* (☎ 961 788, 940 814), León Borja 35-48, is quite good at US$11 per person. Some rooms have TV. The *Hotel Whymper* (☎ 964 575, fax 968 575), Angel León 23-10, has received mixed reviews from readers: friendly, overpriced, clean, dirty bathrooms, great views, noisy, best hot shower we had . . . . Sometimes I wonder if they are all writing about the same hotel! Certainly, rooms vary considerably with regard to the views, but more readers seem satisfied than not. Breakfast is available at an extra cost, and they can arrange tours and transportation to Chimborazo.

Out toward the terminal terrestre, the clean *Zeus Hotel* (☎ 962 292, 968 036/7/8, fax 963 100), León Borja 41-29, has good rooms with private bath, hot water and TV for US$14/27. The *Hotel Riobamba Inn* (☎ 961 696, 940 974), Carabobo 23-20 and Primera Constituyente, is run by the folks who run the Hotel Imperial. They have spacious rooms with private bathroom, hot water, TV and telephone for US$15 per person for gringos; Ecuadorians reportedly pay half as much.

The best hotel in the center is the *Hostal Montecarlo* (☎ 960 557), 10 de Agosto 25-41. Inside an attractively restored, turn-of-the-century house, the Montecarlo has comfortable rooms with TV and phone (US$20/28) and a restaurant.

Two other mid-range hotels are within a block of one another on Avenida Argentinos, about a kilometer west of the center: The *Hotel Chimborazo Internacional* (☎ 963 475, fax 963 473) is at Argentinos and Nogales, and the *Hotel El Galpón* (☎ 960 981/2, fax 960 983) is at Argentinos and Zambrano. Both have restaurants and bars. The Chimborazo charges US$24/34 and, of the two hotels, is a better deal. The El Galpón is a little more expensive but has a swimming pool and sauna (which aren't always in working order); it is not very well managed.

The *Hostería El Troje* (☎ /fax 964 572) is 4½ km southeast of town on the minor road to Chambo. It has a pool, tennis court and restaurant and bar, and charges about US$50 for a double room. Many of the rooms have fireplaces. Another good and similarly priced choice is the newer *Albergue Abraspungo* (☎ 940 820, fax 940 819), which is 3½ km northeast of town on the road to Guano. Although it's new as a hotel, it is built around a traditional hacienda and is quite attractive. Spacious rooms, a restaurant and bar, and horseback riding are all available here. The owners are friends of the famous mountaineer Marco Cruz, and climbing expeditions can be arranged.

About 15 km north of Riobamba on the Panamericana is the *Hostería La Andaluza* (☎ 904 223, fax 904 234). This colonial hacienda has been attractively restored and is now perhaps the best hotel in the province of Chimborazo. There are a pair of restaurants, a small exercise room and sauna, and a bar with a fireplace. Nearly all the antique-furnished rooms have fireplaces, as well as cable TV and telephones. Rates are about US$40/60, and I've heard that if you take a chance and just drop in, you will pay much less than if you make an advance reservation. They are not often full, except possibly at weekends.

Places to Eat

Riobamba's many restaurants are fairly basic and cheap. Budget travelers watching their pennies can try the *Restaurant Los Alamos* or *Restaurant El Paraíso*, two inexpensive places on Lavalle and 10 de Agosto. Nearby, a favorite place for both locals and tourists is the lively *Pizzería San Valentin*, León Borja and Torres, where you have to order pizza at the counter. *Charlie's Pizzería*, García Moreno and 10 de Agosto, is more sedate but very good and has vegetarian pizzas and good lasagna. Two decent chifas are the *Pak Hao*, next to Charlie's Pizzería, and the cheaper *Joy Sing*, on Guayaquil by the railway station. There are several other cheap restaurants near the railway station.

The *Restaurante Bellavista* (☎ 965 861), Buenos Aires 12-34 and Darquea (about four blocks north and nine blocks east of the Plaza Simón Bolívar), is good for above-average Ecuadorian meals at about US$3.

The *Restaurant Candilejas*, 10 de Agosto and Pichincha, looks nice and has been recommended in the past. Recently, meals have been variable in quality and service has been slow and indifferent. It's a nice place that might recover if they can get a consistently good cook and better staff. Nearby *La Cabaña Montecarlo* (☎ 968 609), García Moreno 24-10 and 10 de Agosto, is associated with the good Hostal Montecarlo, and both service and food are satisfactory, though pricey by Riobamba standards (meals around US$5). One of Riobamba's most atmospheric eateries, *El Delirio Restaurant* (☎ 960 029, 965 027), Primera Constituyente 28-16 and Rocafuerte, is in a historic house where Simón

Bolívar stayed. Meals start at about US$4 or US$5; it's definitely recommended. They are closed on Mondays and on Sunday evenings. The *Steak House* (☎ 968 291), Dávalos and Veloz, is good for steaks and other meaty dishes, though it is not particularly cheap.

If you're staying out at the Hostería La Andaluza, you'll find their restaurant is as good as any in Riobamba itself. It is very popular at weekends for lunch, when the wealthier citizens of Riobamba descend upon the hotel, bringing the whole family.

Entertainment

Nightlife is limited. The *Unicornio*, Pichincha 26-70 and Villarroel, has two bars – one with dancing and occasional live music (salsa) at weekends and the other a more sedate piano bar. The *Peña Farahan*, just off León Borja about a half kilometer before the terminal terrestre, is another spot. There are a few other places on León Borja or just north of it west of the center. Otherwise, I could find nothing except the theaters shown on the map, which advertise in *La Prensa*, the local daily paper.

Getting There & Away

Air A secondary airport is used for military and emergency services only.

Bus Riobamba has two long-distance bus terminals. The main terminal is located almost two km northwest of the town center along León Borja. Buses bound for Quito (US$3.30; four hours) and intermediate points are frequent, as are buses for Guayaquil (US$3.80; five hours). There are two night buses for Machala (about US$6; 10 hours) and Huaquillas (12 hours) if you're heading for Peru. There are several buses a day for Cuenca (US$4; five hours). Buses for Alausí leave about every hour with CTA (US$1.20; 1½ hours). Buses for local towns leave from a smaller terminal to the south (see Getting Around).

For buses to Baños and the Oriente you have to go to the Oriente bus terminal on Avenidas Espejo and Luz Elisa Borja almost four km away from the main terminal. There is no direct bus linking the two terminals, but a taxi will only cost about US$0.80. You can walk to the Oriente bus terminal from downtown.

Once in a while there are buses leaving the main terminal for Baños – it's a matter of luck. If you're arriving in Riobamba from the Oriente, you may find that your bus makes a swing through the center before ending up at the Oriente terminal.

A few buses from the Oriente terminal go through Baños and on to Tena (US$4; six hours), but this service is now disrupted because of the road construction between Baños and Puyo.

Train El Niño floods of 1982-83 washed out over 80 km of the track beyond Riobamba, severely disrupting the services to Guayaquil and Cuenca. It was a decade before services resumed.

Train schedules from Riobamba have been changing a great deal in recent years, and you should inquire locally for the latest information (though don't assume that is accurate, either!).

Recently, service from Quito (US$10; seven hours) left at 8 am on Saturday, returning from Riobamba at 8 am on Sunday, but this is liable to change. Service for Durán (Guayaquil, US$14; 12 hours) via Alausí and Bucay leaves daily at 6 am. Roof riding is allowed. Inquire at the train station (☎ 961 909).

Getting Around
North of the terminal terrestre, behind a church with a blue dome, is a local bus stop for the city center nearly two km away. These buses run along León Borja, which turns into 10 de Agosto near the railway station. Here you'll find a good selection of hotels. To return to the terminal terrestre, take any bus marked 'Terminal' on Primera Constituyente; the fare is US$0.10.

Three long blocks south of the terminal terrestre (turn left out of the front entrance) is a smaller terminal with frequent local buses for Cajabamba, Laguna de Colta and Balbanera; the fare is US$0.25. Buses for Guamote also leave from here.

To visit the villages of Guano and Santa Teresita, take a US$0.20 local bus ride from the stop at Avenidas Pichincha and New York.

SOUTHWEST OF RIOBAMBA

The southbound Panamericana actually heads west out of Riobamba until it reaches a cement factory 10 km away. Here the road forks, with the west road continuing to Guaranda and the main highway heading southwest to **Cajabamba**, about seven km farther.

Founded in 1534, Cajabamba was historically important until it was devastated by the 1797 earthquake, which killed several thousands of its inhabitants. Most of the survivors founded nearby Riobamba, but a few remained and their descendants still live here. As you arrive, look up to your right and you'll see a huge scar on the hillside. This is the only sign of the landslide that caused much of the damage two centuries ago.

Most of the buses from Riobamba continue down the Panamericana beyond Cajabamba; if you want to see some of the old town, get off at the junction of the main highway and Avenida 2 de Agosto on the right. Most bus drivers stop here. If you head down 2 de Agosto, you'll soon come

Llamas are still used as beasts of burden in remote highland villages, as they have been since pre-Columbian times.

to a history museum on your right, which contains about a dozen fragments of carved rock dating from before the earthquake. It's not worth seeing, but maybe in the future the museum will have a proper exhibit. Continuing down the road, you come to the earthquake-damaged town church on your left. There are no hotels and there's little else to see.

Returning to the Panamericana, you'll see a few food stalls and very basic restaurants. Heading south on the main highway, you soon pass open fields that are the site of the interesting weekly market. There are no permanent buildings; the Indians just lay out their wares in neat rows. Every Sunday morning the bare fields are transformed by a bustling but surprisingly orderly throng who buy, sell and barter produce. Quechua rather than Spanish is spoken and there are no tourist items; this is one of the more traditional markets in the Ecuadorian highlands. Amazingly, it takes place right by the side of the Panamericana – a measure of just how rural this part of Ecuador is.

Most buses from Riobamba continue about four km beyond Cajabamba to Laguna de Colta. On the way, the road gently climbs to a notch in the hill to the south and the little chapel of **La Balbanera**. It is built on the site of the earliest church in Ecuador, which dates from August 15, 1534, though only a few stones at the front survived the devastating earthquake of 1797. The church has been almost completely rebuilt, and the curious traveler can enter to inspect its simple interior and look at the usual disaster paintings.

In La Balbanera one painting carries the explanation: 'On the 17th of May, 1959, the train derailed, setting the whole convoy on fire. Señor Juan Peñafiel, the brakeman, prayed to the Divine Lady of La Balbanera and her miracle saved the train near Alausí.'

Looking almost due north of the chapel, you can see Chimborazo looming up from 30 km away. Next to the chapel are a few simple restaurants where you can sample local dishes. A little to the south of the chapel there is a fork in the road. You can either continue south on the Panamericana or take the 100-km detour to the right, via the junction of El Triunfo, and then return to the Panamericana at Cañar. Occasional road closures caused by landslides might make the detour impossible to avoid.

Opposite the fork in the road is **Laguna de Colta**. Its blue expanse is often choked up by reeds, which form an important crop for the local Colta Indians. Sometimes you can see the Coltas' rafts on the lake; the Indians cut the reeds for use as cattle fodder or to make the reed mats and baskets for which they are famous.

Some of the more traditional Colta Indian women can be easily identified, as they dye the fringes of their hair a startling golden color. If you have the time or inclination, you could walk around the lake in a couple of hours.

You can visit this area on a day excursion from Riobamba using local buses or hiring a taxi. The views of the volcanoes, especially Chimborazo, are particularly good as you return from Colta to Riobamba along the Panamericana – try to sit near the front of the bus.

CHIMBORAZO

Not only is the 6310-meter extinct Volcán Chimborazo the highest mountain in Ecuador, but its peak is also the farthest point from the center of the earth (due to the earth's equatorial bulge). For insatiable trivia buffs, it is higher than any other mountain in the Americas north of it. Nearby is the ninth highest mountain in Ecuador, the 5020-meter-high Carihuairazo. Climbing either mountain is an adventure only for experienced mountaineers with snow and ice-climbing gear (consult a climbing guide recommended in Facts for the Visitor or contact a local guide) but reaching the refuge on Chimborazo is as simple as hiring a car. The area around these mountains is also suitable for backpacking trips – the walk from Mocha (on the Panamericana north of Riobamba) over the pass between the two mountains and emerging at the Ambato-Guaranda road is as good a choice as any. Allow three days for this hike and bring plenty of warm clothes. June to September is the dry season in this region.

There are two refuges. Most vehicles reach the lower one where you can sometimes buy drinks and sweets. You can sleep at the upper refuge (about a half-hour walk uphill) for US$8 or US$10 per night; there is a fireplace and cooking facilities, but bring your own sleeping bag. Refuge guardians are on duty. The refuge is named after Edward Whymper, the British climber who in 1880 made the first ascent of Chimborazo with the Swiss Carrels as guides.

At 5000 meters this is Ecuador's highest refuge, and altitude sickness is a very real danger. It is essential that you spend several days acclimatizing at the elevation of Riobamba or higher before going to the refuge.

At some of Riobamba's hotels you can rent a pickup (about US$25 and up, depending on the hotel and services requested) for a day trip to the refuges on Chimborazo. The manager of the Hotel Imperial, Carlos Morales, will take you to the refuge for about US$12 per person (minimum three people) and stay there for about three hours while you look around, or come back to pick you up another day. He will also drive you to Ingapirca and other small villages for US$50 for the entire day. The manager of the Hotel Whymper also provides rides to the refuge. Several other hotels can arrange this service.

If you can bargain hard, try hiring a pickup truck from near the Riobamba railway station (about US$20, depending on the vehicle and your bargaining abilities). Pickups are also available from the Plaza Simón Bolívar at Junín and 5 de Junio. If the road is in reasonable shape, you can even get there in an ordinary car. It is also possible to get a truck (with passengers) to the village of San Juan, and from this village rent a pickup for about US$7 to the refuge – assuming that all the vehicles in San Juan haven't gone somewhere else!

GUANO & SANTA TERESITA
These small villages are a few kilometers north of Riobamba and make an ideal day trip. Guano is an important carpet-making center, and although it's unlikely that many travelers will have room in their luggage for a couple of souvenir carpets, it is nevertheless interesting to see this cottage industry. In Guano you should get off the bus at the central plaza, where there are several carpet stores, and then continue down Avenida García Moreno, which will take you past several more. There are no hotels and only a few restaurants. One near the plaza is reportedly OK; look for the topiary garden with El Altar rising in the background – a pretty sight.

From the main plaza you can continue with a US$0.10 bus ride to Santa Teresita a few kilometers away. The bus route terminates at the end of the road. From there turn right and head down the hill for about 20 minutes to the *balneario* (spa), where swimming pools are fed by natural springs. The water is quite cool (22°C), but the views of Tungurahua and El Altar are marvelous. There is a basic cafeteria and camping is permitted.

The roundtrip from Riobamba will take about six hours if you take it leisurely and have a swim in the pool. There are frequent buses during daylight hours, and it's a good chance to see some of the local countryside. A taxi from Riobamba will cost a few dollars. Travelers report that it's easy and pleasant to walk part of the way – take a bus from Riobamba and then walk back. Locals know the way.

GUAMOTE
From the Cajabamba region the southbound Panamericana roughly follows the railway and crosses the tracks quite often. Some 30 km beyond Cajabamba you reach the village of Guamote, which has an interesting and unspoiled Thursday market. There is a basic pensión near the train tracks.

Guamote is the beginning of a new road being built to the southeast, over the Atillo Pass in the Eastern Cordillera, down the eastern slopes of the Andes, past the southern edge of Parque Nacional Sangay and on to Macas in the southern Oriente (see the earlier section on the Parque Nacional Sangay for more details). From Guamote, it is possible to hire a truck as far as Atillo, about 45 km away; there is no bus.

Note that Guamote is located almost one km off the Panamericana in a valley. Unless your bus is actually going to Guamote, you will be dropped off on the Panamericana and will have to walk in.

ALAUSÍ

Almost 50 km south of Guamote you reach Alausí, which is near the head of the Río Chanchán valley, down which the railway runs to the coast. Just below Alausí begins the famous Nariz del Diablo (see the Nariz del Diablo sidebar). Alausí is also a popular highland resort for Guayaquileños wishing to escape the unpleasant heat and humidity of the coast while experiencing one of the world's great feats of railway engineering.

In addition, there is a busy Sunday market. Alausí is an important, albeit brief, destination for travelers.

Orientation & Information

The main street is Avenida 5 de Junio, which is about six blocks long. Buses arrive and depart from this street and most of the hotels are located along it. The train station is at the north end of 5 de Junio. There is an EMETEL office one block to the west of 5 de Junio behind the fire station near the train station. From the train station, head east and wander around to find a plaza, church, cobbled streets and balconied buildings – *tranquilisimo*. There is one movie theater.

Apart from the Sunday market, there is a smaller one on Thursday. The feast of Saints Peter and Paul (June 28) is one of Alausí's major fiestas, and the town is very crowded then.

Places to Stay & Eat

Hotels are often full on Saturday night for the Sunday market and Ecuadorian weekend visitors. There are no first-class hotels; most are along 5 de Junio. The clean, family-run *Hotel Tequendama* (☎ 930 123) has hot water and charges US$3.50 per person. Breakfast is available. Other possibilities are the friendly *Hotel Panamericano* (☎ 930 156), with electric showers and a basic restaurant, charging US$6 for a double; the *Hotel Europa*, which also has a restaurant; and the *Residencial Alausí* (☎ 930 361), on Estaban Orozco just off the south end of 5 de Junio, which is new and has nice rooms.

The *Hotel Gampala* (☎ 930 138) has erratic hot water and tries to rip you off at US$20 for a basic double with private bath. Try to bargain – it's not worth more than US$10. Their restaurant overcharges, too. Your best bet is the *Hotel Americano* (☎ 930 159), García Moreno 159, a block east of 5 de Junio near the train station. Good, clean rooms with private hot bath are about US$7/12.

Apart from the hotel restaurants, there are a couple of basic restaurants along the main street, mostly serving meriendas. There's really not much choice, but the food is quite adequate. *Danielito's* opposite the Tequendama is simple but friendly. *Momentos*, at the south end of 5 de Junio, is quite nice.

Getting There & Away

Bus Buses from Riobamba (US$1.20; 1½ hours) arrive every hour or so. Buses turn off the Panamericana and drop down into town, where they normally stop near the Hotel Panamericano. Buses for Cuenca (US$3; four hours) also leave from here several times a day. Buses between Riobamba and Cuenca don't normally enter town, but they leave passengers on the Panamericana from which it is almost a one-km walk down into town.

Old buses (or pickup trucks acting as buses) leave from 5 de Junio for nearby destinations. Some of the rides can be quite spectacular, especially the one to Achupallas, about 23 km to the southeast. Make sure that any sightseeing ride you take is coming back to Alausí, as there are few, if any, places to stay in these villages.

There are also buses and trucks to the village of **Chunchi**, about 25 km farther south on the Panamericana. Here you'll find a local Sunday market and a few basic places to stay.

Train Alausí used to be a major railroad junction, with tracks heading north to Riobamba and Quito, south to Cuenca and west to Durán (a suburb of Guayaquil). The Cuenca line is now closed, perhaps permanently, but there are daily services to Durán and services on most days to Riobamba. All are subject to occasional cancellation.

The train for Durán leaves Alausí daily at 9 am and tickets go on sale at 7:30 am. This train usually arrives from Riobamba and is often quite full, but ticket sales are orderly. The fare is US$12 for foreigners, or US$10 if you get off in Bucay. Ecuadorians are charged a fraction of this price, but if foreign travelers don't subsidize the train service, it will be shut down. It takes three to four hours to Bucay (see the Nariz del Diablo sidebar) and about eight to Durán.

The train from Durán arrives in Alausí in mid- to late afternoon and continues on to Riobamba. This service is subject to cancellation, especially if the train is running late, and passengers to Riobamba may be told to catch a bus.

BUCAY
OK. I'll finally let you in on the secret: There is no place called Bucay on any map of Ecuador (at least none of the many I have examined). Bucay is the name of the train station in the small town officially known as General Elizalde. Maps mark Gral Elizalde, but, inexplicably, no one knows where Gral Elizalde is – it's Bucay to everybody except Ecuadorian map makers. It took me several years to figure this out. I used to think that Bucay was simply too small to put on the map. Recently the town received some minor fame as the birthplace of cutting-edge feminist Lorena Bobbitt.

Bucay is a small but bustling town. Many people descending from Alausí by train get off here (the most scenic part behind them) and continue by bus. It is two hours to Guayaquil by bus as opposed to four by train, and you end up in the Guayaquil bus terminal rather than Durán. Many travelers wishing to ride the train but not go to Guayaquil at all take buses from Bucay back to the highlands. There are many buses to **El Triunfo** (25 minutes) from

El Nariz del Diablo
The most exciting part of the train ride to Durán is the hair-raising 66-km descent from Alausí to Bucay through the area know as *El Nariz del Diablo* (the Devil's Nose). This is where the landslides caused by the torrential rains of the 1982-83 El Niño did the most damage. These tracks were repaired in the late 1980s, and now the spectacular train ride between Alausí and Guayaquil attracts many travelers. Alausí is at 2607 meters above sea level, according to one tourist brochure; another guidebook puts it at 2356 meters; and a sign at the Alausí train station attests a third altitude: 2347 meters. Whatever the height, the first few kilometers are very steep. At the station of Huigra, about 26 km away, the elevation is given as only 1255 meters, and Bucay's elevation is considerably lower still.

The steep descent is accomplished by a series of switchbacks down the steep mountainside. Occasional rickety-looking bridges cross steep ravines. Daredevils can even ride on the flat roof of the train, with nothing but empty space between you and the valleys far below. The local machos stand up on the roof, especially when going through the tunnels where there is barely enough clearance for the sombrero jammed jauntily on their heads. I was content with sitting on the roof and grinning like an idiot. Actually, the greatest hazard is probably the steam locomotive that blows steam, soot and cinders during the ride, so wear clothes you don't mind getting dirty. (Sometimes, a nonsteam train does the route.) ∎

where you can connect with frequent buses to Cuenca (four hours). El Triunfo is a busy, hot agricultural center in the southern lowlands and has a few basic hotels, though I can see no reason for staying here. Alternately, you can catch a bus back to Riobamba from Bucay. There are plenty of buses leaving in the middle of the day when the train from Alausí arrives.

Usually, the train from Alausí arrives in Bucay before the train from Durán. In that case, you can get off the down train and catch the up one back to Alausí. You can't rely on this, however – the last time I took the train from Alausí we didn't make it to Bucay before the train in the opposite direction left.

I don't particularly recommend staying in Bucay, but if you get stuck here for some reason, try the cheap and basic but clean *Hotel California* or *Hotel Florida* (both with hot showers) and the even more basic *Hotel Central*. At least the people are friendly.

ACHUPALLAS

This village is the starting point for a three-day hike south along the old Inca road to Ingapirca, the most important Inca ruin in Ecuador (see the Cuenca chapter). Occasional trucks leave Alausí for Achupallas, or you can hire a taxi (pickup) for about US$7. Alternately, there is transport from Alausí to Guasuntos (La Moya) from where you can wait for trucks to Achupallas. It is about 10 km from Alausí to La Moya and a further 15 km to Achupallas. There is nowhere to stay at either place.

The hike from Achupallas to Ingapirca is a good one (see the hiking guides recommended in the Books appendix in the back of the book). The Inca road is faint in places, but you could probably find your way to Ingapirca with a compass and map, asking the locals for directions if you don't have a hiking book. Head south and pack some extra food in case you get temporarily lost. The area is remote but inhabited, so don't leave your stuff lying around outside your tent, and be prepared for persistent begging from children. The area is covered by three 1:50,000 topographical maps available from the IGM in Quito. These are the Alausí CT-ÑV-A3, Juncal CT-ÑV-C1 and Cañar CT-ÑV-C3 sheets.

Cuenca & the Southern Highlands

The three southern Sierra provinces, Cañar, Azuay and Loja, are noticeably different from the seven highland provinces to the north. Geographically they are much lower, with very few peaks reaching 4000 meters. The topography is rugged nevertheless, and communications with the rest of Ecuador have been developed only relatively recently.

Cuenca, the major city of the region and Ecuador's third largest, didn't have paved highway connections with Guayaquil and Quito until the 1960s, and even today these highways are not in particularly good shape. Due to its isolation until recent times, the area is rich in history, and the region has a strong flavor of the colonial past.

The southern highlands had a colorful history even before the Spanish conquest. These were the lands of the Cañari Indians, an independent culture with exceptional skill in producing gold jewelry and other metalwork, fine weavings and ceramics.

In the late 15th century the Cañaris were conquered by the Incas, who built several major centers. These included the city of Tomebamba, near present-day Cuenca, and the fortress of Ingapirca, the best preserved pre-colonial ruin found in Ecuador today. The Inca influence was short lived, however, and the Spanish conquistadors under Pizarro took control by the 1530s. Cuenca was (re)founded relatively late in 1557. Several other important towns of the region were founded earlier, such as Loja in 1548.

Remnants of the colonial era are more likely to be seen here than anywhere else in the country, except Quito. Although progress is slowly catching up with the southern Sierra, this area is still a long way behind the coast and northern highlands. Today travelers are struck by the paucity of large cities in the southern highlands.

Cuenca and Loja are the only towns with a population of over 30,000 inhabitants. Many villages have cobbled streets and old houses with balconies, and the tradition of handicrafts ranging from jewelry-making to weaving is strong. A journey through the provinces of the southern highlands is a journey into the past.

CUENCA

Barely half a century before the arrival of the Spaniards, the powerful Inca Tupac (or Topa) Yupanqui was undertaking the difficult conquest of the Cañari Indians, who struggled bravely to stem the expansion of the Inca Empire. After several years of bitter fighting, Tupac Yupanqui's forces prevailed.

The Inca began construction of a major city whose splendor and importance was to rival that of the imperial capital of Cuzco. The Indians told of sun temples covered with gold sheets and palaces built using the finest skill of Cuzqueño stonemasons, but what happened to Tomebamba, as the city was called, is shrouded in mystery.

By the time Spanish chronicler Cieza de León passed through in 1547, Tomebamba lay largely in ruins, although well-stocked storehouses indicated how great it had recently been. Today it is difficult to imagine Tomebamba's splendor, for all that remains are a few recently excavated Inca walls by the river that bears the town's name.

The Río Tomebamba divides Cuenca in half. South of the river are fairly recent suburbs, the stadium and the modern university. To the north is the heart of the colonial city, which lies at about 2530 meters above sea level.

Although Cuenca has expanded to become Ecuador's third largest town with about 200,000 inhabitants (officially, but probably closer to 300,000), it still retains a pleasantly provincial air. The people are more conservative than in Quito (you will find that you will draw attention to yourself if you don't dress conservatively).

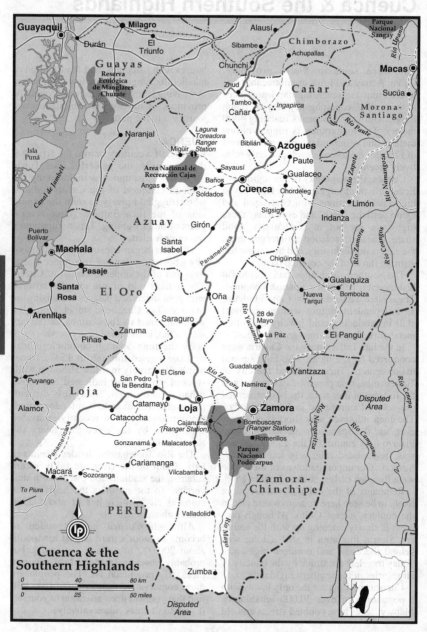

CUENCA

Cuenca &
Southern Highlands

| 0 | 40 | 80 km |
| 0 | 25 | 50 miles |

The old colonial center has churches dating from the 16th and 17th centuries and is a delight to stroll around. The earliest building is the original cathedral, construction of which began in 1557, the year Cuenca was founded by the Spanish conquistador Gil Ramírez Dávalos.

There are cobbled streets and red-tiled roofs, art galleries and flower markets, shady plazas and museums. The majority of the hotels, too, are near the center, so the traveler can conveniently enjoy a relaxing few days in this colonial city.

Cuenca also makes a good base from which to visit the Area Nacional de Recreación Cajas, as well as local thermal baths, villages and markets (described in Around Cuenca). The ruins of Ingapirca are described in the section North of Cuenca.

For a good view of the area, take a taxi south of town along Avenida Fray Vicente Solano to the church at Turi, a southern suburb about four km away from the center. The white church is perched on a hill and Cuenca stretches out below you.

Information

Tourist Offices The CETUR tourist information office (☎ 882 058, fax 831 414) is at Hermano Miguel 6-86 and Córdova. They are friendly and they do try to help with city maps and information. They say that their hours are from 8 am to 4 pm Monday to Friday, but they are usually closed around 1 pm for lunch.

The Asociación Hotelera del Azuay (☎ 821 659, 836 925, fax 826 301), at Córdova and Padre Aguirre, has information about hotels in the region, including rates at all budget levels.

The INEFAN information office (for Area Nacional de Recreación Cajas, described later) is at Bolívar 5-33, 3rd floor. They have some information, but most travelers just go directly to Cajas and get maps and information when they arrive.

The immigration office is in the Municipalidad (City Hall) on Parque Calderón.

Money Both banks and casas de cambio will change money at rates similar to Quito's. Casas de cambio have faster service and longer hours. The several branches of Filanbanco are good for Visa advances.

Cambistral (☎ 822 213), next to the Hotel Paris Internacional on Sucre and Borrero, accepts a few currencies (German, French, Swiss) other than US dollars. Another, VAZ (☎ 833 434, 832 795), is at Gran Colombia 798 and Cordero. There are others around Borrero and Sucre.

Post & Communications The post office is on the corner of Gran Colombia and Borrero. The EMETEL office is at Benigno Malo and Sucre. The area code for Cuenca and the province of Azuay is 07.

Travel Agencies & Guides Several local agencies and guides have been recommended for tours to Ingapirca, Area Nacional de Recreación Cajas, nearby villages and markets, and various other local attractions.

English-speaking Eduardo Quito (☎ 823 018, fax 834 202 or 823 449), Cordero 20-56, is a good local guide who has received several recommendations. He charges about US$60 to take a group to Ingapirca. Expediciones Apullacta (☎ 837 681), Gran Colombia 11-02, has day tours to Ingapirca, Cajas and other places from US$35 per person. These tours are competitively priced and popular, especially among travelers on a budget.

Ecotrek (☎ 842 531, 834 677, fax 835 387), Calle Larga 7-108 at Cordero, is run by well-known local adventurers Daniel Kuperman, Juan Diego Domínguez and Juan Gabriel Carrasco. They speak English and French and are recommended for adventure travel, trekking, mountaineering etc. They also operate the new Huagrahuma Páramo Lodge at the border of Cajas.

English-speaking naturalist guide Edgar Aguirre at Aventuras Río Arriba (☎ 840 031, 830 116, 883 711), Hermano Miguel 7-14, by the CETUR office, is another good choice for a variety of tours. He has, in the past, arranged camping equipment rental. Club Andinismo Sangay (☎ 806 615, 844 313), often has group hikes on

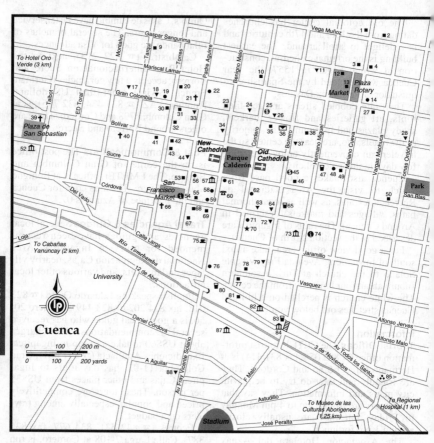

Sunday at a nominal fee. Cajas is often featured. (A camping store at the corner of Gran Colombia and Cordero may have more information.)

Excursiones Santa Ana (☎ /fax 832 340), Córdova and Borrero, and Yroo Tours (☎ 835 533/888), Calle Larga 8-90 and Benigno Malo, are slightly pricier than the above mentioned, and of the two Yroo Tours is cheaper. Metropolitan Touring (☎ 831 185, 842 496), Sucre 6-62 and Borrero, has had expensive tours to Ingapirca by train (part of the way) in the past, and this may resume depending on the

condition of the tracks. These agencies are also useful for straightforward reservations for airlines and better hotels.

English-speaking Humberto Chico at Cabañas Yanuncay (see Places to Stay) organizes overnight tours to Cajas (three days; US$100 per person), the southern Oriente (five days; US$250 per person) and other areas. Tours include food, accommodations and transportation, and are small and personal.

Note that entrance fees, which are not included in many tours, can add a substantial amount – check.

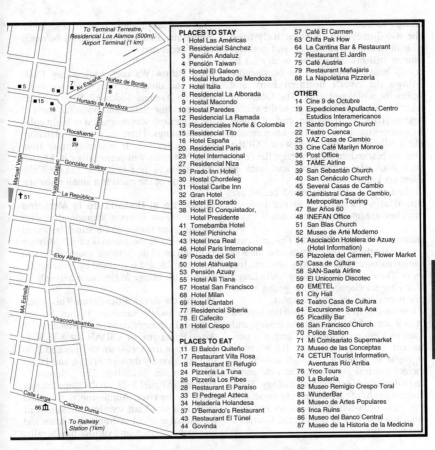

To Terminal Terrestre,
Residencial Los Alamos (500m),
Airport Terminal (1 km)

PLACES TO STAY
1 Hotel Las Américas
2 Residencial Sánchez
3 Pensión Andaluz
4 Pensión Taiwan
5 Hostal El Galeon
6 Hostal Hurtado de Mendoza
7 Hotel Italia
8 Residencial La Alborada
9 Hostal Macondo
10 Hostal Paredes
12 Residencial La Ramada
13 Residenciales Norte & Colombia
15 Residencial Tito
16 Hotel España
20 Residencial Paris
23 Hotel Internacional
27 Residencial Niza
29 Prado Inn Hotel
30 Hostal Chordeleg
31 Hostal Caribe Inn
32 Gran Hotel
35 Hotel El Dorado
38 Hotel El Conquistador,
   Hotel Presidente
41 Tomebamba Hotel
42 Hotel Pichincha
43 Hotel Inca Real
46 Hotel Paris Internacional
49 Posada del Sol
50 Hotel Atahualpa
53 Pensión Azuay
55 Hotel Alli Tiana
67 Hostal San Francisco
68 Hotel Milan
69 Hotel Cantabri
77 Residencial Siberia
78 El Cafecito
81 Hotel Crespo

PLACES TO EAT
11 El Balcón Quiteño
17 Restaurant Villa Rosa
18 Restaurant El Refugio
22 Pizzería La Tuna
26 Pizzería Los Pibes
28 Restaurant El Paraíso
33 El Pedregal Azteca
34 Heladería Holandesa
37 D'Bernardo's Restaurant
43 Restaurant El Túnel
44 Govinda

57 Café El Carmen
63 Chifa Pak How
64 La Cantina Bar & Restaurant
72 Restaurant El Jardín
75 Café Austria
79 Restaurant Mañajaris
88 La Napoletana Pizzería

OTHER
14 Cine 9 de Octubre
19 Expediciones Apullacta, Centro
   Estudios Interamericanos
21 Santo Domingo Church
22 Teatro Cuenca
25 VAZ Casa de Cambio
33 Cine Café Marilyn Monroe
36 Post Office
38 TAME Airline
39 San Sebastián Church
40 San Cenáculo Church
45 Several Casas de Cambio
46 Cambistral Casa de Cambio,
   Metropolitan Touring
47 Bar Años 60
48 INEFAN Office
51 San Blas Church
52 Museo de Arte Moderno
54 Asociación Hotelera de Azuay
   (Hotel Information)
56 Plazoleta del Carmen, Flower Market
57 Casa de Cultura
58 SAN-Saeta Airline
59 El Unicornio Discotec
60 EMETEL
61 City Hall
62 Teatro Casa de Cultura
65 Excursiones Santa Ana
65 Picadilly Bar
66 San Francisco Church
70 Police Station
71 Mi Comisariato Supermarket
73 Museo de las Conceptas
74 CETUR Tourist Information,
   Aventuras Río Arriba
76 Yroo Tours
80 La Bulería
82 Museo Remigio Crespo Toral
83 WunderBar
84 Museo de Artes Populares
85 Inca Ruins
86 Museo del Banco Central
87 Museo de la Historia de la Medicina

CUENCA

Medical Services Of the several hospitals and clinics, Clínica Santa Ana Inés (☎ 817 888), located on Daniel Córdova about two blocks west of Fray Vicente Solano, has had several recommendations. The clinic is staffed by some English-speaking doctors. The regional hospital (☎ 811 299) is on Avenida del Paraíso on the southeastern outskirts of town.

Emergency In an emergency, contact the Red Cross ambulance at ☎ 822 520. The police station (☎ 101 or 810 068) is at Cordero and Córdova.

Dangers & Annoyances For some years, it has been reported that a short, dark, pudgy man asks lone female travelers to write letters for him and then invites them out. He may claim to be a businessman traveling abroad. He is known to ask women to answer questions and to then go with him to meet his female friends or relations by way of thanks. He is a known rapist and should be considered dangerous. Sadly, he seems to have close relations with the police.

Travelers visiting Cuenca in 1995 report that this guy is still around, and this has been corroborated by locals.

Things to See

The Río Tomebamba is attractively lined with old colonial buildings, and washerwomen still lay out clothes to dry on its grassy banks. Avenida 3 de Noviembre follows the river's northern bank and makes for a pleasant walk. The following selection of places of interest to the visitor begins at the southeastern end of town, then moves northwest into the town center, and finally heads out to the west. All the sites are marked on the city map; the complete walk along the river and back is about six km.

Most of the sites described below are closed at weekends or, in the case of churches, are open irregular hours.

Museo del Banco Central This museum is in the southeast part of town near the Río Tomebamba, and is not very obvious (no sign). The entrance gate is on Calle Larga near Huayna Capac, and the guard at the gate may ask to see your passport.

Entrance is free and the museum is open from 9 am to 5 pm Monday to Friday, and 9 am to 1 pm on Saturday. There is a permanent collection of old B&W photographs of Cuenca, a small exhibit of ancient musical instruments and the usual small displays of art and archaeology. Their changing exhibits are often very good, and they have occasional slide shows and cultural movies. This is considered Cuenca's best museum.

Behind the museum is an Inca archaeological site, Pumapungo, which is currently being excavated.

Inca Ruins Walking back along Calle Larga and along the river, you come to the ruins on Avenida Todos los Santos. There are some fine niches and walls but most of the stonework was destroyed to build colonial buildings. There are a few explanatory signs in Spanish. If you're coming from Peru, the ruins will seem rather lackluster. Admission to the site is free. On the Calle Larga side of the ruins is a small museum.

Museo de la Historia de la Medicina This museum is open sporadically, with changing art shows and a small botanical garden. It is in the grounds of the Military Hospital on 12 de Octubre, south of the Río Tomebamba, and is reached by crossing the river on the bridge at Hermano Miguel.

Museo de Artes Populares This small but worthwhile museum is run by the Centro Interamericano de Artesanías y Artes Populares, or CIDAP, (☎ 828 878) and is open from 9:30 am to 1 pm and 2:30 to 5 pm Monday through Friday, and 10 am to 1 pm on Saturday. The address is Hermano Miguel 3-23, on the steps leading down to the river. Admission is free, and there is a small but worthwhile exhibit of traditional musical instruments, native and regional costumes, and various handicrafts.

Museological Muses

If you happen to like museums, the good news is that you'll find quite a selection in Cuenca, although they aren't as good as the museums in Quito or Guayaquil. The bad news is that the wonderful rambling collection of Padre Crespi, once the most famous Cuenca archive, has been closed indefinitely since the Padre's death in 1982. Some of the collection has been taken over by the Banco Central, and other parts are in the hands of the Museo Remigio Crespo Toral, but most of it was not available for viewing when I was last in Cuenca. Of those pieces that are on display, it is hard to tell which can be attributed to Crespi's collection.

Padre Crespi was an eccentric Italian missionary who became a local cleric. He claimed that Ecuador was settled by the Phoenicians who sailed from the eastern Mediterranean, across the Atlantic and up the Amazon – 3000 years ago! The Crespi 'stones,' described in Von Daniken's *Chariots of the Gods*, are now reported to be in a private collection. ■

There is also a changing exhibition that can feature anything from Chinese porcelains to Cuencano pottery.

Museo Remigio Crespo Toral This museum (also known as the Museo Municipal), Calle Larga 7-07 and Borrero, has been under restoration for some years. This is probably just as well, because the creaking old building seemed positively dangerous last time I was there. The collection contains religious sculptures, colonial furniture and paintings, a fine selection of Indian artifacts and relics of the local Saint Miguel who was canonized in 1984. It may have reopened by the time you get there; check with CETUR.

Museo de las Conceptas This museum (☎ 830 625) is housed in the Convent of the Immaculate Conception at Hermano Miguel 6-33, three blocks up from the river and opposite the tourist office. The museum is in what used to be the old infirmary of the convent, which was founded on June 13, 1599. Parts of the building date to the 17th century. The chapel of the infirmary has a display of crucifixes by the noted 19th-century local sculptor, Gaspar Sangurima. Other parts of the building display a variety of religious art: paintings, carvings, statuettes, nativity scenes etc. There is also a display of photographs showing the austere daily life of the nuns. This is considered Cuenca's best religious museum. There is an audio-visual presentation at 11 am and 3 pm. Museum hours are 9 am to 4 pm, Tuesday to Friday, and 9 am to noon on Saturday; admission is US$2.

Church of San Blas Four blocks east of the Museo de las Conceptas is where colonial Cuenca's boundary used to be, marked by the church and plaza of San Blas. Originally built in the late 16th century, the small colonial church has since been replaced by a new early 20th century building. The modern church is one of the city's largest, and is the only one in Cuenca built in the form of a Latin cross.

Parque Calderón The main plaza, or Parque Calderón, is three blocks northwest of the Museo de las Conceptas. The dominant building is the **new cathedral** with its huge blue domes. It is particularly attractive when illuminated, although the lighting hours are unpredictable. The marbled interior is rather stark. Construction began in 1885, and the cathedral was supposed to be much taller than it is – an error in design meant that the tall belltowers could not be supported by the building and so it was not built as originally planned.

Almost unnoticed on the other side of the park is the squat but more interesting **old cathedral** (also known as El Sagrario) which was renovated for the 1985 visit of Pope John Paul II to Ecuador. Construction of this building began in 1557, the year that Cuenca was founded. In 1739 it was used as a triangulation

Elaborately carved wooden doors are found on many colonial churches.

point by La Condamine's expedition to measure the shape of the earth. It is open to the public but hours are variable.

Casa de Cultura At the southwest corner of Parque Calderón is the Casa de Cultura. There is a good art gallery here with frequently changing exhibits. Most paintings are by local artists and are for sale, but there is absolutely no pressure to buy. In fact it's hard to find a salesperson if you should happen to see a work that you're seriously interested in. There's also a bookstore of art-oriented books in Spanish and a coffee shop.

Plazoleta del Carmen A block from the Parque Calderón at the corner of Sucre and Aguirre is the church of El Carmen de la Asunción, founded on August 1, 1682. Although the church itself is open infrequently, there is a colorful and attractive daily **flower market** in the small plaza in front of the church – a pretty sight. Turning left down Aguirre brings you to the 19th-century **San Francisco** church and market, a block away.

Plaza de San Sebastián Continuing west along Sucre for five blocks brings you to this plaza, also known as the Parque Miguel León. This is a quiet and pleasant park with the interesting 17th-century **church of San Sebastián** at the north end and the Museo de Arte Moderno at the south end. In 1739 the Frenchman Juan Seniergues, a member of La Condamine's geodesic expedition, was killed in this plaza during a fiesta, apparently following an affair with a local woman.

Museo de Arte Moderno This is on Sucre and Talbot (☎ 830 499) and is open from 9 am to 1 pm and 3 to 6 pm Monday to Friday – sometimes on weekends. Admission is free. There is a small permanent collection and changing shows of (mainly) local artists and sculptors.

Back into the Center Return to the center along Bolívar and look into the republican

church of San Cenáculo as you go. This has recently been cleaned and has had work done on it – it looks very bare in contrast to the opulent churches of Quito. After San Cenáculo, head north for one block and continue into the center along Gran Colombia, the main handicraft and shopping street in Cuenca. Soon you pass the **church of Santo Domingo** on your left, which has some fine carved wooden doors and colonial paintings inside. Although it looks older, the church was built in the early 20th century. In the next few blocks you pass several arts and crafts stores selling a variety of handicrafts. Parque Calderón is only a block to the south.

Museo de las Culturas Aborígenes This new museum (☎ 811 706, 880 010) is at the southeast end of town at 10 de Agosto 4-70 and JM Sánchez. You can walk there from the center in well under an hour, or take a taxi for about US$1.50. The museum houses a private collection of about 5000 archaeological pieces representative of some 20 pre-Columbian cultures of Ecuador. This collection rivals that of the Banco Central. Hours are 9 am to noon and 3 to 6 pm Monday to Saturday, and admission is US$2. Call ahead to arrange a guided tour in English; tours last about 1½ hours.

Markets

Market day is Thursday, with a smaller market on Saturday. There are two main market areas: one around the **church of San Francisco** and the other at the **Plaza Rotary** by Avenidas Mariscal Lamar and Hermano Miguel. The San Francisco market is mainly for locals rather than tourists, and crafts shoppers will do better to look into the Plaza Rotary market or along Gran Colombia. The markets are lively and interesting, but watch your belongings, as pickpockets have been reported. The market continues on a smaller scale on other days of the week.

Special Events

Cuenca's Independence Day is November 3, which combines with November 1 and 2

(All Saints' Day and All Souls' Day) to form an important holiday period for the city. The markets are in full swing, and there is music and dancing, parades and drinking. Hotel rooms may be very difficult to find at this time and prices may rise. April 12 is the anniversary of the foundation of Cuenca and is similarly celebrated for several days around that date.

Carnaval, as in other parts of Ecuador, is celebrated with boisterous water fights. No one is spared – I saw a whole bucket of water poured from a balcony over an old nun's head! Cuenca seems to be more enamored of these soggy celebrations than the rest of the country; Easter and New Year's are also popular with water-throwers. Protect your camera gear.

There is a colorful city parade on Christmas Eve, starting in the suburbs in late morning and emerging, finally, near the cathedral in the afternoon. It may be held on the Saturday before Christmas. Corpus Christi (usually the 9th Thursday after Easter) is also colorfully celebrated for several days.

Courses & Work
The Centro de Estudios Interamericanos (☎ 839 003, fax 833 593), Gran Colombia 11-02, Casilla 597, Cuenca, offers courses, including Spanish, Quichua, Portuguese, Latin American literature and indigenous culture. Students who already speak Spanish can take internships in areas ranging from ethnomusicology to export. These courses are offered for full semesters and for college credit three times a year, although students wishing to learn Spanish on a 'drop-in' basis can also be accommodated.

The center also offers English classes, which are taught by native English speakers with a college degree. This is an opportunity to work in Ecuador, particularly if you have training in teaching English as a second language, although tutors with a degree in other fields can also find work.

Places to Stay
Hotels seem pricey in Cuenca, partly because they will try to charge as much as they think they can get. Try bargaining. The more expensive hotels have two prices (the one for gringos is about twice what locals pay). This system is trickling down into the mid-priced hotels as well. A reader recently wrote that a double room at one hotel was US$36, but I was quoted US$20 for a double at the same place when I was researching the book. Use the following prices as a rough guideline only. Speaking Spanish and traveling by local transport will probably get you better rates than if you don't speak Spanish and arrive at a hotel in a rented car. Not fair? Maybe, but that's how it is.

Most hotels (except a few of the most desperately cheap) have hot or at least tepid water. There are, however, occasional problems with water supply, so make sure the water is running before you pay extra for a room with private bath.

There are half a dozen hotels within a few hundred meters of the terminal terrestre, but most are a kilometer or more away in the downtown area.

Places to Stay – bottom end
Opposite the terminal terrestre northeast of town is the *Residencial Los Alamos* (☎ 825 644), with its simple restaurant. Clean rooms with shared and private baths are US$3.50 and US$5 per person, respectively. A few minutes' walk towards town is *Residencial La Alborada* (☎ 831 062), Olmedo 13-82, at US$3/5 with shared, hot baths. Nearby, the clean and friendly *Hotel España* (☎ 824 723), Sangurima 1-19, is US$4 per person, or US$7/12 with private bath. Rooms vary in quality – some have TVs; there is a reasonably priced restaurant. On the same block, the *Residencial Tito* (☎ 829 734), Sangurima 1-49, is similar, though many rooms lack windows. The modern, clean *Hostal El Galeón* (☎ 831 827), Sangurima 2-36, has spacious rooms with bath for US$6 per person.

There are cheaper hotels closer to the center. A good number of them are in the market area near Mariscal Lamar and Mariano Cueva, which one reader suggests is a poor area after dark, though it seemed

OK to me. A decent basic place is the *Residencial Norte* (☎ 827 881), Mariano Cueva 11-63, for US$3.50 per person, or US$4.50 with private bath (one reader tells me he got a double with bath for about US$6 off-season). Rooms are large and there's plenty of hot water. Next door, the basic *Residencial Colombia* (☎ 827 851) is similarly priced and also OK. The basic but adequate *Residencial La Ramada* (☎ 833 862), Sangurima 5-51, is friendly and charges from US$3.50/5.50 (shared baths); a few rooms with private baths go for a little more. The *Residencial Sánchez* (☎ 831 519), Vega Muñoz 4-28, is similar. The *Residencial Niza* (☎ 823 284), Mariscal Lamar 4-51, is clean and friendly. Rooms are $3.50 per person, or US$4.50 with private bath. Also in this price range is the recently improved *Pensión Azuay* (☎ 824 119), Padre Aguirre 7-61.

Other basic places that are cheap but not as good include the *Pensión Taiwan*, and *Pensión Andaluz*, both with doubles for about US$4 or US$5. Equally cheap but worse are the *Hostal San Francisco* and the run-down *Hotel Cantabri*.

The hospitable *Hotel Pichincha* (☎ 823 868), on Torres near Bolívar, has large, clean rooms for US$4.75 per person with towels and plenty of hot water in the shared bath. The friendly *Hotel Milan* (☎ 835 351), Córdova 9-89, is popular and charges US$7/12 with bath, or US$4.50/7.50 with shared bath. Some rooms have balconies, there's plenty of hot water and there is a simple restaurant.

The friendly *Gran Hotel* (☎ 831 934, 835 154), Torres 9-70, is US$5/8 without and US$8/14 with bath; some rooms have TVs. There is a restaurant and an attractive courtyard, although rooms near it can be noisy. The clean *Residencial Paris* (☎ 842 656, 827 257), Torres 10-48, has a helpful English-speaking manager. Rooms are US$6 per person with bath, including breakfast. The friendly, helpful and comfortable *Hostal Paredes* (☎ 835 674, fax 834 910), Cordero 11-29, is in an early-20th-century building and is reputedly one of Cuenca's oldest hotels. Spacious rooms

are furnished with colonial-style furniture and there are many flowers. Rates are about US$5 to US$10 per person, depending on the month, whom you talk to and how long you stay. A reader reports that *El Cafecito* (☎ 827 341), owned by the same folks that have the El Cafecito in Quito, recently opened at Honorato Vasquez 7-36 near Cordero, and charges about US$5 per person in rooms with shared hot showers.

The *Hostal Macondo* (☎ 831 198, fax 833 593), Tarqui 11-64, is quiet and friendly, with kitchen privileges and a nice courtyard. This place is affiliated with Hostelling Internacional. Good sized rooms are US$8/12 (shared bath) and a few have private bath for US$12/16. Reservations are recommended in the high season.

Places to Stay – middle

Many of the hotels in this section add 20% tax; I try and include this in the price, but you should check the total rates before booking a room.

Just under three km southwest of the center, you'll find the recommended *Cabañas Yanuncay* (☎ 883 716, ☎ /fax 819 681), Calle Canton Gualaceo 2-149. Take a taxi or bus (they run frequently) out along Avenida Loja and take the first right after 'Arco de la Luz,' 200 meters along the river. Rooms are in a private house or in two cabins in the garden. Rates are US$8 per person with shared bath (three double rooms share one bath), and breakfast is included. Rooms with private bath are US$12. A delicious homemade dinner with organic products from the owner's farm is about US$4. The owner is a recommended local guide, and the place is family-run and friendly; English is spoken.

Back in town, on the corner of Gran Colombia and Torres, the attractive *Hostal Chordeleg* (☎ 824 611, fax 822 536), has a decent restaurant and rooms with TV and telephone for about US$14/24 in a refurbished older building with a nice patio. The similarly priced *Hotel Las Américas* (☎ 831 160, 835 753, fax 833 850), Mariano Cueva 13-59, is a modern hotel with attentive service and a good, reasonably priced restaurant. The back rooms are quieter but the ones in front have large windows. Also modern and slightly cheaper is the *Hostal Hurtado de Mendoza* (☎ 831 909) at Huayna Capac and Sangurima. Another choice in this price-range is the friendly and clean *Hotel Atahualpa* (☎ 826 906, 831 841), Sucre 3-50 and Tomas Ordóñez. The *Residencial Siberia* (☎ 840 672) used to be a decent budget hotel near the market but has now moved to Cordero 4-22 and become rather more upscale.

The *Hotel Alli Tiana* (☎ 831 844), Córdova and Aguirre, has modern rooms, some with balconies and good views, TV and telephone, and is about US$18/25. Also, at about this price is the nice-looking *Hostal Caribe Inn* (☎ 835 175, ☎ /fax 822 710), Gran Colombia 10-51, with TV and telephone in the rooms and a pleasant restaurant.

The *Posada del Sol* (☎ 838 695, fax 838 995), Bolívar 5-03, is a small hotel in an attractive 18th-century house. Comfortable rooms with telephone and plenty of hot water are US$20/26, including continental breakfast; there's a restaurant. The management is friendly and helpful and the hotel is affiliated with Hostelling International. Also affiliated with HI is the *Hotel Internacional* (☎ 831 348, 823 731), Benigno Malo 10-15, which looks nice with its high ceilings and white with pastel painted walls. Some rooms have TV and/or telephones. Rates are in the low US$30s for a double.

At about US$25/30, the *Hotel Inca Real* (☎ 823 636, 825 571, fax 840 699), Torres 8-40, has been charmingly renovated and has attractive carpeted rooms with TV and telephone. There is a nice restaurant. Also at this price is the more modern *Tomebamba Hotel* (☎ 823 797, 831 589), Bolívar 11-19 and Torres, with pleasant, clean rooms with telephone, TV and minifridge; and the similar and newer *Hotel Italia* (☎ 840 060, 842 884, fax 864 475), Avenida España at Huayna Capac. Both of these have restaurants.

Other hotels with rooms for under US$30 include the *Hotel Paris Internacional*

(☎ 842 118, 824 752, fax 831 525), Sucre 6-78, which one reader describes as dirty and overpriced, though another recommends it. I guess you can't please everyone! It looked OK to me. Also try the friendly *Hotel Catedral* (☎ 823 204, ☎ /fax 834 631), Aguirre 8-17 and Sucre. They have a good restaurant. Another is the new *Prado Inn Hotel* (☎ 807 164, 861 614, fax 804 812), Rocafuerte 3-45, which looks OK.

The *Hotel Presidente* (☎ 831 979/066/341, fax 824 704), Gran Colombia 6-59 and Borrero, is a well-run, modern hotel with good-sized, very clean rooms for about US$28/36, which seems like a fair value. Apart from all the usual amenities, it has a 9th-floor bar with a great view of the city. Next door, the modern *Hotel El Conquistador* (☎ 831 788, 834 537, 842 631, fax 831 291), Gran Colombia 6-65 and Hermano Miguel, has a coffee shop, restaurant and bar, and provides room service. They have a disco at weekends. A double room is in the US$40 range, but gringos are often quoted more.

Another possibility is the *Hotel Apart El Jardín* (☎ 808 811, 804 103, fax 800 064), Avenida Pumapungo and Viracochabamba, in the southeastern suburbs about a kilometer east of the Museo del Banco Central. These are apartments with kitchen/dining room and parking, sleeping two, four or six people at about US$18 per person.

Places to Stay – top end

Cuenca's top-end hotels charge foreigners twice the rate that residents pay. If you don't want to pay that much, stay in one of the better mid-range hotels – there really isn't that much difference in quality.

The most worthwhile of the top-end hotels is the *Hotel Crespo* (☎ 827 857, 829 989, fax 835 387), Larga 7-93 and Cordero. It is in an attractive turn-of-the-century building overlooking the Río Tomebamba. Of the 31 rooms, 12 have lovely river views. Rooms are spacious and have high molded ceilings, wood-paneled walls and classical furnishings, though the bathrooms are on the small side. There is a an elegant restaurant (service can be too leisurely for some people) and room service. River-view rooms are about US$50/60; others are US$8 less. More rooms are being added.

The fanciest hotel downtown is the modern *Hotel El Dorado* (☎ 831 390, fax 831 390), Gran Colombia 7-87 and Cordero. There is a good restaurant and piano bar with views from the 7th floor, coffee shop and lobby bar downstairs, a disco and sauna/exercise room. The 92 rooms are modern and spacious at about US$60/72.

Finally, if you want to stay out of town, try the *Hostería El Molino* (☎ 890 150, fax 830 991), 7½ km out of town on the Panamericana Norte (leave town on Avenida España). There is a good pool, restaurant and bar, and rooms are spacious and attractive. Rates are about US$60 for a double. If you want the most expensive, try the Swiss-run *Hotel Oro Verde* (formerly La Laguna, ☎ 831 200, fax 832 849) on Avenida Ordóñez Lazo, at the northwestern edge of Cuenca, just over three km from the city center. The hotel is popular with North Americans (US Embassy staff stay here on their jaunts down to Cuenca) and is set in pleasant gardens with a small pool, a little lake with boats and a kid's playground. There's an expensive restaurant with room service, and a sauna and exercise room. Rates are around US$110 for a double.

For a few other choices, see Baños, below.

Places to Eat

Many restaurants are closed on Sunday, and some on Saturday, too. Several good new restaurants have opened – a few are aimed at the traveler.

The best hotels in town have good restaurants that are among the first to open, and their breakfasts are usually the cheapest meals available – you can relax with coffee and croissants in pleasant surroundings. Set lunches at the cheaper hotels' restaurants are also a good deal.

The coffee shop at the *Hotel El Conquistador* has some of the best coffee in town, and the one at *El Dorado* serves breakfast

from 6:30 am. Both the *Presidente* and El Dorado have top floor restaurant/bars with good city views – go for a snack if you are economizing, but El Dorado is a good value for a tasty meal.

Those on a tight budget will find that the restaurants at the *España* and *Residencial Tito* are cheap and good. There are several other places as you walk into town. One of the best is at the *Hostal Chordeleg*, with a set lunch for under US$2. There are also worthwhile restaurants in the hotels outside of town.

Restaurant El Refugio, Gran Colombia 11-24, is quite elegant and a good value for lunch. They serve Ecuadorian food. Also inexpensive are the vegetarian restaurants: Hare Krishna-run *Govinda*, Aguirre 8-15; Hindu-run *Restaurant Mañajaris*, Borrero 5-33; and *Restaurant El Paraíso*, Tomas Ordóñez 10-19, where a tasty set lunch is just US$1.20.

Slightly pricier choices – US$3 or US$4 for a meal – are the locally popular *El Balcón Quiteño* (☎ 824 281), Gaspar Sangurima 6-49, where good Ecuadorian food is served in a bright, plastic environment; and *Chifa Pak How*, Córdova 5-46, which seems to be the best of the several chifas in town.

The *Heladería Holandesa*, Benigno Malo 9-45, serves up excellent ice cream, cakes, coffee, yogurt and fruit salads, and is a very popular hangout for international travelers. Prices are not low but the food is delectable. Also popular is the *Café Austria*, Benigno Malo 5-45, with delicious Austrian-style cakes and coffee. The *Café El Carmen*, next to the Casa de Cultura on the southwest corner of Parque Calderón, has snacks and meals. Also on the park is *Raymypampa*, under the colonnade in front of the new cathedral. It looks quite nice but receives mixed reviews – some find it overpriced with slow service, while others find it full of character and a good place to relax.

Lovers of Italian food will find plenty to choose from. Two pizzerias on Gran Colombia, on either side of Cordero, are the *Los Pibes* and *La Tuna*. Both have been recommended for pastas and other dishes, as well as for pizza. The best Italian place is said to be *La Napoletana Pizzería* (☎ 823 172), Solanos 3-04, where pizza to feed five hungry travelers runs about US$25. La Napoletana will also deliver pizza to your room. This place is popular with locals and is often full. *Pizza Hut* (☎ 883 693) also delivers.

El Pedregal Azteca (☎ 823 652), Gran Colombia 10-33, is in an attractive old building. It is Mexican-run and serves good Mexican dinners from Monday to Saturday and lunches from Tuesday to Saturday. There is live music some evenings. Although it is popular with travelers (and I like it), the portions aren't big for US$4 or US$5, so this is not for the starving student on a budget.

Another pleasant building with a nice atmosphere is *D'Bernardo's Restaurant* (☎ 829 967), Borrero 9-68 and Bolívar, which serves good and reasonably priced local dishes and rather more expensive international food. The *Restaurant El Túnel* (☎ 823 109), Torres 8-60 and Bolívar, is a small, intimate place with medium-priced local food. Their lunches are a good value.

La Cantina Bar & Restaurant, Córdova and Borrero, has a pleasant, elegant patio and good meals. One traveler reports it to be 'full of US tour groups.' Opposite, and also popular with tourists, is the *Restaurant El Jardín* (☎ 831 120, 824 882), at Córdova 7-23 and Borrero. This restaurant is reputed to be the best in town, and a meal will cost about US$25 for two – not bad. The subdued lighting is either romantic or too dark to read the menu, depending on your mood. They are closed on Sunday and Monday.

Giving the El Jardín some recent competition for 'best restaurant in town' is the *Restaurant Villa Rosa*, Gran Colombia 12-22. It's in a pretty covered courtyard within a colonial house and serves both local and international dishes.

If you're leaving town – or arriving, for that matter – you can eat at the terminal terrestre. They have a 24-hour snack bar and a decent restaurant that is open during the day. Although Sunday is a poor day for restaurants outside the hotels, the terminal area has several inexpensive ones that are open for travelers. Just beyond the airport (a few minutes' walk from the terminal terrestre), the *Rancho Chileno* serves good steaks and seafood – its good enough that Cuencanos sometimes will drive out there from town for a meal.

On Gran Colombia, about one km west off the map, is an area of mid-priced restaurants and bars that are popular with more affluent young locals and those travelers who find their way there. Recommended places include *Doña Charito*, Gran Colombia 20-33, with good Ecuadorian and international food; *El Tequila*, Gran Colombia 20-59, with good Cuencano dishes and occasional live music; and *The Stone Bar*, Gran Colombia 21-130. A few hundred meters further west, Gran Colombia becomes Ordóñez Lazo, with other bars and the Hotel Oro Verde.

Entertainment

Though Cuenca is Ecuador's third largest city, entertainment is quite limited. *El Mercurio* is the Cuenca newspaper for listings of movies at the cinemas. Note that the Teatro Casa de Cultura is not the same place as the Casa de Cultura, which occasionally also has movies or lectures – both are shown on the map.

Apart from the area of restaurants and bars on Gran Colombia, other popular bars for young people include the trendy *WunderBar*, on Hermano Miguel, and the *Cine Café Marilyn Monroe*, Gran Colombia 10-29, which shows music videos. *La Bulería*, Larga 8-49, is a nice bar with a pool table.

The best peñas, with a variety of Latin American music, are usually at *La Morada del Cantor* (☎ 837 197), on Ordóñez Lazo (west extension of Gran Colombia) near the Hotel Oro Verde.

Bar Años 60, Bolívar 5-69, has a disco. Other places to drink and dance include *Blah! Blah!* on Avenida 10 de Agosto, a few blocks south of the stadium; *Saxon*, Ordóñez Lazo and Unidad Nacional; and *El Unicornio*, on Córdova at Benigno Malo, a block from Parque Calderón. The ones away from the center seem better, though, The best downtown hotels also have nightclubs.

Two rather fancy and pricey bars where well-off locals and affluent tourists like to hang out are *La Cantina Bar & Restaurant* (the bar is also called Las Capulies) at Córdova and Borrero, and *Picadilly Bar*, across the street on Borrero. La Cantina sometimes has live music, usually folklórica. Both places are expensive and a bit pretentious, so go for the surroundings, not the drinks.

Things to Buy

Cuenca, the center of the Panama hat industry, is one of the best places to buy these hats. A good place to start is with the well-known Ortega family, who have worked in this industry for generations. Visitors can take a guided tour at the Homero Ortega factory (☎ 808 349, 828 439), Gil Ramírez Dávalos 3-86 (a block north of Avenida España, near the terminal terrestre), or visit one of two shops at Vega Muñoz 9-33 and Hermano Miguel 6-84. Note that these Panama hats are of the highest export quality and are not cheap, though they are a good value.

Other crafts of the Cuenca area include *ikat* textiles that are made with threads that have been tie-dyed before weaving; this method dates to pre-Columbian times. Traditional colors are indigo (a deep blue-violet), but red and black have appeared recently. Handmade ceramic tiles, plates, cups and bowls are also popular as are baskets. Typical Cuencano baskets are huge and come with lids – few people can manage to take one of these home. Gold and silver filigreed jewelry from the nearby village of Chordeleg is for sale, as are the usual weavings, carvings and leatherwork of Ecuador.

Wandering down Gran Colombia and the blocks just north of the Parque Calderón will bring you to most of the best craft stores. One that has been recommended by a local guide is at Gran Colombia 6-97 and Borrero. This is a small souvenir store with a large variety of crafts and an owner

willing to explain where items are made and the difference in quality etc. One of the most upscale places is Artesa, on the corner of Gran Colombia and Cordero. This displays the work of Eduardo Vega, one of Ecuador's best ceramic artists. Interested travelers can also visit his factory – ask at the store.

Other recommended stores are El Tucán Handicrafts Gallery, Borrero 7-35; Cooperativa Madres Azuayas (local mothers' cooperative), Mariscal Lamar 9-76; Galería Pulla, Jaramillo 6-90, with art by a locally famous painter and other work.

The Thursday **market** at Lamar and Hermano Miguel is mainly for locals (which means pigs and polyester, fruit and furniture – just about anything except for used cars). There are a few stalls with crafts for sale. Visitors should watch for pickpockets and purse/camera snatchers – I wouldn't bring a camera to this market unless I was with some friends.

For some utilitarian shopping, try the Mi Comisariato Supermarket on Cordero at Córdova.

Getting There & Away

Air The Aeropuerto Mariscal Lamar passenger terminal is conveniently only two km from the heart of town, on Avenida España. Flight schedules to and from Cuenca change several times a year, so you should make local inquiries about these. As of this writing, only TAME has flights to and from Guayaquil, mid-mornings from Monday to Friday; fares are about US$23.50. From Monday to Friday they fly three times a day to and from Quito for US$29. There are two morning Quito flights on Saturday and one afternoon flight on Sunday. Both TAME and SAN-Saeta service this route. In 1996 Aerogal was also flying to and from Quito – the only route this small airline flies – on Thursday, Friday and Sunday.

For flights to Loja, Machala and some coastal cities, fly into Guayaquil and change; for most other cities, change in Quito.

TAME has an airport desk (☎ 862 193) for inbound/outbound flights, and another office downtown (☎ 827 609), in the alley off of Gran Colombia between the Hotel Presidente and Hotel El Conquistador. Business hours are 9:30 am to 12:30 pm and 2 to 5 pm on weekdays, but are subject to change. SAN-Saeta has an office at the Cuenca airport (☎ 804 033) and another downtown (☎ 823 403, 842 432) at Benigno Malo 7-35 and Córdova. Aerogal (☎ 843 202) is at Cordero and Vega Muñoz (but will probably move).

Bus The well-organized terminal terrestre is on Avenida España on the way to the airport and about 1½ km from the town center.

There are dozens of different bus companies with offices in the terminal. Some run two or three buses every hour, others run two or three every week. Buses used vary widely in size, speed and comfort. One reader suggests that the fast, small buses stop for longer meal stops than the slower coaches, making arrival times about the same.

Buses leave for Guayaquil (US$4; five hours) many times daily. Buses leave for Machala (US$3.50; four hours) about every hour; a few continue to Huaquillas, or you can go to Machala and change.

Buses for Azogues (US$0.50; 45 minutes) leave at least every hour, many continuing to Cañar (US$1; 1½ hours) and Alausí (US$3; four hours). Buses for El Tambo (seven km beyond El Cañar), leave every 30 minutes and get you within eight km of Ingapirca. Direct buses to Ingapirca (US$1.25) from Cuenca recently began running at 9 am and 1 pm on weekdays – this service is subject to change.

For Quito (US$6 to US$10; eight to 11 hours) there are buses about every hour; driving time depends on route and road conditions. For destinations between Alausí and Quito there are several departures every day; it takes six hours to reach Riobamba.

There are six or seven buses a day to Saraguro continuing to Loja (US$4; six hours). For destinations south of Loja it is best to change in Loja.

If you want to go into the southern Oriente, several buses a day go to Macas (US$6; 12 hours) and several others to Gualaquiza (US$4; eight hours).

Buses to the Gualaceo Sunday market depart from the corner of Avenidas España and Benalcázar, about 100 meters southwest of the terminal terrestre. They leave every few minutes on market day and less frequently on weekdays for the 1½ hour ride. Some buses go from the terminal through Gualaceo to Sígsig.

There is a passenger information desk at the terminal where you can ask about other unusual destinations.

Train The station southeast of town used to have trains to Sibambe, connecting to Guayaquil and Alausí, but these have not run for some years and the line is reportedly closed permanently. Inquire locally about possible reopenings.

Getting Around
To/From the Airport Taxis are about US$2 between downtown and the airport. City buses (US$0.10) pass the terminal frequently, although they tend to be rather full just after a plane arrives. Downtown, buses depart from the stop by the flower market on Aguirre – not all are marked so ask the drivers.

To/From the Terminal Terrestre City buses leave from the front of the terminal for the center (US$0.10), and buses for the terminal leave from the bus stop on Aguirre by the flower market. Most – but not all – buses are marked 'Terminal;' ask the driver to be sure.

Bus Local buses (US$0.10) for Baños leave from Avenida Torres by the San Francisco market. Local buses for Turi travel along Fray Vicente Solano.

Car Cuenca Rentacar (☎ 825 318, 822 140, fax 817 869), Huayna Capac at Córdova; International Rentacar (☎ 801 892, 804 063) at the airport; and Hertz at the Hotel Oro Verde (☎ 831 200) provide rental services for drivers over 25.

CUENCA

Bicycle Bikes can be rented for US$15 a day, helmets included, from Explorbike (☎ 833 362), Jaramillo 5-100 at Hermano Miguel. A guide costs an extra US$10.

The Cuenca Area

BAÑOS

This is a much smaller version of the Baños, described in the South of Quito chapter. Here you'll find sulfurous hot springs with public pools and restaurants – a popular getaway for Cuencanos.

The village is about five km southwest of Cuenca. Local buses go there, or take a taxi for US$2 or US$3. Use of the thermal pools costs about US$0.40 or twice that for a private bath.

Places to Stay & Eat

There are a couple of basic residenciales by the baths, charging about US$4 per person in rooms with hot water. A short distance away is the comfortable *Hostería Durán* (☎ 892 485/6, fax 892 488), which has a private thermal swimming pool, sauna, pleasant gardens, and the best restaurant in the area. A spacious double room is about US$45, and, reportedly, camping is permitted.

Apart from the Durán, there are several simple restaurants in the area serving inexpensive Ecuadorian food.

AREA NACIONAL DE RECREACIÓN CAJAS

This 28,800-hectare recreation area lies about 30 km west of Cuenca and is famous for its many beautiful lakes – well over 200 have been named, and there are countless smaller ponds, pools and puddles. There are trout in the lakes and fishing is permitted. The terrain is bleak and rough and the lakes shine like jewels against the harsh countryside. It is rugged hiking and camping country, much of it páramo at around 4000 meters above sea level. None of the area is above

4500 meters, so it doesn't normally snow, although the winds and rains can make it very cold. Hikers and campers should be well prepared with warm, windproof gear and plenty of energy. Several readers have written to say that they underestimated the cold weather and had a very cold trip – bring protective clothing!

Flora & Fauna

In sheltered hollows and natural depressions of the terrain, small forests of the quinua *(Polylepis)* tree are seen. This tree grows at the highest altitudes of any tree in the world, and the quinua thickets provide welcome protection from the elements for all kinds of unusual plants and animals. Everything is on a small, tightly packed scale, and forcing your way into one of these dense dwarf forests is like entering a scene from a Grimm's fairy tale.

Birdwatchers will have a great time looking for the many different species found on the lakes, in the quinua forests and in the surrounding páramo. These are the habitats of such evocatively named birds as the giant conebill, tit-like dacnis and gray-breasted mountain toucan.

A variety of exotically named hummingbirds can also be seen: the rainbow-bearded thornbill, sapphire-vented puffleg and purple-throated sunangel, just to name a few. Raptors, including on rare occasions the Andean condor, lazily flap overhead. Even the LBBs (little brown birds) that hop

Refuge, Area Nacional de Recreación Cajas

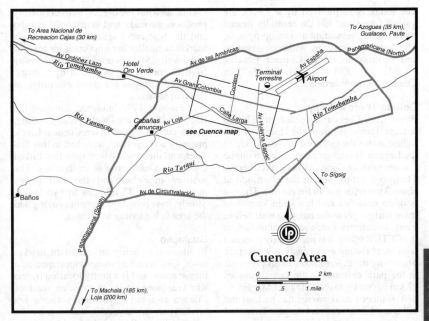

Cuenca Area

0   1   2 km

0   .5   1 mile

CUENCA

unobtrusively through the thickets have interesting names like mouse-colored thistletail. Bring binoculars and a field guide if you have them.

Information

The Laguna Toreadora ranger station is on the northern side of Cajas, a few hundred meters from the park entrance. The entrance fee is US$10 plus US$2 for overnight stays. The INEFAN offices in Cuenca can give you further information, maps and permits – but the maps are very sketchy. You can also obtain maps and information at the ranger station. There are a number of poorly signed trails, but an effort is being made to improve signage. Trails range from short hikes to multiday treks. Hikers may want to buy topographical maps from the IGM in Quito. Four 1:50,000 maps cover the area: Cuenca CT-NV-F4; Chaucha CT-NV-F3; San Felipe de Molleturo CT-NV-F1; and Chiquintad CT-NV-F2.

The driest months are August to January but it can rain anytime – those hundreds of beautiful lakes need to be kept full! During the dry season, daytime temperatures can go into the high teens Centigrade (up to 70s, Fahrenheit); night temperatures can go well below freezing. Wet-season temperatures are less extreme. Annual rainfall is about 1200m. Water temperatures are usually about or below 5°C or 40°F – you can leave your swimming suit at home.

Places to Stay

You can usually sleep for a small fee at the ranger station (but don't rely on it – there are only four beds), and camping is allowed anywhere in the recreation area. The bus passes within a few hundred meters of the ranger station.

Apart from camping in Cajas, you can stay at the new *Huagrahuma Páramo Lodge*, which opened in 1996 on the park boundary at 3700 meters above sea level.

The lodge is surrounded by a 12-hectare quinua forest and has 26 centrally heated rooms, a bar, restaurant and camping area. The lodge is designed with conservation and ecology in mind. Contact Ecotrek (☎ 842 531, 834 677, fax 835 387) in Cuenca for more details.

Getting There & Away

Buses from Cuenca leave at 6 or 6:30 am (except Thursday) from the church of San Sebastián for the cramped two-hour ride to the Laguna Toreadora ranger station on the northern side of Cajas, 34 km from Cuenca. There is a return bus in the afternoon at about 3 pm (check with the driver). The bus is often crowded and has been known to leave early – get to the bus stop well before 6 am. Sometimes a second bus runs – ask at the CETUR office. It is particularly crowded with local fishing enthusiasts at weekends. Make sure the driver knows to drop you off at the park entrance – the bus continues 12 km beyond it to the village of Migüir.

A southern road passes the park at the villages of Soldados and Angas. This road is in very poor shape, but there are buses on Monday, Wednesday, Friday and Saturday leaving from El Vado and Loja in Cuenca at 6 am. It is 34 km to Soldados and 56 km to Angas; the trip takes about four hours. There are no ranger stations or facilities at either of these tiny and remote villages; Cajas lies to the north of you. Buses return to Cuenca in the afternoon.

Apart from the bus, you can take a taxi (about US$25) or go on a day trip with one of the tour agencies in Cuenca. I've received mixed reviews about these – check whether lunch and park entrance fee are included.

GUALACEO, CHORDELEG & SÍGSIG

These villages are all famous for their Sunday markets. If you started from Cuenca early in the morning you could visit all three markets and be back in Cuenca in the afternoon. Buses leave Cuenca from the southwest corner of the terminal terrestre. The best known markets are at Gualaceo and Chordeleg, which are within a few kilometers of one another.

Gualaceo has the biggest market (mainly produce, animals and household goods) and the best hotel selection. Chordeleg's market is smaller but important for textiles and jewelry. Sígsig's market is further away from Cuenca and less visited by tourists. All three villages are good examples of colonial towns.

A massive 1993 landslide dammed the Río Paute and caused widespread flooding, which cut the area off from Cuenca. Lives, property and livestock were lost in this disaster, and the newly paved road that linked Cuenca to Gualaceo was washed out. The journey time between the two towns increased from 45 minutes to two hours. Slowly, travel conditions are improving and the area is beginning to recover.

Gualaceo

In addition to being an important market town, Gualaceo has some importance as a tourist resort and is a pretty location by the Río Gualaceo. It is 25 km due west of Cuenca at about 2370 meters above sea level. There are several restaurants by the river, and a stroll along the banks is a nice way to pass an afternoon. The town is quite progressive, and its spacious, modern church has nice stained-glass windows. There are several restaurants and places to stay, as well as an EMETEL office and a cinema. A casa de cambio has just opened on 3 de Noviembre, a block from the plaza. This is your best bet for changing money.

Market Note that the Sunday market is several blocks from the terminal terrestre in Gualaceo, although there are some souvenir stands near the bus plaza that may fool you into thinking that is the market. There is also an animal market across the covered bridge, on the east bank of the river. The market is not geared to tourists (there are very few crafts for sale), but is colorful and fun to visit. Heavy knitted sweaters are reportedly a good buy.

Despite the paucity of crafts at the Gualaceo market, many of the surrounding villages are known for the manufacture of a variety of handmade goods, ranging from

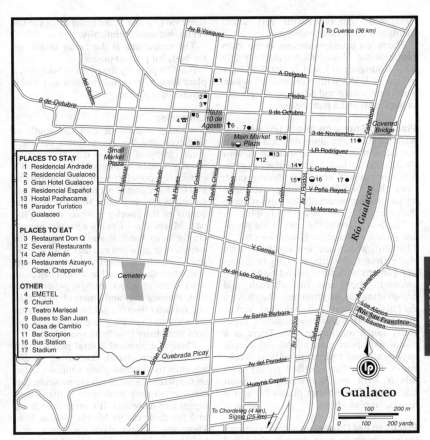

PLACES TO STAY
1 Residencial Andrade
2 Residencial Gualaceo
5 Gran Hotel Gualaceo
8 Residencial Español
13 Hostal Pachacama
18 Parador Turístico
   Gualaceo

PLACES TO EAT
3 Restaurant Don Q
12 Several Restaurants
14 Café Alemán
15 Restaurants Azuayo,
   Cisne, Chapparal

OTHER
4 EMETEL
6 Church
7 Teatro Mariscal
9 Buses to San Juan
10 Casa de Cambio
11 Bar Scorpion
16 Bus Station
17 Stadium

To Cuenca (36 km)

Covered
Bridge

Río Gualaceo

Río San Francisco

Gualaceo

0   100   200 m
0   100   200 yards

To Chordeleg (4 km),
Sigsig (25 km)

CUENCA

---

musical instruments to textiles to hats. It is possible to arrange crafts tours with guides in Cuenca, if this interests you. There is a small display of crafts from the area in the Parador Turístico Gualaceo (see Places to Stay).

Special Events The annual fiesta on June 25 celebrates the cantonization of Gualaceo. The annual peach festival starts on March 4 and goes on for about a week, featuring an agricultural fair (flower and fruit shows, parades). Many fiestas happen east of town, across the Río Santa Barbara via the covered bridge (see map).

Places to Stay – bottom end There are several places to stay in the town center for about US$3 to US$4 per person. The *Gran Hostal Gualaceo* has rooms with a private bath and hot water, but is open only sporadically, during fiestas and perhaps at weekends. The friendly *Residencial Gualaceo* sometimes has hot water and is a basic, reasonably clean, family-run place – you have to walk through their kitchen to reach the rooms. The *Residencial Carlos Andrade* is fairly basic and friendly, and has reasonably large rooms with hot water. There is also the cheaper and more basic

Residencial Español, with very small rooms and questionable showers.

The nicest accommodations in the town center is the *Hostal Pachacama* (☎ 255 229), Rodríguez 317, which costs US$5 per person or US$6 with bath and hot water. They have a café and advertise telephones in the rooms and a parking area.

Places to Stay – middle A few minutes' walk south of town along the road from the bus station is the *Hostería La Ribera* (☎ 255 052), which is by the river and has a restaurant and small swimming pool. They charge US$14/20 with private bath; try bargaining, especially for stays of more than one night. The manager is helpful.

The best place in the area is the pleasant *Parador Turístico Gualaceo* (☎ 255 110/126), about one km south of town along Gran Colombia. It is set in attractive gardens with flowers and birds, has a swimming pool and Turkish bath, and horse riding can be arranged. They have a decent restaurant and bar that serves meals to both guests and visitors, especially lunch on market day. There is a disco that opens on demand (10 people paying a cover charge, usually at weekends). Clean, flower-filled rooms with private bath and hot water are about US$30/40. These better places fill up for fiestas, so plan ahead.

Places to Eat Gualaceo has several cheap, basic restaurants near the bus plaza and around the main market plaza. The *Café Alemán*, near the bus plaza, is good for snacks and desserts rather than meals. Opposite the bus plaza are three inexpensive but decent places.

The stalls in the market on market day serve a variety of local dishes like whole roast pigs (you don't have to eat it all). Around the market, places that have been recommended by readers (and not on the map, but just walk around the market) include the *Europa Bar* for hamburgers and *La Delicia* for good, cheap local food. There are more cheap local places along Cuenca, south of the market. The *Restau-* rant *Don Q* is one of the better places in the center, but opens erratically.

The restaurants at the better hotels are the best, but priciest places.

Bar Scorpion, by the covered bridge, is a place for a beer – single women may find it harrassingly macho.

Chordeleg

Chordeleg is four or five km south of Gualaceo and has many stores selling a great variety of crafts – it is known as a jewelry center throughout Ecuador. It's especially popular with Guayaquileños looking for highland bargains. Some people complain that it is too 'touristy' and the quality of the jewelry is lower than in the past. Maybe it is – I'm not a jewelry expert. On the other hand, if you're shopping for souvenirs or gifts you can choose from gold and silver filigree jewelry (by far the most interesting item) as well as a small selection (look hard) of woodcarvings, pottery, textiles, Panama hats and embroidered clothing. A reader who is a goldsmith writes that the walk to Chordeleg is pleasant, but the gold work there is nothing special.

There is a pleasant central plaza with a small, modern church containing simple but attractive stained-glass windows. Also on the plaza is a small village museum that manages to pack more into it than some bigger city museums. It's open from 8 am to 5 pm daily except Monday and is free. There are displays about the history and techniques of many of the local handicrafts such as filigreed metalwork, Panama hat making and ikat weaving. Some of the locally made work is for sale, and I'm told the money goes directly to the artisans. Guides are available. It helps if you understand Spanish.

Places to Stay & Eat The *Residencial Chordeleg* is reportedly on the plaza opposite the museum, but I haven't checked it out. Beds are US$3.50 per person or US$9 for as double with private shower. There is a restaurant attached and there are a few other simple restaurants, including a café/snack-bar next to the museum and the

Restaurant El Cisne by the market, a couple of blocks from the main plaza.

Sígsig

Sígsig is a pleasant colonial village where little happens apart from Sunday market. It is about 25 km south of Gualaceo and the center of a hat-making region. There are a couple of restaurants on the main market plaza. A few blocks from the plaza is a bus office. Opposite, is a store that will rent you a room, and there is a basic pensión. The ride out here from Cuenca is nice.

Getting There & Away Buses from Cuenca with Cooperativa de Transportes Gualaceo take 1½ to two hours to reach Gualaceo (this may improve when the road is rebuilt). Buses leave every few minutes on market day, and at least every hour on weekdays; the fare is US$1. You can continue the four or five km to Chordeleg on foot or take a local bus. Buses pass the Chordeleg plaza for Sígsig at least once an hour and charge US$0.50 for the 40-minute ride. Sit on the right-hand side of the bus for good views of the river canyon on the way to Sígsig. Buses return from Sígsig to Cuenca about every hour for US$1. There may be occasional buses to Gualaquiza, in the southern Oriente, if the road is passable.

A new road to Gualaquiza is being built via **Chigüinda** – buses go there from Sígsig. In Chigüinda you reportedly can stay with one of the locals and then continue on foot towards Gualaquiza via the remote villages of Aguacate and Río Negro. I haven't gone beyond Sígsig myself, nor know anyone who has. Good luck to adventurous travelers.

PAUTE

Before the 1993 floods the road forked a few kilometers before you reached Gualaceo. The left-hand fork went up the Río Paute valley to the village of Paute, about 30 km from Cuenca. The village was virtually cut off from Cuenca for two years but the road reportedly goes through again. Near Paute is the Distilería Uzhupud, which makes several of the local liquors. There is

an attractive local flower festival to celebrate Paute's cantonization on February 26.

This area is reportedly a knitting center.

Places to Stay

Near the village is the *Hostería Uzhupud* (☎ 250 339, 807 784, ☎ /fax 250 329, 806 521), an excellent tourist resort in pleasant countryside. It was very popular as a getaway for upper-class Cuencanos until the 1993 floods caused it to close. It reopened in late 1995. There is a very good restaurant, a swimming pool, sauna, Turkish bath, tennis courts and an amazing garden that contains hundreds of varieties of flowers, including dozens of species of orchids. Birdlife is also prolific – you can see the 19-cm giant hummingbird, largest of the approximately 320 species of hummingbirds known, all of which are found only in the Americas. Rooms vary in quality and price, but all are comfortable. Rates are in the US$40s for a double.

North of Cuenca

AZOGUES

About 35 km north of Cuenca on the Panamericana lies Azogues, a quiet, small town of some 30,000 inhabitants and the capital of the province of Cañar. Azogues literally means 'quicksilver,' a name derived from the mercury-rich ores supposedly found in the area; I could find no evidence of mercury extraction, although there are reportedly some cement works. The town is important for its Panama hat industry and Saturday market, and is also worth visiting for its church. It is a possible alternative to Cuenca as a base for visiting Biblian, Cañar and Ingapirca to the north.

Information

The EMETEL and post office are on the main plaza. Filanbanco will change traveler's checks and Cambiaria del Cañar will change cash dollars. The provincial hospital

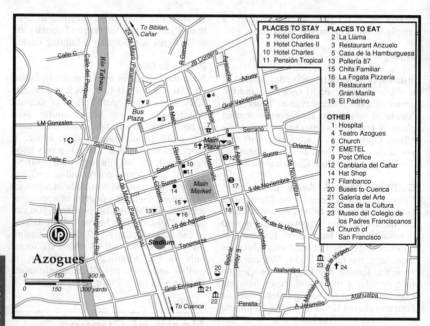

is on the other side of the river, west of town (though Cuenca has better facilities).

Note that there is some reconstruction of the Panamericana on the west side of town, and the road may look a little different from what appears on the map by the time the project is finished.

Things to See

The most interesting place to visit is the **church of San Francisco**, which dominates the town from a hill to the southeast. You can't see it when you arrive at the bus terminal, but if you head generally southeast and then climb up the Avenida de la Virgen, you'll reach it in about half an hour.

From the church there are sweeping views of the town, the surrounding countryside and several other churches perched on the top of nearby hills. Hilltops seem to be the place to build churches in this region. This may be because there used to

be Inca structures on top of the hills and the Spanish built churches over them. Inside San Francisco there is a beautiful gilt altar. The building is sometimes illuminated at night – sitting on the dark hill, it looks almost as if it were floating in midair.

Another church worth visiting is that of **Biblian**. This village is some nine km north of Azogues on the Panamericana; there are plenty of buses from the terminal. The **Santuario de la Virgen del Rocío** (Sanctuary of the Virgin of the Dew) is highly visible to the right (east) of the main highway on a steep hill dominating Biblian. It is one of the most attractive churches I've seen and looks more like a fairy-tale princess's palace than it does a church. Keep your eyes open for it even if you're just driving straight through Biblian. There is an annual pilgrimage here on September 8. There's also a weekly market on Sunday.

Both these churches were renovated for

the Pope's 1985 visit. Strolling the streets of Azogues and admiring the colonial architecture is a pleasant way to pass a few hours. There are also many modern stores and houses, especially on the outskirts.

As you stroll, keep your eyes open for signs of the Panama hat industry. Avenida 3 de Noviembre is a good street to see hats being blocked and sold. One store selling hats is on Sucre near the main marketplace, which is where the bustling **market** is held. It extends down to and across the Panamericana on busy Saturday mornings. There is also a smaller market on the Plaza San Francisco, in front of the church – it's worth going for the view.

There are three small **museums** in Azoguez, but they have erratic opening times. Near the church of San Francisco is the Museo del Colegio de los Padres Franciscanos, where religious art can be seen. Other local artifacts and art are displayed in the Casa de Cultura on Bolívar, which is open weekdays from 8 am to 6 pm and closes for a long lunch break. Around the corner is a local art gallery at Enríquez 243 where artists from the region display and sell their work. The Museo Ignacio Neira in the Colegio Julio María Matovalle is a private collection that you must make an appointment to see.

If you spend the night and want something to do, try the movie theater. There's only one, the Teatro Azogues.

Places to Stay

Despite its provincial-capital status, Azogues does not yet have any particularly good hotels. The reasonably clean *Hotel Charles II* at the corner of Serrano and Emilio Abad, near the main plaza, charges about US$8 per person in rooms with private hot showers, but the staff are reportedly unfriendly. The basic *Hotel Charles* at Rivera and Solano is about US$5 per person and has hot water in the communal showers. Nearby is the more basic and cheaper *Pensión Tropical*. By the bus plaza, the *Hotel Cordillera* offers very cheap beds in noisy and unpleasant surroundings.

The *Hotel Playa* is supposedly by the river, west of town, though I have received conflicting reports about whether it exists or not. It is apparently the best – if it's there!

Places to Eat

Simple, basic restaurants by the bus plaza include *La Llama* and *Restaurant Anzuelo*, but there are better ones in town.

Casa de la Hamburguesa on Veintimilla near Oriente is quite good for hamburgers. The inexpensive *El Padrino* on Bolívar has OK meals for a little over US$1. Opposite, the *Restaurant Gran Manila* is quite good – their lomito saltado has been recommended (this is a dish of chopped, fried beef mixed with vegetables such as onions, tomatoes and French fries, served with rice). The *Pollería 87*, on 3 de Noviembre near the main market, is a clean and family-run chicken restaurant that opened, unsurprisingly, in 1987. They serve other dishes too and have been recommended by one traveler as the best place in town. The *Chifa Familiar* and *La Fogata Pizzería* are nearby and seem OK.

Getting There & Away

Bus The main bus plaza is just off the Panamericana, which is renamed 24 de Mayo as it goes through Azogues. There are many daily departures for Quito, Guayaquil and Machala; for other destinations it is best to go to Cuenca and change buses.

For buses to Cañar it may be best to stand on the highway outside the bus plaza and wait for one to come by – often Cuenca-Cañar buses don't pull into the bus plaza – see what the locals are doing.

For Cuenca there is a local bus terminal on Rivera about three blocks south of the main market. Buses for Cuenca leave as soon as they are full – several times an hour from dawn until about 7 pm. Later on you can catch buses to Cuenca by waiting on the Panamericana outside the main bus plaza. The fare to either Cuenca or Cañar should be about US$0.50.

Train The train station is across the river, almost one km west of town. Trains between Cuenca and Sibambe used to stop

CUENCA

here before the 1993 floods closed the line. I don't know when it might reopen.

CAÑAR

The small town of Cañar, on the Panamericana, is the nearest place to stay for travelers wishing to visit the Inca ruins of Ingapirca. At 66 km north of Cuenca and 3104 meters above sea level, it is a chilly place. There is a very colorful local market on Sunday that is visited by Cañari Indians coming down from the remote villages in the surrounding mountains.

Cañari men wear distinctive belts made by an unusual weaving method that gives rise to designs and motifs appearing on both sides of the belt. These may be available in the market – they are also woven by the local prisoners, and if you head down to the jail, you will be allowed in to make purchases.

Places to Stay & Eat

Cañar has some simple places to stay. The basic *Pensión Ingapirca* (☎ 235 201) on Calle Sucre at 5 de Junio charges US$3 to US$5 per person, depending on the room. The *Residencial Monica* is on the corner of the main plaza and charges about the same. Both places have hot water and are friendly and helpful. If these are all full you can find accommodations in unsigned private houses – ask around. None of the

places to eat are particularly noteworthy, and most close by about 7 pm. One reader recommends *Restaurant Don Pedro* as the best in Cañar.

Getting There & Away

Buses from Cuenca's terminal terrestre leave for Cañar (about US$1; 1½ hours) at least every hour.

INGAPIRCA

The ruins of Ingapirca (see the sidebar, below) are the most important Inca ruins in Ecuador. The ruins are about a km away from the small village of the same name. In the village there are several crafts stores and an occasionally open craft shop/museum by the church on the plaza. A modest hotel and a few simple restaurants cater to tourists. The weekly market is on Friday.

An interesting on-site museum near the entrance to the ruins is informative, particularly if you have a guide. Entrance to the site and museum is US$4; the museum is open from 9 am to 5 pm Monday to Saturday, and the ruins are open daily. Some excavation and reconstruction work is still going on.

Places to Stay & Eat

There is a *shelter* by the entrance with toilet facilities and benches. Officially, you aren't allowed to sleep there, but if you are

---

The Ingapirca Ruins

Ingapirca (3230 meters above sea level) is the major Inca site in Ecuador, but opinions are mixed about the significance of the ruins. They have never been 'lost,' as were the Inca ruins at Machu Picchu in Peru. As a matter of fact, the Frenchman Charles-Marie de La Condamine drew accurate plans of Ingapirca as far back as 1739. The ruins are referred to as a fortress, but its garrison – if there was one – must have been quite small.

Archaeologists think that the main structure, an *usnu* elliptical platform known as the Temple of the Sun, had religious and ceremonial purposes. This building boasts some of the Inca's finest mortarless stonework, including several of the trapezoidal niches and doorways that are hallmarks of Inca construction. The less well preserved buildings were probably storehouses, and the complex may have been used as a *tambo* or a stopping place for runners carrying imperial messages from Quito to Tomebamba.

Unfortunately, the ruins were both well known and lacked protection, and so many of the dressed stones, which comprised the buildings, were stolen over the centuries for use in colonial and modern building projects. Ingapirca's importance is now recognized and the ruins are officially protected. ■

Top: Colonial Cuenca and Río Tomebamba (RR)
Bottom: Cofan Indian house (RR)

Top: Cofan Indian Children (RR)
Left: Oriente Boy (RR)
Right: Group of Cofan Indians passing under a breadfruit tree (RR)

running fox god

stuck in Ingapirca you may be allowed to do so – you would need a sleeping bag. Ask at the entrance to the ruins.

Inti Huasi is a small, clean hotel and restaurant at the entrance to the village. They charge about US$10 for a double room with bath and hot water. Rooms with shared bath are cheaper. The owner is a friendly Cañari woman, and the hotel has a truck that can be used for local transportation if needed.

La Posada is the restaurant of choice for tour groups; it's a little pricey but OK. The building is attractive and they plan to have rooms available for rent by the time you read this. There are a few other cheap local places to eat.

Getting There & Away

A few tourist agencies in Cuenca organize day trips, or you can rent a taxi for the day, which should cost about US$35 – bargain for the best rate. Tours start at about US$35 per person – see Travel Agencies & Guides under Cuenca for details.

To make an economical visit, catch a direct bus from Cuenca (US$1.25) at 9 am or 1 pm Monday to Friday. If you take the morning bus, you can spend a few hours at the ruins and return by the afternoon. This service is quite new and is subject to change. Alternately, take a bus to Cañar (about US$1; 1½ hours from Cuenca). About two km before Cañar there is a signed turnoff to Ingapirca on your right. You can wait here for a passing vehicle to take you the 15 km to the ruins; expect to pay about US$0.50 for the ride if you are

one of a group of passengers (though drivers try to overcharge gringos, especially if they don't speak Spanish and don't seem to know what they are doing!). Vehicles pass by about once an hour. Leave early or you may be stuck without a ride back.

The bus from Cuenca usually continues through Cañar to **El Tambo**. From here there is a shorter (eight km) road to Ingapirca which is the shortest walk from the Panamericana. Pickup trucks travel the road several times a day and act as buses. The fare is anywhere from US$0.40 to US$10! If you wait for a large group and bargain, you'll get the lower fare. If you jump in the first pickup that stops by and don't bother with the routine of bargaining, you'll get stuck with an inflated fare. This route is probably the fastest and most convenient if you don't find the direct bus. I'm told that there is a basic place to stay in El Tambo, but I've never tried it. There are plans to pave this road – I'll believe it when I see it.

Pickup trucks leave Cañar for Ingapirca when they have a load. There are no set departure times or places – ask around.

South of Cuenca

About 20 km south of Cuenca, the road forks. The Panamericana heads to the left and goes south to Loja via the towns of Oña and Saraguro. The right fork heads southwest to Machala.

FROM CUENCA TO MACHALA

This road goes through impressive mountain scenery and is well worth doing in daylight. Some 23 km from the Panamericana, you'll pass the small town of **Girón**. As you look down on it from the road, you'll see a neat-looking town of red-tiled roofs interspersed with brightly colored red, blue and green tin roofs. There is a cheap hostal.

At **Santa Isabel**, 37 km beyond Girón, buses may stop for a meal break. There are several restaurants in this bustling little community and a basic pensión is reported,

CUENCA

though I didn't see it. The town is an agricultural center for tropical fruits grown in the area, which is about 1600 meters above sea level. Banana and papaya plantations are seen interspersed among the cornfields.

Just below Santa Isabel the scenery changes suddenly and dramatically as the road winds through completely barren mountains with no signs of life. Just as suddenly, a forest of columnar cacti appears, which soon gives way to cloud forest mixed with tropical agriculture.

About 35 km beyond Santa Isabel there is a military checkpoint – have your passport ready. Ten km beyond is the town of Pasaje, and 25 km still further is Machala. Both are described in the South Coast chapter.

OÑA

The Panamericana climbs steadily from Cuenca and allows good views of páramo moorlands and the southern Ecuadorian Andes. Oña, 105 km south of Cuenca, is reached after almost three hours and the bus sometimes stops here to refuel. Notice the interesting and ancient generator-driven petrol pump. The attendant has to switch on the generator before he can deliver the fuel, and then switch it off when he's finished – a good measure of how frequently vehicles stop in Oña. It's a small town with a couple of simple restaurants and a basic pensión – there's not much reason to stop here.

SARAGURO

Just beyond Oña, the road crosses the provincial line into Loja and continues rising and falling through the eerie páramo scenery until it reaches Saraguro, almost four hours, 165 km and US$3 south of Cuenca. This small town is named after the Saraguro Indians (see the sidebar). Their interesting market day is Sunday, when local Indians show up in their traditional black clothing.

Places to Stay & Eat

There are a few very basic places to stay, none with private bathrooms. The *Residencial Armigos* and *Pensión Saraguro* are both near the church and are the best places. Both are cheap, and the latter has hot water. Local stores or businesses may rent a room – ask around.

There are two or three basic restaurants, of which the 'best' is the *Salón Cristal*, behind the church, but it reportedly serves only lunch. There are other places on or near the main plaza.

Getting There & Away

Loja, the provincial capital, is 62 km to the south, and buses leave Saraguro every hour or so during the day for the 1½ hour ride, which costs almost US$1. The main bus office is a block from the main plaza. Buses also leave for various small villages in the

---

The Saraguro Indians

These people originally lived in the Lake Titicaca region in Peru, but were forced to colonize this area of Ecuador by the Incas. The Saraguros are readily identifiable by their traditional dress. Both men and women (but especially the women) wear flat white felt hats with wide brims. The men sport a single pigtail and wear a black poncho, but perhaps the most unusual part of their attire is their knee-length black or navy-blue shorts that are sometimes covered with an odd little white apron. They carry double shoulder bags with one pouch in front and one behind for a balanced load. The women wear heavy pleated black skirts and shawls fastened with ornate silver pins. The pins are known as *tupus* and are highly prized, often being passed down from mother to daughter as family heirlooms.

The Saraguros were well known for their jewelry, but this craft seems to be dying out. Today, cattle-raising is their main occupation and the people can be seen on foot driving their herds to tropical pastures in the 28 de Mayo area. Wherever they go, they normally wear their traditional clothing and are the most successful Indian group of the southern Ecuadorian highlands. ■

area. For Cuenca, it is best to wait in the plaza for a northbound bus from Loja to pass by.

LOJA

From Saraguro the road continues to drop steadily to Loja at 2100 meters – a pleasant elevation that leads to a temperate climate. Loja was founded by the Spanish captain Alonso de Mercadillo on December 8, 1548, and so is one of the oldest towns in Ecuador. None of the earliest buildings have survived, although houses from the 18th century can be found.

With about 120,000 inhabitants (some local sources claim 160,000, while the official census of 1990 gives 94,305), Loja is both an important provincial capital and a college town, with two universities, a music conservatory and a law school. A small hydroelectric project became operational in 1897, at the base of Pedestal Hill a short distance west of the town center. It generated 34 kilowatts, and gave Loja the distinction of being the first city in Ecuador to have electric energy.

Although the town itself is not particularly exciting, it is attractive, and travelers on their way to Peru via the border town of Macará find this a convenient place to stop. The highland route to Peru through Loja and Macará is slower and rougher but much more scenic than the more trav-eled route through the coastal towns of Machala and Huaquillas. Loja is also the departure point for visiting Vilcabamba (see below) and Zamora in the Southern Oriente (see the next chapter). The road between Cuenca and Loja is being improved and that between Loja and Machala is also very scenic.

Information

Tourist Offices The CETUR tourist information office (☎ /fax 572 964) is at Bernardo Valdivieso 08-22 just south of 10 de Agosto.

The INEFAN office (☎ 571 534), which is responsible for administering the Parque Nacional Podocarpus, is at Miguel Riofrío 13-54 and Bolívar.

Peruvian Consulate The consulate (☎ 571 668) is at Sucre 10-56 and Azuay. Hours are 8:30 am to 1:30 pm Monday to Friday.

Money Few of the banks change money. Filanbanco and Banco de Azuay, both on the Parque Central, are exceptions. Only Filanbanco takes traveler's checks and their rates aren't very good. Travel agencies and various stores will change cash dollars – shop around for the best rates. Try to change money in Macará or Cuenca. If you are arriving from Peru, get rid of Peruvian

CUENCA

Garden of Ecuador

Loja is very close to the Oriente, and the surrounding countryside is green and pleasant. The people are proud of the great variety of plant species found in the region.

They tell the story of the beautiful Countess of Cinchón, the wife of an early 17th-century Peruvian viceroy, who was dying of malaria. A Franciscan monk cured her with quinine extracted from the bark of a tree found in the Loja area. After her recovery, fame of the 'miraculous' properties of the tree spread throughout the Spanish Empire and the world. Today the scientific name of the tree is *Cinchona succirubra*, after the countess.

German scientist and explorer Alexander von Humboldt visited the area in 1802 and called it 'the garden of Ecuador.' British botanist Richard Spruce also mounted an expedition here in the mid-19th century. In recent times, the area has been recognized for its biological value, and in 1982 the Parque Nacional Podocarpus (see below) was established in the nearby mountains. The proximity of the Oriente influences Loja's climate. June and July are the wettest months, when roads into the Oriente may be closed by landslides caused by the torrential rains, and October through December are considered the most pleasant by local inhabitants. ■

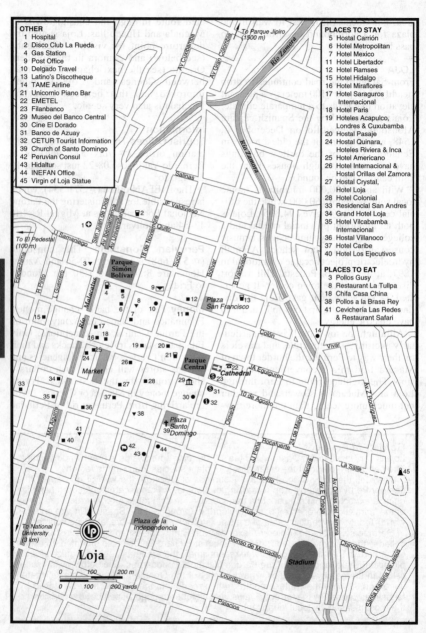

OTHER
1 Hospital
2 Disco Club La Rueda
4 Gas Station
9 Post Office
10 Delgado Travel
13 Latino's Discotheque
14 TAME Airline
21 Unicornio Piano Bar
22 EMETEL
23 Filanbanco
29 Museo del Banco Central
30 Cine El Dorado
31 Banco de Azuay
32 CETUR Tourist Information
39 Church of Santo Domingo
42 Peruvian Consul
43 Hidaltur
44 INEFAN Office
45 Virgin of Loja Statue

PLACES TO STAY
5 Hostal Carrión
6 Hotel Metropolitan
7 Hotel Mexico
11 Hotel Libertador
12 Hotel Ramses
15 Hotel Hidalgo
16 Hotel Miraflores
17 Hotel Saraguros Internacional
18 Hotel Paris
19 Hoteles Acapulco, Londres & Cuxubamba
20 Hostal Pasaje
24 Hostal Quinara, Hoteles Riviera & Inca
25 Hotel Americano
26 Hotel Internacional & Hostal Orillas del Zamora
27 Hostal Crystal, Hotel Loja
28 Hotel Colonial
33 Residencial San Andres
34 Grand Hotel Loja
35 Hotel Vilcabamba Internacional
36 Hostal Villanoco
37 Hotel Caribe
40 Hotel Los Ejecutivos

PLACES TO EAT
3 Pollos Gusy
8 Restaurant La Tullpa
18 Chifa Casa China
38 Pollos a la Brasa Rey
41 Cevichería Las Redes & Restaurant Safari

currency at the border, as it's very hard to change in Loja.

Post & Communications The post office is at the corner of Colón and Sucre. The EMETEL office is a block east of the Parque Central on Eguiguren. The area code for both the city and province of Loja is 07.

Travel Agencies Franklin Hidalgo's Hidaltur (☎ 571 031, fax 573 378), Bolívar 10-33, is recommended for international travel services and local travel information. The agency sells discounted tickets for flights within Peru if you are heading that way. This deal is available only outside of Peru.

Delgado Travel (☎ 573 446), at Sucre and Colón, is another useful travel agent.

Newspapers Two local newspapers, *El Mundo* and *El Siglo*, feature local news only, including movie listings. Guayaquil and Quito newspapers are available by about 9 am.

Emergency The hospital (☎ 570 540) is at Iberoamérica and Quito. The Red Cross ambulance (☎ 570 200) is by the hospital.

Things to See & Do

For most of the year Loja is a quiet but pleasing provincial town with little to do except walk around and enjoy the atmosphere and traditional architecture.

For a short but pleasant walk, head east from the center on Rocafuerte and cross the Río Zamora, where washerwomen can sometimes be seen at work. From there, climb the small hill to see the statue of the **Virgin of Loja**, which is protected by a caged (stone) lion. There is a rather damaged lookout with good city views. Another good lookout point is the hill and church of **El Pedestal**, west of the center off of 10 de Agosto – this area is known as **El Balcón de Loja**.

In the center, both the **cathedral** and the **church of Santo Domingo** have interesting painted interiors and elaborate statues. The cathedral is on the Parque Central and Santo Domingo is on a pretty, traditional

little plaza at Bolívar and Rocafuerte. Also found on the Parque Central are government buildings and the **Museo del Banco Central**, which has a small archaeological collection and is open from 9 am to 4 pm Monday to Friday. Admission is free. The Plaza San Francisco, at Bolívar and Colón, has a **statue** of the city's founder on his horse that is attractively framed by the trees.

The weekly **market** is on Sunday, but Saturday and Monday also seem to be busy and there is some activity every day. The **Plaza de la Independencia** (also known as Plaza San Sebastián) is one of several places where market activities go on. It is a historic spot – this is where the Independence of Loja was declared on November 18, 1820. There are several colonial buildings around the plaza, and an incongruous 32-meter-high modern clock tower.

A couple of kilometers north of the center (head north on Gran Colombia), the **Parque de El Valle** and **Parque Jipiro** are the sites of the annual produce fair. There is also some Sunday market activity here. At other times, the suburban community of El Valle is worth a visit to see the old church and to try some of the typical food sold in comedores around the plaza. The nearby Parque de Jipiro has a small lake with a miniature island adorned by a white statue of a larger than life Venus. This island is sometimes the scene of symphony performances. The musicians cluster around the statue and the audience must content itself with listening from the shores of the lake – the orchestra takes up the entire island.

At the south end of town is the national university (☎ 571 841, 570 252), set in a large park containing a **botanical garden** that can be visited.

Northeast of town is the UTPL (☎ 570 275) that sometimes has demonstrations of how ceramics are made and has items for sale. Ask locally for directions.

Special Events

From late August to the beginning of November, the cathedral is home to La Virgen del Cisne (the Virgin of the Swan), carved in the late 1500s by Diego de

CUENCA

Robles. Throughout the rest of the year the statue is kept some 70 km away in the village of El Cisne (see the sidebar later in this chapter). El Día de La Virgen del Cisne is celebrated in Loja on September 8 with huge processions; an annual international produce fair is held for about four or five days on either side of the 8th (it's called 'international' because Peruvians attend it).

An important fiesta celebrating the independence of Loja takes place on November 18. Festivities may go on for a week, featuring parades and cultural events. The feast of San Sebastián, which coincides with the foundation of Loja, is celebrated on December 8.

Places to Stay
Loja appears to have an excess of accommodations. I counted over two dozen hotels, and many of them were nearly empty when I was there in July – admittedly not the best month for tourism. They probably fill up for the annual fiestas. A few of the hotels were temporarily closed. The lack of guests means that the owners may be willing to bargain during off-peak seasons, especially for two or more people sharing a room. The hotels are close together, so wander around until you find one that appeals to you.

Places to Stay – bottom end
Loja's cheapest hotels are generally more acceptable than the cheapest hotels in many towns. The basic but clean and friendly *Hostal Carrión* (☎ 561 127), Colón 16-30, is a good value at US$2.50 per person, including hot showers. The clean and decent *Hotel Caribe* (☎ 572 902), Rocafuerte 15-52, is another reasonable shoestring choice with hot water at US$2.25 per person.

Other OK places with hot water at about US$2.50 per person include the friendly *Hostal Pasaje*, Eguiguren and Bolívar; the clean *Hotel Mexico* (☎ 570 581), 18 de Noviembre and Eguiguren; the clean *Hotel Londres* (☎ 561 936), Sucre 07-41, with plenty of hot water but flimsy locks (bring your own padlock); the friendly *Hotel Loja* (☎ 570 241), Rocafuerte 15-27, (another

one where a padlock is useful); and the *Hotel Americano*, 10 de Agosto 16-62. The *Residencial San Andres* lacks hot water but may be the cheapest.

At US$3 per person, the *Hotel Hidalgo* has hot water, while the *Hotel Colonial* does not. At US$3.50 per person, the *Hotel Cuxubamba* (☎ 578 570), next to the Hotel Londres, has hot water and some rooms with private bath, as does the *Hostal Orillas del Zamora*, 10 de Agosto and Sucre. Both are adequate.

The friendly *Hotel Paris* (☎ 561 639), 10 de Agosto 16-37, charges about US$3 per person, or US$4.50 with private hot bath and TV. The *Hostal Crystal* (☎ 570 226), Rocafuerte 15-39, looks nice after a recent paint job and charges US$4.50 per person in large rooms with shared hot showers. The *Hotel Internacional* (☎ 570 433), 10 de Agosto 15-28, is friendly and has a restaurant. Rooms with shared bath are about US$3 per person or US$4.50 with private bath and TV. Readers report plenty of hot water. The friendly *Hotel Miraflores* (☎ 570 059), 10 de Agosto 16-65 and Universitaria, charges US$2.50 per person for rooms with shared cold showers, or US$5.75 per person in large, clean rooms with private hot shower.

The *Hotel Acapulco* (☎ 570 651), Sucre 07-49, is clean and safe, with small but satisfactory rooms with TV and private, hot-water bath for US$6/9.50; there is a restaurant. The *Hotel Metropolitan* (☎ 570 007), 18 de Noviembre 6-41, and the *Hotel Los Ejecutivos* (☎ 960 004), Universitaria 10-96, are both similar to the Acapulco and seem OK. The *Hostal Villanoco* (☎ 560 895, 575 845), M Riofrio 16-61, is part of the Hostelling International chain; they charge US$7 per person in clean rooms with shared hot showers. This is a new hostal – feedback is welcomed.

The next step up is to get a color TV instead of B&W, and maybe a telephone in your room. The *Hotel Inca*, Universitaria and 10 de Agosto, is OK and charges US$7 per person in rooms with private bath, hot water, color TV, and telephone, but the rooms themselves, though clean, are still bottom end. The *Hotel Saraguros International* (☎ 960 521), Universitaria 7-24, is similar. Slightly nicer rooms with hot water, color TV and telephone are found at the *Hotel Riviera* (☎ 572 863), Universitaria and 10 de Agosto, which charges US$9/15, and the *Hostal Quinara* (☎ 570 785) on the same block which charges US$9 per person in clean carpeted rooms.

Places to Stay – middle

The oldest of the better hotels is the *Hotel Vilcabamba International* (☎ 573 393, 573 645, fax 561 483), on MA Aguirre and M Riofrio, overlooking the Río Zamora (the river is not very scenic here). Rooms with TV and telephone are clean and comfortable but rather worn. Rates are a reasonable US$15/21.

The other better hotels are newer and plusher, and all have restaurants. The helpful and friendly *Grand Hotel Loja* (☎ 575 200/201, 562 447, 571 803, fax 575 202), MA Aguirre and Rocafuerte, has nice rooms for US$19/26 – a very good deal. One drawback is the noisy street outside. The similarly priced *Hotel Ramses* (☎ 571 402, 579 868, fax 574 186), Colón 14-31 and Bolívar, is a little quieter but otherwise fairly standard. Across the street, the *Hotel Libertador* (☎ 560 779, 578 278, 570 344, fax 572 119), Colón 14-30 and Bolívar, is the most upscale hotel at this time. Rooms with the usual amenities are about US$26/34.

Another mid-range hotel to try is *Hostal Aguilera International* (☎ 563 189), south of town at Sucre 00-44. I haven't been there, but it has been recommended as being clean and quiet.

Places to Eat

The locally popular *Restaurant La Tullpa*, 18 de Noviembre 5-12, is good for inexpensive Chinese and Ecuadorian food. *Chifa Casa China* is also good. *Pollos Gusy* is a chicken restaurant popular with local youngsters. *Pollos a la Brasa Rey* is also OK for chicken. For ice cream, snacks and coffee, try the *Heladería Sinai*, Colón 14-3, in the Hotel Ramses. I like the *Cevichería*

Las Redes, 18 de Noviembre 10-41, with seafood and other dishes in pleasant surroundings for under US$3 – good food at a good price. Nearby, the *Restaurant Safari* is popular with locals.

The best hotels are also good for meals. *La Castellana* in the Libertador is one of Loja's fanciest restaurants, and the restaurant in the Gran Hotel Loja offers a very good, reasonably priced almuerzo that brings in the locals.

Entertainment

Though Lojanos are known as good singers and guitar players, nightlife is fairly low key. For a drink and possibly music at weekends, try the *Unicornio Piano Bar* on the west side of the Parque Central. For dancing, try *Latino's Discotheque*, Imbabura 12-76 and Bernardo Valdivieso, the *Disco Club La Rueda*, Quito 16-33 and Universitaria, or *Sandy's Club* by the bus terminal.

The *Cine El Dorado* may have movies in English with Spanish subtitles. A military band often plays in the *Parque Central* on Sunday evenings – the young population of the town comes to watch the band and each other. *Plaza de la Independencia* sometimes has 'Cultural Thursdays' – free outdoor performances of dance or music.

Getting There & Away

Air Loja is served by La Toma airport in Catamayo (described later in this chapter), some 30 km to the west. TAME has a 6 am flight from Quito (US$32) from Monday to Saturday. On Tuesday, Thursday and Saturday the plane stops at Guayaquil before continuing to Catamayo. The fare from Guayaquil is about US$20. The return is direct to Quito at 7:20 am on Monday, Wednesday and Friday, and via Guayaquil at 8 am on Tuesday, Thursday and Saturday. Though six flights a week have been going for some years, this may change – check with TAME (☎ 573 030) at their office on the east side of town (see map). Note that flights in late August and early September are often booked well ahead of time for the fiestas.

CUENCA

Taxi drivers hang out in front of the TAME office and will arrange to pick you up from your hotel to take you to the airport. They charge about US$3 per person in a shared cab (four passengers). Alternately, you can arrange transportation with the better hotels or take a bus into Catamayo the night before the flight.

Bus The new terminal terrestre opened in the early 1990s, and almost all buses now leave from here. An information booth near the entrance will direct you to where you want to go. Transportes Loja has the most buses, but there are many other companies.

There are several buses per day to Quito (US$9 to US$11; 12 to 14 hours) and points in between like Riobamba and Ambato. There are also several buses a day to Macará, on the Peruvian border, (US$4.50; six hours); Guayaquil (US$6; nine hours); Machala (US$4.50; seven hours); Zamora, for access to the southern Oriente (US$2; three hours); Cuenca (US$4; six hours); and other towns en route to these final destinations. Huaquillas, on the main route to Peru, can also be reached by a night bus in about seven or eight hours, thus avoiding having to backtrack to Machala. Buses also go to small, remote towns in the southern Sierra and southern Oriente where tourists don't go. Ask at the terminal.

Buses for Vilcabamba (US$1) leave once or twice an hour. Two of these continue south as far as Valladolid or Zumba. Buses for Catamayo near the airport (US$0.80) also leave frequently but, as of this writing, not early enough to be sure of catching the flight out. I expect that this will improve, but don't rely on it.

PARQUE NACIONAL PODOCARPUS
Created in 1982, this is the only national park in the southern Andes. Its 146,280 hectares comprise of a wide range of habitats, with altitudes ranging from over 3600 meters in the páramo and lake covered mountains southeast of Loja to about 1000 meters in the rainforests south of Zamora in the southern Oriente. In-between the coun-

tryside is wild and rugged, and home to many rare animal and plant species.

Flora & Fauna
The biological diversity of the area has been remarked upon by a succession of travelers and explorers through the centuries. Currently, a Danish scientific team from the University of Aarhus is working with Ecuadorian biologists to classify the native species. Their findings indicate a high degree of endemism (species found nowhere else), apparently because the complex topography combines with the junction of Andean and Amazonian weather patterns to cause the unique microclimates throughout the park. These areas give rise to many unique habitats within the park.

Some of the most important plants here include three species of the park's namesake genus, *Podocarpus*, Ecuador's only native gymnosperm (a division of plants that includes all conifers and a few smaller classes of trees). Also of interest is *Cinchona succirubra*, locally called *cascarilla*, from which quinine, the drug that cures malaria, is extracted (also see the sidebar Garden of Eden in Loja). Demand for this product has left few cascarillas outside of the park.

Animals include the Andean spectacled bear, mountain tapirs, puma, two species of deer and the Andean fox (locally called a wolf). All of these animals are hard to see but are prized by local poachers who will sometimes burn habitat in an attempt to flush out animals for their 'sport.' Birds, too, are of great interest and are more abundant and easier to see. Scores of species are known to be present, including the usual string of exotic-sounding ones such as lachrymose mountain-tanager, streaked tuftedcheek, superciliaried hemispingus and pearled treerunner. (I promise I am not making these names up!)

Ecology & Conservation
Despite being a national park, Podocarpus faces huge problems in protecting the varied habitats within its boundaries.

Not least of these is that the legal boundaries are not respected by local colonists – by 1990 approximately 800 people were logging and ranching in about 5000 hectares of the northwestern parts of the park. Cattle and horses are permitted within the park. Hunting is not permitted, but poaching is an ever-present problem.

The Nature Conservancy's Latin American Program reports that over 99% of the park has been granted in mining concessions, with gold being the mineral of interest. Mining companies and their armed guards work within the park; meanwhile, the park's staff of eight workers tries to protect the park, carry out local environmental education programs, maintain trails and shelters, collect park fees and provide visitor information.

In 1990 Parque Nacional Podocarpus was named one of Ecuador's four most biologically significant and yet imperiled conservation areas. The Nature Conservancy sponsors the Parks in Peril program, providing financial support and ongoing management and training programs for Ecuadorians wishing to work in the parks – an essential project that is well worth supporting. The Peace Corps is also involved in park projects.

Information

For the eastern part of the park, see under Zamora in the Southern Oriente chapter.

For the western and central parts of the park, information, maps and permits should be obtained from the INEFAN office in Loja. Admission to the park is US$10, and a basic map and verbal information is available both in Loja and at the park. Note that the entrance fee is valid for a week and you can use the ticket to visit the Oriente side (where, because of bureaucratic inconsistencies, the entrance is US$20).

Podocarpus receives a lot of rainfall, so be prepared for it. October through December are the driest months on the west side of the park.

If you are in Quito, you can get topographical maps at the IGM. The western

side of the park is covered by two 1:50,000 maps: Río Sabanilla CT-ÑVII-B2 and Vilcabamba CT-NVII-B4. Alternately the 1:100,000 Gonzanamá CT-ÑVII-B map covers the area in lesser detail. The eastern (Oriente) side of the park is covered by the 1:50,000 maps of Zamora CT-ÑVII-A1 and Cordillera de Tzunantza CT-ÑVII-A3.

Getting There & Around

To get there, take a Vilcabamba-bound bus from Loja and get off at the Cajanuma park entrance, about 10 km south of the city. There is a large sign on the left hand side of the road. From the entrance – which may not be staffed – a driveable track leads 8½ km uphill to the Cajanuma ranger station. There is no public transport here, though you could hire a taxi from Loja to the station (about US$10) and arrange to be picked up at a later time. Make sure the driver is clear about whether you want to go to the Cajanuma park entrance or the ranger station.

The ranger station has bunk beds and a camping area. From the station foot trails head up into the lake and páramo region – a full day of hiking is required to reach the lakes, where you can camp. Birdlife is varied and interesting, both on the dirt road up to the ranger station and around the station, where there are shorter trails. How far you go depends on your equipment and how much food and energy you have. There are few facilities, so you should be entirely self sufficient.

VILCABAMBA

The minor road from Loja passing Podocarpus continues due south and drops steadily through green mountainous scenery to Vilcabamba, some 45 km from Loja. En route you pass through the village of **Malacatos**, distinguished by a large church with three blue domes that are visible from a great distance. Malacatos has a Sunday market and there is a basic restaurant behind the main plaza.

Vilcabamba has for many years been famous as 'the valley of longevity.' Inhabitants supposedly live to be 100 or more, and some have claimed to be 120 years old. This has been attributed to their simple, hard-working lifestyle, nonfatty foods and the excellent local climate. Scientific investigation has been unable to substantiate these beliefs, but the legend persists and gives rise to local tourism. The climate certainly is very pleasant and the surrounding countryside offers lovely walks. Both locals and gringos sometimes complain that there are more foreigners than Ecuadorians, and that the foreigners who do come here may be more interested in sampling local mind-altering plants than in really seeing the area. Please be sensitive and responsible in your travels.

About 1½ km out of town along the main southbound road is the **Area Nacional de Recreación Yamburaro**, which has a small zoo of local animals and a greenhouse with an excellent collection of orchids – some 30 species by one account.

Information

Most of the town surrounds the main square, where there is a local tourist information office, a church, an EMETEL office, a few simple stores and some basic accommodations. Money exchange is poor, so think ahead. Telephone service is unreliable. Many people stay in one of the popular hotels outside of town.

Activities

Orlando Falco, a trained, English-speaking naturalist guide, can be contacted in his craft shop, Primavera, on the plaza. He is well-recommended and leads tours to Parque Nacional Podocarpus and other areas for about US$15 per person, plus US$10 park fee. (Costs depend on the number of people in the group).

The folks at the Cabañas Río Yambala (see Places to Stay) have a private reserve, camping gear, horse rental and plenty of hiking and riding opportunities with or without guides.

Gavilan (contact him at the tourist information office) rents horses for three day treks at US$75 per person. Several other

people rent horses, and hotels will arrange this as well.

Another locally advertised activity is massage – nice after riding or hiking. Spanish lessons are also available; the Hostería Vilcabamba is one place that offers them.

Places to Stay & Eat

The basic, cold-water *Hotel Valle Sagrado* (☎ 673 179), on the plaza, costs US$2.25 per person and often fills with budget travelers; it has a popular vegetarian restaurant. Behind the bus station, the similarly priced *Hostal Mandango* is also becoming increasingly popular with budget travelers. Some rooms have a private bath for US$3.25 per person. Warm showers are available, and there's a cheap restaurant. The clean *Posada Real*, behind the hospital, charges US$5/7 with bath.

For a family stay, call Señora Lydia Toledo (☎ 673 130), a block from the plaza. She charges US$3 per person with shared hot bath and kitchen privileges. Orlando Falco, at the Primavera store, rents a house in a quiet location a few km from town. He calls it 'the pole house' because it is raised up on poles; it has a kitchen, a porch with hammock, and four beds. Daily rates are about US$20.

Almost a kilometer from the square is the *Parador Turístico Vilcabamba* (☎ 673 122, fax 673 167), with a restaurant, where clean rooms with private bath are US$12/19 (ask for low-season discount). Further out on this road is the more expensive *Hostería Vilcabamba* (☎ 673 131, 673 133, fax 673 167), with a good restaurant, pool, massage, hot tub and Spanish lessons available to the general public. Rates are about US$25/35. Nonguests pay about US$1 to use the pool and spa facilities. Both places are recommended and Ecuadorian-run. Nearby is the *Cabañas El Paraíso*, with friendly owners, a restaurant/bar and rooms with warm showers for about US$6 per person. Sometimes they have live music.

The *Hostal Madre Tierra* (☎ 673 123), two km north of town (reservations: PO

Box 354, Loja), is a rustic, laid-back hostal run by an Ecuadorian/Canadian couple. Bus drivers can drop you off at the entrance; the hotel is five or 10 minutes' walk down the lane. (The sign at the entrance is small, so ask.) Rooms are in damp cabins spread over a steep hillside, sometimes reached by long, slippery paths – bring a flashlight. Lodging is US$10 to US$15 (depending on the room) per person, including breakfast and dinner – less without dinner. Showers are shared and there is hot water. Local hiking and riding information, a book exchange, steam bath, video room and table games are available. It's popular and often full, especially with large groups of young backpackers from Israel, who reportedly get a discount. I have received widely varying reports about this place – many people enjoy it; others find it's not their kind of scene and move on to the next place.

About four km southeast of town, the rustic *Cabañas Río Yambala* is run by friendly Charlie and Sarah. You can walk there or hire a taxi or pickup for US$4. Miguel Carpio, half a block from the plaza, is their recommended driver. They have rooms and cabins, some with private baths, from US$3 to US$8 per person. A vegetarian restaurant and kitchen privileges are available, and the owners arrange camping, hiking and horseback riding. They may be full in the high season but accept reservations left at Comercial Karmita (☎ 637 186), a store on the plaza.

Getting There & Away
Transportes Sur-Oriente has buses from Loja's terminal terrestre once or twice an hour. There is a bus office on the main plaza in Vilcabamba and buses return to Loja every hour or so. The trip takes about two hours. Two buses a day continue south to Zumba.

If you are in a hurry to get here, take a taxi from the airport at Catamayo to Vilcabamba for approximately US$20, or from Loja to Vilcabamba for about US$15. Bargain hard for these rates, which are what the locals are charged.

ZUMBA
The all-weather road continues south of Vilcabamba through the village of Valladolid to the small town of Zumba, about 115 km south of Vilcabamba. The drive is through attractive countryside. Zumba is about 10 km north of the (disputed) border with Peru – there are no border-crossing facilities and visitors must return the way they came. There is a basic pensión in Zumba, and two buses a day from Loja.

Since the 1995 border war, you can expect extra attention at military checkpoints, so make sure your passport is handy and don't photograph any areas near military compounds.

CATAMAYO
The Panamericana continues west of Loja through Catamayo, Catacocha and on to the Peruvian border at Macará.

Loja was founded twice. The first time was in 1546, on what is now Catamayo; the second time on its present site two years later. Despite its long history, Catamayo is a totally unremarkable town except for its airport, La Toma, which serves Loja 30 km away.

Places to Stay & Eat
The basic *Hotel San Marcos*, on the plaza, is quite popular; reasonably clean, large rooms go for about US$3 per person. The nearby *Hotel Turista* is similarly priced and has some cheaper rooms without a shower. Other basic places are the *Residencial María Dolores* which is cheaper still, the *Hotel Granada* and the *Hostal El Vergel*, which is a bit more expensive but has better rooms, some with private hot shower.

Two or three km outside Catamayo to the west is the *Hostería Bellavista* (☎ in Loja 677 255, in Catamayo 575 487). They have a pool, restaurant and bar, and can arrange airport transfers or local tours. Rooms are about US$10/15 with private bath. On Sunday they have a popular buffet lunch with traditional dishes such as *caldo de patas* (cow's hoof soup), *seco de chivo* (goat stew) and *cecina* (smoked ham). A taxi from town costs about US$1.

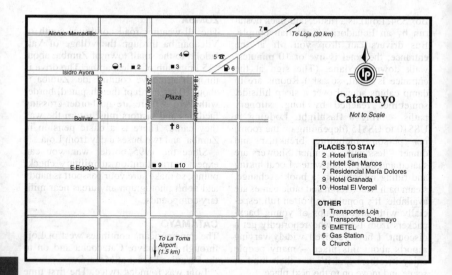

There are several simple restaurants on or near the plaza. I had a merienda washed down with a beer at a table outside a place on the north side of the plaza – watching the activities in the plaza was the extent of the evening's entertainment. The Chinese restaurant opposite the Hotel Turista has been recommended.

Getting There & Away

Air The local La Toma airport is about 1½ km south of town – a taxi will cost almost US$1. Services are described in Getting There & Away under Loja.

Bus Transportes Catamayo, just northeast of the plaza, has frequent buses to and from Loja. Transportes Loja, half a block west of the plaza, has about eight buses a day to Machala (six hours), two night buses to Huaquillas, eight buses a day to Guayaquil (nine hours), four a day to Macará, and six a day to Quito. Local buses from here can take you to the small villages to the north and south of Catamayo. The long-distance buses rarely originate in Catamayo but are just passing through; they usually have limited seating availability. Better services

are available from Loja. Transportes Santa, on the plaza, has a few buses to Quito.

About 25 km west of Catamayo the road forks. The northwest fork goes to Machala and the southwest fork goes through Catacocha to the border town of Macará.

EL CISNE

About 15 km west of Catamayo, the Panamericana passes through the village of San Pedro de la Bendita. From here, a road runs north for a further 22 km to the village of El Cisne, home to the famous Virgin del Cisne.

La Virgen del Cisne

This statue, famous throughout Ecuador, is housed in an enormous church in Gothic style surrounded by unpretentious houses of traditional campesinos. The church is locally referred to as El Santuario.

According to local lore, it was the ancestors of these campesinos who made the long and difficult journey to Quito in the late 1500s in search of a fitting religious statue. They returned in 1594 with the carving of La Virgen del Cisne and installed it in a small shrine. Since that time, this icon has been the 'Queen' of the campesinos.

The major religious festivals in El Cisne are on May 30 and August 15. After the August festival, thousands of pilgrims from Ecuador and northern Peru carry the statue on their shoulders to Loja (70 km away). This is an impressive sight, with many of the pilgrims walking the entire way. The Virgin finally arrives in Loja on August 20, where she is ceremoniously installed in the cathedral. On November 1, the process is repeated in reverse, and the Virgin rests in El Cisne until the following August.

For most of the year, tours and buses make day trips to the village from Loja and Catamayo to see the sanctuary and statue. But on procession days, forget it! You walk like everybody else – the road is so full of pilgrims that vehicles can't get through. This is a very moving religious festival for those who are so inclined.

GONZANAMÁ

About 40 km south of Catamayo, this small town is noted for its weavers and the production of *alforjas* (saddlebags). You can stay in the cold-water *Residencial Jiménez*.

From Gonzanamá the road continues to the villages of Cariamanga and Sozoranga, with basic pensiones, before ending in Macará at the border. This road goes through a remote area seldom visited by gringos.

CATACOCHA

It's a scenic but bumpy seven-hour ride from Loja to Macará. Catacocha is the halfway point on the more frequently used route, and is the only place after Catamayo where you can break the journey. Catacocha is the capital of the canton of Paltas and is only about 1800 meters above sea level. From here, the Panamericana drops towards Macará and the Peruvian coast. It's a rural village, and on market day (Sunday) it seems as if there are almost as many horses as vehicles in town. There is reportedly a small local museum.

Places to Stay & Eat

There are a few basic hotels, all a couple of blocks from the main plaza but in different directions. They charge between US$2 and US$4 per person – one traveler reports that the *Guayaquil* is friendly. There are a few basic restaurants.

MACARÁ

From Catacocha the road continues to drop steadily to Macará at a hot and dusty 450 meters above sea level. Macará is a small, unimportant town on the Peruvian border. The faster and more convenient coastal route carries almost 100% of the international traffic. The main advantage to the Macará route is the scenic descent from Loja. There are two police checkpoints on this road, which are no problem if your passport is in order.

Information

Although there is a bank in Macará, it does not have foreign exchange facilities. Because of the low volume of border traffic, there are few people who will change money. If you ask around, however, you will invariably find someone. There are usually moneychangers hanging out around the market.

Rates for exchanging Peruvian currency into sucres and vice versa are inferior to using US cash dollars, so try to arrive at the border with as little local cash as possible. Exchange rates for cash dollars with Macará street changers are about as good as in Loja. If possible, ascertain exchange rates before arrival at the border by talking with travelers going the other way.

There is an EMETEL office and a ratty movie theater. The Peruvian Consulate (☎ 694 030), Bolívar 127 y 10 de Agosto, is supposedly open from 8:30 am to 1:30 pm Monday to Friday.

Places to Stay & Eat

There are some cheap and basic hotels in the town center. They only have cold water, but the weather is warm enough that it isn't a great hardship. Afternoon water shortages are common, so plan on a morning wash.

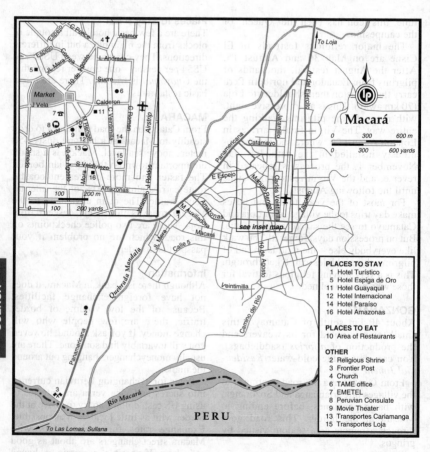

PLACES TO STAY
1 Hotel Turístico
5 Hotel Espiga de Oro
11 Hotel Guayaquil
12 Hotel Internacional
14 Hotel Paraíso
16 Hotel Amazonas

PLACES TO EAT
10 Area of Restaurants

OTHER
2 Religious Shrine
3 Frontier Post
4 Church
6 TAME office
7 EMETEL
8 Peruvian Consulate
9 Movie Theater
13 Transportes Cariamanga
15 Transportes Loja

The cheapest hotel is the poor and dirty *Hotel Guayaquil* (☎ 694 023), which is over a store – ask the store owners for rooms. The *Hotel Amazonas*, Rengel 418, charges about US$2 to US$3 per person and is basic but clean and friendly. The *Hotel Internacional* is OK and similarly priced.

The *Hotel Paraíso*, Veintimilla 553, and *Hotel Espiga de Oro* are both better. They charge about US$3 to US$6 per person for clean rooms with private bath – still cold water, though. The Paraíso also has cheaper rooms without private bath. The Espiga de

Oro has a restaurant with pricey food and very slow service.

There are a few basic restaurants around the intersection of Bolívar and M Rengel, most of which are open only at meal times and have limited menus. One reader recommends the *Restaurant Emperador*.

The best hotel and restaurant is the *Hotel Turístico* (☎ 694 099), on the outskirts of Macará on the way to the border. It has simple, clean rooms with private baths and hot water for about US$16 for doubles. There is a restaurant, which is by far the best (and most expensive) place to eat in Macará, though it is not always open. There is also a swimming pool – again, not always functioning.

Getting There & Away

Air A local airstrip (see map) once had flights to Guayaquil with TAME, using small aircraft such as Twin Otters or Avros. These flights have been suspended for some years now, but something may be available (this is not likely, however). The TAME office, Veintimilla 683, is a few minutes' walk from the town center, near the airstrip. Their hours are erratic.

Bus Transportes Loja is the main bus company. Buses to Loja leave six times a day (US$4.50; six hours), with the last leaving at 3 pm. There are morning buses to Guayaquil and Quito (20 hours). Transportes Cariamanga also has two morning buses to Loja.

These times are rough estimates. The journeys are tiring and uncomfortable, and you are recommended to go to Loja and break up the journey.

To/From Peru

Macará is about three km from the border at the Río Macará. Pickup trucks leave the market once or twice an hour and charge about US$0.40 (Peruvian or Ecuadorian currency). You can take a taxi for US$1. Overcharging is common – bargain hard. Vehicles wait at the border to pick up passengers from Peru.

At the border there are a couple of fly-blown restaurants where you can get a cold drink. Border crossings are from 8 am to 6 pm daily with irregular lunch hours. The formalities are fairly hassle-free, though they can take an hour or more. Make sure your documents are in order.

Travelers entering Ecuador are rarely asked to show exit tickets or money, though a valid passport and tourist card are needed. If arriving, you will be given a tourist card at the border; if leaving, you will be expected to surrender the card you received on arrival to the border authorities.

Travelers entering Peru are occasionally asked for a ticket out of the country, especially those who require a visa. If you don't require a visa you probably won't be asked. If you are, and you don't have an airline ticket out of Lima, you can usually satisfy this requirement by buying a return bus ticket to the nearest large town, Sullana, about 150 km away. The unused portion of the ticket is nonrefundable. Most nationalities need only a valid passport and tourist card, which is obtainable from the border authorities. Gringos who require visas are Australians, New Zealanders, South Africans and Spaniards.

Facilities for accommodations, transport and food are inferior on the Peruvian side; it is best to stay in Macará, if possible. Trucks leave the border for the first Peruvian town of Las Lomas when there are enough passengers (usually about 10 am). The road is bad. From Las Lomas to the main town of Sullana the road is paved. A bus leaves the border for Sullana at 2 pm daily. It is difficult to get transport into Peru later in the afternoon and evening; therefore, crossing the border in the morning is advisable.

Lonely Planet publishes *Peru – travel survival kit* for travelers continuing to that country.

The Southern Oriente

Oriente literally means 'the orient,' or 'east,' and is the term used by Ecuadorians for all of their Amazon basin lowlands east of the Andes. The words *selva* (forest) and *jungla* (jungle) are not used for the area as a whole, although selva can refer to a particular part of the forest of the Oriente. Even though the Amazon River itself does not flow through Ecuador, every one of Ecuador's rivers east of the Andean divide eventually empties into the Amazon, and hence all of the Oriente can properly be considered a part of the upper Amazon basin. The correct term for most of the basin's vegetation is 'rainforest;' popular usage, however, refers to this lush tropical growth as 'jungle.'

A glance at any Ecuadorian map will show Ecuador's claim to a large section of jungle extending beyond Iquitos. The basis of this claim has a long history. After independence in 1822, the new republic claimed lands as far as the Río Marañon to the south, and as far eastward as what is now Brazil. This remote and difficult-to-control area was slowly settled by increasing numbers of Peruvians (as well as a few Colombians and Brazilians). Ecuador gradually lost lands to these countries. In 1941 matters came to a head, and war with Peru broke out. Each country accused the other of beginning the aggression. The following year a treaty signed at Rio de Janeiro ended the war, and Peru was allotted a huge section of what had been Ecuador.

The Ecuadorians have never officially accepted the full terms of this treaty, claiming that it was bulldozed through when most of the world was occupied with WWII; that Peru invaded them; that the limits of the treaty were geographically invalid because a small section in the Cordillera del Cóndor in the southeast was ambiguously defined; and that the land was theirs anyway. However, the border as drawn up by the 1942 treaty is internationally accepted. If you should ever fly from Miami to Iquitos on a regularly scheduled jet service, rest assured that you will land in Peru!

This dispute affects the traveler in several ways. The southeastern border region is still very sensitive, and there are skirmishes every few years. The last major battles were in early 1981, when several soldiers were killed and aircraft shot down, and in early 1995, when several dozen soldiers were killed on both sides. These brief wars tend to be in January and February, coinciding with the anniversary of the signing of the contested treaty. Some political observers suggest that the wars serve politicians by increasing their popularity with citizens of both Ecuador and Peru during either periods of internal crisis or election years.

After the 1995 war, travel through the southern Oriente was temporarily subject to delays and military checks and searches. While journeying through the Oriente, even on the well-traveled tourist routes, you should always have documentation on hand, as passport checks at military checkpoints are not uncommon, even when there is no actual conflict with Peru happening. These checks are usually quick and hassle-free, assuming your papers are in order and you show the proper deference to those running the checkpoints.

The dispute also means that crossing the border into the Peruvian jungle is no longer possible for foreign travelers (though various Indian groups do so all the time). So if you were hoping to descend from Ecuador to the Amazon in riverboats or canoes, forget it. Finally, try not to wave non-Ecuadorian maps of the region under people's noses. One friend had maps of Peru confiscated by customs officers at Quito airport, because the Peruvian maps naturally didn't show the Ecuadorian claim. All the areas described within this chapter are safe to travel in at this time.

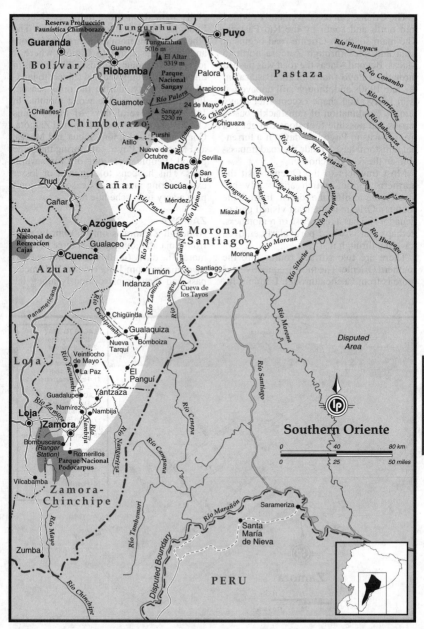

Southern Oriente

0   40   80 km
0   25   50 miles

The Oriente can be conveniently divided into north and south by the Río Pastaza. The main southern Oriente road begins at Loja and goes through Zamora north to Macas. Beyond Macas the road was pushed through to Puyo (north of the Pastaza) in the late 1980s and, though still unpaved, it is in fairly good shape except after heavy rain. A combination of ramshackle buses, ferries and possible foot slogs can get you from Macas to Puyo in a day – if a torrential rainstorm hasn't made the road impassable on the day you choose.

Most travelers to the Oriente visit the northern region, which admittedly has much more to offer the tourist. Indeed, the southern Oriente is the least visited part of Ecuador and has a real sense of remoteness. Perhaps that is why I particularly enjoyed traveling through it.

There are two surface routes into the southern Oriente. The most frequently used route is from Cuenca through Limón (officially named on most maps as General Leonidas Plaza Gutiérrez) to Macas. The other route runs from Loja through Zamora and continues north to Limón, where it joins the first route. Almost all the roads in this region are unpaved and subject to landslides and delays during the rainy season; June to August are the worst months. In July 1991, several days of heavy rains closed the roads between Loja and Zamora, Gualaquiza and Limón, Sucúa and Macas, and Macas and Puyo – all during the same period. People were cut off for several days. This happens to a greater or lesser extent during most rainy seasons, so don't plan a very tight schedule here.

ZAMORA

Although Zamora is only 60 km by road from Loja, the journey takes three hours or more. The dusty (muddy in the wet season) road climbs from Loja over a 2500-meter pass and then drops tortuously along the

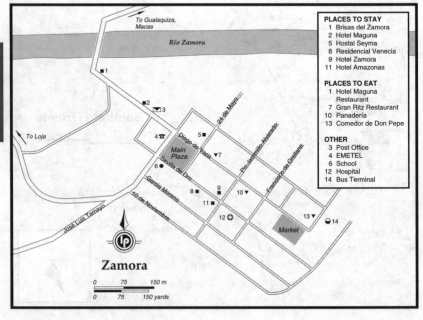

PLACES TO STAY
1 Brisas del Zamora
2 Hotel Maguna
5 Hostal Seyma
8 Residencial Venecia
9 Hotel Zamora
11 Hotel Amazonas

PLACES TO EAT
1 Hotel Maguna Restaurant
7 Gran Ritz Restaurant
10 Panadería
13 Comedor de Don Pepe

OTHER
3 Post Office
4 EMETEL
6 School
12 Hospital
14 Bus Terminal

To Gualaquiza, Macas

Río Zamora

To Loja

Main Plaza

Market

Zamora

0   75   150 m
0   75   150 yards

Río Zamora valley to the town at 970 meters above sea level. The scenery soon becomes tropical and the vegetation thicker, and you begin seeing strange plants such as the giant tree fern. There are good views from both sides of the bus. A paving project, underway as I write this, will cut the journey time substantially when finished. In the meantime, construction crews can shut the road for hours at a time.

Zamora was first founded by the Spanish in 1549, but the colony soon died out because of Indian attacks. It was refounded in 1800 but remained very small. A local old-timer recalls that when he arrived in Zamora in the 1930s, there were only half a dozen buildings. In 1953 it became the provincial capital when the province of Zamora-Chinchipe was created, although it was still extremely small and isolated. The first vehicle did not arrive in town until 1962.

Saraguro Indians, wearing their trademark black shorts, are sometimes seen in the Zamora area. They arrive there on foot, driving their cattle on the trail from Saraguro, through Veintiocho de Mayo, to the Zamora-Yantzaza road. North of Zamora, Shuar Indians may also be seen, as well as colonists and miners.

Over the past few years, Zamora has been experiencing a boom since the rediscovery of gold in Nambija, a few kilometers to the north. The sudden influx of miners has strained the resources of the area somewhat, and food costs are relatively high. The present population of the Zamora area is estimated to be about 15,000, and although the town is growing it still retains somewhat of a frontier feel.

Military Checkpoint

Past conflicts with Peru took place close to Zamora. This, combined with the present gold boom, means that there is a high-profile military presence in Zamora. You may or may not need to show your documents at the military checkpoints on both sides of town, but be prepared to do so if asked.

Information

There is a bank, but it can't be relied on to change foreign currency, so come with sucres. The EMETEL is on the plaza, and the post office is a block to the west. The area code in Zamora-Chinchipe is 07.

The covered indoor market is near the bus terminal.

The weather is not too hot, with daytime temperatures averaging about 20°C and pleasant evenings (with few insects).

Things to Do

There is not much to do. The main plaza is a concrete affair with few trees and little shade, but is improving slowly as the trees grow. There are few foreign travelers. Most come here to see the nearby Parque Nacional Podocarpus (see below) or to continue north to see some of the southern Oriente. From the bridge shown on the map, you can walk east along the river on a dirt road to another bridge. This has little traffic and would make a good choice for early-morning or late-afternoon birdwatching.

Places to Stay

The three cheapest hotels are all clustered together on Sevilla de Oro, a block southeast of the plaza. The best and cleanest of these is the *Hotel Zamora* (☎ 605 253), which charges about US$2 per person. They have some balcony rooms, which you should ask to see. *Hotel Amazonas* (☎ 605 179) and *Residencial Venecia* are not as good. Neither has private bathrooms or hot water, but you have to get used to that in the Oriente. Anyway, cold showers are refreshing in the hot weather.

The *Hostal Seyma* (☎ 605 583), on 24 de Mayo a block northeast of the plaza, has rooms that are a little nicer than those in the three cheapest hotels. The hotel is clean and friendly, though quite noisy – rooms facing the road are quieter than those facing the inner courtyard. They charge about US$3.50 per person, and this is the best low-budget value in town. The newer *Brisas del Zamora* near the river is family-run and friendly. Basic but clean rooms

SOUTH ORIENTE

with private bath are about US$6 per person, and less with shared bath.

The 'best' place in town is the *Hotel Maguna* (☎ 605 113) on Diego de Vaca, northwest of the plaza near the post office. They have basic rooms with private baths, (musty) carpeting, TV and telephone for about US$10 per person. Some of the rooms have excellent balcony views of the Río Zamora; otherwise, none are especially appealing.

Places to Eat

Most restaurants are closed by 8 pm, so eat early. *Comedor de Don Pepe*, opposite the bus terminal, serves good breakfasts and is convenient if you are waiting for a bus. They continue to serve cheap meals throughout the day. There are a few other restaurants near the terminal. Several places are on the main street of Diego de Vaca. The best is the *Hotel Maguna Restaurant*. Other possibilities are the reasonable *Gran Ritz Restaurant* and the unnamed *panadería* (bakery) nearby.

Menus are sometimes limited, and the meal of the day is often the best choice.

Getting There & Away

The bus terminal is at the southeast end of downtown.

Transportes Loja runs buses almost hourly to Loja (US$2; three hours). One bus a day continues through Loja to Cuenca (US$6; 11 hours).

Buses north to Gualaquiza and beyond usually originate in Loja and stop at the bus terminal in Zamora. Enough passengers normally get off at Zamora so that it's not very difficult to get a seat to continue north. Some of these buses go only as far as Yantzaza (1½ hours); only two or three a day continue as far as Gualaquiza (five hours).

Zamora-Chinchipe buses are often open-sided trucks with tiny, uncomfortable bench seats. They provide frequent services to nearby villages as far north as Yantzaza. To visit the wild gold-mining town of Nambija, go to Namirez (roughly halfway between Zamora and Yantzaza) and change there.

For Podocarpus, there are daily buses to Romerillos (two hours) leaving at dawn and early afternoon.

Buses also go up the Río Yacuambi valley as far as the mission town of Guadalupe and, if the rains haven't made the road impassable, on to La Paz. Trucks sometimes continue to the remote village of Veintiocho de Mayo.

PARQUE NACIONAL PODOCARPUS

This national park, more fully described in the previous chapter, has an information center in Zamora and ranger stations nearby. There are less frequently used entrances to the national park.

The INEFAN information office is on the right-hand side of the main road as you enter Zamora from Loja. There is a sign. At the information office you can obtain basic maps and verbal information, and pay the US$20 national park entrance fee. In common with other Ecuadorian national parks, the fee for highland parks is US$10 and for lowland parks is US$20. Entrance tickets can be used for up to a week, so travelers on a budget can use their (US$10) highland park ticket, bought in Loja, for entrance here, thus saving money. Budget travelers can also economize by paying in sucres, as this is currently a 20% saving over US dollars (but may change in the future).

The **Bombuscara** ranger station is at the park entrance about eight km south of Zamora by rough road. The easiest way to get there is by taxi – it shouldn't cost more than US$3, but the road is poor, and you may have to walk the last two or three km. The park rangers are friendly and helpful and can suggest places to camp. There is a good spot about one km into the park. From the ranger station there is a maintained trail suitable for a long day hike through the cloud forest. The birding is reported to be excellent.

Another way into the park is to take a bus from Zamora to the tiny village of **Romerillos**, about 25 km south of Zamora (not the same road as the one going to Bombuscara). There is reportedly a park refuge here, but no ranger station. A rugged three-day loop trek leaves Romerillos, but is recommended for only the hardy, experienced and properly equipped hiker. Be prepared for lots of mud. A mining company was given a concession to survey this part of the national park, but their exploratory work was apparently unsuccessful (from the miners' point of view) and they have reportedly departed, leaving the area relatively unscathed. However, the rumor mill grinds on, and local miners still think that gold can be found in them thar Podocarpus hills, so getting information at the INEFAN office in Zamora is a good idea, for your own safety.

NAMBIJA

This mining village is on the banks of the Río Nambija where gold was discovered around 1980. This led to a gold rush in the area, and Nambija became a wild mining town with heavy drinking, prostitution, gunfights, smelly open sewers, muddy streets and constant, frenzied mining action. A landslide in the late 1980s killed many people, and the town has calmed down somewhat in recent years. Soldiers at the entrance of town now reportedly frisk people to make sure they aren't carrying weapons. A very small number of interested travelers trickle through this gold boom town; a couple of friends told me that it was an interesting place if you want to see what a gold-rush town is like, but they advised visitors to bring no valuables and to have a friendly and open disposition. The miners are a hard-bitten bunch, but a pack of cigarettes will help in making friends.

Although Nambija itself is a new town, the area has been a source of gold for centuries. The Incas used to mine nearby, though few of the modern-day prospectors realize the historical significance of the area.

There is a noisy and basic hotel, or you could come on a day trip from Zamora if you left first thing in the morning. All the locals wear rubber boots – this is the best footwear for the very muddy streets.

YANTZAZA

The northbound road to Yantzaza follows the left bank of the Río Zamora, so the best views are on the right of the bus. There are beautiful vistas of open stretches of the river with heavily forested hills on either side, often with tropical trees flowering in bright reds, yellows and purples. The bus goes through many little Indian hamlets and *fincas* (farms) growing a variety of tropical produce such as coffee, sugarcane and citrus fruit. The road also goes near the Nambija mining area, so the journey is enlivened by the various interesting characters getting on and off the bus. There may be a passport checkpoint between Zamora and Yantzaza; as always in this region, keep your documents handy.

Yantzaza is the first village of any size on the road north of Zamora, 1½ hours away. In 1970 it consisted of only a couple of shacks, but since the Nambija gold boom it has become one of the fastest-growing towns in the province. Its population is now several thousand, and there are restaurants and a couple of basic places to stay near the main square. These are likely to be full of miners, so it's probably best to continue to Gualaquiza.

GUALAQUIZA

North of Yantzaza the population thins and houses are seen infrequently. The road continues to follow the left bank of the gently dropping Río Zamora, and there are fine tropical views. Sit on the right-hand side of the bus. The road continues through the tiny village of **Los Encuentros** and on to **El Pangui**, where there is a basic hotel on the one main street. Just north of this village the road drops suddenly, and a lovely jungle panorama stretches out below. Soon, the road crosses the provincial line into Morona-Santiago Province.

Several kilometers before reaching Gualaquiza, a turnoff to the right leads to **Bomboiza**, where a Salesian mission can be visited. A couple of kilometers beyond the turnoff, the road to Gualaquiza crosses the Río Cuchipamba. A new steel bridge is now open, but recently all traffic had to cross the river by a decrepit wooden raft capable of transporting only a single vehicle at a time. Most passengers got off the bus and crossed on a footbridge.

Gualaquiza is a pretty, little village of about 4000 inhabitants. It is set at an altitude of about 950 meters and surrounded by forested hills. Pleasant walks lead into the surrounding countryside. A rough road heads west out of town for about 15 km to the village of Nueva Tarqui, where caves can be explored. There are reportedly some poorly explored Inca ruins in the Gualaquiza area – ask the locals for guidance.

The church on the main plaza looks like a toy building. There are cobbled streets and houses with attractive balconies, giving the town a Spanish colonial air. Gualaquiza closes down early and is definitely *tranquilo*. The EMETEL office was recently open from 8 to 11 am, 2 to 5 pm, and 7 to 9 pm Monday to Friday only. This will probably improve. There is reportedly one cinema.

Places to Stay & Eat

Accommodations are limited as this is a little-visited town. On the main plaza is the simple *Residencial Amazonas* (☎ 780 183), and *Pensión Oriental* is on the main street, Calle Gonzalo Pezantes Lefebre. Recently opened on the main street is the clean *Hotel Turismo* (☎ 780 113), which charges about US$4 per person and is perhaps the best in town, though still with cold showers. The *Hotel Gualaquiza* (☎ 780 138) is another possibility.

The *Bar Restaurant Gualaquiza* is as good as any of the few restaurants. The Hotel Turismo has an acceptable café. There is a small market just off the main street.

Getting There & Away

There are several bus companies on the main street. Transportes Sucúa, El Cóndor and Oriental each have two or three departures a day for various destinations. Ask around. You can go south (Zamora and Loja), north (Limón, Sucúa and Macas) or west (Cuenca). The next town to the north

is Limón (four hours). Buses to Cuenca go via Indanza (about 10 km before Limón) and take about eight hours, but a new, more direct road via Sígsig should be open soon. To Macas it's about 10 hours and costs US$4.50.

LIMÓN

Limón (General Leonidas Plaza Gutiérrez; population 3000) is a totally unprepossessing town whose primary importance is that it lies near the junction of the roads to Cuenca, Macas and Zamora. It is a typical small Ecuadorian jungle town consisting of one main street (Calle Quito) with a few hotels, several simple restaurants and bus offices. From Gualaquiza the road passes through pretty but sparsely populated countryside until it reaches the missions of San Juan Bosco and Plan de Milagro (also known as Indanza), about an hour before Limón.

Places to Stay & Eat

Both the *Residencial Domínguez* and *Santo Domingo* are basic but clean and each charges about US$2 per person. The *Residencial Limón* (☎ 770-114) has large, clean rooms for about US$8 a double, but only one bathroom for all the guests. Avoid getting rooms on the street as bus drivers park their buses with engines running while they have a midnight snack or early-morning breakfast.

The *Rincón de Taiwan* is as good as any of the several simple restaurants.

Getting There & Away

Several times a day various bus companies, which have their offices along the main street, have bus service from Limón to the north, south and west. Few buses originate in Limón, however, so departure times are at best approximate. The road up to Cuenca climbs steeply from Limón at 1400 meters to a pass over 4000 meters in elevation – the ride is spectacular and should be done in daylight.

If you are going to Macas, sit on the right-hand side of the bus, as there are good views of the Río Upano.

MÉNDEZ

You pass through this quiet little village of 2000 inhabitants on the way to Sucúa. Its official name is Santiago de Méndez and is less than two hours from Limón; the fare is about US$1. The houses have red-tiled roofs and flowery gardens. Half a block from the corner of its shady plaza are three very simple pensiones, the *Anita, Miranda* and *Amazonas*, all charging about US$2 per person. Nearby, the *Hotel Los Ceibos* looks a little better. There are only a couple of restaurants here.

About 1½ hours away on foot, in the hills surrounding the town, is the Centro Kuchiankas – Escuela Kayap. This is a Shuar school and development center and visitors are welcomed, although a donation to the school is requested. Ask in Méndez for directions if you are interested.

MORONA

This remote settlement is on the Río Morona near where it crosses the border with Peru. This border is not recognized by Ecuador, and therefore border crossing is not permitted.

Until the late 1980s, the only way to reach Morona was by plane, but a newly constructed road now links the village with Méndez. The trip takes about 10 hours – ask around in Méndez for trucks going to Morona or take a bus from Macas. There are no places to stay and not much in the way of places to eat, so bring a tent and food. This is a remote and poorly explored area – you are really off the beaten track.

CUEVA DE LOS TAYOS

About halfway on the road between Méndez and Morona lies the settlement of Santiago on the Río Santiago. Here one can hire dugout canoes to go upriver to the Río Coangos for about US$30. From the Coangos there is a trail to the 'Cueva de los Tayos' (the Cave of the Oilbirds – see the

Oilbirds

There is only one species of oilbird, and it is so unusual that it is placed in its own family, the *Steatornithidae,* related to the nightjars. Oilbirds are nocturnal, spending most of the day roosting in caves in colonies that may number thousands of birds. The Cueva de los Tayos is one such cave. At dusk, huge numbers of oilbirds leave the cave in search of fruit, particularly that of palm trees. This makes oilbirds the world's only nocturnal fruit-eating birds.

Palm fruits are known for having a high fat content, which gives the oilbirds a very fatty or oily flesh. In 1799, when oilbirds were first described in Venezuela by Alexander von Humboldt, the local people already knew about these birds. They were captured in their roosting colonies and boiled down into a valuable oil used in cooking and for lighting. This practice is now discouraged although it still occurs occasionally.

Oilbirds feed on the wing, and their feet are poorly developed. They require caves with ledges upon which to build their cone-shaped nests, which are constructed of regurgitated fruit and are enlarged regularly. Two to four eggs are laid, and incubation is a relatively long 32 to 35 days. After hatching, the young are fed regurgitated fruit for up to four months, and during this time a nestling can reach a weight of 1½ times that of an adult. It was these fat chicks that were most highly prized as a source of oil. Once the chicks leave the nest, they lose their accumulated baby fat. Adults weigh about 400 gm and reach a length of about 45 cm.

Oilbirds are adapted to their dark environment by having well-developed eyes and exceptional night vision. They also have a sensitive sense of smell, which may help them detect the palm fruits' distinctive fragrance. The caves they roost in are often pitch-black. To avoid crashing into the cave walls (and into other birds), oilbirds emit audible, frequently repeated clicks that they use for echolocation, much as bats do. In addition they have a loud screaming call which they use for communication. The combination of screams and clicks made by thousands of birds within the confines of a cave can be deafening. ■

sidebar). The trail is in poor condition, and you should hire a guide – it is about a two- or three-hour hike. You will need to be self-sufficient with sleeping gear and food for this expedition.

SUCÚA

Sucúa, population 6000, is one of the more interesting villages in the southern Oriente. It is the major center of the Shuar Indians, who were formerly called the Jivaro and were infamous for shrinking the heads of their defeated enemies. This practice still occurred as recently as two generations ago, and the *tsantsas* (shrunken heads) can be seen in various museums, notably the Municipal Museum in Guayaquil. Most of today's Shuar look very Ecuadorian in jeans and T-shirts, but you still see older Indians, especially women, with elaborate facial or body tattoos.

Information

There is a pleasant main plaza with shady trees, tropical flowers, cicadas and birds. From the plaza, walk down the main street (Avenida Francisco de Orellana) and you'll come to the Shuar Cultural Center on your left, about a kilometer away. Here you can buy booklets and obtain further information about the Shuar. The Shuar have become missionized, as have most of the surviving Oriente Indian groups, so you won't be shown tsantsas; other crafts are, however, on display and there is a small selection for sale. Ask about hiring a guide from the Federación Shuar if you want to visit a traditional Shuar village. This can take a few days to arrange and visitors without guides are not usually welcome.

There is a tiny zoological garden with a few local animals. There is also a mission hospital and a movie theater. Market day is Sunday.

Places to Stay & Eat

The *Hotel Oriente* (☎ 740 107), down the main street close to the Shuar Cultural Center, costs about US$3 per person and has a restaurant. Another place to try is the *Hostal Alborada*, which also has a restau-

rant. The clean *Hotel Karina* on the corner of the plaza is about US$3 per person and is OK. Perhaps the cheapest places in town are the *Residencial Cuenca* and *Residencial Sangay*, both basic and not very clean.

The *Hotel Rincón Oriental* on the main street and the *Hostería Orellana* (☎ 740 193) at the south end of town are a little nicer and charge about US$4 or US$5 per person.

There are several restaurants on the corner of the plaza; *Restaurant La Fuente* is one of the better ones. Typical dishes here feature rice and beans as the mainstay.

Getting There & Away

Air The airstrip at Sucúa has light aircraft available for charter into local villages, but has been superseded by the larger airport in nearby Macas. Villages in the interior are for Indians and missionaries; tourists are not encouraged, and there are no facilities for them unless you travel with local Shuar guides.

Bus Pickup trucks and minibuses for Macas (US$0.50; one hour) leave at frequent intervals from 6 am to 7 pm every day. Departures are from the corner of the main plaza near the Hotel Karina.

Southbound buses pass by the restaurants on the main street at the corner of the plaza. Services are better from Macas.

MACAS

This small (population 14,000 and growing) but important town is the capital of the province of Morona-Santiago. I find it the most dignified, quiet and attractive town in the Oriente. It has four centuries of history as a Spanish trading and missionary outpost, and an old mule trail still joins Macas with the highlands near Riobamba. A road is planned, which will follow this trail, and large segments of it have now been completed. A road north to Puyo has recently been completed but requires crossing two river bridges on foot. Buses meet travelers at either end.

Despite its history, Macas is essentially a modern and developing town. The bus ter-

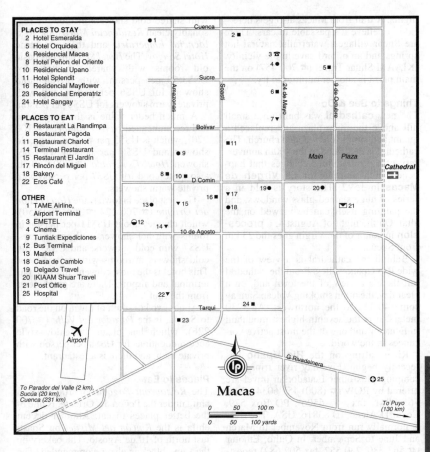

PLACES TO STAY
2 Hotel Esmeralda
5 Hotel Orquidea
6 Residencial Macas
8 Hotel Peñon del Oriente
10 Residencial Upano
11 Hotel Splendit
16 Residencial Mayflower
23 Residencial Emperatriz
24 Hotel Sangay

PLACES TO EAT
7 Restaurant La Randimpa
8 Restaurant Pagoda
11 Restaurant Charlot
14 Terminal Restaurant
15 Restaurant El Jardín
17 Rincón del Miguel
18 Bakery
22 Eros Café

OTHER
1 TAME Airline,
   Airport Terminal
3 EMETEL
4 Cinema
9 Tuntiak Expediciones
12 Bus Terminal
13 Market
18 Casa de Cambio
19 Delgado Travel
20 IKIAAM Shuar Travel
21 Post Office
25 Hospital

Cuenca
Sucre
Bolivar
D Comin
10 de Agosto
Tarqui
G Rivadeinera

Amazonas
Soasti
24 de Mayo
9 de Octubre

Main Plaza
Cathedral

Airport

To Parador del Valle (2 km),
Sucúa (20 km),
Cuenca (231 km)

Macas

0   50   100 m
0   50   100 yards

To Puyo
(130 km)

SOUTH ORIENTE

---

minal and airport are both relatively new, and the main plaza was completed only in 1983.

Information
Money Delgado Travel near the southwest corner of the main plaza and the bakery on Soasti south of D Comin both change US cash dollars. Traveler's checks are harder to change – try the bank on 24 de Mayo a block south of the plaza.

Post & Communications There are both EMETEL and post offices (see map). The EMETEL office is open from 8 am to noon, 2 to 6 pm, and 7 to 10 pm daily.

The area code for Macas and the province of Morona-Santiago is 07.

Travel Agencies & Guides Tuntiak Expediciones de la Selva (☎ 700 185/082), in front of the Hotel Peñon del Oriente, is run by Carlos Arcos and has been well recommended. Carlos is part Shuar and doesn't speak English. His father has simple cabins in the village of **Miazal**, in the jungle about 50 km southeast of Macas as the vulture flies. There is an airstrip here for chartered flights. A trail from Macas also gets here – I don't believe it's passable to cars. There are Shuar villages, waterfalls, natural hot springs and an oilbird cave in the vicinity. IKIAAM Shuar Travel (☎ 700 457) on the main plaza is another outfitter to try.

Things to See & Do

The new **cathedral** was built on a small hill above the main plaza and replaced a quaint and simple old wooden church. The cathedral is dedicated to the 400th anniversary of the miraculous changes that happened in a painting of **La Virgen de Macas** in 1592. The story is told in a series of huge stained-glass windows, and the painting itself can be viewed on the altar. On the night of August 4, a **procession** in honor of the Virgin goes the 23 km from Sucúa.

Behind the cathedral is a view of the wide Río Upano valley. From the cathedral hill there's a view of the town and, on a clear day, the often smoking Volcán Sangay some 40 km to the northwest. At 5230 meters, it is the seventh highest mountain in Ecuador and one of the most active volcanoes in the world.

River rafting on the **Río Upano** has recently begun. Five-day river trips with camping plus other Ecuadorian travel are offered by ROW (☎ (800) 451 6034, (208) 765 0841, fax 667 6506), PO Box 579, Coeur D'Alene, ID 83816, USA. The river is normally run from November to March and June to September. In Quito, Etnotur (☎ 563 380, 230 552, fax 502 682) reportedly offers similar expeditions. The river has Class III and some Class IV rapids.

A movie theater next to the EMETEL office on 24 de Mayo and Sucre shows films on weekends.

Places to Stay

One of the cheapest places is the adequate *Residencial Upano* (☎ 700 057), which is convenient to the bus terminal. They charge about US$3 per person and have shared cold showers. Also cheap is the little *Residencial Mayflower* (☎ 700 704), which has one shared cold shower. Other cheap places

with shared cold showers include the reasonably clean *Residencial Macas*, the *Residencial Emperatriz* and the very basic *Hotel Sangay*. The *Hotel Splendit* has basic old rooms with shared showers for US$3.50 per person, with private cold showers for US$6 per person and with private warm showers for US$8 per person.

A much better value is the very clean and recommended *Hotel Orquidea* (☎ 700 970), which is US$5 per person with cold shower and US$6 per person with hot shower. *Hotel Esmeralda* (☎ 700 160) is also quite good for US$7 per person with private warm showers.

The best place in town is the *Hotel Peñon del Oriente* (☎ 700 124, ☎ /fax 700 450), which charges about US$11 per person in rooms with hot showers and good views, US$7 with cold showers, and US$5 with cold showers in rooms with no windows. This hotel is the most convenient to the bus terminal and airport. There are good views from the roof.

About two km south of town, on the road to Sucúa, is the *Parador del Valle* (☎ 700 226), which has clean, bungalow-style accommodations for US$8 per person with private bath, and there is a restaurant.

Places to Eat

The *Restaurant Pagoda* (☎ 700 280), a chifa under the Peñon del Oriente, is one of the better places to eat. Another decent chifa is the *Rincón del Miguel* on Soasti just north of 10 de Agosto. The bakery on the same block is also recommended. The *Restaurant El Jardín* and the *Restaurant La Randimpa* have both been recommended by locals. The *Restaurant Charlot*, under the Hotel Splendit, and the restaurant under the Residencial Macas are cheap and look clean. The *Eros Café* on Amazonas just north of Tarqui is good for hamburgers, ice cream, snacks and beer, and is popular with local teenagers.

Getting There & Away

Air TAME (☎ 700 162) has flights from and to Quito on Monday, Wednesday and Friday afternoons, leaving Quito at 2 pm and leaving Macas at 3:05 pm. Departure days may change – check with TAME. Tickets cost US$45 (less for Ecuadorians) one way and are obtainable from the TAME office in the Macas airport building. If flying from Macas to Quito, the left-hand side of the plane offers the best mountain views, including Sangay and Cotopaxi if the weather is clear. The aerial photo of Cotopaxi in this book was taken on a Macas to Quito flight.

The last time I flew out of Macas, half the town's population and even people from surrounding villages came to the airport to see the plane land and take off. There was a festive feeling in the air – after all, there's little else to do in Macas.

TAO (☎ 700 174) and the air force have flights on most weekdays to various jungle airstrips. Seating is limited and flights are often booked up several days in advance. Ecuadorians have preference on the (cheaper) flights run by the military and it is hard to get on these.

Bus All departures are from the new terminal terrestre. There are several departures a day for Cuenca (US$6.50; 10 to 12 hours) and Gualaquiza (US$4.25; nine to 10 hours). Buses and pickup trucks to Sucúa (US$0.50; one hour) are frequent. A cricket in the Macas area, which sounded exactly like my travel alarm, kept chirping outside my window all night long, waking me half a dozen times before my early departure for Cuenca.

Buses and trucks go north to Puyo (US$4, five hours) several times a day. About halfway to Puyo the Río Pastaza must be crossed at the settlement of Chuitayo. Cars can cross a small bridge, but buses are too heavy, so passengers have to cross on foot and continue by a second bus waiting on the other side. If it's raining, a covered pickup truck takes passengers across – otherwise, the walk is almost a kilometer.

Transportes Macas runs small buses and pickup trucks to various remote, northern parts of the province, including Chiguaza (two hours), hourly during daylight hours.

Two buses a day go to Nueve de Octubre (for Parque Nacional Sangay) and two a day to Morona.

PARQUE NACIONAL SANGAY

This national park is more fully described in the South of Quito chapter. Most access to the park is from the north and west; access from the south and east is very difficult.

You can get buses from Macas to **Nueve de Octubre**, where you can stay in the school house or camp. The people are friendly and can tell you where the dirt road continues to San Vicente (under construction, no vehicles) and then on to **Purshi** by footpath. Allow about eight hours to hike from Nueve de Octubre to Purshi. This small settlement is the official entrance to Parque Nacional Sangay. There is usually a ranger here, but the local people are also helpful. The entrance fee to the park is US$20 (about US$16 in sucres). Trails lead a short distance into the park, but these peter out fairly quickly and continuing requires a machete and a lot of perseverance – recommended for very experienced explorers only. The rainfall is high, the vegetation thick, and the terrain steep and broken.

It is possible to continue on foot beyond Purshi to Atillo in the highlands, from where a dirt road eventually connects with the Panamericana. This is a several-day trip and most people do it from the highlands down to the jungle. A road is under construction and will eventually link Macas with Cebadas and Guamote in the highlands. Make local inquiries about the status of this road.

There is a park information center by INEFAN in the Macas area. It used to be in Macas itself, then moved to the village of General Proaño, a few km north of Macas on the road to Nueve de Octubre. Ask locally where this office is now.

THE JUNGLE FROM MACAS

There are various ways to see more of the Oriente from Macas. It should be mentioned, however, that the best known center for tourism in the jungle is Misahuallí in the northern Oriente.

Many Ecuadorian maps show tracks or trails leading from Macas into the interior. These often lead to Shuar Indian villages and missions further into the Oriente. The trails are usually overgrown, however, because transportation is mainly by light aircraft these days. It is difficult but not impossible to visit some of these villages.

You can hire an *expreso* light aircraft to take you to some of the better-known centers such as **Taisha**, 70 km due east of Macas by air. There is a basic place to stay here. With luck or the right contacts, flights can be arranged with the Salesian mission aircraft, but flights are often full, and inclement weather may cause days of delay. Hiring your own aircraft is subject to availability of planes and costs about US$60 per person/per hour for a five-seater. Flights between Macas and Shell sometimes stop in Taisha. A Shuar guide, Carlos Arcos (see Travel Agencies & Guides in Macas), is a good contact.

Visiting nearby Shuar centers on foot or bus is fairly straightforward. There are frequent buses to the mission of **Sevilla** (Don Bosco), about an hour's walk away on the other side of the Río Upano.

From Sevilla you can head south on foot along a broad track to the village of San Luis, about a four-hour walk. This makes a good day trip, and en route you'll pass cultivated areas and Indian huts, where you may be invited to try some *chicha de yuca*. This traditional Shuar drink is made by the women, who grind up the yucca by chewing it and then spit it into a bowl where it is left to ferment. If this doesn't

appeal to you, bring a bottle of water. There are no facilities of any kind beyond Sevilla.

Most travelers now go to Puyo by road, crossing Río Pastaza at Chuitayo. A much wilder and more difficult route to Puyo is by bus from Macas north along a fairly good gravel road to various destinations up to and including the Río Chiguaza, beyond which the road continues to **24 de Mayo** (also called Huambuyo) on the Río Palora. The bus passes through Shuar territory, and you can see a few of their oval-shaped, bamboo-caned, thatched huts on the sides of the road. Most of the Indians riding the bus look unremarkably Western, but occasionally a beautifully beaded bracelet or tattooed face is seen. At 24 de Mayo a canoe will ferry you across the Río Palora to Arapicos. Somewhere near here is a village called Pablo VI, which has a basic place to stay. Once across the river, there is a very rough road with occasional trucks to the village of **Palora**, about 25 km from the river, although you may have to walk as far as Palora, as the road is often impassable. There is a basic pensión in Palora.

From Palora several buses a day run to Puyo, in the northern Oriente. Locals say that if you take the first morning bus from Macas to 24 de Mayo (Huambuyo), you can walk to Palora in one long day. I've never tried it.

Finally, if you'd like to experience some of the jungle near Macas in relative comfort, you could try the simple *Cabañas Ecológicas Yuquipa* on the Río Yuquipa, which is a small tributary of the Río Upano a few kilometers east of Macas. Information about the cabins is available from the bakery on Soasti in Macas (see map) or from ☎ /fax 700 071 in Macas.

The Northern Oriente

North of the Río Pastaza are the provinces of Pastaza, Napo and Sucumbíos, which together form the northern Oriente. Unlike the southern Oriente, the northern Oriente is well connected with the capital – there are two roads to Quito and six times as many scheduled flights from Quito. Hence, this is the most visited part of Ecuador's jungle. In one long day of bus riding, you can go from Quito to the oil boom town of Lago Agrio in the far northeastern jungle, or to the tourist center of Misahuallí in the central Oriente.

You can make various roundtrips by bus, boat and air. If your time is limited, the quickest of these is the bus journey from Quito through Ambato, Baños, Puyo, Tena, Baeza and back to Quito. This can be done in two long days and gives a look at the jungle where it meets the eastern slopes of the Andes.

A longer trip can be made by omitting the Tena-Baeza section and going instead to Coca either on the new road from Tena or by motor canoe from Misahuallí down the Río Napo. From Coca one can continue by bus to Lago Agrio and back to Quito through Baeza.

Such an excursion, not beyond anyone's resources, gives a good look at many facets of the Ecuadorian Oriente. It is feasible to do it in four days, but at least a week or more is recommended. The journey could be broken at either Coca or Lago Agrio, both of which have regular air service to Quito.

These areas have been colonized by farmers, ranchers, loggers and oil workers. Therefore, transportation is relatively straightforward on these circuits, but one shouldn't expect to see much in the way of wildlife. For that, tours into the interior are recommended; Misahuallí, Coca and Tena are among the better places from which to begin a more nature-oriented trip.

You should note that during the rainiest months of June to August, roads may be washed out, airports closed, and travel delays common. Always allow leeway of a day or two if you need to return and make important connections in Quito at any time of year, but especially in those months. On the other hand, when I was there for a week in mid-1995, it rained only on one evening, so you can never tell about Ecuador's weather!

THE ROAD TO PUYO

If I were to choose just one stretch of road in Ecuador for the best views of the upper Amazon basin, I would have difficulty improving upon the drive from Baños to Puyo.

The road follows the Río Pastaza canyon as it drops steadily from Baños at 1800 meters to Puyo at 950 meters. This road has recently been rebuilt, and buses now regularly make the journey. Just beyond the famous Agoyan Falls – now the site of a new hydroelectric project – the road passes through a tunnel. A few kilometers further, a waterfall splashes from the overhanging cliff onto the road – quite a surprise if you're hitchhiking in the back of a pickup truck.

Waterfalls frequently cascade into the canyon, and one of the most impressive is by the village of **Río Verde**, 20 km beyond Baños. You have to walk down a short trail to a suspension bridge to appreciate the waterfall properly. There is a sign at the beginning of the trail that reads 'Pailón del Diablo,' or ask at the village for directions.

Next to this sign is another sign for *El Otro Lado*, which literally means 'the other side.' The trail to the waterfall continues by footbridge across the Río Pastaza to El Otro Lado, about a 20-minute walk from the road, where there is a guest farm with bungalows that have private hot showers and good views. It's a tranquil place. Rates are US$35/55/75 for one/two/three people

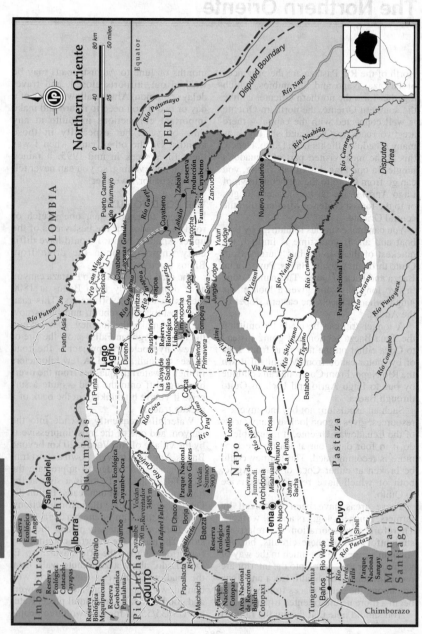

including breakfast and dinner. Reservations can be made at the Café Cultura restaurant in Quito (☎ /fax 224 271) or ask at the SAEC for information.

As the road drops beyond Río Verde, the vegetation rapidly becomes more tropical, and the walls of the Pastaza canyon are covered with bromeliads, giant tree ferns, orchids and flowering trees. The village of Río Negro is passed some 15 km beyond Río Verde, and several kilometers beyond is a bus stop known as La Penal (a few kilometers before Mera). From La Penal, a trail goes down to the Río Pastaza and crosses it on a suspension footbridge, continuing to *El Monasterio de Cumandá* almost an hour from the road. It's not a monastery but a simple guesthouse with tropical forest and waterfalls nearby. Simple cabins and shared cold showers are available for US$15 per person, including breakfast and dinner. Further information is available from Safari Tours in Quito.

Near the small community of Mera the canyon walls spread apart, and you see a breathtaking view of the Río Pastaza meandering away to the southeast through the vast, rolling plains of the Amazon basin. The right side of the bus is best for views. There is no higher land between here and the Atlantic, almost 4000 km to the east.

During the 1990s, a mountain biking craze swept Baños and a descent (mainly) from Baños to Mera or on to Puyo is a popular day trip, returning by bus from Puyo with your bicycle on the roof of the bus. At the end of 1995, this road was closed (reportedly by a landslide) between Agoyan and Río Verde, and construction of a tunnel began. The construction project closed the road to vehicles every day except Monday (open from 6 pm on Sunday to 6 am on Tuesday). Buses go to the tunnel, passengers disembark and have to make their way on foot for about a kilometer through the construction project, and are met by buses on the other side to continue the trip. Bicyclists can get through – but make local inquiry. The project is slated to continue on into 1997.

SHELL

Shell is a few kilometers beyond Mera, and the two communities together are often called Shell-Mera. At Shell is the Pastaza airstrip serving Puyo which is about 10 km away. This is the most important airstrip in the province of Pastaza. There is also a military checkpoint here.

Information

Shell is a US missionary center with schools, churches and hospitals. The missions have flights into the Oriente and may provide emergency services. There is a new Voz Andes missionary hospital. It is reported that they will change US dollars as well as provide medical assistance in an emergency.

There is a 'Cine Militar' (military cinema) where civilians are allowed. Military personnel sit on the right and civilians on the left.

There is a workshop where balsa wood birds are manufactured. It is run by Señor Fabio who is well known in town. You can visit and watch the birds being made.

Military Checkpoint

All foreign travelers arriving in the Oriente through Shell must register with the army. The registration procedure is efficient and straightforward. Buses on the way to Puyo stop by the checkpoint (at the west end of Shell) and wait while foreigners disembark and register. You have to fill out a register with the usual details (age, nationality, etc) and present your passport and the tourist card that you received on entry into Ecuador. You'll be asked your destination and the purpose of your visit. 'Turismo' is the safest and most obvious answer. Your passport will be stamped by the Brigada de Selva No 17, and you'll be free to go.

The whole procedure takes only a minute, and the bus drivers are so used to it that they'll wait as a matter of course. The only possible problem is if you have only a few days left on your visa or tourist card, as they like you to have at least 10 days before going into the Oriente. The stamp is important; it may be inspected in various other places in the Oriente.

If you arrive in Puyo by air you should also register, unless you already did elsewhere in the Oriente. The checkpoint is about a kilometer walk west of the airport on the one main street of town. If you are leaving the Oriente through Puyo, you may or may not have to register.

Places to Stay & Eat

There are three basic hotels that charge about US$2 or US$3 a night. The *Hostal Cordillera* seems to be the best because rooms have private showers, but equally good rooms with shared showers at a cheaper price are available in the *Residencial Azuay*. There are a few simple restaurants. You won't get lost – it's a one-street town with the airport at the west end on the way to Baños. Everything else lies east of the airport.

Getting There & Away

Air Flights with the Ecuadorian Air Force, FAE (Fuerza Aerea Ecuatoriana), leave on weekdays for Quito, towns such as Tena, Coca, Lago Agrio and Macas, and a variety of jungle villages (different destinations on different days). Seating is limited and Ecuadorians are given preference, so be patient – you may have to wait several days to get on a flight. For towns with bus service, it's normally faster to go by bus. Fares are cheap.

Aircraft can be chartered – inquire at the airport. The airport is closed on Sundays.

Bus Most people going through Shell will already be on a bus through to Puyo. Should you need a bus to Puyo, wait on the main road in the middle of town and flag one down. Buses leave every half hour and charge about US$0.20. If you want to go to Baños or Ambato, also wait on the main road for buses from Puyo, which will pick you up if they have room.

PUYO

Puyo, with a growing population of over 20,000, is the provincial capital of Pastaza. Until the early 1970s it had a real 'frontier' atmosphere, and was the most important

town in the Oriente. Since the discovery of oil, however, the frontier has been pushed deep into the jungle, and now Lago Agrio vies for the claim of being Ecuador's most important Oriente town.

It is not a particularly attractive town, but it makes a good stopping point if you need a night's sleep before continuing into the Oriente or returning to the highlands.

Information

Three banks are shown on the map and may change money. There is reportedly a casa de cambio in town, but I couldn't find it – ask around. Try to bring with you as many sucres as you'll need. There are EMETEL and post offices marked on the map. The area code for Puyo and the province of Pastaza is 03.

The hospital is west of town, but the Voz Andes mission hospital in Shell is a better choice for medical emergencies.

Market day is Sunday. Many of the town's businesses are open on that day and closed on Monday.

Things to See & Do

If you can get up at dawn, you'll often see a spectacular view of jagged snow peaks rising up over a jungle covered with rolling morning mist. Later in the morning, the mountains usually disappear into the clouds. The jagged peaks belong to El Altar (5319 meters), the fifth highest mountain in Ecuador, about 50 km to the southeast. Occasionally, you can also catch a glimpse of Sangay (5230 meters). A good view can be had from the main plaza on a clear day (and sometimes from the road to Shell-Mera).

During the day you can go swimming in the river. If you're a birdwatcher, you'll see a variety of jungle species near the river. Alternatively, you can visit La Libertad sports complex just north of the bus terminal about 1.5 km west of town along C Marin. There is a swimming pool open to the public, as well as tennis and volleyball courts. Hours are 10 am to 10 pm daily, except Tuesday, and there is a nominal admission charge.

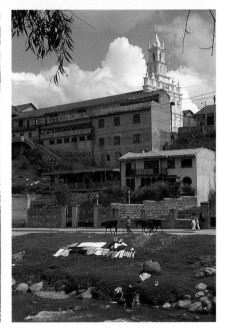

Top: Inca ruins of Ingapirca (RR)
Left: Guayaquil Cathedral and statue of Simon Bolívar (TW)
Right: All Saints Church, Tomebamba River, Cuenca (RR)

Top: Fishermen at work, Atacames (RR)
Left: Domes of La Compañía from Plaza San Francisco, Quito (RR)
Right: Fisherman Monument, Manta (RR)

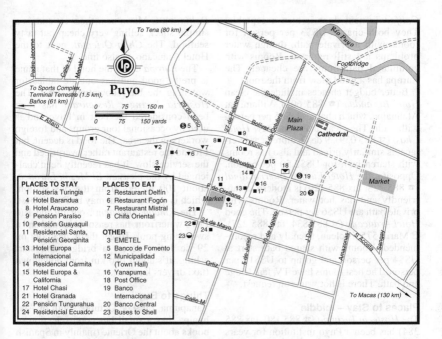

Puyo

To Tena (80 km)

To Sports Complex,
Terminal Terrestre (1.5 km),
Baños (61 km)

0   75   150 m
0   75   150 yards

4 de Enero

Río Puyo

Footbridge

Sucre

Bolívar

Main
Plaza

Cathedral

C. Marín

Atahualpa

F. de Orellana

Market

24 de Mayo

5 de Junio

Ortiz

Calle M

To Macas (130 km)

Market

PLACES TO STAY	PLACES TO EAT
1 Hostería Turingia	2 Restaurant Delfín
4 Hotel Barandua	6 Restaurant Fogón
8 Hotel Araucano	7 Restaurant Mistral
9 Pensión Paraíso	8 Chifa Oriental
10 Pensión Guayaquil	
11 Residencial Santa,	**OTHER**
Pensión Georginita	3 EMETEL
13 Hotel Europa	5 Banco de Fomento
Internacional	12 Municipalidad
14 Residencial Carmita	(Town Hall)
15 Hotel Europa &	16 Yanapuma
California	18 Post Office
17 Hotel Chasi	19 Banco
21 Hotel Granada	Internacional
22 Pensión Tungurahua	20 Banco Central
24 Residencial Ecuador	23 Buses to Shell

A reader reports that there is a small botanical garden with examples of herbs and plants used by local Indian groups for medicinal and ceremonial purposes. The gardens are open from 9 am to 6 pm on weekends, and a guided tour is US$2.50. They are in the Barrio Obrero, near the *balneario* (swimming area) on the river, across the bridge. I haven't substantiated this.

There is not much nightlife. What there is tends to be short-lived – here one year and gone the next. You can usually find the latest fad – video movie theaters. There is sometimes a disco – ask around.

The Fiestas de Fundación are celebrated for a week in early May. The 100th anniversary will be in 1999.

Places to Stay

There's no shortage of accommodations in Puyo, but there are frequent water shortages. If you need a shower, ensure that there is running water before renting a

room. Local hotel owners told me that Tuesday to Thursday are the busiest nights with many businesspeople in town.

Places to Stay – bottom end

Hotel Granada, on 27 de Febrero by the market, charges US$2 per person or US$3.50 with bath and is just OK. The *Residencial Ecuador*, on 24 de Mayo, is old but secure. The *Residencial Carmita* on 9 de Octubre and Atahualpa, is basic but reasonably clean. Other places in this price range include the very basic *Pensión Georginita* and the marginally better *Residencial Santa* and *Pensión Tungurahua*. Closer to the center of town are some cheap and run-down hotels such as the *Pensiones Guayaquil* and *Paraíso*. I must confess to making no more than a cursory examination of these – they don't look very special.

Slightly better cheap hotels to try are the *Hotel Europa* (☎ 885 220), on 9 de Octubre just north of Atahualpa. The *Hotel*

California next door is also acceptable. They both charge US$3 per person for rooms with a private bath, though water problems are still reported. Rooms with communal bathrooms are cheaper. The Europa has a good view from the roof.

Better budget choices include the clean *Hotel Barandua* (☎ 885 604), Villamil at Atahualpa, which charges US$5 per person with bath. The clean and quite new *Hotel Chasi* (☎ 883 059), 9 de Octubre near Orellana, is similarly priced and also has rooms with shared bath for US$2.50 per person. Opposite, the *Hotel Europa Internacional* (☎ 885 228, fax 885 120) is modern, clean, friendly and has hot water. Rooms with private bath are US$6 per person. The good *Hotel Araucano* (☎ 883 834, fax 885 227), C Marin 575, is clean, friendly and recommended. Rooms with shared bath start at US$4 per person and go up to US$12 per person. The best rooms have TV, fan, fridge and bath. There is hot water on request.

Places to Stay – middle

The *Hostería Turingia* (☎ 885 180, fax 885 384) has been a Puyo institution for years and is the best hotel in town. It is on the road to Baños on C Marin 294, on the outskirts of town. They have accommodations in rather cramped bungalows with fans, private bath and hot water for US$18/32 for singles/doubles. The bungalows are set in a tropical garden with many plants and a tiny plunge pool. The restaurant here is quite good but overpriced.

Another reasonable choice is the *Hostería Safari* (☎ 885465/6, fax 823 588) about six km away on the road to Tena. They have a nice garden, a games area, and a simple restaurant and bar. Rooms with private bath and hot water are US$20/36.

Places to Eat

A few restaurants in the center are adequate, if not memorable. The *Restaurant Fogón*, on Atahualpa between Villamil and 27 de Febrero, is quite good for broasted chicken. Nearly opposite is the clean *Restaurant Mistral*, which is good for snacks and light meals. The *Restaurant*

Delfín, on C Marin near the west end, is a simple shack selling very cheap but tasty seafood. The *Chifa Oriental*, next to the Hotel Araucano, is also fine.

The *Europa* under the hotel of that name is pretty good and has outside tables for watching the busy downtown street. The *Hostería Turingia Restaurant* has long been considered the best in Puyo and is used by occasional tour groups and foreign workers in the area. The food is decent, but I found the restaurant rather overpriced and the service slow. It has recently been challenged by the pleasant *El Mesón Europeo*, about 100 meters from the bus station, which is quite new but may be Puyo's best.

The *Rincón Ambateño*, out by the Río Puyo waterfront, has reasonable food and a swimming pool. To get there, head out on 29 de Julio, across a bridge, and start asking. It's about two km from downtown (taxi drivers know it).

Things to Buy

Yanapuma, on 9 de Octubre south of Atahualpa, has a small but good selection of books about the Oriente (mainly in Spanish but a few in English) as well as crafts of the area. It's worth a visit.

The La Casa de Balsa is a larger, more commercial operation on the edge of town on the road to Baños. Here, you can see balsa wood animals being crafted before you buy them.

Getting There & Away

Air The provincial airstrip is in Shell (see above).

Bus The terminal terrestre is southwest of town and became fully operational in 1990. There are frequent buses to Baños (US$1.50; two hours) and to Ambato (US$2.50; three hours), but be sure to check the current road construction situation (see The Road to Puyo, above). There are several buses a day to Quito (US$4; six to seven hours) and Riobamba (four hours). Buses to Tena (US$2; three hours) often originate in Ambato or Baños and may be full or standing room only when they pass through Puyo. Buses that originate in Puyo should be booked a day ahead to ensure a seat. There is a 6 am bus to Guayaquil.

Centinela del Oriente runs ancient buses to various small villages in the surrounding jungle. The most important of these is Palora, where there is a basic pensión and from where you can continue south by pickup truck (if you are lucky), foot and canoe ferry to Chiguaza near Macas in the southern Oriente (for more information about this journey, see Macas in The Southern Oriente chapter). Buses for Palora leave several times a day for the three-hour ride. Various other nearby jungle villages can also be explored with various buses. Although the buses leave from the terminal, they'll stop at the Mercado at Atahualpa and Amazonas for a while to fill up with passengers.

Buses to Macas (US$3.75; five hours) leave five or six times a day. The bus goes as far as the Río Pastaza, where you have to transfer (see under Macas).

Getting Around
Small local buses providing service to Shell (US$0.20; every 30 minutes or so) for the Pastaza airstrip leave from the southwest corner of the market.

A taxi from downtown to the terminal terrestre is about US$0.80.

PUERTO NAPO
The narrow, graveled road from Puyo into the Oriente heads almost due north, passing small homesteads and occasional banana plantations until the road crosses the provincial line into Napo. Puerto Napo is about seven km from Tena. There is a place to stay, the very basic *Hotel Palandacocha*, but few travelers stop here. A road fork to the right leads to Misahuallí, 17 km away, or you can continue north to Tena.

You can wait here for a vehicle to take you to Misahuallí. Many buses/trucks to Misahuallí come from Tena, and there is often a scramble for seats. It is probably easier to get a seat, though slower, if you go into Tena and take a bus back to Misahuallí from there.

TENA
Tena, at about 600 meters above sea level, is the capital of the Napo Province. This province, with an area of 33,930 sq km – almost an eighth of the country – is the largest in Ecuador. Despite its size, only 110,000 people live here, with Tena housing about 14,000 of them.

Tena was founded in 1560, and was the most easterly of Ecuador's early colonial missionary and trading outposts. There were several Indian uprisings in the early days, notably in 1578 when Jumandy, chief of the Quijos, led an unsuccessful revolt against the Spaniards. Tena survived the uprising, though many early Oriente towns were completely wiped out by other Indian attacks. Today the area is largely agricultural, with cattle ranches and coffee or banana plantations. It is at the junction of the Tena and Pano rivers and is a minor, but growing, center for Ecuadorian tourism. The average year-round temperature is 24°C, with the rivers having a moderating effect on the climate.

Information
The CETUR tourist information office on Bolívar is open at irregular hours. There are the usual EMETEL and post offices, the latter difficult to find as there is no sign (see map for location). The area code for Tena and the entire Napo Province is 06.

Money changing facilities are limited; the banks did not change dollars when I was last there, so plan on bringing sucres with you. If you ask around enough, you'll find a store or other business that will change cash dollars at unfavorable rates, but traveler's checks could be a real problem.

The hospital (☎ 886 302/3/4/5) is south of town on the road to Puerto Napo.

Tours & Guides
Amarongachi Tours (☎ 886 372, fax 886 015), 15 de Noviembre 432, is a tour company that opened in 1990 and has been well recommended by numerous readers. The friendly staff will arrange various jungle excursions and book bus tickets for you after the trip. Amarongachi is a source

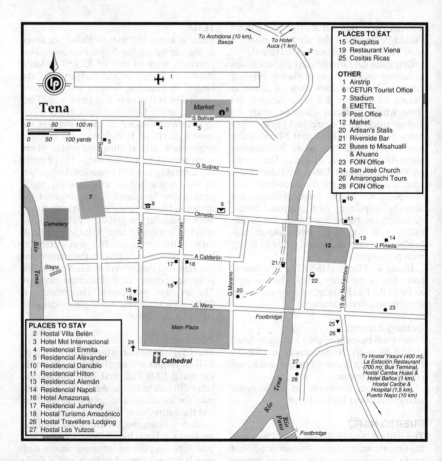

PLACES TO EAT
15 Chuquitos
19 Restaurant Viena
25 Cositas Ricas

OTHER
1 Airstrip
6 CETUR Tourist Office
7 Stadium
8 EMETEL
9 Post Office
12 Market
20 Artisan's Stalls
21 Riverside Bar
22 Buses to Misahuallí & Ahuano
23 FOIN Office
24 San José Church
26 Amarongachi Tours
28 FOIN Office

Tena

To Archidona (10 km), Baeza
To Hotel Auca (1 km)

Market
S Bolívar

Sucre
G Suárez
Olmedo
A Calderón
JL Mera
Footbridge

Cemetery

Río Tena
Steps

J Montalvo
Amazonas
G Moreno
15 de Noviembre
J Pineda

Main Plaza

Cathedral

Río Tena
Río Pano

To Hostal Yasuni (400 m),
La Estación Restaurant (700 m), Bus Terminal,
Hostal Camba Huasi & Hotel Baños (1 km),
Hostal Caribe & Hospital (1.5 km),
Puerto Napo (10 km)

Footbridge

PLACES TO STAY
2 Hostal Villa Belén
3 Hotel Mol Internacional
4 Residencial Enmita
5 Residencial Alexander
10 Residencial Danubio
11 Residencial Hilton
13 Residencial Alemán
14 Residencial Napoli
16 Hotel Amazonas
17 Residencial Jumandy
18 Hostal Turismo Amazónico
26 Hostal Travellers Lodging
27 Hostal Los Yutzos

NORTH ORIENTE

of local information and also owns the Hostal Travellers Lodging and Cositas Ricas restaurant next door. Their tours are about US$35 per person per day (though if you go for several days and with a group, the price drops considerably). Excursions allow you to stay with local families in the jungle, eat good local food, go for nature hikes, pan for gold, swim in the rivers and get a look at the local rainforest. Although much of the land around Tena has been colonized, there are some nearby sections of uncut primary forest that can still be visited nearby. They operate the Shangri

La cabins on a bluff 100 meters above the Río Anzu, with great views of river and forest. It's a good base for jungle exploration. The cabins are simple doubles, and food and services are provided by local families. Many speak Quichua as a first language and Spanish as a second, but few speak English.

Also recommended are local guides listed with the Federación de Organizaciones Indígenas (FOIN; ☎ 886 614) with offices east of town on JL Mera and on the east bank of the Río Pano. FOIN has organized local villages into the Red Indígena de Communidades del Alto Napo para la Convivienca Intercultural y Ecoturismo (RICANCIE – Indigenous Network of Upper Napo Communities for Cultural Coexistence and Ecotourism). Almost all of their guides speak Quichua and/or Spanish, but few speak English. They can arrange stays in local villages as well as the usual jungle trips. They also know the locations of the numerous caves and petroglyphs found in the Tena region. Tarquino Tapuy is a good contact at FOIN. A recommended caving guide is Fernando Noriega Reyes; ask for him locally.

Readers and Peace Corps volunteers recommend the local Quichua guide Delfín Pauchi who owns the Cabañas Pimpilala (☎ 886 434), a 45-minute drive from Tena. He uses these as a base for jungle excursions. Other readers recommend Olmedo and Oswaldo, who can be contacted at Olmedo's daughter's house. Her name is Neli Cerda (☎ 886 419), 9 de Octubre 356 in the Bellavista Baja suburb east of Tena. Rates are generally in the US$20 to US$35 per person/per day range, depending on group size and length of trip.

For a change of pace, you can go rafting and kayaking on whitewater rivers in the Tena area. A new outfitter that has received several recommendations is Ríos Ecuador (☎ 887 438, fax in Quito 568 042, see also Online Services), who have an office in the Hostal Camba Huasi by the bus terminal. They run eight different rivers ranging from easy Class I floats suitable for anybody to very difficult Class V whitewater rapids for experienced river runners. Most rivers are within an hour's drive of Tena, and raft trips of one to three days are offered as well as guided one-day kayaking trips. Genner Coronel, their head guide, is an Ecuadorian who has kayaked in the USA and speaks excellent English. He is one of Ecuador's foremost kayakers and has competed internationally. Rates are US$50 or US$60 for one-day trips. A five-day whitewater kayaking school (suitable for beginners) is offered for US$300 (a bargain compared to rates in the US or Europe). Rental kayaks are available for experienced kayakers. These are available year round, although some of the more difficult rivers are not easily runnable from April to September when choices are more limited.

Things to See & Do

There's not much to do in the town itself, although it is a good base for visiting the nearby village of Archidona and the Cuevas de Jumandí (Caves of Jumandí) described below under Archidona. *The Ecotourist's Guide to the Ecuadorian Amazon*, available in Quito, is a useful book describing 18 caves and 36 petroglyphs in the Tena region; there are undoubtedly many more. Despite it's earthy attractions, more often than not Tena itself is just a resting-up place for a night or two.

If you're interested in looking for tropical birds, the steps leading down to the Río Tena near the cemetery are a good place for birdwatching.

On a clear day, visitors are sometimes puzzled by the sight of a volcano looming up out of the jungle, some 50 km away to the north-northeast. This is Volcán Sumaco (see below).

The anniversary of Tena's foundation is celebrated on November 15, and is the time for celebrations, colorful processions and other festivities (see the sidebar A Fiesta in Tena).

Market days are Friday and Saturday. Although there is nothing specifically aimed at tourists, the market is an interesting, bustling affair.

Places to Stay – bottom end

The cheapest hotels are in the town center, but they have all suffered from water shortages. Make sure there is running water if you don't want to bathe in the river. The basic *Hotel Amazonas*, on the corner of the plaza, is just over US$2 per person and is fine if you can get an outside room. The *Residencial Jumandy*, a block north of the main plaza, and the *Hotel Baños*, near the bus station, are similarly priced and acceptable.

The friendly *Residencial Enmita*, on Bolívar, is about US$4 per person in rooms

A Fiesta in Tena

While visiting the town during one of their November fiestas, I had one of those unusual experiences that make traveling all the more fun. I was sitting quietly in my hotel room, making notes for the Tena city map, when there was a knock on the door. When I opened the door, two officious-looking gentlemen in plain clothes walked in. Perhaps it's the sign of a guilty conscience, but my first thought was, 'Oh, no, what am I in for now?'

To my relief, the gentlemen introduced themselves as the organizers of the annual Tena beauty pageant, which was being held that evening to elect that year's 'Señorita Tena.' They had heard that a Spanish-speaking foreigner was in town and wondered if I would be kind enough to help judge the contest, as they wanted some nonbiased judges for a fair vote!

I don't normally hold beauty contests in very high esteem, but I couldn't refuse. The evening turned out to be riotous fun, with each señorita having her own wildly cheering entourage of relatives, friends and neighbors, and a sound system that screeched maniacally at inopportune moments. Although I enjoyed myself, I haven't changed my opinion of beauty contests. ■

with cold bath (less without). Nearby, the *Residencial Alexander* is also US$4 per person with bath but is not as good.

Across the Río Tena bridge, the clean *Residencial Hilton*, at the north end of 15 de Noviembre, charges US$4 per person with bath, or US$3.25 without. Nearby, the clean *Residencial Napoli* (☎ 886 194) is US$4/6.50 with shared bath. The *Residencial Danubio* is cheaper and OK. The clean and friendly *Residencial Alemán* (☎ 886 409) charges US$4.25 per person in rooms with bath and fans.

The clean and popular *Hostal Travellers Lodging* is operated by Amarongachi Tours (see above) and has rooms with private hot shower for US$14 double, and some cheaper rooms with shared shower or with several beds. It is popular with international travelers and a good place to get information, meet new friends to get a tour group together, etc.

Barely a block south of the bus station, the *Hostal Camba Huasi* (☎ 887 429) charges US$4/7 with cold bath in large, clean, but bare rooms. This is a relatively new place – rooms will either become shabbier with time or the owners will put some work into it and edge the prices up, but they seemed like a good value when I was there. There are also a couple of other places in this price range along the street to the bus terminal – they are cheap and decent.

Also recommended is the *Hostal Villa Belén* (☎ 886 228), north of town, charging about US$8 per person in very clean rooms with hot showers. There is a garden and they have a good, slightly pricey restaurant.

Places to Stay – middle

There are two better hotels near the town center. The *Hotel Turismo Amazónico* (☎ 886 487), Amazonas and Abdón Calderón, charges about US$10 to US$14 per person in rooms with private bath, TV with cable, telephone and mini-fridge. Rooms have fans and some will have air-conditioning. The *Hotel Mol Internacional* (☎ /fax 886 215), at Sucre 432 at the north end of town, charges US$14/22 with private bath and hot water. Rooms have fans and TV, many have a balcony and are quite spacious. A swimming pool was under construction and may be finished by 1997. The hotel is modern and clean, but has been criticized for raising its prices during fiestas.

On the east side of the Río Tena is the new *Hostal Los Yutzos*, which is also in this price range and in a quiet location. I didn't see it, but rooms are reported as clean and modern, with TV, mini-fridge, private bath and river view.

The *Hotel Auca*, about two km northeast of the town center, used to be run by CETUR but is apparently changing hands –

it was closed when I last visited (midweek in the low season) but will probably reopen. They have spacious grounds by the river, a restaurant and bar, a discotheque (which opens for locals on weekends) and a casino. Prices have been similar to the hotels above.

Places to Eat

There are a number of small and inexpensive restaurants. *Cositas Ricas*, next to Amarongachi, is the current favorite of travelers and serves vegetarian and Ecuadorian plates (US$2 to US$4) and good juices made with boiled water. They do a good job with clean food preparation for travelers' finicky stomachs. Also good for Ecuadorian food at reasonable prices is the locally popular *Chuquitos* just off the plaza. One of the cheapest decent places is *Restaurant Viena* with local meals under US$2. *La Estancia*, on the way to the bus terminal has a nice jungle ambience and meals around US$4, but avoid salads and juices here.

Several hotel restaurants have been recommended. *Enmita's* is a perennially popular and friendly place. Both the *Villa Belén* and *Auca* serve good food at slightly higher prices than average for Tena, but will hardly break the bank.

Entertainment

There's not much to do here in the evening but hang out with other travelers. The little *riverside bar* (see map) is a nice place to watch the river flow while drinking an ice-cold beer and listening to the owner's extensive salsa CD selection.

Getting There & Away

Air There is an airstrip at the north end of town. The Ecuadorian Air Force (FAE) has flights to Shell, Coca and Nueva Rocafuerte on Monday and Wednesday. Fares are very cheap, but seats are often booked well in advance and preference is given to Ecuadorians so it is hard to get on these flights – inquire at the airstrip.

While I was in Tena, there was a rumor that TAME may be starting direct flights from Quito in the future. Ask locally.

Bus The main bus terminal is about 1½ km away from the center in the southeastern outskirts of town on the Puerto Napo road. There are several departures a day for Quito (US$4; six hours) via Baeza; the southern route (via Puyo) is longer. Fares to Puyo or Baeza cost about US$2, and to Ambato US$4. Flota Jumandy run several buses a day to Lago Agrio (US$7; 10 hours). Several buses a day go to Coca (US$5.50; seven hours). These times are approximate, as bad roads, old buses and inclement weather all make journey times in the Oriente notoriously unreliable.

Getting Around

Local buses do not leave from the main terminal. For Archidona (US$0.20; 15 minutes), buses leave about every half hour during daylight hours from the hospital and go along 15 de Noviembre to Olmedo and out of town on Bolívar. You can flag it down on its route. Equally frequent services for Misahuallí (US$0.50; one hour) leave from the east side of the river just south of the market. Note that on market days (Friday and Saturday) the market expands southward and these buses leave from the same street but from the north side of the market. There are several buses from this stop to Ahuano (US$0.60; 1½ hours).

ARCHIDONA

Archidona is a small mission village founded in 1560, the same year as Tena, 10 km to the south. Although found on the earliest maps of Ecuador, Archidona has grown little in the intervening centuries and remains a village.

The best reason for visiting is to see the main plaza, which is a small, attractive and well laid out forest of tropical palms, vines, ferns, flowers and trees. Such a pretty plaza is a surprise in so small a village; it is probably the mission's work. Their carefully but strangely painted concrete-block church is also very colorful. A good day to visit Archidona is on Sunday, when the local Quijos Indians come to their weekly market and to hear mass.

NORTH ORIENTE

From the plaza you can take a bus to Cotundo and ask to be dropped at the entrance to the **Cuevas de Jumandí**, about four km north of Archidona. There are three main branches in the cave system, which apparently has not yet been fully explored. There is a snack bar and small amusement park (not always open) by the caves. The entrance to the cave is lighted, but you must bring your own lights and equipment to see the stalagmites and other formations further in. The cave is muddy and rubber boots and old clothes are recommended. If you plan on going deep into the cave you should have a local guide and equipment; entry costs US$0.50.

These are by far the best known of the many caves in the area and there are guides available in Tena to show you others. Some of the caves can be visited fairly casually, but many require crawling or wading or even swimming, and technical spelunking (caving) gear is needed.

The next town of any importance to the north is Baeza, about 100 km away. This is at the junction with the Lago Agrio-Quito road and will be described later in this chapter.

Places to Stay & Eat

There are a couple of cheap and basic hotels near the plaza. *Residencial Regina* (☎ 889 144) has rooms with private baths and has been recommended for its friendly staff. Rates are about US$7/10, or a little less with shared bath. The cheaper *Residencial Carolina* is also OK. There are a few simple and inexpensive places to eat, of which the inexpensive *Restaurant Los Pinos* near the Residencial Regina is a reasonable choice.

A comfortable new lodge, reportedly opening as I write this, is the *Orchids Paradise Lodge* (☎ 889 221, 889 174, fax 886 380) on the main road to Baez about halfway between Archidona and the Cuevas de Jumandí.

A few kilometers east of Archidona, the Quichua Mamallacta family have cabins that are normally rented to visitors taking their all-inclusive four-day tour from Quito

(about US$200 per person). They can be contacted through Safari Tours in Quito.

VOLCÁN SUMACO

The 3900-meter-high cone of Sumaco is surrounded by rainforest, plagued by wet weather, and is the most remote and least known of Ecuador's volcanoes. It is dormant at this time, though volcanologists believe it is potentially active. It lies about 27 km north of the new Tena-Coca road, from which it can be climbed in about five or six days (roundtrip). The road to Coca leaves the Tena-Baeza road to the east about 24 km north of Archidona. About 20 km along the Coca road after turning off from the Tena-Baeza road, a short dirt road leads to the village of Huamaní.

In Huamaní guides can be hired for the climb to the summit, which involves poorly marked trails and chopping through the jungle with a machete. It is easy to get lost and therefore guides are strongly recommended. Two experienced ones are Francisco Chimbo and Benjamin Shiguango, who you should ask for in the village. The going rate is about US$12 per day for a guide, plus you have to provide food and shelter for the guide as well as yourself. In addition, a US$12 fee per climber is charged, which goes to the community of Huamaní.

There are limited facilities in Huamaní so you should bring food and equipment from Tena. The rainiest months of May to August turn the trail into a mud bath, and the mountain views are clouded over. The driest months are reportedly October to December, and these are the best times to go.

The volcano is within the **Parque Nacional Sumaco-Galeras**, the newest and one of the most remote of Ecuador's national parks. Climbing Sumaco is the only way I know of visiting the park.

MISAHUALLÍ

This small village is marked on many maps as Puerto Misahuallí and is at the end of the road running from Puerto Napo along the north bank of the Río Napo. It is a popular place from which to see some of the

Oriente because you can easily get here by bus from Quito in a day, so it is suitable for the traveler with a limited amount of time. Tours from Misahuallí are often cheaper than from many other parts of the Amazon.

However, before you grab your hammock and pith helmet and jump on the next bus, you should realize that this isn't virgin jungle. The area has been colonized for decades, and most mammals (monkey, wild pig, jaguar, capybara) have been either hunted out or had their habitats encroached upon to the point where they cannot survive.

What you will see, if you keep your eyes open – or better still, with a local guide – is a variety of jungle birds, tropical flowers, army ants and other insects, and hundreds of dazzling butterflies.

In addition you will see the people living in the jungle – colonists, gold panners, oil workers, farmers, ranchers, military personnel, people in the tourism industry and entrepreneurs. The remaining Indian tribes live deeper into the jungle and, for the most part, prefer to be left alone. Most of the Indians in the area are either transplanted highlanders or acculturated locals.

The physical geography of this area is still rolling and rather rugged. The elevation is about 400 meters (with hills twice that high within a few kilometers) and there are many more ridges and valleys around here than you'll see by the time you get to the flatlands of Coca at barely 100 meters above sea level. The more complex geography means that there are still some small areas that haven't been disturbed by colonists because they are hard to get to. Tourists also find that these areas are hard to reach!

Buses can usually reach Misahuallí in any weather, but extremely high or low water levels can disrupt river services. The 'dry' season – though it can still rain – is November and December. The wettest period is June to August.

If you want an excursion deep into the jungle, it can be arranged in Misahuallí. This will require time, patience, flexibility and money – but it is still less expensive than jungle expeditions in other countries. Excursions can also be arranged in Coca, Baños, Dureno, Tena and Quito. Finally, if you want a reasonable amount of comfort – or even luxury – look further down the river, but not in Misahuallí.

Information

Money For most trips, both sucres and cash US dollars are accepted. US dollar traveler's checks can sometimes be negotiated, but cash is better. There are no proper exchange facilities in Misahuallí, although locals may change small amounts of cash dollars.

Post & Communications There is no post office as such in Misahuallí, and mail takes months to arrive. Mail sent from Europe to Quito usually takes one to two weeks; from Quito to Misahuallí, one to two months. If you have the time, you can make postal inquiries and reservations with the guide of your choice by writing to Misahuallí, Provincia de Napo, Ecuador.

A few guides (see Jungle Tours, below) now have telephone or fax facilities. Long tours can be arranged in advance in Quito or Baños, or go to Misahuallí at the beginning of your stay in Ecuador and make the arrangements in advance.

Legal Matters Note that anyone heading downriver (on a tour or on public transport) is required to register their passport number at the port captain's office by the waterfront. You should be carrying your passport.

Tours & Guides

Jungle Tours The various restaurants in Misahuallí are good places to meet potential traveling companions for excursions, or to pick the brains of travelers returning from a trip. Any one of the several small restaurants on the plaza is a good place to start. Other places include Douglas Clarke's Restaurant Dayuma, just off the plaza, and the Hotel Albergue Español just beyond the Dayuma. El Paisano restaurant is also popular with travelers.

NORTH ORIENTE

It's a small village, so you'll be able to 'cruise' the likely places in a few minutes. If you want to see some of the river without taking a tour, you can take a passenger boat trip as far as Coca. These go several times a week.

Even if you don't usually enjoy organized tours, you should consider joining one if you want to see some of the jungle, particularly if this is your first visit. There are many guides available in Misahuallí, and they offer a variety of tours ranging from one to 10 days in duration. Usually you have to get a group together to make it economical.

Travelers pass through Misahuallí every day and it's a small place; if you're alone, you'll meet others very soon. Alternatively, get a group together in advance in Quito or Baños. Also, bear in mind that tourism is increasing in the Coca area, where tours may be a little cheaper than from Misahuallí, although there are fewer outfitters.

There are many outfitters and guides in Misahuallí. Make sure that whomever you choose gives you a good deal. Work the details out carefully beforehand to avoid confusion or disappointment. Common sense dictates making sure that costs, food, equipment, itinerary and group numbers are all discussed thoroughly before the tour.

The most important matter to settle is the guide; a good guide will be able to show you much you would have missed on your own, particularly if you convey your enthusiasm and interest by asking questions. An inadequate guide will spoil the trip. Guides should be able to produce a Tourist Guide license on request.

A common problem is that a group makes arrangements with an outfitter and then an inferior guide is supplied at the last moment. Many of the outfitters have been guilty of this to a greater or lesser extent, although it is a problem that appears to be diminishing since the last edition of this book. If you want a specific guide, you may have to wait until he or she is available.

Try to meet with your guide before you leave. Can you communicate adequately?

Has he or she done this before? Can they show you the *achiote* plant (whose red berries are crushed to make decorative body paints)? Can he or she find the vine which, when cut, provides water fit to drink? Can you go for a swim by a waterfall, go fishing from a dugout canoe, go birdwatching or do whatever it is you want? What will be cooked for dinner and breakfast? Will game be hunted for the pot? (The area is overhunted and a no-hunting policy is encouraged.) A few questions like these will soon tell you if you and the guide are going to have a good trip together. Most people have a great time, especially if they plan their excursion carefully.

Tours booked out of Misahuallí cost from US$20 to US$50 per person per day. Trips lasting several days need at least four, and in some cases six or eight, participants. Shop around carefully to get the tour you want at a price that you can afford. On the other hand, by saving yourself money you may find that the standard of guide service, environmental concern, care for the 'client' or quality of the food is other than what you would have liked.

Obviously, I am unable to take trips with all the local outfitters or I would never have time to see the rest of the country and write this book. I would appreciate travelers sending me recommendations and criticisms of guides so that I can include them in the next edition.

One tour provider that has been around for many years is *Douglas Clarke's Expediciones Dayuma*. They have a Quito office (☎ /fax 564 924) at 10 de Agosto 38-15 near Mariana de Jesús, Edificio Villacis Pasos, Office 301, though their tours are cheaper if arranged in Misahuallí, at Casilla 291, Tena, Provincia de Napo. In Misahuallí, Expediciones Dayuma (☎ 571 513) is a block from the plaza.

This outfit's costs are a bit higher than most of the other outfitters, but they'll arrange tours in advance and I have received generally favorable reports about them. Several of their guides speak some English (Douglas' English, despite his name, is limited – he's an Ecuadorian).

They do a simple one-day walk as an introduction to the jungle; various plant and insect species are pointed out, and a swim under a hidden waterfall can be included. They also do four- to eight-day trips, which include camping in their jungle camp, where all necessary equipment is provided. Some canoeing in dugouts as well as hiking is involved.

Other trips go to the Coca region where there is a greater chance of seeing wildlife. These trips can all be organized to leave from Quito.

Finally, they will organize a 10-day trip that takes you far down the Río Napo and back up the Río Aguarico, with a chance of seeing birdlife such as macaws, parrots, toucans and rarer bird species. Animals such as caymans, various monkey species and perhaps wild pigs, anteaters or – with a great deal of luck – a jungle cat are also sometimes seen. This trip must be arranged ahead of time. It is a rugged expedition and there is little comfort. It is not for the faint-hearted.

Note that similar expeditions are offered by some of the outfitters listed below and are often just as good – I don't want to keep repeating the same information. Recommended guides and outfitters include the following.

Fluvial River Tours
Héctor Fiallos (☎ 886 189, or 239 044 in Quito) runs this company (also called Sacha Tours); it has also been here for years. This is Expediciones Dayuma's main competitor, and they run similar tours at slightly lower prices. They have an office on the Misahuallí plaza. Fiallos himself is good, but he has used inferior guides in the past, mixed in with some good ones. This seems to be improving, according to recent reports, but check guides' licenses.

Crucero Fluvial Misahuallí
On the plaza, this agency is run by the cheerful and knowledgeable Carlos Lastra Lasso, who speaks some English. He used to work with Expediciones Dayuma in the early 1980s, then decided to start his own business. Lasso uses good guides who get along well with travelers. I enjoyed my trip with him several years ago.

Crucero Fluvial El Oriente
Also called Ecoselva, this outfit is run by English-speaking Pepe Tapia González, who has a biology background and is recommended. He is just off the plaza.

Ñuca Sacha Tours
This company (☎ 584 964; in Quito 355 590) is on the plaza and the owner, Domingo Andy, is a Quichua Indian and well recommended. The whole staff are Quichuas – none speak English.

Aventuras Amazónicas
Based in the Residencial La Posada on the plaza, this is the only outfit run by a woman, María del Carmen Santander. They do a good job.

Expediciones El Albergue Español
This outfit is based at the hotel of the same name. Several of their guides have been recommended.

Other Guides
All guides should produce a license on request. Recommended ones are Sócrates Nevárez, Alfredo Andrade, Luis Duarte, Billy Clarke (a woman), Marcos Estrada and Elias Arteaga. There are others – their signs are posted on the plaza.

Waterfall Walk This is a short trip offered by some guides as a one-day look at the local jungle. It is one you can do yourself quite easily. First, take a Misahuallí-Puerto Napo bus and ask the driver to leave you off at the Río Latas, about 15 or 20 minutes away from Misahuallí. All the drivers know *el camino a las cascadas* (the trail to the falls). Follow the river upstream to the falls, passing several swimming holes en route. Be prepared to wade. It takes about an hour to reach the falls, depending on how fast you walk. It's a nice place to swim and have a picnic.

Places to Stay & Eat
None of the accommodations in Misahuallí itself are expensive or particularly luxurious. Water and electricity failures are the rule rather than the exception in all these places. Although the cheapest places may look pretty rundown, don't let their appearance make you think they are dangerous. They aren't – they are just cheap, beat-up jungle hotels.

NORTH ORIENTE

Shopping for Jungle Trips
There is a limited amount of equipment available in Misahuallí. Essential items to bring are insect repellent, water-purifying tablets and sun lotion. Sheets of plastic and tarpaulins, which make reasonable rain ponchos, can be bought in Misahuallí. Rubber boots in small and medium sizes and blankets are also available. ■

On the plaza you'll find the *Residencial El Balcón de Napo,* which has small concrete-block rooms, some of which look like jail cells. The rooms with windows are OK. The residencial is fairly clean by jungle standards, though their showers are a bit grungy. They charge just under US$2 per person, making the Balcón de Napo the area's cheapest place to stay. The rambling, old *Residencial La Posada,* nearby, charges about US$2.25 per person and has a hodge-podge arrangement of creaky wooden rooms and somewhat dubious bathroom facilities. There are several others on the plaza that cost around US$2.50 per person; of these, the basic but adequate *Pensión 50* is as good as any. They also have a simple vegetarian restaurant. Other cheap restaurants are found on the plaza, of which the *Abuela* has been recommended for pizza and other meals.

El Paisano hotel and restaurant is popular with travelers. It is 100 meters from the plaza on the road past the military post and is well known. Clean, basic rooms are US$3.50 per person or US$9 for a double with private bath. There is a pleasant garden with hammocks, and the open-air restaurant specializes in vegetarian dishes. This is one of the best vegetarian choices in town.

Half a block from the plaza is Douglas Clarke's *Hostal Dayuma Lodge,* behind the restaurant of the same name. The restaurant is one of the better ones in town. The lodge used to charge about US$6 per person in rooms with private bath, but is being newly renovated so prices are slated to increase two or three times. A pool and rooms with balconies are planned which will make this the most upscale hotel in Misahuallí itself. They are also building a new restaurant on the roof of the hotel – rooftop dining will

probably cost more, but the views may make it worthwhile.

The Spanish-run *Hotel Albergue Español* (☎ /fax 584 912) is about US$20 for a double with private bath – water is heated by solar energy. There is jazz music played in the dining room, which is perhaps the town's best restaurant. There are laundry facilities. The management is helpful, and the hotel is popular and has been recommended by several readers. It is about 200 meters off the plaza past the Dayuma Lodge.

The *Misahuallí Jungle Lodge* is across the Río Misahuallí on the north side of the Río Napo. Reservations can be arranged through their office in Quito (☎ 520 043, fax 454 146), Ramírez Dávalos 251 and Páez. It's a comfortable lodge with nice cabins, electricity, private baths and hot water, and a number of trails. Guides are available. Rates are about US$60 a day in Quito, but if you just show up you can get rooms with meals for half that if they aren't busy.

There are various other lodges downriver from Misahuallí. They are described later in this chapter.

Entertainment
Nightlife is rather limited. There is one video movie theater. Otherwise, there are restaurant/bars to hang out with locals and other travelers, and usually a disco happening somewhere on weekends.

Getting There & Away
Bus Buses leave from the plaza at least every half hour during daylight hours. The main destination is Tena, where you can make connections to other places. The ride costs US$0.50 and takes about one hour. Buses to Ahuano may be available, though

most people take a Tena bus and change at Puerto Napo.

Boat Motorized dugout canoes leave from the port for various destinations downriver. The port is a block away from the plaza. Since the opening of the Tena-Coca road and the construction of roads east along the Río Napo, river traffic has dwindled. It is still possible, however, to travel downriver by occasional public canoes or by private charters. You are required to register with the port captain if heading downriver.

A passenger boat leaves most mornings for the villages or settlements of (in geographical order) Ahuano, Anaconda Island, Hotel Jaguar, Santa Rosa and Bellavista. This last village is about halfway to Coca. Ahuano is near several tourist lodges and the fare there is about US$2.50 if you go on a regular passenger boat. A charter is about US$30 or US$40.

Once or twice a week, a boat departs for Coca if there is enough passenger demand. The fare is around US$20 per person with an eight-person minimum (Ecuadorians travel for less). If there are fewer people, the fare is about US$160 (bargain hard) divided among the passengers and you can leave any day. Rates change (usually upward) so ask around about what the going rate is. The journey to Coca takes about six hours if the river is running normally.

Note that buses now go from Tena to both Ahuano and Coca and most of the locals go by bus because it is cheaper and more reliable. There are locals who want to travel by river because they need to be dropped off at remote settlements that aren't easily reached by road, but boats for Coca are often full of gringos wanting the experience of traveling by river.

The front seats of the boats to Coca give better forward views but are the narrowest; the middle seats are wider and are more comfortable; and the back seats are closest to the noise and fumes of the engine. Read the section on traveling by dugout canoe in the Getting Around chapter for further information.

Even on the second half of the trip down to Coca you won't see much wildlife, as the area is heavily colonized. Little houses on stilts huddle on the bank, prospectors pan for gold by the river's edge, and colonists wave and whistle for a ride. Impossibly tiny dugout canoes, loaded to the gunwales with an Indian family perched on a pile of bananas, are steadily and gracefully poled upriver. A sudden rain shower forces passengers to hurriedly dig out sheets of plastic but can enhance the beauty of the river. The jungle glows green in the late afternoon sun, and a few pure white clouds suspended in a perfectly blue sky contrast dramatically with the muddy flowing river. The scenery is worth the discomfort.

JATUN SACHA

This is a biological station and rainforest reserve on the south side of the Río Napo, roughly midway between Misahuallí and Ahuano (described below). It is run by the Fundación Jatun Sacha (☎ /fax 250 976, 441 592, 253 266, see also Online Services), Río Coca 1734, Casilla 17-12-897, Quito, a nonprofit Ecuadorian organization founded in 1985 with the goals of promoting rainforest research, conservation and education. The foundation also operates the Reserva Biológica Bilsa in the Western lowlands and the Reserva Biológica Guandera in the Andes north of Quito. Both are described in the appropriate chapters of the book.

At Jatun Sacha scientists are currently carrying out surveys of what species are present. This may appear to be a simple task, but it is complicated by the fact that the Jatun Sacha area is one of the most species-rich regions on earth. Some of the plants and animals found here are unknown to science – exciting stuff. Herpetologists (scientists who study reptiles) claim that there are more different species of 'herps' here than almost anywhere on the globe. Botanists echo this with flowering plants. The preserve covers about 1300 hectares, most of it virgin rainforest. There are several kilometers of trails. Jatun Sacha means 'big forest' in the Quichua language.

Visiting the Huaorani – Ecotourism or Exploitation?

Trips are sometimes offered in Misahuallí or Coca to visit the villages of 'primitive' Huaorani (Auca) Indians, two or three days' walk into the jungle.

I feel strongly that these kind of tours are not to be encouraged. The guides are rarely sensitive to the needs of the Indians, who are undergoing the painful process of integration into 20th-century life. Many guides are just inexperienced local youngsters trying to make a living, and through simple ignorance or sheer bravado the Indians are treated in a degrading or abusive manner.

As often as twice a week, groups of tourists are taken to gawk at 'real' Indians in the 'real' jungle. The Indians stare miserably and with little interest at the frequent hordes of tourists and the parade of goods that to us seems basic: backpacks, not one but two pairs of shoes and a change of clothing, sleeping bag, rain gear, sunglasses, cameras, penknives, cigarette lighters, plastic water bottles, canned food and so on.

The tourists expect and demand the basic necessities of water and a place to sleep, while the Indians' experience is ignored and little is given in return. I recently read an open letter to the public from Moi Vicente Enomenga, the coordinator of the first Huaorani National Assembly held in 1990. In his letter Enomenga writes:

> We don't want to see tour guides or tourists because they bring diseases that the Huaorani can't cure; tour guides and tourists enter our houses when we are working in the fields, they hunt and fish for the food we need, they leave garbage. Tourists are paying US$20 to $30 per day for this and we are being exploited and receive nothing. Therefore we resist tourism and want the tours to leave us alone. If necessary, we will oppose tourism with our spears.

If you want to see the Indians, it is best to wait until they come to you. A few of the more adventurous and acculturated Huaoranis usually come to trade in Misahuallí or Coca, where you can see them and they, in turn, can see you in an unstrained and uncompromising atmosphere.

Although most Huaorani villages don't want to see tourists, in the last few years some villages have made arrangements with particular guides whom they trust. A good source of information about this is Randy Smith (☎ 880 606, 880 451), a Canadian who has several years of experience living and working with the Huaorani and is an advocate for them. Randy works with Amazon Jungle Adventures in Coca. This company employs Huaorani staff with the support of the tribe. Safari Tours in Quito can put you in contact with this outfit or you can ask at Pappa Dan's restaurant in Coca.

Other guides who have positive relationships with the Huaorani are Ernesto Juanka at Pankitour Alternativo (☎ /fax 880 405), 6 de Diciembre and García Moreno in Coca; Julio Jarrín (☎ 880 251) of Ejarsytur opposite the Hotel Oasis in Coca; and Juan Enomenga – ask for him on the Coca waterfront. They don't speak English. ∎

Unfortunately, neighboring areas are being rapidly cleared for logging and agriculture, and it is not known how long the incredible biodiversity of Jatun Sacha will remain intact. One of the goals of the Foundation, however, is the furthering of rural development projects, which will help residents engage in economically viable and sustainable activities as an alternative to deforestation. Training and providing facilities for Ecuadorian students and researchers as well as visiting international scientists are

also an important goal. Volunteers are welcome to apply for a variety of projects – the minimum stay is usually a month. The reserve has recently expanded in size from an original 300 hectares, and a final total of about 4500 hectares is hoped for.

Jatun Sacha is one of the longest-standing and best local conservation and environmental projects in Ecuador. Tax-deductible (for US citizens) donations can be made to Los Amigos de Jatun Sacha, 540 Sussex Drive, Janesville, WI 53546, USA.

Places to Stay & Eat

At the *research station* itself there are four unscreened buildings that sleep about two dozen people. Accommodations are primitive – bunk beds, outdoor showers and latrines. You need insect repellent or mosquito nets, plus a sleeping bag or blankets – the beds only have a bare mattress. A dining room and meals are available. Researchers, students and tourists (the last on a space-available basis as the station is often full with the former) can stay here for US$20 a day, including meals and access to the reserve trail system. Volunteers stay here at a very modest cost – about US$6 a day including food.

Most tourists stay at the *Cabañas Aliñahui* (also called the Butterfly Lodge), which is owned and operated by the Fundación Jatun Sacha in partnership with Health & Habitat, a nonprofit organization from California. Aliñahui is about three km east of the research station. There are about 10 simple but comfortable screened cabins with electricity (solar panels), most of which have two double rooms sharing one bathroom with a solar-heated shower.

Each cabin has a shady patio with a hammock. There is a good open-sided restaurant, bar and gift shop. The site is on a bluff above the river and there are several thatched shelters with excellent views of the river and, on clear days, four of the Andean volcanoes (hence the name Aliñahui, which means 'good view' in Quichua). These shelters are great places to relax in. A variety of jungle hikes and boat trips can be arranged to the Jatun Sacha reserve, to visit those local villages that do have ecotourism programs, or to try your hand at gold panning. Some of the staff and guides speak English, German or French. The food is plentiful, homemade and good. Several readers have recommended this place as one of Ecuador's best environmentally conscious lodges.

Rates are US$62 per person per day including three meals or US$71 per day with guided tours. Multi-day packages can also be arranged. Reservations can be made at Fundación Jatun Sacha (see above) for both the research station and Aliñahui, or c/o Missouri Botanical Gardens, PO Box 299, St Louis, MO 63166-0299, USA (☎ (314) 577 5100) for the research station only, or at Health & Habitat (☎ (415) 383 6130, fax 381 9214), 76 Lee St, Mill Valley, CA 94941, USA.

Getting There & Away

Boat Motor canoes can be hired from Misahuallí for the approximately 10 km downriver trip to Aliñahui or the reserve. Most visitors come by land.

Bus Jatun Sacha can help arrange transportation from Quito if your group takes one of their multi-day tours. Otherwise, the best way is to go to Tena and take the Tena-Ahuano bus. Jatun Sacha is about 21 km east of Puerto Napo or seven km before you reach Ahuano.

AHUANO

This small mission village is about one hour downriver from Misahuallí and can also be reached by bus from Tena. This is the end of the road – beyond Ahuano you must travel by boat on the Río Napo as far as Coca, where you can rejoin the road again. There is not much to do in Ahuano itself, though there are some nearby jungle lodges.

On a tributary of the Río Napo about two or three km east of Ahuano, is the

Poison-arrow frogs, such as this (*Phyllobates spp*), have colorful markings to warn predators not to eat them.

AmaZOOnico (fax 887 304), founded in 1994 by Remigio Canelos and Angelika Raimann (a Quichua/Swiss couple). This is a rehabilitation center for rainforest animals that have been confiscated from illegal traffickers or otherwise injured. Animals are cared for and then released back into the rainforest. There are dozens of animals on the premises at any time, ranging from toucans to tapirs. The center is run on a bare-bones budget, and donations and volunteers (with veterinary skills for several months) are welcomed. More information is available by writing to Apartado 202, Tena, Provincia de Napo, Ecuador. The center is reached by a 15-minute boat ride from the Ahuano dock (about US$20 for a half day, split between the passengers, and allowing the boatman to wait for you and then bring you back). Admission to the center is about US$1 per visitor.

Places to Stay

In the village itself, there is a basic pensión (no sign) run by a friendly woman with who charges about US$3.50 per person. Ask in the village.

Near AmaZOOnico and run by the same people is the new *Cabañas Runa Huasi*. Simple rooms are US$8 per person, and basic meals are available. They have local guides that are registered with FOIN (see Tena for details).

On the outskirts of Ahuano is the comfortable *Casa del Suizo*, a jungle lodge that has recently been expanded to accommodate up to 150 guests. The cabins and rooms are very pleasant, with private showers, hot water, electricity and all modern comforts. There is a pool and a good restaurant and bar, all in a pleasant location by the river. The place is clean, comfortable and has been recommended by travelers who want just a taste of the rainforest without discomfort, although some folks may find it a bit tame. There is a variety of tours available including river trips, jungle hikes, visits to missions and local communities, and wildlife walks, after which you can return to the comfort of the lodge. Rates depend on group size and services requested, but average about US$75 per person including meals. Drop-in guests can probably get a better price, but aren't guaranteed a bed.

The *Cabañas Anaconda* (☎ /fax in Quito 545 426) is on Anaconda Island, about an hour from Misahuallí and just a few minutes from Ahuano. This is a fairly comfortable jungle-style lodge (bamboo walls and thatched roofs), but there is no electricity or hot water. Rooms come with private bathrooms and mosquito screens, and the meals (included in the price) are good. They charge about US$45 per person per day, including meals, and transportation from Quito is available (though pricey). Canoe trips and jungle excursions from the island are available at extra cost; guides don't speak English unless requested in advance. You'll see pet animals such as monkeys and peccaries.

Getting There & Away

Bus Buses from Tena run several times a day to Ahuano, which is about 28 km east of Puerto Napo. If you are driving, note that the road to Ahuano is on the south side of the Río Napo from Puerto Napo; the road on the north side of the river goes to Misahuallí; the roads are dirt. The bus can drop you off at the entrance to the Cabañas Aliñahui, just a one-km walk to the cabins themselves. The bus goes as far as La Punta, on the south side of the Río Napo. From here, you have to cross to the north side of the river by boat to get to Ahuano and the other jungle lodges. Even though the bus doesn't actually go to Ahuano, it's still called the Ahuano bus locally because there isn't much happening at La Punta. There is little problem crossing the Río Napo from La Punta to Ahuano.

Boat Dugout canoes wait at La Punta to take you across to Ahuano. The fare is about US$1 or less per person and there are frequent boats, particularly after a bus arrives. Chartering your own boat costs more. These boats can drop you off at La Casa del Suizo. Boats to the Hotel Anaconda and AmaZOOnico can also be arranged but are more expensive.

You can also get to Ahuano or any of the lodges by boat from Misahuallí. For more information, see under Misahuallí. Most people go via bus to La Punta because it's a more frequent and cheaper service.

TO COCA ON THE RÍO NAPO

There are two more lodges on the Río Napo between Ahuano and Coca but travelers must reach them by boat. Whereas the lodges around Ahuano accept drop-in visitors, most of the guests beyond Ahuano arrive on prearranged tours that take care of the boat transportation (and ensure that there is enough food and staff for the group). Most visitors arrive by boat from Misahuallí, where there are more boats than in Ahuano.

The *Hotel Jaguar* (☎ in Quito 239 400, 230 552, 564 565, fax 502 682), with an office in Quito at L Cordero 1313 and JL Mera, is about 1½ hours from Misahuallí. This is a comfortable, modern hotel on the banks of the Río Napo and, because it is beyond the road, the surrounding rainforest has been less impacted than the previous lodges. There are about a dozen rooms with private bath (hot water and electricity are available when the generator is running) and an attractive main lodge with good views and a decent restaurant and bar. Spanish-speaking guides are available for a variety of guided tours. Rates are about US$30 to US$80 a day, depending on the size of the group, services needed and number of days you stay.

A new cabaña complex called the *Yachana Lodge* has been built in the tiny community of Mondaña, almost halfway between Misahuallí and Coca on the Río Napo. The lodge is a project of the nonprofit Fundación para la Educación y Desarrollo de las Nacionalidades Indígenas (FUNEDESIN, ☎ 541 862, 543 851, fax 220 362, see also Online Services), Andrade Marín 188 and Diego de Almagro, Casilla 17-17-92, Quito. The lodge opened in 1995, and proceeds will be used to help fund FUNEDESIN's education and development program for local Indian groups. Beekeeping and organic farming are two of the programs taught to local people, while learning about medicinal plants is a sort of reciprocal education for tourists. A program for foreign students who want to learn about the rainforest is being developed – contact FUNEDESIN for information.

When it opened, Yachana Lodge had eight double rooms with shared bathrooms, but this may well expand. A balcony with hammocks, a dining room, a meeting room and river views complete the picture. Rates are US$40 with meals, and there are discounts for long stays or students.

COCA

All Ecuadorian maps show this town's official name, Puerto Francisco de Orellana, but I've never heard of it referred to by any name other than Coca. It is located at the junction of the Río Napo and the Río Coca (hence its popular name). Its official name derives from the fact that Francisco de Orellana came through here on his way to 'discover' the Amazon in 1542.

The Río Napo is Ecuador's major tributary into the Amazon. Indeed, it is at the point where Ecuador's Río Napo and Peru's Río Marañon meet that the Amazon continues as a single river.

The Coca of today is a sprawling oil town with little to recommend it. There are no street signs, and every road is unpaved and hence covered with dust, puddles or mud, depending on the season. People say that to 'alleviate' this inconvenience, the roads are sometimes slicked down with oil. Most of the buildings are just shacks, and the place has a real shanty-town appearance – they don't even have a town plaza. There's not much to do apart from drink beer or go to bed. The population is about 25,000 (1996 estimate) and growing, and Coca can be expected to improve in the future. A local tourist industry is developing because Coca is closer to primary rainforest than Misahuallí. Coca itself may not be especially attractive, but it is the haunt of oil workers and tourists looking for expeditions further into the jungle.

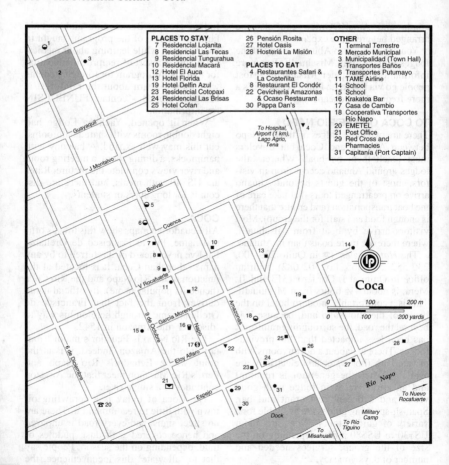

PLACES TO STAY
7 Residencial Lojanita
8 Residencial Las Tecas
9 Residencial Tungurahua
10 Residencial Macará
12 Hotel El Auca
13 Hotel Florida
19 Hotel Delfin Azul
23 Residencial Cotopaxi
24 Residencial Las Brisas
25 Hotel Cofan

26 Pensión Rosita
27 Hotel Oasis
28 Hostería La Misión

PLACES TO EAT
4 Restaurantes Safari &
   La Costeñita
8 Restaurant El Condór
22 Cevichería Amazonas
   & Ocaso Restaurant
30 Pappa Dan's

OTHER
1 Terminal Terrestre
2 Mercado Municipal
3 Municipalidad (Town Hall)
5 Transportes Baños
6 Transportes Putumayo
11 TAME Airline
14 School
15 School
16 Krakatoa Bar
17 Casa de Cambio
18 Cooperativa Transportes
   Río Napo
20 EMETEL
21 Post Office
29 Red Cross and
   Pharmacies
31 Capitanía (Port Captain)

To Hospital,
Airport (1 km),
Lago Agrio,
Tena

Guayaquil
J Montalvo
Bolívar
Cuenca
V Rocafuerte
García Moreno
9 de Octubre
6 de Diciembre
Eloy Alfaro
Espejo
Amazonas
Napo

Coca

0   100   200 m
0   100   200 yards

Río Napo

To Nuevo
Rocafuerte

Military
Camp

To Río
Tiguino

Dock

To
Misahuallí

Information

There is no official CETUR office, although a tourist information office is intermittently open at the dock on the Río Napo. The EMETEL office, unlike most of Ecuador, is open only from 8 to 11 am, 1 to 5 pm, and 6 to 9 pm Monday to Saturday. On Sunday it is open during the morning and evening hours only. The area code for Coca (which is in the Province of Napo) is 06. There is a post office, but service is very slow. A casa de cambio (see map) changes money, but I couldn't find a bank that would. This may change in the future,

but your best bet is still to bring plenty of sucres with you.

All travelers arriving and departing by river must register with the port captain at the Capitanía by the landing dock. I was treated extremely courteously here.

Jungle Tours

Read the section on Jungle Tours under Misahuallí for general information, which is also useful for tours out of Coca. A growing number of guides are leaving Misahuallí to work out of Coca, where there is less competition. Some of the guides listed under Misahuallí may well have moved to Coca by the time you read this.

Coca is closer to the Huaorani (Auca) Indian villages than any major town in the Oriente, and tours are available to visit these villages. These have a negative impact on the Indians, who themselves prefer to be left alone in most cases – I do not recommend any tour that involves visits to the Huaorani unless the guides have been approved by the tribe (see the Visiting the Huaorani sidebar).

Guides charge around US$30 per person per day and group sizes are usually four to six people. Smaller groups have to pay more per person. It is easier to find people to make up a group in Quito or Misahuallí than it is in Coca. Trips are usually from three to 10 days. You may have to bargain to get the best rate, but make sure everything you expect to be included is.

Guides who have been recommended for travel outside of Huaorani territory include Whymper Torres of Selva Tour (☎ 880 336). He is entertaining, but I've also read that he hunts for tourists' meals and catches animals for photo opportunities – activities that should not be encouraged. Also try Braulio Llori of Multitravel (☎ 880 166) who speaks some English and has an office near the Hotel Auca, or César Andy, a Quichua, who has an office out beyond the Hostería La Misión.

Places to Stay – bottom end

Hotels in Coca sometimes suffer from water shortages in the showers and lavatories. The *Hotel El Auca* (☎ 880 127, 880 600, in Quito ☎ /fax 240 392, 435 399) is popular and often full by mid-afternoon. It isn't bad for US$10 a double (shared showers) or in cabins for US$10/18 (or nicer new cabins for US$12.50/22) with bath and cold water. They have the nicest garden in Coca and an acceptable restaurant. This is the best budget choice, but there are cheaper places.

The *Lojanita, Las Tecas* and *Tungurahua* are three very basic residenciales on the block northeast from the Auca. They charge US$2.50 to US$3.50 per person,

are popular with oil workers and are not recommended for women traveling alone. The similarly priced *Pensión Rosita* (☎ 880 167) is one of the hotels nearest to the port and is often crowded and noisy. It has variously been described (by readers who have stayed there) as musty, dirty and barely habitable and is also a poor choice for single women. Other cheapies are the *Residencial Macará, Hotel Cofan* and the *Residencial Las Brisas*.

A better budget place is the *Residencial Cotopaxi* at US$4.50 per person with bath. The *Hotel Oasis* (☎ 880 174) costs US$10 per double with bath and fan. Because of its quieter location on the river, some people prefer it to the noisier El Auca in the center, though the rooms are less attractive. The similarly priced *Hotel Florida* (☎ 880 177) is in a horribly ugly building (concrete blocks looking like a jail) but is OK. Another decent choice at this price is the *Hotel Delfín Azul*.

Places to Stay – middle

The *Hostería La Misión* (☎ 880 260, 880 544, 880 261, fax 880 547) on the riverfront is the best hotel at US$16/20 for rooms with fan or US$25/30 with air-conditioning. All rooms have a mini-fridge and private baths with hot water. There is a good, slightly pricey restaurant (American breakfast US$4, set lunch US$7) and bar. There is also a pool with a waterslide and river views.

Places to Eat & Drink

The restaurants at the hotels *La Misión* and *El Auca* are considered the best in town. Locals recommend the *Cevichería Amazonas* and *Ocaso Restaurant* as the best places to eat outside the hotels. They are conveniently next to one another so you can look them over and make your choice. Most visitors go for the Ocaso because it has air-conditioning.

The *Restaurant Safari* and *Restaurant La Costeñita* are cheaper choices and quite good, too. The basic *Restaurant El Condór* serves roast chicken (not condors).

Pappa Dan's opens at 4 pm and is a recommended US-run bar/restaurant. They are clean and serve salads, burgers and similar food that goes well with a cold beer. This is the best and safest place for drinking at night and a good spot to get local information and make contacts.

Another good place to enjoy a cold drink is the *Krakatoa Bar*, on Napo, which has a shaded porch outside. As is true of all bars in Coca, unaccompanied females may receive unwanted attention.

Getting There & Around

Air TAME offers regular service from and to Quito. There are two flights a day from Quito on most days except Wednesday (one flight) and Sunday (no service). Flights leave Quito between 8:30 am and 1 pm, depending on the day, and return from Coca to Quito 45 minutes later. Tickets cost about US$46 and are available from the TAME office opposite the Hotel El Auca. Tickets can be bought in Quito but TAME will only confirm reservations from Coca in Coca. If you are on a tour or staying at a lodge that provided you with the ticket, they will reconfirm your return flight from Coca to Quito for you.

Independent travelers should confirm as far in advance as possible and reconfirm their flight the day before, if possible. Flights are not always full, however, and you can sometimes buy tickets at the airport before the flight if the TAME office is closed when you arrive. Even if there are seats available, TAME office personnel are often reluctant to sell seats until the very last minute – hang around the TAME office looking forlorn until they relent.

FAE (the air force) has cheap flights to Nuevo Rocafuerte, Tena and Shell on Monday and Wednesday. Ask about these at the airport control tower. These flights are usually full and Ecuadorians get priority. You might get lucky, but don't count on it.

The airport is almost two km north of town on the left-hand side of the road to Lago Agrio.

Bus A new terminal terrestre is at the north end of town, but some buses still leave from offices in the town center. The situation is changeable, so make careful inquiry about the departure point of your bus.

Transportes Baños has several daily buses to Quito (US$10; about nine hours via Loreto, 14 hours via Lago Agrio) and an overnight bus to both Ambato and Santo Domingo. Transportes Turismo Jumandy in the terminal terrestre has several buses a day on the new road to Tena (US$6; six hours). Both companies have buses to Lago Agrio (US$2; three hours). Transportes Putumayo has buses to Quito via Loreto. Flota Pelileo has a nightly bus to Ambato.

Open-sided trucks called *rancheras* leave from the market for various destinations between Coca and Lago Agrio, and to Río Tiputini to the south. Pickup trucks parked at Cooperativa Transportes Río Napo provide service to just about anywhere you want to pay to go.

Boat Since the completion of the new Tena-Coca road, it is difficult to get boats to Misahuallí. Usually at least 10 passengers are required and the trip takes about 14 hours, so you are advised to take the trip in the opposite direction, from Misahuallí to Coca, which takes only six hours. The upriver trip is sometimes broken, and passengers camp out by the river – be prepared. The boat fare is about US$20 and so the bus (to Tena and change) is much cheaper and quicker.

The Capitanía may be able to give you information about getting a boat further downriver. Destinations of interest downriver include the Hacienda Primavera, Pompeya, Limoncocha, Sacha Lodge, La Selva Jungle Lodge, Pañacocha, Yuturi Lodge and Nuevo Rocafuerte on the Peruvian border, about 12 hours away from Coca (all these places are described later in this chapter).

Boat services to these destinations are irregular, infrequent and comparatively expensive. A weekly passenger boat leaves Coca for Nuevo Rocafuerte on Monday morning, returning on Friday. The fare is US$25. Otherwise, you have to hire your own boat, which is expensive. Note that a military permit is required for travel to Nuevo Rocafuerte.

HACIENDA PRIMAVERA

This small lodge is a one-hour trip downriver from Coca on the Río Napo. There are pleasant walks and lakes in the nearby jungle. The hotel and surrounding jungle have been recommended by travelers on a budget (rates are about US$20 for a double room), though I have never been there. I have, however, received an unconfirmed report indicating that this lodge closed indefinitely in 1996. Information is available in Quito (☎ 565 999, fax 525 774), José Trevinio 114 and 12 de Octubre.

Provided they are open, the main problem with this place (and others further downriver) is getting there. Transport can be arranged in advance in Quito, but it is more difficult to arrange for the independent traveler already in the Oriente. The Monday boat from Coca to Nuevo Rocafuerte may take you if there is room (they prefer long-distance passengers). Other boats leave at irregular intervals.

It costs US$30 to hire your own boat from Coca, but they can take several passengers for that price. Returning to Coca is more of a problem – either you have to rent your own boat or you may have to wait days for a passing passenger boat. Be prepared with either extra time or money.

POMPEYA & LIMONCOCHA AREA

Pompeya is a Catholic mission about two hours downriver from Coca on the Río Napo. There is a school and small archaeology museum here, and basic food and lodging can be arranged. The museum reputedly has the best collection of indigenous artifacts from the Río Napo area and has pre-Columbian ceramics on display. A small admission fee is charged. Some archaeologists believe that before the arrival of Europeans the indigenous population of the Río Napo (and other parts of the Amazon Basin) was many times greater than it is today.

Opposite Pompeya is **Monkey Island**, which can be reached by canoe in a few minutes. The troops of monkeys living on this island used to be spotted relatively frequently, though a recent report claims that they haven't been seen recently, so you should inquire before going there.

From Pompeya you can walk eight km north on a new road to the ex-North American mission of Limoncocha where there is a basic place to stay (US$2.50 per person) and eat. Nearby, the locally run **Limoncocha Biological Reserve** has a lake recommended for birdwatching at dawn and dusk. Oil company operations jeopardized the lake and the birds in the 1980s and early 1990s. However, the creation of the reserve lead to an improvement of the oil company operations, and the birds are reportedly recovering in numbers. There is a rustic lodge here with about a dozen rooms, each with four beds and a cold shower. Food is available, and local guides can take you around the lake, although they do not speak English.

No Keys in the Jungle

Many of the remoter lodges in the Oriente have a 'no key' policy. This means that none of the rooms has a lock and key. The idea is that you are so far away from civilization that there is no reason to worry about theft. The lodge employees are completely trustworthy (and even if they weren't, they'd have keys to your room, anyway!). Generally speaking, this relaxed policy works just fine but, once in a while, something valuable disappears. It is easy to get lulled into a sense of false security by the laid-back attitude in these lodges. Even if you can't lock the room, don't leave your valuables lying around in plain sight – it is simply tempting fate too much. I usually keep my camera and binoculars around my neck, but if I leave them in my room after dark, I put them in my locked duffle bag to deter light fingers. I have never had a problem with a 'no key' policy, but I have heard stories of occasional losses. ■

A visit costs US$16 per person (including meals). Reservations can be made at Asociación Indígena de Limoncocha, c/o CONFENIAE (☎ 220 326, fax 543 973), 6 de Diciembre 159, Quito.

South of the Pompeya area is the Río Tiputini, and south of this river is the **Reserva Huaorani**, where thousands of Huaorani people hunt and gather in a traditional manner. Access for non-Huaorani is limited, although oil companies seem to be able to get around this. The reserve acts as a buffer zone for the nearby Parque Nacional Yasuní, further east, which is largely uninhabited.

To get to Pompeya, take a boat from Coca (see under Hacienda Primavera for more information). Limoncocha can also be reached by bus (several a day) from the oil town of **Shushufindi**, a two- or three-hour trip from either Coca or Lago Agrio. Among several basic places to stay, the most reputable seems to be the *Hotel Shushufundi*. A local guide charmingly describes the town as having 40 prostitutes and no medical doctors. The police in this area are said to be particularly corrupt and, at a passport checkpoint on this road, have been known to steal valuables. Keep alert. One daily bus from Shushufindi to Limoncocha continues to Pompeya.

SACHA LODGE

Opened in 1992, this Swiss-run lodge now has an enviable reputation as being one of the two best rainforest lodges in the country, competing with the older and more established La Selva Jungle Lodge (see below). Several readers have praised this place enthusiastically.

The lodge is built on the banks of the Laguna El Pilche, a lake about one km north of the Río Napo. Getting there is half the fun – a three-hour ride in a fast motor-canoe from Coca is followed by a walk through the forest on an elevated boardwalk, and then a 15-minute paddle in a dugout canoe to the lodge.

The main building is three stories high and has a little observation deck at the top. This is where you'll find the restaurant, bar and small library. It is linked by boardwalks to seven cabins, each with two rooms. Each room has a private bath and hot water (a rarity in this neck of the woods) as well as a deck and hammock with fine forest views. All rooms are screened (though mosquitoes seem not to be a problem), and a generator provides electricity from 6 am until 10 pm. Buffet-style meals are plentiful and delicious, and both vegetarians and meat-eaters are well catered to.

Activities available from the lodge include hiking, canoeing and swimming. Hikes and canoe trips are made in small groups, typically consisting of about five tourists and two guides. One guide is a local and the other is usually North American or British (French- and German-speaking guides are usually available, especially if requested in advance). A fine network of trails ensures that you get to explore different places every day. Trails vary in length, and destinations include flat rainforest, hilly rainforest and various lakes, rivers and swamps, which each have different types of flora and fauna. A 35-meter-high observation deck atop a huge ceiba tree (reached by stairs built around the tree trunk) is a few minutes walk away from the main lodge. A second tower for birding is under construction and should be open in 1997. A new butterfly farm has recently opened. Special interests such as birdwatching, photography, plants or fishing can be easily accommodated, and a birding list is available. Tours to Indian villages are not arranged because the locals simply don't want them.

Most guests come on a four-day/three-night or five-day/four-night package – the first is Friday-Monday and the second is Monday-Friday. Once you arrive, you won't be disturbed by a new influx of guests until it's time to leave. On your arrival day, you arrive early enough for a short afternoon hike, but on your departure day you leave before dawn. High-season rates are US$683/1050 on the former program, or US$853/1312 for the latter. The two can be combined for a seven-night/eight-day program for US$1430/2200.

These rates are for advance reservations, but last-minute walk-in travelers can get a discount at the Quito office on a space-available basis. You can arrange to be met at the Coca airport.

Reservations should be made with Explorer Tours (☎ 509 115, 522 220, 508 871, fax 508 872), Reina Victoria 1235 and L García, Apartado 1608, Quito.

LA SELVA JUNGLE LODGE

This is the most expensive but also the most celebrated and well-run jungle lodge in Ecuador. If you can afford it, you'll enjoy it. I have heard reports ranging from positive to raving – no negative reports have been received.

The lodge is run by a North American-Ecuadorian couple, Eric and Magdalena Schwartz, who are interested both in providing a first-class ecotourism experience and in responsible tourism. They hire as many local people as possible, offer excursions into the rainforest with informed and interested guides, incorporate local food into their cuisine and avoid annoying visits to the unacculturated Indians living in the vicinity. In 1992, the lodge won the World Congress on Tourism and the Environment award – one of the highest ecotourism awards available.

Accommodations are in 16 double cabins, each with private cold-water bath and mosquito screens. Lighting is by kerosene lanterns, which avoids the noise of a generator outside your bedroom window. This place is therefore more rustic than the nearby Sacha Lodge, which may be the deciding factor for many people who are trying to choose between the two. Personally, I like rustic, but have no quibbles with people wanting a warm shower. Meals are excellent by any standards, and absolutely outstanding for Oriente standards.

There is also a small research facility where scientists and students can work on their projects. Discounted accommodations are available for researchers if arranged well in advance – often, researchers pay off part of their expenses by giving guided jungle excursions to interested visitors.

One project that has been successful is the breeding of butterflies in a 'butterfly farm' near the lodge. Visitors are able to see this operation, which affords excellent opportunities to photograph rainforest butterflies as well as learn about their life cycles.

Excursions are both by dugout canoe and on foot along several kilometers of trails. There is a 35-meter-high canopy platform about 20 minutes' walk from the lodge. Birdwatching is a highlight – over 500 species have been recorded in the La Selva area, including the rare zigzag heron, which birdwatchers from all over the world come to see. About half of Ecuador's 44 species of parrots have been recorded near here, as well as a host of other exotic tropical birds: toucans and trogons, jacamars and tanagers, antbirds and fruitcrows, just to name a few. Monkeys are frequently seen, and other mammals are occasionally sighted. Of course, there are tens of thousands of species of plants and insects.

Small groups of tourists are accompanied by a local indigenous guide and an English-speaking guide (often North American or European). Although the indigenous guides speak no English, my guide had a remarkable 500-word English vocabulary consisting of 'OK' and the names, in English, of all the birds that are seen near the lodge. Our conversations were never very long – 'Zigzag heron, OK?' 'OK!!' was about the extent of one – but I certainly got a lot out of the experience.

The lodge is five to six hours downriver from Coca by regular passenger canoe, but visitors usually pay for a complete package from Quito. This includes air transport to Coca and river transportation in La Selva's private launches, which go twice as fast as the ordinary passenger boats. The lodge is on Laguna Garzacocha, reached by a one-km boardwalk through the forest on the north shore of the Río Napo. Then a half-hour paddle in a dugout canoe takes you to the lodge – this part of the journey is my favorite. Garzacocha, with its several tributaries and varying vegetation, must surely be one of the prettiest small jungle lakes anywhere.

Visitors are required to spend a four-day/three-night minimum at the lodge. Prices include roundtrip airfare from Quito to Coca, river travel, accommodations, all meals and all guide services. The bar tab is extra.

The three-night package (Wednesday to Saturday) costs about US$675 per person; the four-night package (Saturday to Wednesday) costs US$800 per person. You can combine any number of three- and four-day packages to make seven, 10, 11 or 14-day stays – these are discounted. They also arrange a one-week 'Light Brigade' tour, which involves camping in the jungle – but in style! Ask them for details.

Visits can be made at any time of year. Keep in mind that June and July are the wettest months. Information and reservations are available from La Selva (☎ 554 686, 550 995, fax 563 814), PO Box 635, Sucursal 12 de Octubre, Quito. The street address is 6 de Diciembre 2816 and James Orton, in Quito.

KAPAWI LODGE

This is a new lodge under construction in this area. I'm told it is being built by a local NGO concerned with rainforest conservation and indigenous human rights, and profits will go to support these causes. The lodge should be open by 1997 and is expected to be comfortable and good. Information will no doubt be available at the better travel agencies in Quito.

PAÑACOCHA

Pañacocha is Quichua for 'the Lake of the Piranhas.' There is a small community near the lake where you can stay. Pañacocha is about five hours downstream from Coca, or about halfway to Nuevo Rocafuerte.

Cheap accommodations are available at a variety of small local places and private houses where rates start as low as US$5 a double. *Cabañas Pañacocha*, which are run by the same people that own the Hacienda Primavera (see that section for information), are right by the lake and away from the village. They charge US$20 per person, including food. The more expensive *Paña-*

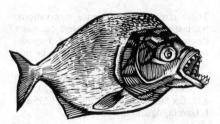

Several species of piranha inhabit Ecuadorian rivers. Not all are flesh eaters - some prefer to eat fruit!

cocha Lodge (☎ in Quito 541 972, 541 977), Robles 610 and JL Mera, is another possibility. The very rustic (bathe in the river) *Cabañas Jarrín* can be reserved through Ejarsytur (☎ 880 251) in Coca.

A popular activity is to go piranha fishing – the fish are fairly easy to catch and make good eating, but don't let them get their razor-sharp jaws around your finger, or you might lose it.

YUTURI LODGE

This lodge is built on the Río Yuturi, a tributary of the Río Napo, about 20 minutes beyond Pañacocha. It is the only place that is south of the lower Napo. There are 15 rustic cabins with private cold-water showers, mosquito netting and good views. All the guides here are indigenous, so you have to speak Spanish. The usual foot and canoe trips are available. The food is reportedly good, though I haven't been by here. Reservations can be made at Yuturi Jungle Adventure (in Quito ☎ /fax 504 037, 503 225, 544 166, 507 056), Amazonas 1324 and Colón, Quito. Rates are about US$500 for four days/three nights, including roundtrip airfare from Quito, and longer stays are available.

NUEVO ROCAFUERTE

This small river town is on the Peruvian border, about 12 hours from Coca along the Río Napo. Entering Peru at this point is prohibited. Since the 1981 war between Peru and Ecuador, you need a military permit to be allowed to travel to this area.

NORTH ORIENTE

This became more difficult to arrange since the 1995 war, but if you can get the permit it'll give you the opportunity to see life on the frontier of the Oriente.

One way to get the permit is to apply at the *Comandancia General del Ejercito* (the General Army Command) at the *Ministerio de Defensa* (Ministry of Defence) in Quito. If a permit is refused, you can try again at the military camp by the bridge in Coca, where you have to speak to the *comandante*. Being able to speak Spanish helps.

If you are a writer on assignment or are doing scientific research, you may find it easier to get a permit, particularly if you have some kind of professional credentials and a letter from your embassy. If you are simply a tourist, you may be allowed to do the trip if you hire a local guide (expensive). Tourists traveling alone are generally refused permission – this is a remote and politically sensitive area. I have heard of travelers being accused of drug smuggling when they tried to go to Nuevo Rocafuerte. If you are allowed to go, you will have to leave your passport with the commandante in Coca. My advice is to hire a local guide if you want to go – but I've never been beyond the Pañacocha area myself.

Guides are also available in Nuevo Rocafuerte for trips into Parque Nacional Yasuní.

Places to Stay & Eat
There is a basic pensión in Nuevo Rocafuerte. Rooms are about US$3.50 per person. There is a small store with basic supplies, but you should bring everything you need with you. There is no restaurant, but by asking around you can find someone to cook simple and inexpensive meals for you.

Getting There & Away
The weekly canoe from Coca departs early on Monday morning. The 12-hour trip is usually broken at Pañacocha for a meal.

The return canoe leaves Nuevo Rocafuerte early on Friday morning. Because travel is against the flow of the river, the return trip may require an overnight stop. The fare is about US$25 each way.

PARQUE NACIONAL YASUNÍ
Yasuní lies south of the Río Napo and includes most of the watersheds of the Río Yasuní and Río Nashiño, as well as substantial parts of the Río Tiputini. This 679,730-hectare national park is by far the largest in mainland Ecuador and was established in 1979 to conserve a wide variety of different rainforest habitats.

These can be divided into three major groups: 'terra firme,' or forested hills, which are never inundated even by the highest floods; 'varzea,' or lowlands, which are periodically inundated by flooding rivers; and 'igapó,' which are lowlands that are semipermanently inundated. Thus, Parque Nacional Yasuní has wetlands, marshes, swamps, lakes, river systems and rainforest.

The biodiversity of this varied and remote tropical landscape is staggeringly high. Not many scientists have had the opportunity to visit the park, but those that have report much higher species counts than they had expected, including many new species. The animals present include some of the rarer and more difficult to see jungle wildlife such as the jaguar, harpy eagle, puma and tapir.

Because of the importance of the park's incredible biodiversity, UNESCO (United Nations Educational, Scientific and Cultural Organization) has declared Yasuní an international biosphere reserve.

The national park is almost uninhabited, except for about 20 Huaorani Indian families. Most Huaoranis live outside the park boundaries, especially in the Reserva Huaorani, which acts as an ecological buffer zone for the national park. This was created in 1991, encompassing much of what used to be the western part of Yasuní and providing the Huaorani with a suitable area of rainforest in which to live in a traditional manner. Meanwhile, the eastern and southern borders of Parque Nacional Yasuní were extended to the Río Cururay, so that the size of the park remains about the same.

On the face of it, then, this huge, remote national park, surrounded by a buffer zone, is a modern conservation success story.

Unfortunately, this is not entirely the case. Oil has been discovered within the boundaries of the park. In 1991, despite Yasuní's protected status, the Ecuadorian government gave the US-based oil company Conoco the right to begin oil exploitation. Conoco was soon replaced by the Maxus Oil Consortium, a subsidiary of Du Pont. It is understandable that the Ecuadorian government wants to make money from its oil reserves, but much of the profit will benefit foreign interests rather than Ecuador.

Where drilling begins, a road soon follows, thus opening up pristine rainforest to colonization, deforestation and degradation. It is the roads and the subsequent colonization that causes greater long-term damage than the oil drilling itself. A 110-km road has been built into the park but, in an attempt to avoid the problems associated with colonization, the road is open only to oil company workers, local indigenous people and a few scientists with permits. The Universidad Católica in Quito runs a research station in Yasuní that is reached by this road. I have recently heard that some classes will be taught here, but I have no details. Inquire at the university.

Degradation caused by the oil drilling process itself does occur. This includes contamination of soil and drainage systems by oil and the waste products associated with oil exploitation, as well as the noise pollution and destruction of vegetation causing the exodus of wildlife from the region. Nevertheless, this degradation has so far been reasonably well-contained, and wildlife is reportedly very abundant – though you can't go there to see it unless you're a researcher or an oil worker.

Various international organizations, such as the Nature Conservancy, Conservation International and Natural Resources Defense Council, in coalition with Ecuadorian groups such as the Fundación Natura and local grassroots conservation groups, have worked hard to minimize the oil company's impact in Yasuní. Although Parque Nacional Yasuní remains threatened by oil exploitation, there is now hope that the threat will not develop into as destructive a pattern as has occurred in other parts of the Amazon.

In common with the majority of Ecuador's preserved areas, Yasuní is woefully understaffed. In 1990, they had only one ranger. Poaching of game for sale to pet traders is a growing concern. Most of the organizations mentioned above are working to train and fund an Ecuadorian park staff consisting of administrators, rangers and management technicians to combat the various threats facing Yasuní.

At present, the only staffed ranger station is at Nuevo Rocafuerte, which is difficult to reach. Sacha and La Selva Jungle Lodges lie near the northwestern boundary of the park, and visitors to these lodges can make brief forays into the edges of the park. Some of the guides in Coca can take you on trips into the park.

The annual rainfall is about 3500 mm depending on which part of the park you are in. May to July are the wettest months; January to March are the driest. This is one of the few remaining true wildernesses in Ecuador. The beauty of this area is its remoteness and inaccessibility, which allows the wildlife to remain in the region relatively undisturbed. I hope that it will be able to remain so.

VÍA AUCA

A road from Coca crosses the Río Napo and continues south across the Río Tiputini and the Río Shiripuno and ends at the small community of Bataboro on the Río Tiguino. There are daily rancheras and buses as far as Bataboro. This used to be Huaorani territory and virgin jungle. The Vía Auca is an oil exploitation road built in the 1980s. The Huaorani have left, pushed eastward into their new reserve. The jungle is being colonized, and cattle ranches and oil rigs are replacing the jungle. This is what happens when an oil exploitation road goes in. Conservationists are trying to prevent this from happening along the road built by Maxus in the Parque Nacional Yasuní.

The rivers crossed by the road provide access to remote parts of both the Huaorani Reserve and Yasuní, but you should seek the local advice of authorized guides about the advisability of taking trips down these rivers. Some tours may be possible but others enter the territories of Huaoranis who either are strongly opposed to tourism or want to manage it on their own terms. Taking the road to Bataboro in the morning and returning to Coca is no problem if you are interested in seeing what it looks like. The trip takes about three or four hours and costs about US$3. If you leave first thing in the morning, you will have no problem doing the roundtrip. There is nowhere to stay in Bataboro.

LAGO AGRIO

Lago Agrio's official name is 'Nueva Loja,' because many of the early Ecuadorians who colonized the area came from Loja. But US oil workers working for Texaco nicknamed the town 'Lago Agrio' after a small oil town in Texas called Sour Lake, and the nickname has stuck. Many locals simply call the town 'Lago.'

The bus ride from Coca to Lago Agrio gives an interesting view of how the discovery of oil has changed the Oriente. In the early 1970s, this was all virgin jungle, and communications were limited to

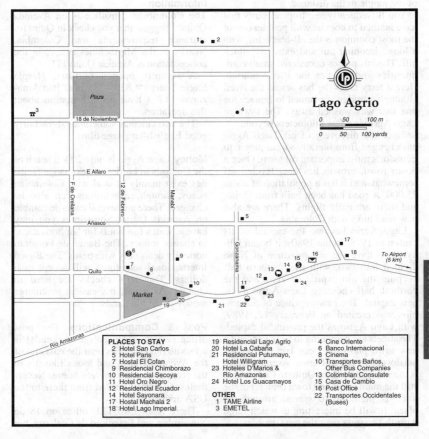

PLACES TO STAY
2 Hotel San Carlos
5 Hotel Paris
7 Hostal El Cofan
9 Residencial Chimborazo
10 Residencial Secoya
11 Hotel Oro Negro
12 Residencial Ecuador
14 Hotel Sayonara
17 Hostal Machala 2
18 Hotel Lago Imperial

19 Residencial Lago Agrio
20 Hotel La Cabaña
21 Residencial Putumayo,
    Hotel Willigram
23 Hoteles D'Marios &
    Río Amazonas
24 Hotel Los Guacamayos

OTHER
1 TAME Airline
3 EMETEL

4 Cine Oriente
6 Banco Internacional
8 Cinema
10 Transportes Baños,
    Other Bus Companies
13 Colombian Consulate
15 Casa de Cambio
16 Post Office
22 Transportes Occidentales
    (Buses)

NORTH ORIENTE

mission airstrips and river travel. Today there are roads and buses, and there are always signs of the oil industry – the pipelines, oil wells or trucks.

A short way north of Coca the bus heads east and passes the belching wells of the Sacha oil works. It continues through the small oil town of **La Joya de las Sachas**, where there are a few restaurants and two basic residenciales (the *Carmita* and *Zaruma*), neither of which are recommended. The road is narrow but in good condition and almost entirely paved. It follows the oil pipeline for most of the way, and there are several stretches with vistas of the jungle in the distance.

You'll frequently see tropical birds that have learned to coexist with people; one of the most common is the all-black ani, with a long, drooping tail and extremely thick bill. The bus passes occasional small communities and reaches the Río Aguarico. Here a ferry takes the bus across the river, although a bridge is planned to replace the one that was washed away. The town of Lago Agrio is a few kilometers beyond.

Since the discovery of oil, Lago Agrio has changed from literally virgin jungle to Ecuador's most important oil town. Once a boom town, growth has now leveled off somewhat, and it has a population of about 25,000. A road has been built from Quito, and there are daily flights. There are also new road links with Colombia.

Lago Agrio became the capital of its canton in 1979. In the 1980s, it began lobbying to have the old province of Napo divided into two, with the southern half keeping the old capital of Tena and the northern half choosing Lago Agrio as its new capital. The new province of Sucumbíos was created on February 12, 1989, with Lago Agrio as the provincial capital. The streets are beginning to be paved, and a new town plaza has been laid out on the northwestern edge of town. Avenida Quito is the main route from Quito to Coca and is still the main street and town center, but the town is planning to spread around the plaza. It will be interesting to watch Lago Agrio's progress over the next decades.

Although it's the oldest, biggest and 'best' of Ecuador's oil towns, Lago Agrio is still just an oil town, and an oil town is an oil town. Most travelers spend as little time here as possible; it's simply an overnight stop. The drive from the jungle up into the Andes is very beautiful, and it's a good idea to rest in Lago Agrio and leave refreshed on a morning bus if you're headed to Quito, so that you can appreciate the scenery. Also, you can use Lago Agrio as a base for further excursions into the jungle on the road that is being pushed ever deeper into the Oriente.

Information

The Colombian consulate is on Avenida Quito; I suggest that you check in Quito for entrance requirements into Colombia. Nearby is the Migraciones office, in the police station at Avenida Quito 111.

A recently opened outfitter, Harpía Eagle Tours (☎ 830 438), is at Río Amazonas 117. I have no information about this operation.

The two cinemas sometimes show fairly good English-language films.

Money Lago Agrio is only 20 km south of the Colombian border and exchange facilities exist mainly to deal with Colombian pesos, though cash dollars can also be changed. There are several casas de cambio on Avenida Quito. Sometimes you may have to wait a few hours for 'authorization' to change money. The Banco de Fomento normally deals only with pesos. The Banco Internacional sometimes will accept cash dollars. Traveler's checks are hard to change. As usual, it's easiest to change money in the highlands.

Post & Communications The post office (which is closed on weekends) is up some rickety stairs near the east end of the Avenida Quito, and looks like it's in the front room of a private home. Nevertheless, a letter I mailed from there to the USA arrived safely.

There is an EMETEL office on 18 de Noviembre and Francisco de Orellana, but it suffers from occasional communication breakdowns. The area code for Lago Agrio and the province of Sucumbíos is 06.

Things to See

There's a Sunday-morning market that can be quite interesting when the local Cofan Indians come into town to buy staples and sell their handicrafts, such as necklaces made of seeds and iridescent beetle wings.

The Cofan men often wear a typical one-piece, knee-length smock called a *kushma*, along with a headband around their short hair. This latter may be made of porcupine quills. The women wear very brightly patterned flounced skirts, short blouses that expose an inch of midriff, bright-red lipstick, and have beautiful, long, dark hair.

The Cofan Indians are related to the Secoya people, and there used to be tens of thousands of them before early contacts with whites decimated them, mainly by disease. This, unfortunately, is the history of most Amazonian Indian groups. Before the discovery of oil, most Cofans' exposure to non-Indian people was limited to the occasional missionary, and they still remain quite shy, as opposed to the Otavaleño Indians, for example. They live in several river villages near Lago Agrio, but there are no restaurants or accommodations there. Their main village is Dureno, and jungle tours can be arranged.

Places to Stay

Lago Agrio is a fast-growing town, and new hotels open every year. Some hotels are expanding upward, in which case the top floor has the advantage of being newer and cleaner, but then there's the disadvantage of being closer to the roof, with the sun and the heat. It's worth looking at different rooms in the same hotel to see what's best for you.

Most hotels provide a fan or mosquito net. Although spraying keeps the mosquito population in Lago Agrio down to a minimum, you should look for rooms with fans or nets, especially if you're not taking malaria pills.

Note that water shortages are common.

Places to Stay – bottom end

There are plenty of budget hotels that are cheap and basic, but they usually look horrible because the rate of deterioration of cheap architecture in the humid jungle is very fast. Some of the oldest and cheapest places are getting a bit rank, so the sensitive shoestring traveler might consider it worthwhile staying somewhere more expensive. Most of the hotels are on Avenida Quito.

The cheapest places are about US$3.50 per person but are very basic and run down. These include the *Residenciales Chimborazo, Putumayo* and *Lago Agrio* and the *Hotel Río Amazonas*.

Better places at US$4.50 per person include the *Hotel Willigram*, where rooms are basic but not too bad, as long as you bring your own padlock for the doors, and the *Hotel Oro Negro*, which is one of the town's oldest hotels and seems well-run, although the rooms don't look very inspiring. Also at this price, the *Residencial Secoya* looks decent. The clean *Hotel San Carlos* has some simple rooms at US$4.50 per person, and rooms with air-conditioning and bath for US$12/16 (make sure that the facilities you are paying for are in working order). The *Residencial Ecuador* is US$4.50 per person or US$7 with bath.

The secure *Hotel D'Marios* is US$7 per person with bath and is clean and a fair value for this price. They are often full, and I suspect their prices will go up. Their restaurant is one of the town's better places to eat. The friendly *Hostal Machala 2* (☎ 830 073) is also quite good at US$9 per person with bath and TV (not many channels). The *Hotel Sayonara* (☎ 830 562) is US$6 per person with bath and fan, US$8 with air-conditioning and US$10 with TV. Others at this price are the *Hotels Paris, Los Guacamayos* and *La Cabaña*. I haven't stayed in them or received feedback from readers, but they look OK.

The friendly *Hotel Lago Imperial* (☎ 830 453, ☎ /fax 830 460), Quito at Colombia, has clean rooms with private bath, fans and TV for US$11/18. They advertise air-conditioning, but it wasn't yet installed when I stopped by. As soon as they get organized, this could become the best budget hotel in town.

Places to Stay – middle

There are two better hotels. The modern *Hostal El Cofan* (☎ 830 009/109), on Avenida Quito and 12 de Febrero, charges about US$25/42 for clean but boring rooms with private bath, hot water and fan. Rooms with air-conditioning or TV cost a little more. The hotel is often full, so get there early or call ahead. It was recently under renovation, so prices may go up.

The newer *Hostal Gran Lago* is almost a kilometer west of downtown heading out along J Añasco. I didn't get to check it out, but I'm told this place has a restaurant and bungalows set in pleasant surroundings. Prices are about the same as the El Cofan.

Places to Eat

There are several chifas, and some of the hotels have reasonable and cheap restaurants attached – try along Avenida Quito east of the market. The *Hostal El Cofan* restaurant is supposedly the best in town and is not too expensive, but was closed for remodeling on my last visit. I found that the restaurant under the *Hotel D'Marios* was both the best and the most popular, and had a good choice of dishes reasonably priced at about US$3.

Getting There & Around

Air TAME has a daily flight (except Sunday) from Quito at 10:30 am returning from Lago Agrio to Quito at 11:30 am. The one-way fare is US$46 for foreigners. Flights are often full, but it's always worth getting on the waiting list and going to the airport in the hope of cancellations. Tour companies sometimes book up more seats than they can use. The TAME office (☎ 830 113) is next to the Hotel San Carlos in Lago Agrio. It is usually open on weekdays, but their hours are quite erratic. Often everyone packs up and goes to the airport.

A Colombian company called Aires

Crossing the Colombian Border

It's certainly possible to enter Colombia from Lago Agrio; the border is less than 20 km to the north, and there are always a few Colombians in town. Although the area is notorious for smugglers, and the Colombian side has been called 'dangerous' by Ecuadorian locals, several readers have written to me about crossing the border (in both directions), and none of them experienced any problems or felt there was any danger. However, there were numerous passport and baggage checks by the Colombian military, so you needed to have your passport handy. The military say that the road is safe enough during the day but should be avoided at night.

Note that there are no Ecuadorian border crossing posts at the border itself. If you are entering or leaving Ecuador, you should get your passport stamped at the immigration office in Lago Agrio. If you are entering Colombia, ask at the Colombian Consulate if they need to stamp your passport.

The most frequently used route from Lago Agrio is to take a Transportes Putumayo bus to La Punta (about 1½ hours) on the Río San Miguel. Then take a motorized canoe for the short river crossing (about 30 minutes) to Puerto Colón on the Colombian side of the river. When you arrive in Puerto Colón, you'll find several buses each day to take you to Puerto Asís (about six hours by unpaved road) where there are places to stay and road, air and river transportation to other parts of Colombia. (Puerto Asís is on the Río Putumayo, and you can take a boat from here to Leticia at the tri-border of Colombia, Peru and Brazil on the Amazon. Boats aren't frequent, though, and the trip takes several days.) If you leave Lago Agrio at dawn, you should be in Puerto Asís by mid-afternoon. A larger town with more facilities is Mocoa, three hours north of Puerto Asís by paved road. Mocoa has the Colombian migraciones where you should get a passport stamp both if arriving and leaving Colombia.

There are other routes from Lago Agrio into Colombia, but they are rarely used. ■

began flying from Puerto Asis, Colombia, to Lago Agrio and back three times a week in 1994. The flight supposedly took about 10 minutes and cost US$16. This service didn't last, but you never know when it may be reinstated. Ask at the TAME office for information.

The airport is about five km east of town, and there is a TAME pickup truck that may take people from the office to the airport for US$0.80 about an hour before the flight. Taxis (which are usually yellow pickup trucks) cost about US$2, depending on how well you bargain.

If you are arriving in Lago Agrio by air, it's likely you'll see several buses waiting at the airstrip. Unfortunately, most of these are oil company vehicles picking up workers on the flight, and they can't or won't give you a ride. If you ask around, however, you'll eventually find something. One of the buses is usually a public bus, and the TAME people often take passengers back in their truck. There are usually taxis hanging around – see if you can share a ride with someone. The muggy or wet five-km walk is not recommended.

Bus There is no main bus terminal, and most bus companies have their offices on or near the main street, Avenida Quito. Buses to Quito cost about US$8.50 and take eight hours. Transportes Baños has several buses a day, and there are a number of other companies with less frequent departures. Each company has a variety of buses ranging from slow, noisy old monsters to smaller and faster buses; they all seem to break down periodically, so I can't recommend one in particular because you'll only blame me if your bus breaks down!

You can continue further into the Oriente with buses and rancheras that leave from the market area. Ask around on the west side. Look for Transportes Jumandy and Transportes Putumayo, which go east to the Colombian border or to Tarapoa and Cuayabeno. These routes give access to the Reserva Producción Faunísta Cuyabeno. Also on the Río San Miguel is a bus to Tetetes. Buses to the oil town of Shushufindi

are available. The roads into the Oriente from Lago Agrio are constantly being improved and expanded; ask at Transportes Putumayo for the most recent information.

DURENO

There are two Durenos. The Cofan village of Dureno (described in this section) lies on the south banks of the Río Aguarico about an hour east of Lago Agrio by bus or dugout canoe. The Cofan village is 23 km east of Lago Agrio; if you miss the turnoff for it, you will end up at the colonists' village of Dureno, 27 km east of Lago Agrio. There are basic comedores here, and you could find floor space to sleep on if you asked around.

River transportation is infrequent, but Transportes Putumayo have several buses a day to Tarapoa or Tipishca, which pass the Dureno (Cofan village) turnoff, 23 km from Lago Agrio. It is marked with a small sign that is not very obvious; it's best to ask the driver for the 'Comuna Cofan Dureno.' From the turnoff follow the path until you reach the Río Aguarico about 100 meters away. From the river bank yell and whistle to attract the attention of the villagers on the other side – somebody will come and get you in a dugout. It may take an hour or more before somebody comes over – keep whistling and yelling.

In the village, you'll be given a roof over your head in an Indian-style hut – bring a hammock or sleeping mat as there are no beds. Bring your own food and stove as supplies are not available in Dureno. There is a modest fee for the river crossing and a place to sleep.

The Cofans are excellent wilderness guides and know much about medicinal and practical uses of jungle plants. You can hire a guide with a dugout canoe for about US$25 per day. Up to six people can be accommodated in a dugout, so it's cheaper in a group. One of the best guides is Emerihildo Criollo. If he's not around, ask for Elias Lucitante. The guides Delfín and Lauriano have also been recommended by readers. They speak Cofan, with Spanish as their second language, but

NORTH ORIENTE

First Flight

I had an eye-opening experience once while flying from Quito to Lago Agrio. At the Quito airport I ran into an anthropologist I knew. She was accompanying a Cofan couple who had been in a hospital in Quito and were returning home. She explained that it was their first flight and that they spoke a lot of Cofan and very little Spanish, and asked if I could keep an eye on them. I said I would be delighted to do so, though I couldn't imagine that there would be any problems. And so off I set with my new Cofan friends.

Our first problem was with the X-ray machine. I convinced them that no harm would come to their little bundles, so they put them onto the conveyer belt and then walked to the waiting plane. They didn't realize that the X-ray machine didn't automatically deliver all hand luggage to the plane – after all, with all the automated devices they had seen in Quito, why not? So I called them back for their bundles and they looked at me with some disgust; obviously, this fancy machine was no good at all.

We clambered aboard the aircraft, and the next thing we had to deal with were the seat belts. They couldn't quite understand why the flight attendant was buckling them in, and they seemed rather worried when they couldn't unbuckle their belts. A brief demonstration of the quick-release device on the seat belts seemed in order. Then, once we were airborne, they started to complain of earaches. I tried to show them how to equalize the pressure in their ears, and there followed a hilarious episode as we held our noses and swallowed and blew and snorted and sprayed. Finally, through the giggles and general uproar, I managed to convey, in sign language, how to get rid of the pain in their ears.

It was a short flight, and soon we were preparing to land at Lago Agrio. I had made sure that the couple got window seats, thinking that they would enjoy the views. Instead, as we were about to land, the wife firmly covered the window with a blanket and then took a couple of very quick, tentative peeks before closing her eyes tightly shut.

We landed safely. ■

English is not understood. This is off-the-beaten-path tourism and is not for those expecting any comfort.

They have one- to four-day trips within the area, but they don't go to Cuyabeno. Although you won't see much wildlife, jungle plants will be shown and explained to you. These trips are more a cultural experience than wildlife watching. Ask questions!

An American missionary family works in the village – although they don't arrange trips or provide services for travelers, they can be of assistance in an emergency.

You can look for Cofans in Lago Agrio at weekends. They are there to sell their handicrafts and to do some shopping, so look for them around the market area. They often wear their distinctive traditional clothing (described under Lago Agrio) and are easy to spot. Ask them if you could join them after the Sunday morning market when they return to Dureno – they will then be able to show you where to get off the bus, and you can cross the river with them.

FLOTEL ORELLANA

This large, flat-bottomed river boat has three decks, 20 double cabins and two quadruples, each with private bath and hot water. The *Flotel* cruises the Río Aguarico in the sections close to the Peruvian border and provides a comfortable base from which to tour the region and to visit the Cuyabeno Reserve. These tours are operated by Ecuador Amazon Expeditions, a subsidiary of Metropolitan Touring, Ecuador's biggest travel agency, and the prices and quality are commensurate with this. Bilingual naturalist guides accompany the boat to explain the wildlife and surroundings. Day trips to shore are taken in dugout canoes, and short nature hikes (often on boardwalks) and canoe rides on a lake are part of the adventure. Nights are spent in relative luxury aboard the Flotel, which provides good food, a bar and lectures about the jungle. Metropolitan Touring is taking an increasingly active role in promoting responsible ecotourism, using local guides, trying to minimize impact on the culture and environment of the region, and educating their passengers about the rainforest. I have heard good reports about the tours.

Voyages on the Flotel are for three or four nights and are all-inclusive from Quito (you arrive and leave by air via Tarapoa or Lago Agrio, included in the price). The three-night trip is from Tuesday to Friday, and the four-night trip is from Friday to Tuesday. Rates are about US$660/720 for three/four nights (per person for double occupancy, including airfare from Quito and all meals and guiding services). Low season (April to early June, and September to November) discounts of about US$120 apply.

You can get full information from Metropolitan Touring (☎ 463 680, 464 780, fax 464 702, 465 868), República de El Salvador 970 (mail: PO Box 17-12-0310), Quito. Or contact their US representative, Adventure Associates (☎ (214) 907 0414, (800) 527 2500, fax 783 1826), 13150 Coit Rd, Suite 110, Dallas, TX 75240.

ZABALO

This is a small Cofan community on the Río Aguarico near the confluence of the Aguarico with the smaller Río Zabalo.

Randy Borman, born and raised in the Oriente as the son of American missionaries, lives at Zabalo with his Cofan wife and family along with a handful of other Cofan families. Randy speaks and lives as a Cofan and guides occasional groups on excursions into the jungle. Metropolitan Touring's Flotel sometimes makes a stop near here, and you can visit an area across the river from the village where they have an interpretive center with a Cofan guide. Souvenirs are sold, and a rainforest walk to see medicinal and other plants, accompanied by the Cofan guide, are part of the program, but entering and visiting the village itself and taking photographs are not allowed.

For an exceptional, in-depth jungle expedition with the Cofans (where you sleep in Indian-style huts, trek through the Cuyabeno Reserve, bathe in the river and travel by foot or in dugout canoes) contact Randy through Wilderness Travel (☎ (510) 548 0420, (800) 368 2794, fax 548 0347, see also Online Services), 801 Allston Way, Berkeley, CA 94710, USA.

A 14-day tour of Ecuador, including nine days with the Cofans, costs about US$2700 plus airfare and is limited to 10 participants.

TARAPOA

This oil center, about 85 km by road east of Lago Agrio, is a possible jumping-off point for visiting the Reserva Producción Faunísta Cuyabeno or joining a tour on the Flotel. There is a guard station for the Cuyabeno in Tarapoa. There are two basic places to stay.

Getting There & Away

Air Since the mid-1980s, TAME have had morning flights from Quito several days a week. These have recently stopped, but may start again. Chartered flights are available.

Bus There are several buses a day to Lago Agrio (US$2; two hours).

RESERVA PRODUCCIÓN FAUNÍSTICA CUYABENO

This reserve covers 603,380 hectares of rainforest around the Río Cuyabeno, north of the Río Napo and almost to the Colombian border in northeastern Ecuador. The boundaries of Cuyabeno have been changed several times, and it is now substantially larger than it originally was.

The reserve was created in 1979 with the goals of protecting this area of rainforest, conserving its wildlife and providing a sanctuary in which the traditional inhabitants of the area, the Siona, Secoya and Cofan Indians, could lead their customary way of life. There are several lakes and swamps in Cuyabeno, and some of the most interesting animals found here are aquatic species such as freshwater dolphins, manatees, caiman and anaconda. Monkeys abound, and tapirs, peccaries, agoutis and several cat species have been recorded. The birdlife is prolific.

Its protected status notwithstanding, Cuyabeno was opened to oil exploitation almost immediately after its creation. The new oil towns of Tarapoa and Cuyabeno were built on tributaries of the Río Cuyabeno, and both of these towns and segments of the trans-Ecuadorian oil pipeline were within the reserve boundaries. Roads were built, colonists followed and tens of thousands of hectares of the reserve were logged or degraded by spills of oil and toxic waste.

At least six oil spills were recorded between 1984 and 1989, and others occurred unnoticed. Many of the spills found their way into the Río Cuyabeno itself, which is precisely the river basin that the preserve was supposed to protect.

It was interesting to see how MAG, the government body originally charged with overseeing the reserve, managed to remain apparently oblivious to oil development in the midst of the protected area. An informative leaflet published in 1991 by MAG's Division of Natural Areas and Wildlife urged the visitor: 'We must contribute to a national ecological conscience!' Ten rules for visiting Cuyabeno were listed. The No 1 rule is 'Put litter in its place.' Other rules include: avoid getting lost, do not molest the wildlife, do not make unnecessary noise, do not damage the trees, and inform the authorities of any 'irregularities.' Yet the leaflet made no mention whatsoever of oil exploitation and colonization within the reserve!

Various international and local agencies set to work to try and protect these areas which, although legally protected, were in reality open to development. Conservation International funded projects to establish more guard stations in Cuyabeno, to train local Siona and Secoya Indians to work in wildlife management, and to support CORDAVI, an Ecuadorian environmental law group that challenged the legality of allowing oil exploitation in protected areas.

Finally, in late 1991, the government shifted the borders of the reserve further east and south and enlarged the area it covered. The new reserve is both more remote and better protected. Vocal local indigenous groups, supported by Ecuadorian and international NGOs, tourists, travel agencies and conservation groups, are doing a better job of keeping the area protected than the government did in the original reserve. Although the threat of oil development and subsequent colonization is always present, there is now a solid infrastructure in place to prevent uncontrolled development from ruining the reserve. This is due, in part, because of the hard work of the local people but also because of the positive economic impact of tourism.

The Cuyabeno Reserve has now become a tourist destination. It is quite easy to visit the reserve without being aware of the problems it has faced, and many large areas of the reserve remain quite pristine. It is an excellent place to experience the rainforest, and I hope the new reserve will remain protected.

Several tour companies in Quito offer tours of Cuyabeno. These go far beyond the colonized areas, and there is a good chance of seeing some of the wildlife, such as monkeys and freshwater dolphins. Travel is mainly by canoes and on foot, except from December to February when low water levels may limit the areas accessible by canoes. Ask at the tour companies about details.

One company is Nuevo Mundo Expeditions (☎ 552 617/816, fax 565 261), PO Box 402-A, Quito. Their street address is Amazonas 2468, Quito. Their tours are among the best; they are marked by a conservationist attitude and led by well-informed, bilingual guides. Their tours use the *Cuyabeno River Lodge* as a base for further exploration. The lodge has comfortable cabins built in native style but with private (cold water) bathrooms. You can arrange trips further into the jungle where they have a camp near the Laguna Grande. 'Ecofishing' trips with a biologist guide are also available. Rates for five days/four nights are US$700, including flights from Quito and all food and guiding services.

Metropolitan Touring (see above under Flotel Orellana) also operate the *Iripari*

Camp and the *Imuya Camp*, both located on the shores of lakes of the same name as the camps. Iripari is south of the Río Aguarico about halfway between Zabalo and the Peruvian border and Imuya is north of the Aguarico off Río Lagartococha, which forms the border of Peru. Both are in remote areas. Both camps are quite small and rustic, with private screened double rooms and shared bathrooms. Good food and experienced naturalist guides are part of the programs to these lodges, which can be combined with a Flotel excursion for a longer stay in the jungle. Metropolitan Touring also has a couple of more primitive camps where you sleep on hammocks or floor mats. Costs are similar to that of the Flotel program.

Several other companies in Quito and Baños offer cheaper tours to the Cuyabeno Reserve, but check carefully that they offer you the type of experience that you are after. Some recommended agencies are Latin Tour (☎ 508 811, 508 800, fax 568 657), Diego de Almagro 1219 and La Niña, Quito; and Native Life Travels (☎ 550 836, fax 569 741), J Pinto 446 and Amazonas, Quito. These companies charge from about US$300 for a five- or six-day trip (usually with a minimum of about six passengers), with the first and last day spent traveling from and to Quito by bus. Shorter, more expensive trips traveling by air and spending the same amount of time in the reserve can be arranged. Note that while these companies can make arrangements for you in advance, the best rates can usually be obtained by going to their offices and seeing when their next trip is leaving and if there is room on it. This is particularly true of single travelers or couples who may wish to join a larger group and save money.

It is possible to visit Cuyabeno independently but, since the borders have been pushed further south and east and since the increase in local indigenous control over tourism in the area, this is no longer a recommended or inexpensive option. Most visitors go with an organized group, which is the best way to go to get the most out of your visit.

Entry to the reserve costs US$20 per person (less for Ecuadorians). This is usually added to the cost of any tour – ask in advance if you are on a tight budget. There is a guard post in Tarapoa where you can pay the fee and ask for information. There are a few other guard posts within the reserve.

Most visitors come during the wetter months of March to September. In the less rainy months, river levels may be too low to allow easy navigation. Annual rainfall is between 2000 and 4000 mm depending on location, and humidity is often between 90% and 100%. Be prepared with sun protection, rain gear, insect repellent, water-purification tablets and food.

SAN RAFAEL FALLS & VOLCÁN REVENTADOR

The road west of Lago Agrio roughly follows the Río Aguarico for about 50 km before turning southwest and beginning the long climb up into the Andes by following the valley of the Río Quijos. There are two major landmarks on this ascent: On the left of the road, some 95 km from Lago Agrio, are the San Rafael Falls (also called the Coca Falls), about 145 meters high and the biggest in Ecuador. To the right of the road is the 3485-meter Volcán Reventador, which means 'the exploder' and which had a period of major activity in the late 1970s. Unfortunately, it's obscured by cloud cover more often than not.

You can glimpse the San Rafael Falls briefly from the road. To see them properly, get off the bus just beyond the bridge crossing Río Reventador, at a concrete-block hut on the left side of the road. Make sure you get off the bus at the Río Reventador and not at the bigger community of **El Reventador**, which is about 15 km away in the direction of Lago Agrio (and has a cheap hotel). A new metal bridge has been built by Río Reventador, and a correspondent writes that the bridge has a plaque proclaiming *Obra de Norman*, meaning 'Norman's Work.' Most bus drivers know *La entrada para la cascada de San Rafael*.

From the hut it's about 2½ km down a steep track to the falls. Near the top of the track is the *San Rafael Lodge* and beyond is the track to the falls, which may or may not be passable to vehicles for some or all of its length. The lodge is operated by the Hotel Quito in Quito where you can make reservations. Rates from Quito include transportation to the lodge, all meals, a visit to the falls and transportation back again, and this runs over US$100 a night. Some travelers told me that they just dropped in and were charged US$5 per person to sleep there, and had to bring all their own food. I'm told you can camp within sight of the falls for US$1.50 per person. The rooms at the lodge have shared bathrooms, and hot water is available when they turn it on. Once back on the road, flag a bus down when you want to go on, but be prepared to wait, as buses are sometimes full.

The falls are quite impressive, but the best thing about them, at least from some people's point of view, is the great bird-watching in the area. The Andean cock-of-the-rock is one of the more spectacular species regularly seen here.

Just north of the Río Reventador bridge there are a couple of houses, and just north of that there is a trail that climbs up Volcán Reventador, on the northwest side of the road. It is hard to find the beginning of the trail, and there are various confusing little paths, so you should ask anyone you see (note that there are very few people around here). After a few minutes, the trail crosses the river, and about half an hour later the trail goes through a grove of palm trees. Beyond that there is only one trail to the summit, but it is steep and slippery in places. There is almost no water, and the climb takes two days – it's only for experienced hikers with plenty of extra water bottles and camping gear. Technical climbing is not involved, but it's easy to get lost in the lower slopes, so I recommend hiring a guide. Try Guillermo Vásquez in the community of Pampas, about three km west of the San Rafael Falls; Edgar Ortiz at the Hotel Amazonas in El Reventador; or Lucho Viteri in Baeza.

This area is within the eastern boundaries of **Reserva Ecológica Cayambe-**

Coca, described in the North of Quito chapter. There are no signs or entrance stations. There is reportedly a guard station in the village of **El Chaco** about 20 km beyond the Río Reventador bridge on the way to Baeza. In El Chaco there are a couple of very basic residenciales.

Bus drivers on the Lago Agrio-Quito run usually know the San Rafael Falls, but few of them know about the Río Reventador bridge or climbing the volcano. So ask about the falls, even if you plan on climbing Reventador.

BAEZA

Beyond Río Reventador the road continues climbing, following the trans-Ecuadorian oil pipeline and the Río Quijos all the way. There are enchanting views of beautiful cloud forest full of strange species of birds and plants. You pass several small communities with little to recommend them, and in six hours you reach Baeza, 170 km from Lago Agrio.

Baeza is on the junction with the road to Tena and is the most important village between Lago Agrio and Quito. It was an old Spanish missionary and trading outpost, having been first founded in 1548 and re-founded three more times since. The pass from Baeza via Papallacta to the Quito valley was known well before the conquest, but the road from Baeza to Lago Agrio has been opened only by the oil boom, so Baeza is both a historical and geographical junction. It is also recommended as a good, quiet and inexpensive spot to stay for walks in the surrounding hills. The plants of the Andean foothills and the bird life are outstanding.

Places to Stay & Eat

Facilities are very limited. There is a gas station, basic hotel and restaurant in the *Oro Negro* complex at the junction of the road going to Tena.

About two km away from the junction, heading toward Tena, you reach the village of Baeza proper. Here you'll find the basic but clean *Hotel Samay* in the center, which charges about US$4 a night. The *Hostería El Nogal de Jumandy* is at the west end (the end nearest the road junction) and also cheap but used by truck drivers and prostitutes (according to one reader, who stayed there nevertheless). At the east end (the end toward Tena) is the newer *Hostal San Rafael* with good, clean rooms for US$6 per person. Restaurant *El Viejo* is one of the better of the simple restaurants.

About 17 km south of Baeza on the road to Tena is the village of **Cosanga** on the outskirts of which is the *Cabañas San Isidro Labrador* (☎ in Quito 465 578, 547 403, fax 228 902), Carrión 555 and JL Mera. It is an Ecuadorian-owned cattle ranch on the eastern slopes of the Andes at about 2000 meters. Some of the land has been left undisturbed, and the birding here is reportedly first class, according to a local bird guide who brings birding groups here. You can stay here by advance reservation for only about US$80 per person, including meals served by the friendly family who owns the place. Rooms have private baths and hot water.

Getting There & Away
There are no bus stations in these villages. You must flag down passing buses and hope that they have room. Buses to and from Lago Agrio, Tena and Quito pass through regularly. If coming from one of these towns, you may find that bus companies will only sell you a ticket for the whole journey (eg, Lago Agrio-Quito). If you don't want to pay full price, you have to jump on the bus just after it leaves the terminal, hope you can get a seat and pay the driver a prorated fare.

PAPALLACTA
The westbound road from Baeza continues climbing steadily for some 40 km until the village of Papallacta. About 1½ km beyond the village, on the right as you head to Quito, are the Baños Termales or natural **hot springs** of Papallacta.

Their setting is grand; on a clear day you can see the snow-capped Antisana (5704 meters) about 15 km to the south. The hottest spring is very hot, and there's a refreshing cold plunge pool as well as other pools at various temperatures. The complex recently has been developed and costs about US$2.50 to get in, with nice changing rooms and toilet facilities provided. The area is beautiful, the pools are clean and there aren't too many visitors midweek, although it's busy with Quiteños at weekends. Papallacta is a nice place to relax and soak away the aches and pains of a jungle expedition.

Quito is only 60 km away, but the drive is difficult and spectacular. The road climbs over the Eastern Cordillera of the Andes via a sometimes snow-covered pass nearly 4100 meters high. This pass is literally the rim of the Amazon basin. If you're driving up from the Oriente, be prepared for the cold. Beyond the pass is the valley of Quito.

Places to Stay & Eat
In the village of Papallacta, the *Residencial Viajero* has simple rooms for under US$3 per person. The shared showers are heated (naturally), rooms have good views and the friendly owners cook meals on request. The slightly cheaper *Hotel Quito* also serves food.

At the Baños Termales there is a good but slightly pricey restaurant (trout is a highlight of the menu), and a new cabaña and hotel opened in 1996 – I don't have telephone numbers or prices but they are mid- to high-end.

Getting There & Away
Making you way to Papallacta from Quito isn't straightforward. Most bus companies going to Tena or Lago Agrio will sell tickets for the entire journey only. You have to wait until departure time and then hop onto the bus and buy a prorated ticket from the driver. This is usually not a problem except at weekends when the buses may be full. One company that can be persuaded to sell you tickets to Papallacta is Centinela del Norte.

To leave Papallacta, wait for a bus to Quito, Tena or Lago Agrio and flag it down. Ask locals about the best place to wait.

The Western Lowlands

A physical map of Ecuador shows the country divided neatly into two by the massive range of the Andes. To the east lie the jungles of the upper Amazon basin, and to the west are the coastal lowlands. The western drop of the Andes is dramatic and steeper than the eastern side. Lowlands at below 300 meters are soon reached; from Ecuador's highest peak (Chimborazo at 6310 meters) it is only 50 km due west to the 300-meter contour, a gradient of about 12%. It does not stay low all the way to the coast, however. After dropping to almost sea level, the land rises again in a barren, scrubby and almost uninhabited range of 700-meter-high hills before dropping to the coast. Thus, the coastal lowlands are subdivided into the coast itself, west of the coastal hills, and the flat lowlands lying east of the hills and west of the Andes. The latter is described here in addition to the descent down the steep western slopes of the Andes.

The western lowlands were once forest, but well over 90% of these forests have now been cleared to develop banana plantations and other forms of agriculture, predominantly cacao and African oil palm. The forests that used to exist here were very different from those found in the Oriente – indeed, botanists estimate that about half the plant species that once grew in these western Andean slopes and lowlands were found nowhere else! Almost no forest is left in the flat lowlands but, in the more difficult to reach areas of the steep western slopes of the Andes, a few areas have become belatedly protected, thus preserving small parts of a unique ecosystem that is on the verge of disappearing from the globe. The small Reserva Biológica Maquipucuna, the Río Palenque Science Center and a couple of other private reserves are included in this chapter. The larger Reserva Ecológica Cotacachi-Cayapas protects some of the northern parts of the western lowlands, but access is very difficult from here. The reserve can be more easily accessed from the area north of Quito and from the north coast, and so it is described under those chapters.

Some travelers think of Ecuador as a 'banana republic' – one of those tropical countries that produces bananas and little else. Indeed, until the export of oil began in 1972, bananas were Ecuador's most important product, and they remain the country's major agricultural export.

Fortunately for agriculturalists and the Ecuadorian economy, the western lowlands are fertile, and huge banana and palm tree plantations can be seen through this area. It has not been developed much for tourists, and many people rush through it on their way to the coast or highlands. If you're interested in seeing some of the tropical banana republic Ecuador – the kind of countryside that was typically Ecuadorian before the recent oil boom – then it is worth taking a couple of days to travel slowly through this area.

MINDO

This small village, about a three- or four-hour drive west of Quito, has recently become a popular destination for bird-watchers and travelers interested in natural history who want to see some of Ecuador's western forests at a reasonable cost. Mindo is at about 1300 meters elevation and has an area of premontane forest nearby, called the **Bosque Protector Mindo-Nambillo**. A local private group is trying to preserve the area, which is very beautiful and excellent for birdwatching.

Beyond Mindo, the poor road drops further to **San Miguel de los Bancos** (locally called Los Bancos), shortly beyond which the road improves and continues through Puerto Quito and on to intersect with the main road between Santo Domingo de los Colorados and the north coast port of

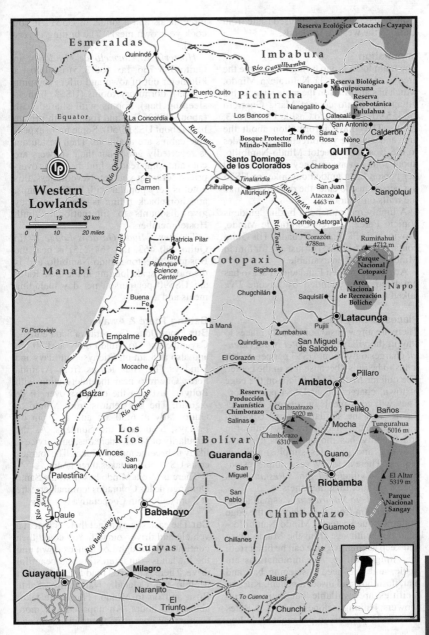

Esmeraldas. This is a little used route from Quito to the western lowlands.

Information

The main local group trying to preserve the area is Amigos de la Naturaleza-Mindo, which has an office on the main street in the village. In Quito contact María Guerrero (☎ 455 907) or write to Casilla 17-03-1673, Quito. They have information about the area and can give you directions and guides to the Bosque Protector Mindo-Nambillo, about km away. They charge US$10 per person for a guided day hike, or US$5 per person just to enter the reserve and hike the trails on your own.

A highly recommended birding guide is Vinicio Perez, Correo Central de Mindo, Provincia de Pichincha, Ecuador. His Quito contact is (☎ 612 955) or just ask for him in Mindo – he's often available.

An agency named Fundación Pacaso has not been recommended by anyone I've talked to.

Places to Stay & Eat

There are a few basic but friendly places to stay in the village. The *Hotel Noroccidental* charges only about US$3 per person but tends to be noisy because it is in the center. The quieter *Hostería El Bijao*, on the edge of town, charges about US$4 per person. They will cook meals on request. A reader reports that the similarly priced *Guadual Inn*, also on the edge of town, is family-run and friendly, has mosquito nets and cold showers, and provides simple meals on request. There are a few very simple restaurants in the village; *Elenita's Restaurant* is open a bit later than the others.

Amigos de la Naturaleza is a small lodge about four km from the village on the edge of the Bosque Protector Mindo-Nambillo – head out southwest from the Mindo plaza and keep asking. A guide can be hired from the Amigos office. Accommodations are rustic, and you need a sleeping bag and mat, flashlight and insect repellent. Kitchen facilities are available but there are no showers; bathing is done in a bucket. Rates are US$25 per person per night including three meals and a guide, or US$17 if you cook your own meals. The birding is very good.

Hostería El Carmelo de Mindo (☎ in Quito 538 756, fax 408 355) is almost a kilometer out of town and offers camping (US$5), dormitory rooms (US$8; bring a sleeping bag), rooms with shared bath (about US$25/30) and rooms with private bath (about US$35/50). Some more expensive cabins are available. Their restaurant is reportedly good, but their showers are cold and some readers find the rooms overpriced for what you get. Nevertheless, this hotel is very popular with birding groups, and horseback riding is available. They give discounts to International Youth Hostel members.

The new *Mindo Gardens Lodge* (☎ in Quito 230 463, fax 564 235) is near the Bosque-Protector Mindo-Nambillo and is the most upscale lodging in the area. Rates are US$90 per person per day including meals and a guide.

Getting There & Away

Bus From Quito, Cooperativa San Pedro de Cayambe goes to Mindo daily at 3:30 pm and also at 8 am on Fridays, Saturdays and Sundays. The bus leaves from Avenida Perez Guerrero near the intersection with Bolivia, just past the overpass over 10 de Agosto. The bus returns from Mindo to Quito daily at 6:30 am and at 2 pm on Fridays, Saturdays and Sundays. As the popularity of Mindo increases, bus service is likely to become more frequent. The journey costs US$1.50 and takes three hours.

There is also a Mindo bus from the Santo Domingo de los Colorados terminal terrestre at 2 pm daily with Cooperativa Kennedy.

Car The easiest way to get there is to rent a vehicle and drive yourself. You could then continue on through Los Bancos down into the lowlands – an interesting and beautiful drive. There is a paved road from Mitad del Mundo via Calacalí, Nanegalito, Santa Rosa and on to Mindo. This route takes about two hours. An unpaved and more scenic road goes from Quito via Nono and joins the paved road near Santa Rosa. This road is in poor condition and 4WD is advised in the wet months (the driest months are June to September). Allow about four hours for this route.

RESERVA BIOLÓGICA MAQUIPUCUNA

This 3000-plus hectare reserve is only about 30 km northwest of Quito as the condor flies but, because of the topography of the land, Maquipucuna lies on the western slopes of the Andes. It protects a variety of premontane and montane cloud forests in the headwaters of the Río Guayllabamba at elevations ranging from about 1200 to 2800 meters. The reserve was purchased in 1987 by The Nature Conservancy and is administered by the Fundación Maquipucuna, a nonprofit conservation organization.

About 80% of the reserve (some reports say over 90%, but I'm skeptical) is undisturbed primary forest – the remainder is secondary growth and includes a research station. The reserve and research station were established to investigate, among other things, sustainable use of the tropical forests, as well as to provide conservation education to Ecuadorians. The biggest problem facing the reserve is uncontrolled colonization, which is often condoned or actively supported by the government. Colonists are deforesting the areas bounding the reserve and this, combined with indiscriminate hunting, has severely reduced the plant and animal life in the area around Maquipucuna, as well as the western lowlands in general. Nevertheless, the story would be much worse if it were not for the efforts of the Fundación, which is doing an admirable job in the face of these difficulties.

Information

A rustic lodge where researchers and visitors can stay with reservations is available, through the Fundación Maquipucuna. There are about a dozen beds in four rooms, a dining room and kitchen (bring your own food unless you have requested meals in advance), and two bathrooms with hot showers. There are basic laboratory facilities, such as a plant drier and work benches, and a small electric generator. Otherwise there is little development in the reserve, and researchers should bring their own equipment. Overnight stays and use of the facilities are about US$40 with meals, considerably less without.

Further information is available from Fundación Maquipucuna (☎ 507 200, fax 507 201), Baquerizo 238 and Tamayo, La Floresta, Quito, or write to Casilla 17-12-167, Quito, Ecuador. Preliminary plant lists (about 2000 species) and bird lists (about 250 species) have been prepared by Ecuadorian, Latin American, North American and British workers. A more complete plant inventory is currently being written. Several conservation workshops have been held, some in collaboration with the University of California Research Expeditions Program or with the US Peace Corps. These have been aimed particularly at the local people. This education, inventory and research work is urgently in need of financial support – contributions are welcomed at the address above.

Getting There & Away

A bus from Quito's Cotocollao Plaza leaves at 12:30 pm daily for Nanegalito and on to Nanegal (2½ hours). Shortly before Nanegal, at a place locally called 'Las Delicias,' you get off the bus and walk on the road to your right for about 1½ hours to the reserve. At Las Delicias there is a country store and a 'Departamento Forestal' sign.

If you are driving, head west of Quito via the Mindo road. About 30 km past Nono, turn right to the village of Nanegalito about eight km away and continue about 12 km to Las Delicias. The reserve cabin is about seveb km away by a very bad road, so 4WD is recommended.

You can also reach Nanegalito from the village of Calacalí, which is about eight km beyond the Mitad del Mundo monument. From Calacalí it is about 31 km to Nanegalito.

Hitchhiking is possible, but there is very little traffic indeed.

RESERVA BELLAVISTA

This small 110-hectare reserve is in the same western Andean slopes as Maquipucuna (see above) at about 2000 meters above sea level. About 25% is primary forest, and the rest has been selectively or completely logged but is being reforested. Various conservation projects are underway, and the owner is looking to expand. A geodesic dome has been built containing five rooms with private baths, a dormitory sleeping platform, a restaurant and a 360° balcony. Camping is permitted. The area has received several very enthusiastic recommendations by birders. Accommodations are about US$30 per person, including all meals, and transport can be arranged from Quito through the owner.

For more information, call Richard Parsons (☎ 242 929, 242 993, 490 891, fax 447 090), República de El Salvador 635 and Portugal, Quito. It may be hard to get through on the phone; if so, leave a message and he'll call you back.

LOS CEDROS BIOLOGICAL RESERVE

This remote area covers 6400 hectares of cloud forest to the north of the two reserves described above. It is recommended by the South American Explorers Club, though I have never talked to anyone who has been there, let alone gone myself. It can be reached by hiking for about six hours from the end of the road from Nanegal – obviously not a casual trip. Rates are reportedly US$20 a day including meals – this might be just the adventure for you.

For further information, contact Los Cedros (☎ 221 324), Casilla 17-07-8726, Quito. Apparently, four buses a week go from Quito to the road head, or you can arrange transport through Safari Tours in Quito. Let me know how it goes.

QUITO TO SANTO DOMINGO
The Old Road

This little used gravel road is an alternate route to Santo Domingo de los Colorados – one that is a favorite of birders who like to spend the entire day driving and birding the 55 or 60 km from Quito until the new

main road to Santo Domingo is reached. The trans-Ecuadorian pipeline follows the old road, and thus it is kept in reasonably good shape. Because few vehicles travel along it, you can easily view the relatively undisturbed premontane habitat as the road drops from over 3000 meters to 1200 meters above sea level. You have to have your own transport.

To get onto this road, head south on the highway on the west side of Quito, Avenida Occidental, continue under the tunnels, through the one-way system on the west side of the old town, and out on Avenida Vencedores de Pichincha. About half a kilometer before the end of this road, just beyond a CEPE petrol station, the old road to Santo Domingo de los Colorados goes to the right.

There are a few villages along the road but no accommodations. You should bring some food. The first village to ask for is **San Juan**, about 10 km outside of Quito. After this, ask for **Chiriboga**, the halfway point on the road and the largest village. Once you are beyond San Juan, it's hard to get lost. A few kilometers beyond Chiriboga, you cross the Río Guajalito. Reportedly, the **Reserva Río Guajalito** is near here – a small reserve with mixed pasture, secondary growth and virgin forest. Dr. Jaramillo of the botany department at the Catholic University in Quito is a contact for the area.

The Main Road

The most frequently used route from the highlands to the western lowlands is the main road from Quito to Santo Domingo de los Colorados. From Santo Domingo you can head south, through Quevedo and Babahoyo in the lowland province of Los Ríos, to Guayaquil on the coast. This is the travelers' route I follow in the rest of this chapter.

From Quito, the bus heads south through the 'Avenue of the Volcanoes' to **Aloag**, where the road to Santo Domingo branches off from the Panamericana. Since the bus often refuels here, a common sight is the hordes of snack sellers lustily hawking their delicacies.

The descent into the lowlands is a spectacular and sometimes terrifying one. It is best to make the journey in the morning, as in the afternoon both the passengers' and the driver's views are often obscured by fog. Despite almost nonexistent visibility, the drivers hurtle down the western slopes of the Andes at breakneck speeds. Amazingly, accidents are very rare, but near misses are somewhat more common.

The road begins in high páramo, with views of the extinct volcanoes Atacazo and Corazón to the north and south. The tortuous descent follows the left bank of the Río Pilatón, and occasionally waterfalls cascade into the narrow gorge. The road passes the village of **Cornejo Astorga** (also known as Tandapi) and follows the Río Toachi valley. The vegetation becomes increasingly tropical, and if you're lucky you may see orchids growing on the sides of the road. Higher temperatures are noticeable by the time you pull into the village of **Alluriquín**.

Shortly before reaching Santo Domingo you pass an oil pressure station. The road follows the trans-Ecuadorian oil pipeline for the last third of its distance. If your bus is continuing beyond Santo Domingo, it may avoid the town altogether because there are a couple of bypasses; normally, however, even long-distance buses pull into the town for a break.

Places to Stay & Eat Both Cornejo Astorga and Alluriquín have basic hotels and restaurants; the best of these is the *Hotel Florida* in Alluriquín, but few travelers stay in these villages. They seem to be overnight stops for truck drivers doing the long, slow haul from the lowlands up to Quito.

About 10 km from Cornejo Astorga is *Hacienda La Hesperia* within the Toachi Pilatón Forest Preserve. There is a new ecotourism project here, with accommodations for naturalists and birdwatchers at prices well below that of Tinalandia (see below). The hacienda is at 1400 meters above sea level, and the birding is reportedly good. Horseback riding and hiking are available on forest trails. Recently, there were six rooms with a total of 18 beds, separate bathrooms (each with two hot showers) for men and women, and a restaurant, but this may well change. Further information and reservations are available through Nuevo Mundo Expediciones in Quito, who are joint partners in this new venture. Safari Tours in Quito also has information on the hacienda.

TINALANDIA

About 16 km outside of Santo Domingo is a famous hotel owned by Señora Tina Garzón, who emigrated to Ecuador from Russia many years ago. The hotel, named *Tinalandia*, appropriately enough, is now run by her son, Sergio, and is the haunt of birders and naturalists. There is a (rarely used) nine-hole golf course next to the hotel, but otherwise the extensive grounds have been left largely undisturbed except for a few nature trails. The birding is excellent, and the grounds of Tinalandia boast more than 150 subtropical plant species. The vegetation is premontane wet forest at an elevation of about 600 meters.

Accommodations consist of bungalows or cabins with private baths and hot showers. Rates are US$60/100 for singles/doubles including three meals. The hotel is sometimes booked by birdwatching groups so you have to take your chances if you don't have a reservation – there are about 16 rooms. The driest months of May and June are particularly popular with birders. Make reservations at ☎ 247 461, fax 442 638 in Quito, or write to Tinalandia, Apartado 8, Santo Domingo de los Colorados, Provincia de Pichincha, Ecuador. Major travel agencies in Ecuador can make reservations for you. You can make day visits to the grounds for US$10.

Tinalandia is about 86 km after turning off the Panamericana in Aloag. There is a small stone sign on the right side of the road as you drive from Quito, and the hotel itself is about half a kilometer up a track on the left side of the road. If you are on a bus to Santo Domingo, ask the driver to let you off at Tinalandia – all the drivers know it.

SANTO DOMINGO DE LOS COLORADOS

Santo Domingo de los Colorados, as the town is officially known, is one of the fastest growing cities in Ecuador, with a population of 115,000 according to the 1990 census. It is important as a transportation hub with major roads heading north, south, east and west. Just 500 meters above sea level and only 130 km from Quito, this is the nearest lowland tropical town easily accessible from the capital and hence it is a popular weekend destination for Quiteños.

Information

Because Sunday is the main market day, the town closes down on Monday. There are the usual EMETEL and post offices, and the Filanbanco (open Tuesday to Saturday) will exchange US dollars and traveler's checks at rates close to Quito's. Banco del Pichincha changes cash dollars only. The area code is 02.

Things to See & Do

Santo Domingo is a convenient city in which to make bus connections or break a long journey. There are lively street markets (see map) and a busy Sunday market, but otherwise it's not a particularly interesting town. There are two cinemas.

The Río Toachi is nearby, and city buses go there. Just across the river is a modest resort village with a few restaurants, a swimming pool (you may prefer to swim in the river) and some games courts.

Santo Domingo is the capital of its canton and celebrates its cantonization day on July 3 when there are street fairs and an Industrial & Agricultural Festival – the town and the hotels are quite crowded then.

Places to Stay

During the July 3 celebrations the town is crowded, as it also is on weekends, with shoppers at the Sunday market and with weekend visitors from Quito. You will have a better choice of hotels midweek. Most of the cheapest hotels have only cold-water showers and don't look like much. Some hotels don't turn on water to your room unless you ask at the front desk.

Places to Stay – bottom end

The basic but clean and helpful *Residencial San Martín* (☎ 750 813), on 29 de Mayo

---

Tsachila (Colorado) Indians

Santo Domingo used to be famous for the Tsachila Indians (better known by their Spanish name, the Colorado Indians, after whom the town is named), who painted their faces with black stripes and dyed their bowl-shaped haircuts a brilliant red using a natural dye from the achiote plant. You can buy postcards of them all over Ecuador, but the Indians are now fairly westernized and you are unlikely to see them in their traditional finery except by going to one of their nearby villages and paying them to dress up. Photographers are expected to give 'tips,' but the Tsachilas are becoming increasingly unhappy with their role as models for foreign photographers. Please be sensitive to this.

The best known village is **Chihuilpe**, about seven km south of Santo Domingo on the road to Quevedo and then about three km east on a dirt road. Some of the older Indians, notably the headman Abraham Calazacon (who died in the 1980s) and his brother Gabriel, earned reputations as *curanderos* (medicine men), and people still come from all over Ecuador to be cured. The present *gobernador* (headman) is Abraham's son, Nicanor Calazacon, who continues the traditional work of a curandero. Nearby, the house of Agosto Calazacon is a tourist center, and there is now a small museum here that describes Tsachila history and culture. Reportedly, you can ask here about locals posing for your camera, though I didn't look into this myself.

There are other Colorado villages in the area south of Santo Domingo but, for the most part, the villagers prefer to be left alone. Apart from going to the tourist center in Chihuilpe, I do not recommend visits to see the Colorados. A taxi from Santo Domingo to Chihuilpe will cost about US$15 for a two- to three-hour trip. ■

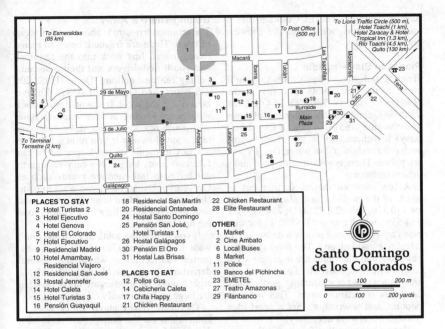

Santo Domingo de los Colorados

0   100   200 m
0   100   200 yards

PLACES TO STAY
2 Hotel Turistas 2
3 Hotel Ejecutivo
4 Hotel Genova
5 Hotel El Colorado
7 Hotel Ejecutivo
9 Residencial Madrid
10 Hotel Amambay,
   Residencial Viajero
12 Residencial San José
13 Hostal Jennefer
14 Hotel Caleta
15 Hotel Turistas 3
16 Pensión Guayaquil
18 Residencial San Martín
20 Residencial Ontaneda
24 Hostal Santo Domingo
25 Pensión San José,
   Hotel Turistas 1
26 Hostal Galápagos
30 Pensión El Oro
31 Hostal Las Brisas

PLACES TO EAT
12 Pollos Gus
14 Cebichería Caleta
17 Chifa Happy
21 Chicken Restaurant
22 Chicken Restaurant
28 Elite Restaurant

OTHER
1 Market
2 Cine Ambato
6 Local Buses
8 Market
11 Police
19 Banco del Pichincha
23 EMETEL
27 Teatro Amazonas
29 Filanbanco

and Tulcán, is US$2.50 per person and seems like a reasonable low-budget choice. The basic *Hotel Turistas 1, 2* and *3* (at three locations) claim to have hot water and charge US$2.25 per person. The *Hostal Santo Domingo* (☎ 754 078), Quito 715 and Cuenca, is also OK at US$2.50 per person without bath or US$4.50 with bath. The *Pensión Guayaquil*, 3 de Julio and Tulcán, is acceptable at US$3 per person. Other basic cheapies for under US$3 per person are the *Residencial San José, Pensión San José, Ontaneda, Viajero, El Oro* and *Madrid* – nothing to recommend about these except their cheap rooms. Perhaps the best budget choice is the *Hostal Jennefer* (☎ 750 577), 29 de Mayo at Latacunga, at US$3.50 per person with warm electric shower.

Also acceptable is *Hotel Ejecutivo*, with two locations. The one on 29 de Mayo east of Cuenca (☎ 751 943) is about US$4.50 per person with bath – the rooms facing the

street are noisy. Slightly better rooms are available at the Hotel Ejecutivo on 29 de Mayo west of Cuenca , at US$5 per person with bath. They also have rooms for US$8/15, but they aren't much better than the cheaper rooms except they have a TV. *Hostal Las Brisas* (☎ 750 560), on Quito near Iturralde, and the *Hostal Galápagos*, on Calle Galápagos and Tulcán, are both about US$4.50 per person with bath. The *Hotel Amambay* (☎ 750 696), 29 de Mayo near Ambato, is also this price but looks a bit rundown.

For something a bit more upscale, the *Hotel Genova* (☎ 759 694), 29 de Mayo and Ibarra, is clean and friendly and costs US$9/13 for rooms with hot bath (seems like a good value), or an extra US$4 for rooms with a TV. For about US$8/12, the *Hotel Caleta* (☎ 750 277), Ibarra 137 and 29 de Mayo, and the large *Hotel El Colorado* (☎ 750 226, 754 299), 29 de Mayo and Esmeraldas, are both good choices and have restaurants. The El Colorado has a variety of rooms, some with hot showers and telephones.

Places to Stay – middle

Heading out along Avenida Quito, you'll come to the best hotels. The first is the *Hotel del Toachi* (☎ 750 295, 754 689, fax 754 688), almost a kilometer out of town and charging US$18/24 (less if they aren't busy) for characterless but clean rooms with private shower, hot water, fan, TV and telephone. There is a swimming pool and a decent restaurant.

A few hundred meters further out of town is the well-known *Hotel Zaracay* (☎ 750 316, 750 429, 751 023, 754 873, fax 754 535), which charges US$30/42 for spacious air-conditioned rooms with bath, TV, telephone and balcony. The food is pricey but good, and the rooms are in jungle-style cabins with thatched roofs. There are pleasant gardens and a swimming pool. Their casino is sometimes open. This hotel is popular, and reservations are a good idea (though not always necessary).

Nearly opposite the Zaracay is the new *Hotel Tropical Inn* (☎ 761 771/2/3/4, fax 761 775), which I haven't checked out but is reportedly about as good as and similarly priced to the Zaracay; it also has a decent restaurant.

Places to Eat

Pollos Gus is a plastic but clean US-style fried chicken restaurant on Latacunga just off 29 de Mayo. At the east end of 29 de Mayo there are a couple of other cheap chicken places.

On the main plaza, *Chifa Happy* for Chinese food and *Elite Restaurant* for general Ecuadorian food are both reasonably priced and recommended.

The *Cebichería Caleta*, in the Hotel Caleta on Ibarra between 29 de Mayo and 3 de Julio, has tables on the street and is a good place for a snack and a cold beer as you watch the goings on. Meals are also available. It's not very cheap but it's popular.

The best restaurants are found in the better hotels.

Getting There & Away

The terminal terrestre is about two km west of town. There are frequent buses to many major towns. Just walk into the terminal and you'll find drivers and their assistants yelling out destinations. Quito (US$2.20; 2½ hours) and Guayaquil (US$4.40; five hours) are the most frequent destinations with buses leaving at least once an hour with various companies. Make sure you take a small *buseta* if you're in a hurry to get to Guayaquil, as the larger buses can take two hours longer. It's easy enough to get buses to intermediate points such as Quevedo or Daule, but if you want to go to Babahoyo you'll find fewer buses, as most southbound buses take the Daule road beyond Quevedo.

If you're heading south to Peru and don't want to change at Guayaquil, try Transportes Occidentales, which have several departures a day to Machala (US$5.50; eight hours). Their buses are fairly slow but are large and reasonably comfortable.

There are buses about every hour to Esmeraldas on the north coast (US$2.20; 3½ hours) stopping at La Concordia and Quinindé. Some of these buses may continue to Atacames or Muisne.

Buses also go to the central coast but not as frequently as to Esmeraldas. Bahía de Caráquez (US$3.50; six hours) and Manta (US$4.30; seven hours) are both served by several companies.

Express Sucre has five daily buses to Cuenca (US$5; 10 hours). There are also buses to Latacunga, Ambato and Riobamba (US$3.50; five hours).

There is a local bus plaza at the west end of Avenida 3 de Julio where you can find beat-up old bone-shakers to take you to nearby villages. It can be interesting to take one of these buses just to see the countryside, but make sure that there is a return bus, as these villages often don't have restaurants, let alone a place to stay. You can also find buses here returning to Quito via La Concordia and (San Miguel de) Los Bancos, an uncomfortable eight-hour ride, but with beautiful scenery. Buses to Mindo may leave from here or the main terminal; ask locally.

Getting Around

Bus The most useful city bus is signed 'Centro' and runs east from the terminal terrestre, through the center and out along Avenida Quito past the hotels Toachi and Zaracay on the way to the Río Toachi swimming area. The fare is US$0.10. The return bus, signed 'Terminal Terrestre,' heads west along 29 de Mayo picking up passengers for the terminal.

Taxi A taxi from the terminal terrestre to the center costs just under US$1.

NORTHWEST OF SANTO DOMINGO

This roads goes to the port of Esmeraldas (see the North Coast chapter) almost 200 km away. Most people go straight through, but the area is not devoid of interest.

The **Bosque Protectora La Perla** forest reserve (☎ 725 344, 759 115), Casilla 17-24-128, Santo Domingo, is about 42 km northwest of Santo Domingo. This 250 hectare reserve is a good spot for birding and nature walks; guided hikes and camping are also possible. Visits are US$5 per person (including a guide), and a maximum of 10 visitors are allowed on any day. Advance reservations are requested and exact directions will be given.

A few kilometers beyond is the village of **La Concordia** with a basic hostal. About 50 km northwest of Santo Domingo (just past La Concordia), a road to the right leads to **Puerto Quito**, about 20 km east of the main Santo Domingo-Esmeraldas highway. Buses go by occasionally. About two km before reaching Puerto Quito, a sign points to *Aldea Salamandra*, about half a km away on the banks of the Río Caoni. This is a very tranquil, rustic hideaway with swimming and canoeing on the river, birdwatching and relaxing. There are no showers and no flush toilets. Beds are US$4 to US$7 per person depending on the room. Food is available. The place is part of the Hostelling International chain and is gaining popularity among young budget travelers, though it is far from discovered. Further information is available from Katie in Quito (☎ 519 910), Guayaquil 1228 and Olmedo, office 107,

between 1 and 5 pm, Monday to Friday. Also ask at the Youth Hostel in Quito or at the SAEC for more details.

About 87 km northwest of Santo Domingo, is the small town of **Quinindé** (also known as Rosa Zarate). Here there are a couple of basic hotels, of which the *Paraíso* has been suggested. Approximately 40 km west of Quinindé is the Reserva Biológica Bilsa.

Reserva Biológica Bilsa

This 1400-hectare reserve lies in the Montañas de Mache (a small range of coastal mountains) between 300 and 600 meters in elevation and preserves some of the last remaining stands of premontane tropical wet forests. The biodiversity here is exceptionally high – it is rated as one of the world's megadiversity hot spots. Howler monkeys are common, jaguars and pumas have been recently recorded, isolated populations of endangered birds found, and new species of plants discovered. Clearly, the area holds a lot of potential for conservation, research and education, the primary goals of the Fundación Jatun Sacha, which founded the reserve in 1994. Jatun Sacha is one of Ecuador's primary research and conservation organizations.

Bilsa was founded in memory of US ornithologist Ted Parker, botanist Al Gentry, and Ecuadorian conservationist Eduardo Aspiazu, three noted scientists who died near here in 1993 in an aircraft accident while carrying out research to inventory the flora and fauna of the area.

During the wet months of January to June, access is via a 25 km muddy trail (foot or mule only), but vehicular access may be possible in the dry months. This difficulty of access is what has contributed to the preservation of the area in the first place, so don't feel bad about it! There is a rustic field station that accommodates visiting researchers and natural history visitors for US$10 a day plus food. As of yet, this remains a fledgling operation, but better facilities are planned. Various research and volunteer programs are underway. Reservations should be made with the reserve manager Michael McColm through Jatun Sacha (☎/fax 441 592, email mccolm@jsacha.ecx.ec), Casilla 17-12-867, Quito.

RÍO PALENQUE SCIENCE CENTER

Río Palenque Research Center is just off the main Santo Domingo-Quevedo road, about 46 km south of Santo Domingo and 56 km north of Quevedo. This small, privately owned preserve of 180 hectares contains about 100 hectares of primary rainforest. Although this is not a very large area, it is one of the largest tracts of western lowland forest left. It forms a habitat island and is surrounded by agricultural land. There are about 70 hectares of African oil palm plantation within the science center, and more palm, banana, cacao and other crops are grown for many kilometers around the center. The elevation is about 200 meters, and it is hot and humid for much of the year, particularly from December to July. It is drier the rest of the year.

There are facilities for researchers, including a small laboratory and a small library of books and papers relevant to the area. A flora checklist published in 1978 mentions 1100 plants at the center, and of these about 100 species were new to science. This gives an indication of how important it is to preserve what little there is left of this unique habitat. Bird lists include over 360 species from the area, and insect lists are equally impressive. Because of the small size of the preserve, however, there are no large mammals and few small ones present. Slowly, the pressure of the surrounding agricultural lands is lowering the species counts for the science center – if a species dies out or leaves, it is unlikely to come back again.

There are about three km of trails at the center, and the birdwatching is excellent. A day use fee of US$5 is charged.

Places to Stay & Eat

The field station has six quadruple rooms, shower and toilet facilities, and an equipped kitchen. Accommodations are adequate but not luxurious. Rates are US$15 per person per night if you bring your own food or US$30 if you have the caretaker prepare meals for you. The nearest store is in the village of Patricia Pilar, about two km north of the entrance to the science center.

Reservations and information are available from the owner, renowned orchid expert Dr Calaway Dodson (☎ 561 646) in Quito. If the place is not full of researchers (it usually isn't), you can just show up.

Getting There & Away

If you are coming from Santo Domingo, you pass through the small village of Patricia Pilar about two km before reaching the sign 'Centro Científico Río Palenque' on the left. From here a dirt road leads about 1½ km to the field station. The road is usually locked with a chain, but the caretaker has the key.

Any bus between Santo Domingo and Quevedo can drop you off or pick you up at the entrance road to the center.

QUEVEDO

It's a little over 100 km from Santo Domingo to Quevedo on a gently descending paved road. During the first 15 km you see frequent signs on the sides of the road advertising the homes of Colorado Indian *curanderos* (medicine men). This is where you go if you want to see them, but expect to pay for both cures and photography.

There are little villages about every 20 km along this road. The most important is the small market town of **Buena Fe**, about 15 km before Quevedo. Buena Fe has a couple of basic hotels on the main street. The land is agricultural with many banana plantations and, as you get closer to Quevedo, African palm and papaya groves. The palm is important for vegetable oil.

One of the first things I noticed in Quevedo was a strange smell, rather like stale beer. I thought there was a brewery in town, but I was told that it was *tamarindo*, a brown, bean-like fruit popular in fruit juices. Quevedo, with over 80,000 inhabitants, is an important road hub and market town; tamarindo and many other products

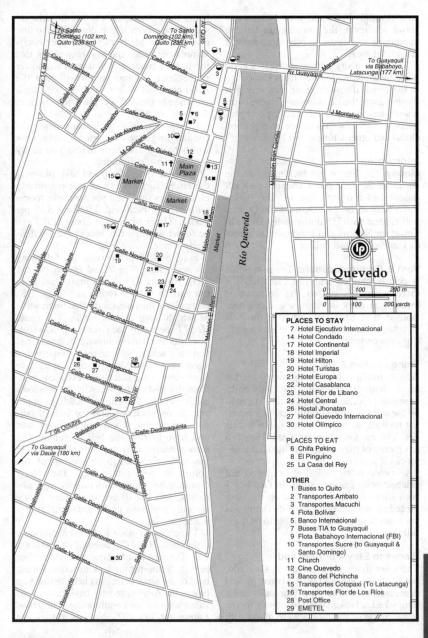

Quevedo

0   100   200 m
0   100   200 yards

PLACES TO STAY
7 Hotel Ejecutivo Internacional
14 Hotel Condado
17 Hotel Continental
18 Hotel Imperial
19 Hotel Hilton
20 Hotel Turistas
21 Hotel Europa
22 Hotel Casablanca
23 Hotel Flor de Libano
24 Hotel Central
26 Hostal Jhonatan
27 Hotel Quevedo Internacional
30 Hotel Olímpico

PLACES TO EAT
6 Chifa Peking
8 El Pinguino
25 La Casa del Rey

OTHER
1 Buses to Quito
2 Transportes Ambato
3 Transportes Macuchi
4 Flota Bolívar
5 Banco Internacional
7 Buses TIA to Guayaquil
9 Flota Babahoyo Internacional (FBI)
10 Transportes Sucre (to Guayaquil &
   Santo Domingo)
11 Church
12 Cine Quevedo
13 Banco del Pichincha
15 Transportes Cotopaxi (To Latacunga)
16 Transportes Flor de Los Ríos
28 Post Office
29 EMETEL

W LOWLANDS

pass through here. At only 145 meters above sea level, the town is hot but the mountains with their cooler temperatures are not far away.

There are many hotels, and it is a good place to break the journey from Latacunga to the coast, if you're going that way. For some reason, the Ecuadorian Chinese community has settled in this bustling and progressive town, so there are many good chifas and other Chinese-run businesses.

Information
Money The Banco del Pichincha, on the corner of the main plaza, changes cash US dollars and traveler's checks. The Banco Internacional, on 7 de Octubre and Quarta, will change cash US dollars only. Delgado Travel on Novena and Progreso has a casa de cambio for cash dollars.

Post & Communications The post office is poorly marked and you can't tell it's there when it's closed. Its entrance is through an alley in a business block near Bolívar. The EMETEL office is on 7 de Octubre at the southeast end of downtown. The area code is 05.

Things to See & Do
As you might expect in a growing market town, there are markets. The daily early morning produce market on the Malecón by the river is quite colorful, and it's pleasant to walk along the river before it gets hot. The market at Septima and Progreso has plenty of plastic junk but also has hammocks if you need one.

Quevedo is the capital of its canton and celebrates its cantonization on October 7 with street parades and a fair on the days preceding the 7th. (Avenida 7 de Octubre is the main drag.) Hotels are liable to be quite full then.

Places to Stay – bottom end
There are many cheap hotels in Quevedo, but the half dozen or so I visited looked depressingly similar – peeling walls and a lumpy bed, a broken window or no window at all. Some of the rooms were marginally better than others, so it is worth asking to see another room if you don't like the first one you see. Many of the cheaper hotels suffer from water shortages, so check that the water's running if you want to shower immediately. Some hotels will turn the water pump off to save water but will turn it on when requested. People often swim in the river.

Cheaper hotels with fans and air-conditioning have basic rooms, and it's not worth paying for them unless you really want the air-conditioning.

The best of the cheap and basic places is the *Hotel Turistas*, which has reasonably clean rooms for US$3 per person or rooms with private bath and TV for US$6 per person. Other places for about US$3 can be found within a few blocks but are definitely worse.

For US$4.50 per person, the following are acceptable. The *Hotel Hilton* (☎ 751 359), Novena 429, looks pretty bad from the outside but the rooms inside are OK, particularly the ones on the 2nd floor, some of which have private baths. The clean *Hotel Imperial* by the river is a good value. The rooms all have private bathrooms (I had cold water, but one reader reports hot water) and fans. Many of the rooms have river views (and there's an excellent view from the roof), which is why the windows lack curtains – there are no buildings opposite. Some readers found the lack of curtains unnerving. The hotel is secure and you have to ring the bell to get in. The market nearby may preclude sleep early in the morning, though the views of the goings-on are interesting. The *Hotel Condado* has rooms with rather dank bathrooms, and the disco below may create sleeping problems on Saturday nights, but it's not too bad.

The cheapest place with air-conditioning is the basic *Hotel Continental* (☎ 750 080), 7 de Octubre and Octava, at US$5.50 per person. Some rooms lack air-conditioning but are the same price, so check before you pay as the rooms are very basic and a poor value without air-conditioning. The *Hotel Europa* (☎ 751 202), Novena 311, is just

OK at US$6.50/11 for rooms with bath. The *Hotel Flor de Libano* (☎ 755 500) is marginally better at US$6.50 per person with bath and fan.

Places to Stay – middle
The *Hotel Central* (☎ 750 701, 757 579), Bolívar 925, has quite nice rooms with bath, TV and fan for US$9 per person. The *Hotel Jhonatan* (☎ 750 483, 752 298, 752 296), Progreso at Decimasegunda, has similar rooms with a telephone for US$11/17 and one room with air-conditioning for US$22 a double. The *Hotel Ejecutivo Internacional* (☎ 751 780, 751 781, fax 750 596), 7 de Octubre and Quarta, has reasonably sized air-conditioned rooms that vary somewhat in quality – the interior rooms are nicer and quieter. Rates are about US$10/15.

The *Hotel Quevedo Internacional* (☎ 751 875, 751 876), Decimasegunda 207, has fair rooms with air-conditioning, TV, telephone and private hot showers for about US$22 single or double. The restaurant is quite good.

Finally, the best place to stay is on the eastern edge of town – *Hotel Olímpico* (☎ 750 455, 750 965, fax 751 314), on Decimanovena at Bolívar. This is a tourist complex, complete with Olympic swimming pool, waterslides, tennis courts, casino, a good restaurant and bar. Rooms are around US$45/60. It is popular and often full, so call ahead.

Places to Eat
With its large Chinese community, Quevedo has plenty of chifas. There are several along Avenida 7 de Octubre of which the *Chifa Peking* is popular with locals. Just over a block away on Tercera is *El Pinguino* for good ice cream. *La Casa del Rey*, Bolívar at Novena, is another inexpensive, locally popular place.

Another cheap place to go is across the river. If you keep going straight after the bridge, you'll be walking along Avenida Guayaquil which, after half a dozen blocks, makes a large Y; one road goes to Latacunga and the other to Babahoyo. Between the bridge and the Y are dozens of restaurants, ranging from little street stands to bigger comedores and fish restaurants. It's worth a look – there's a good choice of places, and it's colorful.

The restaurant in the Hotel Olímpico has been recommended as the best in town. The restaurants in the Quevedo Internacional and Ejecutivo Internacional are also acceptable.

Entertainment
The disco below the Hotel Condado is loud and cheap, and the one in the Hotel Olímpico is loud and pricey. There is a cinema.

Getting There & Away
Bus There is no central bus terminal so you have to roam the streets looking for the various terminals; the main ones are on the map. Quevedo is 180 km from Guayaquil by flat road and 235 km from Quito by mountainous road, so it's not surprising that the bus situation heavily favors Guayaquil. In fact, there are only two companies with direct buses to Quito (US$3.25; four hours). Transportes Macuchi has the most buses to Quito. You can also stand at the town exit at the end of Avenida 7 de Octubre and wait for a bus heading for Quito, or take one of the frequent Transportes Sucre buses to Santo Domingo, where you can change to equally frequent buses to Quito. Transportes Sucre also has buses to Portoviejo. Transportes Ambato, near the bridge, has several buses a day to Ambato (US$3.75; six hours) via Santo Domingo.

Buses to Guayaquil (US$2.25) are very frequent and take from 2½ to four hours depending on the bus. Ask at Transportes Sucre or TIA companies, which normally go via Daule. If you want to go via Babahoyo (US$1.30; 1½ to two hours), you should go with FBI – which translates, inoffensively, into Flota Babahoyo Internacional and has a bus stop at Bolívar and Tercera.

Other bus companies you should know about are Transportes Cotopaxi and Flota Bolívar. The first runs 10 buses a day to Latacunga (US$3), about five hours by unpaved road. The second has an 8 am and a 1 pm bus to Portoviejo (US$3.50), which takes about four hours. This route, from Latacunga via Quevedo to Portoviejo, is one of the least frequently traveled and also one of the prettiest highland-to-coast routes. The buses are old, crowded and uncomfortable, but the journey is more interesting than the standard routes.

Transportes Flor de los Ríos has local buses every hour to **Mocache**, a small agricultural community about 20 km south of Quevedo and off any main road. They also have a daily 9 am bus to Guayaquil.

Boat Although the Río Quevedo is wide and deep enough for boats and eventually runs into the Pacific at Guayaquil, there is little river traffic. It is much cheaper and more convenient to use the good road connections to the coast. A few dugouts chug up and down and there's usually a raft of bamboo logs floating through, but figure on using the bus to get anywhere.

SOUTH OF QUEVEDO
If your southbound bus crosses the Río Quevedo bridge, then you are going to Babahoyo; if it doesn't, then you are heading to Daule, which is the most frequent route to Guayaquil and described here.

About 20 km away from Quevedo you reach **Empalme** – or Velasco Ibarra, as it's officially called. Here the road forks, westbound on an unpaved road to Portoviejo and southbound on a paved road to Guayaquil. Empalme is a busy little junction town with several basic restaurants and pensiones. You're in the heart of banana country here and it continues that way to **Balzar**, another small market town with a basic hotel.

Near **Palestina** the banana plantations give way to rice paddies, and *piladoras* are frequently seen along the road. These are husking and drying factories with tons of rice spread out on huge concrete slabs to dry in the sun (assuming you're traveling in the dry season). Not everyone can afford the commercial piladoras, and often you see a poor campesino spreading out his few

bushels of rice to dry on the tarmac at the side of the road. In other areas, similar piladoras are used to dry various crops such as coffee.

About three quarters of the way to Guayaquil, you'll reach **Daule**. This is another small commercial and agricultural center with basic hotels. As you cross the Río Daule you may see a few outboard-powered dugouts. Few people travel to Guayaquil that way as it is prohibitively expensive compared to the bus. Three hours after leaving Quevedo, the bus gets to Guayaquil, Ecuador's major port and largest city, described in the chapter on the South Coast.

BABAHOYO
With about 50,000 inhabitants, Babahoyo is the capital of the flat agricultural province of Los Ríos. North of it lie banana and palm plantations, south of it are rice paddies and some cattle raising. Huge flocks of white cattle egrets can make the ride from Babahoyo to Guayaquil very pretty.

Babahoyo was an important town on the route between Guayaquil and Quito. In the 19th century, passenger and cargo boats regularly steamed up the Río Babahoyo as far as this town, and then transferred to mules for the ride up to Quito. Perhaps because of its low elevation and propensity to flooding, the area was called Babahoyo which, literally, translates into 'slimepit.'

Although it's not exactly exciting, Babahoyo is a bustling and energetic town with much commercial activity. The central streets are very busy and, for some strange reason, I found myself liking this town with the slimy name. I didn't see any other gringos here.

Things to See & Do
Babahoyo, only seven meters above sea level and on the banks of the Río Babahoyo, was badly flooded during the 1982-83 El Niño. To get some idea of what the flood was like, go to the library at the edge of the river. The flood-retaining walls, some six meters high in the dry season, were completely washed away in places. The

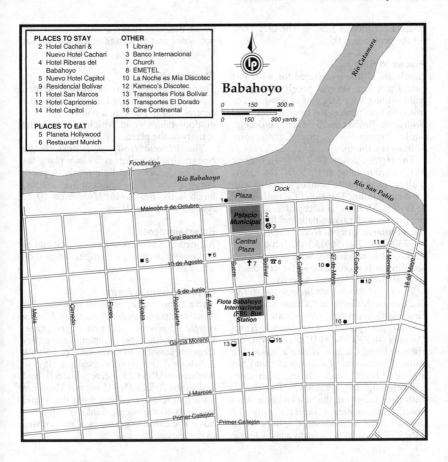

Babahoyo

PLACES TO STAY
2 Hotel Cachari &
   Nuevo Hotel Cachari
4 Hotel Riberas del
   Babahoyo
5 Nuevo Hotel Capitol
9 Residencial Bolívar
11 Hotel San Marcos
12 Hotel Capricornio
14 Hotel Capitol

PLACES TO EAT
5 Planeta Hollywood
6 Restaurant Munich

OTHER
1 Library
3 Banco Internacional
7 Church
8 EMETEL
10 La Noche es Mía Discotec
12 Kameco's Discotec
13 Transportes Flota Bolívar
15 Transportes El Dorado
16 Cine Continental

0   150   300 m
0   150   300 yards

Río Catamara

Footbridge

Río Babahoyo

Dock

Río San Pablo

Plaza

Malecón 9 de Octubre

Palacio
Municipal

Central
Plaza

Gral Barona

10 de Agosto

5 de Junio

Flota Babahoyo
Internacional
(FBI) Bus
Station

García Moreno

J Marcos

Primer Callejón

Primer Callejón

Sucre

Bolívar

A Calderón

27 de Mayo

P Carbo

J Montalvo

18 de Mayo

Mejía

Olmedo

Flores

M Icaza

Rocafuerte

P Alfaro

---

water level reached the library entrance, which is on a small patio about half a meter higher than the surrounding streets – all of which were flooded for several weeks. The inhabitants waded knee-deep from house to house or used canoes.

Before the floods there were floating houses on the river; they just rose and fell with the waters. A few drifted loose but most remained undamaged. You can cross the river for a nominal fee; there are frequent departures from the dock.

The church on the central plaza has a large, modern mural of the Virgin and

Child decorating the entire front. The otherwise pleasing effect is marred somewhat by the massive, rusty iron doors, which look more like the doors of a maximum security prison than the entrance to a place of worship.

Babahoyo was officially founded on May 27, 1869. The day is celebrated with parades.

Information

The Banco Internacional changes both traveler's checks and cash US dollars. The post office is found in the government buildings on the central plaza, and the

EMETEL office is nearby. The area code for the province is 05.

Places to Stay

Hotels are a little overpriced for what you get. There are several hotels to choose from – none very fancy or expensive. For just US$2 per person, the basic *Residencial Bolívar* on Bolívar and 5 de Junio is decent, while the similarily priced *Hotel San Marcos* is a dump.

The *Hotel Cachari* (☎ 730 749), Bolívar 111, is a fair value at US$6/10 for rooms with fans and private bath, or US$8/14 with air-conditioning. The *Hotel Capital*, Sucre at García Moreno, is acceptable at US$6 per person with private bath and fan, while the similarily priced *Hotel Capricornio* (☎ 730 413, 730 564), 5 de Junio and P Carbo, also has rooms with private bath and fan but is more basic and over a disco, so likely to be noisy at weekends.

The *Hotel Riberas de Babahoyo* (☎ 730 082), on the Malecón at P Carbo, has clean, air-conditioned rooms with private bath for US$10 per person. The *Nuevo Hotel Cachari* (☎ 730 734 443), next door to the cheaper Hotel Cachari, is also a reasonable value. Rooms with TV, hot water and fan are US$14/20 and those with air-conditioning are US$18/30. The rooms with river views are the best in town. Also good, but smaller (currently only 12 rooms), is the *Nuevo Hotel Capitol* (☎ 730 446, 733 368), 10 de Agosto and M Icaza, which has large rooms with TV, telephone, hot water and air-conditioning that go for US$18/30.

Places to Eat

There are many *chifas* in the town center, especially on General Barona east of the central plaza. There is a corner *café* with outdoor tables from which to watch the activity of the plaza.

The *Planeta Hollywood*, next to the Nuevo Hotel Capitol, is a clean place for breakfast, snacks and light meals. A good, cheap place for an outdoor (or indoor) lunch is the *Restaurant Munich* on 10 de Agosto and Eloy Alfaro.

Entertainment

A cinema and two discos at the east end of downtown (see map) might keep you amused.

Getting There & Away

There is no proper terminal terrestre, but most companies have departures from a couple of blocks southwest of the plaza. Between them, these companies have very frequent services to Guayaquil (US$0.80; 1½ hours) and several buses a day to Ambato (US$3.25; five hours) and Riobamba (US$3.25; 4½ hours). These are attractive routes climbing from the humid lowlands to the scenic flanks of Chimborazo. You can also get buses to most towns in the province.

The North Coast

Unlike the coast of Peru to the south, Ecuador has warm water bathing its coast, and swimming is pleasant year round. There are palm-fringed, sandy beaches that, unfortunately, suffered greatly during the 1982-83 El Niño floods. Many of the beaches were destroyed (palm trees uprooted, the sand washed away and ocean-front buildings and streets damaged) but they are now recovering.

According to Cárdenas and Greiner, who recently completed the noteworthy (if slightly mad) project of *Walking the Beaches of Ecuador* (see the Books appendix in the back of the book), the Ecuadorian coastline is approximately 2790 km in length, of which less than one-third is beaches. The rest is a combination of mangroves, estuaries, river deltas and other geographic features.

There are two definite seasons on the coast. The rainy season lasts from December to June and the dry season the rest of the year. The rainy season is hot and humid as well as wet, and the climate in the lowlands is uncomfortable. At this time, local people flock to the beaches. I suppose that if it is hot, humid, wet and stickily uncomfortable, you may as well go to the beach and cool off in the sea. January to March seem to be popular months because the water temperature, influenced by El Niño currents, is warmer than the rest of the year.

The biggest problem during the wet months is that the rain can make roads slow or impassable, but generally the main roads remain open year round. During the dry season there are often fewer Ecuadorian tourists than during the wet, because they don't like the cooler water, but there are plenty of foreign visitors.

Having said all this, I should point out that visiting Ecuador just for the beaches can be disappointing – they don't compare with the beaches of the Caribbean. The Andes, Amazon and Galápagos are all

much more worthwhile destinations for foreign travelers. If you have some time on your hands and just love the coast, then by all means, come. But the beaches are not the highlight of a trip to Ecuador, not for me at any rate.

Traveling along the coast is varied and exciting. If you were to begin in the north and work your way southward, you would travel by motorized dugout, normal bus, ranchera, poled dugout and on foot.

This chapter describes the north coastal provinces of Esmeraldas and Manabí. Esmeraldas is the most northerly province in Ecuador, reaching a latitude of 1°25′ North. It is also the wettest and most humid of the coastal provinces, with tropical rainforest in the far north coastal areas and inland regions of the province. The south coastal areas of Esmeraldas and on into Manabí become drier and less humid. Here, there are some remnants of tropical dry forest.

Note that the north coast has a higher incidence of malaria than the Oriente, so come prepared, especially during the wet months when mosquitoes abound. Also note that lobster, served in some coastal seafood restaurants, is locally overfished and endangered. Restaurants are not legally allowed to serve lobster fished in Ecuador until the species recovers, but many places still have it on the menu. Possibly, it is imported or it may have been caught during the few short weeks of lobster season, but generally it is being served illegally and is best avoided.

SAN LORENZO

A new road from Ibarra to San Lorenzo was built in late 1995, though construction is not complete and bus transportation is still irregular, especially in the wet season. Meanwhile, most travelers arrive by train or boat. The train ride down from Ibarra in the highlands is rough but beautiful and

NORTH COAST

takes all day. San Lorenzo itself is not very attractive as there are no beaches; most people use it just as an overnight stop before continuing to Esmeraldas.

San Lorenzo is a small town with a few streets centered around the railway tracks. A couple of the most central streets are paved, but there are very few vehicles (until the road arrives). The town is not very well laid out but is small and most everyone knows where everything is. *Marimba* music can sometimes be heard in town but there are no special bars or nightclubs; ask around. There are approximately 20,000

inhabitants in the town and surrounding area, but I expect there to be a boom when the road is finally finished.

Eventually, the coastal road from Esmeraldas to Borbón will be elongated to San Lorenzo, making a Quito-Esmeraldas-San Lorenzo-Ibarra-Quito roundtrip possible by bus or car. Then, there are plans to continue the coastal road north to the Colombian border, a few kilometers beyond which is a Colombian road. Thus San Lorenzo's former isolation will soon be a memory and the face of this region will change dramatically by the end of the century.

Orientation & Information

The center is a 15-minute walk from the railway station and a few minutes from the port. It is possible to arrive in San Lorenzo by boat from Tumaco in Colombia, but there is no immigration office here. You have to go to Esmeraldas' immigration office, Ibarra's police station or maybe even Quito to get your passport stamped.

There are no proper money changing facilities, though if you ask around you'll find people will change small amounts of Colombian currency or US dollars. The EMETEL office is near the train station. The area code for San Lorenzo and the province of Esmeraldas is 06.

Excursiones El Refugio (☎/fax 780 134), 30 meters from the EMETEL office, has local beach, mangrove and cultural excursions from US$10 per day, depending on group size. In addition, they have various volunteer projects in the area ranging from reforestation to teaching English. This new company has been recommended as being culturally and environmentally sensitive.

The Catholic hospital in San Lorenzo is reputedly the best in the area north of Esmeraldas.

Places to Stay & Eat

None of the few hotels in San Lorenzo are of high quality, so if you like some comforts you will be uncomfortable here. None of the rooms have hot water, air-conditioning or other amenities, and very few have private bathrooms. They should, however, have a bed and a mosquito net or fan; the mosquitoes can be bad, especially in the wet months. Bring insect repellent or mosquito coils. The town suffers from occasional water shortages, so take showers when you can.

If arriving by train, try to find a place to stay quickly because everyone else will be looking. At the train station friendly but persistent kids badger travelers for tips to take you to a hotel. Several of these kids are becoming very entrepreneurial – they'll walk down the railway track to a station up from San Lorenzo and, by boarding the train before it arrives in San Lorenzo, begin to look for prospective customers early. Some travelers find the kids amusing, friendly and helpful (which they are), while others feel put-out by the kids' insistence. These young 'guides' will also hang out in front of hotels in order to show you where the restaurants are – another tip expected.

The best place is the *Gran Hotel San Carlos* (☎ 780 267, 780 284), Imbabura and Garces (near the train station), with clean rooms for US$5 per person and US$7 with tepid shower. Most rooms have TV, fan and mosquito nets. Also decent is the *Hotel Imperial* (☎ 780 242, 780 221), on the right on Calle Imbabura as you walk in from the station, and the *Hotel Continental* (☎ 780 125) on the left. They charge US$5 per person for rooms with private bath. The owners of the Imperial also own the OK *Hotel San Lorenzo* at US$2.50 per person. In town the basic but adequate *Hotel Ecuador* (☎ 780 137) is US$2 per person or US$3.50 with bath. The friendly *Hotel Carondolet* (☎ 780 202), across from the Parque Central, has clean rooms with mosquito nets and baths for US$4.50 per person and some cheaper ones. The *Yeaniny* is new and similarly priced.

Meals are not cheap. The *Hotel Ecuador* has a decent restaurant. The set meals are the cheapest. The nearby *El Fogón* is considered the 'best' but is more expensive.

Getting There & Away

Bus The service on the new road is erratic in the wet months but, as I write in the 1996 dry season, there are two buses every day to and from Ibarra, and a daily bus continuing to Quito. This service is bound to become more regular in 1997.

Train The railway station is just over one km from the town center. The autoferro leaves daily at 7 am from San Lorenzo for Ibarra. Services are often disrupted – sometimes trains run every other day, although they ran daily when I was in town. The train continues to run because of the higher rates paid by foreign travelers.

They won't sell you tickets until the day of departure. People start lining up around 6 am, the ticket office opens at 6:30 am, and the train usually leaves late. The fare is US$15. The train is almost always full and people often ride on the top. The scenery is great and the rooftop ride is recommended for good views and photography. Remember to always look ahead when the train is underway or you will be hit by low-hanging branches.

Most travelers do this trip from Ibarra down to San Lorenzo and then south along the coast as is described in this chapter. There are fewer people doing it the other way and so it is a little less crowded from San Lorenzo up to Ibarra. The first half of the journey is relatively flat, and a 15-minute lunch break is often made at **Lita** (at 450 meters above sea level), where there are a couple of simple restaurants by the train station and a basic place to stay on the main street. You may be asked to register your passport here, so be prepared.

North of Lita is the little-known **Awa Ethnic & Forestry Preserve**, which protects some of the lowland forests on the Ecuadorian-Colombian border. The preserve is managed by INEFAN and is the home of a few remaining Awa Indians.

The World Wildlife Fund was involved in the implementation of a management plan for the area and provided financial grants of US$119,000 in 1990 and US$70,000 in 1991 for this purpose. I do not know of any way to visit the preserve at this time.

Beyond Lita the train begins to climb noticeably, and there are many tunnels and gorgeous views of luxuriant forest – but watch those branches if riding on top!

Boat General inquiries about boat services are best directed to the Capitanía on the waterfront. They have lists of departing and arriving boats.

The most frequent travelers' destinations are Limones (officially called Valdéz, US$3.50; 1¼ hours), Borbón (US$6; 3½ hours) and La Tola (US$4.50; 2½ hours). As with the trains, there is a two-tier pricing system and locals pay less.

La Tola is the most frequent destination of most travelers and is served by two companies: Transportes San Lorenzo del Pailón (known locally as La Costeñita) and Ecuador/Pacífico Tours. They take turns and, between them, have departures every hour from 5:30 am to 2:30 pm daily. Most boats to La Tola stop at Limones en route, but few travelers stop there. If you take an early morning boat to La Tola you can connect with a bus on to Esmeraldas. Tickets are sold in San Lorenzo for the complete journey, or you can buy the bus portion when you get to La Tola. The bus takes about four or five hours from La Tola to Esmeraldas, so the whole trip from San Lorenzo to Esmeraldas can be done in one day and costs about US$7.

A new route has opened to Esmeraldas from Borbón at the confluence of the Río Cayapas and Río Santiago. Motorized dugouts go from San Lorenzo via Limones to Borbón from where there are buses going to Esmeraldas several times a day. Service from San Lorenzo to Borbón is at 7 am and 1 pm daily.

There are boats most days at 7 am to Tumaco in Colombia, but make sure you have all the necessary visas (see Facts for the Visitor). Few foreigners take this route; the journey is done in motorized dugouts, costs about US$4 (local prices – there is no two-tier price system because hardly any gringos go this way) and takes most of the day. It can get both very wet and sunny, so protect yourself and your gear. Border crossing facilities are not geared to foreign tourists and you may have difficulty entering Colombia. Esmeraldas is probably the best place to get your exit stamp from Ecuador.

You can hire a motorized dugout to San Pedro, which is a completely undeveloped beach on an island north of San Lorenzo. You can camp here if you bring everything you need – a trip for the adventurous and prepared traveler. Excursiones El Refugio organizes tours here.

It is supposedly possible to take a steamer all the way from San Lorenzo to

Esmeraldas, but this isn't recommended. You don't see much of the countryside and the boats are cargo vessels that are dirty, hot and uncomfortable. Service is irregular – about twice a week.

The motorized dugout journey via Limones and on to Borbón or La Tola is much nicer. The dugouts are small enough to travel through the coastal mangrove swamps and you'll see much more scenery than you would from a larger steamer.

Keep your eyes open for the black scissor-tailed frigatebirds circling overhead, squadrons of pelicans gliding by and schools of jellyfish floating past the boat. And don't forget protection against sun, wind, rain and spray.

LIMONES

Limones is a small town at the mouth of the deltas of Río Santiago and Río Cayapas. It has a population of about 7000 and is economically more important than San Lorenzo, despite the latter's railway connections.

Timber is logged in this area and floated down the river to Limones, where there is a sawmill. There are few amenities in town, and the two hotels are pretty rough.

The only way into Limones is by boat and you can sometimes see Chachi Indians (formerly known as the Cayapas) here, although more can be seen at Borbón and further up the Río Cayapas.

About twice a week a cargo steamer leaves Limones for Esmeraldas – if you want to sail on it, ask the captain. Passengers are not normally carried, but the captain will allow you to go if you are interested. It's cheap, but dirty and uncomfortable.

BORBÓN

This small river port on Río Cayapas has about 5000 inhabitants, most of whom are the descendants of African slaves brought here by the Spanish. The town now has road connections to Esmeraldas and is also the best place to get boats up the Cayapas and to continue up the Río San Miguel to the Reserva Ecológica Cotacachi-Cayapas – an interesting trip to a remote area. It is also the entry point for trips up the equally interesting Río Santiago. Borbón is beginning to compete in importance with Limones. Market day is Sunday.

Information

Angel Ceron is the principal (headmaster) of the local school, Colegio Luz y Libertad. He also runs the Pampa de Oro Hotel in Borbón. Ceron is a good source of information about the area; he can tell you how to get to some of the local archaeological sites that pertain to the Tolita culture, which existed here around 2000 years ago. There is not much to be seen - these sites are mainly of interest to professional archaeologists.

Riches from the Rainforest

In the rainforests around Borbón a small tagua nut industry is developing. Known as 'vegetable ivory,' tagua nuts come from a palm tree that grows in the local forest. The nuts are relatively tender when first harvested but soon become extremely hard and can be carved into small ornaments, buttons and other trinkets.

Harvesting the nuts is a sustainable and economically attractive alternative to harvesting the whole rainforest. With the help of Conservation International, the local industry has started finding buyers in North American clothing markets. If you shop in Canadian or US stores, you may find clothes labeled with a 'Tagua Initiative' tag, which explains to consumers how the buttons used on the clothing help make tropical forests worth more standing up than cut down.

You may also find tagua nut products for sale in the Borbón market, Esmeraldas, Riobamba and in Quito gift shops. I bought a beautiful tagua nut carving of a leaping dolphin – it was reminiscent of scrimshaw. The ornaments do make good souvenirs of the rainforest – and buying them helps to preserve that forest. ∎

A local NGO, SUBIR (Sustainable Uses of Biological Resources) has an office in Borbón. It's funded by USAID and guided by CARE International and the Corporación de Conservación y Desarollo (CCD, ☎ /fax 465 845, see also Online Services), Apartado 17-16-1855, Quito, and is developing local ecotourism projects on the Río Santiago and in San Miguel (see Excursions from Borbón). CARE International is a charity concerned with giving food and medical relief to the poor of various third-world countries, and this project will help to fund its local relief efforts as well as provide employment and preserve the rainforest. Reportedly, there is also an INEFAN office with information about the Cotachai-Cayapas reserve.

Opposite the SUBIR office, a well-known local musician, Papá Roncón, gives marimba demonstrations for a couple of beers (so I'm told).

The US-run mission in Borbón can be of assistance to travelers. If you are driving, they may let you park your vehicle in their parking lot while you take river trips or whatever. Ask for directions in town – most people know where it is.

Places to Stay & Eat

All of the hotels are very basic. The best place is the friendly *La Tolita Pampa de Oro*, charging about US$4 per person - it's also a good source of visitor information. The *Residencial Capri* charges US$2.50 per person in basic but clean rooms with mosquito nets – toilet facilities are primitive. *Hotel Panama City* and *Residencial Anny Christina* are other cheap places to stay.

There are comfortable jungle lodges some distance away by river (see Excursions from Borbón, below).

Most restaurants are basic comedores that don't bother with a menu – ask them what they have. There are places to eat on the waterfront by the dock and others a block behind the waterfront in the 'town center.' Some can get raucous with checker or domino playing and beer drinking in the evening.

Getting There & Away

Bus La Costeñita runs several buses or *rancheras* (flat-bed trucks mounted with excruciatingly narrow and uncomfortable benches) every day to Esmeraldas (US$2.50; four hours). The road is subject to temporary closures during the wet months (January to May), but is being paved.

Boat Passenger boats to San Lorenzo (via Limones) leave daily at 7 and 11 am. The fare is US$6 for the three-hour trip. A daily passenger boat leaves at 11 am for San Miguel (US$8; five hours). This boat can drop you at any location on the Cayapas or San Miguel rivers (see Excursions from Borbón). Other boats run irregularly to other destinations – ask around at the docks.

Fletes or private boats can be hired any time to take you anywhere if you have the money. These are not cheap – expect to pay about 15 times the fare that you would be charged in a passenger boat. Of course, this is not a problem if there is a group of you.

About twice a month there are cargo boats leaving Borbón for Esmeraldas or even Guayaquil. Although the boats don't have passenger cabins, you may be allowed to travel as a passenger if you ask the captain. The fares are low and conditions primitive.

Excursions from Borbón

Occasional passenger boats or fletes will take you up Río Santiago, via the community of Maldonado, to the small village of **Concepción**. This is about a two-hour trip – a flete will cost about US$20 if you bargain. In Concepción, villagers can show you the beginning of a well-beaten path through the forest to the San Lorenzo-Ibarra railroad, about a 12-km walk away. Turn left when you reach the tracks and, in about two km, you'll come to the little village of San Javier de Cachavi, where you can wait for the train coming from Ibarra. The train passes through sometime in the mid to late afternoon, though reportedly a local San Javier-San Lorenzo train leaves at 2 pm. If you left Borbón first thing in the morning, you should have no trouble getting to the railway in time to catch a train to San Lorenzo that afternoon – an interesting and infrequently traveled route.

Further up the Río Santiago (about five hours by boat from Borbón) near the border of the Cotacachi-Cayapas reserve is the remote community of **Playa de Oro**, so named because gold has been panned in the region for centuries. Here, there is a new lodge operated by SUBIR. There are eight clean rooms with comfortable beds and mosquito nets. Bathroom facilities are shared. SUBIR organizes biocultural tours based at the lodge and visiting the nearby rainforest and people. The guides are knowledgeable locals but don't necessarily speak English. Tours from Borbón cost about US$50 per person per night, including meals and guided hikes, boat rides and village visits.

The most reliable boat service from Borbón is the daily passenger boat to San Miguel, (see below), which is used more often by travelers – though you certainly won't find hordes of tourists. There are several possible stopping places along the way.

The first is **Steve's Lodge** at the mouth of the Río Onzole, about an hour from Borbón. Run by a friendly Hungarian, Steve Tarjanyi, the lodge has six comfortable double rooms with great river views. Rates are US$50 per person including meals, or US$300 per person for a three-night stay including meals and a guided boat tour up Río Cayapas to the Reserva Ecológica Cotacachi-Cayapas (optional camping in the reserve is possible). There are discounts for groups of four or more. Guides speak English and the tours have been recommended.

Reservations can be made in Quito with Antonio or Judy Nagy (☎ 431 555, 447 709, fax 431 556) at Avenida 10 de Agosto 4341. Alternately, write to Steve Tarjanyi, Casilla 187, Esmeraldas or the Nagys, Casilla 5148 CCI, Quito. These people all speak excellent English. If you just show up, you can sleep at the lodge or take a tour on a space available basis (available more often than not). The passenger canoe costs

US$2 or a flete is about US$20 from Borbón. A reader writes that there is an inexpensive place to stay across the river from Steve's Lodge.

Beyond Steve's Lodge the boat to San Miguel stops at a number of communities and missions. River travel is made interesting by passengers ranging from Catholic nuns to Chachi (Cayapas) Indians embarking or disembarking in the various tiny ports – usually no more than a few planks at the water's edge.

The first mission is the Catholic **Santa María**. Here, there is a clean dormitory that sleeps up to six people; ask for Señora Pastora, who will show you where to sleep and cook meals if requested. There is also a basic residencial or you can camp. The next mission is the Protestant **Zapallo Grande**. You can find a basic place to sleep here, too. Chachi crafts are often for sale. Both missions have medical clinics and local people will offer to take you on tours. There are also a number of other communities such as Pichiyacu, Playa Grande, Atahualpa and Telembi that are the homes of mainly Chachi Indians or black people.

Finally, you'll reach San Miguel.

SAN MIGUEL

This small, friendly village is the main base from which to visit the lowland sections of the Reserva Ecológica Cotacachi-Cayapas. There is a ranger station on a small hill overlooking the village – the view of the rainforest and river from here is quite spectacular. There are about 20 houses in the village, one of which is a small store selling soft drinks, crackers, sardines, candy, oatmeal and little else. The inhabitants of the village are Afro-Ecuadorians. Chachi Indians' houses are scattered along the shores of the river nearby.

The grass in front of the ranger station has been macheted into a rough lawn – but it is a haven for chiggers. I forgot to put insect repellent on until a couple of hours after I arrived because there were so few mosquitoes. I didn't realize how bad the chiggers were until that evening, when I started itching. The next morning I counted over 100 bites just on one ankle. Put on repellent, especially around your ankles, before you disembark at San Miguel.

Places to Stay & Eat
The *guardaparque* (park ranger) will let you stay in the ranger station for US$3 per person per night. There are four beds, but no running water or mosquito nets. Larger groups can sleep on the floor or camp outside. The station has a cold shower, toilet and kitchen facilities. A shop sells a few very simple food supplies or you can buy basic meals (rice and fried bananas, with a little soup) for about US$5. The people are friendly.

SUBIR has recently opened a lodge here. Facilities and costs are similar to their lodge in Playa de Oro (see Escursions from Borbón, above) or ask for details in their office at Borbón. These facilities are much more comfortable than the park ranger station.

Getting There & Away
The driver of the daily passenger canoe from Borbón spends the night about 15 minutes downriver from San Miguel. He will not come back to San Miguel unless he knows for sure that he has a passenger. It is essential to make arrangements with the boatman about the day you want to be picked up. The canoe leaves San Miguel around 5 am, when it is still dark. Dawn on the river makes this a nice trip.

RESERVA ECOLÓGICA COTACACHI-CAYAPAS
This 204,420-hectare reserve is by far the largest protected area of western Andean habitats in Ecuador. It covers an altitudinal range from about 200 meters above sea level in the San Miguel area to 4939 meters above sea level at the summit of Cotacachi. Thus the type of habitat changes rapidly from lowland tropical wet forest to premontane and montane cloud forest to páramo, with many intermediate habitat types. This rapid change of habitat produces the so-called 'edge effect' that gives rise to an incredible diversity of flora and fauna.

These are the haunts of such rarely seen mammals as the giant anteater, Baird's tapir, jaguar and, in the upper reaches of the reserve, the spectacled bear. The chances of seeing these are remote, however. You may see monkeys, squirrels, sloths, the nine-banded armadillo, bats and a huge variety of bird species. It is certainly a great area for birding.

There are two principal ways to visit the reserve. You can go in from the highlands (as described in the North of Quito chapter) or you can go in from San Miguel, as described below. Whichever way you elect to go, you will find it extremely difficult to descend from the highlands to the lowlands or climb up in the opposite direction. The areas near the reserve boundaries can be visited in both the lowlands and the highlands; the steep and thickly vegetated western slopes of the Andes in between are largely trackless and almost impenetrable. This is bad news if you want to visit the interior of the reserve but good news for the species existing there – they will probably be left alone for a little while longer.

Both the lower reaches of the reserve and the rivers leading into this area are the home of Chachi (Cayapas) Indians, of which about 5000 remain. The Chachis are famous for their basketwork and there are stores in Borbón, Limones, Esmeraldas and Quito selling their crafts. You can buy them far more cheaply direct from the Indians on the river – however, be warned that the baskets tend to be very large, so getting them home may be a minor problem. Many of the Chachis live in traditional style in breezy, open-sided, thatched-roof houses built on stilts near the river. Fishing and subsistence agriculture is their main source of food, and many of the Indians speak only the Chachi tongue. Some groups now live on or close to missions; others are largely beyond missionary influence. In these groups, both men and women go bare breasted.

Over the last few decades the Chachi Indians have been swept by a form of river blindness that is supposedly carried by a blackfly, which is particularly prevalent in

April and May. Some 80% of the Indians have the disease to a greater or lesser extent. Insect repellent works to keep the insects off you, and taking chloroquine as a malarial prophylactic also works to prevent the disease.

The area is very rainy, with up to 5000 mm of rain being reported in some of the more inland areas, although it is somewhat less wet around San Miguel. The rainy season is December to May and the river levels are high then, which makes the local people consider it to be the best time to travel. It is also the season with the highest concentrations of mosquitoes, blackflies and other insects, but they tend to be really bad only at dawn and dusk, so cover up then. Even during the rainy months, mornings are often clear. The drier months of September to December are usually less buggy and there is a better chance of seeing wildlife, though river navigation may be limited.

Entrance into the reserve costs, officially, US$20, payable at the ranger station in San Miguel. If you pay in sucres, the cost is a little less. The rangers will act as guides. They charge about US$10 per day plus food, and two guides are needed for many trips – one for each end of the dugout canoe. These canoes are paddled and poled – they don't have outboard engines – not many people have engines out here. Alternately, you can visit on a guided tour with one of the lodges. Note that the SUBIR lodge in Playa de Oro is also an access point for the reserve, although a less frequently used one than from San Miguel.

It is about two or three hours by canoe from San Miguel to the park limits proper. A further one or two hours brings the visitor to a small but pretty waterfall in the jungle. There are a few poorly marked trails, for which a guide is almost essential. There are places to camp if you have tents and all necessary gear. There are plans to build a hut by the waterfall and another somewhere within the reserve – ask the guides about whether these plans have materialized.

LA TOLA

Most people traveling between San Lorenzo and Esmeraldas take the boat to La Tola and continue by bus to Esmeraldas. There is one extremely poor, basic *residencial* (my friend Randy writes, 'You'd have to be desperate or stupid to stay here.') in La Tola, but local people will help stranded travelers find somewhere to sleep. There are a few stores where you can buy snacks. Near the EMETEL office, the *Comedor Maurita* looks simple but OK. The annual fiesta is on July 16. There is a Tolita archaeological site on the nearby island of Manta de Oro, but the gold ornaments that were found here are now in museums and there is not much to see unless you are an archaeologist. There is a small museum. A few people live on the island and can offer guiding services.

Getting There & Away

There are two transportation companies; both run buses to and from Esmeraldas and boats to and from San Lorenzo. You can buy a single straight-through ticket from San Lorenzo to Esmeraldas. There are a few buses, but most transport is on rancheras. Try to get an end seat so you can at least stretch one leg. Buses or rancheras take four hours to Esmeraldas and cost US$2.50. If you take a morning bus from Esmeraldas you will connect with a boat to San Lorenzo and vice versa, so there is no reason to stay in La Tola.

La Tolita gold mask

THE ROAD TO ESMERALDAS

The bus journey to Esmeraldas from either Borbón or La Tola is bumpy and uncomfortable. It is very dusty in the dry season and muddy in the wet. The first half of the road is very bad and may be impassable during the rainy season. The halfway point is the Río Lagarto – if you are coming from Borbón you cross the river inland and if you are coming from La Tola you cross it close to the river mouth. In both cases, there is a village called **Lagarto**, where there's a basic residencial and a restaurant. There is also a military checkpoint at the Río Lagarto on the Borbón-Esmeraldas route. The soldiers are an oafish bunch, who have been known to search luggage and hold up women's underwear to the delight of their colleagues and disgust of the passengers. Have your passport available for these 'gentlemen.'

After crossing Río Lagarto the paved road begins and the routes from Borbón and La Tola unite. Beyond, the road passes through the village of **Montalvo** and on to the coastal village of **Rocafuerte**, which has a very basic residencial and simple restaurants selling tasty fresh seafood. People from Esmeraldas drive out here on weekends for a good meal in a rural setting. Rocafuerte celebrates its annual fiesta on August 31.

A few kilometers further, the road passes through the coastal village of **Río Verde**, again with a cheap hotel and restaurants. Río Verde was the setting of Moritz Thomsen's *Living Poor* (see Books appendix). Almost 20 km beyond Río Verde is the village of **Camarones**, which sells, as its name implies, delicious shrimp dishes in the simple beachfront restaurants. Ask around about cabins for rent if you want to stay by the beach – it's off the beaten track but close enough to the road that buses to Esmeraldas are easy to catch. A few kilometers beyond Camarones, the road passes the Esmeraldas Airport on the east side of the Río Esmeraldas. The city is on the west side but there is no bridge until San Mateo, about 10 km upriver. It is a half-hour drive from the airport to Esmeraldas.

The drive gives good views of the coastal scenery and I persuaded the driver to let me ride on the roof of the bus, which was better than being squashed inside (there was no extra charge for the air-conditioning). I don't recommend this during the rainy season! Also, watch out for sunburn during the dry season. The bird-life along the coast is varied and spectacular; I enjoyed looking at trees filled with hundreds of roosting white cattle egrets.

ESMERALDAS

This important city of about 100,000 inhabitants (official 1990 census; there are probably around 150,000) is capital of the province of Esmeraldas. It was near here that the Spanish conquistadors made their first landfall in Ecuador. Esmeraldas has been an influential port town throughout Ecuador's history, and it is now the largest port in northern Ecuador. Although fishing and shipping are important, the recent construction of an oil refinery near the terminal of the trans-Andean oil pipeline has given Esmeraldas a new source of income and employment, as well as its share of noise and pollution.

Most tourists just spend the night (if they have to) and continue southwest to the towns of Atacames, Súa and Muisne, where the best beaches are to be found. Esmeraldas also has beaches in the northern suburb of Las Palmas, but they are not as good and are reportedly dirty.

Information

Tourist Offices The tourist office, half a block from the main plaza, has a small sign reading *Comisión Provincial de Turismo*. Hours are erratic – it was recently closed because they didn't have enough funds to pay the rent!

Immigration The immigration office (☎ 710 156) is at the Policía Civil Nacional, three km south of town (think about taking a cab). You should have your passport stamped here if you are leaving or entering Ecuador via the little-used coastal route to Colombia.

Top: Boats off Islas Plazas, Galápagos Islands (TW)
Bottom: Isla Bartolomé, Galápagos Islands (TW)

Top: Boat building in Puerto Ayora, Galápagos Islands (TW)
Bottom: Brachycereus cactus on pahoehoe lava, Isla San Salvador,
Galápagos Islands (RR)

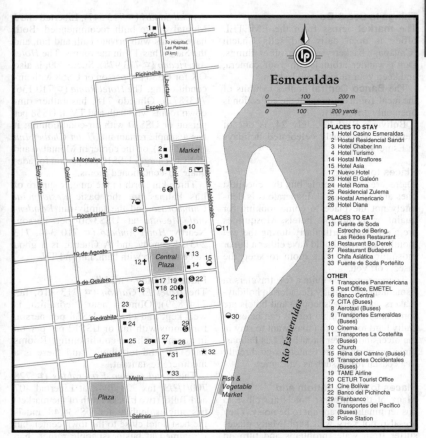

Esmeraldas

PLACES TO STAY
1 Hotel Casino Esmeraldas
2 Hostal Residencial Sandri
3 Hotel Chaber Inn
4 Hotel Turismo
14 Hostal Miraflores
15 Hotel Asia
17 Nuevo Hotel
23 Hotel El Galeón
24 Hotel Roma
25 Residencial Zulema
26 Hostal Americano
28 Hotel Diana

PLACES TO EAT
13 Fuente de Soda
Estrecho de Bering,
Las Redes Restaurant
18 Restaurant Bo Derek
27 Restaurant Budapest
31 Chifa Asiática
33 Fuente de Soda Porteñito

OTHER
1 Transportes Panamericana
5 Post Office, EMETEL
6 Banco Central
7 CITA (Buses)
8 Aerotaxi (Buses)
9 Transportes Esmeraldas (Buses)
10 Cinema
11 Transportes La Costeñita (Buses)
12 Church
15 Reina del Camino (Buses)
16 Transportes Occidentales (Buses)
19 TAME Airline
20 CETUR Tourist Office
21 Cine Bolívar
22 Banco del Pichincha
29 Filanbanco
30 Transportes del Pacífico (Buses)
32 Police Station

Money Banco del Pichincha and Filanbanco change cash US dollars and traveler's checks.

Post & Communications The post office is at the corner of J Montalvo and the Malecón. EMETEL is upstairs, and there is a good view from the EMETEL balcony of the Río Esmeraldas and the riverside market. The area code for the city and province of Esmeraldas is 06.

Medical Services The public hospital (☎ 710 012) is found on Avenida Libertad between Esmeraldas and Las Palmas on the north end of town.

Dangers & Annoyances Be careful in the market areas (especially the south end of the Malecón) and anywhere away from the main streets. There are drug problems and thieves. Avoid arriving in Esmeraldas after dark and keep to well-lit streets to avoid these problems. Electricity and water supply are erratic. The incidence of malaria is high during the wet months. Single women have reported that they get hassled more often in Esmeraldas than elsewhere.

Things to See & Do

The **market** across from the EMETEL office is open daily and sells Chachi (Cayapas) basketry among other things. Don't wander around with your camera, and keep your money well hidden.

The **Banco Central** houses exhibits of the local Tolita culture, but the collection is open only erratically.

Bolívar's Birthday, July 24, is one of the more vigorously celebrated holidays in Esmeraldas.

Places to Stay

There are many hotels but the cheapest ones are not too good. Esmeraldas is definitely not the place to come looking for quaint or memorable hotels. Mosquitoes are a problem, particularly during the wet months, and you should have either a fan or mosquito net in your room to keep the insects off you.

There seem to be quite a few travelers in Esmeraldas (especially Ecuadorian holiday-makers and businesspeople) and hotels are sometimes full. Single rooms can be especially hard to find. You may want to stay in the nicer and pricier suburb of Las Palmas, three km north of the center, or go directly to a coastal resort such as Atacames.

Places to Stay – bottom end

Many of the cheapest hotels are close to bus terminals and are apt to be noisy. They are also not very well kept. Many places suffer from water problems and turn on water when requested only. For about US$3 per person, try *Hostal Miraflores* or *Hotel Turismo* (☎ 712 700), which are just OK. The *Nuevo Hotel* (☎ 711 327) is US$3.50 per person or US$5.50 with a poor private bath. The *Residencial Zulema* (☎ 711 789, 710 910, 712 424), Olmedo near Cañizares, isn't bad at US$9 for a double with bath. The clean *Hotel Asia* (☎ 714 594, 710 648, 711 852), 9 de Octubre 116, is OK for US$4 to US$6 per person, (some rooms with bath).

For US$6 per person, the friendly and helpful *Hotel Diana* (☎ 710 333), Cañizares 224, and the clean *Hostal Residencial Sandri* (☎ 713 547), Libertad and J Montalvo, are both recommended. Both have rooms with private bath and fan, and the Sandri has TV in the rooms. The *Hotel Americano* (☎ 713 978), Sucre 709, is also OK for US$6 per person or US$8 with air-conditioning. The *Hotel Roma* (☎ 710 136, 713 872), Olmedo 718, has rather run-down rooms with bath and TV at US$8 per person or US$10 with air-conditioning; it has a simple restaurant. *Hotel Chaber Inn* (☎ 712 438), on the corner of Montalvo and Bolívar, charges US$10 per person for adequate air-conditioned rooms.

Three km north in the quieter suburb of Las Palmas are the basic *Residencial Chimborazo* and the family-run *Residencial Mechita* at US$3.50 per person. Nearby, *Hotel Ambato* (☎ 710 344, 713 293), Kennedy and A Guerra, is a good value at US$6 with bath, fan and TV.

Places to Stay – middle

The *Hotel El Galeón* (☎ 713 116, fax 714 839), Olmedo near Piedrahita, is well kept and charges US$8 per person for rooms with fan or US$12 per person in rooms with air-conditioning. Rooms have TV and telephone, and there is a mediocre restaurant.

The *Hotel Casino Esmeraldas* (☎ 728 700/1/2/3, fax 728 704), at Libertad 407 and Tello, (two blocks north of the market) has singles/doubles for US$34/48 and is the best hotel close to the town center, but it's aimed at businesspeople rather than tourists. Air-conditioned rooms have minifridges, telephone, TV and room service. There is a casino, guarded parking lot and restaurant/bar. Locals come to the US$11 Sunday buffet brunch.

Some blocks further north along Libertad on the way to Las Palmas is the *Hotel Estuario Internacional* (☎ 713 930, 714 849, fax 714 785). Again, this is a business hotel and is therefore busy during the week but has bargain rates at weekends. Monday to Thursday rates are US$32/40, but at weekends you pay US$24/30 for clean, modern, air-conditioned but small rooms.

In Las Palmas, almost all of the hotels are

on Avenida Kennedy, which is the main street and parallels the beach. Reach it by heading north on Libertad. The *Hotel del Mar* (☎ 713 910, 711 916) is close to the beach at the end of Avenida Kennedy. Rooms are about US\$12/20 but vary widely in quality – some have ocean views. The *Hotel Cayapas* (☎ 711 022/77, ☎ /fax 710 838) has a pleasant garden. Nice rooms with air-conditioning, minifridge, telephone and TV are US\$20/28 and there is a restaurant with room service. The best hotel in this area is the *Costa Verde Suites* (☎ 728 714, fax 728 716), Luis Tello 809 and H Padilla, just a couple minutes' walk from the beach. Rooms have air-conditioning, a kitchenette, balcony, TV, phone and room service. I believe it is the only hotel in the Esmeraldas area with a pool (albeit a small one), and there is a sauna. There is a restaurant and bar. Rates are US\$65 for a double, including breakfast.

Places to Eat

There are many dishes typical of the coast and sometimes found only in this province. Fish and other seafood are more common than meat and are usually served with a mountain of plain white rice, boiled beans and plantains. The plantains are sometimes boiled whole (very stodgy to my taste) or are sliced and fried to make *patacones* – very tasty. Raw seafood is often marinated to make ceviche, which is very good. *Cocado* is any seafood cooked with coconut to impart a delicate flavor; camarones cocado is a particularly typical north coast dish. *Cocadas*, on the other hand, are sweet bars of grated coconut cooked in sugar and sold on bus journeys throughout the province.

The better hotels in Esmeraldas and Las Palmas have decent restaurants, with the Hotel Cayapas (see above) being above average. The food in the many small and cheap pavement cafés and comedores is often very good – try the places along Olmedo between Mejía and Piedrahita. On the east side of the central plaza *Las Redes Restaurant* is good for seafood, and the nearby *Fuente de Soda Estrecho de Bering*

is a good place for snacks and ice cream and for watching the busy goings-on in the plaza. The *Chifa Asiatica*, on Cañizares near Sucre, is the best place for Chinese food. The Hungarian-run *Restaurant Budapest*, Cañizares 214, has also been recommended by travelers for good food at reasonable prices. The *Fuente de Soda Porteñito*, Sucre and Mejía, is locally popular and has good coffee. The *Restaurant Bo Derek*, on Sucre just south of the plaza, has been recommended for cheap meals. Delicious fresh seafood is served at very moderate prices in the unpretentious but recommended *La Sultana del Valle* (☎ 712 988) on Libertad at Parada, on the way to Las Palmas.

There are a few more expensive and elegant restaurants near the Las Palmas hotels, such as the *Restaurant Tiffany* (☎ 710 263), Kennedy 707, a couple of blocks from the Costa Verde Suites. This international restaurant is one of the very best in Esmeraldas, and its prices are reasonable.

Entertainment

The coast is known for its lively African-influenced music. There are no particular places where you can go to listen to shows; impromptu gatherings are the norm. The best way is to make friends with the locals and ask them. There are a couple of cinemas, of which the *Ciné Bolívar* is the most comfortable. There are several discos, most away from the center in Las Palmas. There is a good salsateca at the Hotel Cayapas and a disco at the Hotel Casino Esmeraldas. Women should not go to any of these places unescorted.

Getting There & Away

Air TAME has flights from Quito late every morning, Monday to Friday. The recent schedule was the following: Monday, Wednesday and Friday depart Quito at 10:30 am and leave Esmeraldas at 11:30 am; Tuesday and Thursday depart Quito 11:30 am and leave Esmeraldas at 1:30 pm. They also have a late afternoon flight on Sunday. The fare is US\$21. Sometimes there is also a Friday afternoon flight, especially during the high season.

The TAME office (☎ 712 663) is on Bolívar just off the corner of the central plaza. You can also buy a ticket at the airport if the flight is not full. Make sure you get a seat assignment at the airport or you won't get on – there are different windows for ticket buying and seat assignments, so you have to wait in line twice. It's not very organized.

TAME also provides flights (in conjunction with Intercontinental of Colombia) to Cali, Colombia, on Monday and Friday. The plane departs Cali at noon and departs Esmeraldas at 1:30 pm. The fare is US$78.50 one way.

In the past, AECA had coastal flights from Guayaquil stopping in towns such as Pedernales, Bahía de Caráquez or Manta en route to Esmeraldas. Service was in small aircraft. These services were not available recently but may be available if there is demand (during the beach high season). Call AECA (☎ 711 506, fax 714 416 in Esmeraldas; ☎ 288 580, in Guayaquil 288 110).

Bus There is no central bus terminal, although there are plans to build one during the late 1990s. The map indicates where you need to go to catch the different companies' buses until then. There is a direct road to Quito via Santo Domingo. The fastest service to Quito is with Aerotaxi (US$6; five hours) but they drive suicidally fast. Transportes Occidentales and Transportes Esmeraldas are slower and a little cheaper. Transportes Panamericana (under the Hotel Casino Esmeraldas) has the most luxurious buses to Quito but are a couple of dollars more expensive. Buses are frequent.

Transportes Occidentales and Transportes Esmeraldas also have frequent buses to Guayaquil (US$5.50 to US$7; eight hours). Transportes Occidentales has an early morning and early evening bus to Machala (US$8; 11 hours) if you want to go to Peru the next day. CITA has several buses a day to Ambato (US$5; eight hours). Reina del Camino has five buses a day to

Manta (US$6.20; nine hours) and one to Bahía de Caráquez (US$6.20; eight hours).

For provincial buses go to Transportes La Costeñita or Transportes del Pacífico. Buses for Atacames and Súa (US$0.60; less than an hour) leave frequently from 6:30 am to 8 pm. There are several buses a day to Muisne (US$1.40; 2½ hours). Buses to La Tola leave several times a day and the US$7 ticket includes the boat to San Lorenzo. Take a morning bus to ensure that you don't have to overnight in La Tola. There are also several buses a day to Borbón (US$2.75; four hours). Buses also go to other small provincial villages.

Note that buses from Esmeraldas to La Tola or Borbón pass the airport, and passengers arriving by air and continuing to these towns by bus don't need to backtrack to Esmeraldas.

Taxi Taxis (☎ 711 020) will take you from Esmeraldas to Atacames for US$16, to Muisne for US$28, to La Tola for US$60 and to Quito for US$120.

Boat The Capitanía is on the right side of the road linking downtown with Las Palmas, just before you get to Las Palmas. They can give information about which boats are going where, and then you have to talk to the captain of the boat directly. Boats occasionally go to Guayaquil and other coastal ports but the most frequent sailings are for Limones. Boat travel from Esmeraldas is not recommended because it is cheaper and more convenient to travel by land – besides, you see more.

Getting Around
The airport is about 25 km away from town across the Río Esmeraldas. Passengers and cab drivers gather in front of the TAME office a couple of hours before the flight, and four or five passengers are crammed into each taxi at a cost of about US$4 per person. Incoming passengers get together to do the same thing at the airport. At the airport you can hire a taxi for about US$25 to take you directly to Atacames and can thus avoid Esmeraldas completely.

To get to the airport cheaply, take a La Costeñita bus or ranchera heading for La Tola. They may not sell you a ticket at the office, so board without a ticket and pay the driver – about US$0.50 to the airport. If you leave Esmeraldas by 9 am, you should get to the airport in good time to catch the flight.

Take a Selectivo bus signed 'Las Palmas' northbound along Avenida Bolívar to get to the port of Esmeraldas and beaches of Las Palmas. The fare is US$0.20. A taxi charges US$0.80.

TONSUPA

This small coastal village is just off the Esmeraldas-Atacames road, about 5 km before reaching the better-known resort town of Atacames. It is a much quieter resort than Atacames.

Places to Stay

Most of the hotels have cabins renting for about US$30 to US$70, usually sleeping four to six and geared to family groups. The hotels tend to be self-contained resorts (with restaurant, bar and perhaps a pool or other activities), though there are a few simple restaurants near the beach. During high-season weekends most of the hotels are booked in advance by Ecuadorian families but can be almost dead midweek, when prices are lower but services may be lacking. The resorts are OK, but nothing I could get excited about.

Try *Hotel Club de Pacífico* (☎ 731 053/056, fax 731 368), with a large pool and international restaurant, or *Conjunto Vacacional Vista Azul* (☎ in Quito 227 018, 528 564, fax 545 663), with a pool and kitchenettes.

ATACAMES

This small resort town, almost 30 km west of Esmeraldas, has built up a reputation among young international travelers as one of the best places to go for a relaxed and moderately priced beach vacation. Simple accommodations can be found right on the ocean front, so you can walk straight out of your room onto the beach. Atacames is also popular with visitors from Colombia and

Quito, and can get extremely crowded, particularly on weekends and national holidays. The wet-season weekends (especially Christmas, Carnaval and Easter) are very popular with locals, and the months of April to October are more popular with foreign visitors.

Nightlife is variable. I've been here when nothing was happening and other times when every bar was hopping. I can't recommend anywhere in particular; if there's anything going on, you'll hear it!

There is nothing to do in Atacames apart from sunbathe and swim, eat and drink, and hang out in bars and discos with new-found friends. Some travelers love it and stay for days or weeks. It's fine if that's what you want to do, but I get tired of Atacames very quickly. After a couple of days, all the discos sound the same, all the restaurants seem to have the same stuff on the menu and I get bored. Ho hum. Bring a good novel.

Orientation & Information

The main road from Esmeraldas goes through the center of town. The center and the beach area are separated by the Río Atacames. To get to the ocean and beach hotels, you have to walk a few blocks and cross the Río Atacames on a wooden footbridge. Buses do not go down to the beach.

There is no reason to go into the town center except to catch a bus, change cash or traveler's checks at the Banco del Pichincha or go to the EMETEL office to make a phone call.

Dangers & Annoyances

The beach has a powerful undertow and no lifeguards. People drown every year, so stay within your limits.

Thieves thrive wherever there is a conglomeration of travelers. This is certainly true of beach areas, and Atacames is no exception. Camping is definitely not recommended because thieves cut through the tent material and rob you even while you're asleep inside. Stay in a beach cabin or hotel, and make sure that it has secure locks on the doors and shutters on the windows.

Assaults have been reported by people

walking the beaches at night. Stay in front of the hotel area – women have been raped and travelers have been mugged just a short distance away from the hotel area. It is safe if you stay in well-lighted areas in front of the hotels – it is definitely dangerous beyond these areas. Even during the day, you shouldn't walk the beaches alone or even as a couple.

Bring insect repellent or mosquito coils, especially in the wet season (though the insects aren't bad in the dry months). The cheapest hotels may have rats, so stay in a medium-priced hotel to minimize the chance of seeing them.

Although the chance of being bitten by a sea snake is remote, every once in a while they get washed up on the beaches. Don't pick them up – they are venomous.

Places to Stay

Atacames can get very full at weekends, especially holiday weekends, when prices rise to what the market will bear and single rooms are unavailable unless you want to pay for a double. Therefore the rates given below are an approximate guideline only. You are advised to arrive Sunday to Wednesday when you can try bargaining, especially if you plan on staying a few days. Rooms are often geared to families and have several beds, so go in a group to economize.

New hotels, or old hotels under new management and name, open frequently. There are about 20 or 30 hotels to choose from within a few blocks of the beach. Always check your room or cabin for security before you rent it.

Most showers have brackish water (which is quite salty) – only the more expensive hotels have fresh-water showers.

Places to Stay – bottom end

The cheapest is *Hotel Doña Pichu* (☎ 731 441), on the main street in the village, not on the beach. Basic rooms are US$2.50 per person and bathrooms are primitive. There are other basic places in the village.

On the beach, US$10 for a double is rock-bottom cheap. *Cabañas Rincón del Mar* (☎ 731 064), to the left after crossing

the footbridge to the beach, is clean, secure but small and charges US$10 for a double with bath; they double their rates at weekends. The owners speak English and German. *La Casa del Manglar*, by the footbridge, is clean and friendly; rates are US$8 to US$16 for a double with bath.

More hotels are to the right of the footbridge. The *Cabañas Los Bohios* (☎ 731 089) has quite nice little double cabins with bath at US$10, and has singles midweek. The *Rincón Sage* (☎ 731 246) has decent rooms with bath for US$8/12, and there is a nice roof-top patio. The *Hostal Jennifer* (☎ 710 482, 731 055), has some singles and charges about US$8 per person with bath, less without. Rooms are a bit bigger than in most bottom-end hotels. The popular *Hotel Galerías Atacames* (☎ 731 149) has English-speaking owners and rooms for US$16 a double with bath at weekends. They also have a good restaurant.

The *Hotel Chavalito* (☎ 731 113) is run by an ex-merchant marine who has a fund of good stories to keep you entertained. Rooms with private baths cost from US$12 to US$20, depending on the room. The two best rooms at the front of the hotel have ocean-view balconies. Others to try with doubles in the teens include the *Hotel Rodelu* (☎ 731 033), the *Hotel El Tiburon* and the *Hostería Cayapas*.

Places to Stay – middle

For families or groups the following can be recommended. *Cabañas Caida del Sol* (☎ / fax 731 479) has German owners and nice little cabins with a fan and minifridge for US$20 to US$40 for two to four people. Away from the center, the quiet *Villas Arco Iris* (☎ 731 069) provide clean and comfortable cabins with private bath and kitchen facilities, and a little porch with hammock. Rates are US$20 to US$40 for one to four people. *Casitas Familiares Marbella* (☎ 731 129) aren't bad at US$12 per person.

The *Hotel Casa Blanca* (☎ /fax 731 031/096) has clean air-conditioned rooms with TV, telephone and minifridge for US$60 at weekends, US$40 during the week. Rooms with fans are about US$10 cheaper. The *Hotel Castel Nuevo* (☎ in Quito 223 608/262, fax 223 452) has similarly priced rooms with fans but no air-conditioning, and has the largest swimming pool in Atacames.

Places to Eat

There are many simple comedores close to the beach near the footbridge. They all tend to serve the same thing – whatever was caught that morning. Make sure you ask the price before you get served, or you may be overcharged. A whole fish dinner will start at around US$3. All the comedores seem to be alike, which is why I don't describe them individually. Wander around till you find one that suits your fancy. Many of them double as bars or dancing places in the evenings, and their popularity changes with the seasons. Keep your ears open and you'll soon hear where it's happening.

Getting There & Away

All buses stop on the main road near the road to the footbridge; there is no bus terminal. Buses also stop at the HeladoBar Pinguino, on the main road, where you can have a beer, coffee or ice cream as you wait for a bus. If leaving Atacames, you pay for your ticket after you board the bus. Buses for Esmeraldas (US$0.60; 45 minutes) normally begin from Súa, and there are plenty of seats. Most buses from Esmeraldas to Atacames continue to Súa, Same and Tonchigüe for about USD$0.50. Buses for Muisne (US$1.20; 1½ hours further down the coast) are often full when they come from Esmeraldas, and you may find it easier to return to Esmeraldas and then retrace your route. Alternately, be prepared to ride on the roof or stand the whole way.

SÚA

This small fishing village is more bustling than Atacames. It's an interesting place to stay if you'd rather watch the boats at work than just hang out on the beach. The fishing industry attracts its attendant frigatebirds, pelicans and other sea birds and the general setting is attractive.

Because it is quieter and less popular than Atacames, it is easier to find uninflated prices at weekends. There is an EMETEL office with one phone.

Súa is about a six-km walk by road from Atacames. I've heard that you can walk along the beach at the lowest tides, but if you try this be careful not to get cut off by the tide and go with several friends to avoid getting robbed.

Places to Stay & Eat

There's much less to choose from than in Atacames, but prices are lower. On the road into town, *Residencial Quito* is a very basic hotel that charges US$3 per person and is barely worth even that. The good-value *Hotel Chagra Ramos* (☎ 731 006, 731 070), has a little beach, nice views and charges US$5 or US$6 per person for pleasant rooms with bath. They have a good, inexpensive restaurant. *Hotel El Peñón de Súa* (☎ 731 013), is 300 meters away from the beach but has nice rooms with private shower and a little patio for US$4 per person. Other decent places at this price are the friendly little *Hostal Le Weekend* with six rooms sharing hot showers and a cheap restaurant, and the *Hostal Mar y Sol* (☎ 731 293) where rooms vary in quality. Much better rooms, some with ocean view, are in the nearby *Hotel Las Buganvillas* (☎ 731 008), which charges US$6 per person. The *Hotel Súa* (☎ 731 004) is US$16 a double with hot shower and has a good restaurant serving both simple fish almuerzos and upscale French dinners. Some rooms have balconies with ocean views.

Getting There & Away

Buses to and from Esmeraldas run about every 45 minutes and arrive and leave from in front of the Residencial Mar y Sol. It takes 10 minutes to Atacames (US$0.35) and about an hour to Esmeraldas (US$0.60). You pay on the bus.

If you want to go further along the coast to Muisne you have to wait out of town along the main road for a bus passing from Esmeraldas (often full).

SAME

This small village (pronounced 'SA-may') is a quiet beach resort about five or six km southwest of Súa. Same lacks the crowds of Atacames and is slightly more expensive. The attractive gray sand beach is palm-fringed and clean.

Places to Stay

La Terraza (☎ 544 507 in Quito) near the beach charges US$8 per person and is the cheapest choice. It's good value and recommended. Their restaurant and bar is popular and the service reportedly slow.

The *Cabañas Isla del Sol* (☎ /fax 731 151) at the end of the beach, has simple but adequate cabins sleeping four to six people for about US$14 per person. There is a restaurant and pool. Also on the beach is the *Hostería El Rampiral* (in Quito ☎ 246 341, 435 003, fax 472 038), at US$17 per person. There is a pool and restaurant and rooms reportedly have TVs and minifridges.

El Acantilado (in Quito ☎ 235 034, 453 606) is located on a cliff overlooking a small but private beach. They have cabins for four to eight people, each with kitchen facilities and daily maid service. Rates were about US$18 per person when the book was researched (although a reader who was there earlier writes he was charged US$60 a double).

Hotel Club Casablanca is a first-class resort with swimming pool and games facilities. Reservations can be made through Metropolitan Touring in Quito. Rates are about US$70 to US$100 for a double. I haven't checked it out.

TONCHIGÜE

This beach is a continuation of the Same beach (see above). The *El Acantilado* hotel is between Same and Tonchigüe. There is also the cheaper *Hotel Luz del Mar* and other cheaper places to stay on the main street with rooms around US$4 per person.

MUISNE

This small port is fairly important for banana shipping. It is on an island at the end of the road from Esmeraldas. It is relatively remote and far fewer people come here than the more popular beaches such as Atacames. There are some mangroves remaining in the area and this is one of the few places where the remains are, to some extent, protected (see the sidebar The Mangroves of Muisne).

Orientation & Information

At the end of the road from Esmeraldas, you have to take a motorized dugout across the Río Muisne to the island. Boat owners will meet the bus and take you to their boat – just follow other passengers. The fare is about US$0.20 per passenger when the boat is full. Don't let the boatman leave early unless you are in a hurry and want to pay several fares. Boats leave every few minutes. When you disembark at Muisne you'll see the main road heading southwest directly away from the pier into the town 'center.' There is an EMETEL office here but it's often closed. It's best to continue on the main road, past the town square, and towards the ocean. The 'main road' deteriorates into a grassy lane, and it's about 1½ km to the beach.

Some of the hotels will change or accept cash dollars – try the Hotel Galápagos.

Dangers & Annoyances

There have been reports of thefts from beach cabins, some of which are not very secure. Bring your own padlock and check the windows. Single travelers, particularly women, are advised not to wander along the beach away from the hotels and restaurants – rapes and muggings have been reported.

Note that water shortages occur frequently in Muisne.

Places to Stay

There are only bottom-end hotels. The basic *Residencial Nuevo Muisne* is on the mainland side of the river, near the dock and last bus stop. Most travelers elect to cross the river to the island. The cheapest looks like the *Residencial Reina*, in the

The Mangroves of Muisne

Ecuador's coastal mangroves are an important habitat providing homes, protection and nutrients for numerous fish, bird, mollusk and crustacean species (see Flora & Fauna in Facts for the Country) as well as controlling erosion of the coast. Unfortunately, mangroves have been in a legal no-man's-land, and it has been difficult to say who owns these coastal tropical forests that are semipermanently inundated. Squatters took over areas of mangroves as their own, but this was not, in itself, a problem because they were able to use the mangroves sustainably. Only small sections were cut for charcoal production or building materials. The mangroves also supported cottage industries such as fishing, shrimping and crabbing, as well as some sport fishing. Thousands of families along the coast were gainfully employed in these industries without impacting the mangroves.

This all changed in the 1980s with the arrival of shrimp farms. These produced shrimp in artificial conditions in numbers many times greater than could be caught by ordinary shrimping methods in the wild. To build these shrimp farms, it was necessary to cut down the mangroves. The prospective owner of a shrimp farm simply took over an area of mangroves, paid off anyone who was living there with what seemed like a sizable sum, cut down the mangroves, and began the shrimp farming process. The net profits of the shrimp farms were very high, and the idea soon caught on and spread rapidly along the coast, resulting in the complete destruction of 80% to 90% of Ecuador's mangroves during the 1980s and early 1990s.

Although there are now laws controlling this destruction, it continues because the laws are difficult to enforce in the remote coastal areas. The short and long term effects of the shrimp farms have been negative in many ways. Where previously many families could find a sustainable livelihood in the mangroves, now there are shrimp farms employing only a handful of seasonal workers. Where before there were mangroves protecting a large diversity of species, now there are just commercial shrimp. Where before there were mangroves controlling coastal erosion, now there is erosion plus pollution from the wastes of the shrimp farms. It is another case of a handful of entrepreneurs getting very rich at the expense of thousands of families' livelihoods and severe ecological damage.

In Muisne, the Fundación de Defensa Ecológica (FUNDECOL) is working to save the mangroves remaining in that area through campaigns to increase public awareness and by an ecotourism program. They have a balcony restaurant in the midst of the mangroves, 20 minutes by boat from Muisne, and an experimental farm (not for shrimp!) two hours upriver. Also upriver is a bird sanctuary and undisturbed coastal rainforest inhabited by Chachi Indians. FUNDECOL organizes guided day trips for US$20 to US$30 per person or three-day trips (overnighting in Muisne's Hotel Galápagos) for US$80 to US$110 per person (costs depend on group size, six maximum).

The FUNDECOL contact in Muisne is Bernardo Lourdes (☎ 480 167) who runs a bicycle repair shop in a two-story white house, one block from Muisne's main plaza in the direction of the beach. In Quito, the contact is Jason Spensley (☎ 224 271). ■

town center, at US$2.50 per person. Another choice is the *Residencial Isla de Baños* at U$3 per person, which looks a bit less run down. Also in the center, the basic *Hotel Ginger* charges US$3 per person or US$4 with bath. The marginally better *Pensión Sarita* charges about US$4 per person and has some rooms with private baths and mosquito nets.

About 750 meters before arriving at the beach, and one block to the right of the 'main road,' you pass the *Hotel Galápagos* (☎ 480 158). This is the most hotel expensive in Muisne at US$6 per person in rooms with private bathroom. The rooms on the left-hand side of the hotel (as you face it) are quieter. The Galápagos is the best and most secure place to stay (though take the usual precautions against theft).

Closer to the beach are the *Cabinas Ipanema*, which charge US$5.50 for a basic cabin with private bath (one or two people). It seems like a decent enough place for this price. On the beach itself, the friendly *Hotel Calade* charges US$4 per person in clean but basic rooms with mosquito nets. There are a couple of other cheap places on the beach.

Places to Eat

The *Bambu Bar*, on the corner of the main plaza, has good, reasonably priced food. Several inexpensive comedores are on the beach – names, owners and popularity among travelers seem to change every year. You can buy simple foodstuffs at the basic store by the beach. Some travelers opt to collect some of the driftwood on the beach and cook their own food.

Entertainment

There's usually a basic bar on or near the beach, with music and dancing on weekend evenings. Single women are advised not to go unescorted.

Getting There & Away

Bus La Costeñita and Transportes del Pacífico have buses about every hour to Esmeraldas (US$1.40; 2½ hours), passing Same, Súa and Atacames en route. Transportes Occidentales has overnight buses to both Quito (11 pm, US$6, seven hours) and Guayaquil (10 pm, US$7, eight hours), but these services are subject to change.

Boat There are two or three boats a day to Cojimíes (US$6; two hours). They leave from the dock at the end of the road from Esmeraldas. Recently, departures were at 9:30 am and 1:30 pm, but I wouldn't base your itinerary on these times!

Excursions around Muisne

You can take a boat trip up the Río Muisne to see the mangrove forests (see the sidebar The Mangroves of Muisne). Passenger canoes go once or twice a day to **San Gregorio** (1½ hours). You can get information about the area at the red house on the left side of the church on the main plaza. To get back to Muisne, stand by the river and flag down any boat heading downriver.

SOUTH OF MUISNE

There is no road south of Muisne (though one is under construction), so if you want to travel further you have to take a boat or walk. The boat trip takes you out past the mangroves of the Río Muisne and into the open ocean. Crossing from the river mouth into the ocean can be tricky and exciting and the open section can get very wet because of spray, so be prepared. The boat rounds Punta Portete and heads in towards a protected river delta near Bolívar before continuing 'inland' past Daule and on to Cojimíes.

You can also head south on foot and get to Cojimíes in one day, but you'll need to leave at dawn, as there are no hotels between Muisne and Cojimíes, and you may have to wait several hours to get boat rides. At low tide, pickup trucks sometimes act as buses on some sections and you may get a ride, but don't rely on them. There are several rivers to cross but you can find dugouts to ferry you for a few hundred sucres. Bring change. Leave when the tide is falling to make sure you are not cut off by a high tide later in the day. From Muisne, walk south along the beach for about five km (this first section can be avoided by taking a boat to Las Manchas on the way to San Gregorio); take a dugout across the river and continue seven km along the beach past Mompiche (small store); follow a jeep track over the headland four km to Punta Suspiro; make the dugout crossing to Portete (small store); walk five km to Bolívar.

Although you can sometimes catch rides, be prepared to walk the whole distance. I've done this walk twice and seen sea snakes, a beached whale, crabs galore, jellyfish, seabirds and other sea creatures along the beach.

The town of **Bolívar** has a little port where you can ask around about getting a boat ride to Cojimíes; this should run about US$2 or US$3 (in a passenger boat). There are no hotels here. If you can't get a ride, you can rent a boat for about US$25 to take you to Cojimíes.

COJIMÍES

Cojimíes, a small port with road connections to the south, is the northernmost point of the province of Manabí. It is sometimes cut off by heavy rains in the wet season (January to May). Because it is so isolated, food prices in Cojimíes tend to be expensive. The locals party late on Saturday night.

The village is on a headland that is constantly being washed away into the ocean. Consequently, the village has to keep moving inland and the houses closest to the sea get washed away every few years. The locals say that the cemetery, now near the shoreline, was once way at the back of the town. There is an EMETEL office.

Places to Stay & Eat

There are a few very basic (wash in a bucket) places to stay on or just off the one main street. The best place is *Hotel Costa Azul* at US$4 per person.

The *Hotel Coco Solo* (☎ in Quito 240 404, 461 677 or reserve through Guacamayo Adventures in Bahía de Caráquez) is 14 km south of Cojimíes – a hotel lost in the coconut groves. It's for lovers of deserted beaches and the noise of the wind clattering through the palm leaves. Rates are about US$16 per person in the cabins; there is a restaurant with a limited menu. Horseback riding can be arranged.

There are a few basic restaurants with pricey meals. Ask around to eat in small comedores in people's houses – the meals are cheaper and often better.

Getting There & Away

Air There is a small airstrip with occasional flights to and from Pedernales during the wet season (see Pedernales, below).

Bus The Costa del Norte bus office is on the main street and can give transportation information. Trucks to the next village of Pedernales cost US$2 and take about an hour – they simply run along the beach for much of the way. Departures depend on low tide – if the tide is rising, you could be in town for 12 hours or more before the next vehicle can make it out. Buses sometimes go further, depending on the state of the 'road.'

Boat At a shack by the beach you can buy tickets for the boat to Muisne (US$6; two hours). Although a posted schedule lists daily departures, boats don't stick to schedule. My boat left 1½ hours early because all the seats had already been sold. If a boat isn't full at departure time, the captain may hang around for an extra hour.

PEDERNALES

Pedernales is about 40 km south of Cojimíes and, with some 10,000 inhabitants, it is the most important market town between Muisne and Bahía de Caráquez. Until recently, fishing and agriculture (especially bananas, cacao and coffee) were the main industries. Now the shrimp industry, expanded from the south, is the main industry, and there are many shrimp ponds and hatcheries in the area. This new industry has given Pedernales a free-wheeling boomtown atmosphere. The people are hard-working but will cheerfully overcharge you if you give them half a chance.

Pedernales is about eight km north of the equator. At the appropriate spot, a monument near the beach marks the equator.

Places to Stay

The best hotel in town is the *Hotel Playas*, which is clean and friendly – but you have to bargain hard. Rooms with private bath and TV rent for US$6 per person for Ecuadorians – but gringos are often charged twice that! Being friendly and speaking Spanish is the best approach to avoid being overcharged.

There are several cheaper places that aren't as good but will be OK for most budget travelers.

Getting There & Away

Air AECA (☎ 288 110, 288 580 in Guayaquil) has flights in small aircraft from Guayaquil (possibly stopping at other coastal towns), subject to passenger demand, which is higher in the wet season.

NICA (☎ 690 377 in Bahía de Caráquez) has flights in three or five passenger aircraft between Pedernales and Bahía de Caráquez, depending on passenger demand. These small aircraft have very limited luggage space – 10 kg is the usual maximum. Aircraft can be chartered to various towns along the coast. These coastal flights give a good look at the coastline, shrimp hatcheries, banana plantations and villages of the area.

Bus A Costa del Norte bus office on the main street sells tickets for Cojimíes (northbound) or San Vicente (southbound; US$3.50; four hours). Southbound departures are on the hour from 5 am to 5 pm. The buses (often trucks or rancheras) usually follow the beach, and the ride is very fast on the hard-packed sand, especially between Pedernales and Cojimíes. There are some rougher stretches south of Pedernales. Bus travel to Cojimíes depends on tides and road conditions, and delays are frequent during the wet months of January to May.

An inland dirt road (between San Vicente and Pedernales and on to Cojimíes) avoids the beach, but is very rough and seldom used. There is also a recently improved road that heads inland to El Carmen and on to Santo Domingo de los Colorados. Opposite the Costa del Norte office is Transportes Santo Domingo with five buses a day (US$3) to Santo Domingo de los Colorados.

JAMA

This village is a small market town midway between Pedernales and San Vicente. Several shrimp hatcheries are in the area. There are a couple of basic places to stay of which the *Hotel Jamaica* has showers and is as good as any.

Buses (trucks) between Pedernales and San Vicente pass through Jama in either direction but may be full when they come through. If so, ride on the roof.

CANOA

This village is about 18 km north of San Vicente and has a wide quiet beach, con-

sidered one of the best in the area. There is a basic pensión, and a few beachfront comedores. The good *Posada de Daniel B&B* (reservations through Guacamayo Adventures in Bahía de Caráquez) charges US$6 per person. It is fairly straightforward to get here by bus or truck going up the beach from San Vicente.

SAN VICENTE

A short ferry ride across the Río Chone from the more important town of Bahía de Caráquez, San Vicente has beaches, a few hotels, and the regional airport. The beaches to the north are the area's most pleasant.

Places to Stay & Eat

If you turn right from the pier you'll find the basic *Hostal San Vicente* (☎ 674 182), charging US$2.50 per person, with a restaurant below. There are a few other basic places, but this is the best one.

Closer to the pier is the more expensive but quite good *Hotel Vacaciones* (☎ 690 671, 674 116), which charges US$11 per person or more during busy weekends for air-conditioned rooms. They have a pool and decent restaurant. On the northern outskirts of town and on the way to Canoa are several self-contained resort hotels, such as *Cabañas Alcatraz* (☎ 690 842, fax 674 179), which has a sauna, and *Hotel Las Hamacas* (☎ 674 134, or 542 700 in Quito). Both have a pool, a private beach and charge US$10 to US$20 per person, depending on group size and season, in bungalows or cabins sleeping five or more with private bathroom. Three km north of San Vicente on the beach is *Cabañas La Playa* (☎ 674 148) also with family bungalows and a restaurant. Also try *Hostal El Montés* (☎ 674 201) and *Hotel El Velero* (☎ 674 122).

Some cheap and clean comedores, such as *Yessenia*, are behind the market. The best hotels have the best restaurants.

Getting There & Away

Air The main regional airport, also serving Bahía de Caráquez, is behind the market. The airline offices are in Bahía; further information is given under that town.

Bus San Vicente is the main office of the Costa del Norte company and they have buses, trucks or rancheras leaving hourly to Pedernales, with one or two continuing to Cojimíes. They also have two daily buses going inland to Chone. The bus office is close to the boat pier.

Boat Passenger launches take 10 minutes to reach Bahía de Caráquez and leave several times an hour all day long. The fare is US$0.20. After 9 pm it costs about US$1.50 to hire a boat to take you across (four passengers maximum). A car ferry leaves about every half hour – foot passengers can cross at no charge. You can hire boats for trips anywhere you want for US$6 an hour.

BAHÍA DE CARÁQUEZ

This small (18,000 inhabitants) but nevertheless fairly important port and holiday resort is locally referred to simply as 'Bahía.' There are beaches here, though

most of the ones in Bahía have been eroded away and the San Vicente-to-Canoa coastline has much better ones. To get to the beaches, go north on Avenida Montúfar for about 500 meters. For some reason, this whole area is rarely visited by foreign travelers although the beaches are as good as elsewhere and the hotels adequate. The Río Chone entrance is quite busy and you can laze around at a riverside café and watch the boats go by, or go for a ferry ride. The outgoing president, Sixto Ballén Durán, has a holiday home here. One reader met and chatted with the president, clad in red swimming shorts and sunglasses, on the beach in Bahía.

Information
Tourist Office CETUR has an office near the north end of the Malecón. Also see Travel Agencies.

Money The Banco Comercial de Manabí

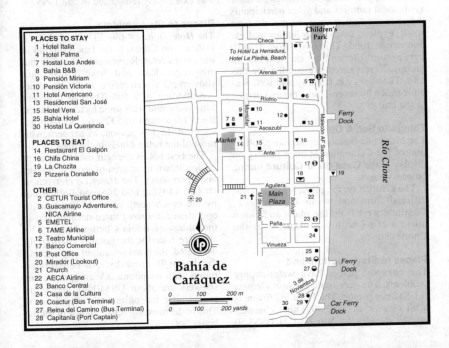

PLACES TO STAY
1 Hotel Italia
4 Hotel Palma
7 Hostal Los Andes
8 Bahía B&B
9 Pensión Miriam
10 Pensión Victoria
11 Hotel Americano
13 Residencial San José
15 Hotel Vera
25 Bahía Hotel
30 Hostal La Querencia

PLACES TO EAT
14 Restaurant El Galpón
16 Chifa China
19 La Chozita
29 Pizzería Donatello

OTHER
2 CETUR Tourist Office
3 Guacamayo Adventures,
    NICA Airline
5 EMETEL
6 TAME Airline
12 Teatro Municipal
17 Banco Comercial
18 Post Office
20 Mirador (Lookout)
21 Church
22 AECA Airline
23 Banco Central
24 Casa de la Cultura
26 Coactur (Bus Terminal)
27 Reina del Camino (Bus Terminal)
28 Capitanía (Port Captain)

Bahía de Caráquez

Río Chone

(on the Malecón) changes US dollars and traveler's checks.

Post & Communications Both post and EMETEL offices are shown on the map. The area code for Bahía de Caráquez and the province of Manabí is 05.

Travel Agencies Guacamayo Adventures (☎ 691 412, fax 691 280), Avenida Bolívar and Arenas, is a good source of local information and arranges tours. You can visit islands with seabird colonies, coastal forests, local villages and other areas (mostly outside of the national parks, thereby saving the US$20 entrance fee for travelers on a tight budget). Some of the islands visited give excellent opportunities to view and photograph frigate-bird colonies at a fraction of the cost of the Galápagos! Cultural tours, boat and kayak trips, horseback riding and mountain bike rentals are available. A three-day/two-night cultural exchange tour visits local families and gives participants the chance to catch river shrimp, do farm work, explore caves, ride horses and eat homemade food. This costs from US$70 per person (depending on number in group). Reservations are needed for this tour. The agency is friendly and well recommended by several travelers and people in the know.

Things to See & Do

The Museo de Banco Central has a collection of pre-Columbian Manabí pottery on display at the **Casa de la Cultura** during business hours.

The **church** on the plaza is built in traditional form and worth a quick look. Continue west from the plaza and climb up to a cross with a **lookout** over the Chone estuary.

Places to Stay – bottom end

The cheapest places have water-supply problems. The very basic *Pensión Victoria* is US$2 per person. The *Pensión Miriam* is a bit cleaner at US$2.50. Other cheapies are the *Residencial San José*, at US$3.50 each, and the better *Hotel Vera*, which has some rooms with bath.

The most popular low budget choice is the OK *Hotel Palma* (☎ 690 467), Bolívar 910, at US$4 per person with basic shared baths or US$6 with a better private bath and fan, but many rooms lack windows. The *Hostal Los Andes* (☎ 690 587) is basic but clean at US$6.

The *Hostal La Querencia* (☎ 690 009), Malecón 1800, is good value for Bahía at US$8 or US$10 per person in pleasant rooms, some with private bath. The *Bahía Hotel* is also OK at US$10 per person with private bath. The simple but friendly *Bahía B&B* (☎ 690 146), Ascazubi 322, is also about US$10 per person and includes breakfast. Rooms have fans and private baths with hot water. Some rooms have TV. The *Hotel Americano* (☎ 690 524/594, 691 324), on Ascazubi and Montúfar, has rooms with a private bath, air-conditioning and telephone for about US$20 a double. It was extensively remodeled in late 1995.

Places to Stay – middle

The *Hotel Italia* (☎ 691 137, fax 691 092), Bolívar and Checa, is the fanciest hotel in the town center. Rooms aren't too big but are very clean and have private hot showers, TV, telephone and either air-conditioning or a fan. There is a decent little restaurant with some local specialties. Rates are around US$32, with a small discount in the low season, as happens with most of the better hotels in the area.

The best hotels are near the beach north of downtown in an area of modern houses and apartments. The *Hotel La Herradura* (☎ 690 446, fax 690 265), on Bolívar out by the beach north of town, has been in operation for almost three decades and is the oldest of Bahía's better hotels. The staff are friendly, the hotel is charmingly decorated, the hotel restaurant is good, and the beach is close by. Air-conditioned rooms with telephone, TV and private hot showers are about US$40/50, and some rooms have balconies with ocean views. This is the most attractive choice of all the better hotels.

Places to Stay – top end
The new *Hotel La Piedra* (☎ 690 780, 691 473, fax 690 154), on the beach just beyond the end of Bolívar, is the most luxurious hotel in Bahía. They have a swimming pool, a 'semiprivate' beach, and a good restaurant and bar. Rooms with private bath, air-conditioning, telephone and TV cost US$50/70.

Places to Eat
The *Restaurant El Galpón*, on Montúfar near the market, is cheap and good. There are also a couple of cheap chifas, of which the *Chifa China* is simple but has been recommended.

Check out the reasonable and inexpensive cafés and parrilladas by the river. *La Chozita* has a nice location overlooking the river and seems as good as any. At the south end of town, the *Pizzería Donatello* is quite good. The better hotels serve decent food, particularly La Herradura and La Piedra.

Getting There & Away
Air The regional airport is across the river in San Vicente. Some ferries cross directly to the airport if there are enough passengers; otherwise the ferry drops you off near the San Vicente market and you have to walk to the right, behind the market, to the airport. It's about a 10- to 15-minute walk.

Both AECA (in Guayaquil ☎ 288 580, 288 110), Aguilera near the Malecón, and NICA (☎ 690 377), Bolívar and Arenas, have coastal flights in small aircraft. The baggage allowance is 10 kg. AECA flies from Guayaquil to Bahía and back on most days. Some flights may continue to Pedernales or stop at Manta or Portoviejo en route. NICA has light planes to Pedernales (occasionally continuing to Cojimíes). Flights normally depend on passenger demand. Ask at the Bahía offices or go over to the airport and ask there first thing in the morning. Light planes are available for charter.

TAME recently began flying between Quito and Bahía on Friday and Sunday afternoons. The fare is US$26. Their new office is shown on the map, but if it moves, ask at Guacamayo Adventures for flight information.

Bus The two bus companies have offices next to one another on the south end of the Malecón. All buses out of Bahía climb a hill, which gives good views of the Río Chone estuary; sit on the left when leaving town and look back. Coactur have buses to Portoviejo (US$1.50; two hours) and Manta (US$2; 2½ hours) every hour. Reina del Camino has several buses a day to Portoviejo, Quito (US$6; eight hours), Esmeraldas (US$6; eight hours), Santo Domingo de los Colorados (US$3.75) and Guayaquil (US$5; six hours).

Boat Passenger launches to San Vicente leave from two docks several times an hour during daylight (US$0.20; 10 minutes). There is also a car ferry to San Vicente about every half hour, on which passengers ride for free. San Vicente has more boats for hire to other areas.

PORTOVIEJO
This large city of over 130,000 inhabitants, founded on March 12, 1535, is one of the oldest cities in Ecuador and is the fifth largest. It is the capital of Manabí Province, which is important for coffee and cattle. Portoviejo has a thriving agricultural processing industry and is an important commercial center with good road connections to Quito and Guayaquil. Though it is a bustling town, Portoviejo is not visited much by tourists, who prefer to head to the coast.

Orientation
Most travelers arrive at the bus terminal one km west of downtown. The streets have both names and numbers but locals tend to use the names more frequently.

Information
Tourist Office CETUR (☎ 630 877), Morales 613, can give tourist information. The Banco Comercial de Manabí (☎ 653 888) or Banco del Pichincha (☎ 651 900)

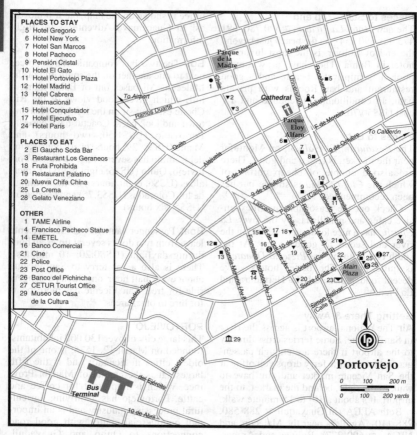

PLACES TO STAY
5 Hotel Gregorio
6 Hotel New York
7 Hotel San Marcos
8 Hotel Pacheco
9 Pensión Cristal
10 Hotel El Gato
11 Hotel Portoviejo Plaza
12 Hotel Madrid
13 Hotel Cabrera Internacional
15 Hotel Conquistador
17 Hotel Ejecutivo
24 Hotel Paris

PLACES TO EAT
2 El Gaucho Soda Bar
3 Restaurant Los Geraneos
18 Fruta Prohibida
19 Restaurant Palatino
20 Nueva Chifa China
25 La Crema
28 Gelato Veneziano

OTHER
1 TAME Airline
4 Francisco Pacheco Statue
14 EMETEL
16 Banco Comercial
21 Cine
22 Police
23 Post Office
26 Banco del Pichincha
27 CETUR Tourist Office
29 Museo de Casa de la Cultura

Portoviejo

are the most likely places to change cash dollars, but not traveler's checks.

The post office (☎ 652 384) is on the main plaza and the EMETEL office is a few blocks to the west. The area code for Portoviejo and Manabí Province is 05.

The public hospital (☎ 630 766) is out of town; take a taxi there or call the Red Cross ambulance (☎ 652 555). The police (☎ 630 094, 630 086) are on the main plaza.

Things to See
Despite the town's colonial history, there are few old buildings. There is a **Museo de**

Casa de la Cultura (☎ 631 753), on Sucre near García Moreno, with an exhibit of traditional musical instruments, but opening hours are erratic and unpredictable. You can wander down to the pleasant **Parque Eloy Alfaro**, where you'll find the starkest, barest modern **cathedral** that I've seen in Ecuador. It's quite an impressive building but takes the wind out of the sails of those people who complain that the Catholic church in Latin America spends all of its money on gold ornaments. Next to the cathedral you will find a **statue** of Francisco Pacheco, the founder of Portoviejo.

Places to Stay – bottom end

The basic *Pensión Cristal*, on Ricaurte and Pedro Gual, charges only US$1.80 per person but is often full by mid-afternoon and is not recommended for single women. *Hotel Portoviejo Plaza* (☎ 634 442), on Universitaria and Pedro Gual, has small but clean rooms for US$3/5, or US$5/8 with a private bath. Unfortunately, its nicest rooms look out on the street and are noisy, but it's not a bad cheap choice.

The friendly *Hotel Paris* (☎ 657 272), Sucre 513 and Olmedo, is simple, safe and clean, but rather dilapidated looking. Rooms with private baths are US$4 per person and this is a recommended choice for budget travelers. Many of the rooms at the *Hotel Pacheco* (☎ 651 788), 9 de Octubre 512 near Universitaria, are without windows but they do at least have fans. The staff seems indifferent and charges US$4 per person or a bit more in rooms with a private bath. The good, clean *Hotel Gregorio* (☎ 652 567), on Rocafuerte near Alajuela, charges US$5 per person in rooms with private baths and US$4 without.

Places to Stay – middle

Hotel Madrid (☎ 631 326), on Pedro Gual and García Moreno, has clean and spacious rooms with fans and private bath for US$7/12 or US$12/20 with air-conditioning, TV and phone. Across the street, the *Hotel Cabrera Internacional* (☎ 633 199/201/250), García Moreno 102, charges US$8 per person in rooms with private bath and fan or US$13/20 with air-conditioning. They have larger rooms ('suites') at US$18/32.

Hotel Conquistador (☎ 651 472, 633 259, 631 678), 18 de Octubre 407, has quite nice rooms with private bath, fan, TV and telephone for US$10/15 or US$14/22 with air-conditioning. The *Hotel San Marcos* (☎ 630 650/1), on Olmedo and 9 de Octubre, has rooms with phone, fan and private bath for US$11/15. Better rooms with air-conditioning cost US$15/20. The *Hostal Zucasa* is by the bus terminal, and charges in the teens for a double. All these hotels are OK, though nothing special.

The *Hotel El Gato* (☎ 636 908, 632 856, fax 632 850), Pedro Gual and Olmedo, has good clean rooms with cold showers, TV, telephone and fan for US$10/15, or rooms with air-conditioning and hot water for US$22/26. The *Hotel New York* (☎ 632 037, 631 998, 632 006, fax 632 044) on Olmedo and F de Moreira, is quite new and has a decent restaurant. Inside rooms with fans, hot showers, TV are US$20/28 and rooms with outside windows, refrigerator and air-conditioning are US$32/35. They have some 'suites' for US$52 a double.

Places to Stay – top end

The *Hotel Ejecutivo* (☎ 632 105/235/398, 630 840/872, fax 630 876), 18 de Octubre near 10 de Agosto, charges US$45/55. This is the best in town but the staff have been described as provincial snobs. It has a restaurant. The similarly priced *Hotel Concorde* (☎ 631 909, fax 636 877), is a kilometer north of town on the road to Crucita (cab drivers know it). This is probably the best in the area and, unlike the other hotels (which are geared to businesspeople) is a tourist complex. The grounds are pleasant with two swimming pools with waterslides, tennis courts, volleyball, a restaurant, bar and disco. Rooms are comfortable with air-conditioning and hot showers.

Places to Eat

There is an inexpensive chifa below the *Hotel Paris* and the *La Crema* restaurant next door is also OK. The *Nueva Chifa China* on 18 de Octubre and Sucre is another reasonably priced chifa. At the north end of Chile *Restaurant Los Geraneos* and *El Gaucho Soda Bar* have both been recommended for good inexpensive lunches. The *Gelato Veneziano*, on Sucre near Rocafuerte, is clean and has the best (and most expensive) ice cream in town. *Fruta Prohibida*, Chile at 10 de Agosto, has indoor and outdoor tables and serves a good variety of snacks including fruit salads and drinks, hamburgers, ice cream and desserts. *Restaurant Palatino*, 10 de Agosto and Chile, is a good, locally popular place, but they have been known to inflate the bill for gringos. I've read that they have good coffee – it's Nescafé from the jar.

Getting There & Away

Air The TAME office (☎ 633 600, 632 429) is on Avenida América at the north end of the town center. The airport (☎ 650 361) is about two km northwest of town (taxi US$1.25). TAME has flights on Monday, Wednesday and Friday from Quito at 4 pm, returning from Portoviejo to Quito at 5 pm. The one-way fare is US$26. Although Portoviejo is the provincial capital, the beach resort of Manta, 35 km away, has daily flights to Quito.

AECA (☎ 294 711 in Guayaquil) has flights to and from Guayaquil on most days in light aircraft. Ask at the airport.

Bus The terminal terrestre (central bus terminal) is about one km west of town along Pedro Gual, beyond the Río Portoviejo. A taxi will take you downtown for about US$0.80.

Coactur runs several buses an hour to Manta (US$0.70; 50 minutes). They also have buses for Bahía de Caráquez (US$1.25; two hours) and Guayaquil (US$3.75; four hours). CTM Aerotaxi also has buses for Manta. Rutas Ecuatorianas has frequent service to Guayaquil (US$3.75; 3½ hours). Carlos A Aray has many buses to Santo Domingo de los Colorados (US$4; five hours) with some buses continuing to Quito (US$5.50; eight hours) or going to Guayaquil. Reina del Camino has buses to Quito (US$5.75), Santo Domingo, Esmeraldas (US$6; nine hours), Bahía de Caráquez and Guayaquil. Flota Bolívar has two slow old buses leaving at 8 am and 1 pm for Quevedo. Ciudad de Calceta has buses to Calceta.

Co-op 15 de Octubre and Co-op Jipijapa have buses to Jipijapa about every 45 minutes. Other small nearby villages, including the beaches of San Clemente and Crucita in the Bahía de Manta region, are served by small bus companies that often use open-sided rancheras.

INLAND FROM PORTOVIEJO

Manabí is an important agricultural province, and a relatively good road system links Portoviejo with a number of canton capitals. The towns, often quite large, act as market centers for coffee, cattle, citrus, corn, cotton, yucca and bananas. They are colorful and bustling, and the people are hard-working and friendly. Tourists rarely visit these towns, even though the region is quite easy to travel in using the small local buses and rancheras, and you can find cheap and basic hotels in the bigger towns. This area provides a great glimpse of rural and provincial Ecuadorian life for those travelers who want to get off the beaten track.

Approximately 20 km north of Portoviejo, **Rocafuerte** is known for its confectionery made of coconuts and caramel. **Calceta**, 43 km northeast of Portoviejo, is known for sisal production. Sisal is the fiber gathered from the spiny-leaved agave plant that grows in the region. The sisal fibers are used for ropes and sandals, among other things.

From Calceta, a good road continues about 25 km northeast to the sizable town of **Chone**. From here, an important but not frequently traveled road continues northeast, linking the coastal lowlands with Santo Domingo de los Colorados, 155 km away. This road climbs to over 600 meters above sea level as it crosses the coastal mountains, then drops back down on the eastern side of these mountains to the canton capitals and market towns of **Flavio Alfaro** and **El Carmen**, en route to Santo Domingo. See Getting There & Away in Portoviejo for buses that go to some of these towns.

MANTA

Manta, with 126,000 inhabitants in the official 1990 census (though probably close to 200,000 including outlying areas), is the major port along the central Ecuadorian coast and an important local tourist resort and commercial center. Despite its popularity among (mainly Ecuadorian) tourists, the city's beaches are not very good, though

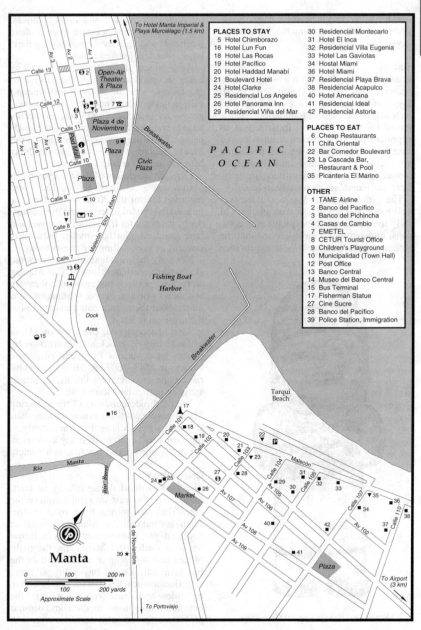

PLACES TO STAY

5 Hotel Chimborazo
16 Hotel Lun Fun
18 Hotel Las Rocas
19 Hotel Pacífico
20 Hotel Haddad Manabí
21 Boulevard Hotel
24 Hotel Clarke
25 Residencial Los Angeles
26 Hotel Panorama Inn
29 Residencial Viña del Mar
30 Residencial Montecarlo
31 Hotel El Inca
32 Residencial Villa Eugenia
33 Hotel Las Gaviotas
34 Hostal Miami
36 Hotel Miami
37 Residencial Playa Brava
38 Residencial Acapulco
40 Hotel Americana
41 Residencial Ideal
42 Residencial Astoria

PLACES TO EAT

6 Cheap Restaurants
11 Chifa Oriental
22 Bar Comedor Boulevard
23 La Cascada Bar,
   Restaurant & Pool
35 Picantería El Marino

OTHER

1 TAME Airline
2 Banco del Pacífico
3 Banco del Pichincha
4 Casas de Cambio
7 EMETEL
8 CETUR Tourist Office
9 Children's Playground
10 Municipalidad (Town Hall)
12 Post Office
13 Banco Central
14 Museo del Banco Central
15 Bus Terminal
17 Fisherman Statue
27 Cine Sucre
28 Banco del Pacífico
39 Police Station, Immigration

To Hotel Manta Imperial &
Playa Murciélago (1.5 km)

Open-Air
Theater
& Plaza

Plaza 4 de
Noviembre

Ped Mall

Plaza

Plaza

Civic
Plaza

Breakwater

PACIFIC
OCEAN

Fishing Boat
Harbor

Dock
Area

Malecón Eloy Alfaro

Breakwater

Tarqui
Beach

Rio   Manta

Rio Burro

4 de Noviembre

Market

Manta

0   100   200 m
0   100   200 yards
Approximate Scale

To Portoviejo

To Airport
(3 km)

Plaza

Malecón

there are better ones in nearby villages. Some of the beachfront restaurants, however, do serve good seafood.

History

Manta has a long history. It was founded by Francisco Pacheco on March 2, 1535, 10 days before he founded Portoviejo. But even before its Spanish foundation, Manta, named Jocay by the local Indians, was an important port. The Manta culture thrived throughout the whole western peninsula from about 500 AD until the arrival of the conquistadors, and many artifacts made by these early inhabitants have been found.

The pottery of the Manta culture was well made and decorated with pictures of daily life. Through these pictorial decorations, archaeologists have learned that the Manta people enhanced their appearance

Mother and child figure, Bahía culture

by skull deformation and tooth removal, thus increasing the backward slope of their foreheads and chins and emphasizing their large, rounded, hooked noses.

Also evident in their pottery, as well as being recorded in detail by the early conquistadors, was the Mantas' astonishing skill in navigation. They were able to navigate as far as Panama and Peru, and claims have been made that they reached the Galápagos. There are records claiming that the Manta seafarers sailed as far north as Mexico and as far south as Chile.

Capitán Bartolomé Ruiz captured a Manta balsa sailing raft in 1526 and recorded that of the 20 crew members, 11 jumped overboard in terror, and the remainder he captured for translating purposes and later freed. Similar but smaller balsa rafts can still be seen sailing the coasts today.

Not only their navigational and ceramic skills were well developed. The Mantas were also skilled stonemasons, weavers and metal workers. People wishing to learn more about the Manta culture should visit the museum in town.

After the conquest, the town of Manta had a history of attack and destruction by pirates from various European countries. Attacks in 1543, 1607 and 1628 left the city ruined and the survivors fleeing for inland areas, in particular Montecristi.

Today, the descendants of the seafaring Manta people continue to demonstrate their superb marine skills as fishermen, navigating their small open boats many kilometers out in the open ocean for days at a stretch.

Orientation

The town is divided into two by an inlet. Manta is on the west side and Tarqui on the east. They are joined by a road bridge. Avenidas and calles in Manta are single or double digits; Avenidas or calles in Tarqui begin at Calle 101. Manta has the main offices and shopping areas, as well as the bus terminal. Tarqui has a bigger hotel selection and beaches, but the hotels tend to be older and more run-down, and the beaches more prone to theft and similar problems. Streets with numbers over 110 are said to be in a particularly unsalubrious neighborhood. The main residential areas are to the southwest of Manta business district, while the best beaches are to the northwest of Manta.

Information
You can extend your tourist card at the police station on 4 de Noviembre.

Tourist Office In Manta there is a CETUR tourist information office (☎ 622 944) on Avenida 3 between Calle 10 and Calle 11. This whole block is a pedestrian precinct with no traffic allowed.

Money The Banco del Pacífico (☎ 623 212), on Calle 13 near Avenida 2, the nearby Banco del Pichincha and several casas de cambio change money and traveler's checks. There is also a Banco del Pacífico in Tarqui. Rates vary from day to day and place to place, so shop around. They are usually a fraction lower than in Quito.

Post & Communications The post office (☎ 621 994) is on Calle 8. DHL International (☎ 622 155, 621 186) has air courier service from Manta. There is an impressive modern EMETEL building on the waterfront in Manta. The area code is 05.

Travel Agencies Principal travel agents include Metropolitan Touring (☎ 621 600), Avenida 4, 1239 and Calle 13, Ecuadorian Tours (☎ 621 796), Avenida 11 between Calle 12 and 13, and Delgado Travel (☎ 622 813, fax 624 614), Avenida 2 and Calle 13. This last one will also change cash dollars at good rates, provide international telephone and fax service, rent cars and arrange airline ticketing.

Medical Services The public hospital (☎ 611 849, 611 515) is on Avenida 24 and Calle 13. The Clínica Manta (☎ 921 566) has doctors of various specialties, including plastic surgeons and dentists. Dr Oscar Pico Santos is a recommended physician who works at the Clínica Manta. There are many pharmacies around town.

Emergency Contact the police on ☎ 101 or 920 900, the fire department on ☎ 610 300 and the Red Cross ambulance service on ☎ 623 904.

Things to See & Do
The **Museo del Banco Central** (☎ 622 878) by the Banco Central on the Malecón is worth a visit to understand more of the Manta culture. The exhibit is small, but is well laid out and labeled in Spanish. Hours are Monday to Friday from 8:30 am to 4:30 pm.

Manta's **fishing boat harbor** is busy and picturesque. To get over to Tarqui, don't follow the harbor around or you'll have to swim. Cross on the bridge set back from the harbor. In Tarqui there is a huge **statue** of a Manabí fisherman and beyond it the protected sandy **Tarqui Beach**. At the end of the beach there are many more fishing boats. It's interesting to watch in the early morning while the fishermen unload their cargo, but don't bring valuables. There is a bustling market in Tarqui and a cinema nearby.

The **Playa Murciélago** (beach) in Manta is less protected and has bigger waves (though still not very big). There is a powerful undertow, which can sweep swimmers away even when the beach appears fairly calm. It is a couple of kilometers northwest of the town center along the

The Manta culture was marked by skillful stone-carving, as seen from this seat or throne.

waterfront and less locally popular than Tarqui, though safer. Further northwest is the **Playa Barbasquillo**, which is quieter still and has a tourist resort complex.

Places to Stay – bottom end

Prices tend to rise during holiday weekends and during the December to March and June to August high seasons. Single rooms are hard to find, unless you want to pay for a double. Travel with a friend or partner to economize. At other times of the year, particularly mid-week in the low season, hotels can be almost empty and you can bargain for cheaper rates.

The *Hotel Chimborazo* at US$6 a double is pretty poor but the only cheap place in Manta. Most budget travelers stay in Tarqui.

In Tarqui, the clean and secure *Residencial Villa Eugenia*, on the Malecón near Calle 105, is a good budget choice for US$4 per person. It's poorly marked, but it's there. The very basic *Residencial Playa Brava*, Calle 110, is just US$2 per person. The *Residencial Los Angeles*, on Avenida 108 near Calle 102, is reasonably clean and charges US$4/6. The *Residencial Viña del Mar*, on Calle 104, is OK for US$8 a double. Other cheap but basic residenciales at US$3 or US$4 per person are the *Acapulco, Montecarlo, Astoria* and *Ideal*.

The student and youth-group-oriented *Boulevard Hotel* (☎ 625 333, 620 627, 621 836), on Calle 103 near Avenida 105, is OK and charges US$6 per person in the high season. *Hostal Miami* (☎ 622 055), Calle 107 and Avenida 102, has simple rooms with private bath for US$6 per person. The similarly priced *Hotel Miami*, on the east end of the Malecón in Tarqui, has simple rooms with private bathrooms and cockroaches. Some rooms have good ocean views. The safe *Hotel Clarke* (☎ 625 835, 623 201), on Avenida 108 near Calle 102, is US$6 per person for clean, basic rooms with private bath. The clean *Hotel Americana* (☎ 623 069), on Calle 105 near Avenida 106, is US$20 for a basic double with private bath and air-conditioning; rooms with fans are cheaper but still overpriced.

Places to Stay – middle

Hotel El Inca (☎ 620 440, 610 986, fax 622 447), on Calle 105 near the Malecón, charges US$17/24 with air-conditioning and bath, TV and phone. Some rooms have ocean views. There is a restaurant attached. The *Hotel Pacífico* (☎ 623 584, 622 475), on Avenida 106 near Calle 102, has quite nice rooms with fans for US$10 per person or US$13 per person with air-conditioning.

Hotel Panorama Inn (☎ 611 552), on Calle 103 near Avenida 105, has rooms from US$10 to US$20 per person, depending on the amenities you choose. Rooms are rather worn but clean and spacious, all with private bathrooms, many with air-conditioning, and some with TV, telephone and good views. They give you pool privileges for the pool at La Cascada restaurant across the street.

Hotel Las Rocas (☎ 612 856, 610 299, 620 607), on Calle 101 at Avenida 105, is a favorite of Ecuadorian tour groups. Rooms are US$13/22 with bath and fans, and almost twice as much with air-conditioning. Their rooms are clean but their restaurant is nothing special. *Hotel Las Gaviotas* (☎ 620 140, 620 940, 625 899, fax 611 840), on the Malecón near Calle 107, has adequate air-conditioned rooms with bath and phone, some with an ocean view, for US$42/50. They have a restaurant, though I prefer their café and bar. Also in this price range is the *Hotel Haddad Manabí* (☎ 622 710/712, fax 624 876), on Calle 102 near the Malecón, which dates from 1931 and is Manta's oldest good hotel.

In Manta the *Hotel Lun Fun* (☎ 622 966), on Calle 2 near the Malecón, is good and comfortable. It is the best hotel close to the bus terminal but can be noisy because of traffic. Rates are US$30/40 for good-sized clean rooms with bathroom and hot water, air-conditioning, minifridge and telephone. They have a good Chinese restaurant.

The *Hotel Manta Imperial* (☎ 621 955, 622 016, fax 623 016) is next to Manta's Playa Murciélago. It has air-conditioning, a swimming pool, a small gym, a disco at weekends and a somewhat mediocre restaurant. The rooms are clean with private bath, minifridge and TV, but aren't anything special unless you get one with a beach view. Rates are about US$40/50.

On the next beach northwest of Murcielago is the *Centro Turístico Barbasquillo* (☎ 620 718, 625 976, fax 622 456). They have private beach access and a beach bar, a pool, disco, kid's playground and a restaurant. It's a new place – they plan on opening a sauna, spa and gym as well. Rates for air-conditioned rooms with TV and telephone are US$32/40, including breakfast, or about US$10 less with fans instead of air-conditioning. They also have family cabins with kitchenettes sleeping four or five for US$50; breakfast is extra.

Places to Stay – top end

The *Hotel Cabañas Balandra* (☎ 620 316, 620 915, fax 620 545), north of downtown Manta at Avenida 8 and Calle 20, is also a new place. Although they are not on the beach, the ocean is a few minutes' walk away. Very comfortable two-bedroom cabins have air-conditioning, minifridge, TV, bath, telephone and balconies with views of the ocean. There are also double rooms. The complex has a restaurant, pool, public fax and a guarded parking lot. Rooms start at US$60.

The new *Hotel María José* (☎ 612 294) is a small luxury hotel at Calle 29 and Calle Flavio Reyes to the northwest of downtown. I don't have any details about the facilities, but the rates are about US$75/100, including continental breakfast.

Places to Eat

Many cheap outdoor comedores on the east end of Tarqui Beach serve fresh seafood. The *Picantería El Marino* is a good, locally popular and inexpensive one. The market is also a center for cheap food. Several restaurants and bars are along the Tarqui waterfront, of which *Bar Comedor Boulevard* has large servings of reasonably priced food. Some other restaurants nearby are cheaper and serve good seafood. For a night out you can have a slightly expensive but good meal in the more elegant *La Cascada* (which has a swimming pool).

Near the bridge joining Tarqui with Manta is *Chifa Popular* (☎ 621 346) at 4 de Noviembre and Avenida 109. It's cheap and good. In Manta, there is the cheap *Chifa Oriental* on Calle 8 at Avenida 4. There are also cheap restaurants near the Hotel Chimborazo by the Plaza 4 de Noviembre. The restaurant at the *Hotel Lun Fun* serves Chinese and other food and is popular with the locals.

Near Playa Murcielago, *Pizzería Topi* (☎ 621 180), on the Malecón near Avenida 15, is open late and has a good variety of pizza and other Italian dishes. The *Restaurant Charlot* (☎ 611 320), west of the Malecón around Avenida 18 (best to take a cab because it's hard to find) is one of the best established upscale restaurants. Right opposite the Playa Murcielago, *Restaurant Cheers* (☎ 620 779) is a popular steak and seafood restaurant with an outdoor courtyard. Way west of town (again take a cab) is Manta's best steak house, *La Parrillada del Che Marcelo* (☎ 620 664), Avenida 24 and Calle 20. Also good for international food in a nice setting is the *Club Ejecutivo Restaurant* (☎ 620 113), on the top floor of the Banco del Pichincha on Avenida 2 near Calle 11.

Entertainment

El Descanso del Pirata (☎ 620 779), is a peña opposite Playa Murcielago. *Escandal Ho!* (☎ 623 653) is a Manta discoteca near the corner of Calle 12 and Avenida 2; another is *Madera Fina* (☎ 626 573) northwest of town on Calle Flavio Reyes near Calle 23. There is a cinema near the market in Taqui.

The open-air theater in Manta occasionally has performances, especially during the annual agriculture, fishing and tourism exposition, held from October 14 to 18. Portoviejo has a similar event at the same time. You can get more information on what's going on then from the CETUR office in Manta.

Getting There & Away

Air The TAME office (☎ 622 006, 613 210) is on the Manta waterfront, past the open-air theater. TAME has flights from Quito at 8:30 am, returning from Manta to Quito at 9:40 am daily except Sunday. On Sunday, they have a flight from Quito at 3:15 pm, returning to Quito at 4:15 pm. The one-way fare is US$26. You can buy tickets at the airport on the morning of the flight, but the planes tend to be full at weekends and holidays.

If you can't get on a flight from Manta, you could try flying from Portoviejo, 35 km away, where there are afternoon flights to Quito on Monday, Wednesday and Friday.

AECA (☎ 288 810, 288 580 in Guayaquil) has flights from Guayaquil in light aircraft when there is passenger demand.

The airport (☎ 621 580) is some three km east of Tarqui and a taxi costs about US$1.20 if you bargain hard.

Bus There is a large central bus terminal in front of the fishing boat harbor in Manta, and almost all buses leave from here, which makes things easy. There are several companies with buses to most major Ecuadorian cities. Journey times and prices are similar to Portoviejo's (see above). Some of the smaller companies running buses to nearby Manabí towns and villages don't have an office in the terminal, but their buses leave from there anyway and you pay aboard the bus.

BAHÍA DE MANTA

Although Manta itself does not have good beaches, several coastal villages on the large Bahía de Manta (Manta Bay), have pleasant beaches and are local resorts. You can get to these villages by local buses and rancheras that take the inland road to Portoviejo and then backtrack to the coast. During low tide, however, vehicles often drive northeast of Manta along the beach. This makes the journey less than half the distance and much quicker. Taxis can be hired to these destinations – the price depends on whether you have to go inland or can drive along the beach. Ecuadorian

tourists often go to these villages on day trips to bathe in the ocean and eat seafood, and then return to their hotel in Manta at night. Gringo travelers, on the other hand, are seldom seen on these beaches.

About eight km east of Manta by road is **Jaramijó**, a picturesque fishing village of about 7000 inhabitants. It is said to be one of the oldest fishing villages in Ecuador and was called Xamaxejo before the conquest. There are some cheap restaurants selling decent seafood, but no hotels. It is popular at Easter and Carnaval time and is quiet for most of the rest of the year. They have an annual fiesta on August 24.

Beyond Jaramijó the road stops, although vehicles often drive along the beach at low tide. (A recent report says this is prohibited because of a military base en route. Ask locally.) The next fishing village is **Crucita**, about 16 km beyond Jaramijó. Here, you'll find several good seafood restaurants, a very long beach and hang gliders (with competitions every few months). The beach in front of town is not very clean, but heading north or south brings you to much better ones. The village is experiencing a local tourism boom and several new hotels are under construction. Right now, the best seems to be *La Zucasa* with a pool and rooms around US$20, but there are several cheaper ones. Buses from Portoviejo (US$0.60; 45 minutes) leave several times an hour during daylight.

The next villages are **San Jacinto**, about 13 km beyond Crucita and slightly inland, and **San Clemente**, about three km beyond and on the coast. There are good, sandy beaches between these villages, both of which have restaurants and cheap to mid-range places to stay. In San Jacinto, *Hotel San Jacinto* is one of the best ones.

On the outskirts of San Clemente, there is the *Hostería San Clemente*, with a swimming pool, and the *Cabañas Tío Gerardo*, which has cabins with sleeping space for two to six people. There are a bunch of other places. Beyond San Clemente, a good new road (not marked on Ecuadorian road maps) continues northeast along the coast to Bahía de Caráquez, about 20 km away.

Crucita, San Jacinto and San Clemente can all be easily reached from Portoviejo. All have been developing a tourist industry in the 1990s, and there are new hotels (bottom-end and midrange) opening every year. Most visitors are Ecuadorians – the place has yet to be discovered by foreign travelers. Beware of walking barefoot in these places – a worm infection has been reported.

MONTECRISTI
This small, interesting town can be reached during the day by frequent buses (US$0.20; 15 minutes) from the terminal terrestre in Manta.

Montecristi is an important center for both the Panama hat industry and wickerwork. There are many stores along the main road and along the road leading into the town center. If you go in towards the center and ask around, you can see the manufacturing of Panama hats in various stages.

The town is an old colonial one; it was founded around 1628, when many of the inhabitants of Manta fled inland to avoid the frequent pirate plundering to which the port was subjected. The many unrestored colonial houses give the village a rather tumble-down and ghostly atmosphere.

The main plaza has a beautiful church dating back to the early part of the last century. It contains a statue of the Virgin to

which miracles have been attributed, and is worth a visit. In the plaza is a statue of Eloy Alfaro, who was born in Montecristi and was president of Ecuador at the beginning of the century. His tomb is in the town hall by the plaza.

I didn't see any hotels and only a couple of basic comedores, so it's best to stay in Manta and visit Montecristi on a day trip.

JIPIJAPA
The 'j' is pronounced as 'h' in Spanish, so this town's name is pronounced 'Hipihapa.' Jipijapa has a population of over 30,000 and is an important center for the Panama hat industry as well as for coffee and cotton. The town market is a good place to buy Panama hats. Sunday is market day and the town is very busy – there are signs outside many merchants' stores reading 'Compro Café' (Coffee Bought Here). There's not much else to see or do.

Jipijapa is the main town on the good road linking Manta and Portoviejo with Guayaquil. The road crosses the coastal hills and through Jipijapa at an elevation of about 350 meters above sea level. Manta is about 60 km to the north and Guayaquil is about 140 km to the southeast. Parque Nacional Machalilla is a short distance to the southwest.

Information
The Banco del Pichincha changes cash dollars but not traveler's checks. EMETEL is on the southwest corner of the plaza. The area code is 05.

Places to Stay & Eat
Jipijapa is not a particularly pleasant place to stay but there are very basic pensiones if you get stuck here. The *Pensión Mejía* on Rocafuerte is just acceptable for about US$3 or US$4 per person in cramped rooms with bath. The poor *Pensión Venezuela* on 10 de Agosto near V Rendon is cheaper, dirty and unfriendly. About a kilometer from town is the *Hostal Jipijapa* with rooms with private bath for about US$9/12. They offer tours to the national park.

Weaving Panama hats

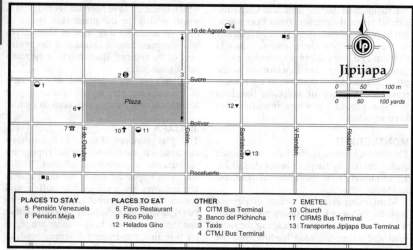

PLACES TO STAY
5 Pensión Venezuela
8 Pensión Mejía

PLACES TO EAT
6 Pavo Restaurant
9 Rico Pollo
12 Helados Gino

OTHER
1 CITM Bus Terminal
2 Banco del Pichincha
3 Taxis
4 CTMJ Bus Terminal

7 EMETEL
10 Church
11 CIRMS Bus Terminal
13 Transportes Jipijapa Bus Terminal

The simple *Pavo Restaurant* on the plaza is a locally popular place for lunch and dinner; chicken is the main feature. *Rico Pollo*, another chicken place, is down a block on 9 de Octubre. *Helados Gino* just east of the plaza, serves good ice cream. It's hard to find a restaurant open for early breakfast.

Getting There & Away

There is no central bus terminal. CTMJ, on 10 de Agosto near Santistevan, has frequent buses to Manta (US$0.90; 1¼ hours). CITMS, on the plaza by the church, has several buses a day for Puerto López (for Parque Nacional Machalilla). CITM, on Sucre a block west of the plaza, has several buses a day through Puerto López (US$1; 1¼ hours) and on down the coast past Alandaluz (US$1.60) to La Libertad (US$3.75; three to four hours). Transportes Jipijapa, on Santistevan just south of Bolívar, has buses to Quito (US$6.50; seven hours) and Guayaquil (US$2; 2½ hours).

Other companies have buses to Guayaquil passing through from Manta or Portoviejo – ask locals which street corners are the best places to flag them down.

PUERTO DE CAYO

About 30 km west of Jipijapa, the road reaches the Pacific Ocean at the small town of Puerto de Cayo. The only telephones in town are at the EMETEL office. *Hostería Luz de Luna* and the *Hotel Torremolinos* are a couple of small mid-priced hotels in town. There are also some more basic places.

PARQUE NACIONAL MACHALILLA

This is the only coastal national park in Ecuador, so it is of particular importance in preserving a very small part of the rapidly disappearing coastal habitats of the country. The park was created in 1979 to protect about 50 km of beach (less than 2% of Ecuador's coastline), some 40,000 hectares of tropical dry forest and cloud forest, and about 20,000 hectares of ocean, including two offshore islands and the only coral formations found on the Ecuadorian mainland coast.

From December to June it is sunny and hot, with rainstorms most days. From June to November it does not rain much and is cooler and usually overcast.

The number of archaeological sites within and near the park mainly date from the Manta period, from 500 AD to the conquest. There are also remains of the much older Machalilla and Chorrera cultures, dating from about 1500 to 500 BC, and the Salango culture from 3000 BC.

The tropical dry forest found in much of the inland sectors of the park forms a strange and wonderful landscape of characteristically bottle-shaped trees with small crowns and heavy spines – a protection against herbivores. Some of the most common species include the leguminous algarrobo, *Prosopsis juliflora*, which has green bark and is able to photosynthesize even when it loses its leaves.

The kapok tree, *Ceiba pentandra*, which has huge plank-like buttresses surrounding the base of the gray trunk, has fruits that yield a fiber that floats and doesn't get waterlogged. The kapok fiber was used in life jackets before the advent of modern synthetics.

Fig *(Ficus* species), laurel *(Cordia* species) and palo santo *(Pursera graveolens)* trees are also commonly seen.

The tall spindly cactus that grows profusely on some hillsides belongs to the genus *Armatocereus*. The prickly pear, of the genus *Opuntia*, is also common.

Within this strange-looking forest, a variety of bird and animal life is found. Well over 200 species of birds have been recorded, including a variety of coastal parrots, parrotlets and parakeets, as well seabirds, such as frigatebirds, pelicans and boobies, some of which nest in the offshore islands.

Other animals include deer, squirrels, howler monkeys, guantas, anteaters and a variety of lizards, snakes and iguanas.

This interesting and unusual tropical dry forest once stretched along much of the Pacific coast of Central and South America, but has suffered from human interference as much as or more than other tropical forest types. It has now almost entirely disappeared and is one of the most threatened tropical forests in the world. It is particularly vulnerable to fire and to grazing by goats, which eat young trees before they have developed their protective spines and the full complement of chemicals that make the mature trees less palatable to herbivores.

The Nature Conservancy recently estimated that there were about 1000 cows and 1500 goats grazing within the mainland confines of the national park. Some of these animals belonged to people living in small communities within the park, and their grazing was, for the most part, relatively controlled. Many of the goats, however, belonged to people living outside the park who illegally introduced their animals into ungrazed sectors of the park. Some of these people are poor campesinos who don't have other land to graze their animals on. This is typical of the management problems facing the Ecuadorian national park system as a whole.

Fortunately, Machalilla has been identified as an area deserving of immediate and special protection because of its uniqueness. Its staff includes a park superintendent and several seasonal and full-time rangers who work with the local people to establish better protection of the park. Locals work as tourist guides and maintain a museum and archaeological area. Also, alternative agricultural projects such as bee-keeping and pig-raising are being developed to replace goat grazing.

Orientation & Information

The national park is in the southernmost part of coastal Manabí Province. The coastal road goes through the park and provides the main access. It is also possible to enter the park from the inland side by taking the road south from Jipijapa.

The **park headquarters and museum** are in Puerto López, a coastal village on the south side of the park. The museum is open daily from 8 am to 4 pm. Here, there are informative exhibits and a good map of the park. Staff can answer questions, and brochures and maps are available. Entrance fees to any or all sectors of the park are US$20 (a little less if you pay in sucres), and the entrance is valid for several days, so you can visit both mainland and coastal sectors.

About six or seven km north of Puerto López you come to the **park entrance** on the right side of the road. There is a sign and an entrance booth where you pay the US$20 admission if you have not already done so.

Agua Blanca & Around

A dirt road goes through tropical dry forest to Agua Blanca, five km from the entrance. This little village has an **archaeological museum** (US$1.25, 8 am to 6 pm) explaining the excavation of the Manta site, which is about a half-hour walk away. The site can be visited, but a local guide (US$8) is required. Only the bases of the buildings can be seen, but there are plans to restore some of the approximately 400 buildings excavated at the site, which is thought to have been an important political capital of the Manta people.

From Agua Blanca, a four-hour hike to the southeast goes up through a transition zone to a remnant area of cloud forest at **San Sebastian**, about 600 meters above sea level. Guides are required and are available in Agua Blanca to take you to either the archaeological site or San Sebastian. Horses can be hired if you don't want to hike. Camping or staying with local people are the only accommodations at present.

The dirt road to Agua Blanca continues up the Río Julcuy valley to the northeast. From the village, it is a six- to seven-hour hike up this road through the park, coming out at the village of **Julcuy**, just beyond the park boundary. From Julcuy, it's about another three hours to the main Jipijapa-Guayaquil road.

Los Frailes

About 10 km north of Puerto López, just before reaching the village of Machalilla, a poor dirt road goes three km to the coast at **Los Frailes**. There is a good beach here and sport fishing is a possibility. Nearby, there are seabird nesting colonies.

Offshore Islands

Boats can be hired from Puerto López to take you out to the offshore islands. The one most frequently visited is **Isla de la Plata**, about 40 km northwest of Puerto López. The name (Silver Island) derives from the local legend that Sir Francis Drake buried some treasure here. The island has nesting colonies of seabirds – blue-footed boobies are usually seen. Red-footed boobies, frigatebirds and pelicans have also been frequently recorded, as well as a variety of gulls, terns, petrels and other seabirds. There are a few coral reefs as well, and you can snorkel if you bring gear or take a tour that features snorkeling. From mid-June to mid-October (especially in July), whales and dolphins have been sighted on the trip over to the island, which has been locally and aptly dubbed as 'the poor person's Galápagos.' (Some scientists don't like this term, claiming there are biological differences. I find it appropriate from the lay-travelers point of view.) The island is used as a resting or overnighting place by the local fisherfolk. A closer island is **Isla Salango**, which is about 1½ km west of Salango or about eight km southwest of Puerto López.

Places to Stay

You can camp in several places within the park, but check with park authorities about the availability of water, particularly during the May-to-December dry season.

People in Agua Blanca will put you up in their houses if asked. Basic food is available on request, but it's best to bring some of your own. You can also camp near Agua Blanca.

Most people stay in hotels at Puerto López or at the nearby Alandaluz Ecological Tourist Center (see Alandaluz, below).

Getting There & Away

Bus Every hour buses run up and down the coast between Puerto López and Jipijapa. You should have no difficulty, therefore, in getting a bus to drop you off at the park entrance (note that it is a five km walk from here to Agua Blanca) or in finding one to pick you up when you are ready to leave.

Trucks occasionally go from the main road to Agua Blanca and back; most likely, you'll have to walk or hire a taxi in Puerto López. This costs about US$8.

Buses south from Jipijapa can drop you at the settlement of San Dimas, about 11 km south of town. From here, the dirt road goes west to Guarango, three km away, and on through Julcuy to the park. Few people take this route.

Boat You can arrange boat trips to Isla de la Plata through the tour agencies in Puerto López (see below). The park service may know of other boats or tours.

PUERTO LÓPEZ

This is a busy fishing village, with a population of about 10,000. You can watch the fishermen come in and unload their catch most mornings – the fish are gutted on the spot and the air is full of wheeling frigatebirds and vultures trying to grab the scraps. If you make friends with the local fishers, they may take you out on a fishing trip.

Buses running from La Libertad to Jipijapa often stop here for about 10 minutes while passengers buy snacks. Sometimes, children get on the bus yelling 'Corviche Caliente!' This snack, found only in this region, consists of a dough made of flour and banana paste and stuffed with salty fish. Served hot, maybe with a dash of salsa, it will give your taste buds something new to think about.

Puerto López is the nearest town of any size to Parque Nacional Machalilla and houses the park headquarters.

Orientation & Information

The bus stops in the center of town, about a block away from the EMETEL office, which is on the right side of the main road if you are northbound. The national park museum and administrative center is a block behind the EMETEL, away from the main road. The ocean is about five blocks to the left of the main road. Money changing facilities are poor.

Organized Tours

Pacarina Travel (☎ 604 173) uses small boats to Isla de la Plata for about US$200,

which includes snorkeling. The boat holds up to eight passengers, so it's not very expensive if you can get a group together. The ride out takes from two to 3½ hours one way, depending on the boat and the winds, tides and weather. Be prepared to get wet and take motion sickness pills if you are susceptible – the crossing can get very rough.

Pacarina Travel is also a general travel agency and can arrange a variety of other tours or arrange for taxi pickups. They also have an office at the Alandaluz (see below).

Salangome (☎ 604 120) has guided boat tours for US$35 per person in larger boats. They will also arrange tours to the mainland part of the park and other areas.

Note that the park entry fee is not included in any of these tours. Both the above agencies are well known and easy to find. As this book goes to press, I hear that a third agency is planning to open with a PADI-recognized dive shop.

Places to Stay & Eat

There are two or three cheap pensiones in various states of disrepair. The owners are generally friendly, but the accommodations are poor. Rooms are about US$3 to US$4 per person. *Carmita's*, on the shorefront, is a good, cheap restaurant and they have a few simple rooms with bath for US$6 per person. Next door, the *Mayflower* is a locally popular restaurant. The *Hotel Pacífico* (☎ 604 133, fax 604 147) is the most comfortable place, with good rooms, hot baths and air-conditioning at US$16/24 and cabins with shared bath for US$9/14.

Many people prefer to stay at the Alandaluz (see below).

Getting There & Away

Cooperativa Manglaralto and CITM have buses running between La Libertad and Jipijapa – they stop in Puerto López about every 45 minutes. It is about 2½ hours to La Libertad and 1½ hours to Jipijapa (US$1.60). CITMS also has buses between Puerto López and Jipijapa. These buses will drop you off at any point you want along the coast. Buses stop running in late afternoon.

MACHALILLA

This village is about 10 km north of Puerto López. There is a decent beach and you can stay at the mid-priced *Hotel Internacional Machalilla*.

SALANGO

This little fishing village is about five km south of Puerto López. Isla Salango is less than two km out to sea – you could go on a tour or hire a fishing boat to take you out and see the seabirds, but they are not as numerous as on Isla de la Plata.

The small, modern and well-laid-out **archaeological museum** was founded by the Banco Central and has exhibits about the local archaeological sites – a worthwhile stop. Admission is about US$0.80 and hours are 8 am to 6 pm.

El Delfín is a decent seafood restaurant, but there are no hotels in the village. A couple of kilometers away, *Los Piqueros* charges about US$50 for cabins that sleep up to six.

ALANDALUZ

About five km south of Salango, the road passes through the village of Puerto Rico. The **Alandaluz Ecocultural Tourist Center** is about one km further south. This is an alternative Ecuadorian-run hotel, built entirely of local fast-growing and easily replenishable materials, such as bamboo and palm thatch. The result is an interesting-looking building with grassy, overhanging eaves and a slightly contorted appearance. Each room is different: twisted beams, uneven floors and rough wooden beds make for a truly rustic decor.

The main building is surrounded by organic gardens that produce many of the spices, herbs, fruits, and vegetables served at meal times. The lavatories are also organic and, by using sawdust, it is possible to convert human waste to (more or less) odor-free fertilizers and conserve water. Everything that can be is recycled and local communities are encouraged to follow suit. The idea is to create a self-sustaining hotel that, as much as is possible, has a minimal impact on the environment.

There is a bar and dining room that serves good meals (with a predominantly seafood and vegetarian menu). The nightly set meals are usually a better bet than ordering à la carte. There is a volleyball area and a small games room. The beach is close by, and you can bathe undisturbed, although the waves are rather wild. Don't go out far unless you are a very confident swimmer.

The management is laid-back and friendly. They work with Pacarina Tours and will try to help travelers organize trips to Machalilla, the museums and the offshore islands (though this depends on how many people are staying there). The ambiance is very relaxed, and some people end up staying for days as they unwind from a fast-paced travel schedule. Others find the place too laid-back and move on quickly. It's definitely a unique place that most travelers have strong opinions about, usually positive.

Communal showers are heated by the sun – you get a hot shower sometimes. Rooms are inside the main building or outside, in strangely shaped private cabins. Rates are US$4 per person to stay in a hammock on the porch or to camp. Beds are US$12 per person (shared bathrooms) or US$14 (private bathrooms); there are few singles. Meals are US$3 for breakfast, US$4 to US$6 for lunch or dinner.

Reservations can be made in Quito (☎ / fax 543 042, see also Online Services), Baqueadano 330 and Reina Victoria, 2nd floor. You need to pay half of the fee in advance – you can do this by paying into an account at any branch of the Banco del Pichincha (if you can't get to their Quito office). Often they have space available if you just show up at the hotel, although they are occasionally booked full for Friday and Saturday nights. Try to get there early in the day.

Any bus going up or down the coast can drop you off in front of the hotel (see Puerto López for more details).

AYAMPE

This small village is about three km south of Alandaluz. A couple of kilometers south of the village is the most comfortable hotel on the stretch of coast between Manta and Salinas. The German-run *Hotel Atamari* (in Quito ☎ 228 470, 227 896, fax 508 369) sits on a bluff overlooking the mouth of the Río Ayampe. Like the Alandaluz, recycling and conservation are important issues but, unlike the Alandaluz, the hotel is far from rustic, with elegant and spacious sea-view rooms with large modern bathrooms and

attractive furnishings and decor. Their restaurant is pricey but very good. Rooms are close to US$100 for a double and are often booked well in advance – it's a small hotel and reservations are advised.

The Río Ayampe forms the provincial line between Manabí and Guayas. The south coastal provinces of Guayas and El Oro are described in the next chapter.

The South Coast

The south coast, consisting of the provinces of Guayas and El Oro, is generally much drier and more barren than the north coast. The weather pattern changes, and the rainy season, which in the north lasts from December to May, is only from January to April in Guayaquil. Further west and south it becomes drier still, and at the Peruvian border the South American coastal desert begins.

The agriculturally important lowlands of Los Ríos Province continue into the provinces of Guayas and El Oro. Bananas are the most important crop, and irrigation in the dry south means that plantations can continue beyond Machala. Rice, coffee, cacao and African palm are other important crops of the region.

West of Guayaquil is the dry, infertile and scrubby Santa Elena Peninsula with not enough rivers for irrigation. Archaeological investigation shows that the land used to be as wet and fertile as it is now in the northern coastal areas, but drought and deforestation over the last 5000 years have wrought severe changes. Decorations on pottery shards and other excavated remains indicate that early farmers living in the area from 3000 to 1500 BC cultivated maize (corn), manioc, avocados, beans, squash, chilies, papayas, pineapples, palms and the bottle gourd. Bananas, Ecuador's most important crop, were introduced after the Spanish conquest.

The heart of the south coast is Guayaquil, Ecuador's largest city. To the west are the popular beach resorts of Playas and Salinas and to the south another important port city, Machala, which is the common gateway to Peru.

GUAYAQUIL

This is by far the most important port in Ecuador. More exports and imports pass through Guayaquil than through all the other ports combined. It is also the most populous city in the country.

Travelers to Ecuador tend to avoid Guayaquil because of its reputation as a hot and humid port (oppressively so from January to April) with too many inhabitants (two million) and little of interest to do.

I spent over two years traveling in Ecuador before I finally visited Guayaquil, and I must admit to having been pleasantly surprised. I discovered that it does have its attractions. There is a pleasant walk along the river front, shady plazas, colonial buildings, friendly people and interesting museums. It's definitely worth spending a day or two.

The province of Guayas is named after the Puna Indian chief of the same name who fought bravely against first the Incas and then the Spanish. The capital of the province, Guayaquil, is named after the chief, Guayas, and his wife, Quill, whom he is said to have killed before drowning himself, rather than allowing her to be captured by the Spanish conquistadors.

Orientation

Most travelers stay in the city center, which is organized in a grid-like fashion on the west bank of the Río Guayas. The main east-west street is Avenida 9 de Octubre, terminating at the river by 'La Rotonda,' the famous statue of the liberators, Bolívar and San Martín.

The airport is about five km north of the center, and the bus terminal is about two km north of the airport (seven km north of the center). The railway station is in the suburb of Durán, which is on the east side of the Río Guayas and reached either by river ferries or by a huge three-km bridge to the north of the city center. One suburb that is frequently visited for its good restaurants and nightlife is Urdesa, three or four km to the northwest of the center. There are many other suburbs, most of them residential or industrial, many of them poor and dangerous for the average tourist.

Top: Male frigatebird with inflated neck pouch, Galápagos Islands (TW)
Bottom: Marine Iguana (RR)

Top: Climber descending from Chimborazo, (6310 metres), the paramo far below (JW)
Bottom: Chimborazo, with the climber's refuge in the foreground (JW)

Reserva
Producción
Faunística
Chimborazo

Manta
San Jacinto
Calceta
Rocafuerte
Portoviejo
Quevedo

Isla de
la Plata
Parque
Nacional
Machalilla
Puerto
Cayo
Jipijapa
Manabí

Río Daule
Río Quevedo
*Los
Ríos*

Machalilla
Agua Blanca
Parque Nacional
Machalilla
Vinces
San Juan
Bolívar
Guaranda

Puerto López
Isla Salango
Alandaluz
Palestina
Riobamba

Olón
Montañito
Manglaralto
Daule
Babahoyo
Chillanes

Valdivia
Ayangue
Palmar
Guayas
Río Daule
Guayas
Chimborazo

La Libertad
Milagro
Naranjito
Alausí

Salinas
Santa Elena
San Vicente
Guayaquil
Durán
El
Triunfo
Bucay
Guasuntos

Punta Carnero
Anconcito
Río Babahoyo
Puerto
Nuevo
Reserva
Ecológica
de Manglares
Churute
Chunchi
Cañar

Chanduy
Progreso
La Troncal
Cañar
Ingapirca

Punta
Pelada
El
Morro
Naranjal
Azogues
Biblián

*PACIFIC
OCEAN*
Playas
Posorja
Data
Area Nacional de
Recreación Cajas
Cuenca

Isla
Puná
Sígsig

*Golfo de
Guayaquil*
Azuay
Girón

Canal de Jambelí
Santa
Isabel
Panamericana

South Coast
Puerto
Bolívar
Machala
Jambelí
Costa Rica
Pasaje
Oña
Macas

0   25   50 km
0   15   30 miles
Huaquillas
**Santa
Rosa**
El Oro
Zaruma
Saraguro
La Paz
Río Yacuambi

Tumbes
Arenillas
Palmales
Piñas
Portovelo
Guadalupe
Namírez
Nambija

*Disputed
Area*
Puyango
El Cisne
Río Zamora
Zamora

Alamor
San Pedro
de la Bendita
Catacocha
Catamayo
Loja
Bombuscara
Romerillos

Celica
Parque
Nacional
Podocarpus
Malacatos

Loja
Cariamanga
Vilcabamba
*Zamora-
Chinchipe*

PERU
Macará
Panamericana
La Tina

To Lima
To Piura

SOUTH COAST

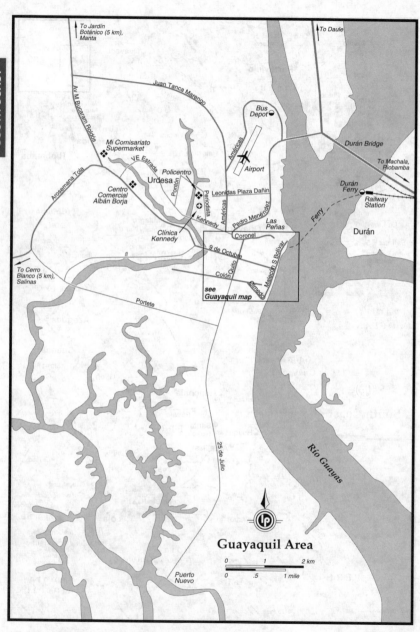

To Jardín
Botánico (5 km),
Manta

To Daule

Juan Tanca Marengo

Bus
Depot

Durán Bridge

Av M Bucaram Polotos

Mi Comisariato
Supermarket

VE Estrada

Policentro

Américas

Airport

To Machala,
Riobamba

Durán
Ferry

Railway
Station

Arosemana Tola

Urdesa

Centro
Comercial
Albán Borja

Prontón

Leonidas Plaza Dañín

Periodista

Kennedy

Américas

Pedro Menéndez

Las
Peñas

Ferry

Durán

Clínica
Kennedy

Coronel

9 de Octubre

Colón

Quito

Olmedo

Malecón S Bolívar

To Cerro
Blanco (5 km),
Salinas

Portete

see
Guayaquil map

25 de Julio

Río Guayas

LP

Guayaquil Area

0   1   2 km

0   .5   1 mile

Puerto
Nuevo

Information

Tourist Offices The CETUR information office (☎ 328 312) is on the waterfront at the Malecón and Aguirre. They are officially open from 8:30 am to 5 pm Monday to Friday, have some English-speaking staff and try to be helpful – although travelers sometimes complain that the tourist office is not very useful. It depends on whom you talk to. There is also a CETUR office at the airport. The better travel agencies are also sources of information.

Foreign Embassies In accordance with Guayaquil's status as Ecuador's major port and city, there are many embassies and consulates. Their office hours tend to be short, so try to call in advance to find out when they are open – or if they have recently changed addresses. Most countries also have diplomatic representatives in Quito. Travelers heading for Peru may want to visit the Peruvian Consulate – their hours recently were 8:30 am to 1 pm, Monday to Friday.

Most embassies and consulates are listed below – there may be a few more so check in the phone book or at a tourist office. To avoid cluttering the Guayaquil map with too many symbols, I have omitted embassies and consulates. Those marked below with an asterisk (*) have street addresses that are on my map; those without are off the map.

Argentina*
Aguirre 104 and Malecón
(☎ 530 767, fax 323 574)
Australia
Calle San Roque and Avenida Orellana,
Ciudadela Kennedy Norte
(☎ 298 823, fax 298 822)
Austria*
9 de Octubre 1312 and Quito
(☎ /fax 282 303)
Belgium
L García 301 and Vélez
(☎ 454 429, 454 077, fax 454 234)
Bolivia*
F Paula de Icaza 302 and Córdova, office
601 (☎ 564 260, 565 888, fax 560 144)
Brazil
Km 7.5, Vía a Daule
(☎ 252 899, fax 251 615)

Canada*
Córdova 812 and VM Rendón, 21st floor
(☎ 563 580, 566 747, fax 314 562)
Chile
JA Campos 101 and García Aviles
(☎ 562 995, ☎ 564 619, fax 565 151)
Colombia*
Córdova 812 and VA Rendón, 2nd floor
(☎ 563 308, fax 565 854)
Costa Rica*
Pichincha 105 and P de Icaza, 5th floor
(☎ 311 285, fax 561 373)
Denmark*
Córdova 604 and Mendiburo
(☎ 308 020, fax 204 591)
Finland*
Urdaneta 212 and Córdova
(☎ 564 381, 564 268, fax 566 291)
France*
Aguirre 503 and Chimborazo
(☎ 328 159, fax 322 887)
Germany
Avenida CJ Arosemena, Km 2.5, Edificio
Berlin (☎ 200 500, 202 688, fax 202 554)
Holland*
P de Icaza 454 and B Moreno
(☎ 562 777, fax 313 710)
Israel*
9 de Octubre 727 and Avilés
(☎ 322 555, fax 328 196)
Italy*
Baquerizo Moreno 1120 and 9 de Octubre
(☎ 563 136, 563 140, fax 408 255)
Mexico*
Tulcán 1600 and Colón
(☎ 372 928, fax 250 151)
Norway*
9 de Octubre 109 and Malecón
(☎ 329 661, fax 329 253)
Panama*
Aguirre 509 and Chimborazo, 9th floor
(☎ /fax 512 158)
Peru*
9 de Octubre 411 and Chile, 6th floor
(☎ 322 738, 327 639, fax 325 679)
Spain
Urdesa (☎ 380 265, fax 881 134)
Sweden
Km 6.5 on Daule Road
(☎ 254 111, fax 254 159)
Switzerland*
9 de Octubre 2105 and Tulcán
(453 607, fax 394 023)
UK*
Córdova 623 and Solano
(☎ 560 400, 563 850, fax 562 641)

Uruguay*
  Aguirre 512 and Escobedo
  (☎ 320 658, 513 461)
USA*
  9 de Octubre and García Moreno
  (☎ 323 570, fax 325 286)
Venezuela*
  Chile 329 and Aguirre, 2nd floor
  (☎ 326 579, 326 566, fax 320 751)

Immigration & Documents To extend
your tourist card, go to the immigration
office (☎ 322 539, 290 502) in the government building (Palacio de Gobierno) on
Aguirre and the Malecón.

Money Along with Quito and Cuenca,
Guayaquil has the best foreign exchange
rates in Ecuador. The easiest places to
change money are the casas de cambio, of
which there are over a dozen on the first
couple of blocks of Avenida 9 de Octubre
by the waterfront and along the first few
blocks of Avenida Pichincha. All casas de
cambio are closed on Sunday, and a few are
open on Saturday morning. The airport has
a casa de cambio that is open at weekends
to meet incoming international flights.

Banks will also change money and traveler's checks. The Banco del Pacífico on
Plaza de San Francisco has been recommended, but there are several others in
the vicinity.

Post & Communications The EMETEL
(☎ 560 200) and main post office (☎ 531
713, 514 710) are in the same huge building occupying the block bounded by
Avenidas Ballén and P Carbo. There are
agencies on the streets nearby that will
send faxes for a fee.

Courier companies will insure and send
important packets and documents from
Guayaquil to major cities of the world.
Delivery is within 24 to 48 hours to places
served by air from Guayaquil (eg, Miami,
New York, Frankfurt, London, most Latin
American capitals) and longer to cities
needing connecting flights. Costs are about
US$40 for a small package. Companies
include DHL International (☎ 287 044),

UPS (☎ 451 003) and World Courier
(☎ 326 050/353).

Travel Agencies Anybody who has anything to do with travel will try to sell you a
Galápagos trip. One of the cheapest agencies
is Economic Galápagos Tours (☎ 312 447,
fax 313 351), 9 de Octubre 424 and Córdova,
office 1106 (they also have an office in
Quito). Metropolitan Touring (☎ 320 300,
320 748, fax 323 050), José de Antepara 915
and 9 de Octubre, has its main office in Quito
and has good middle- to luxury-priced tours,
including both small boats and cruise ships.
Canodros (☎ 285 711, 280 143, fax 287 651),
Urdaneta 1418 and Ejército, is the agent for
the *Galápagos Explorer*, the newest and
most expensive cruise ship. Many offices
offer low-budget tours, but often they simply
broker for the Economic Galápagos Tours
boats. Tours to the Galápagos are generally
expensive, and these agencies cover the price
spectrum. More information is given in the
Galápagos section.

Ecuadorian Tours (☎ 287 111, fax 280
851), at 9 de Octubre 1900, is the American
Express agent. Delgado Travel (☎ 560
680), at Córdova and 9 de Octubre, and
(☎ 389 687/337), G Moreno 917 and 9 de
Octubre, are good all-around travel agents.
Chasquitur (☎ 281 084/5), Urdaneta 1418,
is reportedly good for ecotourism.

City tours are available. Tours to nearby
beaches are also available, but for small
groups I suggest a bus or hiring a taxi for
the day to be more economical.

Bookstores For English-language (and
other) books, the best store is the Librería
Científica (☎ 328 569), at Luque 225 and
Chile. The Bookshop on VE Estrada in
Urdesa also sells books in English. Librería
Minis (☎ 888 642), in the Centro Comercial Plaza Mayor, is a good bet for travel-
related books and information; their hours
are noon to 8 pm.

There is a public library (☎ 533 134) at
the Museo Municipal. Use the back
entrance on Avenida 10 de Agosto for the
library and the front entrance on Avenida
Sucre for the museum.

Medical Services The best hospital in Guayaquil (and the whole coastal region) is reputedly the Clínica Kennedy (☎ 286 963, 289 666), Avenida del Periodista (also known as San Jorge), by the Policentro shopping center in the Nueva Kennedy suburb, near Urdesa. They have specialists for almost everything. Take a taxi there if you're sick.

Recommended physicians in Guayaquil include Dr Carlos Albán Cárdenas (☎ 294 874), 1 de Mayo 1019, Dr Alfonso Guim León (☎ 532 179, 531 793), Boyacá 1320 and Luque, and Dr Angel Sáenz Serrano (☎ 561 785), Boyacá 821 and Junín.

I have never had reason to visit a hospital or doctor in Guayaquil (there are limits to what I will do to research this book), but a resident of the city recommends that patients be prepared to pay at the time of treatment. For example, an X-ray and treatment for a simple fracture (no hospitalization) might run US$30 to US$40.

Good dental care is available from Clínica Dental Urdesa Central, in Urdesa. Another good choice is Clínica de Odontología Integral (☎ 398 791, 293 620) in Guayaquil.

There are many pharmacies. Among the best is Farmacia Fybeca (☎ 510 584), Moncayo 938.

Emergency You can reach the Red Cross ambulance at ☎ 560 674, or the CEAMSA ambulance center at ☎ 445 406. The police are at ☎ 101, or 392 221/30. The fire department is at ☎ 102, or 526 666.

Dangers & Annoyances Guayaquil has a reputation for theft problems. Take the normal precautions of visiting any large city: Avoid walking in ill-lit areas at night. At all times, keep money and valuables well hidden. Avoid wearing expensive watches or jewelry and dress in simple clothing in public. If arriving or departing from the bus terminal or airport with luggage, taxis are safer than public buses. Public buses are usually OK if you just have hand luggage, which you can easily keep your eagle eye and firm hand-

hold on, or if you are with a couple of other travelers.

Always be alert for pickpockets and bag snatchers, especially near hotel entrances. Well-dressed thieves may even enter hotel lobbies in search of poorly attended bags or bulging pockets.

Having said all this, I don't think that visiting Guayaquil is necessarily any more dangerous than visiting New York or Rome.

Walking Tour

The majority of interesting sights are on or within a few blocks of the waterfront, locally called the Malecón Simón Bolívar, or the Malecón for short. Because of their proximity to one another, I devised the following walking tour, which I certainly don't expect you to follow slavishly! Choose the bits that sound the most interesting to you. It is a good idea to begin your sightseeing walk near the CETUR tourist information office at Olmedo and the waterfront. CETUR may be able to provide a guide to accompany you for a fee.

The whole walk as described in this section can be done in two or three hours, but if you want to enjoy the sights thoroughly, you could spend one whole day, or even two. Keep your eyes open for plaques and signs. Guayaquil is full of them, and they give interesting historic information (if you read Spanish).

Sunday is a good day to take your walking tour because there isn't much traffic (though some museums may be closed). On other days, start as early in the day as practical to avoid the heat.

The Malecón At the south end of the Malecón and Olmedo there is an imposing **statue** of José Joaquín Olmedo Maruri, an Ecuadorian poet and politician born in Guayaquil on March 19, 1789. He sits, bard-like, in a colonial armchair.

Heading north along the Malecón, with the Río Guayas to your right, you pass several **monuments**. One is to the UN, known in Spanish as the ONU (Organización de Naciones Unidas) and another is the famous Moorish-style **clock tower**,

SOUTH COAST

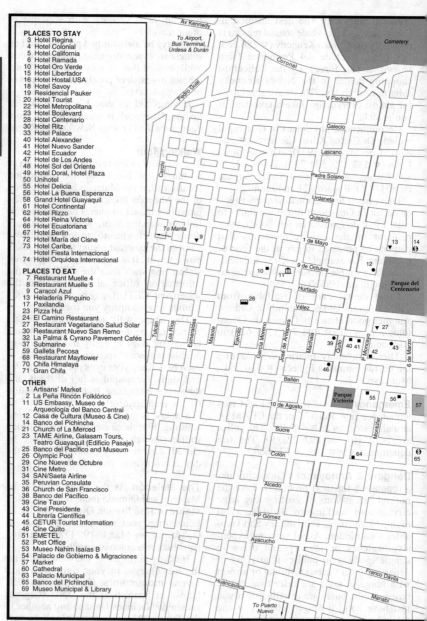

PLACES TO STAY
3 Hotel Regina
4 Hotel Colonial
5 Hotel California
6 Hotel Ramada
10 Hotel Oro Verde
15 Hotel Libertador
16 Hotel Hostal USA
18 Hotel Savoy
19 Residencial Pauker
20 Hotel Tourist
22 Hotel Metropolitana
23 Hotel Boulevard
28 Hotel Centenario
30 Hotel Ritz
33 Hotel Palace
40 Hotel Alexander
41 Hotel Nuevo Sander
42 Hotel Ecuador
47 Hotel de Los Andes
48 Hotel Sol del Oriente
49 Hotel Doral, Hotel Plaza
50 Unihotel
55 Hotel Delicia
56 Hotel La Buena Esperanza
58 Grand Hotel Guayaquil
61 Hotel Continental
62 Hotel Rizzo
64 Hotel Reina Victoria
66 Hotel Ecuatoriana
67 Hotel Berlin
72 Hotel María del Cisne
73 Hotel Caribe,
   Hotel Fiesta Internacional
74 Hotel Orquidea Internacional

PLACES TO EAT
7 Restaurant Muelle 4
8 Restaurant Muelle 5
9 Caracol Azul
13 Heladería Pinguino
17 Paxilandia
23 Pizza Hut
24 El Camino Restaurant
27 Restaurant Vegetariano Salud Solar
30 Restaurant Nuevo San Remo
32 La Palma & Cyrano Pavement Cafés
37 Submarine
59 Galleta Pecosa
68 Restaurant Mayflower
70 Chifa Himalaya
71 Gran Chifa

OTHER
1 Artisans' Market
2 La Peña Rincón Folklórico
11 US Embassy, Museo de
   Arqueología del Banco Central
12 Casa de Cultura (Museo & Cine)
14 Banco del Pichincha
21 Church of La Merced
23 TAME Airline, Galasam Tours,
   Teatro Guayaquil (Edificio Pasaje)
25 Banco del Pacífico and Museum
26 Olympic Pool
29 Cine Nueve de Octubre
31 Cine Metro
34 SAN/Saeta Airline
35 Peruvian Consulate
36 Church of San Francisco
38 Banco del Pacífico
39 Cine Tauro
43 Cine Presidente
44 Librería Científica
45 CETUR Tourist Information
46 Cine Quito
51 EMETEL
52 Post Office
53 Museo Nahim Isaías B
54 Palacio de Gobierno & Migraciones
57 Market
60 Cathedral
63 Palacio Municipal
65 Banco del Pichincha
69 Museo Municipal & Library

SOUTH COAST

To Las Peñas
(100 m)

Ferry to Durán

Coronel

1

Loja

J Montalvo

2

V Piedrahita

Galecio

Lascano

Padre Aguirre

Martínez

Imbabura

3

Riobamba

Jimena

Boyacá

Escobedo

Baquerizo Moreno

Mendiburo

Córdova

Rocafuerte

Orellana

Panamá

6

Pier 4
7

Padre Solano

4

Roca

8
Pier 5

5

Junín

16

19   20

21

22

15

VM Rendón
17

18

Paula de Icaza

Plaza de
La Merced

El Pirata Restaurant

9 de Octubre

24

28   29   30

23

25

31

35
34   36   37

Vélez

Plaza de
San Francisco

38

La Rotonda

32

33

Luque

Río

Garaycoa

Rumichaca

Avilés

Boyacá

Escobedo

Chimborazo

Chile

44

P Carbo

Pichincha

45

Guayas

Aguirre

47

48

49

Ballén

51 52

53

54

Maleón Simón Bolívar

Capitanía (Port Captain)

58
59   60

Parque
Bolívar

62
61

63

10 de Agosto

Clock Tower

Sucre

69

66   67

68

70
71

Colón

72

Chiriboga

Guayaquil

Lavayen

Romero

Olmedo

Chimborazo

Chile

Luzarraga

73

Villamil

Eloy Alfaro

74

0   100   200 m
0   100   200 yards

which dates originally from 1770 but has been replaced several times. Occasionally, the tower is open to visitors who can climb the narrow spiral staircase inside.

Across the street from the clock tower is the **Palacio Municipal**, an ornate gray building that is separated from the simple and solid **Palacio de Gobierno** by a small but pleasant plaza. In the plaza there is a statue commemorating some of the victories of the liberator, General Sucre. Both buildings were built in the 1920s, but the Palacio de Gobierno replaces the original wooden structure, which was destroyed in the great fire of 1917. The CETUR office is nearby.

Continuing along the Malecón, you soon come to the famous statue of **La Rotonda**, one of Guayaquil's more impressive monuments (particularly when it is illuminated at night). It shows the historic but enigmatic meeting between Bolívar and San Martín in 1822.

Bolívar was the Venezuelan who liberated Venezuela, Colombia and Ecuador from Spanish colonial rule. San Martín was the Argentinian liberator who defeated the Spanish in Chile and Peru. After their

secret meeting in Guayaquil, San Martín returned to Argentina before moving to France, while Bolívar continued his triumphs in Bolivia.

From La Rotonda there are good views north, along the river front, of the colonial district of Las Peñas at the foot of Cerro El Carmen and, far beyond, the impressive Guayaquil-Durán bridge, the biggest in the country.

Many people like to continue along the waterfront to the picturesque colonial district of Las Peñas. Several piers are passed en route, some of which are working docks and others with restaurant boats. You can eat seafood and sip a beer while you watch the busy traffic of the Malecón on one side and Guayaquil's river traffic on the other. Fragile craft paddled by banana peddlers bob close to shore, and huge ocean-going vessels lumber by in mid-channel. Pleasure craft and fishing trawlers abound, and frigatebirds, terns and seagulls fly by in a constant stream.

Soon after passing the **Durán ferry** pier you reach the end of the Malecón. This north end has a reputation for being a poor neighborhood, and tourists are advised to guard their belongings against pickpockets, especially those working the passenger exits from the Durán ferry. The ferry to Durán makes a very inexpensive and enjoyable sightseeing trip across the Río Guayas. A couple of hundred meters beyond the Durán ferry dock one enters the Las Peñas district.

Las Peñas At the end of the Malecón you'll see a short flight of stairs leading up to the small **Plaza Colón**, which has two cannons pointing out toward the river, commemorating a battle against Dutch pirates in 1624. The narrow, winding **Calle Numa Pompillo Llona**, named after the Guayaquileño (1832-1907) who wrote the national anthem, begins from the corner of the plaza. This street is one of my favorite sights in Las Peñas. Walking up this historic

José de San Martín

street, you'll see several unobtrusive plaques set into the walls of some houses. The plaques indicate the simple residences of past presidents. The colonial architecture has not been restored per se, but it has been well looked after and is interesting to see.

Several artists now live in the area and there are a few art galleries; the one at No 186 is the best known and belongs to the painter Luis Lara. Take your time – it's a short street. At the end of the street is the **National Brewery**, which is open from 7 am to 12 noon and 2 to 5 pm Monday to Friday. Brewery tours can be arranged.

Calle Numa Pompillo Llona is a dead-end street, so you retrace your footsteps to the Plaza Colón and, instead of continuing back along the Malecón, you turn right and walk past a small plaza with a brightly painted statue of a fireman (there are two fire stations nearby), and past a statue of the conquistador Orellana, to the open-air theater Bogotá. Behind the theater is the oldest church in Guayaquil, **Santo Domingo**, which was founded in 1548, restored in 1938, and is worth a visit.

You can continue by climbing the stairs to the right of the church and then heading left up the steep Calle Buitrón (the Street of the Vulture!), which will soon take you to the top of the hill, **Cerro El Carmen**. From here is a good view of the north section of the river and the impressive **Durán Bridge**, which is almost four-km long.

It is important to note, however, that Las Peñas is unfortunately not a very safe district, though Ecuadorian guide publications continue to describe the Las Peñas area as a 'typical colonial section.' It's worth asking at the CETUR information office about the area's safety and also to go with a group of friends or on a guided tour. In 1990, the government got a grant of US$750,000 to renovate the area, which has made it safer, and a police post has reportedly opened in order to maintain safety. Nevertheless, avoid the area at dusk and at night.

Downtown Area From Las Peñas walk back along Calle Rocafuerte to the downtown area. The colonial buildings blend into modern ones and after a few blocks you pass the church of **La Merced**. Although this building is comparatively modern (constructed in 1938), the original wooden church dated back to 1787 but, like most of Guayaquil's colonial buildings, was destroyed by fire. The modern version is worth seeing for its richly decorated golden altar. There's a pleasant plaza in front of the church.

Just over a block beyond La Merced you reach the **Museo Arqueológico del Banco del Pacífico** (☎ 566 010, 563 744), P de Icaza 113. This fine private museum is air-conditioned and quiet, which in itself is a welcome break from the hot hustle and bustle of downtown. The collections are good and well laid out with labels in both Spanish and English. The main exhibit has ceramics and other artifacts documenting the development of Ecuadorian cultures from 3000 BC to 1500 AD. There is also a contemporary art gallery with shows changing every few weeks. Hours are 10 am to 6 pm, Monday to Friday. Weekend hours recently were 11 am to 1 pm, but are subject to change. Admission is free.

Another block to the south you cross the busy **Avenida 9 de Octubre**, downtown Guayaquil's major thoroughfare. Here

Strange deity image in clay

Calle Rocafuerte becomes Calle P Carbo and you find the church of **San Francisco**, originally built in the early 1700s, burnt in 1896, reconstructed in 1902 and now beautifully restored. The plaza in front is notable for containing Guayaquil's **first public monument**, unveiled on New Year's Day 1880. It is a statue of Ecuador's first native president, Vicente Rocafuerte, who held office from 1835-39. (Ecuador's first president, Juan Flores, was a Venezuelan.)

Parque Bolívar Area The Parque Bolívar (also known as the Parque Seminario), three blocks south of the Plaza de San Francisco along Chile, is one of Guayaquil's most famous plazas. In its small but well-laid-out ornamental gardens live prehistoric-looking land iguanas of up to a meter in length, and of a species different from those found in the Galápagos. They're a surprising sight here, right in the center of the city. Around Parque Bolívar are many of Guayaquil's first-class hotels.

On the west side of the Parque Bolívar is the **cathedral**. The original building on this site dates from 1547 but, as is common with most of Guayaquil's original wooden buildings, it burnt down. The present structure was completed in 1948 and renovated in 1978. The front entrance is extremely ornately decorated, but inside it is simple, high-vaulted and modern. High up on the white walls are some fine stained-glass windows.

A couple of blocks east of Parque Bolívar over to Pichincha brings you to the **Museo Nahim Isaías B**. This museum has a small display of religious art and some archaeological pieces. It is open from 10 am to 5 pm daily.

A block south of Parque Bolívar on Sucre you find the **Museo Municipal** (☎ 516 391) and the municipal library. The museum is small but has varied exhibits. On the ground floor there is an archaeology room, a colonial room and a changing display of modern art. The archaeology room has mainly Inca and pre-Inca ceramics, with some particularly fine pieces from the Huancavilca period (circa 500 AD) and several figurines

from the oldest culture in Ecuador, the Valdivia (circa 3200 BC). The colonial room has mainly religious paintings and a few household items from colonial times.

Upstairs there are modern art and ethnography rooms, inexplicably joined. Here you might see the famous *tsantsas*, or shrunken heads (but a reader recently reported that they are no longer on display). Other jungle artifacts include beadwork, featherwork, tools and weapons, but unfortunately very few labels. There are also regional costumes and handicrafts. Another room on this floor contains paintings of presidents and famous men, of which my favorite is a wild and eccentric-looking Theodor Wolf, the geologist after whom the highest active volcano in the Galápagos is named. All in all, a varied collection with which to pass the time.

The Museo Municipal is open 9 am to noon and 3 to 8 pm Monday to Friday, and 9 am to noon and 3 to 6 pm on Saturday.

Parque del Centenario From the Parque Bolívar you can head north a few blocks and then walk west along the modern Avenida 9 de Octubre to the huge Parque del Centenario, the city's largest plaza. A more colorful walk is along 10 de Agosto to the main **market** area, which is so crowded with street stalls, people and traffic that your pace slows to a crawl. Watch your belongings – pickpockets are common in market areas. In the Parque del Centenario, which covers four city blocks, there are many monuments. The most important is the great central column topped by Liberty and surrounded by the founding fathers of the country – a monument to patriotism.

Casa de Cultura Avenida 9 de Octubre continues beyond the Parque del Centenario. At its junction with the west side of the park is the archaeology museum of the Casa de Cultura (☎ 300 500). The main attraction at this museum was the gold collection, but the building was damaged by fire in 1987 and the museum was closed for some time. It has now reopened and hours are 10 am to 5 pm, Tuesday to Friday. There is also a cinema on the premises that shows good movies. Recently, the cinema had a foreign film season, with different films showing at 7:30 pm on Monday, Wednesday and Friday. Foreign films are very popular, and the cinema is small – get there early to buy a ticket (about US$1). Other cultural events such as art shows and lectures occur regularly.

Museo de Arqueología del Banco Central Three blocks west of the Parque del Centenario you reach this museum (☎ 327 402), at 9 de Octubre and José de Antepara (half a block from the US Embassy). This excellent archaeology museum is open from 10 am to 6 pm Monday to Friday, and 9 am to 2 pm on Saturday. It is free, well-laid-out, and has a varied and changing display of ceramics, textiles, metallurgy (some gold) and ceremonial masks. The descriptions are good but are only in Spanish. There is also an art gallery with changing shows.

City Cemetery If you continue north of the Parque del Centenario along P Moncayo, you'll come to the city cemetery, which is worth a visit. It is a dazzling white and contains hundreds of tombs, monuments and huge mausoleums. A palm tree–lined walk leads to the impressive grave of President Vicente Rocafuerte.

A traveler writes that the area north of the Parque Central is becoming increasingly dangerous, so go with friends and be alert.

Jardín Botánico
About a half hour drive north of town is a botanical garden (☎ 416 975, 417 004), which has recently gained recognition for its fine orchid collection (as well as hundreds of other plants). Paths and trails lead you past labeled plant exhibits, and there is a gift shop, café, butterfly garden and auditorium.

Insect repellent is recommended in the rainy months. The garden is open from 8:30 am to 4 pm daily, and admission is about US$3.50 for foreigners (rather less

for Ecuadorians, otherwise very few would come!). This is a new place and will probably improve; comments from readers are welcomed.

Call the gardens for information about getting there (it's a bit complicated on public bus and involves a couple of changes) or take a taxi and ask for Urbanización de Los Orquideas. The Chasquitur travel agency reportedly runs tours and has information.

Special Events
All the national holidays are celebrated vigorously in Guayaquil, but one stands out as the major annual festival. This is, in fact, a combination of two holidays: Simón Bolívar's birthday on July 24 (1783) and the Founding of Guayaquil on July 25 (1538). The already lively city goes wild with parades, art shows, beauty pageants, fireworks and plenty of drinking and dancing – a carnival atmosphere. Hotels are booked up well in advance – the evening of July 24 is not a good time to arrive in Guayaquil without a hotel reservation. The festivities often begin on July 23 or even July 22, depending on which day of the week the holiday falls in any particular year. Banking and other services are usually disrupted.

Other important dates are Guayaquil's Independence Day on October 9 (1820), which combines with Día de la Raza celebrated on October 12 to create another long holiday, though much less exciting than the July festivities. New Year's Eve is celebrated with bonfires. Life-sized puppets called *viejos* (the old ones) are made by stuffing old clothes – they represent the old year. The viejos are displayed on the main streets of the city, especially the Malecón, and they are burnt in midnight bonfires – fun for all the family. Less fun is the annual carnival (a movable feast held on the days immediately preceding Ash Wednesday and Lent) which, in addition to the traditional throwing of water, is 'celebrated' by dousing passers-by with all manner of unpleasant liquids – no one is exempt.

Locals say that holidays, especially July 24 and 25, are a good time to visit areas such as Las Peñas because of the sheer number of visitors. Generally, the locals are very friendly to foreign visitors during the holidays. Pickpockets still abound, but they are looking for easy targets like drunks. Leave your camera in your room and come out to enjoy yourself.

Places to Stay

The Guayaquil Tourist Board controls hotel prices, and each hotel is required to post its approved prices near the entrance. Perhaps surprisingly, most hotels do have the price list prominently displayed. You may be charged up to 20% tax on the listed price, though most of the cheaper hotels don't bother.

During holiday periods finding a room can be problematic, especially in the better hotels, and prices are usually higher than the listed price. Most hotels, including the budget ones, are registered at the CETUR tourist office where you can complain if you get gouged. Hotel prices change frequently.

For some reason there are not many single rooms to be had. In the cheaper hotels I usually had two or more beds in my room when I was traveling alone. If it's not the holiday season, you can persuade many hotel owners to give you a double or triple at the price of a single. During fiesta time, travel with a friend or be prepared to pay for a double.

Unfortunately, water shortages occur frequently. Most top-end hotels have fairly reliable water supplies (though unfortunately this is because they can afford to pay premium prices for water, which is supposedly destined for the poor areas of town). The cheaper hotels may lack water at times, so grab a shower when you can.

Guayaquil has unfortunately begun the practice of having a two-tier pricing system in the better hotels. Foreign tourists are charged about twice as much as residents, particularly in the top-end hotels.

Places to Stay – bottom end

Bottom-end hotels in Guayaquil are generally of a higher price and lower standard when compared to other cities. One of the best cheap hotels is the *Hotel Delicia* (☎ 524 925), at Ballén 1105 and Montúfar. The hotel is secure and clean and charges about US$2 per person but is often full. Opposite is the *Residencial Baños*, which charges about US$2.50 per person and is also often full.

For people on a very tight budget, the very basic *Hotel La Buena Esperanza*, on the corner of the market at Ballén and 6 de Marzo, and *Hotel Ecuatoriana* (☎ 518 105), Rumichaca 1502 and Sucre, are both US$3 per person. There are several worse ones at or below this price near the market and in the dodgy area between Olmedo and Sucre. Some of the cheap hotels in these areas double as brothels, and lone females may be improperly treated or molested.

The clean, secure *Hotel Delicia* (☎ 324 925), Ballén 1105, is US$4 per person and recommended. The *Hotel Ecuador* (☎ 321 460, 518 680), P Moncayo 1117, is a decent place at US$7.50 for a double with bath and TV; singles cost the same. The clean *Hotel Berlin*, at Rumichaca and Sucre, is quite good at US$3.75 per person. The similarly priced *Hotel Reina Victoria* (☎ 322 188), Colón near P Moncayo, is basic but OK. Other acceptable places for about US$4 per person are the *Hotel Savoy* (☎ 308 296), VM Rendón and Boyaca, and the *Residencial Pauker* (☎ 565 385), Baquerizo Moreno 902 and Junín. The Pauker is reasonably secure, though the rooms are basic and rundown. Across the street is the *Hotel Tourist*, which is no better and overpriced at US$7.50 per person.

The *Hotel Hostal USA* (☎ 307 804), Quisquis 305, has small, windowless rooms with fans for US$4/6 for singles/ doubles and better rooms with bath and TV for US$5/8. The *Hotel Caribe* (☎ 526 162), Olmedo 250, is OK at US$8 for a double with bath and fan or US$10 with TV and air-conditioning. Next door, the OK *Hotel Fiesta Internacional* (☎ 329 813) is US$2 more. The *Hotel Libertador* (☎ 304 637), on Garaycoa on the corner of the Parque del Centenario, isn't bad for US$5 per person. The *Hotel Colonial*,

Rumichaca at Urdaneta, is safe, clean and friendly at US$8/10 with bath, TV and air-conditioning.

The *Hotel Alexander* (☎ 532 000), Luque 1107, is a very good value at US$11/14 for rooms with bath, air-conditioning, hot water, telephone and a decent restaurant. The similarly priced *Hotel Metropolitana* (☎ 565 250/1), VM Rendón 120, safely up on the 4th floor, also has air-conditioning and hot water and is a good deal. The reasonable *Hotel Nuevo Sander* (☎ 320 030), at Luque 1101, has air-conditioning and cold-water private baths at US$11 for one or two people. The decent *Hotel Regina* (☎ 312 893), Garaycoa 423, is US$13 (one or two people) with air-conditioning, hot water and TV. The *Hotel Centenario* (☎ 524 467), Vélez 726, is about US$14 for one or two people. Rooms vary: Some have fans, others air-conditioning, some have TVs. All have cold baths, and some are nicer than others.

Hostal Ecuahogar (☎ 248 357, 240 388) is near the airport on Isidro Ayora in front of the Banco Ecuatoriana de Vivienda. It is part of the Hostelling International chain and charges US$10/18 or US$8 in dorms. There is a discount for hostel members. Private hot baths, kitchen privileges, a café, information and airport or bus pick-up service is available. The 22 city bus goes by from the bus terminal.

Places to Stay – middle

The *Hotel California* (☎ 302 538, fax 562 548), Urdaneta 529 and Jimena, has adequate rooms with private baths, hot water, air-conditioning, TV and telephone for US$15/22. The *Hotel Orquidea Internacional* (☎ 402 686, 406 968, fax 403 121), Olmedo 309 and Chile, is adequate at US$17/20 for rooms with private bath, hot water, TV and fan; rooms with air-conditioning are US$3 more. They have a restaurant with room service. The newer *Hotel María del Cisne* (☎ 323 563, 532 586, 532 610), Chiriboga 224 and Chimborazo, has clean rooms with air-conditioning, hot water, TV and telephone for US$26 a double. Singles lack air-

conditioning and are US$18. It's a decent enough place, although the neighborhood is not very good. Rooms in these hotels are OK but I think a tad overpriced.

In the hotels below, expect private baths, hot water, air-conditioning, telephone, TV, restaurants on the premises and similar amenities. The *Hotel de Los Andes* (☎ 329 793, 329 741, 329 773, fax 329 796), Garaycoa 1233 and Ballén, calls itself a first-class hotel but is merely adequate. Rooms with the usual features are US$24/30, which isn't too bad, though you may get charged a higher gringo rate, which is definitely not worth it. The similarly priced *Hotel Ritz* (☎ 530 120/122/123, 324 134, fax 322 151), 9 de Octubre 709, is also OK. Better rooms in the mid US$30s are found in the modern *Hotel Plaza* (☎ 327 140, fax 324 195), Chile 414 and Ballén, PO Box 10299, Guayaquil. Rooms have mini-fridges, and there are a few junior suites. Another decent choice for rooms in the US$30s is the *Hotel Rizzo* (☎ 325 210, fax 326 209), Ballén 319 and Chile. They include breakfast in their rates.

Out in the suburbs fairly close to the airport is the *Tangara Guest House* (☎ 284 445, fax 285 872), Ciudadela Bolivariana, Manuela Sáenz and O'Leary, Block F, Casa 1. This is a quiet, friendly, family-run guest house with simple but clean, bright rooms with private bath, hot water and fans. There is a TV room and kitchen privileges. Some rooms have air-conditioning. Rates are about US$30 for a double, and weekly/monthly discounts are available. Breakfast is available for US$4. Take a taxi the first time, then the owners can help you figure out the bus system.

A good mid-priced choice is the *Hotel Doral* (☎ 327 133/75, 328 002, fax 327 088), Chile 402 and Aguirre, PO Box 10938, Guayaquil. This hotel is clean and secure and has a good restaurant. Above-average (for Guayaquil!) rooms are about US$48 a double, including breakfast.

The *Hotel Palace* (☎ 321 080, fax 322 887), Chile 216 and Luque, is clean and secure and, with almost 200 rooms, usually has space available at short notice. The hotel has business and fax services and a travel agency. The street-side rooms suffer from road noise, though if you live in a big city, perhaps you're used to it! Rates are about US$50/70. Also good at about this price range is the *Hotel Sol del Oriente* (☎ 325 500, 328 049, fax 329 352), Aguirre 603 and Escobedo. Rooms are spacious and have a mini-fridge, and the hotel has a decent Chinese restaurant and a sauna.

Places to Stay – top end

There seems to be a big jump in hotel prices between middle- and top-end hotels. This is artificially created by the top-end hotels themselves, who consider themselves luxury class and charge nonresident tourists twice the rate for residents.

If you have any kind of residency status, use it. The prices I give below are for non-residents and include the obligatory 20% tax. All these hotels have good restaurants.

Perhaps the least expensive of the top-end hotels is the *Hotel Boulevard* (☎ 562 888, fax 560 076), 9 de Octubre 432 and Chile, PO Box 7524, Guayaquil. The hotel is popular for business travelers because of its location by the financial district. There is a casino. Rooms are about US$75/95.

The following four hotels all charge about US$100 to US$160 for a double or single room. More expensive suites are often available.

The *Hotel Ramada* (☎ 565 555, fax 563 036), on the Malecón at Orellana, PO Box 10964, Guayaquil, overlooks the Río Guayas. There is an indoor pool, a sauna and a casino. If you stay here, bear in mind that the Malecón north of the hotel is not a good place to wander around at night.

The *Unihotel* (☎ 327 100, 324 046, fax 328 352), Ballén 406 and Chile, PO Box 563, Guayaquil, is centrally located. They have numerous facilities, including a sauna and gym, a games room for children, a shopping mall with scores of stores and a casino. One of their restaurants has delightful views into the Parque Bolívar.

The *Grand Hotel Guayaquil* (☎ 329 690, ☎ 327 251, or toll-free in the USA and Canada (800) 223 9868, or in the USA

(800) 528 5568), Boyacá and 10 de Agosto, PO Box 9282, Guayaquil, is behind the cathedral. This hotel has plenty of sporting facilities for the energetic: pool, two squash courts, gym, two saunas, massage. They have outdoor barbecues by the pool as well as three other restaurants.

The *Hotel Continental* (☎ 329 270, fax 325 454 or toll-free in the USA and Canada (800) 333 1212, (800) 223 0888), Chile and 10 de Agosto, PO Box 4510, Guayaquil, is right on the Parque Bolívar. It is the oldest of the city's luxury hotels. If you want to swim or work out, this is not the place for you. The hotel is known for its restaurants: One has won international gastronomy awards, another specializes in Ecuadorian cuisine, and a third is open 24 hours.

The *Hotel Oro Verde* (☎ 327 999, fax 329 350), 9 de Octubre and García Moreno, PO Box 9636, Guayaquil, is the largest hotel in town. It is also considered the best place to stay, although rooms aren't really much better for the price. It is slightly away from the center, out by the US Embassy. They have a pool, gym, sauna, casino, shops and several restaurants. Rooms are US$240/265 for singles/doubles, and suites go up to US$420.

Places to Eat

For breakfast I like *La Palma*, a pavement café on Escobedo and Vélez. They sell good coffee and warm croissants, and it's a good place at which to wake up and ease into the day. This is also a good place for snacks and light meals throughout the day. Next door, the *Cyrano* serves much the same, though the coffee is not as good. Both of these are locally popular places and a good place for a beer after work.

Many of the city's best restaurants are in the better hotels (all open to the public). The *Gran Hotel Guayaquil* has breakfast specials from US$4 and up. The coffee is excellent, and coffee addicts can get many refills. Several more of the better hotels offer good breakfasts – even if you are on a budget, this might be the chance for a lovely breakfast in comfortable surroundings. Relax, read the newspaper or catch up on your journal. Cheaper breakfasts with good coffee are served at the *Hotel Doral Cafeteria*, which has a pleasant outside patio, and at the *Café Jambeli* in the Hotel Rizzo.

El Parque restaurant (on the 4th floor of the Unicentro building – enter through Unihotel) overlooks the Parque Bolívar and is recommended for dinner – good value and good views but not cheap. They also have less expensive buffet lunches – help yourself to seconds and thirds. In the Hotel Continental, the expensive *Restaurant El Fortín* has won international gastronomic awards, and the less expensive *Restaurant La Canoa* serves Ecuadorian specialties. *El Patio* in the Hotel Oro Verde serves delicious Ecuadorian dishes but at very upscale prices. Still, it's cheaper than the hotel's French restaurant, *Le Gourmet*. The restaurants in the other top-end hotels are also very good, if pricey.

A chifa is often a reasonable choice for the hungry budget traveler, and there are several on and around Avenida Colón. One of the very best – ornate and expensive-looking but in fact very reasonably priced – is the *Gran Chifa* (☎ 530 784, 512 488), on P Carbo 1016 near Sucre. Around the corner, on Sucre 308 and P Carbo, is the cheaper *Chifa Himalaya* (☎ 329 593), which is as good and popular as the nearby *Restaurant Mayflower*, on Colón near Chimborazo. There are many other chifas to choose from.

There are many modern cafeterias, restaurants and fast-food places on Avenida 9 de Octubre, but they are not very cheap. There's even an authentic *Burger King* at 9 de Octubre and Escobedo – the burgers are OK and the 'soft serve' chocolate ice cream has been recommended by none other than Betsy Wagenhauser, founder of the Quito office of the South American Explorers Club and self-professed dessert expert. (Betsy also recommends the *Galleta Pecosa* bakery, at 10 de Agosto and Boyacá, for the best cookies and cakes in Ecuador.) *Heladería Pinguino*, on the Parque del Centenario, is good for ice cream.

Other places on 9 de Octubre include the *Submarine* near the intersection with P Carbo – this restaurant is highly recommended for sandwiches. *Pizza Hut* (☎ 563 050) is at 9 de Octubre 404 and Córdova and serves what you might expect plus other Italian dishes. The *Restaurant Nuevo San Remo* (☎ 510 620), 9 de Octubre 737 and Boyacá, is a popular spot for business lunches. There's good Italian and Ecuadorian food for about US$5 to US$8 for a full meal.

One of my favorite places to eat or snack is on a boat moored on the riverbank. There are several piers along the Malecón where restaurant boats are moored, and it is fun to spend some time watching the busy river traffic. A medium-priced place is *El Pirata*, a couple of blocks from La Rotonda statue. They have an indoor section and an open top deck with sunshades for when the weather is good. North of El Pirata there are fancier and more expensive restaurants at *Muelle 4* and *Muelle 5* (☎ 561 128). These all serve good seafood.

Paxilandia, VM Rendón 751, is a good, cheap vegetarian restaurant open for lunch. The *Restaurant Vegetariano Salud Solar*, at Luque and P Moncayo, serves good, simple and cheap food. *El Camino* restaurant, at Paula de Icaza and Cordova, used to be called El Camino Vegetariano, but it struggled as a purely vegetarian restaurant. Now it serves a wider variety of inexpensive dishes, including a few meatless ones. It is a good place for an inexpensive lunch but is often closed by supper time. Vegetarianism isn't big in Guayaquil.

The expensive *Caracol Azul* (☎ 280 461), 9 de Octubre 1918 and Los Ríos, has often been described as the best (and most expensive) seafood restaurant in the city. I keep meaning to try the food but, inexplicably, have never made it out there. You'll have to decide for yourself whether it merits the description. Meat dishes are also served.

If you are adventurous enough to explore beyond the hotels and restaurants of the downtown area, you'll be well rewarded. The suburb of Urdesa, six or seven km northwest of the city center, is one of the best restaurant areas and worth the trip if

SOUTH COAST

you like to eat well. The main drag here is VE Estrada and most of the restaurants, bars and nightlife are found along this street. Also check out *El Viejo Barrio* in Urdesa Norte – this is one structure housing many good restaurants.

La Parrillada del Ñato (☎ 387 098), VE Estrada 1219 and Laureles, serves huge and juicy steaks, grills and barbecues as well as pizzas – prices are fairly high. A couple of blocks away, *Pizzería Ch'Enano*, VE Estrada 1320, also serves good pizzas. Other Italian restaurants include *Pizza Hut* (☎ 381 167), VE Estrada 472 and Ebanos, *La Carbonara*, Bálsamos 108 and VE Estrada, and *La Trattoría de Enrico* (☎ 387 079), Bálsamos 504. For Mexican dinners try *Paco's* (☎ 442 112), Acacias 725 and Guayacanes. They sometimes have mariachi bands playing. *El Caribe* on VE Estrada has been recommended for Caribbean food – I don't know the cross street. *La Balandra* (☎ 384 256), Calle Quinta 504 and Las Monjas, is one of Urdesa's most recommended seafood restaurants.

The Japanese restaurant *Tsuji* (☎ 881 183, 380 040), VE Estrada 816 and Guaycanes, is not cheap but serves excellent food. There are two excellent and expensive restaurants just off VE Estrada at the entrance to Urdesa. The *Barandua Inn* (☎ 389 407, 387 366), Circunvalación Norte 528B, serves delicious seafood, and *La Posada de las Garzas* (☎ 383 256), Circunvalación Norte 536, has international cuisine.

Entertainment

Read the local newspapers *El Telégrafo* and *El Universo* to find out more about what's going on. They give cinema listings for the approximately 18 cinemas in Guayaquil, of which about half are downtown and are listed below. If you're buying the newspaper for the cinema listings, make sure that the newspaper has them. Occasionally, even the best papers omit the listing if there's been no change. English-language movies with Spanish subtitles are often shown.

Cine Casa de la Cultura
    9 de Octubre and Parque del Centenario
Cine (Teatro) Guayaquil
    9 de Octubre 424 (☎ 305 867)
Cine Imperio
    6 de Marzo and Ballén
Cine Metro
    Boyacá 1221 and Vélez (☎ 322 301)
Cine Nueve de Octubre
    9 de Octubre 815 and Avilés (☎ 531 788)
Cine Presidente
    Luque 715 and 6 de Marzo (☎ 325 180)
Cine Quito
    Aguirre and Quito (☎ 328 570)
Cine Tauro
    Quito and Luque (☎ 323 381)
Policine 1 & 2
    CC Policentro Shopping Center,
    Kennedy suburb (☎ 288 313)

Friday newspapers advertise peñas, which are normally held on weekends. They are rarely cheap and always start late. A good one is *La Peña Rincón Folklórico*, at Malecón 208 and Montalvo (take a cab – it's not a very safe area at night). They open around 10 pm for food and drinks, and the show gets underway about midnight and continues until the early hours. Cover is US$4 and drinks aren't cheap. *Los Checitos*, PP Gómez and Garaycoa, has live salsa bands and dancing from Wednesday to Sunday. A US$6 cover charge includes five beers! It's a lively spot.

VE Estrada in Urdesa is a good street to hang out on Friday and Saturday nights, along with the more affluent Guayaquileño kids. The *Tequilala* in Urdesa Norte is currently popular and has a US$6 cover. The *Infinity Club*, VE Estrada 505, is popular for disco dancing. It's reportedly best at weekends from midnight to 6 am, and single women might think twice about going there alone. There are several dance floors, one for American-style rock, another for Latin music. One reader recommends the *Peña Amnesia* on VE Estrada – he had so much fun that he couldn't remember where it was. There are other places in the area with waxing and waning popularity. In Guayaquil, there are discos in some of the better hotels, especially the Oro Verde. Other places to dance include *Flashdance* at Aguirre 221.

Gamblers will want to try their luck at the casinos found at the Ramada, Unihotel, Boulevard and Oro Verde hotels. These top-end hotels will also help guests spend a day at a club with golf, tennis or sailing.

If you're the athletic type, visit the *Olympic Pool*, which costs US$0.30 for a two-hour period. Inquire at the entrance for times.

Things to Buy

Guayaquileños like to shop at the outdoor black market called La Bahía, located on P Carbo and Villamil between Olmedo and Colón. It's crowded, busy and colorful. Anything from blue jeans to video cameras can be found here – some of it at bargain prices, much of it counterfeit. There are pickpockets, naturally, but the area has a high police profile and is not especially dangerous.

If you prefer a more sedate shopping atmosphere, try one of the several indoor shopping centers, styled like North American shopping malls. The Unicentro, downtown by the Parque Bolívar, is the smallest. The Policentro, in the Kennedy suburb at the end of the Avenida del Periodista (San Jorge), is one of the biggest and has many modern stores as well as restaurants and a movie theater. The Central Comercial Urdesa is similar. Just outside Urdesa is the Centro Comercial Albán Borja.

On the first block of Chile off 9 de Octubre you'll find Otavaleños selling handicrafts and souvenirs, though the quality isn't high. Better quality can be found in the Mercado de Artesanía (Artisans' Market) in a warehouse at Loja and Escobedo. It's on the edge of the Las Peñas district, however, so go with a couple of friends for added security. Other craft and souvenir stores include the government-run OCEPA at VM Rendón 405 and Córdova and several on the first block of 9 de Octubre by the waterfront.

The shopping centers are mainly geared to general shopping, but usually have one or two souvenir shops. The better hotels have stores selling good-quality and higher-priced crafts.

Getting There & Away

Air Guayaquil's Simón Bolívar Airport is one of Ecuador's two major international airports, and it is about as busy as Quito's. There are three terminals. The international and main national terminals adjoin one another and are on the east side of Avenida de las Américas, about five km north of the city center. The *Avioneta* (small aircraft) terminal is about one km south of the main terminal. It can be reached by turning left out of the main terminal and walking south along the busy Avenida de las Américas.

The main national terminal deals with most internal TAME, SAN and Saeta flights. Passengers for the Galápagos may go through the international terminal, however, particularly if they are changing in Guayaquil on a Quito-Guayaquil-Galápagos flight. The main terminal has a casa de cambio, which pays about as much as the downtown rate. It is open for most incoming international flights. There are also the usual cafeteria, car rental, gift shop and international telephone facilities.

Air – domestic There are many internal flights to all parts of the country. The most frequent are to Quito with TAME and SAN-Saeta. If you buy your ticket with cash, the companies will honor each other's tickets so you can arrive at the airport and leave on the next available flight if it isn't full. There are about eight to 14 flights a day, most often on weekdays. Tickets cost about US$29. For the best views sit on the right side when flying to Quito.

Only TAME has flights from Guayaquil to Cuenca at 10:30 am from Monday to Friday for US$24. Only TAME operates flights between Guayaquil and Loja (Tuesday, Thursday and Saturday at 7 am, US$20), Machala (Monday to Friday at 10:45 am, US$18) and Salinas (holiday season weekends subject to aircraft availability and passenger demand). Fares and departure times are subject to change. Flights have been known to leave early so get to the airport early.

TAME operates the only scheduled flights to Baltra Airport in the Galápagos.

They leave daily at 9:50 am and cost US$333 for the roundtrip. Cheaper fares are available to Ecuadorian residents. SAN-Saeta operates the only scheduled flights to San Cristóbal airport in the Galápagos. They leave daily except Sunday during the low season at noon for the same fare.

All the above flights (TAME, SAN-Saeta) leave from the main national terminal. Several small airlines have flights leaving from the Avioneta terminal, one km from the main terminal. These airlines use small aircraft to service various coastal towns such as Manta, Portoviejo, Bahía de Caráquez, Pedernales and Esmeraldas. Flights are subject to passenger demand, but there is usually a flight every day (except Sunday) to most of these towns leaving early in the morning. Flights may be more frequent in the wet season. Fares are reasonably low.

Flights to other destinations (Machala, Santa Rosa, other coastal destinations) may be available if there is passenger demand. Charters are possible. Bear in mind that because some of these flights are in five-passenger aircraft, baggage is limited to a small 10-kg bag and passenger weight is limited to 100 kg.

AECA
    Avioneta Terminal (☎ 294 711)
AvioPacífico
    Avioneta Terminal (☎ 283 304/5)
CEDTA
    Avioneta Terminal
    Escobedo 924 and VM Rendón
    (☎ 561 954, 301 165)
SAN & Saeta
    Vélez 226 and Chile (☎ 329 855, 326 466)
TAME
    9 de Octubre 424, Gran Pasaje
    (☎ 561 751, 563 993, 565 806)

Air – international If you are leaving on an international flight, there is a US$25 departure tax, payable in sucres or dollars.

The following airlines have offices in Guayaquil. Those marked with an asterisk have direct flights into and out of Ecuador. Some airlines fly to Quito, but it is a simple matter to connect between Quito

and Guayaquil on the many domestic flights. Only the most important airlines are listed; see also Online Services in Facts for the Visitor.

Aerolineas Argentinas*
    P Moncayo 707 and VM Rendón
    (☎ 562 141)
AeroPerú*
    Chile 329 and Aguirre, 8th floor
    (☎ 513 676)
Air France*
    Aguirre 106 and Malecón (☎ 320 313)
American Airlines* (USA)
    Córdova 1021 and 9 de Octubre, 20th floor
    (☎ 564 111, 566 902)
Americana de Aviación (Peru)
    Quisquis 1064 and Tungurahua
    (☎ 290 337/8)
Avensa* (Venezuela)
    9 de Octubre 424, 9th floor
    (☎ 561 658, 560 851, 566 355)
Avianca* (Colombia)
    VM Rendón 416 and Córdova
    (☎ 314 091, 312 736)
British Airways
    Vélez 206 and Chile (☎ 325 080, 323 834)
Continental Airlines* (USA)
    9 de Octubre 1911 and Esmeraldas,
    11th floor (☎ 453 600)
Copa* (Panama)
    Circunvalación Sur 631-A and Ficus,
    Urdesa (☎ 883 751/2/3)
Iberia* (Spain)
    9 de Octubre 101 and Malecón
    (☎ 320 664, 329 558)
Icelandair
    Malecón 1203 and 9 de Octubre
    (☎ 531 210)
JAL (Japan)
    9 de Octubre 410 and Chile, 4th floor
    (☎ 310 818/21)
KLM* (Netherlands)
    Aguirre 411 (☎ 328 028)
Korean Air
    Córdova 1013 and 9 de Octubre, 3rd floor
    (☎ 320 908, 566 390)
Lacsa* (Costa Rica)
    Córdova 1040 and 9 de Octubre, 7th floor
    (☎ 562 950, 293 879)
Ladeco* (Chile)
    Malecón 1400 and Illingworth
    (☎ 324 360, 328 692)
LanChile
    Antepara 921 and Hurtado (☎ 320 342/3)
Lufthansa* (Germany)
    Malecón 1400 and Illingworth (☎ 324 360)

Saeta Internacional* (Ecuador)
  Vélez 226 and Chile (☎ 329 855, 326 466)
Swissair
  Martínez 102 and Malecón (563 333)
Varig* (Brazil)
  P Carbo and 9 de Octubre
  (☎ 562 877, 560 876)
Viasa* (Venezuela)
  P Moncayo 707 and VM Rendón
  (☎ 562 141)

Note that Americana de Aviación is a domestic Peruvian airline that offers discounted flight coupons for its domestic flights within Peru, only if they are bought outside of the country. If you are heading to Peru next, you can save up to 40% on your Peruvian fares if you buy them through this airline in advance.

Bus The terminal terrestre opened in late 1986 just beyond the airport. It is modern and efficient and boasts many stores, restaurants, tourist information, a bank, a hairdresser, etc. There are scores of bus company offices, and you can get just about anywhere from here. The following selection gives an idea of what's available – there are many more options. Fares will almost certainly change but not drastically.

For the Santa Elena Peninsula you can take Transportes Villamil or Co-op Posorja, which have frequent buses to Playas (US$1.75; 1¾ hours) and Posorja (US$2, two hours). Co-op Libertad Peninsular and CICA have buses to Salinas (US$2.20; 2½ hours) every 15 minutes.

If you're headed southbound or to Peru, take CIFA, Transportes Rutas Orenses or Ecuatoriana Pullman to Machala (US$2.50; 3½ hours) and Huaquillas (US$3.40; five hours). CIFA and Rutas Orenses run frequent small buses; the others run larger coaches. Transportes Loja has one bus at 6:30 pm to the border at Macará (US$8; 12 hours), and seven buses to Loja (US$6; nine hours).

Several companies run buses to Cuenca (US$4; five to seven hours). Supertaxis Cuenca and Buses San Luis run faster small buses, while Transportes Oriental run

larger, slower and cheaper buses. All three companies run buses about every hour.

Babahoyo (US$0.90; 1½ hours) is served by Transportes Urdaneta and Flota Babahoyo Interprovincial (or FBI). Flota Bolívar has many slow buses every day to Guaranda via Babahoyo.

For Riobamba and Ambato there are many companies taking as little as 3½ hours to Riobamba if the road is OK. These include: Transportes Andino, Transportes Patria, CITA, Transportes Gran Colombia and Transportes Chimborazo. One of the fastest is probably Transportes Andino.

Santo Domingo de los Colorados and Quevedo are served by Transportes Sucre, Transportes Zaracay and others.

Quito (US$7.50; seven to nine hours) is served by frequent buses with Flota Imbabura, Transportes Ecuador and Transportes Panamericanaa. All three are close to one another so check around for what's best for you.

Transportes Esmeraldas, Transportes Occidental and AeroTaxi have, between them, many buses a day to Esmeraldas (US$5.50; seven hours).

Rutas Ecuatorianas and Reina del Camino have many departures for Portoviejo or Manta (US$3.80; four hours) and Bahía de Caráquez (US$5, 5½ hours).

It's easy enough to buy tickets in advance if you want to assure yourself of a place. Otherwise, if you just show up at the terminal, you'll most likely find a bus to your destination within an hour or so. Friday nights and holidays can get booked up, so plan in advance if traveling then.

Train Trains leave from the Durán railway station, which is best reached by taking the Durán ferry from Guayaquil. Details are given under Durán.

Boat Cruise lines occasionally call at Guayaquil, and passengers may make brief forays ashore. A few cargo boats will take passengers to and from North America or Europe (see the Getting There & Away chapter). Generally, sailing between

Guayaquil and a foreign port is more expensive and less convenient than flying.

Ecuadorian cargo ships ply the coastal routes down to Puerto Bolívar (Machala) and up to Manta, Bahía de Caráquez and Esmeraldas. These working boats are not very attractive and don't normally have passenger facilities – though occasionally a captain will take passengers. Hanging out by the waterfront and asking around for the captain may yield the opportunity of a fairly inexpensive coastal trip – very few people do this, however. Most cargo boats work from the docks in the new port, about 12 km south of downtown.

Cargo boats steam for the Galápagos about once or twice a month. The roundtrip from Guayaquil takes about 12 to 20 days, of which about three to four days are spent crossing the ocean from Guayaquil to the islands and the rest is spent in the archipelago. The trips are designed to deliver and pick up cargo from various Galápagos ports and are not very comfortable. Passengers are accepted, however, and though this is not a recommended way of getting to the islands, it is possible. See Getting There & Away in the Galápagos chapter for more details.

Getting Around

To/From the Airport The airport is on Avenida de las Américas, about four or five km north of the center of town. A taxi from the airport to the center will cost about US$2.50. Taxi drivers are supposed to use meters but many try to charge higher fares from the airport – bargain. If you cross the street in front of the airport, you can take a bus downtown, and from the center of town the best bus to take to the airport is the No 2 Especial, which costs US$0.20 and takes about a half hour. It runs along the Malecón but is sometimes full, so you should leave yourself plenty of time or take a taxi – often less from downtown than it is from the airport, which should tell you something . . . .

To/From the Terminal Terrestre From the airport to the terminal terrestre is about two or three km. You can walk the distance

if you want – turn right out of the airport terminal and head for the obvious huge terminal. Or take a bus or taxi.

Buses from the center to the terminal terrestre leave from Parque Victoria (near 10 de Agosto and P Moncayo).

Several buses leave from the terminal for the center. The 71 charges a few cents more and is a little less crowded than the others. A taxi to the center is about US$2.50.

Bus City buses are cheap (US$0.20 to US$0.30) but are always crowded and the system is complicated. They are mainly designed to get workers and commuters from the housing districts to downtown and back again, and are not much use for riding around the city center. They never seem to go exactly where you want to go, and what with waiting for them and battling the traffic, you'd be better off walking, which is what I always do. The downtown area is less than two sq km, so it's easy to walk anywhere.

The CETUR information office can help you with bus information if you want to go out into the suburbs, though there isn't much to see there except for the suburb of Urdesa, which has good restaurants and nightlife. The No 52 Policentro bus goes along the Malecón and can drop you off at the beginning of Urdesa. The No 54 bus also goes to Urdesa.

Car If you're feeling affluent, you can rent a car; if you're not, then forget it because it's not cheap. There are several car rental agencies at the airport. Make sure that insurance, tax and mileage are included in your rate. If you find a cheap deal, ensure that the car you get isn't about to break down. Read the Getting Around chapter for more details.

Taxi If you really must get somewhere in a hurry, you won't get there much quicker on a city bus than on foot. Take a taxi but make sure the meter is working because Guayaquil taxi drivers have the worst reputation in the country for overcharging. You should be able to get between any two points downtown for about US$1, and to the airport, the terminal terrestre or Urdesa for under US$3.

If you need a taxi to pick you up at your door, call Radio Taxis El Paraíso (☎ 204 232, 201 877) or Cooperativa de Taxis Carrusel (☎ 250 610).

Boat The Durán ferry across the Río Guayas leaves three or four times an hour from 7 am to 6:30 pm daily. The crossing lasts 15 minutes and costs US$0.15 – a cheap sightseeing trip! The ferry dock is on the Malecón at the foot of Avenida J Montalvo. It makes a nice trip around sunset – but make sure you don't miss the last ferry back at 6:30 pm.

DURÁN

This suburb of Guayaquil is on the east bank of the Río Guayas and easily reached by ferry (see the previous reference). The main reasons for coming here are to enjoy the ferry ride across the river or to catch the train from Durán to the highlands.

It's a small town and you won't have any difficulty finding your way around. Two blocks inland from the river is the main street of Loja, where you'll find a bank, a cinema, stores and a hotel or two.

Places to Stay & Eat

There are several places near the ferry dock serving seafood and beer – not fancy but certainly adequate. There are a number of cheap and basic hotels used by 'short-stay guests' (a sign in one – 'No Guests Under 18 years' – gives you the picture). Nevertheless, unless you are a single woman, spending the night is not out of the question, and overnight guests are welcome. Probably the best are the *Hotel Paris* (☎ 800 403) or *Residencial La Paz* (☎ 803 465) at about US$6 for a double room. There are others nearby.

Getting There & Away

Most people get here by ferry, taxi or train – the dock is less than a block from the railway station. It used to be easy to get from one to the other, but the first ferry

from Guayaquil now arrives after the train leaves and the train from the highlands arrives about the time the last ferry leaves, so you might miss it. Most train passengers catch a taxi to and from Guayaquil for about US$5 or spend the night in Durán. Getting off (or on) the train at Bucay is a popular alternative.

See under Alausí for more description of the train ride. The train leaves Durán daily at 6:25 am. Sometimes the train is canceled. The fare is US$12 to Alausí and US$14 to Riobamba and you ride all day. The first section to Bucay is mostly flat and not very interesting. It takes about four hours. You could take a bus from Guayaquil to Bucay in two hours and catch the train there for the ascent to Alausí, which is the most interesting part of the trip.

West of Guayaquil

This region is a fairly dry, relatively barren and sparsely populated area, but one containing Guayaquileños' favorite beach resorts. It is busy during the high season (Christmas to April, especially weekends, and also July to September to a lesser extent) but is very quiet at other times. These beaches are infrequently visited by foreign travelers, who prefer the more northerly areas.

BOSQUE PROTECTOR CERRO BLANCO

About 15 km west of Guayaquil is the Balrosario Cemento Nacional factory, which owns over 2000 hectares of protected tropical dry forest on the Cerro Blanco, north of the main coastal highway. This is a private reserve administered by Fundación Pro-Bosque in cooperation with the cement works, and there are several trails (one a short loop, another taking a half day, etc) that take you into this area of tolling coastal hills. Although fairly small in area, the reserve contains over 200 species of birds (including the endangered great green macaw) as well as animals like howler monkeys, peccaries, kinkajous and even ocelots and jaguars. There are stands of dry forest with huge ceiba trees and views of coastal mangrove forests in the distance. This is one of the most interesting places to visit close to Guayaquil if you are interested in natural history.

Information

Cerro Blanco has a visitor center and a campground with barbeque grills, bathrooms and running water (even showers!). The visitor center sells a bird list and booklets and dispenses information and trail maps. There is also a plant nursery. Backcountry camping may be permitted. There are rangers who patrol the area.

The reserve is open daily from 8:30 am to 5 pm, though earlier entry can be arranged in advance. Admission is about US$1 for day use or US$4 for overnight stays (which is a bargain compared to the national parks!). The low fees are partly because of support from the cement factory who have an enlightened approach to using the land that they own.

Guides are available but it is best to arrange one in advance through Fundación Pro-Bosque (☎ 871 900, 416 975, 417 004), Office 91, Edificio Multicomercio, Eloy Alfaro and Cuenca, Guayaquil, or write to Apartado 09-01-04243, Guayaquil.

During the wet season, there are lots of mosquitoes so bring repellent. There are few insects in the dry season and it is easier to see wildlife as it concentrates in the remaining wet areas and the vegetation is less thick. Early morning and late afternoon are, as always, the best times to see wildlife.

Getting There & Away

Buses from Guayaquil's terminal terrestre heading west (to any of the towns below) can drop you off at the entrance at km 15 on the north side. There is a sign and the cement factory is also in evidence, just beyond it (get off before the factory!). Local buses marked 'Chongón' also pass the entrance. Chongón buses leave from the Parque Victoria in central Guayaquil. A

taxi will charge about US$10, depending on your bargaining ability.

From the reserve entrance, it is about a 15-minute walk to the information center and camping area.

PUERTO HONDO

A little west of Cerro Blanco is the small community of Puerto Hondo, at km 17 on the south side of the Guayaquil-Salinas highway. It can be reached the same way as Cerro Blanco. There are basic stores and supplies. The Club Ecológico Puerto Hondo will take visitors on boat rides into the mangroves in the area, which can be arranged in advance through Fundación Pro-Bosque (see above).

PROGRESO

Progreso is officially known as Gómez Rendón and is a village almost 70 km southeast of Guayaquil. Here the road forks and you head west to Salinas and the Santa Elena Peninsula or south to the resort of Playas. The road fork is Progreso's claim to fame; there's no reason to stop here except to change buses.

From Guayaquil to Progreso the paved road passes through very dry scrubland. It is amazing how quickly the land changes from the wet rice-growing areas in the regions north and east of Guayaquil to the dry lands of the west. Despite the dryness, the scenery is quite attractive and interesting, with strange, bottle-shaped kapok trees and bright flowers dotting the hilly landscape.

PLAYAS

From Progreso the paved road heads due south for 30 km to Playas (called General Villamil on some maps), the beach resort nearest Guayaquil.

Playas is also an important fishing village. A generation ago, many of the fishing craft were small balsa rafts with one sail – similar in design to the boats used up and down the coast for many centuries before the Spanish conquest. Now, motor-driven dugouts and other more modern craft are most frequently used, but you can still

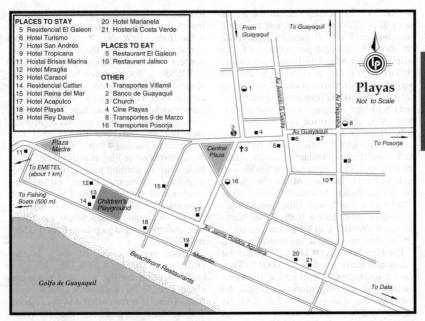

PLACES TO STAY
5   Residencial El Galeon
6   Hotel Turismo
7   Hotel San Andrés
9   Hotel Tropicana
11 Hostal Brisas Marina
12 Hotel Miraglia
13 Hotel Caracol
14 Residencial Cattan
15 Hotel Reina del Mar
17 Hotel Acapulco
18 Hotel Playas
19 Hotel Rey David
20 Hotel Marianela
21 Hostería Costa Verde

PLACES TO EAT
5   Restaurant El Galeon
10 Restaurant Jalisco

OTHER
1   Transportes Villamil
2   Banco de Guayaquil
3   Church
4   Cine Playas
8   Transportes 9 de Marzo
16 Transportes Posorja

Playas
Not to Scale

SOUTH COAST

see a few of the old balsa rafts in action. This is one of the most interesting things to look for in Playas. They usually come in at the west end of the beach, but this depends on winds and tides. Large flocks of frigate-birds and pelicans hoping for scraps wheel spectacularly around the fishing fleet as it comes in to unload the catch.

Because of its proximity to Guayaquil, there are many holiday homes in Playas. It is quite a bustling little resort during the busy seasons but is very quiet at other times of year. Weekends are much busier than midweek. Thieves try to take advantage of careless vacationers – do not leave anything unattended on the beach and exercise normal safety precautions. Nevertheless, I find it more appealing than Salinas and the other south coast resorts.

In the high season all the hotels are open and prices may rise a little; in other months many of the hotels, especially the cheaper ones, may close down. Those that

are open have few guests and will sometimes lower their prices to have you stay there – try bargaining.

The Cine Playas movie theater is often closed in the low season.

Information
The Banco de Guayaquil changes cash dollars, but traveler's checks are hard to negotiate. EMETEL is one km west of town on Jaime Roldos Aguilera. The area code is 04.

Places to Stay – bottom end
The cheapest places may lack running water on occasion and are pretty basic. Mosquitoes can be a problem in Playas, so try to get a room with mosquito netting or a fan. Prices are given for high-season weekends. The cheapest are the basic *Hotel Turismo* at US$3 per person and the similar *Hotel Caracol*, which also has rooms with bath at US$6 a person. The *Hotel Acapulco*

(☎ 760 343) has a cheap restaurant and is just OK at US$4 per person, and the basic but clean and safe *Hostería Costa Verde* (☎ 760 645) is US$4 per person or US$6 with bath and nets. The *Hotel San Andrés* (☎ 761 209) is OK at US$6 with bath per person. The similarly priced *Hotel Reina del Mar* (☎ 760 882) can get loud on weekends with the attached disco and restaurant. Also at this price is the basic and noisy *Hotel Tropicana*.

The *Residencial El Galeon* (☎ 760 270), with a good, cheap restaurant, is clean and friendly at US$5 per person or US$6 with bath and nets. The best of the cheapies is the *Hostal Brisas Marina* (☎ 760 324) at US$15 for a double with bath, fan and mosquito nets. Also decent is the *Hotel Marianela* (☎ 760 058), at US$4 per person or US$6 with private bath and mosquito nets.

The *Hotel Playas* (☎ 760 121) is near the beach and quite good for US$8/12. They have a restaurant. About half a kilometer southeast of the map, along the beach, the *Hostería La Gaviota* (☎ 760 133) is friendly and has a decent restaurant, though the rooms are very basic at US$7 per person with bath. The *Hotel Rey David* (☎ 760 024) is on the beach and has characterless rooms at US$12/16. The *Hostería El Delfín* (☎ 760 125) is a kilometer southeast of the center and has decent rooms, some with a sea view, for US$20 a double with bath. They have a restaurant and bar. Nearby is the good *Hosteria Estrella del Mar* (☎ 760 430) charging US$16 for a double with hot water. They, too, have a restaurant.

The sprawling old *Hotel Miraglia* (☎ 760 154) is only open in the high season when it charges an overpriced US$12 per person in rooms with private bath. *Residencial Cattan* (☎ 760 179), on the Malecón, provides a bed and three meals a day for US$16 per person but the rooms themselves, at US$11 per person, are basic, though they do have private showers with brackish water. Their restaurant isn't bad.

Places to Stay – middle

The best hotels are out of town a short way to the southeast along Avenida Jaime Roldos Aguilera (also called Via Data, or the road to Data). The first one you come to is the *Hotel Los Redes* (☎ 760 222) which, perhaps because it's the closest, is the poorest value in the high season when rates of US$50 a double have been reported. Rooms have hot showers and some are air-conditioned, but they aren't worth US$50. Low season rates are half this. They have a restaurant. Next is the *Hostería La Gaviota* (see bottom end) and then comes the *Hostería El Tucán* (☎ /fax 760 127), which is the best hotel in Playas at this time. They have a big swimming pool, sauna, spa and a pricey restaurant. Large, clean, air-conditioned rooms with TV and hot showers are US$40 to US$50 for single or double occupancy, depending on room size. Rooms sleeping up to five are US$60 to US$70.

About one km out of town is the *Hostería El Delfín* (☎ 760 125). It's in a quiet location by the sea, and rates are about US$20 for a pleasant double with bath. There is a restaurant and bar. About 200 meters beyond are the *Hostería Estrella del Mar* (☎ 760 430) and *Hostería Los Patios* (☎ 760 039). Both are decent places with double rooms with hot showers in the US$16 to US$20 range. Both have a restaurant, a bar and beach access.

Finally, the *Hostería Bellavista* (☎ 760 600) is about two km southwest of town on the beachfront. The place is very popular with Swiss and German tourists. Ordinary rooms and three-bedroom villas are available, all with hot showers. Some have kitchenettes and dining areas, and discounts are offered for weekly stays. There's a restaurant and bar if you don't want to cook. Rates go from about US$20 for a single to US$75 for a villa sleeping six. Reservations are suggested, and bikes, canoes and surfboards are reportedly available for rent.

Places to Eat

The better hotels have good, if slightly pricey, restaurants. Cheaper good ones include the one below the *Residencial Galeon* and the one in *Hotel Playas*, which is popular with locals. Several others are cheap and OK but didn't seem very busy on a recent visit. Cheap food is also available at the *Restaurant Jalisco*.

There are plenty of cheap, beachfront restaurants with views of the ocean where you can eat a freshly caught fish from about US$2, washed down with a cold beer. The hygiene standards of these places aren't high, so stick to hot food and ask the servers not to give you the little side salad that often comes with it.

Entertainment
There are places to dance on weekend nights in the high season, usually near the waterfront. It's pretty dead at other times.

Getting There & Away
Transportes Villamil and Transportes Posorja are the bus companies with services to Guayaquil (US$1.70; 1¾ hours). Buses leave every half hour with Transportes Villamil and they often pass the corner of Avenida Paquisha and Avenida Guayaquil. This is where locals wait to get on the next bus out of town.

Transportes Posorja picks up passengers for Posorja if the bus from Guayaquil is continuing there. Transportes 9 de Marzo and other companies have frequent pickup trucks to Posorja (US$0.60; 30 minutes) leaving from Avenida Paquisha – see the map.

Services are normally to Guayaquil, though occasionally a bus may go to the Santa Elena Peninsula. The easiest way to get to Santa Elena is to go to Progreso and change, but buses from Guayaquil to Santa Elena are often full during holidays.

A reader reports that on Sunday afternoons in the January to April high season everybody is returning to Guayaquil and that the road becomes a one-way bus-fest, with no vehicles traveling south into Playas.

PUNTA PELADA
This is a long and fairly deserted beach stretching northwest from Playas. Salt flats, cliffs and cacti provide an interesting-looking backdrop. There is reportedly

good surfing here. The dirt road along the beach is a popular drive for those with their own vehicles – no public transport here. Bring food and water and don't leave anything unattended.

POSORJA
Posorja is an attractive little fishing village with many working boats and hundreds of seabirds wheeling overhead, but the beach is dirty and not good for swimming. Shrimping is becoming increasingly important. Posorja is best visited on a day trip – it is about 20 km southeast of Playas.

There are two roads between Playas and Posorja – one follows the coast, and the other heads inland. The coastal road goes through the villages of Data de Villamil and Data de Posorja, which are often collectively called Data. These places are known for boat building. The inland road passes through the old village of El Morro, which is less important than it used to be. There is a huge old wooden church with dilapidated bamboo walls and three white wooden towers.

Places to Stay
There are two very basic pensiones. One is literally on the point of disintegrating, and the other looks like a particularly sleazy whorehouse – neither are recommended. There is also the *Hostería Posorja* (☎ 764 115), which charges US$6 per person or US$8 in rooms with bath. It has a restaurant and seems decent enough.

Getting There & Away
Pickup trucks serve as a frequent public bus service between Playas and Posorja.

SANTA ELENA PENINSULA
As you continue westward from Progreso, the land becomes increasingly dry and scrubby, the ceiba (kapok) trees giving way to interminable forests of five-meter-high cacti. Few people and little animal life is seen, though herds of tough, half-wild goats seem to thrive. Some of the few inhabitants scratch a living from burning the scrub to make charcoal, and once in a

while you see someone on the side of the road with bags of charcoal.

A little over halfway between Progreso and Santa Elena a road to the left leads to the coastal village of **Chanduy**, some 15 km from the main road. Archaeological excavations nearby have led to the opening of a small museum on the outskirts of the village. This place is not easy to find or get to. You can get to Chanduy by bus from La Libertad.

About 15 km before reaching Santa Elena, a road to the right leads seven km to **Baños de San Vicente**, where there are thermal pools and mud baths. A government-operated tourist complex has been built here, and visitors can enjoy therapeutic and rejuvenating mud packs, hot tubs, massages or swims. Daily entrance to the complex is about US$0.50. There is one place to spend the night, the *Hotel Florida* (☎ 353 016, 352 221 for information and reservations), which is quite inexpensive, although the clientele is mostly upper-class

Guayaquileños on day trips. Go early or late in the day to avoid the crowds on weekends.

As you arrive in Santa Elena the landscape changes. Not that it becomes any less dry; it is simply more built-up. There are three towns near the end of the peninsula, and they all seem to run into one another, making the area almost one complete dusty urban zone with few open spaces.

Santa Elena itself is the least important of the towns from the traveler's point of view, though it does have a nearby oil refinery and is the home of the peninsula's radio station. *Residencial El Cisne* is a clean, basic hotel on the main square. The other towns on the peninsula are La Libertad and Salinas (which is the main resort town for Guayaquileños).

LA LIBERTAD
La Libertad, the largest town on the peninsula, has about 50,000 inhabitants. It is a fishing port of some importance, has an

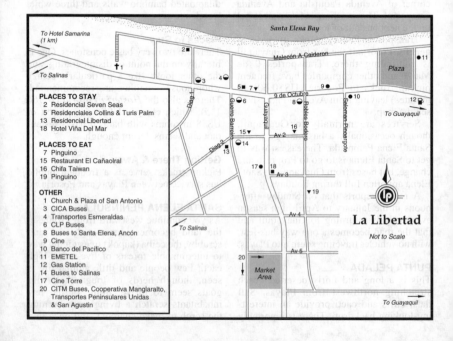

PLACES TO STAY
2   Residencial Seven Seas
5   Residenciales Collins & Turis Palm
13 Residencial Libertad
18 Hotel Viña Del Mar

PLACES TO EAT
7   Pinguino
15 Restaurant El Cañaolral
16 Chifa Taiwan
19 Pinguino

OTHER
1   Church & Plaza of San Antonio
3   CICA Buses
4   Transportes Esmeraldas
6   CLP Buses
8   Buses to Santa Elena, Ancón
9   Cine
10 Banco del Pacífico
11 EMETEL
12 Gas Station
14 Buses to Salinas
17 Cine Torre
20 CITM Buses, Cooperativa Manglaralto, Transportes Peninsulares Unidas & San Agustin

La Libertad
Not to Scale

refinery nearby and is the transportation hub for the area. It is a busy town and is more interesting to visit (especially in the low season) than Salinas, though it is also noisy and dirty. Few travelers like it, but it has an undeniably lively air. The El Niño floods caused severe damage to the waterfront. Most of the Malecón has been washed away, and the beach is mainly rubble.

The Banco del Pacífico near the plaza at the east end will change US cash dollars and traveler's checks. The modern EMETEL office is found on this plaza. For arriving sailors, there is a Migraciones office next to Transportes Esmeraldas on Guerro Barreiro. There is a bustling market and two cinemas.

Places to Stay – bottom end

One of the cheapest hotels on the whole peninsula is the very basic and ugly but friendly *Residencial Libertad*, which costs US$2 per person or US$4/6 with a dank private shower. Another cheapie is the *Residencial Collins*, which costs US$2 per person or US$8 for a double with bath, but the rooms are rather horrible little boxes. Nearby, the *Turis Palm* is slightly better at US$4 each or US$8 with private bath. The basic *Residencial Seven Seas* on the Malecón is US$3 or US$5 per person with bath. *Hotel Viña del Mar* (☎ 785 979), Avenida 3 and Guayaquil, is US$12/20 with bath and the only decent cheap hotel. They have parking available.

Places to Stay – middle

The best places are away from the town center. *Hotel Samarina* (☎ 785 167, ☎ /fax 784 100), on 9 de Octubre at the waterfront about 1.5 km northwest of the town, has an adequate restaurant, a swimming pool and rooms and bungalows for about US$30/45. The ocean is in front of the hotel, though there's not much of a beach.

About half a kilometer further is the better *Hotel Valdivia* (☎ /fax 775 144), which has a swimming pool, very good restaurant and friendly staff. They charge US$45 for a clean room for one or two people and US$90 for a room for six people.

Places to Eat

On Avenida 2 the *Restaurant El Cañaolral* is not expensive and is popular with locals. A block away, the *Chifa Taiwan* is OK. There are a couple of *Pinguinos* that have good ice-cream, and other cheap restaurants can be found on Avenida 9 de Octubre or Guayaquil. The better hotels have the best restaurants.

Getting There & Away

La Libertad is the center of bus services on the peninsula. For Guayaquil (US$2; 2½ to three hours) there are several choices. Cooperativa Libertad Peninsular (CLP), on the corner of 9 de Octubre and Guerro Barreiro, has buses about every hour all day long. Cooperativa Intercantonal Costa Azul (CICA), at 9 de Octubre and Diagonal 2, has the fastest and most frequent service. Their buses often leave from opposite the Residencial Turis Palm on Avenida 9 de Octubre. The CICA buses from Guayaquil continue to Salinas and then return to Guayaquil from Salinas via La Libertad.

To get to Santa Elena you flag down one of the minibuses that run frequently along 9 de Octubre. Frequent buses to Salinas run all day from Calle 8 and Avenida 2.

To visit Punta Carnero, the fishing village of Anconcito or the oil town of Ancón, take one of the frequent buses or pickup trucks leaving from near the market on the north side. Near here is Transportes San Agustín, which has minibuses running further east along the coast to the fishing village of Chanduy. Various small coastal villages are served by transport from the market area – ask around. Apart from at Punta Carnero there are no accommodations in these places.

For going north along the coast to the fishing villages of Palmar, Ayangue, Manglaralto (US$1; 1½ hours) and Puerto López (US$2.80; 2½ to three hours) you take minibuses with Transportes Peninsulares Unidas, Cooperativa Manglaralto or CITM. The first one has departures about every half hour but few of the vehicles make it as far as Manglaralto. Most go as far as Palmar and some go to Ayangue. The other two companies have several buses a day that go through Puerto López and on to Jipijapa (US$3.50; four hours). The drivers all know the Alandaluz. Note that buses may be booked up in advance during weekends in the high season.

Transportes Esmeraldas has one morning and two overnight buses to Quito (US$8) going through Babahoyo, Quevedo and Santo Domingo.

PUNTA CARNERO

This is a point of land in the middle of a wild and largely deserted beach, some 15 km in length. There is a resort hotel on the point, the *Punta Carnero Inn* (☎ 775 450, 775 537, fax 775 337), which overlooks the ocean from a clifftop. Comfortable, balconied rooms cost about US$80 (high season) for a double with bath and air-conditioning. There is a restaurant, swimming pool and play area for kids. Reservations can be made at the Plaza Hotel in Guayaquil. Nearby the *Hostería Vista del Mar* (☎ 775 370) has cheaper rooms and cabins with or without air-conditioning, all with hot showers, for US$30 to US$60 a double. There is a restaurant and swimming pool, and they also have a tennis court.

The ocean in front of the hotels may be too wild for swimming, but the beach is good for walks. The sea abounds with fish, and sport-fishing is a popular activity.

Boats and equipment can be chartered from Salinas. The area has also been recommended for birdwatching – some unusual arid land birds and shorebirds like the Chilean flamingo have been reported from the area. Salt lagoons, some made to evaporate salt, are seen along this coast. Whales may be observed in July, August and September.

Buses from La Libertad will get you to Punta Carnero, but most visitors come with their own vehicle.

SALINAS

This important resort town with a permanent population of over 20,000 inhabitants is on the tip of the Santa Elena Peninsula. About 150 km west of Guayaquil, it is the most westerly town on the Ecuadorian mainland. The westernmost point is a hill called La Choclatera, within a military base. Reportedly, you can visit it by taxi if you tip the guards at the entrance to the base, though I haven't tried this myself. One report indicates that you have to leave identification until you leave.

Salinas is called the 'best' resort in Ecuador, and its modern hotels and high-rise condos make it the seasonal haunt of affluent Ecuadorians. It's relatively overpriced yet quite crowded during the season and still fairly expensive and dead in the off-season. The water is warmest for swimming from January to March. The beaches

---

Sport-Fishing from Salinas

On the Salinas waterfront, Pesca Tour (☎ 772 391, in Guayaquil ☎ 443 365, fax 443 142) does deep-sea fishing trips and provides all the equipment. They have a fleet of boats and have been recommended by people who enjoy sport-fishing. Day charters run about US$350 per day (boat for six) to US$550 (boat for 10 people). Longer charters can also be arranged.

The continental shelf drops from about 400 meters, 13 km offshore, to over 3000 meters about 40 km offshore and so a short one-hour sail can take you out into really deep water. Swordfish, sailfish, tuna, dorados and marlin are some of the fish to go after – the black marlin occasionally weigh over 600 kg. Black marlin are the world's third biggest sport fish, after a couple of shark species. The world black marlin record is 707 kg, set in 1953 in neighboring Peru. Locals claim that there is an 800-kg black marlin on the Ecuadorian coast.

Salinas occasionally hosts world fishing competitions. The best fishing is from October to December, when boats may be booked up several days in advance. ∎

oilare not spectacular and are basically rather spoiled by the high-rise backdrop. I prefer the less-developed beaches of Playas or the north coast. The place is overcast, dreary and really dead in July and August.

There is a Yacht Club and, should you arrive in your own boat, you'll find Migración in La Libertad. Foreign sailors say that the Yacht Club is not very accommodating and 'yachties' hang out in other places – a French café on the waterfront has recently been popular. There is a Capitanía on the west end of the waterfront where you are supposed to register if you want to leave by yacht. During the January to April high season, international yachts come through and occasionally need a crew member.

A CETUR tourist office functions during the high season on the Malecón near Calle 36, east of the center. On this block is Seretur (☎ 772 800), which arranges local tours. Banco del Pacífico in the center changes cash

US dollars and traveler's checks. The streets are haphazardly arranged and poorly signed. Most locals go by landmarks rather than street names. The EMETEL office and post office are shown on the map.

Places to Stay – bottom end
Many local tourists stay at holiday homes rather than hotels. There are no very cheap accommodations, and hotels may close down in the off-season.

The cheapest budget hotels are about US$6 per person in the low and US$10 in the high season. Try the family-run *Hotel Florida* (☎ 772 780), which is clean but out of town near the naval base. Some rooms have sea views. *Hotel Albita* (☎ 773 211, 773 042, 773 662), Avenida 7 between Calle 22 and 23, is OK and has slightly musty rooms with fans and private baths. *Residencial Rachel* (☎ 772 501, 772 526), Calle 17 and Avenida 5, has rooms with shared baths for US$6 per person and

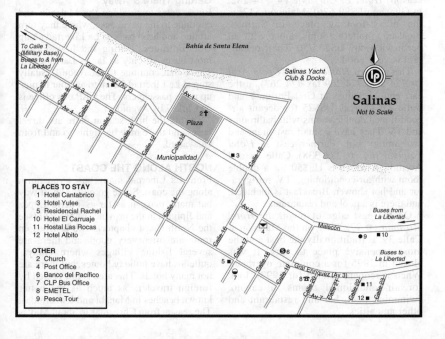

PLACES TO STAY
1 Hotel Cantábrico
3 Hotel Yulee
5 Residencial Rachel
10 Hotel El Carruaje
11 Hostal Las Rocas
12 Hotel Albito

OTHER
2 Church
4 Post Office
6 Banco del Pacífico
7 CLP Bus Office
8 EMETEL
9 Pesca Tour

rooms with private baths and TV for US$16/22. *Hostal Las Rocas* (☎ 774 219), Calle 22 and Gral Enríquez, is US$10 per person in clean rooms with cold shower and fan.

Hotel Cantabrico (☎ 772 026) is somewhat rundown but isn't a bad value if you eat all your meals there. They charge US$12 per person in basic but clean rooms with private bathrooms, and all three meals are included. They have a rather dusty garden with hammocks to lie around in.

The friendly *Hotel Yulee* (☎ 772 028, in Quito 446 651, 446 649), in an old, rambling building near the main plaza, charges US$22/30 in rooms with private bath, hot water and TV. There are cheaper upstairs rooms, and rooms with shared showers are US$14/18. Rates drop by 50% in the low season. They have a restaurant and a garden.

Places to Stay – middle

The small (and usually full in the high season) *Hotel El Carruaje* (☎ 774 282, in Guayaquil 389 676), Malecón 517, is the nicest-looking place in Salinas. Pleasant, modern rooms, most with an ocean view, are US$35/50. Their restaurant is very good.

The modern *Hotel Salinas Costa Azul* (☎ 774 268, 774 269 fax 774 267), at the east end of Salinas at Gral Enríquez and Calle 27, charges US$25 for decent air-conditioned double rooms with bathrooms and TV. They have a small restaurant and swimming pool. Further east is *Hotel Tropikal Inn* (☎ 773 338), Calle 38 and Avenida 3, which is US$50 for a double room with air-conditioning, TV, refrigerator and hot shower. Breakfast is included, and there is a pool and restaurant.

On the east edge of town, the *Hotel Miramar* (☎ 772 115), on the Malecón at Calle 39, is traditionally the best and the most expensive place to stay. It was closed in 1995 for a complete overhaul. When it reopens (slated for 1997), look for air-conditioned rooms, a casino, swimming pool, bar and restaurant and other amenities.

Places to Eat

The cheap local places are found in the area around Calles 17 and 19 south of the Malecón, near the market. Others are found on Gral Enríquez near Calle 23. They are popular with locals, but I don't mark any of them – look around and take your pick.

There are various restaurants, bars and discos along the waterfront east of the center, but they're mostly closed in the low season. Near the Hotel Miramar is the pricey but popular *Mar y Tierra*; a few blocks away is the cheaper and simpler *Flipper*. Both are recommended for – what else? – seafood.

Entertainment

During weekends in the high season, the place comes alive with discos and clubs, mainly near the Malecón. South of town on Avenida 7 near Calle 19 is *Tequilala*, a locally popular spot. Salinas is pretty dead from May to September.

Getting There & Away

Buses enter town along the Malecón and continue to the naval base, where they turn around and head back to La Libertad along Gral Enriquez. During the low season, most buses go only as far as La Libertad. Those that continue to Guayaquil usually stop at La Libertad for up to an hour to pick up more passengers. The CLP bus office is on Calle 7 by Avenida 5.

During the high season there are direct buses and there may be flights to and from Guayaquil.

NORTH ALONG THE COAST

From La Libertad many buses run north along the coast. Some go only a short way but many make it as far as Puerto López and Jipijapa in the province of Manabí (see the North Coast chapter). The beaches en route are often very good, and there are several fishing villages where Guayaquileños have holiday homes, but there are not many hotels. This area is not visited by foreign travelers as much as the better known beaches in Manabí and Esmeraldas. The season from Christmas to about May is hot and sunny but wet – the scenery is lush and pretty between rain showers. The ocean is warmest during January to March. The rest of the year is dry, cooler and cloudier. It can sometimes be gray and miserable during the dry months, especially July and August.

The coast views are good, so sit on the left or ocean side of the bus. The most interesting sight is the literally hundreds of local fishermen surf-fishing. They catch shrimp with hand nets stretched between a framework of two crossed poles, at the end of which a couple of floats are attached. Wading knee-deep in the surf, they push these hand nets up and down the beach. It looks ridiculous – like a lawn-mowing convention gone crazy.

The first place of particular interest is the **Valdivia** area, which is the site of Ecuador's oldest culture. There is a small museum in the little village of Valdivia, about 50 km north of La Libertad, but the best pieces of antiquity are in Guayaquil museums. About five km before reaching Valdivia, the fishing village of **Ayangue** is passed, and five km before that (40 km north of La Libertad), the village of **Palmar**. Both are close to pleasant beaches and have attracted Guayaquileños into buying holiday homes there. The area is fairly crowded with visitors during high season weekends, but only Ayangue has a couple of small hotels.

North of Valdivia the dry landscape begins to get a little wetter. The cactus and scrub give way to stunted trees and the occasional banana plantation.

Manglaralto

About 60 km north of La Libertad, this is the main village on the coast of Guayas Province north of La Libertad. There is a nice beach with decent surf but little shade. There are a few simple pensiones, particularly near the north end of the beach, or ask around for accommodations. I managed to find a place to stay with a friendly local family for US$4. *Señor Ramon's house*, south of the plaza, has been recommended by travelers as a place to stay. The *Restaurant Las Tangas* is quite good, and they also have a few rooms available. You can find beds with families in the other villages, too. There are a couple of basic comedores and an EMETEL and post office on Manglaralto's main square.

A few kilometers inland from Manglaralto is the village of **Dos Mangas**. Here, the land begins to rise into the Cordillera de Colonche, coastal hills reaching an elevation of 834 meters. By asking around in Dos Mangas, you can find guides and horses for excursions into these hills, where you will find waterfalls during the rainy season.

Montañita

Approximately four or five km north of Manglaralto is the village of Montañita. Like other places along the coast, it is a pleasant little fishing village with nice

---

Pre-Columbian Coastal Ceramics

Some of Ecuador's oldest archaeological sites, dating back to about 3000 BC, are found in the Valdivia-Manglaralto area. Although there is little to see for the traveler, villagers in the Valdivia area will offer genuine pre-Columbian artifacts for sale. Many of these are replicas and those that are genuine are illegal to export out of Ecuador (or import into most other countries).

I recommend buying ceramics that are advertised as replicas – many are very attractive and quite authentic-looking. Their purchase not only makes a good souvenir, but encourages and supports the work of local artisans and discourages the removal and exploitation of genuine archaeological artifacts.

Next to the Corona del Mar restaurant in Manglaralto there is a small cultural center with an explanation of the archaeology and ceramics of the area. You can purchase good replicas here. ■

Red de Posadas Comunitarias

This new project (the name means 'Community Lodging Network') is found in small communities of the coastal areas of Guayas and southern Manabí provinces. The network will provide travelers with simple but clean huts for accommodations when visiting remote villages off the beaten track. Local families will provide meals.

It is planned for the villages involved to be about a day's walk or mountain bike ride away from one another and will give travelers a chance to experience some rural hospitality and lifestyle while putting tourist dollars into the pockets of villagers. This project was reported to me by Jean Brown of Safari Tours in Quito. Ask there for more information. ∎

beaches. The surfing is reputedly the best in Ecuador, and new hotels are being built (and will be open by the time this book goes to press).

Meanwhile, *El Rincón del Amigo* (☎ 223 720, fax 225 907) and *Vitos* (☎ 241 975) have both been recommended by budget travelers. Both are friendly and charge about US$6 to US$8 for a double room. There may be cheaper dorm space available, though things are slowly becoming more developed. Some rooms have beach views, and all beds should have mosquito nets – essential during the wet months. Both places have decent restaurants. Other places to eat include *Blancas* for ceviche, *El Pelicano* for Italian food and *Las Olas* run by surfers. Surfboards are reportedly available for rent at Vitos.

A few kilometers further north is the coastal village of **Olón**. This, too, has a decent beach and a couple of inexpensive hotels, which I haven't visited.

Six or seven km north of Olón, the provincial line between Guayas and Manabí is crossed – see the North Coast for further travel.

You can easily do a roundtrip from La Libertad in a day if you just want to sightsee and swim at some beaches.

South of Guayaquil

Guayas Province south of Guayaquil is of little interest to Guayaquileño holiday-makers, compared to west of the city. For the most part, this route is taken by travelers on their way to Peru.

RESERVA ECOLÓGICA MANGLARES CHURUTE

This 35,000-hectare reserve protects an area of mangroves southeast of Guayaquil. Much of the coast used to be mangrove forest – an important and unique habitat (see the Facts about the Country chapter). This is one of the few remaining mangrove coastlands left – the rest have been destroyed by the shrimp industry. About a quarter of the area of the reserve is mangrove, and inland is some tropical dry forest on hills reaching 700 meters above sea level.

This is a poorly known region, but preliminary studies of the area indicate that the changing habitat from coastal mangroves to hilly forest supports a wide biodiversity with a high degree of endemism within the reserve. This is a rarely visited place, partly because there is still relatively little infrastructure for tourism and partly because it is not much publicized. Nevertheless, Manglares Churute is well worth a visit and the few people who go have enjoyed it, especially during the dry season when there are few biting insects. Dolphins have frequently been reported on the coast, and many other animal and bird species are seen by wildlife watchers.

Information

The reserve entrance is on the main Guayaquil-Machala highway about 56 km south of Guayaquil. At the entrance is an information center where you pay the entrance fee, which, because this is part of the national park chain, is US$20 (about US$16 if you pay in sucres). The park rangers can arrange boats for you (a recent report said the fee is US$60 for the whole day, and the boat can take four or five people) to visit the mangroves; there are also several kilometers of hiking trails. Maps are available at the information center. There is room for a few people to sleep here, and a campground is planned.

Getting There & Away
Any bus between Guayaquil and Naranjal or Machala can drop you off at the information center. When you are ready to leave, you can flag buses down. There is a big sign on the road if you are driving.

MACHALA
South of Guayaquil is the important city of Machala, with about 150,000 inhabitants. The capital of the province of El Oro, it lies in an important banana-growing area, and during the 200-km drive from Guayaquil you pass many plantations of bananas, coffee, pineapple and citrus fruits. About halfway to Machala you pass through Naranjal, an important agricultural center but otherwise of little interest.

Despite its economic importance, Machala is not of great tourist interest. Most travelers on their way to and from Peru pass through here, but few people stay more than a night.

It is not totally devoid of interest, however, as the local international port of Puerto Bolívar, only seven km away, is worth visiting. There are beaches nearby. Machala also has a highly touted International Banana & Agricultural Festival during the third week in September, which the Ecuadorian tourist authorities assure me is of great interest to tourists. I'm afraid I missed it.

On the main road to Machala, southeast of the city, stands a huge **statue of El Bananero** – a man carrying a large branch of bananas. This is Machala's most important monument. Watch for it as you arrive in town.

Information
Tourist Offices Most streets in Machala are both named and numbered (I use names). The CETUR information office

(☎ 932 106) is upstairs at 9 de Mayo and Pichincha. It is open somewhat erratically on weekdays.

Peruvian Consulate There is a Peruvian Consulate (☎ 930 680), at Bolívar and Colón, open from 9 am to 1:30 pm Monday through Friday.

Money Banco del Pacífico, Rocafuerte at Junín, and Delagado Travel, 9 de Mayo near the plaza, change both US cash dollars and traveler's checks at rates only a little lower than in Guayaquil and Quito.

Post & Communications The Post Office is on Montalvo near Bolívar. The EMETEL office is several blocks away from the center on 9 de Octubre by the sports stadium. The area code for Machala and the province of El Oro is 07.

Places to Stay
Machala has a better variety of hotels than does the border town of Huaquillas, so travelers are better off staying here. The border is not open until 8 am, so by taking a dawn bus you can still be in Huaquillas by the time the border opens.

Places to Stay – bottom end
Most of the cheap hotels have only cold water, but the weather is hot enough that it's not a great hardship. In fact, fans and air-conditioning are much more appealing than a hot shower!

The cheapest places are the very basic *Residencial Machala*, Sucre and Guayas, at US$2 per person, and the marginally better *Residencial Almache*, Sucre and Montalvo, and *Residencial Pichincha*, Sucre near 9 de Mayo, at US$2.50 per person.

Somewhat better are the *Hotel Molina* (☎ 938 365), Montalvo near Olmedo, at US$4/6 for singles and doubles, the acceptable *Residencial Pesantez*, 9 de Mayo at 3 Norte, and *Hotel La Delicia*, Olmedo near Páez, both at US$3.50 per person, and the friendly *Residencial La Internacional*, Guayas near Olmedo, at US$4 per person. The *Hostal La Bahía* (☎ 920 518), Olmedo

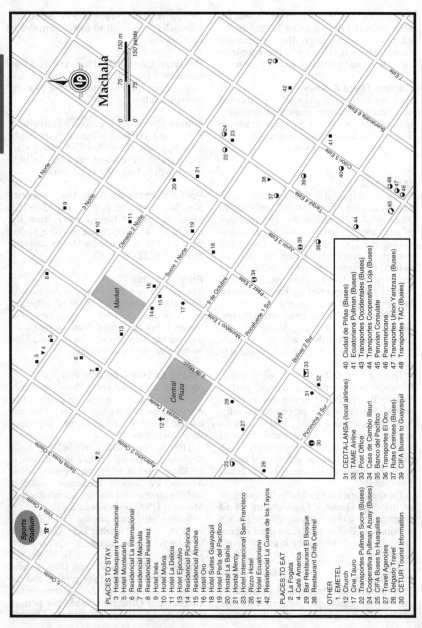

Machala

SOUTH COAST

PLACES TO STAY
3   Hotel Mosquera Internacional
5   Hotel Montecario
6   Residencial La Internacional
7   Residencial Pesantez
8   Residencial Pesantez
9   Hotel Inés
10 Hotel Molina
11 Hotel La Delicia
13 Hotel Ejecutivo
14 Residencial Pichincha
15 Residencial Almache
16 Hotel Oro
18 Hotel Suites Guayaquil
19 Hotel Perla del Pacífico
20 Hostal La Bahía
21 Hostal Mercy
23 Hotel Internacional San Francisco
26 Rizzo Hotel
41 Hotel Ecuatoriano
42 Residencial La Cueva de los Tayos

PLACES TO EAT
2   La Fogata
4   Café América
29 Bar Restaurant El Bosque
38 Restaurant Chifa Central

OTHER
1   EMETEL
12 Church
17 Cine Tauro
22 Transportes Pullman Sucre (Buses)
24 Cooperativa Pullman Azuay (Buses)
25 CIFA Buses to Huaquillas
27 Travel Agencies
28 Delgado Travel
30 CETUR Tourist Information
31 CEDTA-LANSA (local airlines)
32 TAME Airline
33 Post Office
34 Casa de Cambio Illauri
35 Banco del Pacífico
36 Transportes El Oro
37 Rutas Orenses (Buses)
39 CIFA Buses to Guayaquil
40 Ciudad de Piñas
41 Ecuatoriana Pullman (Buses)
43 Transportes Occidentales (Buses)
44 Transportes Cooperativa Loja (Buses)
45 Peruvian Consulate
46 Panamericana
47 Transportes Union Yantzaza (Buses)
48 Transportes TAC (Buses)

at Junín, is a good place at US$4.50 for a double or US$4.50 per person with bath.

One of the best cheap hotels, often full by lunch, is the very good and clean *Hostal Mercy* (☎ 920 116), Junín 609 and Sucre, at US$4.50 per person with bath or US$6 with bath and air-conditioning. The friendly *Residencial La Cueva de los Tayos* (☎ 935 600), Sucre near Buenavista, is clean at US$4.50 per person or US$5.50 with bath and fan. The *Hotel Ecuatoriano* (☎ 930 197), 9 de Octubre 912 and Colón, is rather noisy but convenient if you are arriving late at the adjoining bus terminal. Reasonably clean but shabby rooms, some with air-conditioning, are US$5 per person. The *Hotel Suites Guayaquil* (☎ 922 570, 937 557), 9 de Octubre and Páez, is a fair value for US$6.50 per person with bath, air-conditioning and, in some rooms, TV and telephone. The satisfactory *Hotel Mosquera Internacional* (☎ 931 752, 931 140, 930 210, 930 392, fax 930 390), Olmedo near Ayacucho, is US$8/13 in small, clean rooms with fan and US$10/18 with air-conditioning. All have private hot showers and most have TV and telephone.

Also with hot showers are the decent *Hotel Inés* (☎ 932 301, fax 931 473), Montalvo 1509 and 3 Norte, at US$10/15 with air-conditioning and TV, and the very clean *Hotel Internacional San Francisco* (☎ 922 395, 930 441, 930 457), Tarqui near Sucre, at US$9/16 with fan and US$14/22 with air-conditioning, TV and phone. The *Hotel Perla de Pacífico* (☎ 931 472, 930 915, 931 474), Sucre 613 and Páez, charges US$13/21 and has clean though worn air-conditioned rooms with TV and telephone, but the hot water reportedly doesn't work. All three of these have good restaurants. Also in this price range is the *Hotel Ejecutivo* (☎ 923 162, 933 992, fax 933 987), Sucre and 9 de Mayo, which has rather worn rooms but all the amenities – air-conditioning, cable TV, telephone, hot water and a little café.

Places to Stay – middle

All the hotels in this price range have clean rooms with private bathrooms, hot water

and air-conditioning. The *Hotel Montecarlo* (☎ 931 901, 933 462, fax 933 104), Guayas at Olmedo, has pretty nice rooms with cable TV and telephone. Rates are US$17/27. The *Hotel Oro* (☎ 937 569, 930 783, 932 408, fax 933 751), Sucre and Montalvo, charges US$28/34 in pleasant rooms with cable TV and telephone. There is a restaurant.

The best hotel in town, complete with decent restaurant, swimming pool, sauna and casino, is the *Rizzo Hotel* (☎ 921 511, 921 906, fax 933 651), Guayas near Pichincha. It's traditionally the best because it's the oldest, but the rooms aren't anything special, though they are away from the center and quiet. Rates are about US$32/40.

Places to Stay – top end

In the suburbs outside of town, the new *Oro Verde* (☎ 933 140, fax 933 150) is Machala's only luxury hotel at this time. Spacious rooms start around US$100, and the hotel has all the expected amenities including car rental and travel office and a small shopping mall. It's a 10-minute cab ride from the center of town.

Places To Eat

There are many chifas, and the locally popular *Restaurant Chifa Central*, Tarqui near 9 de Octubre, is recommended as having a wide variety of good and reasonably priced meals. Budget travelers should try the chaulafan, which is a cheap but filling rice dish. The chop suey mixto (beef, pork, shrimp) is also good for about US$2.50. *La Fogata*, on 9 de Octubre near Ayacucho, is good for cheap grilled chicken. There are a number of other cheap places along 9 de Octubre between the Chifa Central and EMETEL, including chifas and chicken restaurants – take your pick.

For a pleasant outdoor ambiance try the *Bar Restaurant El Bosque*, 9 de Mayo near Bolívar, which has simple but decent meals for about US$2.25 and up. The *Café America*, on Olmedo near Guayas, is quite good and open until midnight. Also open late is *Don Angelo's*, on 9 de Mayo just south of the Central Plaza. It's cheap but good and popular with the locals.

The best hotels have more expensive restaurants, but the food is good. The *Hotel Perla del Pacífico* serves vegetarian food. The *Hotel Oro Verde* has the best (and most expensive) restaurants in town.

If you have some spare time, consider heading over to Puerto Bolívar for super-fresh seafood.

Getting There & Away

Air TAME flights from Guayaquil to Machala and back leave Machala at 11:35 am, Monday to Friday, subject to change. The fare is US$18. You can connect with a Guayaquil-Quito flight to be in the capital the same evening for about US$38. TAME has a downtown office (☎ 930 130) on Montalvo near Pichincha. Opposite is a CEDTA-LANSA office. They have light aircraft for flights to Guayaquil.

The airport is barely one km from the town center, and a taxi will cost about US$1. If you are on foot, walk southwest along Montalvo.

Bus There is no central bus terminal. Several of the following companies change their offices frustratingly often, so if you can't find one, ask – it has probably moved a couple of blocks.

To get to the Peruvian border at Huaquillas (US$1.20; two hours) it's best to go with CIFA, who leave at very frequent intervals from the corner of Bolívar and Guayas. They go through Santa Rosa and Arenillas. Make sure your documents are in order and not packed deep in your luggage as there are two or three passport checks en route. You will be asked to leave the bus to register, but the driver is used to this and will wait for you.

CIFA buses also go to Guayaquil (US$3; 3½ hours) from their depot on 9 de Octubre near Tarqui. There are several other companies in the area. Rutas Orenses, 9 de Octubre near Tarqui, has efficient and frequent services to Guayaquil. Ecuatoriana Pullman, 9 de Octubre near Colón, goes there in larger air-conditioned coaches.

Panamericana, Colón and Bolívar, has several large coaches that run daily to Quito (US$7.50; 10 to 12 hours). Transportes Occidentales, Buenavista and Olmedo, has afternoon and night buses to Quito, and a night bus to Esmeraldas (US$6.50; nine hours).

Ciudad de Piñas, Colón and Rocafuerte, has several buses a day to Piñas, of which the 6 am departure continues to Loja. They also have one or two buses to Cuenca (US$3.50; 4½ hours).

Transportes Pullman Azuay and Transportes Pullman Sucre, Tarqui and Olmedo, have many buses daily to Cuenca. Transportes Union Yantzaza, Colón and Bolívar, has a slow old daily bus leaving at 8:30 pm for Yantzaza (US$6.50; 11 hours) in the Southern Oriente.

Transportes Cooperativa Loja, Tarqui near Rocafuerte, goes to Loja (US$4.50; six hours) – ask the driver to set you down at the Puente Nuevo de Alamor to connect with buses to Puyango. Nearby, Transportes TAC has several buses a day to Zaruma.

Getting Around

Bus The most important local bus for travelers is the No 1 bus, which goes northwest from the central plaza along 9 de Octubre to Puerto Bolívar (US$0.20; 15 minutes, crowded). A taxi will cost under US$2. The No 1 bus returns into town along Pichincha and goes southeast as far as the El Bananero monument, almost two km from the center.

Car You can rent a Hertz car (☎ 933 140) at their office in the Hotel Oro Verde.

PUERTO BOLÍVAR

The international port, Puerto Bolívar, is about six km from Machala and is that city's maritime outlet for the south coast's banana and shrimp exports. There are some simple seafood restaurants by the waterfront where you can enjoy a beer among cool sea breezes while watching seabirds wheeling overhead and ocean ships sailing by. I've heard claims that Puerto Bolívar has some coastal nightlife, but I didn't discover any.

The port is protected from the ocean by islands and mangroves. Motorized dugouts can be hired for cruising the mangroves to watch the birdlife or to go to the nearby island beach at Jambelí.

Places to Stay & Eat
There are a couple of cheap and basic hotels, though most people stay in Machala. The seafood restaurants on the pier are not fancy but are pleasant enough. If you are on a tight budget, you'll find the same food to be cheaper in restaurants a block or two away from the waterfront.

Getting There & Around
Bus The No 1 bus from Machala's central plaza runs frequently. The last stop is about two blocks away from the pier and boat dock.

Boat Boats leave Puerto Bolívar for Jambelí at 7 and 10 am, and 3 pm from Monday to Friday. Boats return from Jambelí about an hour later. There are many more departures, dependent on passenger demand, on weekends and holidays. The fare for the half-hour trip is about US$1 per person, or you can hire a boat carrying up to 20 passengers to take you from Puerto Bolívar to Jambelí anytime.

Boats can also be hired to other beaches, with the furthest being at Costa Rica near the Peruvian border (carry your passport). These beaches offer little shade and, with the exception of Jambelí, are undeveloped, so carry food, drink, sunscreen and insect repellent – the mosquitoes can be nasty in the wet season.

JAMBELÍ
This long beach is on the ocean side of the island sheltering Puerto Bolívar. This is the favorite resort of holidaymakers from Machala and can be (relatively) busy at weekends – though it is not particularly well developed. There is little shade and abundant mosquitoes in the wet months. A good reason to visit, if you are a birder, is

to see the wide variety of coastal and pelagic birds and to search for the rufous-necked wood-rail, a rarely seen bird of the mangroves (low tide is the best time to spot them).

Places to Stay & Eat
There are a couple of cheap and basic places to stay. There are plenty of 'restaurants' serving seafood at weekends, but many are closed midweek.

Getting There & Away
See the information given for Puerto Bolívar.

PASAJE
This small town, about 25 km east of Machala, is the capital of its canton and the center of a banana-growing region. It is the last town of any size before the attractive road from Machala to Cuenca (see under Cuenca) begins to rise into the mountains.

Places to Stay
The *Hotel San Martín* (☎ 910 434), at Piedrahita and Olmedo, has rooms with private bathrooms for about US$7/10 for single/doubles. Rooms that have air-conditioning are about US$2 more. The *Hotel Pasaje* (☎ 910 118), at 10 de Agosto 629 and San Martín, has cheaper rooms with private bath.

ZARUMA AREA
This old gold-mining town in the mountains is to the southeast of Machala. Now, the gold is almost all worked out although visits to a mine can be arranged by asking for permission at the Municipalidad (town hall). Some archaeological ruins have been discovered in the area – people have probably been mining gold here since pre-Columbian times.

The town is a small one, and the best reasons to visit are to see the turn-of-the-century architecture (quaint wooden buildings with elaborate balconies) and admire the mountainous views. The nearby towns of Piñas (15 km away) and Portovelo (seven km away) can also be visited.

Places to Stay

There are a couple of basic hotels in Zaruma. The best place to stay in town itself is probably the inexpensive old *Hotel Municipal*, which charges about US$3 per person in rooms with private bath and good views. The better *Hotel Roland* is a little more expensive but is a couple of kilometers from the center. There is an inexpensive country hotel, the *Pedregal*, about three km outside Zaruma. Roughly 12 km north of Zaruma is a good country resort, *Los Rosales de Machay* (☎ 931 898, 924 478 for reservations). This resort boasts a pool, pretty gardens, a decent restaurant and comfortable rooms for US$40 a double.

Getting There & Away

Transportes TAC has several buses a day between Machala and Zaruma.

PIÑAS

Piñas is known as a coffee-producing area. It was near Piñas where, in 1980, a new bird species was discovered – El Oro parakeet. Few travelers come here, however – this is off-the-beaten-track travel.

Places to Stay & Eat

There are a couple of basic hotels. The best place in Piñas is the *Residencial Dumari* in the town center – clean rooms are about US$3 per person, and hot water should be available.

There are several simple restaurants, and the *Restaurant El Tunel* is recommended.

Getting There & Away

Ciudad de Piñas bus company has buses between Machala and Piñas.

PUYANGO PETRIFIED FOREST

This small reserve was created in 1988 to protect the fossil remains and wildlife of the area. Despite its small size of 2659 hectares, Puyango is known for its birds, and over 130 species have been listed since the recent creation of the reserve – there are undoubtedly more. FEPROTUR has published a booklet on the birds of Puyango, containing a bird checklist. The flora and

geology is also of great interest, and research is underway in the area. Fossilized Araucaria tree trunks, many millions of years old and up to 11 meters long and 1.6 meters in diameter, have been found. Various other fossilized trees, ferns and extinct plants are present. This is the largest petrified forest in Ecuador and perhaps in the whole continent.

Puyango is in a valley at about 360 meters above sea level, some 55 km inland from the coast. The valley is separated from the ocean by the Cordillera Larga, which reaches over 900 meters above sea level. Despite the separation, the area experiences a coastal weather pattern, with warm temperatures and most of the annual 1000 mm of rainfall occurring from January to May.

Camping is allowed, and a lookout point and trails have been constructed, though the planned visitor interpretation center has yet to materialize.

The nearby village of Puyango is composed of some 20 families. There is nowhere to stay (except to camp), although the villagers may give you floor space if asked. The local people have been taught about the reserve, and some of the locals will act as guides – ask around. I recommend hiring a local as a guide. They'll show you where to see the fossilized trees and tell you about them, give you some ideas about where to look for the local wildlife, etc. Even better, they will tell you about themselves, their interests and their families.

Entrance to the reserve is US$5. For more information call the Machala office (☎ 930 012).

Getting There & Away

If you are driving, head from Machala to Arenillas, and from there take a unpaved road south through Palmales (22 km from Arenillas) and on to Puyango (38 km south of Palmales). Alternatively, a road heads west from the Loja-Macará (on the Peruvian border) highway, about halfway between Macará and Catacocha (see the Cuenca & the Southern Highlands chapter).

SOUTH COAST

This road goes via Celica and Alamor to Puyango and is less frequently used.

Buses with Transportes Cooperativa Loja leave from Machala and Loja and will enable you to go through Puyango. The service is irregular, but you should be able to get to Puyango from either city within a day if you start in the morning.

TO/FROM THE PERUVIAN BORDER
It is about an 80-km drive from Machala to the border town of Huaquillas – this is the route taken by most overland travelers to Peru. The bus from Machala passes through banana and palm plantations and the dusty market towns of **Santa Rosa** and **Arenillas**, of which Santa Rosa is the most important. There are two or three passport checks en route, but these take only a minute (assuming your passport is in order). Foreign travelers have to get off the bus and register their passports at a control booth – the drivers know the routine and will wait for you.

Places to Stay
There are a couple of fairly cheap and basic hotels in Santa Rosa. The *Hotel América* (☎ 915 130), at Colón and El Oro, is probably the best. The *Residencial Dos Piños* (☎ 915 338), at Cuenca and Libertad, is cheaper.

Getting There & Away
Santa Rosa is about 30 km closer to the border than Machala, and there is an airport with light aircraft flying to Guayaquil – CEDTA and EDSAN are reportedly the companies doing this route at present. Most people coming from Peru continue on to Machala by bus and make connections there for onward transport. Buses to Huaquillas pass by frequently.

HUAQUILLAS
This dusty one-street town (well, there are a few side streets) is of importance only because it is at Ecuador's border with Peru. It has a population of about 20,000 (though it doesn't look it). There is a busy street market by the border, and the place is full

of Peruvians shopping on day passes. It's a rundown and dirty town and not a particularly attractive introduction to Ecuador if you're arriving from Peru. Although almost everything happens on the one long main street, the town is growing and civic amenities like a plaza and park are planned.

Huaquillas continues across the border into Peru where it becomes known as Aguas Verdes.

Money
Banks in Huaquillas or Aguas Verdes do not normally do foreign exchange, so you have to rely on street money changers. They may try to give you a very bad rate, use 'fixed' calculators, offer out-dated (and worthless) bills and are generally pushy and obnoxious. It helps if you know what the real rate is. Check with other travelers going the opposite way for up-to-date exchange rates and currency information.

If you are leaving Ecuador for Peru, it is best to try to get rid of as many sucres as you can in Ecuador and arrive in Peru with US dollars. The Peruvian currency is frequently devalued and changes names every few years. If heading to Peru, ask travelers from Peru or at the South American Explorer's Club in Quito about the current situation. Peruvian money changers will give you better rates for dollars than you'll get in Ecuador, and exchange rates should be almost as good as in Lima – but short-changing is common. Count carefully and change only what you need.

If you're just arriving in Ecuador, you can get within 2% of the Quito rate from street changers if you bargain hard. Again, it is best to use dollars. Other major foreign currencies can be exchanged, but less favorably, and fewer changers want to deal with them. Traveler's checks can also be exchanged, though with some difficulty – usually cash is preferred and gets a better rate.

Places to Stay & Eat
There are several basic hotels on the main street near the Migraciones office. None of them are particularly good, so I can't work

up much enthusiasm for any of them. Hotels tend to be full by early afternoon, and you may have to take whatever is available or go to Machala. Most travelers go on to Machala (or to Tumbes if heading to Peru – less than an hour from the border and with plenty of hotels).

Of the cheap but poor hotels (about US$3 per person) near the immigration office, the *Residencial Huaquillas* is the best. There are cheap and basic restaurants nearby.

For about US$9 a double with bath, the *Hotel Rodey*, Teniente Cordovez and 10 de Agosto, is clean and reasonable. Also good is the *Parador Turístico Huaquillas* (☎ 907 374), 1½ km from the border on the main road out of town, with the town's best restaurant and simple, clean doubles with bath and fans for US$14. The *Hotel Vanessa*, 1 de Mayo 323, has clean, air-conditioned doubles with bath for US$18.

Getting There & Away
CIFA buses run frequently to Machala (US$1.20; two hours). There is no main bus office, but you'll see buses on the main street a block or two beyond the Migraciones office if you're heading into Ecuador away from the border. Panamericana, behind Migraciones, has four buses a day to Quito (US$8; 13 hours). Ecuatoriana Pullman, a couple of blocks past Migraciones (walking away from the border), has buses to Guayaquil (US$4; 5½ hours), but it's often easier to go to Machala and change. A few buses go to Loja and Cuenca.

Crossing the Peruvian Border
The border is the Río Zarumilla, which is crossed by an international bridge. As you enter Ecuador from the bridge, you'll find yourself on the main road, crowded with market stalls, that stretches out through Huaquillas.

The Ecuadorian Migraciones office is on the left side about 200 meters from the bridge and is identified by the yellow, blue and red-striped Ecuadorian flag. All entrance and exit formalities are carried out here. The Ecuadorian office is open daily from 8 am to noon and 2 to 5 pm.

You won't have any difficulty in finding the office. Dozens of small boys will offer their services as luggage carriers and guides, and the many money changers (identified by the ubiquitous black attaché case) will show you the way and pester you to change money with them.

Arriving in Ecuador If you are arriving in Ecuador, you first need an exit stamp in your passport from the Peruvian authorities. After walking across the international bridge, continue 200 meters to the Ecuadorian Migraciones office. Entrance formalities are usually straightforward. No tourists need visas but everyone needs a T3 tourist card, available free at the office. If you're not entering as a tourist, you need a student, resident, worker or business visa, which must be obtained from an Ecuadorian embassy, usually the one that serves your home country.

Exit tickets from Ecuador and sufficient funds (US$20 per day) are legally required but are very rarely asked for. You will receive your T3 card (keep it for when you leave) and an identical stamp in your passport allowing you up to 90 days' stay. Usually, only 30 days are given, but it is easy to obtain a renewal in Quito or Guayaquil.

Note that you are allowed only 90 days per year in Ecuador. If you've already been in the country for 90 days and try to return, you will be refused entry. If you have an exit ticket from Quito or Guayaquil international airports, you can usually get a 72-hour transit visa just to get you to the airport and out of the country.

Leaving Ecuador If you are leaving Ecuador, the procedure is as follows. Go to the Ecuadorian Migraciones office and present your passport and T3 tourist card (the duplicate copy of the small document you filled out on arrival). You will receive an exit stamp in your passport, and the immigration authorities will keep your T3 card. You must have an exit stamp to legally leave (and later re-enter) Ecuador. There are no costs involved. If you have lost your T3 card, you should be able to get a free replacement at the border, assuming that the stamp in your passport has not expired.

As you cross the international bridge, you will be asked to show the exit stamp in your passport to the Ecuadorian bridge guard. On the Peruvian side (now called Aguas Verdes instead of Huaquillas) you normally have to show your passport to the bridge guard, but full entrance formalities are carried out in the immigration building about two km from the border. Taxis and mototaxis are available for about US$0.50 per person.

Most European nationalities and North Americans don't need a visa for Peru, but Australians and New Zealanders do. Visas are not obtainable in either Aguas Verdes or Huaquillas, and you have to go back to the Peruvian Consulate in Machala if you haven't got one. Other nationalities normally just need a tourist card, available at the Peruvian immigration office.

Although an exit ticket out of Peru is officially required, gringo travelers are rarely asked for this unless they look thoroughly disreputable. Other Latin American travelers are often asked for an exit ticket, however, so if you're a non-Peruvian Latin American (or traveling with one) be prepared for this eventuality. If necessary, there is a bus office in Aguas Verdes that sells (nonrefundable) bus tickets out of Peru. The immigration official will tell you where it is.

From the immigration building, shared colectivos (about US$1 per person) go to Tumbes – beware of overcharging. Tumbes has plenty of hotels and transportation further into Peru. See Lonely Planet's *Peru – travel survival kit.*

The Galápagos Islands

The Galápagos Archipelago is world famous for its incredibly fearless and unique wildlife. Here, you can swim with sea lions, float eye-to-eye with a penguin, stand next to a blue-footed booby feeding its young, watch a giant 200-kg tortoise lumbering through a cactus forest, and try to avoid stepping on iguanas scurrying over the lava. The wildlife is truly phenomenal. The scenery is barren and volcanic, and has a haunting beauty all its own – though some find it bare and ugly. A visit to the Galápagos is for the wilderness and wildlife enthusiast, not for the average sun-seeker.

Compared to the rest of Ecuador, the Galápagos are very expensive to visit. Flying from Quito and spending a week cruising the islands during the high season will cost a minimum of US$900, even for the most thrifty of budget travelers. You can pay over three times that for the most expensive of the top-end tours. Even on the expensive boats, conditions are comfortable but austere; therefore, the trip is recommended only for those truly interested in wildlife. The environment is fragile, and the islands don't need bored visitors tramping around and wondering why they've spent hundreds of dollars to sit on a rocky piece of lava under a searing equatorial sun to look at some squawking seabirds. However, if you are interested in natural history, visiting the Galápagos will be the highlight of your trip to Ecuador.

This chapter is essentially divided into two sections: Facts about the Galápagos introduces you to the archipelago and gives background information, while Facts for the Visitor gives you the practical details necessary to visit the Galápagos and describes the individual islands and visitor sites. The following chapter, an illustrated wildlife guide, helps you to identify and learn something about the islands' animals.

FACTS ABOUT THE GALÁPAGOS
History

The Galápagos Archipelago was discovered by accident in 1535, when Tomás de Berlanga, the Bishop of Panama, drifted off course while sailing from Panama to Peru. The bishop reported his discovery to King Charles V of Spain and included in his report a description of the giant *galápago* (tortoise) from which the islands received their name.

It is possible that the Indian inhabitants of South America were aware of the islands' existence before 1535, but we have no definite record of this. In 1953 Norwegian explorer Thor Heyerdahl discovered pottery shards that he thought may be pre-Columbian on the islands, but the evidence seems inconclusive.

For more than three centuries after their discovery, the Galápagos were used as a base by a succession of buccaneers, sealers and whalers. The islands provided sheltered anchorage, firewood, water and an abundance of fresh food in the form of the giant Galápagos tortoises, which were caught by the thousands and stacked, alive, in ships' holds. The tortoises could survive for a year or more and thus provided fresh meat for the sailors long after they had left the islands.

The first rough charts of the archipelago were made by buccaneers in the late 1600s, and scientific exploration began in the late 1700s. The Galápagos' most famous visitor was Charles Darwin, who arrived in 1835, exactly 300 years after the Bishop of Panama. Darwin stayed for five weeks, making notes and wildlife collections that provided important evidence for his theory of evolution, which he was just then beginning to develop.

Ecuador officially claimed the Galápagos archipelago in 1832. For roughly one century thereafter the islands were inhabited by a few settlers and were used as penal colonies, the last of which was closed in 1959.

Some islands were declared wildlife sanctuaries in 1934, and the archipelago officially became a national park in 1959. Organized tourism began in the late 1960s, and now an estimated 50,000 to 60,000 people visit the islands each year.

Geography

The Galápagos are an isolated group of volcanic islands that lie in the Pacific Ocean on the equator about 90° west of Greenwich. The nearest mainland is Ecuador, some 1000 km to the east, and Costa Rica, almost 1100 km to the northeast. The land mass of the archipelago covers 7882 sq km, of which well over half consists of Isla Isabela, the largest island in the archipelago and the 12th largest in the South Pacific. There are 13 major islands (from 14 to 4588 sq km), six small islands (from one to five sq km) and scores of islets, of which only some are named. The islands are spread over roughly 50,000 sq km of ocean. The highest point in the Galápagos is Volcán Wolf (1707 meters) on Isabela.

Most of the islands have two – and sometimes three – names. The earliest charts gave the islands both Spanish and English names, and the Ecuadorian government assigned official names in 1892. An island can thus have a Spanish, English and official name. The official names are used here in most cases; the few exceptions will be indicated.

Geology

The earliest of the islands visible today were formed roughly four to five million years ago by underwater volcanoes erupting and rising above the ocean's surface (the islands were never connected to the mainland). The Galápagos region is volcanically very active; over 50 eruptions have been recorded since their discovery in 1535. In 1991 the infrequently visited northern island of Marchena erupted, as did the westernmost large island of Fernandina in 1995. Thus the formation of the islands is an ongoing process; the archipelago is

relatively young compared to the age of the earth (which is about 1000 times older).

Geologists generally agree that two relatively new geological theories explain the islands' formation. The theory of plate tectonics holds that the earth's crust consists of several rigid plates that, over geological time, move relative to one another over the surface of the earth. The Galápagos lie on the northern edge of the Nazca Plate, close to its junction with the Cocos Plate. These two plates are spreading apart at a rate of about one km every 14,000 years, and the Galápagos Islands are slowly moving southeast. How fast is one km every 14,000 years? It's about the same rate at which your fingernails grow – pretty fast by plate-tectonic standards.

The hotspot theory states that deep within the earth (below the moving tectonic plates) are certain superheated areas that remain stationary. At frequent intervals (measured in geological time) the heat from these hotspots increases enough to melt the earth's crust and produce a volcanic eruption of sufficient magnitude to cause molten lava to rise above the ocean floor and, eventually, above the ocean surface.

The Galápagos are moving slowly to the southeast over a stationary hotspot, so one would expect the southeastern islands to have been formed first and the northwestern islands to have been formed most recently. This has proven to be the case. The most ancient rocks yet discovered on the islands are about 3¼ million years old and come from Isla Española in the southeast. In comparison, the oldest rocks on the western islands of Isla Fernandina and Isla Isabela are less than three-quarters of a million years old. The northwestern islands are still in the process of formation and contain active volcanoes, particularly on Isabela and Fernandina. In addition to the gradual southeast drift of the Nazca Plate, the northern drift of the Cocos Plate complicates the matter, so the islands do not get uniformly older from northwest to southeast.

Most of the Galápagos are surrounded by very deep ocean. Less than 20 km off the coasts of the western islands the ocean is

GALÁPAGOS

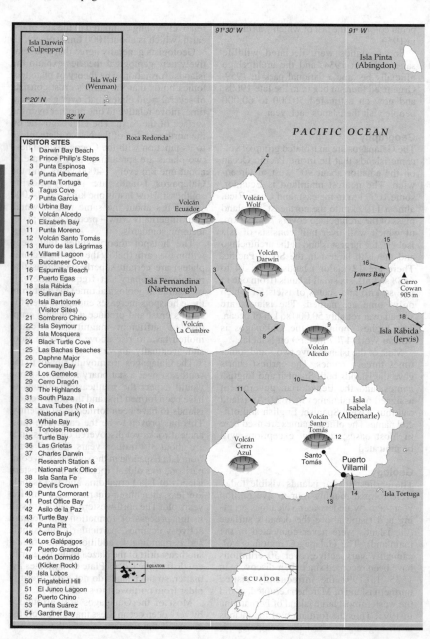

VISITOR SITES

1 Darwin Bay Beach
2 Prince Philip's Steps
3 Punta Espinosa
4 Punta Albemarle
5 Punta Tortuga
6 Tagus Cove
7 Punta García
8 Urbina Bay
9 Volcán Alcedo
10 Elizabeth Bay
11 Punta Moreno
12 Volcán Santo Tomás
13 Muro de las Lágrimas
14 Villamil Lagoon
15 Buccaneer Cove
16 Espumilla Beach
17 Puerto Egas
18 Isla Rábida
19 Sullivan Bay
20 Isla Bartolomé (Visitor Sites)
21 Sombrero Chino
22 Isla Seymour
23 Isla Mosquera
24 Black Turtle Cove
25 Las Bachas Beaches
26 Daphne Major
27 Conway Bay
28 Los Gemelos
29 Cerro Dragón
30 The Highlands
31 South Plaza
32 Lava Tubes (Not in National Park)
33 Whale Bay
34 Tortoise Reserve
35 Turtle Bay
36 Las Grietas
37 Charles Darwin Research Station & National Park Office
38 Isla Santa Fe
39 Devil's Crown
40 Punta Cormorant
41 Post Office Bay
42 Asilo de la Paz
43 Turtle Bay
44 Punta Pitt
45 Cerro Brujo
46 Los Galápagos
47 Puerto Grande
48 León Dormido (Kicker Rock)
49 Isla Lobos
50 Frigatebird Hill
51 El Junco Lagoon
52 Puerto Chino
53 Punta Suárez
54 Gardner Bay

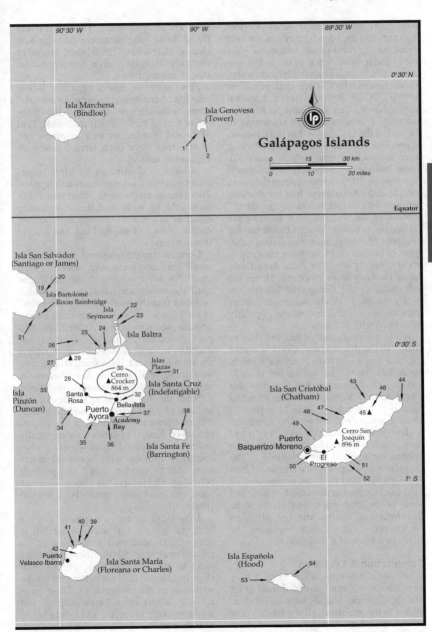

90° 30' W

90° W

89° 30' W

0° 30' N

Isla Marchena
(Bindloe)

Isla Genovesa
(Tower)

1

2

Galápagos Islands

0   15   30 km

0   10   20 miles

Equator

Isla San Salvador
(Santiago or James)

20

19

Isla Bartolomé
Rocas Bainbridge

21

25

24

22

23

Isla
Seymour

Isla Baltra

26

27

29

30

Cerro
Crocker
864 m

Islas
Plazas

31

28

32

Isla Santa Cruz
(Indefatigable)

Isla
Pinzón
(Duncan)

33

Santa
Rosa

Bellavista

38

Puerto
Ayora

37

34

Academy
Bay

35

36

Isla Santa Fe
(Barrington)

0° 30' S

Isla San Cristóbal
(Chatham)

43

46

44

48

47

45

49

Cerro San
Joaquín
896 m

Puerto
Baquerizo Moreno

El
Progreso

50

51

52

1° S

41

40

39

42

Puerto
Velasco Ibarra

Isla Santa María
(Floreana or Charles)

Isla Española
(Hood)

54

53

over 3000 meters deep. When visitors cruise around the islands, they can see only about the top third of the volcanoes – the rest is underwater. Some of the oldest volcanoes are, in fact, completely underwater. Recent research by Christie et al, published in 1992 in the British scientific journal *Nature*, shows that the Carnegie Ridge, a submerged mountain range stretching to the east of the Galápagos, has the remnants of previous volcanic islands, some of which were as much as nine million years old. These have been completely eroded away; they now lie 2000 meters beneath the ocean surface and stretch about half the distance between the Galápagos and the mainland.

Most of the volcanic rock forming the Galápagos is basalt. Molten basalt has the property of being more fluid than other types of volcanic rock, so when an eruption occurs, basalt tends to form lava flows rather than explosive eruptions. Hence the volcanoes of the Galápagos Islands are gently rounded 'shield volcanoes' rather than the ice-cream-cone shape popularly associated with volcanoes.

While not every visitor has the time or energy to climb a volcano, a visit to one of the lava flows is within everyone's reach. Several can be visited, but the one at Sullivan Bay on the east end of San Salvador (also known as Santiago or James Island) is especially rewarding. This lava flow is about a century old and remains uneroded.

Here you can see *pahoehoe*, or 'ropy,' lava, which is formed by the cooling of the molten surface and the wrinkling of the skin into ropy shapes by the continued flow of the molten lava beneath. Impressions of trees can be found in the solidified lava, and some of the first colonizing plants – the *Brachycereus* cactus and the *Mollugo* carpetweed – can be seen beginning the slow conversion of a lava field to soil.

Colonization & Evolution

When the Galápagos were formed they were barren volcanic islands, devoid of all life. Because the islands were never connected to the mainland, all the species now present must have somehow crossed about

1000 km of open ocean. Those that could fly or swim long distances had the best chance of reaching the islands, but other methods of colonization were possible, though more difficult.

Plant seeds or insect eggs and larvae may have been brought over in an animals' stomach contents or attached to the feathers or feet of birds. Small mammals, land birds and reptiles, as well as plants and insects may have been ferried across on vegetation rafts.

Wildlife is dominated by birds (especially seabirds), sea mammals and reptiles. There are no amphibians – their moist skin is unable to withstand the dehydrating effect of salt water – though there are, of course, plenty of tropical fish and marine invertebrates.

Compared to the mainland, there are few small land mammals and insects. Large predators never colonized the Galápagos until the recent arrival of people, which suggests that the well-known fearlessness of the islands' animals comes from having no such predators to fear. At least, not until pigs, goats, cats, donkeys etc were introduced by human colonists. Escaped domestic animals found little competition, and now these feral animals have become a major problem for the islands' inhabitants.

When the first migrating species arrived millions of years ago they found the islands different from the mainland in two important ways: First, the islands were physically different, and second, there were few other species to compete with. Some colonizers were able to survive, breed and produce offspring. Obviously, the young were the same species as their parents, but some had subtle differences.

A classic Galápagos example of this is a bird that produces a chick whose bill is very slightly different from those of its parents or siblings. In the different environment of the islands, some chicks with slightly different bills are better able to take advantage of the environment. These birds are said to have been 'better adapted' and are more likely to survive and raise a brood of their own.

These better-adapted survivors may pass on favorable genetic traits (in this case a slightly better adapted bill) to the genes of their offspring, and thus, over many generations, certain favorable traits are selected for and other less favorable traits were selected against. Eventually the difference between the original colonizers and their distant descendants is so great that the descendants can be considered a different species altogether. This is the essence of Darwin's theory of evolution by natural selection.

Because the earliest colonizers had little competition and a variety of different habitats to choose from, adaptive changes could occur in different ways to take advantage of different habitats or islands. Thus it wasn't only that a longer or broader or smaller bill would be better adapted – it could be that various types of bills could confer adaptive advantages to birds in different ecological niches. One ancestral species could therefore give rise to several modern species in the evolutionary process called adaptive radiation. This explains the presence in the Galápagos of 13 similar species of finches, called Darwin's finches in honor of the founder of evolutionary theory.

Charles Darwin, during his visit in 1835, noted the differences in bills in these 13 species of finches; he also noted similar differences in other groups of animals. These observations, combined with many others, lead to the publication, in 1859, of Darwin's *On the Origin of Species*, which is one of the most influential books ever published and remains the mainstay of modern biological thought.

These evolutionary processes take thousands or millions of generations – species don't normally appear over a single generation (though, as with everything, there are exceptions). For many years, evolutionary biologists were puzzled over how so many unique species could have evolved in the Galápagos over the relatively short period of about four million years (the age of the oldest islands). The answer has recently been provided by the geologists and oceanographers who found nine-million-year-old remnants of islands under the ocean to the east of the existing islands. Presumably, the ancestors of the present wildlife once lived on these lost islands, and therefore had at least nine million years to evolve – a figure that evolutionary biologists find acceptable.

Conservation Problems

As early as 1934, the Ecuadorian government set aside some of the islands as wildlife sanctuaries, but it was not until 1959 that the Galápagos was declared a national park. The construction of the Charles Darwin Research Station on Isla Santa Cruz began soon after, and the station began operating in 1964 as an international NGO (nongovernment organization). The Galápagos National Park Service began operating in 1968 and is the key institution of the Ecuadorian government responsible for the park. The National Park Service and the Charles Darwin Research Station work together to manage the islands. In 1986 the Ecuadorian government granted further protection to the islands by creating the Galápagos Marine Resources Reserve.

The national park covers approximately 97% of the islands' 7882-sq-km land mass – the rest is taken up by urban areas and farms that existed prior to the creation of the park. The Marine Resources Reserve covers the 50,000 sq km of ocean and seabed within which the islands are located, plus a further 20,000-sq-km buffer zone. The function of the park and reserve is to protect and conserve the islands and surrounding ocean, and to encourage educational and scientific research.

Few tourists had visited the islands before the station opened, but by the mid-1960s organized tourism began with a little over 1000 visitors a year. This figure soon increased dramatically. In 1970 an estimated 4500 tourists arrived, and by 1971 there were six small boats and one large cruise ship operating in the islands. In less than two decades, the number of visitors had increased tenfold; in the 1990s an estimated 60,000 visit annually. Roughly half of the visitors are mainland Ecuadorians.

GALÁPAGOS

To cope with the increased demands of tourism, a second airport with regular flights to the mainland opened in the mid-1980s and a third is being discussed. The number of hotels in Puerto Ayora and Puerto Baquerizo Moreno doubled from 15 in 1981 to about 30 a decade later. There are now two large cruise ships (carrying 96 passengers each) and several dozen smaller boats (carrying from four to 40 passengers). The resident population of the islands is growing at about 10% annually to provide labor for the booming tourism industry.

While this is good for the economy of Ecuador, inevitable problems have resulted. Among the more serious are entrepreneurial proposals of building luxurious high-rise hotels and introducing as many more cruise ships into the islands as possible. Fortunately, the Ecuadorian government has seen the sense of preventing these projects, at least until a comprehensive and enlightened tourism policy is developed.

The wildlife of the Galápagos is, literally, unique. The islands have been called 'a laboratory of evolution' and are of immense importance to our understanding of the natural world. The incredible assemblage of wildlife is threatened not only by tourism, but also by the increased colonization that accompanies the booming tourist industry.

The increasing number of tourists has led to trail erosion and litter, and to feeding and frightening the animals. Most tourists are concerned enough to avoid disturbing the wildlife or spoiling the scenery, but with tens of thousands of visitors there is inevitable degradation. Large resort hotels would compound the problem by attracting a greater proportion of tourists who care less for the wildlife than for the 'exotic' vacation site afforded by the islands. Clearly, it is important that tourism is sensibly regulated; the number of visitors is not the real issue – education and environmental awareness is. One thoughtless or uncaring visitor can cause more damage than one hundred people who are aware of their potential impact on the fragile resources and work to minimize that impact.

Earlier colonization created problems with the introduction of domestic species, such as goats, pigs and rats, which can easily cause the extinction of an island species in a matter of years. For example, three goats were introduced to Isla Pinta by colonists as a source of food in the late 1950s; by 1973 the goat population had increased to 15,000 animals who were destroying the vegetation of the island. A determined hunting program was thought to have eradicated the feral goats in 1990, but in 1995 goats were again seen on Pinta and another hunting program is currently underway. It is not clear whether the 1995 goats were a new introduction or remnants of the 1990 campaign. As one of the smaller islands, Pinta's problems are easier to contain; eradication programs on larger islands like Santiago are more difficult. Santiago is estimated to have about 50,000 goats, roughly half the number of a decade ago. In addition, about 1000 wild pigs (down from 5000 in the 1980s) cause serious problems by eating bird and reptile eggs. These numbers can be controlled but probably not eliminated.

The introduction of domestic animals into the islands is only one of various difficulties the archipelago faces. One of the most recent animal immigrants has been the wasp, which arrived on Isla Floreana in the late 1980s, probably with some food items brought in by visitors or residents. Now, the wasps are all over the island and control is difficult, especially during the warm months of January to June.

Some recently arrived islanders see the national park as a barrier to making a living; their arson fires burned about 10,000 hectares on Isla Isabela in 1994.

Overfishing has been a major problem in recent years. One of the most notorious examples was the taking of a reported seven million sea cucumbers in two months during 1994, after the Ecuadorian government authorized a quota of 550,000. Although sea cucumber fishing became illegal in December 1994, the Charles Darwin Foundation reports that close to one million sea cucumbers per month continued to be exported in 1995, chiefly for their purported aphrodisiac properties. Other illegal fishing activities include the taking of shark fins for shark-fin soup, the killing of sea lions to be used as bait and the overhunting of lobsters (whose populations have dropped far below normal numbers) to feed tourists and locals.

Fishermen hoping to make money fast have reacted in a hostile and violent manner to the government ban on fishing sea cucumbers and other animals. In January and September of 1995, armed fishermen, urged on by two unscrupulous local government officials, occupied the Charles Darwin Research Station and threatened to kill tortoises, beat up station personnel and burn portions of the park. Fortunately, these very tense situations were defused with help from the Ecuadorian military and pressure from the US embassy (who sent several people to the islands). During the occupations, the administrative and research activities of the station were severely disrupted, but the personnel living on the station managed to prevent the loss of any life, animal or human.

Conservation for the Future

There are various solutions to the problems facing the Galápagos Islands. One extreme view is to prohibit all colonization and tourism – an option that appeals to few. Many colonists act responsibly and oppose actively the disruptive and dangerous tactics of the protesting fishermen. The tourist industry is important for Ecuador's economy, and the best solution will be an enlightened mixture of environmental education for both residents and visitors, and a program of responsible tourism. Unfortunately, the number of park rangers fell from 75 to 46 during the 1980s and essential equipment, such as patrol boats, is lacking.

The situation is slowly improving, and optimism endures for the survival of the islands and their wildlife. One result of the violent protests of 1995 has been the forging of an even stronger partnership between the National Park Service and the Charles Darwin Research Station. More

park rangers are being trained and a newly arrived vessel, the 101-foot-long MV *Guadalupe River*, has been converted into a 20-knot patrol boat with a crew of eight and an armed Ecuadorian military escort. Since late 1995 the boat has gone on several successful patrols and has also served as a floating school for Ecuadorian students and teachers.

Management of tourism is an important part of the function of the park service. Various successful programs have been implemented to minimize the impact of tourism on the national park while increasing the tourists' enjoyment and learning during their visits. Most visitors understand that these regulations protect the islands as a unique living laboratory.

Camping (for tourists) is not allowed on the islands, except on Volcán Alcedo by permit. All tour boats, by law, must be accompanied by certified naturalist guides that have been trained by the National Park Service. On the better boats, these are 'Naturalist III Guides' – bilingual, university-educated biologists with a very real interest in preserving and explaining the wildlife. On the cheapest boats, 'Naturalist II Guides' are provided who speak little English and know relatively little about the wildlife but will, at least in principle, keep visitors from littering or molesting the wildlife and be able to identify what is seen. Visits to the islands are restricted to the official visitor sites in order to protect the islands as a unique, living laboratory.

There are basically two types of tours around the islands: One goes from island to island, with visitors sleeping aboard a boat and occasionally in a hotel. The other is hotel-based and goes out to visitor sites on day trips. The first system staggers excursions over different times of day, allowing dawn and dusk visits, and more outlying islands can be reached. The day trips, on the other hand, tend to cram large numbers of tourists onto a few nearby destinations around the middle of the day. These trips are the ones that tend to cause the greatest amount of erosion, litter and strain on the wildlife.

GALÁPAGOS

Charles Darwin Foundation

Most tourists have the opportunity to visit the Charles Darwin Research Station and are invited and encouraged to make donations to that worthwhile organization's efforts to carry out research in the islands and advise government and tourist agencies on how to cause minimum impact on the islands. (None of the US$80 park fee goes to the research station.)

Outside of the islands, the research station is supported by contributions to the Charles Darwin Foundation. Donors contributing US$25 or more each year receive the English-language journal *Noticias de Galápagos* twice a year and the *Galápagos Bulletin* three times a year, both published by the Charles Darwin Foundation. These journals are great for keeping up with the latest happenings on the islands, including information about the conservation issues outlined above, as well as interesting recent research and unusual wildlife observations. I would like every visitor to the islands to support this organization.

Donations are tax deductible for US citizens; contact the Charles Darwin Foundation at 100 N Washington St, Suite 311, Falls Church, VA 22046, USA.

European contributors can send donations marked 'for the Galápagos' to the following organizations. Donations may be tax deductible, depending on local laws.

Germany
Zoologische Gesellschaft
Frankfurt Von 1858
Alfred-Brehm Platz 16 D-6000,
Frankfurt, Main 1, Germany

Account: Hilfe Fuer die Bedrohte Tierwelt
1 Postgiroamt Frankfurt/Main,
Postgirokonto Nr 47, BLZ 500 100 60
2 Schweizerische Kreditanstalt
(Deutschland) AG, Frankfurt/Main Nr
35556.9, BLZ 501 207 17

Holland
Vrienden van de Galápagos Eilanden
ABN/AMRO Bank Driebergen
Account: 44.75.03.332

Luxembourg
Foundation The Galápagos
Darwin Trust ASBL
Banque Internationale à Luxembourg
Account: 1-100/9071
2, Boulevard Royal, L-2953

Switzerland
Verein Freunde der Galápagos
Inseln Schweiz Anwaltskanzlei
Heern Marcello Weber
Gartenstracht 2, CH-6300 ZUG

UK
Galápagos Conservation Trust
Registered Charity No 1043470
PO Box 50, Shaftesbury,
Dorset SP7 8SB

All foreign visitors must pay a US$80 park entrance fee upon arrival. This goes to the Ecuadorian government and is used partly to train guides and rangers to protect the Galápagos and other parks on the Ecuadorian mainland. Upon paying the entrance fee, you are given a full set of park rules and other informative leaflets. The rules are for the protection of the wildlife and environment, and are mostly a matter of courtesy and common sense. Don't feed or handle the animals; don't litter; don't remove any natural object, whether living or dead; do not bring pets; do not buy objects made of sea lion teeth, black coral, tortoise or turtle shells, or other artifacts made from plants and animals; show a conservationist attitude. You are not allowed to enter the visitor sites after dark or without a qualified guide, and a guide will accompany every boat. On all shore trips, the guide will be there to answer your questions and show you the best sites, and also to ensure that you stay on the trails and don't molest the animals.

With approximately 60,000 annual visitors, it is essential to have a system of protection for the islands. The above rules are sensible and necessary, and do not infringe on your enjoyment of the Galápagos. The wildlife is so prolific that you'll see just as much on the trail as anywhere else, and staying on the trails helps ensure that other areas are properly protected.

Population & People
Five of the islands are inhabited; the total population is fast approaching 20,000 people and is growing annually. The inhabitants make a living mainly from tourism, fishing and farming. About half the residents live in Puerto Ayora.

In the early 1980s the population was much less than half of what it is today, and the islands are now reaching their saturation point if their national park status is to remain unchanged. Serious discussion has begun of limiting migration to the islands from the mainland.

FACTS FOR THE VISITOR
Orientation
The most important island (from the travelers' point of view) is Isla Santa Cruz in the middle of the archipelago. On the south side of this island is Puerto Ayora, the largest town in the Galápagos and the place from which most tours are based. North of Santa Cruz, separated by a narrow strait, is Isla Baltra, with the islands' major airport. A public bus and a ferry connect the Isla Baltra airport with Puerto Ayora (see Getting Around).

Isla San Cristóbal, the easternmost island, has the provincial capital, Puerto Baquerizo Moreno, a few hotels and an airport. Despite its political status, relatively few tours begin from here, save for some preorganized ones. Most travelers fly into Baltra.

The other inhabited islands are Isla Isabela, with the small port of Puerto Villamil, and Isla Santa María (Floreana), with Puerto Velasco Ibarra – both have places to stay. Inter-island transportation is by infrequent public ferries or private boat (see Getting Around).

The remaining islands are not inhabited by people but are visited on tours.

Further descriptions are given under Visitor Sites, below.

When to Go
The Galápagos are a year-round travel destination, but peak tourist periods are June to August, December to January and around Easter. The wildlife is always there, and birds of different species breed at different times, so you can see courting behavior and young in their nests during any month.

The big exception is the waved albatross. These birds leave en masse in mid-December and spend until late March at sea – avoid that period if seeing the albatrosses is important to you.

The islands have two seasons: The rainy season lasts from January to about June, and the dry season from June to December. The rainy season has many warm, sunny periods interspersed by rain showers and an occasional heavy downpour – it is generally pleasant. February is the hottest month; March and April are milder.

Water temperatures are a balmy 23°C or 24°C and are great for snorkeling. The water is usually fairly calm. Temperatures drop to around 18°C to 20°C between May and July.

The dry season is generally cooler and often misty, and a fog called the *garúa* sometimes envelopes the islands. A warm sweater or jacket is needed at night. The ocean tends to become choppy in July and is often at its roughest from August to October.

Droughts or heavy rains can occur at unpredictable and irregular intervals, often associated with the El Niño climatic phenomenon. Rainfall can vary tremendously between the wettest and driest years – one report claims that the wettest year on record had 100 times as much rain as the driest.

What to Bring
You can purchase most things in Puerto Ayora, but at a price. Little or nothing is available aboard the boats. You should bring all the film, suntan lotion, insect repellent, books and medical supplies

Total Eclipse of the Sun

Of the nine planets and 60 moons in our solar system, it is only from the planet Earth that an exact alignment of sun, moon and planet allows a total eclipse of the sun to be seen. The phenomenon of seeing the sun disappear in the middle of the day is both amazing and disconcerting. Animals stop whatever they are doing and become very quiet as the moon's shadow darkens the Earth. People travel great distances to view a total eclipse, and some folks don't want to miss a single one. They occur an average of a little less than once per year.

Three total solar eclipses remain to be seen this century. One will be visible on February 26, 1998, and will sweep across the central Pacific Ocean, over the Galápagos Islands and the north coast of South America, and on out into the mid-Atlantic. The path of totality in the Galápagos Islands will include the northernmost part of Isla Isabela (including Volcán Wolf), Isla Pinta and some isolated rocky islets.

Many people have already made reservations to be on the islands on February 26, 1998, and remaining tour spaces are filling up fast. If you want to see the eclipse from the islands, make a reservation immediately. Otherwise, don't even think about going there in late February 1998. ■

(including motion sickness medication) that you need. Sunglasses and a shade hat are also recommended.

If you plan on doing a lot of snorkeling – and I recommend that you do (see Activities later in this chapter) – I strongly suggest bringing your own snorkel and mask. Likewise, avid birders should bring binoculars. Shipboard life is casual, so dress accordingly. Be prepared to get wet during landings – shorts are a good idea. Trails can be very rocky and the lava is extremely rough; sturdy shoes that can get wet are important (old tennis shoes are ideal). Bring a spare pair of footwear to keep dry and wear on the boat.

Books & Maps

Dozens of excellent books have been published about the fascinating wildlife of these islands. They are listed in the Books appendix at the end of the book.

A map of the Galápagos at 1:500,000 scale is available from IGM in Ecuador. A better map at the same scale, full of useful information about wildlife, history and tourism, is *Galapagos Islands Map 312*, jointly published in 1993 by Bradt Publications, UK, and ITMB, Canada. A very expensive 1:100,000 map is reportedly available from INGALA (Instituto Nacional Galápagos), Espejo 935, Quito, that costs

about US$25 per sheet – it is probably of little use to anyone other than researchers. Other maps are available locally.

Time

The Galápagos Islands are one hour behind the Ecuadorian mainland.

VISITOR SITES

To protect the islands from haphazard tourism, the national park service allows access to over 50 visitor sites, in addition to the towns and public areas. These visitor sites are found in places where the most interesting features and most varied wildlife can be seen; other areas are off limits to tourism. Almost all of the visitor sites are reached by boat, and normally landings are made in a *panga* (small dinghy), which every boat carries for shore trips (the larger boats carry several).

Most landing sites are sandy or rocky beaches – there are few docks. Landings are called 'wet' or 'dry'. During a wet landing you will have to wade ashore in shallow water, sometimes up to your knees (occasionally deeper if you don't pay attention to your guide and what the waves are doing). Dry landings are made onto rocky outcrops or jetties – you probably won't get wet unless a rogue wave comes up and splashes you, or you slip on some seaweed and fall into the ocean (I've seen it happen). Boat captains will not take groups to places other than designated visitor sites. Occasionally, a new site is added to the list.

Here follows a brief description of all the islands and their visitor sites (which are highlighted in boldface). Further information about the towns is given later. I begin with the central island of Santa Cruz, which is the most often visited, and radiate out from there. More detailed descriptions and maps of some of the visitor sites can be found in the *Guide to the Visitor Sites of Galápagos National Park* by Alan & Tui Moore (Galápagos National Park Service, 1980, now out of print). This book is not easy to find outside of the Galápagos. A more recent book is *Galápagos, Field Observations* by Mauricio García and Raúl Gavela (Quito, 1994), which is available in Quito and the islands and has useful checklists, sketch maps, and brief descriptions of 19 of the most commonly visited sites. The authors are both highly qualified naturalist guides and the book is approved by the Galápagos National Park Service.

Your trip to the Galápagos will enable you to visit some of the following.

Isla Santa Cruz

This island is rarely referred to by its lesser known English name of Indefatigable; most people call it Santa Cruz. With an area of 986 sq km, it is the second largest island in the archipelago. A road crosses Santa Cruz from north to south and gives the visitor the easiest opportunity of seeing some of the highland interior of an island. The highest point is Cerro Crocker, at 864 meters.

This island has the highest population and the greatest number of tourist facilities. The main town is Puerto Ayora on the south coast, and most visitors either stay here while arranging a boat, or anchor in the town's famous harbor, Academy Bay, sometime during their cruise. In addition to the tourist facilities, there are about 10 national park visitor sites and one privately owned visitor site on Santa Cruz. More park visitor sites are planned.

About a 20-minute walk by road northeast of Puerto Ayora, the **Charles Darwin Research Station** can also be reached by dry landing from Academy Bay. It contains a national park information center; an informative museum in the Van Straelen Exhibition Center (where slide shows with English, Spanish, German and French narration are screened several times a day); a baby tortoise house with incubators, where you can see hatchlings and young tortoises; and a walk-in adult tortoise enclosure, where you can meet these Galápagos giants face to face. The tiny tortoises in the baby tortoise house are repatriated to their home islands when they weigh about 1.5 kg (when they are about four years old) – some 2000 have been repatriated so far. In the adult enclosures, you can get close enough to touch the tortoises, but please refrain from doing so. Handling the tortoises is not allowed, as they suffer from being petted by dozens of people each day. An elevated wooden boardwalk goes through the most interesting areas.

Several of the 11 remaining subspecies of tortoise can be seen here. Lonesome George, the only surviving member of the Isla Pinta subspecies, is also here and can be viewed from the boardwalk. There is apparently a US$10,000 reward for finding a Pinta female, but before you go rushing off to try and find one, remember that Isla Pinta is off-limits to visitors (except scientists and researchers). Although the chances of finding a Pinta female to breed with George are remote, attempts are being made to allow him to mate with a female from a closely related subspecies from Volcán Wolf. So far, he hasn't shown much interest, but things move slowly in the tortoise world and something may happen any decade now.

Other attractions include paths through arid-zone vegetation such as prickly pear and other cacti, salt bush, and mangroves. A variety of land birds, including Darwin's finches, can be seen. T-shirts and other souvenirs are sold to support the research station.

A three-km trail takes you to **Turtle Bay**, southwest of Puerto Ayora, where you'll find a very fine white-sand beach and a spit of land giving protected swimming (there are strong currents on the exposed side of the spit). There are sharks, marine iguanas and a variety of water birds, including pelicans and the occasional flamingo. There are also mangroves.

This is one of the few visitor sites where you can go without a guide, although there is no drinking water or other facilities. To get there, find the trail that goes from just before the EMETEL office (see Puerto Ayora map) and hike out for about half an hour.

Several sites of interest in the highlands of Santa Cruz can be reached from the trans-island road. Access to some sites is through colonized areas, so respect private property. From the village of Bellavista, seven km north of Puerto Ayora by road, one can turn either west on the main road continuing to Isla Baltra or east on a road leading in about two km to the **lava tubes**. These underground tunnels are over a kilometer in length and were formed by the solidifying of the outside skin of a molten lava flow. When the lava flow ceased, the molten lava inside the flow kept going, emptying out of the solidified skin and thus leaving tunnels. As they are on private property and are not administered by the national park authorities, they can therefore be visited without an official guide. The owners of the land provide information, guides and flashlights (bring your own flashlight to be sure) for an entrance fee of about US$2. Tours to the lava tubes are offered in Puerto Ayora.

North of Bellavista is the national park land known as **the highlands**. A footpath from Bellavista leads towards Cerro Crocker and other hills and extinct volcanoes. This is a good chance to see the vegetation of the Scalesia, Miconia and fern-sedge zones, and to look for the vermilion flycatcher or the elusive Galápagos rail and paint-billed crake. It is about five km from Bellavista to the crescent-shaped hill of Media Luna, and three km further to the base of Cerro Crocker. Because this is national park land, a guide is required.

A part of the highlands that can be visited from the road are the twin craters called **Los Gemelos**. These are actually sink holes rather than volcanic craters and they are surrounded by Scalesia forest. Vermilion flycatchers are often seen here, and short-eared owls on occasion. Los Gemelos are reached by taking the road to the village of Santa Rosa, about 12 km west of Bellavista, and continuing about two km beyond Santa Rosa on the trans-island road. Although the craters lie only 25 meters and 125 meters on either side of the road, they are hidden by vegetation, so ask your driver to stop at the short trailhead.

Near Santa Rosa there is a **tortoise reserve** where you can observe giant tortoises in the wild. The reserve is also a good place to look for short-eared owls, Darwin's finches, yellow warblers, Galápagos rails and paint-billed crakes (these last two are difficult to see in the long grass). A trail from Santa Rosa leads through private property to park land about three km away. The trail is downhill and often quite muddy. Horses can be hired in Santa Rosa – ask at the store/bar on the main road for directions to the outfitter's house. The trail forks at the park boundary, with the right fork going up to the small hill

Giant tortoises *(Geochelone elephantopus)* are the only native grazers of the Galápagos' reptiles.

of Cerro Chato (three more km) and the left fork going to La Caseta (two km). The trails can be hard to follow, and you should carry drinking water. The reserve is part of the national park and a guide is required. In 1991 a tourist entered the reserve without a guide, got hopelessly lost and died of thirst. Since then another tourist almost suffered a similar fate but was rescued after nine days.

Next to the reserve is a private ranch owned by the Devine family. This place often has dozens of giant tortoises on it and you can wander around at will and take photos for a US$2 fee. The entrance is beyond Santa Rosa off the main road – ask locals for directions. Stay on the main tracks to avoid getting lost. Remember to close any gates that you go through. They have a café selling cold drinks and hot tea, which is welcome if the highland *garúa* (mist) has soaked you.

The remaining Santa Cruz visitor sites are reached by boat and with guides. On the west coast are **Whale Bay** and **Conway Bay**, and on the north coast are **Black Turtle Cove** (Caleta Tortuga Negra) and **Las Bachas beaches**. Between these two areas is the relatively new visitor site of **Cerro Dragón**. Conway Bay has a 1½-km trail passing a lagoon with flamingos; Whale Bay is less often visited. North of Conway Bay, Cerro Dragón has two small lagoons that may have flamingos and a 1.75-km trail, through a forest of palo santo trees and opuntia cacti, to a small hill with good views. There are some large, repatriated land iguanas here.

There is no landing site in Black Turtle Cove, which is normally visited by panga ride. The cove has many little inlets and is surrounded by mangroves, where you can see lava herons and pelicans. The main attraction is in the water: Marine turtles are sometimes seen mating, schools of golden mustard rays are often present and white-tipped sharks may be seen basking in the shallows. It makes a very pleasant change to visit a marine site in a panga instead of walking. This site is occasionally visited by day boats from Puerto Ayora. The nearby

Las Bachas beach, though it is popular for sunbathing and swimming, is often deserted.

Islas Plazas

These two small islands are just off the east coast of Santa Cruz and can be visited by day trip from Puerto Ayora. Therefore visitors on a cruise would do well to visit in the early morning or late afternoon to avoid the day groups. The heavy volume of visitors has led to some trail erosion – please be extra careful to stay on the path and not disturb the wildlife.

The two islands were formed by uplift due to faulting. Boats anchor between them, and visitors can land on **South Plaza** (the larger of the islands), which is only about 13 hectares in area. A dry landing on a jetty brings you to an opuntia cactus forest where there are many land iguanas. A one-km trail circuit leads visitors through sea lion colonies and along a cliff-top walk where swallow-tailed gulls and other species nest. The 25-meter-high cliffs are a superb vantage point to watch various seabirds, such as red-billed tropic-birds, frigatebirds, pelicans and Audubon's shearwaters. Snorkeling with the sea lions is a possibility and out to sea you may glimpse a manta ray 'flying.' Cactus forest, land iguanas, sea lions, seabirds galore – no wonder this is a favorite wildlife-watching site.

Isla Baltra

Most visitors to the Galápagos arrive by air to the Isla Baltra airport. Baltra is a fairly small island (27 sq km) off the north coast of Santa Cruz. There are no visitor sites or accommodations here, but both public and private transport from the airport to Puerto Ayora (the biggest town) are available. People on a prearranged tour are often met at the airport and taken to their boats a few minutes' drive away – a host of pelicans and noddies will greet you as you arrive at the harbor and you can begin your wildlife watching within minutes of leaving the airport. Public transport is described under Puerto Ayora.

GALÁPAGOS

Isla Seymour

Separated from Baltra by a channel, Isla Seymour is a 1.9-sq-km uplifted island with a dry landing. There is a circular trail (about 2.5 km) leading through some of the largest and most active seabird breeding colonies in the islands. Magnificent frigatebirds and blue-footed boobies are the main attractions. Whatever time of year you come, there is always some kind of courtship, mating, nesting or chick rearing to observe. You can get close to the nests, as there is always at least one pair of boobies that chooses the middle of the trail as the best place to build their nest.

Swallow-tailed gulls also nest here, and other birds are often seen. Sea lions and marine iguanas are common, and occasional fur seals and lava lizards are seen as well. I saw a Galápagos snake here on a recent visit. This is a small island but is well worth visiting for the wildlife.

Isla Mosquera

This tiny sandy island (about 120 meters wide by 600 meters long) lies in the channel between Baltra and Seymour. There is no trail, but visitors can land on the sandy beach to see the sea lion colony. Swimming and snorkeling with the sea lions is a popular activity.

Islas Daphne

These two islands of obviously volcanic origin are roughly 10 km west of Seymour. Daphne Minor is the one that is very eroded, while **Daphne Major** retains most of its typically volcanic shape, which is called a tuff cone. A short but steep trail leads to the 120-meter-high summit of this tiny island.

There are two small craters at the top of the cone, which contain hundreds of blue-footed booby nests. Masked boobies nest on the crater rims, and a few red-billed tropicbirds nest in rocky crevices in the steep sides of the islands.

The island is difficult to visit because of the acrobatic landing – visitors have to jump from a moving panga onto a vertical cliff and scramble their way up the rocks.

The steep slopes are fragile and susceptible to erosion, which has lead the national park authorities to limit visits to the island. Either you have to be lucky or you'll have arrange your visit well in advance.

Isla Santa Fe

This 24-sq-km island, about 20 km southeast of Santa Cruz, is a popular destination for day trips. Its infrequently used English name is Barrington. There is a good anchorage in an attractive bay on the northeast coast and a wet landing gives the visitor a choice of two trails. A 300-meter trail takes you to one of the tallest stands of opuntia cactus in the islands. Some of the cacti here are over 10 meters high. A somewhat more strenuous 1½-km rough trail goes into the highlands, where the Santa Fe land iguana may be seen, if you are lucky. This species of iguana is found nowhere else in the world. The endemic rice rat is sometimes seen under bushes by the coast – I saw several on a recent visit. Other attractions include a sea lion colony, excellent snorkeling, marine iguanas and, of course, birds.

Isla San Cristóbal

Also known as Chatham, this island of 558 sq km is the fifth largest in the archipelago and has the second largest population. The provincial capital of Puerto Baquerizo Moreno is found on the southwest point. Despite being the capital, there was little tourist activity here until the recent introduction of regular flights from the mainland, the commencement of which has resulted in an increase in boats and hotels. Nevertheless, most people still use Puerto Ayora as a base.

There are several visitor sites on or near San Cristóbal, but they are not frequently visited by boats from Santa Cruz. The Chatham mockingbird, a species found nowhere else, is common throughout the island.

Frigatebird Hill (*Cerro de las Tijeretas*) is about 1½ km southeast of Puerto Baquerizo Moreno and can be reached via foot trail without a guide. From the hill there is a view of a bay below and the town behind. Both species of frigatebirds have nested here, but pressure from the nearby town appears to be driving them away.

A road leads from the capital to the village of El Progreso, about eight km to the east and at the base of the 896-meter-high Cerro San Joaquín, the highest point on San Cristóbal (buses go here several times a day from Puerto Baquerizo Moreno). Rent a jeep or walk east along a dirt road about 10 km farther to **El Junco Lagoon**, a freshwater lake at about 700 meters above sea level and one of the few permanent freshwater bodies in the Galápagos. Here you can see white-cheeked pintails and common gallinules, and observe the typical highland Miconia vegetation and endemic tree ferns. The weather is often misty or rainy – one reader writes that there was nothing to see but drizzling rain.

Smaller than its name suggests, **Puerto Grande** is also known as Bahía Stephens or Caleta Sappho, and is a well protected little cove on San Cristóbal's northwestern coast. There is a good, sandy beach suitable for swimming, where the island's fishermen sometimes beach their boats in order to work on the hulls. Various seabirds can be seen, but the site is not known for any special colonies.

About an hour northeast of Puerto Baquerizo Moreno by boat is the tiny, rocky **Isla Lobos**, the main sea lion and blue-footed booby colony for visitors to San Cristóbal. There is a 300-meter-long trail where lava lizards are often seen. Both the boat crossing and the trail tend to be rough, and there are better wildlife colonies elsewhere.

About a two-hour boatride northeast of Puerto Baquerizo Moreno, is another little rocky island that, because of a fanciful resemblance to a sleeping lion, is named **León Dormido**. The English name is Kicker Rock. The island is a sheer-walled tuff cone that has been eroded in half; smaller boats can sail between the two rocks. Because the sheer walls provide no place to land, this site can only be seen from a passing boat.

At the north end of the island is **Los Galápagos**, one of the newest areas to have been opened to visitors. Here, you can often see the giant Galápagos tortoises in the wild, though it takes some effort to get to the highland area where they live. One way to get there is to land in a bay at the north end of the island and hike up – it takes about two hours to reach the tortoise area by the trail. I have heard reports that there were no tortoises to be seen; however, I saw about three dozen animals on my last visit. Good luck!

The road from Puerto Baquerizo Moreno through El Progreso and on to El Junco Lagoon is slowly being pushed northeast. It may be possible to get to the Galápagos tortoise area by taking this road to the end and hiking in – ask in town.

The northeasternmost point of the island is **Punta Pitt**, another new visitor site. The volcanic tuff formations are of interest to geologists (and attractive in their own right), but the unique feature of this site is that it is the only one on which you can see all three Galápagos booby species nesting. The walk is a little strenuous, but it is rewarding.

The newest visitor sites on this island include **Cerro Brujo**, near the coast, and **Turtle Bay**; both are at the northeast end and can be visited in association with Punta Pitt and Los Galápagos. Flamingos and turtles are among the attractions. Also new is **Puerto Chino**, on the south side, which I have yet to visit.

Isla Española

This island, often called by its English name of Hood, is the most southerly in the archipelago. It is a medium-sized island of 61 sq km, and there are two visitor sites. Because Española is somewhat outlying (about 90 km southeast of Santa Cruz), reaching it requires a fairly long sea passage; captains of some of the smallest boats may be reluctant to go this far. The better boats will often do the long crossing as an overnight passage. The island is well worth visiting from late March to December because it has the only colony of the waved albatross, one of the Galápagos' most spectacular seabirds.

The best visitor site on Española is **Punta Suárez**, at the western end of the island; a wet landing is necessary. A trail of about two km in length takes visitors through masked and blue-footed booby colonies and past a beach full of marine iguanas before reaching the main attraction, the waved albatross colony.

Just beyond the colony is a blow hole through which the waves force water to spout about 20 meters into the air. If you sit on top of the cliffs between the waved albatrosses and the blow hole, you can watch seabirds performing their aerial ballet (and their less elegant attempts to land and take off).

Other birds to look out for are the Hood mockingbird, found nowhere else; swallow-tailed gulls; red-billed tropicbirds and oystercatchers. The large cactus finch can also be seen and is found on few other islands. This is one of my favorite visitor sites in the Galápagos.

The beautiful white-sand beach of **Gardner Bay**, at the east end of Española, is reached with a wet landing and there is good swimming and a sea lion colony. An island a short distance offshore provides good snorkeling – there's one rock that often has white-tipped reef sharks basking under it.

Isla Santa María

Officially known as Santa María but more often called Floreana or Charles, this is the sixth largest of the islands at 173 sq km.

From the village of Puerto Velasco Ibarra a road runs inland for a few km to an area where you can see the endemic medium tree finch (this finch exists only on Floreana). Early settlers once lived in the nearby caves. This area, called **Asilo de la Paz**, is an official visitor site.

It is an all-day hike up there and back – I went with local biologist/guide Felipe Cruz, who rented the town's dumptruck for the trip. There are no taxis.

There are three visitor sites on the north coast of Floreana. **Post Office Bay** used to have a barrel where whalers left mail. Any captain of a boat that was heading to where

---

Chronicles of Floreana

This island has had an interesting history. The first resident of the Galápagos was Patrick Watkins, an Irishman who was marooned on Floreana in 1807 and spent two years living there, growing vegetables and trading his produce for rum from passing boats. The story goes that he managed to remain drunk for most of his stay, then stole a ship's boat and set out for Guayaquil accompanied by five slaves. No one knows what happened to the slaves – only Watkins reached the mainland.

After Watkins' departure, the island was turned into an Ecuadorian penal colony for some years. In the 1930s three groups of German settlers arrived on Floreana, and strange stories have been told about them ever since.

The most colorful of the settlers was a baroness who arrived with three lovers. Another settler, Dr Friedrich Ritter, an eccentric who had all of his teeth removed before arriving so as to avoid having dental problems, was accompanied by his mistress. The third group was a young couple from Cologne, the Wittmers.

Despite their common nationality there was a great deal of friction among the groups, and mysteriously, one by one, the settlers died. The baroness and one of her lovers simply disappeared, while another lover died in a boating accident. The vegetarian Dr Ritter died of food poisoning after eating chicken. The only ones to survive were the Wittmers.

Margaret Wittmer, one of the original settlers, is now in her 90s and lives in the tiny village of Puerto Velasco Ibarra with her children and grandchildren. They run a small hotel and restaurant. Although several books and articles have been written about the strange happenings on Floreana (including one by Wittmer, herself), no one is really sure of the truth. ■

the mail was addressed would deliver it. The site continues to be used, though obviously the barrel has been changed many times. About 300 meters behind the barrel is a lava cave that can be descended with the aid of a short piece of rope. Nearby is a pleasant swimming beach and the remains of a canning factory; a wet landing is necessary. I have heard talk of building a trail to the baroness' old house (see the Chronicles of Floreana sidebar) – you might ask about this.

Also reached with a wet landing is **Punta Cormorant**. There is a greenish beach (green because it contains crystals of the mineral olivine) where sea lions play and the swimming and snorkeling are good.

A 400-meter trail leads across an isthmus to a white-sand beach where turtles sometimes lay their eggs. The beach is also good for swimming, but beware of stingrays – shuffle your feet when entering the water.

Between the two beaches is a flamingo lagoon, which is probably the main attraction of this visitor site. Several dozen flamingos are normally seen. This is also a good place to see other wading birds such as the black-necked stilt, oystercatchers, willets and whimbrels. White-cheeked pintail ducks are often seen in the lagoon and Galápagos hawks wheel overhead.

Another Floreana visitor site is the remains of a half-submerged volcanic cone poking up out of the ocean a few hundred meters from Punta Cormorant. Aptly named the **Devil's Crown**, this ragged semicircle of rocks is one of the most outstanding marine sites in the Galápagos.

A panga ride around the cone will give views of red-billed tropicbirds, pelicans, herons and lava gulls nesting on the rocks, but the greater attraction is snorkeling in and around the crater. There are thousands of bright tropical fish, a small coral formation, sea lions and, if you are lucky, sharks.

I've heard rumors of a fourth visitor site being added to the east coast of the island – a site that features a green-sand beach, caves and a blue-footed booby colony.

Isla San Salvador

The official name is used less often than the old Spanish name, Santiago, or the English name, James. Santiago is the fourth largest of the islands and has several excellent visitor sites within its 585 sq km. The best site is **Puerto Egas**, on James Bay on the west side of Santiago.

Here, there is a long, flat, black lava shoreline where eroded shapes form lava pools, caves and inlets that house a great variety of wildlife. This is a great place to see colonies of marine iguanas basking in the sun. The tide pools contain hundreds of red Sally Lightfoot crabs, which attract hunting herons of all the commonly found species.

The inlets are favorite haunts of the Galápagos fur seal, and this is one of the best places in the islands to see them. You can snorkel here with fur seals and many species of tropical fish. I have seen moray eels, sharks and octopuses during snorkeling trips here.

Behind the black lava shoreline is Sugarloaf Volcano, which can be reached via a two-km footpath. Lava lizards, Darwin's finches and Galápagos doves are often seen on this path. It peters out near the top of the 395-meter summit, but from here the views are stupendous. There is an extinct crater in which feral goats are often seen (the wild goats are a major problem on Santiago), and Galápagos hawks often hover a few meters above the top of the volcano. North of the volcano is a crater where a salt mine used to be; its remains can be visited by walking along a three-km trail from the coast.

Puerto Egas is one of the most popular sites in the islands. So popular, in fact, that in late 1995 it was temporarily closed by the National Park Service because too many people were visiting it. Ask locally about its current status.

At the north end of James Bay, about five km from Puerto Egas, is the brown-sand **Espumilla Beach**, which can be reached with a wet landing. The swimming is good here, and by the small lagoon behind the beach you can see various wading birds, including, at times, flamingos. A two-km trail leads inland through transitional vegetation where there are various finches and the Galápagos flycatcher.

At the northwestern end of Santiago, another site that is normally visited by boat is **Buccaneer Cove**, so called because it was a popular place for 17th- and 18th-century buccaneers to careen their vessels. The beautiful cliffs and pinnacles, which are used as nesting areas by several species of seabirds, are the main attraction these days. This is best appreciated from the sea, but it is possible to land in the cove where there are beaches.

Sullivan Bay is on Santiago's east coast. Here, a huge, black lava flow from the turn of the century has solidified into a sheet that reaches to the edge of the sea. A dry landing enables visitors to step onto the flow and follow a trail of white posts in a two-km circuit on the lava. You can see uneroded volcanic formations such as pahoehoe lava, lava bubbles and tree-trunk molds in the surface. A few pioneer colonizing plants such as *Brachycereus* cactus and *Mollugo* carpetweed can be seen. This site is of particular interest to those interested in volcanology or geology.

As with several of the other islands, there have been proposals for new visitor sites – ask your guide.

Isla Bartolomé

Just off Sullivan Bay (see above) is Isla Bartolomé with an area of 1.2 sq km. Here you can see the most frequently photographed and hence most famous vista in the islands. There are two visitor sites and footpaths. One begins from a jetty (dry landing) from where it is about 600 meters to the 114-meter summit of the island. This good but sandy trail leads through a wild and unearthly looking lava landscape; a wooden boardwalk and stairs have been built on the last (steepest) section, both to aid visitors and to protect the trail from erosion. There are a few pioneering plants on either side of the trail but the main attraction is the view towards Santiago, which is just as dramatic as the photographs suggest.

The other visitor site is a small, sandy beach in a cove (wet landing). Here you have good snorkeling and swimming opportunities, including a chance to swim with the endemic Galápagos penguins that frequent this cove. Marine turtles and a gaudy variety of tropical fish are also frequently seen.

The best way to see and photograph the penguins is by taking a panga ride close to the rocks on either side of the cove and particularly around the aptly named Pinnacle Rock to the right of the cove from the seaward side. You can often get within a few meters of these fascinating birds – the closest point to Puerto Ayora where you can do so. Other penguin colonies are on the western side of Isabela.

From the beach a 100-meter trail leads across the narrowest part of Bartolomé to another sandy beach on the opposite side of the island. Marine turtles may nest here between January and March. Both beaches are clearly visible from the viewpoint described above.

Sombrero Chino

This tiny island just off the southeastern tip of Santiago is less than a quarter of one sq km in size. It is a fairly recent volcanic cone, which accounts for its descriptive name that translates to 'Chinese Hat.' The hat shape is best appreciated from the north. There is a small sea lion cove on the north shore, where you can anchor and land at the visitor site. Opposite Sombrero Chino, on the rocky shoreline of nearby Isla Santiago, penguins are often seen.

A 400-meter trail goes around the cove and through a sea lion colony – marine iguanas scurry everywhere. The volcanic landscape is attractive and there are good views of the cone. There are snorkeling and swimming opportunities in the cove.

Isla Rábida

Also known as Jervis, this approximately five-sq-km island lies five km south of Santiago. There is a wet landing onto a dark red beach where sea lions haul out and pelicans nest. This is one of the best places for seeing these birds nesting.

Behind the beach there is a salt-water lagoon where flamingos and white-cheeked pintails are sometimes seen (though the flamingos have not been seen much during the 1990s). This lagoon is also the site of a sea lion bachelor colony where the *solteros*, deposed by the dominant bull, while away their days.

There is a three-quarter-km trail with good views of the island's 367-meter volcanic peak, covered with palo santo trees. At the end of this, there is a great snorkeling spot.

Isla Genovesa

This island is known more often by its English name of Tower. It covers 14-sq-km and is the northeasternmost of the Galápagos Islands. As it is an outlying island, Tower is infrequently included on a one-week itinerary. If you have the time, however, and are interested in seabirds, this island is well worth the long trip. It is the best place to see a red-footed booby colony, as well as giving the opportunity to visit colonies of masked boobies, great frigatebirds, red-billed tropicbirds, swallow-tailed gulls and many thousands of storm petrels. Other bird attractions include Galápagos doves and short-eared owls. Both sea lions and fur seals are present, and there are exciting snorkeling opportunities – I have seen hammerhead sharks here.

The island is fairly flat and round, with a large, almost landlocked cove named Darwin Bay on the south side. There are two visitor sites, both on Darwin Bay. **Prince Philip's Steps** (also called El Barranco) is on the eastern arm of the bay and can be reached with a dry landing. A steep and rocky path leads to the top of 25 meter-high cliffs, and nesting seabirds are sometimes found right on the narrow path.

At the top of the cliffs the one-km long trail leads inland, past dry forest vegetation and various seabird colonies, to a cracked expanse of lava where thousands of storm petrels make their nests and wheel overhead. Short-eared owls are often seen here and it is an excellent hike for the bird enthusiast.

The second visitor site, **Darwin Bay beach**, is a coral beach reached by a wet landing. There is a three-quarter-km trail along the beach that passes through more seabird colonies.

You can take a pleasant panga ride along the cliffs. The panga is often followed by playful sea lions. This recommended excursion gives a good view from the seaward side of the cliffs and of the birds nesting on them.

Finally, this is the only regularly visited island that lies entirely north of the equator (the northernmost part of Isabela also pokes above the line). Cruises to Tower may well involve various ceremonies for passengers who have never crossed the equator at sea before.

Isla Marchena

This island is also known as Bindloe. At 130 sq km, this is the seventh largest island in the archipelago and the largest one to have no official visitor sites. There are some good scuba-diving sites, however, so you may get to see the island up close if you are on a dive trip. There are landing sites, and there has been talk of opening an official visitor site in the future.

The 343-meter-high volcano in the middle of the island was very active during 1991 – ask your guide about its current degree of activity. In the past it was possible to see the eruptions from boats cruising in the northern part of the islands.

Isla Pinta

This is the original home of Lonesome George, the tortoise described above in the Isla Santa Cruz section. Pinta is the ninth largest of the Galápagos Islands and is farther north than any of the bigger islands. Its English name is Abingdon. There are landing sites, but the island has no visitor sites, and researchers require a permit to visit.

The island is in the path of the total solar eclipse that will occur on February 26, 1998 (see the sidebar Total Eclipse of the Sun). Landings may be permitted for tourists to view the eclipse.

GALÁPAGOS

Isla Isabela

The largest island in the archipelago is the 4588-sq-km Isabela (occasionally called Albemarle), which occupies over 58% of the entire land mass of the Galápagos. It is a relatively recent island and consists of a chain of five fairly young and intermittently active volcanoes, one of which, Volcán Wolf, is the highest point in the Galápagos at 1707 meters (some sources claim 1646 meters). There is also one small older volcano, Volcán Ecuador.

Although Isabela's volcanoes dominate the westward view during passages to the west of Santa Cruz, the island itself is not frequently visited by smaller boats because most of the best visitor sites are on the west side of the island. The reverse 'C' shape of the island means that the visitor sites on the west side are reached only after a very long passage (over 200 km) from Santa Cruz, and so either you have to make a two-week cruise or you visit Isabela without seeing many of the other islands.

I've heard of a proposal to open a visitor site on Bahía Cartago, on the eastern side of Isabela, which would make it a little more accessible to shorter cruises. As of this writing, this has yet to come about.

There are many visitor sites on Isabela. One of these is the summit of **Volcán Alcedo** (1128 meters), which is famous for its seven-km-wide caldera and steaming fumaroles, where hundreds of giant tortoises can be seen, especially from June to December. The view is fantastic.

Reaching this site is quite an undertaking, however, and needs some preparation and effort. A wet landing at Shipton Cove brings you to the start of a steep, strenuous 10-km trail to the edge of the caldera, and from there it is six km farther to the fumaroles. All food and water must be carried. There is a camp site at the beach, another halfway up the volcano and three more on the caldera rim. One of these is at the point where the trail first reaches the caldera, another is at the fumarole and the third is in between.

You should inquire in the national park office for up-to-date information and a camping permit, although these take days or weeks to obtain. It is easier to sign up for a prearranged tour that already has the necessary permits. This is a rewarding trip, if you can afford the time, and is well worth the hassle and hard work. At the very least it is an overnight trip, and two nights are better still.

Day trips are offered – but spending six or seven strenuous hours to get there and then having to return almost immediately is not a good idea – you really need to spend a night near the rim to appreciate it properly.

A few kilometers north of the landing for Alcedo is **Punta García**, which consists mainly of very rough *aa* lava; there are no proper trails, though you can land. Until recently this was the only place where you could see the endemic flightless cormorant without having to take the long passage around to the west side. Recently, however, these birds have been present only intermittently and visits to this site have declined.

At the northern tip of Isabela is **Punta Albemarle**, which used to be a US radar base during WWII. There are no trails, and the site is known for the flightless cormorants, which normally are not found farther to the east. This is the only established visitor site that will be in the path of the total solar eclipse of February 26, 1998 (see the sidebar Total Eclipse of the Sun).

Farther west are several points where flightless cormorants, Galápagos penguins and other seabirds can be seen, but there are no visitor sites. You must view the birds from your boat.

At the west end of the northern arm of Isabela is the small, old Volcán Ecuador (610 meters), which comes down almost to the sea. Punta Vicente Roca, at the volcano's base, is a rocky point with a good snorkeling area.

The first official visitor site on the western side of Isabela is **Punta Tortuga**, a beach at the base of Volcán Darwin (1280 meters). Part of the land here was formed through a recent uplift. Locals report that one day in 1975 the uplift just appeared.

One day there was nothing and the next day there was an uplifted ledge – no one saw it happen.

Although there is no trail, you can land on the beach and explore the mangroves for the mangrove finch, which is present here, though not always easy to see. This finch is found only on Isabela and Fernandina Islands.

Just south of the point is **Tagus Cove**, where early sailors frequently anchored. You can still see some of the names of the vessels scratched into the cliffs around the cove.

A dry landing will bring you to a trail, which you follow for two km past a saltwater lagoon and onto the lower lava slopes of Volcán Darwin, where various volcanic formations can be observed. There are some steep sections on this trail. A panga ride along the cliffs will enable you to see the historical graffiti and various seabirds, usually including the Galápagos penguin and flightless cormorant. There are snorkeling opportunities in the cove.

Urbina Bay lies around the middle of the western shore of Isabela and is a flat area formed by an uplift from the sea in 1954. Evidence of the uplift includes a coral reef on the land. Flightless cormorants, pelicans and marine iguanas can be observed on land, and rays and turtles can be seen in the bay. A wet landing onto a beach brings you to a one-km-long trail leading to the corals. There is a good view of Volcán Alcedo.

Near where the western shoreline of Isabela bends sharply towards the lower 'arm' of the island there is a visitor site known for its marine life. **Elizabeth Bay** is best visited by a panga ride, as there are no landing sites. The Mariela Islands are at the entrance of the bay and are frequented by penguins. The end of the bay itself is a long, narrow and convoluted arm of the sea surrounded by three species of mangroves. Marine turtles and rays are usually seen in the water, and various sea and shore birds are present.

West of Elizabeth Bay is **Punta Moreno**, where you can make a dry landing onto a

lava flow where there are some brackish pools. Flamingos, white-cheeked pintails and common gallinules are sometimes seen, and various pioneer plants and insects are found in the area. There is a rough trail.

On the southeastern corner of Isabela there is the small village of Puerto Villamil. Behind and to the west of the village there is the **Villamil Lagoon**. This visitor site is known for its migrant birds, especially waders. Michael Harris (see Books appendix at the end of the book) writes that over 20 species of migrant waders have been reported here, and the lagoon is by far the best water bird area in the Galápagos. The surrounding vegetation is dense and without trails, though the road to the highlands and the open beach do give reasonable access to the lagoons. Also west of Puerto Villamil is the new visitor site of **Muro de las Lágrimas** (the Wall of Tears), which, I'm told, is the historical site of a wall built by convicts. I've yet to see it.

The massive **Volcán Santo Tomás** (1490 meters, also known as Volcán Sierra Negra) lies to the northwest. The tiny settlement of Santo Tomás is on the lower flanks of the volcano. Trucks or jeeps can be hired for the 18-km ride from Puerto Villamil. From Santo Tomás it is nine km farther up a steep trail to the rim of the volcano – horses can be hired in the village.

The caldera is roughly 10 km in diameter and is a spectacular site with magnificent views. An eight-km trail leads around the east side of the volcano to some active fumaroles. It is possible to walk all the way around the caldera, but the trail peters out. You should carry all your food and water or hire horses. Galápagos hawks, short-eared owls, finches and flycatchers are among the birds commonly seen on this trip. The summit is often foggy, especially during the June-to-December garúa season, and it is easy to get lost – stay in a group. Nearby is Volcán Chico, a sub-crater where you can see more fumaroles. These volcanoes are very infrequently visited.

Isla Fernandina

At 642 sq km, Fernandina (infrequently called Narborough) is the third largest island and the westernmost of the islands that receive the most visitors. It is considered the youngest of the main islands and the recently formed volcanic landscapes are most impressive. Many eruptions have been recorded since 1813, the most recent being 1995. This is the island on which you are most likely to see a volcanic eruption.

There is one visitor site at **Punta Espinosa**, just across from Tagus Cove on Isabela. The point is known for one of the greatest concentrations of the endemic marine iguanas, which are found by the thousands. Also, flightless cormorants, Galápagos penguins and sea lions are common here.

A dry landing brings you to two trails: a quarter-km trail to the point and a three-quarter-km trail to recently formed lava fields. Here you can see various pioneering plants, such as the *Brachycereus* cactus, as well as pahoehoe and aa lava formations.

Other Islands

The one sizable island in the central part of the archipelago that has no visitor sites is **Isla Pinzón**, also called Duncan. It is a cliff-bound island, which makes landing difficult, and a permit is required to visit it (usually reserved for scientists and researchers).

The northernmost islands are the two tiny islands of **Isla Wolf** (Wenman) and **Isla Darwin** (Culpepper). They are about 100 km northeast of the rest of the archipelago and are very seldom visited, except occasionally on scuba-diving trips. Both have nearly vertical cliffs that make landing difficult; Isla Darwin was first visited in 1964, when a helicopter expedition landed on the summit. Various other rocks and islets are present in the archipelago, but all are extremely small.

ACTIVITIES
Snorkeling

You don't have to be a great swimmer to be able to snorkel. Donning a mask and snorkel will expose you to a completely new world. Baby sea lions may come up and stare at you through your mask, various species of rays come slowly undulating by and penguins dart past you in a stream of bubbles. The hundreds of species of fish are spectacularly colorful, and you can watch the round, flapping shapes of sea turtles as they circle you. This won't, of course, happen immediately after you enter the water, but you do stand a good chance of seeing most of these things if you spend, say, half an hour per day in the water during a week of cruising the islands.

A mask and snorkel also let you observe more sedentary forms of life. Sea urchins, starfish, sea anemones, algae and crustaceans all colorfully combine in an exotic display of underwater life. If I were to give only one piece of advice to someone visiting the Galápagos, I would say, 'Bring a snorkel and mask.' You may be able to buy them in sporting goods stores in Quito or Guayaquil, and they can sometimes be borrowed in the Galápagos, but if you definitely plan to visit the islands, you should bring a mask from home to ensure a good fit and to enable you to snorkel when you feel like it.

The water temperature is generally around 22°C from January to April and about 18°C during the rest of the year. If you plan on spending a lot of time in the water you may want to bring a 'shorty' wet suit with you.

Scuba Diving

There is a professional dive center in Puerto Ayora. This is Galápagos Sub-Aqua (☎/fax 526 350) on Avenida Charles Darwin by Pelican Bay. They also have an information office in Guayaquil (☎ 304 132, fax 314 510) at Dátiles 506 and Quinta.

Galápagos Sub-Aqua is a full-service dive center. If you have never dived before, they can supply you with all the equipment and teach you what you need to know. An all-inclusive, seven-day course leading to full certification starts at US$770, including all gear, student materials, instructor, boat, meals and accommodations. If you want to dive but aren't certified and don't want to take a week-long course, you can go on beginner dives for US$115 a day (including all gear, two dives and an instructor). If you are already a certified diver, you can dive from US$75 a day or take a variety of diving programs including both hotel-based and live-aboard trips. Costs range from about US$1000 to US$2100 per week, depending on the quality of hotels or boats and whether or not you need to rent gear. Tours of various numbers of days are easily arranged. (Park fees and airline flights are extra.)

When I stopped by to visit Sub-Aqua, I was impressed to see a group of dive instructors listening to a biology lecture about submarine wildlife. They seem to take their jobs seriously. The head dive-master, Francisco Zembrano, is very experienced, enthusiastic and friendly. He is also a licensed Galápagos guide and speaks English (as do most of the instructors). I have received several recommendations about this operation.

Diving companies all over the world can also arrange diving tours on boats in the Galápagos.

Diving in the islands is quite spectacular, and you have excellent opportunities of seeing some really dramatic underwater wildlife – I saw hammerhead sharks, which was pretty exciting. Other sightings may include other sharks, a variety of rays (occasionally a manta ray), turtles, penguins, sea lions, moray eels, huge numbers of fish of many kinds and, if you're very lucky, dolphins or even whales.

Photography
Any kind of camera will enable an amateur photographer to get satisfying pictures – the animals will stay near the trails and can often be approached within two or three meters.

Advanced photographers will already have their own favorite lenses and equipment. A few suggestions: First, I have seen nonprofessional photographers use two 36-exposure rolls of film per day in the Galápagos – and then complain that they didn't really bring enough film. Film is not available on the boats, and the selection may be limited in the Galápagos towns; make sure you bring enough. If you happen to have some left over towards the end of your trip, selling film will be very easy.

Don't forget spare batteries for camera and flash unit. If your camera battery goes dead, you may not find another in the islands. Also bring resealable plastic bags for wet panga rides. Specially designed waterproof camera bags are available from photography stores, but plastic bags are an adequate and much cheaper alternative. Lead foil bags are a good idea to protect your film from airport X-ray machines.

A zoom lens is very useful. You can change from a wide angle landscape shot to a telephoto opportunity of a pelican flying over your head without having to change lenses.

Finally, remember to make note of what you photographed after each island excursion and label each film cannister. Otherwise, when you get home you'll find you can't remember which island is which. You'll know the difference between your red-footed and blue-footed booby shots, but you'll have a hard time telling the difference between the four endemic mockingbirds.

ORGANIZED TOURS
There are basically three kinds of tours in the Galápagos: day trips returning to the same hotel each night, hotel-based trips staying on different islands, and boat-based trips with nights spent aboard. Once you have decided on what kind of tour you want, you can either fly to the islands and find a tour there, or make reservations in advance on the mainland or through a travel agent in your home country. Public transport around the islands is very limited, so visiting the islands without taking a tour is a waste of time and money.

Day Trips
More often based in Puerto Ayora, a few day-trip operators are now operating out of Puerto Baquerizo Moreno, though I hear that they are more expensive and that

choices are limited. A typical day trip begins at dawn, with either a walk down to the dock or a bus ride across the island to meet a boat at the north side of Santa Cruz. Several hours are spent sailing to the day's visitor site(s), which you'll visit during the middle of the day with a large group. Only a few central islands are close enough to be visited on day trips.

Because a lot of time is spent going back and forth, and because there is no chance to visit the islands early or late in the day, I do not enjoy this type of tour. The cheapest boats may be slow and overcrowded, their visits to the islands may be too brief, the guides poorly informed and the crew lacking an adequate conservationist attitude. Therefore, I do not recommend the cheapest day trips. Nevertheless, day trips are useful for people who cannot stand the idea of sleeping in a small rocking boat at night.

There are plenty of day-trip operators in Puerto Ayora who charge around US$40 per person per day. The one you choose will depend on which destinations they offer. Ask other travelers about the quality of the guides and boats of the local agencies.

Better and more expensive day trips, using fast boats with knowledgeable guides, and staying in good hotels, can be arranged on the mainland. These trips are normally booked as a series of day trips lasting a week; they give a greater choice of islands to visit and are OK if you must take day trips. Prices range from US$700 to US$1000 per week, including guided trips, hotel and meals, but not airfare or park fee. Book through Metropolitan Touring (see Quito), which uses the Hotel Delfin in Puerto Ayora, or through the Hotel Galápagos and the Red Mangrove Inn (both in Puerto Ayora).

Hotel-Based Trips

These tours go from island to island and you sleep in hotels on three or four different islands (Santa Cruz, San Cristóbal, Floreana, Isabela). Tours typically last a week and cost US$700 to US$1000 per person, plus airfare and park fee. Personally, I find this preferable to day trips out of one hotel, but few companies offer this kind of tour. Ask the agencies in Quito until you find one that does. This kind of tour may be possible to arrange more cheaply in Puerto Ayora, but again, only a few boats do this. The Red Mangrove Inn (see Places to Stay in Puerto Ayora) arranges trips, mixing both hotel nights in different islands with some nights aboard a boat.

Boat Tours

Most visitors (non-Ecuadorians, in particular) tour the Galápagos on boat tours, sleeping aboard the boat. Tours can last from three days to three weeks, though tours from four to eight days are the most common. I don't think you can do the Galápagos justice on a tour lasting less than a week, though five days is just acceptable. If you want to visit the outlying islands of Isabela and Fernandina, a two-week cruise is recommended. On the first day of a tour, you arrive from the mainland by air at about lunchtime, so this is only half a day in the Galápagos, and on the last day you have to be at the airport in the morning. Thus a five-day tour gives only three full days in the islands. Shorter tours are advertised, but with the travel time at either end, they are not recommended.

Boats used for tours range from small yachts to large cruise ships. By far the most common type of boat is the motor sailer, which carries about eight to 16 passengers.

Locally Arranged Tours

Most people arrive in the islands with a prearranged tour, though some come hoping to hook up with a tour when they get there. It is cheaper to arrange a tour for yourself in Puerto Ayora than it is to pay for a prearranged tour from the mainland. Only the cheaper boats are available in the Galápagos; the better boats are almost always booked. Therefore, don't fly to the Galápagos hoping to get on a really good boat for less money – though you might get lucky, it rarely works that way.

Flying to the Galápagos and arranging a tour is not uncommon, but neither is it as straightforward as it sounds. It can take several days – sometimes a week or more – though you may get very lucky and find a suitable boat leaving the next day. This is not an option for people with a limited amount of time, nor for people wanting a very comfortable boat. It is, however, a reasonable option for those with extra time and limited funds.

The best place to organize a tour for yourself is from Puerto Ayora. It is sometimes possible to do this in Puerto Baquerizo Moreno, as well, but there are fewer boats available; I recommend that you try in Puerto Ayora.

Once you arrive in Puerto Ayora, first find somewhere to sleep (especially during the high season, when the choice of rooms may be limited) and then start looking for a boat. If you are alone or with a friend, you'll need to find more people, as even the smallest boats take no fewer than four passengers. There are usually people in Puerto Ayora looking for boats, and you should be able to get a group together in a few days. Check the hotels and restaurants for other travelers and ask around for boats. If they have no business lined up, captains will be looking for passengers. Your hotel manager can often introduce you to someone. After all, it's a small community, so word will quickly get around. Try the Adatur Boat Co-operative on Avenida Charles Darwin.

Finding boats in August and around Christmas and Easter is especially difficult. The less busy months have fewer travelers on the islands, but boats are often being repaired or overhauled at this time, particularly in October. Despite the caveats, travelers who arrive in Puerto Ayora looking for a boat can almost always find one within a week (often in just a few days) if they work at it.

The cheapest and most basic boats are available for about US$50 per person per day, which should include everything except park fees, alcohol and tips. The cheaper the boat, the more rice and fish you can expect to eat and the more crowded the accommodations. A few boats even charge for bottled water. Check this before you leave.

Boats will not sail unless all passenger berths are taken or at least paid for – empty spots add to group space and comfort doesn't come cheap. Bargaining over the price is acceptable and sometimes necessary.

Conditions on the cheapest boats can be cramped and primitive. Washing facilities vary from a bucket of sea water on the very cheapest boats (and there are increasingly few of these) to fresh-water deck hoses or showers on the better boats. If you don't want to stay salty for a week, ask about washing facilities. You should also inquire about drinking water. I'd recommend treating the water on the cheaper boats or bringing your own large containers of fresh water. Bottled drinks are carried, but they cost extra – agree on the price before you leave port and make sure that enough beer and soda is loaded aboard if you don't want to run out of your favorite refreshments. There's nothing to stop you bringing your own supply.

The most important thing to find is a boat crew with whom you get along and a good and enthusiastic naturalist guide who will be able to point out and discuss the wildlife and other items of interest. It is worth paying a little more for a good guide. The cheapest boats may have Spanish-speaking 'Naturalist II Guides,' whose function is to fulfill the captain's legal obligation to have a certified guide aboard. Some Naturalist II Guides know very little about the wildlife and simply act as rangers, making sure that groups stay together on the trails and don't disturb the animals. The better 'Naturalist III' guides have a degree in a biological science, a great deal of training and a command of Spanish, English and some other language. All guides must carry a license.

Owners, captains, guides and cooks change frequently, and, in addition, many boats make changes and improvements from year to year. Generally speaking, a boat is only as good as its crew. You should be able to meet the naturalist guide and captain, and to inspect the boat before you leave; always have an itinerary agreed upon

GALÁPAGOS

with the boat owner or captain. You can deal with a crew member or boat representative during your search, but don't hand over any money until you have an agreed itinerary, and then pay only the captain.

It is recommended that you have the itinerary in writing to avoid disagreements with other passengers and the crew during the cruise. Boats must register their itineraries with the National Park Service and with the port captain. Almost all itineraries are fixed several weeks in advance and cannot be changed. Despite this, you'll find that itineraries are generally good, visiting some of the best visitor sites described earlier in this chapter.

Prearranged Tours

Most visitors arrange tours before arriving in the islands. You can do this in your home country (expensive but efficient) or you can arrange something in Quito or Guayaquil (cheaper but you sometimes have to wait several days or weeks during the high season).

If you are trying to economize, you may find that you can get a substantial discount by checking various agencies and seeing if they have any spaces to fill on departures leaving in the next day or two. This applies both to the cheaper tours and to some of the more expensive ones. Particularly out of the high season, agencies may well let you travel cheaply at the last minute rather than leave berths unfilled. This depends on luck and your skill at bargaining. Safari Tours (see Quito) has a database of tours and can often get you on a boat quickly at a reasonable price. They have a US$25 flat fee to cover their expenses in searching out the best tour for you. This seems like money well spent – I welcome feed back from readers.

The cheapest prearranged tours that I know of are sold by César Gavela at the Hotel Gran Casino Internacional in Quito. Departures are on limited dates and getting something suitable is largely a matter of luck – don't expect any luxury.

A little more expensive but with more frequent departure dates are the economy tours run by Galasam (Economic Galápagos Tours).They might sell you just an air ticket even if you don't want a tour. Galasam has offices in Quito and Guayaquil (see these sections for addresses). Their economy tours are suitable for budget travelers who don't want to organize their own tour once they get to the islands. Their boats are similar to those used by César Gavela.

Galasam has three standards of tours: economy, tourist and luxury. Seven-day economy tours use small boats with six to 12 bunks in double, triple and quadruple cabins. All bedding is provided, and accommodations are clean but spartan, with little privacy. Plenty of simple, fresh food and juice is served at all meals. Guides may be Naturalist II with little English or biology.

There are toilets aboard both companies' boats, and fresh water is available for washing your face and drinking. Bathing facilities may be buckets of sea water, though showers are available on some. Itineraries are preset and visit most of the central islands, allowing enough time to see the wildlife.

One-week (eight days) economy tours cost about US$500 to US$600 per person. There are weekly departures. Shorter, cheaper tours are available – four days for US$300 and five days for US$350. The US$80 park fee, city tax, airfare and bottled drinks are not included. There are weekly departures. Typically, for a one week tour, you'll leave Quito on a specific morning (say Monday) and begin the boat tour on Monday afternoon or evening. The tour may finish on Sunday night or, possibly, Monday morning at the airport for your flight back. Shorter and cheaper tours are available. Sometimes, a one-week tour is a combination of two shorter tours; for example, a Monday-to-Thursday tour combined with a Thursday-to-Monday tour. People on the full week spend most of Thursday dropping off and picking up passengers. Try to avoid one-week trips like this.

If you add up the cost of the cheapest

one-week tour plus airfare and park fees, you get almost no change out of US$1000. Sorry, budget travelers, that's the way it is. My feeling is that if you're going to spend this much, then seeing the Galápagos is probably important to you and you will want to get as much out of it as possible. If economy class is all you can afford and you really want to see the Galápagos, go! It'll probably be the adventure of a lifetime. But you might consider spending an extra few hundred dollars to go on a more comfortable, reliable boat and get a decent guide (though more expensive boats have their problems too!)

For about US$800 for eight days, you can take a tourist-class tour with Galasam or several other companies – the usual extra costs (airfare, fees and taxes) apply. Many companies in Quito offer tours at about this price.

More luxurious tours are also available with agencies in Quito and Guayaquil. These typically over US$1000 per person per week, plus the usual extras. The most expensive boats are reasonably comfortable, have superb food and excellent crews. Many of these boats run pre-arranged tours with foreign groups; you are not likely to find them available for budget or independent travel. If you want this kind of luxury, a good travel agent in Ecuador or at home will be able to help you with information.

There are two large cruise ships carrying 96 passengers. These have the advantage of having comfortable double cabins with private showers, and are spacious and more stable than the smaller boats. Each ship carries (at least) four Naturalist III guides, and passengers divide into four groups and land on the islands at half-hour intervals, thus avoiding the horrendous scene of 96 other people trooping around a visitor site all at once. Tours can be for three, four or seven nights. Rates are approximately US$200 per person per night, depending on your cabin and whether or not you share it. Information and reservations are available from any major travel agent in Quito or Guayaquil.

Dangers & Annoyances

I have received a few letters criticizing both the Gran Casino trips and the economy-class Galasam tours, and even people traveling on more expensive boats have reported problems – anything from sinking boats to sexual harassment. The more common complaints include last-minute changes of boat (which the contractual small print allows), poor crew, lack of bottled drinks, not sticking to the agreed itinerary, mechanical breakdowns and overbooking. Passengers share cabins and are not guaranteed that their cabinmates will be of the same gender; if you are uncomfortable with sharing a cabin with a stranger of the opposite sex, make sure you are guaranteed in writing that you won't have to do this. None of the problems reported to me have resulted in death or rape.

Because a boat is only as good as the crew running it, and because crews change relatively often, it is difficult for me to make blanket recommendations. I have not received consistently poor reports about any one boat, which suggests that problems are usually solved in the long run. Things go wrong occasionally, and when they do a refund is extremely difficult to obtain. If you have a problem, report it to the port captain at the Capitanía in Puerto Ayora. If you are unable to do so while in the islands, reports can be mailed to El Capitán del Puerto, La Capitanía, Puerto Ayora, Galápagos, Ecuador. Reports are taken seriously, and repeat offenders do get their comeuppance – voice your complaints.

Tipping

It is customary to tip the crew at the end of a trip. A tip may be anywhere between US$20 and US$50 per passenger per week, depending on the quality and cost of the tour. On an exceptionally good boat, you might tip more than US$50; on some of the cheapest boats, passengers tip less than US$20.

The total tip is divided among the crew; the guide (if an experienced bilingual naturalist) may get as much as half (definitely less for non-English-speaking guides who

GALÁPAGOS

know little natural history). The cook and captain both get larger portions than the other crew members. It is best for the passengers to do the dividing – giving the money to one crew member and having that person deal with it is asking for complaints from other crew members.

Suggested Itineraries

You can go to almost any island, but it takes time to reach the more outlying ones. It is best to visit a few central islands and inspect them closely, rather than try to cram as many ports of call as possible into your cruise. Inter-island cruising takes up valuable time, and you don't see very much while at sea. Boats now have fixed itineraries so you need to think far ahead if you want a tour that visits a specific island. Most fixed itineraries go to several of the most interesting visitor sites. Make sure you aren't stuck in Puerto Ayora for more than one night at the most.

The following islands are particularly worth visiting: South Plaza, off the east coast of Santa Cruz, has sea lion, land iguana and swallow-tailed gull colonies, a cactus forest and good snorkeling; Isla Seymour, just north of Baltra, has both blue-footed booby and magnificent frigate-bird nesting colonies; and Black Turtle Cove, on the north shore of Santa Cruz, has marine turtles and white-tipped reef sharks.

Isla Bartolomé, on the east side of San Salvador, has a small volcanic cone that you can easily climb for one of the best views of the islands. There are also penguins and sea lions, and the snorkeling is good.

On San Salvador you can walk on a lava flow by Sullivan Bay, and observe marine iguanas, sea lions, fur seals, Galápagos hawks and many kinds of seabirds near Puerto Egas.

In addition to the species mentioned, you'll see common species almost everywhere. Masked and blue-footed boobies, pelicans, mockingbirds, finches, Galápagos doves, frigatebirds, lava lizards and red Sally Lightfoot crabs are so frequently seen that they will become part of the normal surroundings to you.

If you have more time (say a full week) you could visit some of the other islands. The red-footed booby is found only on the more outlying islands such as Genovesa, San Cristóbal and the small islets surrounding Santa María.

The waved albatross breeds only on Española, and the flightless Galápagos cormorant is found on the western islands of Isabela and Fernandina, which require a two-week trip.

GETTING THERE & AWAY

You can either go by boat or by air from the Ecuadorian mainland. If you go by boat you will normally waste a lot of time in Guayaquil securing a place on one of the infrequent passages. The money you spend on hotels and food in Guayaquil, plus the hassles involved, means that you really end up saving very little money, if any at all, unless you are lucky.

Air

Rather than spend frustrating days and weeks looking for boat passage in Guayaquil, I recommend that you just get on a plane and have done with it. TAME operates morning flights daily from Quito and Guayaquil to the Isla Baltra airport, about two hours away from Puerto Ayora by public transport (see Getting Around under Puerto Ayora). Sunday flights are cut in the low season. SAN-Saeta flies daily (except Sunday) from Quito and Guayaquil at 11 am for San Cristóbal. Thursday flights are cut in the low season.

Flights from Guayaquil cost US$333 roundtrip and take 1½ hours to the Galápagos. From Quito flights costs US$377 for the roundtrip, and you have to check in again in Guayaquil and may have to board another aircraft, though not necessarily. Follow the flight attendants' instructions. Flights cost 25% less in the low season (usually about September to November and April to early June).

Students with a school ID can get a discount during the low season (variously reported as 10% to 25% in the past, most recently as 15%); discounts are reportedly easier to get with TAME than with SAN-Saeta. If you have a bona fide student card, ask at the airline office and be prepared for plenty of red tape. Finally, researchers, biologists and others affiliated with a university can also get discounts, but don't leave it until the last minute.

If you buy tickets to the Galápagos in the US with Saeta and fly with them from Miami, you can save US$100 on the Galápagos fare. It is important to realize TAME and SAN-Saeta usually do not honor one another's tickets to the Galápagos (they fly to different islands), so you must know which airport you want to fly into and out of beforehand. Discounted tickets, for the most part, are an incentive to book an organized tour out of San Cristóbal. If you do buy these tickets in advance, make sure that your name is on the computer when you get to Ecuador.

Ecuadorian nationals can fly from Guayaquil for half the price foreigners pay, and Galápagos residents pay half that again. Some foreign residents of Ecuador or workers in the islands are also eligible so if you have a residence visa you should make inquiries.

Cheap flights to the islands are very difficult to get unless you are a resident. Nevertheless, rumors about such 'good deals' float around periodically – none are reliable or recommended.

There is a military logistic flight on Saturday that occasionally has room for passengers. Ecuadorians are given priority, but they get cheap flights with TAME anyway and so there are sometimes seats available for foreigners. Make inquiries at the Ministry of Defense in Quito (ask for Departamento de Operaciones, Fuerza Aerea del Ecuador). Travelers with official-looking letters from universities, embassies, presidents etc will have the best chance. I have never met anyone who has done this, but I keep hearing that it is possible. Rates are lower than the commercial airlines, but not much lower.

I suppose that as long as the flights are expensive there will be people who will happily waste a month of their time trying to beat the system; if you're not eligible for cheap flights and you think the airfare is too expensive, then maybe you shouldn't be visiting the islands anyway.

Flights to the Galápagos are sometimes booked solid well in advance, but you'll often find that there are many no-shows. Travel agencies book blocks of seats for their all-inclusive Galápagos tours. First they sell them to people taking their tours; they will release the seats on the day of the flight when there is no longer any hope of selling their tour. If you are tied into a definite itinerary, you should make a reservation; if you're flexible, you can buy your ticket at the airport when you want to fly. You have a better-than-even chance of getting a ticket, and it's unlikely that you'll be turned away two days in a row. During the high season, large cruise ships pick up passengers at Baltra on Monday, Wednesday, Thursday and Sunday – the busiest days. Tuesday is the quietest day to fly.

Some travel agencies will offer you a 'discount' on an airline ticket if you buy their tour of the Galápagos, which is OK if their tour happens to be what you want. Sometimes you can persuade an agency to sell you a discount ticket because they can't fill their tour space.

There are no air connections between Baltra and other islands. However, there is talk locally of beginning a service with a five-passenger light aircraft between San Cristóbal and Santa Cruz. There is also talk of expanding the Santa Cruz airport so that it can take jets (thus eliminating Baltra as the main airport in the islands) and of building an airport on Isabela. None of this has come about, as of this writing.

Fees & Taxes The US$80 Galápagos national park fee must be paid at one of the airports – either on the mainland before your flight or in the islands after you arrive. You will not be allowed to leave the airport until you pay. Cash only is accepted in the islands, though you can pay with travelers' checks on the mainland. Children under 12 pay US$40; students under 26 with a bona fide student ID card also received this discount as late as 1995, but recent reports indicate that even students now have to pay the full price.

In addition, there's a city tax of US$30 per person at Puerto Baquerizo Moreno (on San Cristóbal) and a US$12 tax at Puerto Ayora (the latter may rise to US$30 in the near future). Again, you can't leave the airport until the fee is paid.

Make sure you have your passport available when you pay your fees and taxes.

Boat

If you really insist on avoiding air transport, there are four ways to get to the islands by boat: with the navy, on a cargo boat, on a cruise ship or on your own vessel. None of the first three are very reliable; therefore, I do not recommend boat transport.

Naval vessels leave Guayaquil every few weeks and may be able to take passengers. Try at Transnave (☎ 561 453), 9 de Octubre 416 and Chile, in Guayaquil. Cargo ships leave irregularly and charge about US$150 to US$200. Conditions are tolerable. The journey to the islands takes about 3½ days, and you should be prepared to bring a sleeping bag or hammock, though a bunk in a cabin may well be available. These ships are mainly for cargo purposes, not for wildlife viewing. If you stay aboard while the boat spends about a week making deliveries around the islands, you are charged about US$50 a day, or you can get off and return later. The most reliable boat is the *Piquero*, which leaves Guayaquil around the 25th of every month; contact Acotramar (☎ 401 004, 401 711, 402 371), at Général Gómez 522 and Coronel, Guayaquil. Also ask at the Capitanía in Guayaquil, or at the boats, which anchor near dock No 4. Be prepared to wait weeks for a boat – though you might get lucky.

The 'best' boats to the islands are the cruise ships. They are more comfortable and have a regular schedule, better food and guide service. They are also much more expensive. Cruise ships accommodate 96 passengers in comfortable double cabins (see the descriptions under Prearranged Tours, above). These seven-day

tours usually cost US$200 or more per person per day and go one way by boat and return by air. Note that the cruise to or from Guayaquil is not offered frequently because the ships spend most of their time in the Galápagos; they usually return to Guayaquil about once a year for maintenance.

You can travel to the Galápagos in your own boat, but the Ecuadorian authorities give only seven-day transit passes to non-Galápagos boats, and you can't normally cruise the islands in your own boat unless you arrange it in advance – a difficult and time-consuming process. If you succeed in getting a permit, you must hire a licensed guide to accompany you in the islands. In the recent past, boats were only given 72-hour transit passes – the situation is liable to change.

There is a US$35 port entrance fee charged to visiting yachts. You can moor the boat in Puerto Ayora and hire a Galápagos boat to visit the islands. If you do this, you'll also have to pay a US$80 national park fee as well as the boat hire.

GETTING AROUND
To/From Baltra Airport

Most visitors arrive by air and land on Isla Baltra. Outside the airport you will be met by a boat representative (if you are on a prearranged tour) and taken by bus on a five-minute drive to the boat dock.

If you are traveling independently, do not take the bus to the boat dock. Instead, take the bus (10- to 15-minute ride) to the dock for the ferry to Isla Santa Cruz. A 10-minute ferry ride will take you across to Santa Cruz, where you will be met by a bus to take you to Puerto Ayora, about 1½ hours away. This drive provides a good look at the interior and highlands of Santa Cruz – dusty and dry in the north and greener and wetter in the highlands and on the south slopes. The ferry and second bus are scheduled to coincide with the departure of the first bus from the airport, so there isn't much waiting involved. You should be in Puerto Ayora within two hours of leaving the airport.

The combined bus/ferry/bus trip costs about US$4. There is a ticket booth at the airport in the departure lounge to your left as you leave the arrival area. Buy your ticket as soon as you arrive, as there is normally only one bus (although a second bus may run if there is enough passenger demand). The journey is often very crowded, and numbered seats are supposedly sold to combat this problem.

Buses from Puerto Ayora to Baltra (via the ferry) leave at 7:30 am every morning that there are flights from the park (see map). Tickets are sold at the supermarket (see map). These same buses return from the airport after the plane from the mainland has landed. A second and third bus will run if there is enough demand.

To/From Puerto Baquerizo Moreno Airport

This airport is on the edge of the small town and is a short walk away from hotels and services.

Bus

Isla Santa Cruz You can have the buses that leave for the Isla Baltra airport (see above) drop you off at the villages of Bellavista or Santa Rosa to explore some of the interior. Also, buses to Santa Rosa (US$1) leave from the corner of Padre Julio Herrera and Charles Binford at 6:30 am, 12:30 and 4:30 pm Monday to Saturday. These hours are subject to change.

Note that neither of these villages has hotels at this time. The most convenient way of seeing the interior and ensuring that you don't get stuck is to hire a bus or truck for the day with a group of other travelers. Ask at your hotel about this.

Isla San Cristóbal There are a few buses that leave each day from Puerto Baquerizo Moreno and go to the farming center of El Progreso, about eight km into the highlands. From here you can rent jeeps for the final 10-km ride to the visitor site of El Junco Lagoon. The road is being pushed eastward, and there are some buses that go farther than El Progreso.

Boat

INGALA (☎ 526 151 in Puerto Ayora) can give you up-to-date details of their inter-island passenger boat services. Buy your tickets a day in advance. Priority is given to islanders and Ecuadorians, so it may take some days to be able to get on a boat; however, in 1995 a new, larger vessel was introduced, which has alleviated some of the past problems in obtaining tickets. If the larger boat is down for maintenance, the old 24-passenger vessel is used (and tends to be full).

Recently, boat schedules were as follows.

Tuesday 10 am
　Puerto Ayora to Puerto Baquerizo Moreno
Wednesday 10 am
　Puerto Baquerizo Moreno to Puerto Ayora
Thursday 8 am
　Puerto Ayora to Puerto Velasco Ibarra (Isla Floreana), continuing to Puerto Villamil (Isla Isabela)
Friday 10 am
　Puerto Villamil to Puerto Ayora
Saturday 8 am
　Puerto Ayora to Puerto Baquerizo Moreno
Monday 10 am
　Puerto Baquerizo Moreno to Puerto Ayora

Fares are US$36 on any passage (US$24 for locals). If you can't get on an INGALA boat, ask around for private trips, which are more expensive. Marcos Martínez in Puerto Ayora reportedly organizes tours to Isabela. The port captain usually knows who is going where.

At time of writing, it is not a good idea to rely on inter-island boats to get you to San Cristóbal or Santa Cruz if time is a concern, such as for a flight.

PUERTO AYORA

This town is on the central island of Santa Cruz and is where most visitors stay and visit. The population, currently over 7000, is growing fast. There are the usual amenities: hotels, bars and restaurants, stores, an EMETEL office, a post office, a CETUR tourist information center, a TAME office, a basic hospital, churches, a movie theater, a dive center and a radio station.

GALÁPAGOS

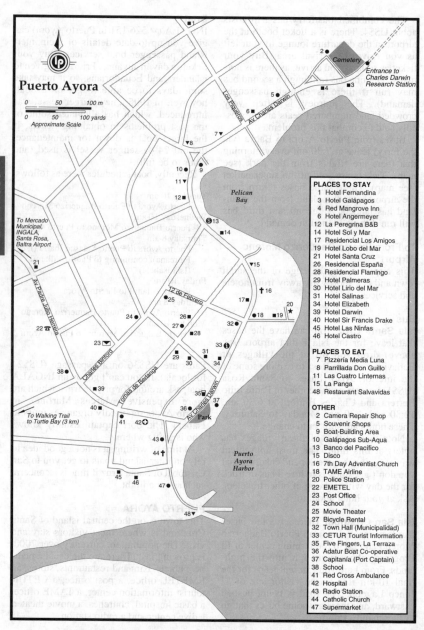

Puerto Ayora

PLACES TO STAY
1 Hotel Fernandina
3 Hotel Galápagos
4 Red Mangrove Inn
6 Hotel Angermeyer
12 La Peregrina B&B
14 Hotel Sol y Mar
17 Residencial Los Amigos
19 Hotel Lobo del Mar
21 Hotel Santa Cruz
26 Residencial España
28 Residencial Flamingo
29 Hotel Palmeras
30 Hotel Lirio del Mar
31 Hotel Salinas
34 Hotel Elizabeth
39 Hotel Darwin
40 Hotel Sir Francis Drake
45 Hotel Las Ninfas
46 Hotel Castro

PLACES TO EAT
7 Pizzería Media Luna
8 Parrillada Don Guillo
11 Las Cuatro Linternas
15 La Panga
48 Restaurant Salvavidas

OTHER
2 Camera Repair Shop
5 Souvenir Shops
9 Boat-Building Area
10 Galápagos Sub-Aqua
13 Banco del Pacífico
15 Disco
16 7th Day Adventist Church
18 TAME Airline
20 Police Station
22 EMETEL
23 Post Office
24 School
25 Movie Theater
27 Bicycle Rental
32 Town Hall (Municipalidad)
33 CETUR Tourist Information
35 Five Fingers, La Terraza
36 Adatur Boat Co-operative
37 Capitanía (Port Captain)
38 School
41 Red Cross Ambulance
42 Hospital
43 Radio Station
44 Catholic Church
47 Supermarket

The town's harbor is named Academy Bay, after the boat *Academy*, which arrived here in 1905 carrying an expedition sent by the California Academy of Sciences. Recently, the town imposed a US$2 per person port tax on passengers entering Academy Bay – this may or may not be included in the cost of your tour.

Note that the nearest airport, Baltra, is two hours away by bus and ferry.

Information

See the description of Isla Santa Cruz, earlier in this chapter, for information on places to visit on the island.

Tourist Offices Tourist information is available at CETUR, on the waterfront a short walk from the docks. There are several self-styled 'information centers' nearby that will give you information about their day trips and boat charters. The best is Adatur, which is a cooperative of about 20 boats of different prices. Most have a capacity of eight to 12 passengers.

The Charles Darwin Research Station, about a km east of town, has an exhibition hall, information kiosk, scientific library and tortoise-raising pens. Walk the grounds at your own pace – tours are not organized.

Travel Information INGALA (☎ 526 151) can give you information about inter-island ferries (see Getting Around). Their office is about a kilometer northwest of town along Avenida Padre Julio Herrera and is open from 7:30 am to 12:30 pm and 1:30 to 4 pm Monday to Friday. The Capitanía, on the waterfront, can give you information about (infrequent) boats to the mainland.

The TAME office is open from 7 am to noon Monday to Saturday and from 1 to 4 pm Monday to Friday. Reconfirming your departures is essential. Flights are often full, and there is sometimes difficulty in changing your reservation or buying a ticket. Be persistent.

Money The Banco del Pacífico gives the best rates for traveler's checks or cash US dollars. Advances on credit cards are

reportedly possible. You can usually pay for tours with cash US dollars.

Post & Communications The EMETEL office is sometimes out of service for phone calls. In an emergency, radio messages are sent from the INGALA office.

The post office is slow in sending mail out of the islands. Make sure your letters are stamped and postmarked – I once sent a dozen postcards and not one was delivered. The larcenous postmistress took my money but kept the stamps.

Medical Services The hospital is not very sophisticated and is poorly supplied. Most sick people go back to the mainland.

Electricity Recently, electricity was turned off at 11 pm (though some places have generators and may stay open later). Carry a flashlight on late-night forays.

Activities

Bicycles can be rented (see map) for about US$12 a day. Scuba-diving gear can be rented from Galápagos Sub-Aqua (see Activities, above, for further information).

Courses & Work

The National Park Service runs guide training courses that last about six weeks (usually beginning around September). The courses are often taught by staff from the Charles Darwin Research Station, but the research station does not accept applications for the course; participants are selected by the National Park Service, to which applications should be sent. It is necessary to pass this course before you can work as a tour guide on the boats.

Only the Naturalist III course is open to foreigners, who must speak fluent Spanish and English, and have some command of a third language. They must also have a degree in a life science and a written agreement with a Galápagos tour operator stating that the operator will give the participant a (paid) job upon successful completion of the course. Usually, a one-year commitment is expected. Metropolita

GALÁPAGOS

Touring has, in the past, sponsored a number of qualified applicants. Each course is limited to six foreign participants, as well as several Ecuadorians. Further information on the course is available in Spanish from Encargado, Curso de Guías, Parque Nacional Galápagos, Puerto Ayora, Santa Cruz, Galápagos, Ecuador.

If you are a biologist, it is possible to work as a volunteer with one of the ongoing projects in the islands. Send resumes and work/project suggestions or requests (in Spanish) to the director of the Charles Darwin Research Station, Puerto Ayora, Galápagos, Ecuador. Note that the research station has a goal of building a cadre of well-trained Ecuadorian conservation professionals to manage the country's natural resources in the future, and Ecuadorians are therefore given priority. Qualified foreign volunteers are accepted if they speak Spanish, pay their own expenses and stay for a minimum of six months. If you are working or studying on the islands, you can normally qualify for the discounted Ecuadorian airfare to the Galápagos.

Places to Stay

Hotels in Puerto Ayora range from cheap and basic to first class . . . by Galápagos standards, at least. There are no luxury hotels. Prices tend to rise during the heaviest tourist seasons (December to January and June to August).

It cannot be over-emphasized that a cheap 'tour' based at a hotel and visiting other islands on day trips gives you only a superficial look at the Galápagos. Stay in Puerto Ayora by all means, but make every effort to visit the islands by taking a cruise of at least several days' duration – preferably a full week or more.

Places to Stay – bottom end

Camping, which was possible during the 1980s, is no longer allowed on this island, except on private property if you have the owner's permission.

There are several cheap and basic hotels, some of which are a better value than the more expensive places. Although facilities are basic, the following are clean and friendly, and are good places to meet other budget travelers.

The *Residencial Los Amigos* is a popular budget hotel with clean rooms for US$3 per person. Also popular is *La Peregrina B&B*, which, at US$4 per person, includes a good breakfast. It is run by Jehovah's Witnesses. The *Residencial Flamingo* is fine for US$3/5 for singles/doubles with bath. The *Hotel Sir Francis Drake* has a decent restaurant, and is quite good at about US$3.50 per person. Other cheap places include the *Hotel Santa Cruz* and *Residencial España*.

The *Hotel Darwin* charges US$5/8 with private bath, and has a restaurant. The *Hotel Lobo del Mar* is popular with Ecuadorian tour groups and tends to be noisy. Rooms are basic but reasonably clean at US$8/10 with bath. There are some triples and quadruples, which are not much more. For about US$5 extra per person, they include three meals a day. The hotel organizes day trips to various islands for about US$40 per passenger.

The *Hotel Las Palmeras* is quite good but often full. Prices are around US$10/15 for clean rooms with private bath. Slightly cheaper and also clean and modern-looking are the *Hotel Salinas* (☎ 526 107) and *Hotel Lirio del Mar*, nearby. The *Hotel Elizabeth* has improved since being remodeled.

The *Hotel Las Ninfas* charges about US$15 per person and has private (cold) baths in all rooms. They arrange tours and can provide full board on request. Next door, the *Hotel Castro* is used for tour groups booked with Señor Miguel Castro, but you can always try it if you have no luck elsewhere.

The *Hotel Sol y Mar* (☎ 526 281) is very pleasantly situated right on the waterfront – marine iguanas sunbathe with the guests on the deck and walk over your feet while you're having breakfast. The owner is Señor Jimmy Pérez, a rather colorful character who speaks English and runs Trans-Galápagos Tourism. He can also help you get a boat. Clean rooms with private bath are US$12/18 in the high season and less at other times; extra people are about US$4 per person. Good meals are available for US$1.50 (breakfast), US$3.50 (lunch) and US$5 (dinner). The bar and restaurant have been recommended.

Also in this price range is the new, family-run *Hotel Fernandina* (☎ 526 122, 526 499), which has been recommended as being friendly and helpful. Rooms have hot private showers and full board is available.

Casa de Iguana is a B&B slated to open in the fall of 1996. Rates are US$15/25, including breakfast, and there are six rooms. The Iguana is near Las Cuatro Linternas restaurant; ask in Puerto Ayora.

Places to Stay – middle to top end

The new *Red Mangrove Inn* (☎ /fax 526 564) is small and intimate. There are three double rooms and a cottage sleeping three adults, all with private baths. Guests leave their shoes at the door. The inn is aimed at providing a relaxing place to stay; there is a Jacuzzi, bar and views of the bay. Rooms are US$50/70, including continental breakfast. A 20% tax is added, but this is negotiable in the low season. Other meals are available on request. The inn runs a variety of tour packages in its 'The Other Galápagos' program. They can arrange overnight camping on their ranch in the highlands (US$60 for two days, one night, meals and transportation included), as well as longer tours. Kayaking, scuba diving and mountain biking are also options.

The *Hotel Angermeyer* (☎ 526 186, 526 570, fax 526 571) was once famous as a budget hotel owned and operated by one of the first families to settle in the islands. Recently, it has been transformed by new owners into a modern hotel, with 29 rooms with private baths heated by solar panels. There is a small but pretty pool and a good restaurant and bar with room service. Rates are roughly US$100 per room, some of which have air-conditioning.

The best hotel in Puerto Ayora is the well-recommended *Hotel Galápagos* (☎ 526 330, ☎ /fax 526 296), which charges US$75/120/135 (including tax) for 14 comfortable single/double/triple cabins

with private bath, hot water and ocean views. They serve excellent meals (about US$8/16/20 for breakfast/lunch/dinner). A pleasant bar and a paperback book library are on the premises. They also provide hot showers to the public for US$1.25, including soap and towels.

Across the bay from Puerto Ayora is the *Hotel Delfín* (☎ 526 297) with a private beach. All rooms have a beach view, private bathrooms and hot shower, and rates are less than those of the other good hotels. There is also a restaurant. This is a very private location – you need a boat to get to this hotel from Puerto Ayora. The hotel is used as a base for day tours organized by Metropolitan Touring in Quito, and they can make reservations for you.

Places to Eat

There are a number of restaurants and bars in Puerto Ayora and they are good places to meet people. Some of these places change hands or names quite often, as places frequented by seasonal influxes of people tend to do, so don't be surprised to find a differently named place at these locations. Service is leisurely. You can buy food and drinks in stores, but the choice is also limited and comparatively expensive. Lobster is sold in some restaurants and, although still legal, it has been dramatically overfished and you are encouraged to forego lobster meals on the islands.

Down by the dock, *Restaurant Salvavidas* (Lifejacket Restaurant!) has, under various names, been the standard daytime meeting place for years. You can grab a beer, snack or meal here while waiting for your panga. *Las Cuatro Linternas* has a variety of Italian and other food, as well as snacks and coffee. It has received several recommendations, but is a bit pricey. Nearby, *Pizzería Media Luna* is also good. *Parrillada Don Guillo* has a small selection of meaty dishes. *La Panga* is a popular restaurant with good, though not particularly cheap, meals.

More places to eat are found out along Avenida Padre Julio Herrera. Some of these are inexpensive, if unremarkable – look for places where locals are eating, especially at lunch. The newly opened *Iguana Café and Bar* (I don't know where it is) has been recommended for healthy home-cooked food and salads, and the bar occasionally has live music.

The restaurants at the better hotels are generally good, pricey and open to the public.

Entertainment

The *Five Fingers* is a popular drinking and dancing spot on Avenida Charles Darwin. Nearby, *La Terraza* is a long-standing nightspot that varies from dead to packed with dancers. On that block is a consistently changing variety of places to eat. Next door to La Panga (see Places to Eat) is a bar and disco, where, local guides assure me 'the landings are always wet.'

Things to Buy

You can purchase the famous Galápagos T-shirts in most souvenir shops, but the profits from those sold at the Charles Darwin Research Station go to support that worthwhile institution. Other available 'souvenirs' include objects made from black coral, turtle and tortoise shell. These threatened animals are protected, and it is illegal to use these animal products for the manufacture of novelties. The practice still continues, unfortunately. The most effective way of stamping it out is to avoid buying such items. The sale of objects made from black coral is a particularly serious problem. Please do not purchase these articles.

Most other things (T-shirts excepted) are either expensive or unavailable, and you are strongly advised to stock up on suntan lotion, insect repellent, toiletries, film and medications on the mainland. These have become increasingly available in recent years, but selection is still not as wide as on the mainland.

A good selection of postcards is available at the post office. Many of these are photographs or drawings by Tui de Roy, a resident famous for her beautifully illustrated books on the wildlife of the islands.

Her books are also for sale at the Libri Mundi bookstore in Quito. Her mother, Jacqueline de Roy, makes exquisite silver jewelry of the Galápagos animals. The work is not cheap but is well worth the money. It is sold in some of the local jewelry stores.

PUERTO BAQUERIZO MORENO

This is the political capital of the Galápagos and is on Isla San Cristóbal. Few travelers came here until SAN-Saeta recently started operating a regular jet service. Although it is the second largest town in the islands, with a population of about 3000, many of the inhabitants work in government-related jobs or fishing and the town is still a long way behind Puerto Ayora for tourism. Facilities are improving, however, and aggressive marketing by SAN-Saeta is steadily making this an increasingly important tourist town.

Information

The CETUR information office is on the short road between the airport and the center, but no English is spoken. Banco del Pacífico changes money.

There is a small museum with a statue of Darwin, a small hospital and a post office. Frigatebird Hill is a short walk from town, and other local visitor sites are described under Isla San Cristóbal, earlier in this chapter.

Don't forget that you will be charged a US$30 municipal tax in addition to the US$80 park fee when you land at the airport here.

Places to Stay & Eat

The cheapest hotels include the *Hotel San Francisco* (☎ 520 104), which is reportedly clean and a good value for US$9 per double with bath. Cheaper places to stay include the *Northia Hotel, Residencial Miramar* and the *Cabañas Don Jorge* (☎ 520 208).

The best and most expensive hotel is run in conjunction with SAN-Saeta airlines. This is the *Grand Hotel San Cristóbal* (☎ 520 179), where a double room with bath is about US$65. It faces a beach at the east end of town and has a decent restaurant. Other hotels somewhere between these two price extremes include the *Hotel Orca*; the *Hostal Galápagos* (☎ 520 157); the *Mar Azul* (☎ 520 130), with pleasant gardens; and the modern *Hotel Chatham* (☎ 520 137, 520 303).

There are basic restaurants and comedores in town. The best is *Rosita's Restaurant*, which serves tasty *bacalao* (a local fish). The *Casa Blanca* is pricier but also good, and the restaurant at the Grand Hotel has also been recommended. Other hotel restaurants worth checking out are in the Orca, Mar Azul, Chatham and Miramar. There are several other places to eat.

PUERTO VELASCO IBARRA

This port is the only settlement on Isla Santa María (Floreana). There is not much to do in this tiny town – the population is less than 100 – but a black beach nearby boasts a sea lion colony, and there's a flamingo lagoon within walking distance. A road goes into the highlands, with very little traffic but easy walking. See the earlier description of Isla Santa María for further information.

Places to Stay & Eat

The famous Margaret Wittmer (see the Chronicles of Floreana sidebar) and her family run a small hotel and restaurant. They also have a small gift shop and post office. You can write for reservations (Señora Wittmer, Puerto Velasco Ibarra, Santa María, Galápagos – allow a couple of months) or just show up. They are rarely full, and even if they were, you could ask them to show you somewhere to crash. Rates are not very expensive. There is nowhere else.

PUERTO VILLAMIL

This is a small port on Isabela, the largest island, with about 2000 inhabitants. It is not much visited by travelers, although some tours do stop here. There are a few hotels and basic restaurants. This island is a marvelous one, with several active volcanoes and a large number of Galápagos tortoises, and it looks like Isabela is going to become more important in Galápagos tourism in the years to come. From Puerto Villamil, there is an 18-km road to the even tinier village of **Santo Tomás**, where horses can be hired to continue up Volcán Santo Tomás. There are several men in Puerto Villamil who work as guides – ask around.

Places to Stay & Eat

The *Hotel Ballena Azul* (☎ 529 125) is recommended as being one of the best places in town – certainly it is one of the best known – and the owners or representatives can be contacted in Puerto Ayora if you ask around. They charge about US$7 per person and arrange tours. A cheaper place is *Posada San Vicente*, which has rooms with private bath. The owner, Antonio Gil, is a local guide and can take you up the volcano on horseback. Down on the beach are the *Hotel Alexander* and *El Refugio del Capitán*, while on the road to the highlands are the *Tero Real* and *Hotel Loja*. None of these places are expensive and all seem to be OK, from what I've heard. Relatively few tourists go there.

The Hotel Loja has a good restaurant. The *Costa Azul* restaurant, near the Tero Real, has also been recommended. There are some cheap comedores in the port, but you need to ask them in advance to cook a meal for you – which should give you an idea of how few visitors they see.

Galápagos

wildlife guide

Galápagos Wildlife Guide

BIRDS

There are 58 resident bird species on the Galápagos, of which 28 are endemic. A further half a dozen regular migrants are frequently seen and about 25 other migratory species are regularly but not frequently recorded. Several dozen other species are accidental and rarely recorded. Many people are confused between a migrant, resident and endemic species. A resident lives and breeds in the island year round, but the species is also found in other parts of the world. A migrant is found in the island for only part of the year. An endemic species is a resident which does not normally breed anywhere else in the world (except in captivity or by accident).

Seabirds are the birds that make the most lasting impression on most visitors. Highly in evidence, spectacular and amusing, the seabirds of the Galápagos will turn everyone into a birdwatcher.

During a week of touring the islands, most careful observers will see about 40 species of birds. If two weeks are spent and some of the more outlying islands are visited, over 50 birds can be recorded, particularly during the northern winter when migrants are present. Even the most casual visitor will see 20 to 30 species. Enjoy your observations!

The birds described below are listed by family in standard taxonomic order. Latin family names can be recognised because they always end in -idae. Uncommon migrants and accidentals are mentioned in passing but not described. A checklist of the 58 resident birds plus six common migrants is provided at the end for you to record the species you see.

PENGUINS (SPHENISCIDAE)

The penguin family is found exclusively in the southern hemisphere. The single Galápagos species is therefore the most northerly penguin in the world.

Galápagos Penguin

Scientific name: *Spheniscus mendiculus*
Spanish name: *Pingüino de Galápagos*

Most penguins are associated with the colder regions of the southern hemisphere but the cool Humboldt current flowing from Antarctica along the South American coast enables the Galápagos penguin to live here – the most northerly penguin in the world. Although they normally breed on the western part of Isabela and Fernandina, a small colony is often seen by visitors to Bartolomé. They are occasionally present in Floreana or on Santiago (across from the visitor site on Sombrero Chino).

Breeding can occur year-round – two broods a

Galápagos Penguin (RR)

year are possible under good conditions. Colonies are small and not tightly packed with nests.

This flightless bird is one of five endemic seabirds in the islands. Penguins' clumsiness on land belies their skill and speed underwater. The best way to appreciate this is to snorkel with them – it is great fun but don't even think about trying to keep up with an underwater penguin!

ALBATROSSES (DIOMEDEIDAE)

One member of this family is a Galápagos resident but a couple of other species have been recorded.

Waved Albatross pair grooming (RR)

Waved Albatross

Scientific name: *Diomedea irrorata*
Spanish name: *Albatros Ondulado*

One of the world's most magnificently graceful flying birds is the waved albatross which can spend years at sea without touching land. It is the largest bird in the islands, averaging 86 cm in length, up to a 240-cm wingspan, and reaching up to five kg in weight. Apart from a few pairs which have bred on the Isla de la Plata off the Ecuadorian coast, the entire world population of some 12,000 pairs nests on Española. Egg laying occurs from mid-April to late June and the colonies are active with parents feeding their single young through December. When the fledged bird finally leaves the nest, it does not return for four or five years. From January to March, all the birds are at sea.

The waved albatross engages in one of the most spectacular ritualised courtship displays of any bird. Courtship tends to occur in the second half of the breeding season, with October being the busiest month, but you may see it anytime that the colony is occupied. The display involves a perfectly choreographed 'dance' of up to 20 minutes of bowing, bill clicking, bill circling, swaying and freezing, honking and whistling. This is one of the most memorable of Galápagos sights.

TRUE PETRELS & SHEARWATERS (PROCELLARIIDAE)

Eight members of this family have been recorded in the Galápagos; the following two are the only residents and frequently seen.

Dark-rumped Petrel

Scientific name: *Pterodroma phaeopygia*
Spanish names: *Petrel Lomioscuro; Pata Pegada*

Audubon's Shearwater

Scientific name: *Puffinus lherminieri*
Spanish name: *Pardela de Audubon*

Left: Audubon's Shearwater
Right: Hawaiian Petrel

The dark-rumped petrel is also called the Hawaiian petrel – in Hawaii it is in danger of extinction because of introduced predators. It is also endangered in the Galápagos but is better protected here. The Audubon's shearwater is widespread in tropical waters around the globe. Both species breed in the Galápagos, but are most frequently seen feeding at sea.

The birds are quite similar at first glance – black upperparts and white underparts. The dark-rumped petrel is 43 cm long and has a wingspan of over 90 cm – it is much larger than the commoner shearwater with a length of 30 cm and wingspan of less than 70 cm. Also, the petrel has a white cap whilst the shearwater is entirely black on top. These features are difficult to pick out when the birds fly by 100 metres away from your boat.

The best way to tell these birds apart when you see them at sea is by their flight. The petrel characteristically glides over the ocean in a series of swoops and banks, displaying the contrasting black and white body surfaces. It is more likely to be seen far out at sea, where it feeds on fish and squid. Shearwaters skim the waves much more directly, without the diagnostic swoops and banks of the petrel. The shearwaters are most likely seen closer to shore feeding on small crustaceans and fish larvae.

STORM PETRELS (HYDROBATIDAE)
The Galápagos has eight recorded and three commonly-seen species of storm petrels which are among the smallest of seabirds. The largest is only 20 cm long with a wingspan of 30 cm, or about the size of a swallow. Their diminutive size distinguishes storm petrels from the true petrels and shearwaters. They are locally called *golondrinas del mar*.

White-vented (Elliot's) Storm Petrel
Scientific name: *Oceanites gracilis*
Spanish name: *Paíño Gracil*

Wedge-rumped (Galápagos) Storm Petrel
Scientific name: *Oceanodroma tethys*
Spanish name: *Paíño de Galápagos*

Band-rumped (Madeiran) Storm Petrel
Scientific name: *Oceanodroma castro*
Spanish name: *Paíño Lomibandeado*

Storm petrels are dark with a white rump. The three species are distinguished by the differences in the shape of the white area – a job for an experienced birder or a good naturalist guide. They feed by grabbing scraps from the surface of the sea, which makes them look as if they are walking on water. The white-vented storm petrel, in particular, is often seen hanging around boats at anchor, looking for food.

Left: Band-rumped (Madeiran) Storm Petrel
Right: Wedge-rumped (Galápagos) Storm Petrel
Below: White-vented (Elliot's) Storm Petrel

The wedge-rumped and band-rumped storm petrels breed in huge colonies on Genovesa (Tower). These colonies are estimated to number hundreds of thousands but not much is known about them. Breeding colonies of the Elliot's white-vented storm petrel have yet to be discovered.

TROPICBIRDS (PHAETHONTIDAE)

Red-billed Tropicbird
Scientific name: *Phaethon aethereus*
Spanish names: *Rabijunco Piquirrojo, Piloto*

Red-billed Tropicbird on nest (RR)

The unmistakeable red-billed tropicbird is one of the most spectacular of Galápagos seabirds. The most noticeable feature of this splendid white bird is its pair of long tail streamers – two elongated feathers often as long as the rest of the body. The birds are 76 cm long (including the tail feathers) and have a wingspan of just over one metre. They are extremely graceful in the air and often fly by in small groups, uttering a distinctive and piercing shriek. The coral-red bill and black eye stripe are noticeable at closer range. The birds nest in crevices and holes in cliffs or rock piles on most of the islands, but are most frequently seen from trails that follow cliff tops, such as on South Plaza, Genovesa (Tower) and Española (Hood). They feed far out to sea, plunge diving for fish and squid.

PELICANS (PELECANIDAE)

Brown Pelican
Scientific name: *Pelecanus occidentalis*
Spanish name: *Pelícano Pardo*

Brown Pelican on nest (RR)

The brown pelican is instantly recognisable with its huge pouched bill and large size (122 cm long and with a two-metre wingspan) and is often the first bird the visitor identifies. It feeds by shallow plunge diving and scoops up as much as 10 litres of water in its distendable pouch. The water rapidly drains out through the bill and the trapped fish are swallowed. It sounds straightforward but apparently it isn't. Although parents raise frequent broods of two or three chicks, many of the fledged young are unable to learn the scoop-fishing technique quickly enough and so starve to death.

As the name suggests, these pelicans are generally brownish in colour. During the breeding season, however, the adults gain bright white and chestnut markings on their heads and necks. They nest year-round in most of the islands.

The pelicans have wide fingered wings and are good gliders. They are often seen flying in a squadron-like formation, flapping and gliding in unison to create an elegant aerial ballet.

BOOBIES (SULIDAE)

Four species of booby have been recorded and three of them breed in the islands. Although they are not endemic, they are still among the most popular birds visitors want to see. It is easy to understand why – their appearance is amusing and their colonies are among the most approachable in the islands. You can often get within a few feet of an active nest which will provide you with great photographs.

The boobies are in the same family as the gannets and look very much like them; they are fast fliers and exceptional plunge divers. Punta Pitt on San Cristóbal is the only visitor site where all three species are seen together.

Blue-footed Booby

Scientific name: *Sula nebouxii*
Spanish name: *Piquero Patas Azules*

Blue-footed Boobies (female with larger pupil on right) (RR)

The blue-footed booby is perhaps the most famous Galápagos bird and is often the first booby seen by visitors. Large active colonies on Seymour and Española (Hood) are occupied throughout the year.

This large, whitish-brown seabird (length, 74 to 89 cm; wingspan, about 1½ metres) really does have bright blue feet which it picks up in a slow, most dignified fashion when performing a courtship display. Bowing, wing spreading, and sky pointing (with the neck, head, and bill stretched straight upwards) are also features of courtship. Watching this clownish behaviour is one of the highlights of any trip to the Galápagos.

At first glance, the males and females are almost identical but you can tell them apart: the larger females have a slightly bigger pupil and honk, whereas the males whistle. Courtship, mating and nesting occur year round – although nesting is a euphemism for a scrape on the ground surrounded by a ring of guano. The young, of which there may be one, two or three, are covered with fluffy white down which can make them look larger than their parents. In a good year, all three young may survive – otherwise the strongest one or two will outcompete the youngest, which dies of starvation.

Masked Booby

Scientific name: *Sula dactylatra*
Spanish names: *Piquero Enmascarado; Piquero Blanco*

Masked Boobies courtship display (JW)

The masked (white) booby is pure white with a black band at the edges of the wings and the end of the tail. The face mask which gives the bird its name is formed by a blackish area of bare skin surrounding the bill, which can be yellow or pinkish. It is the biggest of the Galápagos boobies (76 to 89 cm long; 152 to 183-cm wingspan). This booby is found on most of the islands.

Breeding is on an annual cycle (unlike the other boobies) but the cycle varies from island to island. On Genovesa (Tower), the birds arrive in May, courtship, mating and nest building ensue and eggs are laid from August to November. Most of the young have fledged by February and the colony is out at sea until May. On Española (Hood), the colony is present from September to May, with egg-laying occurring from November to February.

Males and females look the same but their calls differ – the smaller males whistle whilst the females utter a trumpeting quack. They often nest near cliff tops to give themselves an advantage when taking off – they are large birds. Two eggs are laid but the older sibling ejects the younger from the nest and only one survives, even in a good year with plenty of food.

Red-footed Booby (RR)

Red-footed Booby
Scientific name: *Sula sula*
Spanish name: *Piquero Patas Rojas*

The red-footed booby is the smallest of the Galápagos boobies (74 cm long; 137-cm wingspan) and is readily distinguished by its red feet and blue bill with red base. Most adults are brown, but about 5% are white – this is a different colour phase and does not represent a new, different or hybrid species. The red-footed is the most numerous of the Galápagos boobies but also the least frequently seen; this is because it is found only on the more outlying islands, such as Genovesa (Tower) where there is a sizable colony estimated at 140,000 pairs. It feeds far out to sea and thus avoids competing with the blue-footed booby which feeds close inshore and the masked booby which feeds intermediately.

The nesting behaviour of this booby is quite different from the others. It builds rudimentary nests in trees (as opposed to the guano-ringed scrapes on the ground of the other boobies) and lays only one egg. This usually happens when food is plentiful, and can occur at any time of year.

CORMORANTS (PHALACROCORACIDAE)

Flightless Cormorant
Scientific name: *Nannopterum harrisi*
Spanish name: *Cormorán No Volador*

Apart from the penguins, there is only one other flightless seabird found in the world. This is the flightless cormorant, which is endemic to the Galápagos. At about 90 cm long it is the tallest of the world's 29 species of cormorant and the only one which has lost its ability to fly. It is found only on the coasts of Isabela and Fernandina.

Flightless Cormorant

To see this unique bird, you should plan on a two-week tour. If you think that is a long time, consider the time it must have taken for flightlessness to evolve in this cormorant. Its ancestors were almost certainly able to fly, but when they reached the Galápagos, they found no predators in the rocky inshore shallows where they fed. Therefore they didn't need wings to flee, and the cormorants that survived the best were the streamlined ones which could swim and dive strongly in the surf of the shallows. Thus birds with small wings and strong legs were selected for and eventually the flightless cormorant evolved.

Flightless cormorants nest in small colonies and there are only about 700 to 800 pairs of birds in existence. That number dropped to 400 to 500 pairs after the disastrous El Niño year of 1982/83, though they have recovered since. Flightless cormorants are not endangered, but could become so if predatory feral animals (especially wild dogs) are introduced into the islands where they breed.

The birds can breed year-round, though March to September is favoured for egg-laying. Unlike most seabirds, the adults do not mate for life. Indeed, a female may well leave a brood to be raised by the father whilst she mates with another male; thus a female may have two broods a year.

Male Frigatebird displaying colourful pouch

FRIGATEBIRDS (FREGATIDAE)

Magnificent Frigatebird
Scientific name: *Fregata magnificens*
Spanish name: *Fragata Magna*

Great Frigatebird
Scientific name: *Fregata minor*
Spanish name: *Fragata Grande*

The two frigatebird species in the Galápagos are not easy to tell apart. Both are large, elegant and streamlined black seabirds with long forked tails. They make an acrobatic living by aerial piracy, often harassing smaller birds into dropping or regurgitating their catch and then swooping to catch their stolen meal in midair. This occurs because frigatebirds have a very small preening gland and are not able to secrete enough oils to waterproof their feathers – therefore they cannot dive underwater to catch prey. They are, however, able to catch fish on the surface by snatching them up with their hooked beaks. With their 230 cm wingspan, the birds are magnificent fliers and have the largest wingspan to weight ratio of any bird.

As with many Galápagos seabirds, frigatebird courtship display is quite spectacular. The males have flaps of bright red skin hanging under their necks and these are inflated into football-sized balloons to attract females. It takes about 20 minutes to fully inflate the pouch and the male normally sits on a tree and displays skywards to passing females.

Great Frigatebird (female) (RR)

Occasionally, a male is seen flying overhead with his pouch still distended – a strange sight.

North Seymour Island has a constantly active magnificent frigatebird colony and is the place where most people get a good look at these birds. There are colonies on many of the other islands. Great frigatebirds tend to go further out to sea and are found more often on the outer islands; recommended locations are Isla Genovesa (Tower) and Punta Pitt, Isla San Cristóbal. Telling the all-black males apart is problematical – the magnificent frigatebird, at 107 cm in length, is about 5 cm longer than the great frigatebird. This is almost impossible to tell in the field. Also, the male magnificent has a metallic purplish sheen to its black plumage while the great has a greenish sheen – again, it takes an experienced eye to tell the difference.

Females are easier to tell apart. Magnificent females have white underparts with a black throat and also have a thin blue eye-ring. Great females have white underparts, including the throat, and have a reddish eye-ring. Once you identify the females, you can assume that their mates are of the same species. Immature birds of both species, in addition to white underparts, also have white heads.

Great Frigatebird Colony, male adult with young (RR)

HERONS & EGRETS (ARDEIDAE)
This family has five species resident in the islands and three other species have been recorded. There is controversy among ornithologists about naming and classifying some of these birds.

Great Blue Heron
Scientific name: *Ardea herodias*
Spanish names: *Garzón Azulado, Garza Morena*

This is the largest heron in the Galápagos (138 cm long; almost two-metre wingspan) and will be familiar to visitors from North and Central America. Despite its name, it is a mostly grey bird but is easily recognised with its long legs and great size. Like many members of this family, it often stands with its head hunched into its shoulders – it always flies this way, with the legs trailing behind.

Great blue herons are found along the rocky coasts of most of the islands, often standing motionless as they wait for a fish to swim by, although they also will take lizards, young marine iguanas and birds for food. They tend to be solitary or in pairs, but occasionally form a small colony of up to six nests. They breed year round and often nest in mangroves.

Great Blue Heron (RR)

Common Egret
Scientific name: *Casmerodius albus*
Spanish names: *Garceta Grande, Garza Blanca*

Common Egret (RR)

This bird is also known as the Great Egret or the American Egret. The scientific name of *Egretta alba* has also been assigned to this bird. It is a large (102 cm long; 137-cm wingspan) all-white heron with a yellow bill and black legs and feet. It is less common than the great blue heron but found in similar habitats, and occasionally inland.

Cattle Egret
Scientific name: *Bubulcus ibis*
Spanish names: *Garcilla (Garza) Bueyera*

This small white heron (51 cm long; 91-cm wingspan) is distinguished from the common egret at a distance by its shorter neck and stockier appearance. Closer up, the yellow legs and feet can be seen. This bird came originally from Africa and southern Eurasia and was unknown in the Americas until the 1800s. It was first recorded in the Galápagos in 1965 and is now common in pasturelands, especially in the highlands of Santa Cruz where the birds are most often seen.

Lava Heron (RR)

Lava Heron
Scientific name: *Butorides sundevalli*
Spanish names: *Garcilla de Lava, Garza Verde*

This small (41 cm long; 64-cm wingspan) dark heron is the only endemic one in the Galápagos. Its dark green plumage camouflages it well against the lava shorelines where it stealthily hunts for prey. It has yellow/orange legs. They breed year round, although September to March is the preferred time. Immature birds are brown and streaked. Their nests are usually solitary (occasionally in twos and threes) and found under a lava outcrop or in mangrove trees. They are common on the rocky shores of all the islands, but because of their camouflage and solitary nature, are a little difficult to see – your naturalist guide should be able to show you one with no problem.

The striated heron *(Butorides striatus)* is about the same size but paler than the lava heron. Ornithologists are uncertain if the lava heron is simply a variety of the striated heron, or whether the two can hybridise, or whether they are distinct species.

Yellow-crowned Night Heron
Scientific name: *Nyctanassa violacea*
Spanish names: *Garza Nocturna, Garcilla Coroniamarilla*

This common heron tends to feed at night, but can often be seen during the day in shaded areas along the coasts of all the islands. It is a stocky, grey heron with a black and white head and yellow crown. Because of its nocturnal habits, its eyes are larger than other herons. It is 61 cm long and has a 117-cm

Yellow-crowned Night Heron (RR)

wingspan. They breed in single pairs and build nests year round in mangroves or under rocks.

FLAMINGOS (PHOENICOPTERIDAE)

Greater Flamingo
Scientific name: *Phoenicopterus ruber*
Spanish name: *Flamenco*

These large (122 cm long; 152-cm wingspan), long-necked, pink shorebirds are immediately recognisable. Their wing feathers are black and the birds look spectacular in flight with their long necks stretched out, legs trailing, and black and pink markings flapping contrastingly. They are nervous birds, however, particularly when nesting, and visitors should act quietly when viewing flamingos or they may desert their nests. This is one bird for which a long telephoto lens is very useful in photography.

Flamingos breed in small colonies in salty lagoons. They build cone-shaped nests out of mud and lay a single egg in a depression at the top of the nest. They can breed year-round but prefer moist conditions and so most breeding takes place in the wet season (January to May). There are commonly-visited flamingo lagoons on Santa María (Floreana), Rábida and Santiago (James) islands.

Flamingo feeding behaviour is mildly bizarre – they feed by dangling their long necks into the water and swinging their upside down heads from side to side. Water is sucked in through the front of the highly specialised bill and filtered through sieves before being expelled through the sides of the bill. Food consists of insects, small crabs, shrimps and other crustaceans – the pinkish colour of the shrimps maintains the colour of the birds' plumage.

Greater Flamingo (RR)

DUCKS & GEESE (ANATIDAE)
Three species of ducks have been recorded in the Galápagos; only one breeds here.

White-cheeked Pintail
Scientific name: *Anas bahamensis*
Spanish names: *Patillo, Anade Cariblanco*

If you see a duck in the Galápagos it is usually the white-cheeked pintail which breeds in small numbers on salt lagoons and ponds on most of the major islands. It can be seen year-round.

HAWKS (ACCIPITRIDAE)
Apart from the hawks, ospreys (Pandionidae) and peregrine falcons (Falconidae) visit occasionally.

White-cheeked Pintails (RR)

Galápagos Hawk (RR)

Galápagos Hawk
Scientific name: *Buteo galapagoensis*
Spanish name: *Gavilán de Galápagos*

This endemic hawk is the only raptor which breeds in the islands. It is 56 cm long and has a 122-cm wing-span, and has much broader wings than similarly-sized seabirds. The birds are dark brown with yellow legs, feet and ceres (the fleshy area at the base of the bill). Immature birds are lighter and heavily mottled.

These predatory birds have no natural enemies and are relatively fearless. This has led to their extinction by hunters on several islands, including Santa María (Floreana), San Cristóbal, Seymour, Baltra, Genovesa (Tower) and Daphne. They have been severely reduced on Santa Cruz and just over 100 pairs are estimated to remain in the Galápagos. Santiago (James), Bartolomé, Española (Hood), Santa Fe, Fernandina and Isabela are the best islands on which to see them.

Breeding occurs year-round but is most frequent from May to July. The birds practice cooperative polyandry, where a single female has two or more mates and all the adults help in raising the young. It is not easy to separate the sexes, but the female is generally larger than the males.

RAILS, CRAKES & GALLINULES (RALLIDAE)
The three Galápagos species are common but are rarely seen because they are small and secretive. Brief descriptions of these are given.

Galápagos Rail
Scientific name: *Laterallus spilonotus*
Spanish names: *Pachay, Polluela de Galápagos*

This tiny (15 cm long) dark, endemic bird scurries around in the vegetation of the highlands, particularly Santa Cruz and Santiago (James). It has white spots on its wings. It rarely flies and escapes by running.

Paint-billed Crake
Scientific name: *Neocrex erythrops*
Spanish names: *Gallareta, Pollula Pinta*

Slightly larger (20 cm), this dark bird is similar to the rail but lacks the white wing spots and has red legs and a red and yellow bill. The crake, too, dislikes flying. It is associated with farmlands, particularly on Santa Cruz and Santa María (Floreana). It was first recorded in the islands in 1953.

Common Gallinule
Scientific name: *Gallinula chloropus*
Spanish names: *Gallinula, Gallareta Común*

Paint-billed Crake

This chicken-like waterbird (also called the common moorhen) is 35 cm long and is quite cosmopolitan. It is black, with a red and yellow bill, yellow legs, and a white patch under the tail. It lives on a few ponds and brackish areas of water in all the larger islands except Santiago (James). When swimming, it pumps its head back and forth in a characteristic way.

OYSTERCATCHERS (HAEMATOPODIDAE)

American Oystercatcher
Scientific name: *Haematopus palliatus*
Spanish names: *Ostrero Americano, Cangrejero*

This 46-cm-long black and white shorebird has a stout, red, eight-cm long bill, pink feet and yellow eyes, making it quite unmistakeable. Although there are only between 100 and 200 pairs in the islands, they are spread out along the rocky coasts and you are likely to see them on many of the islands. The first sign of their presence is often their repetitive, high-pitched call, described as 'kleep' in some books.

They nest mainly from October to March and are solitary nesters. One or two precocial young are hatched which join their parents within a few minutes.

PLOVERS (CHARADRIIDAE)
Plovers are small, compact, wading shorebirds which tend to run in short bursts. Their bills are generally small and pigeon-like. Six or seven species

American Oystercatcher (RR)

have been recorded in the Galápagos, all migrants. The two most common ones may remain year-round in small numbers and are described below.

Semi-palmated Plover

Scientific name: *Charadrius semipalmatus*
Spanish name: *Chorlitejo semipalmado*

This 18-cm-long shorebird is mainly brown above except for a white collar, forehead and stripe above the eye. Most of the underneath is white except for a brown chest band. Breeding birds may have a black band and head. The base of the bill is orange and the legs are yellowish. It is most commonly seen on sandy beaches from August to April.

Semi-palmated Plover

Ruddy Turnstone

Scientific name: *Arenaria interpres*
Spanish name: *Vuelvepiedras Rojizo*

This 23-cm-long shorebird is found on rocky coasts where it feeds, as its name suggests, by turning over small stones in search of prey. It is common from August to March and has a brown back, white chin and throat, and white underparts with a brownish breast patch. In breeding plumage (not often seen in the Galápagos) it has a black and white patterned head and chest, bright russet back, and white underparts. The legs are orange. Some authorities suggest that the turnstones are sandpipers, not plovers.

SANDPIPERS (SCOLOPACIDAE)

Sandpipers are an extremely varied family of shorebirds. Most are waders and generally have longer necks and beaks and are slimmer than the plovers. Some 22 species have been recorded from the Galápagos, all migrants which breed in the northern hemisphere. The four species described below are commonly seen from August to April; a few individuals remain year-round.

Wandering Tattler

Scientific name: *Heteroscelus incanus*
Spanish name: *Correlimos Vagabundo*

This 25-cm-long shorebird is the most frequently seen migrant but is rather nondescript. It has dark brownish-grey upperparts and breast, white belly and yellowish-green legs. It prefers rocky shores.

Sanderling

Scientific name: *Calidris alba*
Spanish name: *Correlimos Arenero*

Sanderlings (RR)

These common 20-cm-long shorebirds are the palest of the small Galápagos waders. They prefer sandy beaches where they run along the wave fronts like a flock of clockwork toys. They have light grey backs, dark wing tips, and white underparts. The legs and bill are dark. In breeding plumage, the head and upperparts are a rusty brown.

Whimbrel
Scientific name: *Numenius phaeopus*
Spanish name: *Zarapito Trinador*

This common wader is about 43 cm long and has a characteristic down-curved bill which is as much as 10 cm long. The dark legs are also long – long is the operative word in identifying this shorebird. It has a mottled grey-brown plumage, and light and dark stripes through the head. Unlike most other waders, it shows no wing patterns in flight.

Northern Phalarope
Scientific name: *Phalaropus lobatus*
Spanish name: *Falaropo Picofino*

These birds (also called red-necked phalaropes) swim rather than wade and may be seen some way out at sea in 'rafts' of hundreds of birds. These 18-cm-long birds have a blackish back with a pair of whitish longitudinal streaks, and white underparts. There is a conspicuous white wing-bar in flight. The bill is very thin.

STILTS (RECURVIROSTRIDAE)

Black-necked Stilt
Scientific name: *Himantopus himantopus*
Spanish names: *Tero Real, Cigüeñuela Cuellinegra*

This elegant black and white wader is also called the common stilt. It is slightly smaller (38 cm) than the oystercatcher, from which it is easily distinguished by its very slim shape, long red legs, and slim black bill.
It is most frequently seen alone or in pairs, wading in lagoons. Stilts are solitary breeders and lay four eggs in a scrape at lagoon edges during the wet season. They are noisy, especially in flight.

GULLS, TERNS & SKUAS (LARIDAE)
There are two resident gull species, both endemic to the Galápagos, and two resident terns, neither of which are endemic. In addition, three other gull, four other tern and four skua species have been occasionally or rarely recorded.

Swallow-tailed Gull
Scientific name: *Creagrus furcatus*
Spanish name: *Gaviota Blanca, Gaviota Tijereta*

Whimbrel

Northern Phalarope

Swallow-tailed Gulls (RR)

The lovely swallow-tailed gull is grey and white with bright red feet and legs and a crimson eye-ring. It is 51 cm long and has a 114-cm wingspan. This bird feeds at night and is the only nocturnal gull in the world – its eyes are larger than in most other gulls. It is frequently seen perched on cliff tops during the day. Although a few pairs nest on an island off Colombia, almost the entire world population nests in the Galápagos and therefore the swallow-tailed gull is considered endemic.

Swallow-tailed gulls nest in colonies near small cliffs and beaches and can be seen on most major islands except the far western ones. Their breeding cycle lasts about nine or 10 months and so nesting can be seen at any time of year. There are about 10,000 to 15,000 pairs in the islands.

Lava Gull (RR)

Lava Gull
Scientific name: *Larus fuliginosus*
Spanish names: *Gaviota Morena, Gaviota de Lava*

The lava gull is the rarest gull in the world – only about 400 pairs are estimated to exist. Despite this, you have a very good chance of seeing one because they are widely distributed in the Galápagos. They are about 53 cm long and are generally dark grey to black with white eyelids. They are solitary nesters and breed throughout the year.

Brown Noddy
Scientific name: *Anous stolidus*
Spanish names: *Nodi, Charrán Pardo*

Brown Noddy Tern (RR)

The brown noddy tern is, as its name suggests, generally dark brown with a whitish forehead and is often seen feeding with pelicans. It may catch fish scraps from the water draining out of a pelican's bill and even perch on the pelican's head to better enable it to reach the food. This bird is 38 cm long and has a 76-cm wingspan. It nests in small colonies on cliffs and in caves at any time of year.

Sooty Tern
Scientific name: *Sterna fuscata*
Spanish name: *Gaviotín Sombrió*

The black and white sooty tern also breeds in the Galápagos, but is restricted to Isla Darwin in the far north and so is rarely seen.

PIGEONS (COLUMBIDAE)

Galápagos Dove
Scientific name: *Zenaida galapagoensis*
Spanish names: *Paloma, Tórtola de Galápagos*

This pretty little 20-cm-long dove is endemic. The underneath is reddish, the upperparts are brownish, and there are green neck patches, blue eye rings, and red legs and feet – a colourful bird.

Breeding occurs year-round. Two eggs are laid in a haphazard nest of grass and twigs under a rock or in an abandoned nest of another species. When incubating, adults may walk away from a nest feigning injury, to lure predators away from the nest – this behaviour evolved long before doves arrived in the Galápagos and has been retained, even though it was of little advantage in the islands.

Galápagos Dove (RR)

CUCKOOS & ANIS (CUCULIDAE)
Two species of cuckoos and two of anis have been recorded; one of each is common.

Dark-billed Cuckoo
Scientific name: *Coccyzus melacoryphus*
Spanish names: *Cuclillo Piquioscuro, Aguatero*

About half of this 28-cm-long bird is tail – long tails are characteristic of this family. It is a dark brown-grey bird with a light underside with a yellowish wash, white tail tips, and black beak and legs. The cuckoo is reasonably common but secretive – therefore its low, chuckling call is heard more often than the bird is seen. It is commonly found only on Santa Cruz, San Cristóbal, Santa María (Floreana), Isabela and Fernandina. The nesting season is January to May.

Groove-billed Ani
Scientific name: *Crotophaga sulcirostris*
Spanish name: *Garrapatero Piquiestriado*

The groove-billed ani was introduced to the islands in the 1960s and it is now seen regularly in the Santa Cruz highlands where it probably breeds. The similar looking smooth-billed ani *(C. ani)* was recorded in the same area during the 1980s. Both birds are all black, about 30 cm long, and with a distinctively long, floppy tail. Telling them apart is not easy.

OWLS (TYTONIDAE & STRIGIDAE)
The two families of owls are each represented by one species in the Galápagos.

Barn Owl
Scientific name: *Tyto alba*
Spanish names: *Lechuza Campanaria, Lechuza Blanca*

This small (25 cm long) owl is found all over the world. The almost white, heart-shaped facial disk is the most striking feature of this pale owl which, because of its nocturnal habits, is rarely seen. It is most common on

Short-eared Owl (RR)

Vermilion Flycatcher (RR)

Fernandina but also has been recorded from Santa Cruz, Isabela, Santiago (James) and San Cristóbal.

Short-eared Owl
Scientific name: *Asio flammeus*
Spanish names: *Lechuza de Campo, Buho Orejicorto*

This owl is much larger (36 cm long; 94-cm wing-span) and darker than the barn owl. Also, it is diurnal and so is seen much more often. It is found on all the main islands but is least common on Fernandina and most common on Santa Cruz and Genovesa (Tower) where it is frequently seen hunting in the storm petrel colonies. Owls have specialised feathers which enable them to fly and glide soundlessly – a great advantage when hunting small birds, rodents and lizards. They can breed year round but prefer the wet season. They nest on the ground in heavy vegetation and are territorial.

TYRANT FLYCATCHERS (TYRANNIDAE)

Vermilion Flycatcher
Scientific name: *Pyrocephalus rubinus*
Spanish names: *Mosquero Bermellón, Brujo*

This adult male is tiny (about 13 cm long) but quite unmistakeable with its bright red crown and under-parts. The upperparts, tail and eye stripe are almost black. Females are brown above and yellowish beneath; the chest is almost white and lightly streaked.

The vermilion flycatcher is widespread in the high-lands of most islands, though it is occasionally seen by the coast. The trees and shrubs around the collapsed calderas of Los Gemelos, in the Santa Cruz highlands, is a good place to see this bird.

They are territorial and like to breed during the rainy season. Small nests are built in trees in the highlands.

Large-billed (Galápagos) Flycatcher
Scientific name: *Myiarchus magnirostris*
Spanish names: *Papa Moscas, Copetón Piquigrande*

This endemic bird is seen more frequently than the vermilion flycatcher. It is about 15 cm long, and is grey and brown with a yellowish belly, although less yellow than the female vermilion flycatcher. The large-billed flycatcher is found in drier and lower areas than the vermilion flycatcher and is widespread on all the main islands except Genovesa (Tower).

SWALLOWS & MARTINS (HIRUNDINIDAE)
Five species of this family have been recorded, but only one is resident.

Galápagos (Southern) Martin
Scientific name: *Progne modesta*
Spanish names: *Martín Sureño, Golondrina*

This 16-cm-long bird is very dark, with a shallowly forked tail and pointed wings. The female is dark brown; the male is glossy black. They have a characteristic flight of a few quick flaps followed by a glide. The dark plumage, small size, typical flight, and pointed silhouette identify this martin. Martins are less common in the northern islands but are distributed throughout the Galápagos. They hunt for insects on the updrafts from cliffs and highlands.

MOCKINGBIRDS (MIMIDAE)
The fearless and endemic mockingbirds are often seen on all the islands except Pinzón (which has no mockers). These birds are a classic example of adaptive radiation – there are four species descended from a common ancestor which look very similar to one another, except for their bills which differ in size and shape. The mockingbirds are 25 to 30 cm long, streaked grey and brown, with a long tail and curved bill. So how do you tell them apart? Very easily, it turns out. They are most easily separated by their geographic distribution.

The mockingbirds lay from two to four eggs from October to April – two broods may be raised during this period. The birds are territorial and build nests of twigs in trees, shrubs or cacti. Occasionally, they are cooperative breeders, with three or more adults raising a brood.

Galápagos Mockingbird
Scientific name: *Neosomimus parvulus*
Spanish name: *Sinsonte de Galápagos*

This bird is found on all the central and western islands except the ones mentioned later.

Charles Mockingbird
Scientific name: *Nesomimus trifasciatus*
Spanish name: *Sinsonte de Floreana*

This bird was originally found on Santa María (Floreana, Charles) but is now extinct on that island. About 150 birds are left on the nearby islets of Champion and Gardner-near-Floreana.

Hood Mockingbird
Scientific name: *Nesomimus macdonaldi*
Spanish name: *Sinsonte de Española*

Large-billed (Galápagos) Flycatcher
(RR)

Galápagos Mockingbird (RR)

Hood Mockingbird (RR)

Yellow Warbler (RR)

One of Darwin's Finches (RR)

Sharp-beaked Ground Finch

This mocker is the largest of the four species and has a noticeably heavier bill than the others. It is easily found, but only on Española (Hood) and the nearby islet of Gardner-near-Hood.

Chatham Mockingbird
Scientific name: *Nesomimus melanotis*
Spanish name: *Sinsonte de San Cristóbal*

This species is endemic to San Cristóbal (Chatham) where it is common.

WOOD WARBLERS, TANAGERS, BLACKBIRDS etc (EMBERIZIDAE)
There are at least four species of emberizids recorded from the Galápagos, of which only one is resident or commonly seen.

Yellow Warbler
Scientific name: *Dendroica petechia*
Spanish names: *Canario, Reinita Amarillo*

This tiny (only 13 cm long) warbler is the only bright yellow bird in the Galápagos. It is yellow below and greenish olive above; the male has fine reddish streaks on the chest. It occurs throughout the Galápagos, from the coasts to the highlands.
    Although they lay eggs only from December to April, they defend territories throughout the year.

FINCHES (FRINGILLIDAE)
The 13 Darwin's finches are the most famous and biologically important birds of the Galápagos. Some visitors find them disappointing; they certainly are not very spectacular to look at.
    Darwin's finches are all endemic and everyone will see some of them – although it takes an expert to be able to tell them apart. All 13 species are thought to have descended from a common ancestor and their present differences in distribution, body size, plumage, beak size and shape, and feeding habits helped Darwin formulate his evolutionary theories.
    The best islands to separate three of the species is Española (Hood). Here, you'll find only the warbler finch (with its tiny warbler-like bill), the small ground finch (with its small finch-like bill) and the large cactus finch (with a massive bill). After that, the going gets more difficult. There are tree finches which are seen on the ground, ground finches which are seen in the trees, and cactus finches which may be seen in all sorts of places apart from cacti.
    If you want to see all thirteen species, you'll need to do some travelling. The medium tree finch is found only in the highlands of Santa María (Floreana). The mangrove finch is found only on Isabela and Fernandina. The large cactus finch is found only on Genovesa (Tower) and Española (Hood) of the

islands with visitor sites. The other finches are more widely distributed.

The most famous of these birds is the woodpecker finch, which sometimes grasps a twig in its bill and pokes this 'tool' into holes and cracks in dead trees or bark. With some perseverance, the bird may extract a grub or other prey which it would otherwise not have been able to reach. This remarkable example of tool use is very rare among birds. Mangrove finches have also been recorded to do this.

It is beyond the scope of this guide to describe individually all 13 finches adequately enough to enable you to identify them. If your tour guide is a very good naturalist, she or he will help you. Otherwise, get Harris' field guide – he has about 25 pages on the finches alone. And remember what Harris writes: 'It is only a very wise man or a fool who thinks he is able to identify all the finches which he sees.'

Large Cactus Finch (RR)

Cactus Finch on prickly pear cactus flower (RR)

Small Ground Finch
Scientific name: *Geospiza fuliginosa*
Spanish name: *Pinzón Terrestre Chico*

Medium Ground Finch
Scientific name: *Geospiza fortis*
Spanish name: *Pinzón Terrestre Mediano*

Large Ground Finch
Scientific name: *Geospiza magnirostris*
Spanish name: *Pinzón Terrestre Grande*

Sharp-beaked Ground Finch
Scientific name: *Geospiza difficilis*
Spanish name: *Pinzón Terrestre Piquiagudo*

Cactus Finch
Scientific name: *Geospiza scandens*
Spanish name: *Pinzón Cactero Chico*

Large Cactus Finch
Scientific name: *Geospiza conirostris*
Spanish name: *Pinzón Cactero Grande*

Vegetarian Finch
Scientific name: *Platyspiza crassirostris*
Spanish name: *Pinzón Vegetariano*

Small Tree Finch
Scientific name: *Camarhynchus parvulus*
Spanish name: *Pinzón Arbóreo Chico*

Vegetarian Finch

Small Tree Finch

Medium Tree Finch
Scientific name: *Camarhynchus pauper*
Spanish name: *Pinzón Arbóreo Mediano*

Large Tree Finch
Scientific name: *Camarhynchus psittacula*
Spanish name: *Pinzón Arbóreo Grande*

Woodpecker Finch
Scientific name: *Camarhynchus pallidus*
Spanish name: *Pinzón Artesano*

Mangrove Finch
Scientific name: *Camarhynchus heliobates*
Spanish name: *Pinzón Manglero*

Warbler Finch
Scientific name: *Certhidea olivacea*
Spanish name: *Pinzón Reinita*

Warbler Finch (RR)

REPTILES

The prehistoric-looking reptiles found all over the islands are easily approached and observed. There are 22 species, belonging to five families. Of these, all but three species are endemic.

TORTOISES (TESTUDINIDAE)

Giant Tortoise
Scientific name: *Geochelone elephantopus*
Spanish name: *Tortuga Gigante, Galápagos*

The most famous of the reptiles is, of course, the endemic giant tortoise for which the islands are named. There is only one species which has been divided into 14 subspecies – three of these are extinct. One of the best ways to distinguish them (apart from geographic distribution) is by differences in the shape of their carapaces (shells). These differences contributed to Darwin's thoughts whilst he was developing his theory of evolution.

Many thousands of tortoises were killed by whalers and sealers, particularly in the 18th and 19th centuries, and now only some 15,000 remain. A breeding project at the Charles Darwin Research Station appears to be successful and it is hoped to begin re-introduction of animals into the wild. The easiest way to see both tiny yearlings and full-grown adults is at the research station. Although they are in enclosures, visitors are permitted to enter and get a close look at these giants, some of which can reach a weight of 250 kg – or 3000 times more than newborn hatchlings, which weigh only about 80 g. The Research Station is one of the few places where you can actually touch the animals. To see tortoises in the wild you can go to the tortoise reserve on Santa Cruz, visit the Los Galápagos visitor site on San Cristóbal, or climb Volcán Alcedo on Isabela.

The tortoises are vegetarians and have slow digestive systems – a meal can take up to three weeks to pass through. Scientists guess that the tortoises' life span is about 150 years, but records have not been kept for long enough to know for certain. Sexual maturity is reached at about 40 years of age (now you know why they say 'Life begins at forty!') Mating usually occurs towards the end of the rainy season. The males posture and shove other males in contests of dominance and then try to seek out a suitable mate – unsuccessful males have been known to attempt to mate with other males or even with appropriately shaped boulders!

Once mated, the females look for dry and sandy areas in which to make a nest. They dig a hole about 30 cm deep with their hind legs – this may take several days. Anywhere from two to 16 eggs are laid, and covered with a protective layer of mud made from soil mixed with urine. The eggs take about four to five months to develop and hatchlings usually emerge between December and April.

Giant Tortoise (JW)

MARINE TURTLES (CHELONIIDAE)
Leatherback and hawksbill turtles have been occasionally recorded in the Galápagos but only the green sea turtle is a resident breeder.

Pacific Green Sea Turtle
Scientific name: *Chelonia mydas*
Spanish name: *Tortuga Marina*

This marine turtle breeds and lays eggs in the Galápagos, but it is not endemic to the islands. Green sea turtles are quite promiscuous and during the breeding season, especially November to January, much mating activity can be observed in the water.

Nesting occurs at night on many of the sandy beaches of the islands and occurs mainly from December to June, with a peak around February. The females dig a hole in the sand above the high tide mark and deposit several dozen eggs – a process which takes about three hours. Once the eggs hatch, the hatchlings are very vulnerable to predation. They try and get to the ocean and then swim off for years – almost nothing is known about this period of their lives. Turtles seem to have great navigational skills – they return to nest at the same beach where they were hatched. Tagged adults have been recovered as far away as Costa Rica.

Pacific Green Sea Turtle (RR)

The adult turtles are huge and may reach 150 kg in weight. Snorkellers sometimes see them swimming underwater and it is an exciting sight to watch such a large animal come flapping serenely by.

IGUANAS & LIZARDS (IGUANIDAE)

The most frequently seen reptiles are the iguanas, of which there are three species, all endemic. There are seven endemic species of lizards.

Marine Iguana

Scientific name: *Amblyrhynchus cristatus*
Spanish name: *Iguana Marina*

The marine iguana is the only sea-going lizard in the world and is found on the rocky shores of most islands. This iguana has a blackish skin, which in the males can change to startling blues and reds during the breeding season. Breeding occurs at different times on different islands; the males on Española (Hood) are colourful year-round. Marine iguanas are colonial (often piling up one on top of the other) but when breeding, the larger males become territorial and aggressive, butting and pushing their rivals. Mated females lay two to four eggs in a sandy nest – these nests are guarded by the mothers although the hatchlings, which emerge after three or four months, are not given much parental protection.

Marine iguanas feed mainly on intertidal sea-weeds, although mature males have been recorded offshore at depths to 12 metres and can remain

Marine Iguana (RR)

submerged for an hour or more. The row of spines along the entire length of their backs, their scaly skins, their habit of occasionally snorting little clouds of salt spray into the air, and their length – which can reach almost a metre – makes them look like veritable little dragons.

Galápagos Land Iguana
Scientific name: *Conolophus subcristatus*
Spanish name: *Iguana Terrestre*

Santa Fe Land Iguana
Scientific name: *Conolophus pallidus*
Spanish name: *Iguana Terrestre de Santa Fe*

The two species of land iguanas look almost alike. They are yellowish in colour and bigger than their marine relatives – adults weighing six kg have been recorded. The Galápagos land iguana is found on Isabela, Santa Cruz, Fernandina, Seymour and South Plaza islands, with South Plaza being the best place to see them. They were formerly found on most of the other islands but hunting and competition with introduced animals (goats, rats, pigs, dogs), which prey on the eggs, has caused their demise on many islands. The similar looking Santa Fe land iguana is limited to that island only. It is slightly bigger, on average, than the Galápagos land iguana and is somewhat yellower with more pronounced spines. They can exceed a metre in length.

The preferred food of both species is the prickly pear cactus and the iguanas are sometimes seen standing on their rear legs in efforts to reach the succulent pads and yellow flowers. Their mouths are incredibly leathery, enabling them to eat the cactus pads whole without removing the spines.

Land iguanas are known to live for at least sixty years. They reach sexual maturity between six and ten years of age. Mated females lay from five to 15 eggs and, as in the marine iguana, they defend their nests until hatching occurs. Land iguanas breed in different months on different islands.

Galápagos Land Iguana under prickly pear cactus (RR)

Santa Fe Land Iguana (JW)

Lava Lizard
Scientific name: *Tropidurus spp*
Spanish name: *Lagartija de Lava*

Less spectacular than the iguanas, but also endemic, are the seven species of lava lizard which are frequently seen scurrying around. They can reach 30 cm in length but are usually smaller. Their most distinctive behavioural patterns are rapid head-bobbing and push-up stances to defend their territories and assert dominance. The male is larger and strongly patterned with yellow, black, and brown. The female is less strongly patterned but makes up for this by a flaming red throat.

Male Lava Lizard (RR)

It is easy to separate the seven species of lava lizard by geographical distribution. Six islands have their own endemic species that are found nowhere else in the world. These are *T. bivittatus* on San Cristóbal, *T. grayi* on Santa María (Floreana), *T. habellii* on Marchena, *T. delanonis* on Española (Hood), *T. pacificus* on Pinta and *T. duncanensis* on Pinzón. *T. albemarlensis* is found on most of the other islands except for Genovesa (Tower), Wolf and Darwin, which have no lava lizards.

GECKOS (GEKKONIDAE)

Less often seen are the small, harmless, nocturnal lizards called geckos, of which there are seven species (five endemic). They are often associated with human habitations and may be seen near houses at night. Geckos have adhesive pads on their digits and can climb vertical walls and even walk upside down on ceilings. Again, geographical distribution helps with separating the species. *Phyllodactylus bauri* is limited to Santa María (Floreana) and Española (Hood); *P. galapagoensis* is on several islands including Santa Cruz, Isabela, Santiago (James), Daphne Major, Fernandina and Pinzón; *P. barringtonensis* is only on Santa Fe; *P. gilberti* is only on Wolf. All four are endemic. There are three other species of gecko on San Cristóbal, but only one is endemic. These three are *P. tuberculosis, P. leei* and *Gonatodes caudiscutatus* – this last often lives in houses and has recently been introduced. The most recently introduced (I don't have distribution information) are *P. reissi* and *Lepidodactylus lugubris*.

Galápagos Snake (RR)

SNAKES (COLUBRIDAE)

Finally, you may see the Galápagos snake, which is small, drab and non-poisonous. There are three species of the genus *Alsophis* (formerly *Dromicus*), all endemic, all of the constrictor type, and they are difficult to tell apart. The adults reach a length of one meter and are not dangerous. A fourth species is *Philodrys biserialis*. Many visitors spend a week touring the islands without catching a glimpse of even one.

MAMMALS

In the Galápagos the mammals are poorly represented because they had greater difficulty in surviving a long ocean crossing. There are only six native mammals, of which two are seals, two are bats and two are rice rats. Other land mammals are introduced species gone wild; they create a major nuisance to the native species by preying on them and by competing for food resources. They include feral goats, pigs, burros, cats, dogs, rats and mice.

PLAINNOSE BATS (VESPERTILIONIDAE)

There are two bat species, which probably flew across or were blown over in a storm. The hoary bat *(Lasiurus cinereus)* is well known in North America, but the endemic Galápagos bat *(Lasiurus brachyotis)* has been little studied. Bats are occasionally seen flying around lampposts in the island towns. The Spanish word for bat is *murciélago*.

MICE & RATS (CRICETIDAE)

Two endemic species of rice rat are found in the Galápagos. *Nesoryzomys narboroughii* is on Fernandina and *Oryzomys bauri* is on Santa Fe. Visitors occasionally catch a glimpse of these small rodents running around the trails of the appropriate island. These mammals probably floated across on vegetation rafts. It's thought that there were once seven species of rice rat, but five have become extinct since humans introduced the black rat.

EARED SEALS (OTARIIDAE)

Members of this family have external ears, use their front flippers for swimming, and can turn the hind flippers forward to enable them to 'walk' on land (true seals, Phocidae, can't do this). Both seal species found in the islands are members of the Otariidae.

Galápagos Sea Lion

Scientific name: *Zalophus californianus*
Spanish name: *Lobo Marino*

The native mammal you'll see the most of is the Galápagos sea lion, which is a subspecies of the Californian sea lion and found on most islands. There are an estimated 50,000 individuals in the Galápagos. The territorial bulls, which can reach 250 kg, are quite aggressive and sometimes chase swimmers out of the water. They have been known to bite if harassed so don't approach them too closely. The females and young, on the other hand, are extremely playful and you can often watch them swimming around you if you bring a mask and snorkel.

Sea lions live up to 20 years. Females are sexually mature at five years; males are capable of mating then, too, but don't do so until they are older. Dominant males patrol and guard particularly attractive beaches – these territories may contain up to 30 females. The dominant male has mating access to these females, but only for as long as he is able to keep other males away. Defending a territory is very demanding work and males may go for days without getting much food or sleep. After several weeks of this, a fresh new male may challenge and beat a harem-master and take over his position.

Females become sexually receptive once a year. Gestation lasts nine months and the (usually) single

Sea Lion and pup (RR)

Sea Lion and pup on Sombrero Chino (RR)

Galápagos Fur Seals (RR)

Dolphin surfing bow wave (JW)

pup is born around the beginning of the dry season. The mother nurses the pup for almost a week before returning to the water to feed; thereafter, she will continue to nurse the pup after fishing trips until the pup is five or six months old, when it will begin to learn to fish for itself. Even then, pups will continue to supplement their diet with milk, and some females may nurse two pups from different years.

Galápagos Fur Seal
Scientific name: *Arctocephalus galapagoensis*
Spanish name: *Foca Peletera, Lobo de Dos Pelos*

The endemic fur seals are less commonly seen than the sea lions, which superficially they resemble. On closer inspection, however, fur seals are quite different from sea lions. Fur seals are smaller, and have a broader, shorter shape of the head which supposedly resembles a bear's, hence the scientific name. (Arcto means bearlike and cephalus means head in Greek.) Fur seals' ears are a little more prominent and they have larger front flippers than sea lions.
 Their fur is very dense and luxuriant, being made of two layers of hair. This attracted the attention of sealers who decimated the population in the 1800s whilst hunting for the valuable skins. Because of their thick fur, the animals like to hide out in cool caves during the heat of the day and hunt at night. This secretive behavior helped the species survive the sealers depredations. Today, fur seals are fully protected and have recovered – there are almost as many fur seals as sea lions but the more secretive habits of the former explains why fur seals are seen less frequently by visitors.
 Fur seals' social and breeding behavior is quite similar to sea lions' – one difference is that fur seal males tend to defend territory from the land while sea lion males defend from the water.
 The best place to see fur seals is Puerto Egas on Santiago (James).

WHALES & DOLPHINS (Order CETACEA)
Other marine mammals you may see when cruising between the islands are whales and dolphins. There are seven whale species regularly recorded in the archipelago but they are difficult to tell apart because they are normally seen only momentarily and from a distance. The seven species are the finback, sei, humpback, minke, sperm, killer and pilot whales.
 Bottle-nosed dolphins *(Tursiops truncatus)* are often seen surfing the waves of the boats. If seen at night, the dolphins cause the ocean to glow with bioluminescence as they stir up thousands of tiny phosphorescent creatures that glow when disturbed. Less often seen are the common *(Delphinus delphis)* and spinner *(Stenella caerulleoalba)* dolphins.

FISH

Scientists have recorded 307 species of fish from 92 families in the Galápagos and it is expected that more will be discovered. Over 180 of these fish are found in much of the tropical eastern Pacific and about 50 are endemic. Merlen's *Field Guide to the Fishes of Galapagos* is available in Quito and recommended for snorkellers. This booklet describes and illustrates 107 of the most frequently seen species.

It is interesting that many species of tropical fish change their colour and shape as they age and a few can even change their sex midway through life. This certainly makes identification confusing!

Moorish Idol

Snorkelling in the Galápagos is a rewarding experience and schools containing thousands of tropical fish are routinely seen. Some of the naturalist guides working on the boats can help identify the more common species. These include blue-eyed damselfish, white-banded angelfish, yellow-tailed surgeonfish, moorish idols, blue parrotfish, concentric puffer fish, yellow-bellied triggerfish and hieroglyphic hawkfish – to name but a few and to give you some idea of the variety in form and colour.

The one type of fish that swimmers are often the most interested in is the **shark** (in Spanish, tiburón). There are several species found here and the most common are the white-tipped reef shark *(Triaenodon obesus)* and the Galápagos shark *(Carcharhinus galapagensis)*. Hammerheads *(Sphyrna lewini)* are also occasionally seen. For some reason, the sharks of the Galápagos have never been known to attack and injure a human swimmer.

They are often seen by snorkellers and their speed and grace underwater is almost otherworldly. In fact, one of the best reasons to snorkel in the Galápagos is the chance of seeing these magnificent animals in reasonable safety. Despite this reassurance, you should leave the water if you cut or graze yourself.

Another kind of fish which provides the snorkeller with a real thrill is the **ray.** Again, there are several species; all harmless with the exception of the stingray *(Urotrygon spp)*, which sometimes basks on the sandy bottoms of the shallows and can inflict an extremely painful wound to waders and paddlers. It is a good idea to enter the water by shuffling your feet along the sandy bottom – this gives stingrays the chance to swim away before you step on them.

Other rays are found in slightly deeper water and are often camouflaged on the sandy bottom. My first ray sighting was of a spotted eagle ray *(Aetobatus narinari)* which lay on the bottom motionless and almost invisible. As I swam over it, the fish suddenly broke loose of the sand and flapped away giving me a real shock. The sight of a metre-wide ray gently undulating through the water is quite mesmerising. Sizable schools of beautiful golden coloured mustard

White-banded Angelfish

rays *(Rhinoptera steindachneri)* are also seen quite regularly.

Less frequently seen is the giant manta ray *(Manta hamiltoni)* which is found in deeper offshore waters. You are most likely to catch sight of one as it leaps out of the water and falls back with a loud slap – with a maximum spread of six metres they make a huge splash as they hit the water.

INVERTEBRATES

The remaining animals encountered in the Galápagos do not possess a backbone and are hence collectively called invertebrates. The most common phyla include the Poriferans (sponges), Coelenterates or Cnidarians (jellyfish, sea anemones and corals), Molluscs (snails, chitons, shellfish, and octopuses), Arthropods (insects, spiders, barnacles, crabs, and lobsters), and Echinoderms (starfish, sea urchins, and sea cucumbers). There are other phyla which are less frequently encountered.

Sally Lightfoot Crab (RR)

The first invertebrate which most visitors notice is the **Sally Lightfoot crab** *(Grapsus grapsus)*. This small crab is bright red above and blue below and ubiquitous on almost every rock beach.

Also present on rock beaches is a small black crab which blends well with the lava background. These well camouflaged small black crabs are young Sally Lightfoots. The adults are far from camouflaged and rely on their alertness to escape predators. If you try and approach them, they will run away and are even capable of running across the surface of the water in tide pools. The crabs will, however, approach you if you sit as still as a rock. This is the strategy of the herons which prey on the Sally Lightfoots. Often you'll see a lava heron standing motionless on rocky beach. When a crab comes within reach, the bird will lunge forward and, if successful in capturing a crab, will then proceed to shake it and bang it against rocks until the legs fall off before devouring the animal.

Other crabs are found on sandy beaches. These are the pale coloured **ghost crabs** *(Ocypode spp)* which stare at you with unusual eyes at the end of long eye stalks. They leave the characteristic pattern of sand balls which are seen on most sandy beaches. In tide pools, you may see the **hermit crab** *(Calcinus explorator)* which lives in an empty sea shell which it carries around. As a young crab outgrows its protective shell, it finds a larger one to grow into. This 'moving house' occurs several times before the hermit crab reaches adult size.

At low tides, **tide pools** offer a good opportunity to study marine invertebrates. Starfish, sea anemones, sea urchins, marine snails, barnacles, chitons, and limpets are often found.

As you go further into the water with a mask and

snorkel, you can see many more species including sea cucumbers, octopuses, and corals and, if you care to poke around some of the rocky underwater crevices, lobster.

Be careful where you poke though, because you may encounter the **sea urchin**, *Diadema mexicana*, which has beautiful iridescent black spines which are long, brittle and needle sharp.

Less painful encounters with sea urchins can be had with *Eucidaris thouarsii* which has blunt pencil-like spines which often break off and are washed ashore, sometimes forming a large part of a beach.

The endemic green *Lytechnicus semituberculatus* urchin is also common and despite its prickly appearance, can be held quite easily and its tiny tube feet examined.

Sea urchins' prickly ball appearance belies their taxonomic grouping. They are in fact radially symmetrical in five or more planes and are hence members of the same phylum as the starfish and the sand dollar – the **Echinoderms.** The sand dollar looks like a flattened disc which has a starfish pattern on it. The starfish themselves are immediately recognisable but come in a fascinating array of sizes, colours, shapes, and numbers of arms ranging from five to many. The sea cucumbers are also Echinoderms. They lie on the bottom and look unfortunately similar to turds.

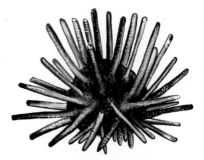

Sea Urchin

The phyla **Coelenterates** are represented by **sea anemones** which are stationary creatures which capture their food by waving stinging tentacles in the water. These tentacles do not create enough sting to hurt you, should you brush against one in a tide pool or shallow area.

Because of their appearance and the fact that they don't move from place to place, they are sometimes nicknamed 'sea-flowers'.

Swimming Coelenterates are represented in the islands by **jellyfish** which also capture prey using stinging tentacles. These can be quite painful should you come into contact with them, but fortunately, jellyfish aren't often seen in the main swimming spots.

Corals are also Coelenterates but there are not many in the Galápagos. The Devil's Crown off Isla Santa María is one of the best places to see living coral.

Dead coral is often found washed up ashore and sometimes forms a large part of a beach.

Insects are the most numerous animals in the world and literally millions of species are found in the tropics. A little over 1000 species are described from the Galápagos, and this comparatively small number reflects the difficulty that insects had in crossing almost 1000 km of ocean to colonise the islands.

There are not many colourful insect species. There are a few species of butterflies, ants, grasshoppers, and wasps, and many more representatives of the beetle and moth groups.

There is one species of bee, one preying mantis,

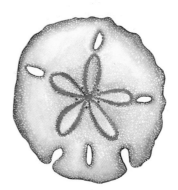

Sea Biscuit or Sand Dollar

and two scorpions in the Galápagos. The scorpions (which are more closely related to spiders than insects but like them are in the Arthropod phyla) are rarely encountered and though their sting can be painful, they are not normally dangerous.

Of the other biting insects, mosquitoes, horse flies, and midges are found and can sometimes make beach sunbathing unpleasant. Fortunately, these insects do not fly far and nights spent aboard a boat anchored several hundred metres off shore will usually be insect free. And if they're not, just anchor a few hundred metres further off.

PLANTS

Between 700 and 800 species of vascular plants have been recorded in the Galápagos, of which over 250 species are endemic. In addition, about 500 non-vascular plants (mosses, lichens, and liverworts) have been described. There are six different vegetation zones, beginning with the shore and ending with the highlands. These zones are the Littoral, Arid, Transition, Scalesia, Miconia, and Fern-Sedge. Each zone supports different and distinctive plant species.

The **littoral zone** contains species such as mangroves, saltbush and sesuvium. These plants are characterised by their ability to tolerate relatively high quantities of salt in their environment.

Immediately beyond the littoral zone is the **arid zone** where many of the islands' cactus species are found, including forests of the giant prickly pear cactus. Trees such as the ghostly looking palo santo, the palo verde, and the spiny acacias are found here as well as the yellow cordia shrub (with yellow flowers).

The **transition zone** has decreasing numbers of the arid zone trees and increasing numbers of lichens, perennial herbs, and smaller shrubs. The vegetation is both varied and thick and no particular plants are dominant.

In the higher islands, the transition zone gives way to a cloud forest type vegetation where the dominant tree is the endemic **Scalesia.** The trees are covered with smaller plants such as mosses, bromeliads, liverworts, ferns, and orchids.

Next is a treeless high altitude layer characterised by dense endemic **Miconia** shrub, liverworts, and ferns. This Miconia zone is found only on the south slopes of Santa Cruz and San Cristóbal.

Finally, the **fern-sedge zone** is the highest and contains mainly ferns and grasses, including the Galápagos tree fern which grows to three metres in height.

It is beyond the scope of this book to delve more deeply into the many hundreds of plant species and the reader is referred to Schofield (1984), Jackson (1985), and Wiggins & Porter (1971).

BIRD SPECIES IN THE GALÁPAGOS

	Species	Sighted	Date	Notes
•	Galápagos Penguin	❏		
•	Waved Albatross	❏		
R	Dark-rumped Petrel	❏		
R	Audubon's Shearwater	❏		
R	White-vented Storm Petrel	❏		
R	Band-rumped Storm Petrel	❏		
R	Wedge-rumped Storm Petrel	❏		
R	Red-billed Tropicbird	❏		
R	Brown Pelican	❏		
R	Blue-footed Booby	❏		
R	Masked Booby	❏		
R	Red-footed Booby	❏		
•	Flightless Cormorant	❏		
R	Great Frigatebird	❏		
R	Magnificent Frigatebird	❏		
R	Great Blue Heron	❏		
R	Common Egret	❏		
R	Cattle Egret	❏		
•	Lava Heron	❏		
R	Yellow-crowned Night Heron	❏		
R	Greater Flamingo	❏		
R	White-cheeked Pintail	❏		
•	Galápagos Hawk	❏		
•	Galápagos Rail	❏		
R	Paint-billed Crake	❏		
R	Common Gallinule	❏		
R	American Oystercatcher	❏		
M	Semi-palmated Plover	❏		
M	Ruddy Turnstone	❏		
M	Wandering Tattler	❏		
M	Sanderling	❏		
M	Whimbrel	❏		
M	Northern Phalarope	❏		
R	Black-necked Stilt	❏		
•	Swallow-tailed Gull	❏		
•	Lava Gull	❏		
R	Brown Noddy	❏		
R	Sooty Tern	❏		
•	Galápagos Dove	❏		
R	Dark-billed Cuckoo	❏		
R?	Groove-billed Ani	❏		
R	Barn Owl	❏		
R	Short-eared Owl	❏		
R	Vermilion Flycatcher	❏		
•	Galápagos Flycatcher	❏		
•	Galápagos Martin	❏		
•	Galápagos Mockingbird	❏		
•	Charles Mockingbird	❏		

•	Hood Mockingbird	❏		
•	Chatham Mockingbird	❏		
R	Yellow Warbler	❏		
•	Small Ground Finch	❏		
•	Medium Ground Finch	❏		
•	Large Ground Finch	❏		
•	Sharp-beaked Ground Finch	❏		
•	Cactus Finch	❏		
•	Large Cactus Finch	❏		
•	Vegetarian Finch	❏		
•	Small Tree Finch	❏		
•	Medium Tree Finch	❏		
•	Large Tree Finch	❏		
•	Woodpecker Finch	❏		
•	Mangrove Finch	❏		
•	Warbler Finch	❏		

REPTILE SPECIES IN THE GALÁPAGOS

	Species	Sighted	Date	Notes
•	Giant Tortoise	❏		
R	Pacific Green Sea Turtle	❏		
•	Marine Iguana	❏		
•	Galápagos Land Iguana	❏		
•	Santa Fe Land Iguana	❏		
•	Lava Lizard (7 species)	❏		
•	Gecko (5 species)	❏		
R	Gecko (2 species)	❏		
•	Galápagos Snake (4 species)	❏		

MAMMAL SPECIES IN THE GALÁPAGOS

	Species	Sighted	Date	Notes
R	Hoary Bat	❏		
•	Galápagos Bat	❏		
•	Santa Fe Rice Rat	❏		
•	Fernandina Rice Rat	❏		
R	Sea Lion	❏		
•	Galápagos Fur Seal	❏		
R	Whales (7 species)	❏		
R	Dolphins (3 species)	❏		

Key: •   Endemic
       R   Resident
       M   Migrant

Appendix: Books

Ecuador Travel Guides

There are few comprehensive guidebooks on Ecuador and most date from the late 1980s or early 1990s – look for new editions of *The Budget Traveller's No Frills Guide to Ecuador* by John Forrest (1989, Bradt Publications) and *Ecuador, the Galápagos & Colombia* by John Paul Rathbone (1991, Cadogan Guides). *Insight Guides Ecuador* edited by Tony Perrottet (1996, APA Publications) makes good background reading and is illustrated with beautiful photographs, but the travel guide section is extremely brief and limited to four cities plus the Galápagos. Read it at home. A newcomer is *The New Key to Ecuador and the Galápagos* by David Pearson and David Middleton (1996, Ulysses Press) which is useful to travelers on a midrange to top-end budget who are interested in natural history. The authors are both experts in that field – one a zoology professor and the other a professional nature photographer.

The Ecotourist's Guide to the Ecuadorian Amazon by Rolf Wesche et al (1995, CEPEIGE, Quito) is a recent and very practical guide to the Napo Province area.

Regional Travel Guides

There are some good general books on South America which have a chapter on Ecuador, and are mainly recommended for the traveler who wants one book for a 'grand tour' of Latin America. *South America on a shoestring* (6th edition, 1997, Lonely Planet) is recommended to the budget traveler for its many maps, detailed travel suggestions and money-saving information.

Another broad approach is available in *The South American Handbook* edited by Ben Box (72nd edition, 1996, Trade & Travel, UK or Passport, USA). *A Traveler's Guide to El Dorado & the Inca Empire* by Lynn Meisch (1984, Penguin Books) is full of interesting details on the crafts, cultures, markets, fiestas and archaeology of Colombia, Ecuador, Peru and Bolivia, and has good background information.

The Outdoors

Edward Whymper's *Travels Amongst the Great Andes of the Equator*, first published in 1891 and now reprinted (1987, Gibbs M Smith, USA and 1990, Peregrine Books, UK), is an exceptional book describing an 1880 mountaineering expedition which made eight first-ascents of Ecuadorian peaks, including the highest, Chimborazo. There are also fascinating descriptions of travel in Ecuador a century ago and the woodcut engravings are pure delight.

Climbing & Hiking in Ecuador by Rob Rachowiecki et al (4th edition, 1997, Bradt Publications) is a detailed guide to climbing Ecuador's mountains and also describes many beautiful hikes, some of which are simple day hikes suitable for the beginner.

If you read Spanish, *Montañas del Sol* by Serrano, Rojas and Landázuri, is a good book for climbers written by three of Ecuador's premier *andinistas*. Another Ecuadorian publication, this one in Spanish with an English translation, is *Cotopaxi – The Mountain of Light* by Freddy Landázuri. This covers Ecuador's most famous mountain in detail, describing routes, wildlife and climbing history. Both books were published by Ediciones Campo Abierto, Quito, in 1994, and more are to follow in this new series of outdoor books.

There is a series of climbing guides to Ecuador's more popular mountains by Jorge Anhalzer. These four-page guides have a sketch map of the *ruta normal* on the back page and are available in Quito. They're lightweight, if nothing else.

If the Pacific coast intrigues you as much as Andean mountains, *Walking the Beaches of Ecuador* by José-Germán Cárdenas and

Karen Marie Greiner (1988, Quito) is for you. The authors walked or jogged the entire length of Ecuador's coastline.

Natural History

Books on Ecuador's wildlife are sadly few. *Birds of Ecuador* by Crespo, Greenfield and Matheus (1990, FEPROTUR, Quito) is a locational checklist. *Birding Ecuador* by Clive Green (2nd edition, 1996, self-published) details the author's several long birdwatching trips to Ecuador. The sketch maps, practical information and checklist are very useful to birdwatchers. The book is available from the American Birding Association (ABA; ☎ (719) 578 0607, (800) 834 7736, fax 578 9705, see also Online Services) PO Box 6599, Colorado Springs, CO 80934, USA, or Natural History Book Source (☎ (0803) 865 913, fax (0803) 865 280) in the UK. Another book in the same vein is *A Guide to Birdwatching in Ecuador and the Galápagos Islands* by R Williams, B Best and T Heijnen (1996, Biosphere Publications).

Aves del valle de Quito y sus alrededores (Birds of the valley of Quito and environs) by Juan Manuel Carrión (1986, Fundación Natura, Quito) is a useful introductory book that illustrates 40 of the area's most common species.

A proper field guide by Ridgely and Greenfield (see Birds in Facts about the Country) will be available in the late 1990s. At almost a decade late, it is going to be a very good book! Meanwhile, ornithologists have to avail themselves of either guides to the whole continent, or to nearby countries. The best of these is Hilty and Brown's *A Guide to the Birds of Colombia* (1986, Princeton University Press), which covers most of Ecuador's species.

Birders will find the cassette tape *Bird Calls of Eastern Ecuador* by English and Parker a very useful audio reference. It's available from the South American Explorers Club or the American Birding Association. Profits aid conservation efforts in Ecuador. The ABA has several other cassette tapes and books of interest, including the US$150 *Birds of the High Andes* by

Fjeldsa and Krabbe (1990, Apollo Books). This is an excellent, detailed, well-illustrated and indispensable guide for those interested in Andean avifauna.

Neotropical Rainforest Mammals – A Field Guide by Louise H Emmons (1990, University of Chicago Press) is essential for those seriously interested in tropical mammals. The book is detailed and portable, with almost 300 species described and illustrated. Although some of the mammals included are found only in other neotropical countries, many of Ecuador's mammals, and certainly all the known rainforest inhabitants, are found within the book's pages.

The only other books on Ecuadorian plants and animals I know of are *Flora del Ecuador* (1985, Quito) and *Fauna del Ecuador* (1989, Quito) both by Erwin Patzelt, in Spanish. The Flora is now out of print (though there is talk of a new edition). The Fauna is a heavy encyclopedic volume covering everything from mammals to mollusks, hence its individual descriptions are not as detailed as those of Emmons' guide.

There are several excellent books on South American natural history which contain some information on Ecuador. One of my favorites is Michael Andrews' *Flight of the Condor* (1982; Little, Brown & Co) which may be out of print.

For the layperson interested in biology, particularly of the rainforest, I recommend the entertaining and readable *Tropical Nature* by Adrian Forsyth and Ken Miyata (1984, Scribner's & Sons). Forsyth is also the author of a children's book *Journey Through a Tropical Jungle* (1988, Simon & Schuster).

Other books of a general nature that have been well received include *A Neotropical Companion* by John C Kricher (1989, Princeton University Press), subtitled 'An Introduction to the Animals, Plants, and Ecosystems of the New World Tropics;' *The Last Rain Forests* edited by Mark Collins (1990, Oxford University Press); and Catherine Caulfield's *In the Rainforest* (1989, University of Chicago

Press), which emphasizes the problems of the loss of the rainforest.

Galápagos Islands

The excellent *A Traveler's Guide to the Galápagos Islands* by Barry Boyce (2nd edition, 1994, Galápagos Travel) is written by an expert tour operator to the islands. It has detailed and lengthy listings of the better boats and tour agencies. Expect a 3rd edition soon.

The best general guide to the history, geology and plant and animal life of these islands is the thorough and highly recommended *Galápagos: A Natural History Guide* by Michael H Jackson, himself a Galápagos guide (2nd edition, 1993, University of Calgary Press). No trip to the Galápagos is complete without this guide.

Avid birders will like *A Field Guide to the Birds of the Galápagos* by Michael Harris (1982, Collins). This excellent handbook illustrates and fully describes every Galápagos bird species.

Amateur botanists will want Eileen Schofield's booklet *Plants of the Galápagos Islands* (1984, Universe Books). This describes 87 common plants and is much more convenient than the classic, encyclopedic *Flora of the Galápagos Islands* by Wiggins and Porter (1971, Stanford University Press).

Snorkelers and divers should look for *Reef Fish Identification – Galápagos* by Paul Humann (1993, New World Publications); *Marine Life of the Galápagos – A guide to the fishes, whales, dolphins & other marine mammals* by Pierre Constant (1992, self-published); or *A Field Guide to the Fishes of Galápagos* by Godfrey Merlen (1988, Libri Mundi, Quito).

Divers will also like *Subtidal Galápagos* by James Cribb (1986, Camden House). This is too big a book to comfortably take with you, but the superb photos are the best underwater Galápagos images I've seen.

Dive and gift shops in oceanographical aquariums and museums in the US sell waterproof cards illustrating common fish of the Pacific. These can be taken underwater and help in identifying some of the Galápagos species. Unfortunately, these cards are not available in Ecuador.

Galápagos Field Observations by Mauricio García and Raúl Gavela (1994, Quito) describes the most popular visitor sites in the islands and provides a checklist of the species most likely to be seen in each one. It's a useful checklist if you want to keep track of what you've seen.

In addition to these guides, there are several good books of a general nature about the Galápagos. The following are particularly recommended: *Islands Lost in Time* by Tui de Roy Moore (1980, Viking Press) is a beautiful book illustrated by Galápagos' premier photographer, Tui de Roy. *Galápagos – Islands of Birds* by Bryan Nelson (1968, William Morrow) has superb descriptions of bird behavior. *Darwin's Islands: A Natural History of the Galápagos* by Ian Thornton (1971, Natural History Press) is one of the earliest natural-history guides – I remember reading it as a teenager when it first appeared and wanting to go immediately to the islands.

The most famous of the visitors to the Galápagos was Charles Darwin who was there in 1835. You can read his *On the Origin of Species by Means of Natural Selection* or his accounts of *The Voyage of the Beagle*. These 19th-century texts are rather dated and make heavy reading today. You may prefer one of the various modern biographies such as Irving Stone's excellent *The Origin* (1980, Doubleday) or Alan Moorehead's illustrated *Darwin & the Beagle* (1969, Harper & Row). Readers interested in a layperson's introduction to evolutionary theory can try the amusingly written but roughly accurate *Darwin for Beginners* by Jonathan Miller and Borin Van Loon (1982, Pantheon Books).

Jonathan Weiner's *The Beak of the Finch* (1994, Knopf) is subtitled 'A Story of Evolution in Our Time' and describes current research on the evolution of Darwin's finches. It's a good read.

A book written for 12- to 16-year-old children is *Galápagos: the enchanted isles* by David Horwell (1988). This 64-page book will teach the young visitor about the

Galápagos, and parents will find it a good introduction, too. It is available only from Galápagos Adventure Tours (see Organized Tours in the Getting There & Away chapter).

Floreana by Margaret Wittmer (various editions and publishers) describes the life of one of the earliest colonists of the islands (Wittmer arrived in 1932 and still lives there).

Indigenous People
Various good books are available about the Indian populations of Ecuador. *The Awakening Valley* by Collier and Buitron (1949, University of Chicago Press) is a photographic anthropological study of the people of the Otavalo region. The Shuar are studied by Michael Harner using their old name, *The Jivaro: People of the Sacred Waterfall* (1973, Doubleday/Anchor). A well-illustrated multilingual book available in Quito is *The Lost World of the Aucas* by KD Gartelmann (1978, Quito). *Otavalo: Weaving, Costume and the Market* by renowned textile expert, Lynn Meisch (1987, Libri Mundi, Quito) is informatively illustrated and written. *Amazon Worlds – Peoples and Cultures of Ecuador's Amazon Region* by Noemi Paymal and Catalina Sosa (1993, Quito) is expensive but well written and beautifully illustrated – a coffee-table book. Other books about Ecuador's and South America's Indian peoples are available at Libri Mundi (see Bookstores in Facts for the Visitor).

History
Going back to the arrival of the Spanish conquistadors, the best book is undoubtedly John Hemming's excellent *The Conquest of the Incas* (1970, Harvest/HBJ). Although this deals mainly with Peru (the heart of the Inca Empire), there are several sections on Ecuador.

Four Years Among the Ecuadorians by Friedrich Hassaurek was originally published in 1867 (republished 1967, Southern Illinois University Press). The author was a US diplomat who traveled widely in the country and vividly reported what he saw.

If archaeology is your interest, look for Karl Dieter's *Digging up Prehistory: the Archaeology of Ecuador* (1989, Libri Mundi, Quito).

Politics
Ecuador – Fragile Democracy by David Corkill and David Cubitt (1988, Latin American Bureau, London) takes a look at historical patterns and current trends in Ecuadorian politics.

Inside the Company: CIA Diary written by former CIA agent Philip Agee and published in 1975, gives a chilling look at US intervention in Ecuador's political affairs. The diary may be difficult to get hold of, but Corkill and Cubitt's book has a few excerpts.

Political Power in Ecuador (1980, University of New Mexico Press) is written by former Ecuadorian president Osvaldo Hurtado.

Amazon Crude (1991, Natural Resources Defense Council, USA) is an environmental look at some of the impacts and problems caused by oil drilling in the Amazon. They don't pull any punches.

General
One of my favorite books about travel in Ecuador is Henri Michaux prose/poetry account of his 1928 visit. Michaux was a Belgian poet and mystic, and his *Ecuador – A Travel Journal* (republished 1970, Peter Owen) is an intriguing look at his impressions of the country more than half a century ago.

Another personal favorite is Tom Miller's *The Panama Hat Trail* (1988, Vintage Departures). If reading about some guy going to Ecuador to look for Panama hats doesn't sound like your cup of tea, think again. This book is well written, fun to read and very informative about Ecuadorian life.

Living Poor by Moritz Thomsen, is a classic account of Peace Corps life in coastal Ecuador during the 1960s. Unlike most volunteers, who are in their 20s, Thomsen was 48 when he arrived for a four-year stint in one of Ecuador's poorest areas. He writes with a mature eloquence and humor about a place and people he obviously grew to love. *Two Wheels & a Taxi* by Virginia Urrutia (1987, The Mountaineers) is the author's story of her bicycling trip around Ecuador, accompanied by a local cab driver for logistical support. Ms Urrutia was 70 when she made the trip – an inspiration to us all.

There are many contemporary writers. A good introduction is *Diez Cuentistas Ecuatorianos* (1990, Libri Mundi, Quito), a book of short stories. Also well recommended is Pablo Cuvi's *In the eyes of my people* (1988, Dinediciones/Grijalbo). See Arts in Facts about the Country for further information.

Index

TEXT

Map references are in **bold** type.

508   Index

LONELY PLANET PRODUCTS

Lonely Planet is known worldwide for publishing practical, reliable and no-nonsense travel information in our guides and on our web site. The Lonely Planet list covers just about every accessible part of the world. Currently there are eight series: *travel guides*, *shoestring guides*, *walking guides*, *city guides*, *phrasebooks*, *audio packs*, *travel atlases* and *Journeys* – a unique collection of travel writing.

EUROPE

Amsterdam • Austria • Baltic States phrasebook • Britain • Central Europe on a shoestring • Central Europe phrasebook • Czech & Slovak Republics • Denmark • Dublin • Eastern Europe on a shoestring • Eastern Europe phrasebook • Estonia, Latvia & Lithuania • Finland • France • French phrasebook • Germany • German phrasebook • Greece • Greek phrasebook • Hungary • Iceland, Greenland & the Faroe Islands • Ireland • Italian phrasebook • Italy • Lisbon • Mediterranean Europe on a shoestring • Mediterranean Europe phrasebook • Paris • Poland • Portugal • Portugal travel atlas • Prague • Russia, Ukraine & Belarus • Russian phrasebook • Scandinavian & Baltic Europe on a shoestring • Scandinavian Europe phrasebook •Slovenia • Spain • Spanish phrasebook • St Petersburg • Switzerland •Trekking in Spain • Ukrainian phrasebook •Vienna •Walking in Britain • Walking in Switzerland • Western Europe on a shoestring • Western Europe phrasebook

Travel Literature: The Olive Grove: Travels in Greece

NORTH AMERICA

Alaska • Backpacking in Alaska • Baja California • California & Nevada • Canada • Florida • Hawaii • Honolulu • Los Angeles • Mexico • Miami • New England • New Orleans • New York City • New York, New Jersey & Pennsylvania • Pacific Northwest USA • Rocky Mountain States • San Francisco • Southwest USA • USA phrasebook • Washington, DC & the Capital Region

CENTRAL AMERICA & THE CARIBBEAN

Bermuda • Central America on a shoestring • Costa Rica • Cuba •Eastern Caribbean •Guatemala, Belize & Yucatán: La Ruta Maya • Jamaica

SOUTH AMERICA

Argentina, Uruguay & Paraguay • Bolivia • Brazil • Brazilian phrasebook • Buenos Aires • Chile & Easter Island • Chile & Easter Island travel atlas • Colombia • Deep South • Ecuador & the Galápagos Islands • Latin American Spanish phrasebook • Peru • Quechua phrasebook • Rio de Janeiro • South America on a shoestring • Trekking in the Patagonian Andes • Venezuela

Travel Literature: Full Circle: A South American Journey

ANTARCTICA

Antarctica

ISLANDS OF THE INDIAN OCEAN

Madagascar & Comoros • Maldives• Mauritius, Réunion & Seychelles

AFRICA

Africa - the South • Africa on a shoestring • Arabic (Moroccan) phrasebook • Cape Town • Central Africa • East Africa • Egypt • Egypt travel atlas• Ethiopian (Amharic) phrasebook • Kenya • Kenya travel atlas • Malawi, Mozambique & Zambia • Morocco • North Africa • South Africa, Lesotho & Swaziland • South Africa, Lesotho & Swaziland travel atlas • Swahili phrasebook • Trekking in East Africa • West Africa • Zimbabwe, Botswana & Namibia • Zimbabwe, Botswana & Namibia travel atlas

Travel Literature: The Rainbird: A Central African Journey • Songs to an African Sunset: A Zimbabwean Story

MAIL ORDER

Lonely Planet products are distributed worldwide.They are also available by mail order from Lonely Planet, so if you have difficulty finding a title please write to us. North American and South American residents should write to Embarcadero West, 155 Filbert St, Suite 251, Oakland CA 94607, USA; European and African residents should write to 10a Spring Place, London NW5 3BH; and residents of other countries to PO Box 617, Hawthorn, Victoria 3122, Australia.

NORTH-EAST ASIA

Beijing • Cantonese phrasebook • China • Hong Kong • Hong Kong, Macau & Guangzhou • Japan • Japanese phrasebook • Japanese audio pack • Korea • Korean phrasebook • Mandarin phrasebook • Mongolia • Mongolian phrasebook • North-East Asia on a shoestring • Seoul • Taiwan • Tibet • Tibet phrasebook • Tokyo

Travel Literature: Lost Japan

INDIAN SUBCONTINENT

Bangladesh • Bengali phrasebook • Delhi • Hindi/Urdu phrasebook • India • India & Bangladesh travel atlas • Indian Himalaya • Karakoram Highway • Nepal • Nepali phrasebook • Pakistan • Rajasthan • Sri Lanka • Sri Lanka phrasebook • Trekking in the Indian Himalaya • Trekking in the Karakoram & Hindukush • Trekking in the Nepal Himalaya

Travel Literature: In Rajasthan • Shopping for Buddhas

SOUTH-EAST ASIA

Bali & Lombok • Bangkok • Burmese phrasebook • Cambodia • Ho Chi Minh City • Indonesia • Indonesian phrasebook • Indonesian audio pack • Jakarta • Java • Laos • Lao phrasebook • Laos travel atlas • Malay phrasebook • Malaysia, Singapore & Brunei • Myanmar (Burma) • Philippines • Pilipino phrasebook • Singapore • South-East Asia on a shoestring • South-East Asia phrasebook • Thailand • Thailand's Islands & Beaches • Thailand travel atlas • Thai phrasebook • Thai audio pack • Thai Hill Tribes phrasebook • Vietnam • Vietnamese phrasebook • Vietnam travel atlas

MIDDLE EAST & CENTRAL ASIA

Arab Gulf States • Arabic (Egyptian) phrasebook • Central Asia • Central Asia phrasebook • Iran • Israel & the Palestinian Territories • Israel & the Palestinian Territories travel atlas • Istanbul • Jerusalem • Jordan & Syria • Jordan, Syria & Lebanon travel atlas • Lebanon • Middle East • Turkey • Turkish phrasebook • Turkey travel atlas • Yemen

Travel Literature: The Gates of Damascus • Kingdom of the Film Stars: Journey into Jordan

ALSO AVAILABLE:

Travel with Children • Traveller's Tales

AUSTRALIA & THE PACIFIC

Australia • Australian phrasebook • Bushwalking in Australia • Bushwalking in Papua New Guinea • Fiji • Fijian phrasebook • Islands of Australia's Great Barrier Reef • Melbourne • Micronesia • New Caledonia • New South Wales • New Zealand • Northern Territory • Outback Australia • Papua New Guinea • Papua New Guinea phrasebook • Queensland • Rarotonga & the Cook Islands • Samoa • Solomon Islands • South Australia • Sydney • Tahiti & French Polynesia • Tasmania • Tonga • Tramping in New Zealand • Vanuatu • Victoria • Western Australia

Travel Literature: Islands in the Clouds • Sean & David's Long Drive

THE LONELY PLANET STORY

Lonely Planet published its first book in 1973 in response to the numerous 'How did you do it?' questions Maureen and Tony Wheeler were asked after driving, bussing, hitching, sailing and railing their way from England to Australia.

Written at a kitchen table and hand collated, trimmed and stapled, *Across Asia on the Cheap* became an instant local bestseller, inspiring thoughts of another book.

Eighteen months in South-East Asia resulted in their second guide, *South-East Asia on a shoestring*, which they put together in a backstreet Chinese hotel in Singapore in 1975. The 'yellow bible', as it quickly became known to backpackers around the world, soon became *the* guide to the region. It has sold well over half a million copies and is now in its 9th edition, still retaining its familiar yellow cover.

Today there are over 240 titles, including travel guides, walking guides, language kits & phrasebooks, travel atlases and travel literature. The company is the largest independent travel publisher in the world. Although Lonely Planet initially specialised in guides to Asia, today there are few corners of the globe that have not been covered.

The emphasis continues to be on travel for independent travellers. Tony and Maureen still travel for several months of each year and play an active part in the writing, updating and quality control of Lonely Planet's guides.

They have been joined by over 70 authors and 170 staff at our offices in Melbourne (Australia), Oakland (USA), London (UK) and Paris (France). Travellers themselves also make a valuable contribution to the guides through the feedback we receive in thousands of letters each year and on our web site.

The people at Lonely Planet strongly believe that travellers can make a positive contribution to the countries they visit, both through their appreciation of the countries' culture, wildlife and natural features, and through the money they spend. In addition, the company makes a direct contribution to the countries and regions it covers. Since 1986 a percentage of the income from each book has been donated to ventures such as famine relief in Africa; aid projects in India; agricultural projects in Central America; Greenpeace's efforts to halt French nuclear testing in the Pacific; and Amnesty International.

'I hope we send people out with the right attitude about travel. You realise when you travel that there are so many different perspectives about the world, so we hope these books will make people more interested in what they see. Guidebooks can't really guide people. All you can do is point them in the right direction.'

– Tony Wheeler

LONELY PLANET PUBLICATIONS

Australia
PO Box 617, Hawthorn 3122, Victoria
tel: (03) 9819 1877 fax: (03) 9819 6459
e-mail: talk2us@lonelyplanet.com.au

USA
Embarcadero West, 155 Filbert St, Suite 251,
Oakland, CA 94607
tel: (510) 893 8555 TOLL FREE: 800 275-8555
fax: (510) 893 8563
e-mail: info@lonelyplanet.com

UK
10a Spring Place,
London NW5 3BH
tel: (0171) 428 4800 fax: (0171) 428 4828
e-mail: go@lonelyplanet.co.uk

France:
71 bis rue du Cardinal Lemoine, 75005 Paris
tel: 1 44 32 06 20 fax: 1 46 34 72 55
e-mail: 100560.415@compuserve.com

**World Wide Web: http://www.lonelyplanet.com
or AOL keyword: lp**